Dictionary of Literary Biography

Dictionary of Literary Biography Documentary Series

Dictionary of Literary Biography Yearbooks

1980 edited by Karen L. Rood, Jean W. Ross, and Richard Ziegfeld (1981)

1981 edited by Karen L. Rood, Jean W. Ross, and Richard Ziegfeld (1982)

1982 edited by Richard Ziegfeld; associate editors: Jean W. Ross and Lynne C. Zeigler (1983)

1983 edited by Mary Bruccoli and Jean W. Ross; associate editor Richard Ziegfeld (1984)

1984 edited by Jean W. Ross (1985)

1985 edited by Jean W. Ross (1986)

1986 edited by J. M. Brook (1987)

1987 edited by J. M. Brook (1988)

1988 edited by J. M. Brook (1989)

1989 edited by J. M. Brook (1990)

1990 edited by James W. Hipp (1991)

1991 edited by James W. Hipp (1992)

1992 edited by James W. Hipp (1993)

1993 edited by James W. Hipp, contributing editor George Garrett (1994)

1994 edited by James W. Hipp, contributing editor George Garrett (1995)

1995 edited by James W. Hipp, contributing editor George Garrett (1996)

1996 edited by Samuel W. Bruce and L. Kay Webster, contributing editor George Garrett (1997)

1997 edited by Matthew J. Bruccoli and George Garrett, with the assistance of L. Kay Webster (1998)

1998 edited by Matthew J. Bruccoli, contributing editor George Garrett, with the assistance of D. W. Thomas (1999)

1999 edited by Matthew J. Bruccoli, contributing editor George Garrett, with the assistance of D. W. Thomas (2000)

2000 edited by Matthew J. Bruccoli, contributing editor George Garrett, with the assistance of George Parker Anderson (2001)

Concise Series

Concise Dictionary of American Literary Biography, 7 volumes (1988-1999): *The New Consciousness, 1941-1968; Colonization to the American Renaissance, 1640-1865; Realism, Naturalism, and Local Color, 1865-1917; The Twenties, 1917-1929; The Age of Maturity, 1929-1941; Broadening Views, 1968-1988; Supplement: Modern Writers, 1900-1998.*

Concise Dictionary of British Literary Biography, 8 volumes (1991-1992): *Writers of the Middle Ages and Renaissance Before 1660; Writers of the Restoration and Eighteenth Century, 1660-1789; Writers of the Romantic Period, 1789-1832; Victorian Writers, 1832-1890; Late-Victorian and Edwardian Writers, 1890-1914; Modern Writers, 1914-1945; Writers After World War II, 1945-1960; Contemporary Writers, 1960 to Present.*

Concise Dictionary of World Literary Biography, 10 volumes projected (1999-): *Ancient Greek and Roman Writers; German Writers; African, Caribbean, and Latin American Writers; South Slavic and Eastern European Writers.*

Dictionary of Literary Biography® • Volume Two Hundred Fifty

Antebellum Writers in New York
Second Series

Dictionary of Literary Biography® • Volume Two Hundred Fifty

Antebellum Writers in New York
Second Series

Edited by
Kent P. Ljungquist
Worcester Polytechnic Institute

A Bruccoli Clark Layman Book
The Gale Group
Detroit • San Francisco • London • Boston • Woodbridge, Conn.

Printed in the United States of America

The paper used in this publication meets the minimum requirements
of American National Standard for Information Sciences–Permanence
Paper for Printed Library Materials, ANSI Z39.48-1984.∞ ™

Library of Congress Cataloging-in-Publication Data

Antebellum writers in New York. Second series / edited by Kent Ljungquist.
    p. cm.–(Dictionary of literary biography; v. 250)
"A Bruccoli Clark Layman book."
Includes bibliographical references and index.
ISBN 0-7876-4667-9 (alk. paper)
1. American literature–New York (State)–Bio-bibliography–Dictionaries. 2. American literature–19th
century–Bio-bibliography–Dictionaries. 3. Authors, American–New York (State)–Biography–
Dictionaries. 4. Authors, American–19th century–Biography–Dictionaries. 5. Southern States–
In literature–Dictionaries. 6. Southern States–Biography–Dictionaries. 1. Ljungquist, Kent, 1948-   .
II. Series.

PS253.N7 A58 2001
810'.9'97471'09034–dc21   2001053164
[B]

10 9 8 7 6 5 4 3 2 1

To the memory of Gladys O. Ljungquist

Contents

Contents

Plan of the Series

. . . Almost the most prodigious asset of a country, and perhaps its most precious possession, is its native literary product—when that product is fine and noble and enduring.

Mark Twain*

The advisory board, the editors, and the publisher of the *Dictionary of Literary Biography* are joined in endorsing Mark Twain's declaration. The literature of a nation provides an inexhaustible resource of permanent worth. Our purpose is to make literature and its creators better understood and more accessible to students and the reading public, while satisfying the needs of teachers and researchers.

To meet these requirements, *literary biography* has been construed in terms of the author's achievement. The most important thing about a writer is his writing. Accordingly, the entries in *DLB* are career biographies, tracing the development of the author's canon and the evolution of his reputation.

The purpose of *DLB* is not only to provide reliable information in a usable format but also to place the figures in the larger perspective of literary history and to offer appraisals of their accomplishments by qualified scholars.

The publication plan for *DLB* resulted from two years of preparation. The project was proposed to Bruccoli Clark by Frederick G. Ruffner, president of the Gale Research Company, in November 1975. After specimen entries were prepared and typeset, an advisory board was formed to refine the entry format and develop the series rationale. In meetings held during 1976, the publisher, series editors, and advisory board approved the scheme for a comprehensive biographical dictionary of persons who contributed to literature. Editorial work on the first volume began in January 1977, and it was published in 1978. In order to make *DLB* more than a dictionary and to compile volumes that individually have claim to status as literary history, it was decided to organize volumes by topic, period, or

From an unpublished section of Mark Twain's autobiography, copyright by the Mark Twain Company

genre. Each of these freestanding volumes provides a biographical-bibliographical guide and overview for a particular area of literature. We are convinced that this organization—as opposed to a single alphabet method—constitutes a valuable innovation in the presentation of reference material. The volume plan necessarily requires many decisions for the placement and treatment of authors. Certain figures will be included in separate volumes, but with different entries emphasizing the aspect of his career appropriate to each volume. Ernest Hemingway, for example, is represented in *American Writers in Paris, 1920–1939* by an entry focusing on his expatriate apprenticeship; he is also in *American Novelists, 1910–1945* with an entry surveying his entire career, as well as in *American Short-Story Writers, 1910–1945, Second Series* with an entry concentrating on his short fiction. Each volume includes a cumulative index of the subject authors and articles.

Since 1981 the series has been further augmented by the *DLB Yearbooks,* which update published entries, add new entries to keep the *DLB* current with contemporary activity, and provide articles on literary history. There have also been nineteen *DLB Documentary Series* volumes which provide illustrations, facsimiles, and biographical and critical source materials for figures, works, or groups judged to have particular interest for students. In 1999 the *Documentary Series* was incorporated into the *DLB* volume numbering system beginning with *DLB 210: Ernest Hemingway.*

We define literature as the *intellectual commerce of a nation:* not merely as belles lettres but as that ample and complex process by which ideas are generated, shaped, and transmitted. *DLB* entries are not limited to "creative writers" but extend to other figures who in their time and in their way influenced the mind of a people. Thus the series encompasses historians, journalists, publishers, book collectors, and screenwriters. By this means readers of *DLB* may be aided to perceive literature not as cult scripture in the keeping of intellectual high priests but firmly positioned at the center of a nation's life.

DLB includes the major writers appropriate to each volume and those standing in the ranks behind them. Scholarly and critical counsel has been sought in deciding which minor figures to include and how full their entries should be. Wherever possible, useful references are made to figures who do not warrant separate entries.

Each *DLB* volume has an expert volume editor responsible for planning the volume, selecting the figures for inclusion, and assigning the entries. Volume editors are also responsible for preparing, where appropriate, appendices surveying the major periodicals and literary and intellectual movements for their volumes, as well as lists of further readings. Work on the series as a whole is coordinated at the Bruccoli Clark Layman editorial center in Columbia, South Carolina, where the editorial staff is responsible for accuracy and utility of the published volumes.

One feature that distinguishes *DLB* is the illustration policy—its concern with the iconography of literature. Just as an author is influenced by his surroundings, so is the reader's understanding of the author enhanced by a knowledge of his environment. Therefore *DLB* volumes include not only drawings, paintings, and photographs of authors, often depicting them at various stages in their careers, but also illustrations of their families and places where they lived. Title pages are regularly reproduced in facsimile along with dust jackets for modern authors. The dust jackets are a special feature of *DLB* because they often document better than anything else the way in which an author's work was perceived in its own time. Specimens of the writers' manuscripts and letters are included when feasible.

Samuel Johnson rightly decreed that "The chief glory of every people arises from its authors." The purpose of the *Dictionary of Literary Biography* is to compile literary history in the surest way available to us—by accurate and comprehensive treatment of the lives and work of those who contributed to it.

The *DLB* Advisory Board

Introduction

The image of antebellum literary history, shaped by the grandiose tone of Ralph Waldo Emerson and his disciples, is perhaps a romantic picture of bustling activity in New England, reinforced by influential volumes, such as Van Wyck Brooks's *The Flowering of New England* (1936) and George Whicher's *Poetry of the New England Renaissance* (1950). Into the 1850s, however, major publishers in New York and Philadelphia remained the most successful arbiters of literary taste. Boston periodicals, moreover, found secure footing only after the durable successes of *The Knickerbocker, The Democratic Review,* and *The Southern Literary Messenger.* The campaign for a distinctive American culture, emancipated from the tyranny of England, was not confined to New England, as reflected in the many articles and manifestos on the subject published in New York. This debate on literary nationalism is perhaps remembered today because two figures, Herman Melville and Walt Whitman, emerged from the clamor surrounding it. It was nevertheless a contentious debate carried out among editors and intellectuals working for periodicals or participating in private salons and clubs in Manhattan or its environs.

New York City, which tripled in size in the 1840s and 1850s, became the publishing center of America in this campaign for a distinctive national literature. Authors, both inexperienced and well traveled in the literary marketplace, flocked to New York during the antebellum period to participate in the activities of the book and periodical trades. After leaving *The Southern Literary Messenger* early in 1837, Edgar Allan Poe, for example, moved to New York City, stayed for more than a year, and pursued magazine work for the "*Monthlies* of Gotham—Their distinguished Editors, and their vigorous Collaborators." Harper and Brothers of New York published Poe's first book of fiction, *The Narrative of Arthur Gordon Pym,* in 1838. The publication of the book had been delayed by the financial crisis of the 1830s, and Poe pursued his literary objectives elsewhere, only to return to New York in 1845 to work as a magazine editor and in 1848 to deliver a lecture on "The Universe."

The circumstances surrounding the publication of Melville's *Typee* (1846), recounted by numerous commentators, offer further perspective on the multiple crosscurrents in the literary world of New York before the Civil War. With the support of Washington Irving, the figure who dominated the New York literary scene, a British publisher had been secured for a narrative of a young sailor's adventures in the Marquesas Islands. If the book first attracted a British imprint, the likelihood of American publication would be enhanced. George Palmer Putnam, soon to become one of the foremost publishers in the United States, arranged to have its proof sheets sent from London back to New York to his firm of Wiley and Putman. *Typee* appeared in 1846 after Evert A. Duyckinck, who later ascended to a leadership role in the "Young America" group of New York, had served as an editorial evaluator. Complemented by the intervention of the most celebrated author of New York, the success of the book was assisted by Putnam, whose name soon rose to prominence with the other great publishing houses of the city—Harper, Scribner, Van Nostrand, and Dodd. By the end of the decade Putnam was underwriting multivolume editions of the works of both Irving and James Fenimore Cooper. The manuscript of *Typee* was read by Duyckinck, who eventually took the helm of *The Literary World,* and it was reviewed by the young Whitman, clearly attracted to the vigor and energy of the city and beginning his literary career as a contributor to *The New York Aurora* and *The Brooklyn Eagle.*

In *The Raven and the Whale: The War of Words and Wits in the Era of Poe and Melville* (1956), a lively and enduring chronicle of the cliquish battles that divided the literary world of the 1840s, Perry Miller may wittily exaggerate in claiming that "Melville's America . . . consisted almost entirely of the city of New York." Whatever the extent of its influence on the young author, there can be little doubt that his reentry into the environs of New York—the Melville family had lived in the city until Melville's father's financial reversals in the 1820s—marked the beginnings of his education into the vagaries of professional authorship. In all likelihood, many of the challenges and disappointments he experienced as a writer were duplicated in the careers of other literary figures who lived and wrote in New York in the 1840s, drawn to opportunities of the expanding book and magazine markets. Hardly at home in urban settings, Henry David Thoreau worked as a tutor at the Staten Island home of William Emerson (several miles outside the city) in 1843, frequented the metropolitan libraries, and tried his hand at placing his pieces with several New York periodicals.

The careers of these authors underscore the centrality of New York to antebellum literary activity, its influence and attraction for both major and minor figures, and its role in enhancing the profession of authorship and the business of publishing. By the time of their entry into the literary world of New York, the booming port city had long ago shed its image as a quaint Dutch town. It had, in fact, become the commercial center of the nation, easily eclipsing Philadelphia—which may have reached the peak of its cultural stature by the War of 1812—for its diversity of publishing ventures. The development of the banking interests of New York and a nascent industrialism were contributing factors in the emergence of a capitalist economy that supplanted the vanished world of Dutch aristocrats. A general drift of people from farms and rural villages to towns and cities altered the demographic and social character of New York—its population rose in the 1840s from just over three hundred thousand to more than half a million. Boston could boast of the prestigious *North American Review,* but by the mid 1840s, New York was three times the size of Boston. "The seat of commerce," reflected a writer in *The Literary World* in 1847, is of necessity "the centre of literary power." By 1850 the city comprised a foreign-born population of 45 percent, as new German and Irish immigrants mixed with original settlers of Dutch, Scotch Irish, English, and Huguenot extraction.

These tangible achievements were obviously a source of pride to local inhabitants. Editor Horace Greeley articulated the feelings of many of them when he boasted of the ways in which New York "towered above her sister cities." Similarly, Whitman referred to New York as "the mainspring of the nation." By the mid 1840s the city had been built solidly from the Battery to Fifteenth Street, and the street system had been laid out extensively, though areas of Manhattan still maintained a rural character. In the face of accelerating and sometimes unsettling geographical, social, and economic changes, however, a more conservative impulse lay behind the work of a group of writers who celebrated the past and local traditions. While businessmen and entrepreneurs trumpeted the commercial prospects of the nation, Irving led a group of New York writers whose satirical essays, histories, and sketches surveyed the past of the region. Irving stood

for a continuity between Old World values and American culture, and his early works reflected the witty, gossipy style of the eighteenth-century British essayists. His early literary efforts were also collaborative ventures, reflecting the sociability and bonhomie of the group of writers for whom he became a model. With his brother William and the young James Kirke Paulding, Irving produced *Salmagundi* (24 January 1807 – 25 January 1808), a volume of letters, verse, and essays. These miscellaneous papers, as they were called, were infused with the town spirit of Old New York, much as were the *Croaker Papers* (March 1819– July 1819) by Fitz-Greene Halleck and Joseph Rodman Drake. For his burlesque *A History of New-York, From the Beginning of the World to the End of the Dutch Dynasty* (1809) Irving chose the pseudonym Diedrich Knickerbocker, an amateur antiquary who delves into the past of the region in a spirit of comic celebration. In a preface Irving eventually added to the volume, he announced that his purpose was "to clothe home scenes and places and familiar names with those imaginative associations so seldom met with in our own country, but which live like charms and old spells about the cities of the old world." This book, which has been overshadowed by *The Sketch Book* (1819–1820), established the tone for the Knickerbocker group of writers, which dominated the literary scene of New York until well after the Civil War. These writers, steeped in the neoclassical traditions of wit and satire, were also attracted to the emerging Romantic movement in Great Britain, whose heroes were Walter Scott and George Gordon, Lord Byron. In addition to Paulding, Drake, and Halleck, other writers sometimes associated with the Knickerbocker school were William Cullen Bryant, Charles Fenno Hoffman, William Leggett, Nathaniel Parker Willis, Park Benjamin, and Samuel Woodworth. Several of these writers—Bryant, Halleck, and Willis—had New England backgrounds, but their literary careers reached maturity in New York, as did that of Richard Henry Dana, who came to the city in 1821 to begin publication of *The Idle Man,* a periodical in the style of *The Sketch Book.* Few writers of the antebellum period could escape the shadow of Irving, whether they imitated, exploited, or burlesqued his narrative voice and strategies. Henry Wadsworth Longfellow, Nathaniel Hawthorne, and John Greenleaf Whittier all contemplated or completed volumes aiming to do for New England what Irving had done for Dutch New York. In surveying the influences on Melville's fiction, scholars have detected Irvingesque echoes even in the audacious *Typee,* and one of Melville's later works was titled "Rip Van Winkle's Lilac."

The Knickerbocker school of writers was loosely organized, but many of them interacted socially in private clubs. Throughout the early part of the century many private clubs and voluntary associations had sprung up, and they helped to define and shape cultural activity. These organizations, depending on their diverse missions, attracted a variety of labels: lyceums, benevolent or humane societies, art or music societies, library societies, debating clubs, and societies for the promotion of useful knowledge. The New York Society Library, the Mercantile Library, and the National Academy of Design attracted the local population as well as visitors from outside the city. The "Club-Mania" of the period, as it was called by the *New-England Galaxy* (16 April 1829), was not confined to New York or New England and was almost as common in towns and cities of the Middle States and the South. The same periodical summarized the phenomenon by noting "the increase in applications for incorporation, this collecting into associations, this clubbing together of all ages and sexes." Perhaps the most famous literary organization in New York was the Bread and Cheese Club, founded by Cooper in 1822. Irving was made an honorary member in 1826, and some of its members gravitated to the Sketch Club, which cultivated an interest in the pictorial arts. Some Knickerbockers were merchants or businessmen, but for respite from the commercial culture of New York, many individuals gravitated to the polite atmosphere of private literary salons where musicians, artists, and poets gathered in a spirit of informal social interchange. The poet Anne Lynch was a hostess at many of these prominent literary soirees.

Both Irving and Bryant were also devotees of the theater, and New Yorkers more easily overcame the moral reservations about plays that may have inhibited the cultural life of other regions, most notably New England. English plays were popular fare, but American playwrights perhaps succeeded in gaining greater recognition in New York, where there were six theaters and where some writers were able to exploit their local ties to the city. There were also two museums offering dramatic entertainment. In addition to Paulding, Willis, and Woodworth, New Yorkers who had plays produced between 1800 and 1840 included Samuel Judah, Anna Mowatt Ritchie, Mordecai M. Noah, George Pope Morris, and Cornelius Mathews. Poe, whose mother had played leading roles in theaters in the North and the South, found reinforcement for his lifelong interest in drama when he served as an editor for the *New-York Mirror* and *The Broadway Journal*. The latter periodical was devoted to the life of the city in all its variety, including the theater, and thus reinforced the image of New York as a cultural alternative to Boston. Just as the club atmosphere of the period stimulated informal literary activity and interchange, these

editorial connections provided access to the lively world of playwrights, actors, and artists. In his role as a magazinist, Poe reviewed Ritchie's comedy *Fashion* (produced in 1845; published in 1849), Willis's melodrama *Tortesa the Usurer* (1839), and Longfellow's closet drama, *The Spanish Student* (1843). Poe's review of Willis's plays, rather than an evaluation of an isolated performance, can be read as a survey of the status of American theater at the time.

By the time Poe assumed his position with the *New-York Mirror*, there were nearly 50 magazines in the city as well as 10 daily newspapers, and many writers supported themselves by editing or contributing to periodicals. Poe commented, "The whole tendency of the age is Magazine-ward," a statement confirmed by the proliferation of periodicals as a staple of Americans' reading habits. In 1825 there were fewer than 100 magazines in the United States; by 1850 there were more than 600. By the time of Poe's death, 54 monthlies appeared in New York alone, and their readership, which extended outside the city limits, approached 500,000.

Many newspapers stressed commerce and politics, but a few, such as *The New York Evening Post*, for which Bryant worked, were hospitable to literature. The *New York American*, edited by Charles King, was among the first newspapers to devote a page exclusively to literary topics. King's values were refined and fastidious if one compares his publication to the journalistic competition represented by James Gordon Bennett's *New York Herald* and Greeley's *New York Tribune*. To King, these papers represented the doctrine "that a newspaper should reflect the living world, as it is, with all its hideous vileness, as well as its rarer virtues—and without too nice repulsion of evil contamination." Some observers thought that papers such as *The Herald* relied on sensationalism—reports of murder and mayhem—to boost circulation. Others thought that the rise of the penny papers and so-called mammoth weeklies—huge folio-sized papers that relied on reprinting foreign authors—ushered in an age of cheap literature. The editor Francis Hawks may have had such fare in mind when he derided the "miserable literary trash which surrounds us." The most notorious of the penny papers was *The New York Sun*, edited by Richard Adams Locke. *The Sun* published sensational and fictitious stories in the guise of fact, and Locke's "Moon-Hoax" (*The Sun*, August 1835), with its narrative of strange creatures and winged bipeds on the lunar surface, was one of the newspaper sensations of the 1830s. Sensing that Locke had ushered in a new and different age in commercial journalism, Poe commented that "the object of the journal professed to be that of 'supplying the public with the news of the day at so cheap a rate as to lie within the means of all.' The consequences of the scheme, in their influence on the whole newspaper business of the country, and through this business on the interests of the country at large, are probably beyond all calculation." Many consumers of the new forms of journalism came from the new immigrant population.

This era of professional metropolitan journalism also ushered in the commercialization of print. In an age of increased sensationalism in journalism, editors might exploit colorful topics or appeal to the reader's sense of excitement or novelty by covering trials and murders, discoveries at sea or on the frontier, and developments in the sciences or pseudosciences. Works of fiction imitated some of the techniques of journalism, and new forms of dissemination included the cheap magazine, the pamphlet, or the pirated novel. In a marketplace in which the written word was seen less as a vehicle of self-expression and more as a commodity, the life of writing seemed uncertain and capricious. If writing were indeed a business, publication was subject to the same economic vagaries that influenced other sectors. Perhaps writers in New York sensed these tensions more acutely; as Willis noted, the city was "the most overstocked market for writers in the country; all the country flock and search here for fame." The business of publishing was hardly immune from economic uncertainty, and during the depression of the late 1830s, several literary ventures were either curtailed or delayed. Working for periodicals might entail low pay, editorial drudgery, and bitter literary warfare. Periodicals nevertheless represented potential sources of recognition, encouragement, and income to budding writers as they aspired to professional status in a sometimes antagonistic literary marketplace. Some writers felt that periodicals could have a civilizing influence. As a contributor to *The Monthly Anthology, and Boston Review* noted, "periodical publications more than any other, contribute toward the forming of the manners of a people. . . . The papers of Addison, as Dr. Johnson informs us, added not a little to the civility of England."

Despite their immersion in urban life, many New York writers participated in a romantic glorification of nature. From writings in periodicals to the major works of the period, repeated references to America as "nature's nation" reflected an exercise in cultural self-definition. If America lacked historical depth and endured European opprobrium for alleged cultural provincialism, native writers could cite nature as a natural birthright. The novels of Cooper, most notably his *Leather-Stocking Tales—The Pioneers* (1823), *The Last of the Mohicans* (1826), *The Prairie* (1827), *The Pathfinder* (1840), and *The Deerslayer* (1841)—reflected strikingly

an alliance between natural landscape and natural virtue. Cooper's heroic Natty Bumppo, while clearly the beneficiary of white, civilized "gifts," served as both a critic of the arbitrary rules of society and as reluctant spectator of the destruction of nature. Like Cooper, Irving attempted to endow natural scenery with storied associations and the stuff of legend, sometimes exploiting European source material, as in "Rip Van Winkle" or "The Legend of Sleepy Hollow." With Cooper and Irving as exemplars, subsequent writers hoped, in the painter Thomas Cole's words, to put landscape in "the great theater of human events" and to develop associations between specific locales and uniquely American achievements. Among Knickerbocker writers, the Catskills, the Adirondacks, and Niagara Falls became favorite settings for short stories or fictional romances. The opposition between nature and civilization perhaps received its most orthodox treatment in the work of Bryant, his poetry reliant on close observation of nature as a stimulus for romantic reverie. In his "Inscription for the Entrance to a Wood," his advice to the reader to forswear worldly complication and misery in favor of the tranquility of nature is explicit:

> Stranger, if thou has learned a truth which needs
> No school of long experience, that the world
> Is full of guilt and misery, and hast seen
> Enough of all its sorrows, crimes, and cares,
> To tire thee of it, enter this wild wood
> And view the haunts of Nature. The calm shade
> Shall bring a kindred calm, and the sweet breeze
> That makes the green leaves dance, shall waft a balm
> To thy sick heart. Thou will find nothing here
> Of all that pained thee in the haunts of men,
> And made thee loathe thy life.

The writings of Irving and Cooper led to celebrations in the region of the paintings of the Hudson River School of artists. The aesthetic principle behind the Hudson River School was simple: The artist should proclaim the "noble subject." These artists chose as settings the crest of a mountain, tall trees on a lengthy slope, or an expansive river. Natural beauty, however, was not its own excuse for being. The handiwork of nature could invoke "moral impressions," which could stimulate artists on the page as well as on the canvas. Thus, in Asher Durand's most celebrated painting, *Kindred Spirits* (1849), the poet Bryant and the painter Cole, perhaps the foremost Hudson River artist, engage with nature in a moment of communal inspiration. As painters, novelists, and poets celebrated the features of individual settings on or near the Hudson River, travelers—many of whom were from the city—flocked to them. Romantic nature became linked with romantic tourism in an uneasy tension, reflecting the dilemma facing writers of the time, the anxious sense that nature was being degraded under the guise of its glorification. Supposedly pure scenes in nature were celebrated just as they were being visited and perhaps corrupted by tourists who brought their urban values with them. There could have been no more artificial urban dandy than Willis, but he maintained a "country estate" at Idlewild on the banks of the Hudson River. Like other urban aesthetes who cultivated a love for picturesque scenery, he observed how riverfront acreage was being bought up for handsome prices by wealthy businessmen. He sensed the commercial value in romantic nature when he compiled and edited *American Scenery* (1840), a collection of engravings of favorite rustic scenes clearly targeted for middle-class readers.

The appeal to romantic nature was common in early issues of the foremost literary periodical in New York, *The Knickerbocker,* though its values became increasingly urban, cosmopolitan, and traditional. During the early nineteenth century, magazines functioned as mouthpieces for the opinions of their editors, and once Lewis Gaylord Clark assumed sole editorial control of *The Knickerbocker* in 1834 (the periodical had been briefly called *The Knickerbacker*), he dominated its contents and tone. Like many of Irving's works, from whose Diedrich Knickerbocker the magazine took its title, *The Knickerbocker* constituted a kind of literary miscellany. A typical issue might include fiction, sketches, travel writing, verse, humor, and reviews. Each issue was usually topped off with a serving from Clark's "Editor's Table," a feature with which readers came to identify. This column included literary gossip and topical humor, though the opinionated Clark occasionally deviated from his usually convivial tone by serving barbs and insults from his table. Criticism was often reserved for New England writers, particularly the transcendentalists, whose writings incorporated vague theories or literary fashions imported from Germany. Another of Clark's targets was Poe, and one can learn much about the journalistic wars of the 1840s by scanning the pages of *The Knickerbocker* from that decade.

Any writing that smacked of foreign corruption was explicitly scorned—the works of Edward Bulwer-Lytton seemed to Clark to have a decadent tone—and *The Knickerbocker* sounded a generally patriotic tone in its early years. One of its paradoxical features, however, was that despite these early nationalistic appeals, the magazine became increasingly supportive and attentive to British writers. *Knickerbocker* writers were conversant with the British essay tradition practiced by Joseph Addison and Richard Steele in *The Spectator,* keenly sensitive to the appeal of urban life. They revered Charles Dickens, and they expressed enthusiasm for later British essayists—Robert Southey, William Hazlitt, Leigh Hunt, and Thomas De Quincey. If for clarity and transparency of style the model was Addison, then for tone—genial, gently playful, and compassionate—the model was Charles Lamb, celebrated by editor Clark as well as by other *Knickerbocker* contributors. In "On Wit and Humor," an essay for the magazine, Frederick S. Cozzens, one of Lamb's keenest disciples, distinguished the intellectual appeal and pungency of wit from the warmth and pathos evoked by the humorist. Cozzens, whose works appeared in *The Knickerbocker* throughout Clark's term as editor, adapted these principles in his own *Sparrowgrass Papers* (1856), sketches of city dwellers who embark on a sojourn to the country on the banks of the Hudson. Like Frederick W. Shelton's *Up the River* (1853), Cozzens's sketches supposedly offered the attractions of a life close to nature, but their appeal was to the urban (and perhaps suburban) values of the growing readership of *The Knickerbocker*—New Yorkers or suburbanites who might tour or vacation outside the city. Duyckinck may have summed up the appeal of this new form of sketch writing when he said of Cozzens's work: "There is a peculiar style of book, genial, humorous, and warm-hearted, which a race of New Yorkers seems sent into the world specially to keep up."

In *Dangerous Pilgrimages: Transatlantic Mythologies and the Novel* (1996), Malcolm Bradbury attempts to revitalize Irving's image as "the originator of the transatlantic dimension to American letters." Irving, to be sure, became the first American author to be hailed in England; his *Sketch Book* did much to transform foreign attitudes toward American writing, and his later works popularized an image of the United States abroad. For the other side of this transatlantic dialogue, however, one might consult the pages of *The Knickerbocker* to trace a line of influence from Lamb and the British essayists to Irving and his subsequent American imitators. Clark's editorial hand reinforced this lineage in nonfiction prose by welcoming many British authors. Though his own creative works were sparse, he did publish an early tale that contrasts rural and urban values by portraying New York as the "London of America." Through his editorial choices at *The Knickerbocker,* particularly by his championing of an Anglo-American tradition, he did much to transform New York into a cosmopolitan cultural center with London as a model.

In early issues of *The Knickerbocker,* Clark had supported an international copyright law, but he was a moderate on this point, compared to figures in the Young America group, whose most radical spokesman was Mathews. Mathews used the pages of the short-lived *Arcturus* to set forth his fervent opinions on copyright laws and the cause of literary nationalism.

The journal included serial publication of Mathews's *The Career of Puffer Hopkins* (1841–1842), which aimed to establish New York City as a legitimate setting for works of native genius. Though Mathews and his co-editor Duyckinck attracted New England authors such as Longfellow, James Russell Lowell, and Hawthorne as contributors, they wanted to make the vigorous cultural life of New York their focus. In his preface to *The Politicians* (1840), Mathews had directed American writers to "the crowded life of cities, the customs, habitudes, and actions of men dwelling in contact . . . amalgamated into a close but motley society . . . and forming a web infinitely diversified." Rather than the Whig values of polish and refinement, Mathews felt that spontaneity and natural energy were uniquely American traits, which should be hallmarks of American literature. All this was heresy to the conservative Clark and his supporters, and Mathews and Young America were ridiculed in *The Knickerbocker*. Clark, after all, had spent his editorial career praising the career of Irving, whose works represented continuity between Europe and America rather than a distinctive native culture that scorned Old World roots.

After the failure of *Arcturus,* Duyckinck enlisted a young Southerner who had fallen out with Clark, William Gilmore Simms, to the cause of Young America. In addition to a detestation for Clark, they shared a common allegiance to the Democratic Party. After a stint as literary editor of *The New York Morning News,* Duyckinck became an unofficial contributor to *The Democratic Review,* edited by John O'Sullivan. Perhaps more than Duyckinck, whose radical impulses may have been tempered by his family's old Dutch roots, his high church Episcopalianism, and his reverence for British authors, O'Sullivan possessed a firm commitment to a democratic culture for the masses. The better-educated classes, O'Sullivan felt, absorbed antidemocratic sentiments because of their obeisance to English culture. In addition to an unwavering espousal of limited government, *The Democratic Review* focused much attention on literary topics and was unwavering in its opposition to the domination by British writers. The best known of O'Sullivan's contributors was Hawthorne, whose *Mosses from an Old Manse* (1842–1846) appeared in *The Democratic Review.* Works by Bryant, Lynch, Simms, and the young Whitman also appeared in its pages.

Duyckinck continued to promote his brand of literary nationalism in *The Literary World,* which printed Melville's famous "Hawthorne and His *Mosses*" in 1850, although that periodical moderated its stance on the issue after its first year. When Duyckinck began *The Literary World* in 1847, he was editing two series of books for Wiley and Putnam, and he maintained close ties with the major authors of the period. When Rufus W. Griswold's *The Prose Writers of America*–an anthology that included Irving, Cooper, Simms, and Mathews–appeared in 1847, he included a preface in which he offered a reformulation of the principles of literary nationalism. A work could promote the cause of nationalism by being American in spirit, not necessarily in subject matter. An excess of patriotic zeal, he implied, might be a hindrance to artistic expression. One need not resort to a specific kind of vocabulary or particular subject–for example, the American landscape–in order to promote the cause of American letters. Griswold included in his anthology many popular *Knickerbocker* writers, and he scorned two of the pet writers of Young America, Mathews and Simms. Duyckinck responded defensively, but as Miller has noted, *The Prose Writers of America* may have blunted the program and extreme rhetoric of Young America by articulating a conservative brand of literary nationalism, more palatable to the popular taste.

As an anthologist and editor, Griswold was a fairly accurate barometer of popular literary values, and in his role as cultural arbiter, he did not limit himself to the genre of prose fiction. Even before *The Prose Writers of America* he had published a similar collection, *The Poets and Poetry of America* (1842), among other gift books and miscellanies. Few critics today would include Bryant and Halleck in a list of foremost American poets, but in the 1840s they were known as two of "The Copperplate Five," their likenesses reproduced along with those of Longfellow, Dana, and the now forgotten Charles Sprague on the frontispiece of Griswold's volume. Although his brand of Americanism won the praise of Clark, Griswold's safe editorial choices did not sit well with the adherents of the Young America group, nor did they win the approval of those excluded from or slighted in his collections. Poe attacked Griswold on the lecture platform in 1843 and 1844, contributing further to what was already a tense relationship. Their conflicts developed into total rupture as the decade ended, and later resulted in Griswold's calumnies against Poe's reputation after the poet's death in 1849.

Personal animus prevented Griswold from acknowledging Poe's talents, nor could Duyckinck fully grasp the extent of Melville's genius. As influential editors, both men were in the position to mold literary reputations, but they fell short of taking the measure of two writers now considered central to the American Renaissance. The term "American Renaissance" was coined by F. O. Matthiessen as the title for his landmark 1941 book, long regarded as the classic description of an unprecedented outburst of imaginative and creative expression in the 1840s and 1850s.

Matthiessen correlated American literature with European and classical models. Putting his case for native authors straightforwardly, he noted how so many masterworks of American literature were produced in a condensed time span of the antebellum period. In the 1850s alone, Emerson's *Representative Men* (1850) and *English Traits* (1856) appeared along with Thoreau's *Walden* (1854) and Hawthorne's major romances—*The Scarlet Letter* (1850), *The Blithedale Romance* (1851), and *The House of the Seven Gables* (1852). In addition to these works by New England authors, Melville's *Moby-Dick* (1851) and *The Piazza Tales* (1856), and Whitman's first edition of *Leaves of Grass* (1855) also appeared. Matthiessen used the term "renaissance" rather loosely, but the term invoked the great writers of the English Renaissance, thus imposing greater respectability on the study of American literature. If Griswold and his fellow editors had striven to establish standards of taste for their own period, with Matthiessen's book a new canon of major writings in American literature had been formed.

Though *American Renaissance* had a huge influence on the academic study of American literature in the 1950s and 1960s, scholars, especially in the last two decades, have debated Matthiessen's criteria for inclusion, his nearly exclusive focus on five major authors, and the importance of those writers excluded from his overall discussion. Notable by his absence in *American Renaissance* was Poe, who represented to Matthiessen the tragic consequences of isolation, a contrast to those writers who consciously or unconsciously confronted a larger social world. If Whitman's poetry represented an engagement with the ordinary experiences of the common man, Poe's works, according to Matthiessen, suggested an escape from such concerns, a retreat into a realm out of space and out of time. Poe's oeuvre suggested the trappings of an abnormal Romantic temperament, a horror and anxiety generated by a tortured sensibility.

If Matthiessen's treatment of Poe approached caricature, he was fully aware of his own principles of exclusion, as noted in the preface to *American Renaissance*. He noted that his volume could have been titled "The Age of Swedenborg," testimony to a figure whose mystical philosophy inspired Emerson and his circle. The transcendentalists, of course, were influenced by the spirit of reform that gave rise to a host of social experiments and utopian schemes, several of which were centered in New England communities but which also influenced writers and thinkers in New York. New York might have its conservative Knickerbockers, but perhaps its most influential editor was Greeley, a Free Soiler who founded the *New York Tribune* in 1841 with a firm commitment to antislavery

principles. It also had its more radical proponents of Association, that is, supporters of socialist communes following the theories of Fourier. Perhaps the most notable American Fourierist was Albert Brisbane, author of *Social Destiny of Man* (1840) and *Association* (1843). Fourier's ideas also asserted an influence on Charles A. Dana, Parke Godwin, and Stephen Pearl Andrews. Many American works, including Harriet Beecher Stowe's *Uncle Tom's Cabin* (1851–1852) were directly affected by radical social theories that sparked social upheaval in Europe, particularly the revolutions of 1848. Matthiessen invoked a moderate spirit of democracy consonant with the perceived political ideals of the United States. Of the writers covered in *American Renaissance* perhaps only Whitman embraced radical social change, though Matthiessen acknowledged that a book on antebellum letters might well be titled "The Age of Fourier."

Though subsequent scholars of the American Renaissance have critiqued the limits of Matthiessen's treatment, they inevitably use his book as a starting point for their explorations. If he imposed on American literature lines of influence from classical and romantic writing—that is, from Homer to Samuel Taylor Coleridge—subsequent scholars have broadened his perspective on antebellum writing by including humorous and popular authors—for example, T. S. Arthur, Joseph Glover Baldwin, George Washington Harris, and Susan Warner. Matthiessen, noting that his book stressed serious treatments of the common man, acknowledged that the five best-sellers of the antebellum period would not be discussed in *American Renaissance*. Of the scholars who have explored "another American Renaissance," one that gives just dues to women writers and popular authors, perhaps David S. Reynolds's *Beneath the American Renaissance* (1988) offers the fullest complement to Matthiessen in its investigation of formulae rooted in the antebellum cultural context.

Another feature of *American Renaissance* was its focus on three New England authors and two New York authors to the nearly total exclusion of Southern literature. The South, to be sure, was less cosmopolitan and more inner-directed during the antebellum period than was the North—the region of manufacturing and commerce. If Northern writers faced challenges in gaining a foothold for literary ventures, there were even more severe constraints on those who pursued publishing projects in the South. If Southerners, particularly Virginians, had played a pivotal role in the founding of the new nation, the antebellum period marked a withdrawal to defend regional institutions. As Brooks has noted, the South "was committed to a patriarchal mode of life and a primitive system of industry and labor system where progress was the watchword everywhere else, while its economic mainstay, slavery, an obsolete institution, was opposed to the conscience and professions of the American people." The Nat Turner insurrection of 1831 and growing Northern opposition to slavery hardened the will of many Southerners to defend their institutions.

In economic terms Virginia and much of the South retained its colonial character after the American Revolution and perhaps until after the Civil War. The South, in large measure, retained agriculture as the basis of its economy. If consumer goods were needed, they were procured elsewhere—either from abroad or from Northern manufacturers. The South, moreover, lacked urban centers that possessed the commercial status or the cultural amenities to be found in either New York or Boston. If the printing industry did develop—as it did in Richmond, for example—its purpose was to assist in the modest commercial development of the city. In addition to ephemeral imprints—newspapers heavy with advertising, handbills, broadsides, and the like—religious and political tracts that responded to local needs constituted the common fare of Southern publishing. Improved distribution of periodicals in an expanding postal system and in an increasing number of Northern periodicals—many with political views inimical to the plantation system of the South—put Southern writers and editors on the defensive or at a great disadvantage. *The Southern Literary Messenger* of Richmond has justifiably been called the first literary periodical to succeed in the South, but whatever success it achieved must be gauged against the dozens of other failures in periodical ventures in the region. Following *The Southern Literary Messenger,* other Southern periodicals—the *Southern Quarterly Review; The Southern Review,* which helped to give Charleston literary prominence; and later, *De Bow's Review*—served to counter Northern propaganda. To the extent that literary content surfaced in these periodicals, it served to complement the political message of the editors.

A cavalier strain seemed to have been kept alive in Maryland, where a spirit of amusement and merrymaking pervaded some of the clubs and private organizations. Unlike the more-sober debating clubs and library societies of the North, songs of the cavalier poets, for example, might be heard in the Delphian Club of Baltimore, which served as a model for a projected volume of satires by Poe, "Tales of the Folio Club." At the Delphian or at the Thespian Club, where Poe's father had gathered with his traveling theatrical companions, those in attendance met for personal enjoyment as well as for supposed public edification. Members gathered in a spirit of conviviality, consumed ample food and drink, and exchanged ideas on literary topics and cultural fashions. Lectures, perhaps more specialized and occasionally more jocular than those sponsored by local lyceums or library societies, were delivered on topics that derived from the interests of club members. Via his Baltimore connections, Poe got to know the verses of Philip Pendleton Cooke and Edward Coote Pinkney—the latter quoted at length in "The Poetic Principle" (1850).

A more significant Baltimore author who also gave Poe encouragement was John Pendleton Kennedy. Though active in the public life of Baltimore as a lawyer and promoter of its culture, Kennedy maintained ties, via his family connections, with plantations in Virginia—he was related to the Cookes, poet Philip Pendleton, and the romancer John Esten. If Irving had evoked the mythic past of the region near the Hudson River, Kennedy established a similar spirit of nostalgia for the post–Revolutionary world of the Old Dominion (Virginia)—in this case, the area near the James River. Indeed, a clear model for Kennedy's *Swallow Barn* (1851) was Irving's *Bracebridge Hall* (1822). Really a loosely connected series of travel sketches colored by Kennedy's love for the picturesque, *Swallow Barn* celebrates plantation life through the career of his central character, Frank Meriwether, a country squire. The book includes vaguely chivalric episodes of romance, hunting, and horsemanship, but Meriwether is more of a down-to-earth planter-gentleman rather than a larger-than-life hero. The atmosphere of the book is relaxed and sunny, though at its conclusion Kennedy includes a defense of slavery, which the author sees as beneficial to both races and crucial to the survival of a cherished way of life. Perhaps unwittingly, Kennedy's book marked a divergence with the North, for he included in his leisurely tour of the South an argument that was countered in later years by *Uncle Tom's Cabin* and other works.

Swallow Barn established a formula for subsequent literary treatments of the Southern plantation, but Kennedy turned to the genre of historical romance in *Horse-Shoe Robinson* (1835) and *Rob of the Bowl* (1838). The conventions of the historical novel in the United States had been formed with the publication of Cooper's *The Spy* in 1821. If Cooper offered a homegrown model for historical fiction, Kennedy also absorbed the romances of Scott. As heroic events of the past were celebrated, the historical novel became a vehicle for furthering the cause of literary nationalism. The public clearly had an appetite for books based on actual circumstances, and no event could outshine the Revolution in importance, especially in the years before and after the semicentennial of the new nation in 1826. For *Horse-Shoe Robinson* Kennedy chose a setting in the Carolinas and Virginia, based on a journey he had made in 1819.

Swallow Barn was a series of sketches joined together by the "hooks and eyes of a traveler's notes," and Horse-Shoe Robinson was based on his actual travels. Both books may have capitalized on the growing interest in Southern topics and ways of life, part of a vogue of travel literature. The New Yorker Paulding published Letters from the South (1817), and popular novelist Joseph Holt Ingraham offered The South-West, by a Yankee (1835). Such fare won ready acceptance with Northern audiences. The perceived gentility of the South appealed to many Northern readers, since the region represented, according to Paul Zweig in Walt Whitman: The Making of a Poet, "an escape from the arduousness of change, too much busy self-reliance." Some wealthy New Yorkers even looked to the South as a region of polite manners, suggestive of a displaced English tone. During the Civil War, in fact, New York acquired the label of a "Copperhead city," sympathetic to the Southern cause. Despite growing tensions between North and South, Southern romances won the approval of influential editors such as Clark, who liked the wholesome message of national pride they inculcated. Of Kennedy's Rob of the Bowl, Clark commented, "we rise with a stronger detestation of vice, and a new love of virtue; which make us love our country and our fellow creatures better."

About Simms's The Yemassee (1835), Clark was even more enthusiastic: "a successful effort to embody the genuine materials of American Romance—such, indeed, as may not well be furnished by the histories of any other country." This tentative and temporary alliance between Northern editor and Southern romancer is not that surprising, since Simms had close relations with many Northern authors. Though he maintained a plantation on the banks of the Edisto River in South Carolina, he frequented New York in the summers—when he was not in New Haven—and he was an admirer of both Cooper, a pioneer in the use of historical materials, and Bryant, who influenced Simms's verse. Simms styled himself a Southern ambassador in the North, and his alliance with Clark became stronger when his Knickerbocker friends joined him in his opposition to the perceived preeminence of New England authors. Tensions erupted when influential editors such as Griswold omitted Southern writers from landmark anthologies such as The Prose Writers of America. Simms and Clark would eventually have a complete falling out over the issue of literary nationalism, but the former's Views and Reviews in American Literature, History and Fiction (1845) offers essential documents in the Knickerbocker–Young America contest and in its defense of the use of native materials.

Simms's voluminous works are diverse in genre—poems, plays, histories, and biographies—and in setting, American as well as European scenery and manners. After submitting verses with a neoclassical flavor to journals when he was a teenager, he produced two volumes of poetry, a genre for which he manifested affection throughout his lengthy career. He tried his hand at Gothic fiction, and he wrote sketches in imitation of Irving. Some of his stories in The Wigwam and the Cabin (1845) anticipate the techniques of realism, and Poe thought Simms's "Grayling, or Murder Will Out" a superior ghost story. Simms's career hit its stride, however, when he took as his subject matter his native South. He had lived in Charleston, absorbed much of its history, and had long been a student of the past of his region. On his travels he had also been exposed to another aspect of Southern experience—life on the frontier. Inspired by the examples of Scott and Cooper, he wrote a series of "border romances" dealing with historical materials. The first was Guy Rivers (1834), soon to be followed by The Yemassee, his most widely read work of fiction. In his preface he insisted his work was a romance rather than a novel and thus shied away from domestic scenes in favor of a wilder setting. In comparing the romance to the epic in his preface, moreover, Simms perhaps sensed that he was adopting the role of myth-maker for his region, much as Irving had done for New York. In the same year that he published The Yemassee, Simms also published The Partisan (1835), the first of his series that cover the vast historical sweep of the American Revolution in South Carolina, although A. B. Longstreet's Georgia Scenes was also published in 1835.

Perhaps because the economic and social systems of the South and the North were so different, there has been a tendency to study the literary histories of each region separately. Many nineteenth-century anthologies tended to exclude Southern authors, and during the antebellum period, perhaps only Evert A. Duyckinck and George L. Duyckinck's Cyclopædia of American Literature gave any generous recognition to Southern writers. As has already been noted, Matthiessen excluded Southern authors from American Renaissance. The editor hopes that the suggestions for further reading at the end of this volume will invite further investigation of antebellum authors in regional and national contexts.

DLB 250: Antebellum Writers in New York, Second Series, and a companion volume, DLB 248: Antebellum Writers in the South, Second Series, complement DLB 3: Antebellum Writers in New York and the South (1978), edited by Joel Myerson. DLB 3 provided the initial logistical direction, reflected in Myerson's vast editorial and bibliographical experience, for DLB 250.

The editor is grateful to those contributors from *DLB 3* who agreed to expand, revise, or update their entries for this volume: Clifford E. Clark Jr. and Stephen Railton.

Many colleagues from universities across the United States recommended contributors, and the editor owes special thanks to Ralph M. Aderman, Benjamin F. Fisher, Richard Fusco, Kevin J. Hayes, Etta Madden, Katharine McKee, Joel Myerson, Jack Wills, and S. J. Wolfe.

The completion of this project would not have been possible without the cooperation and collaboration of Wesley T. Mott of Worcester Polytechnic Institute (WPI). Throughout the initial phases of planning the table of contents for his own *DLB* volumes on The American Renaissance in New England, Professor Mott shared useful information and helpful suggestions. He also read draft material, and his criticisms helped the editor to construct a stronger introduction for this volume. His gentlemanly assistance, along with the generous help provided by Penny Rock, Margaret Brodmerkle, and Joseph Kaupu at WPI proved invaluable.

The editor also benefited from attending the International Edgar Allan Poe Conference, held in Richmond, Virginia, in October 1999. Individual papers and sessions on antebellum publishing provided background information and insights that were useful in preparing the introduction and supporting materials for this volume. In his role as author and editor, Poe once contemplated using his "The Literati of New York City" in a more-comprehensive series of biographical and critical articles on American writers. In "The Literati of New York City" he offered "honest opinions at random" about his contemporaries in New York City. Hoping eventually to produce a more systematic appraisal of the antebellum literary scene, he envisioned sketches that constituted portraits of "every person of literary note in America," crafted with sensitivity to the individual merits of these authors and written with "rigorous impartiality." Although *DLB 250* does not include entries on every notable author or minor Knickerbocker who practiced in the vicinity of New York City, the editor is confident that the essential values implicit in Poe's lofty plan are reflected in the biographical profiles prepared by his contributors. He hopes as well that their diligence, care, and, above all, their patience will be rewarded in the publication of *DLB 250*.

–Kent P. Ljungquist

Acknowledgments

This book was produced by Bruccoli Clark Layman, Inc. Karen L. Rood is senior editor. Penelope M. Hope was the in-house editor. She was assisted by Nikki La Rocque and Angela Shaw-Thornburg.

Production manager is Philip B. Dematteis.

Administrative support was provided by Ann M. Cheschi, Amber L. Coker, and Angi Pleasant.

Accountant is Ann-Marie Holland.

Copyediting supervisor is Sally R. Evans. The copyediting staff includes Phyllis A. Avant, Brenda Carol Blanton, Worthy B. Evans, Melissa D. Hinton, Charles Loughlin, William Tobias Mathes, Rebecca Mayo, Nancy E. Smith, and Elizabeth Jo Ann Sumner. Freelance copyeditors are Brenda Cabra and Thom Harman.

Editorial associates are Michael S. Allen, Michael S. Martin, and Pamela A. Warren.

Database manager is José A. Juarez.

Layout and graphics supervisor is Janet E. Hill. The graphics staff includes Karla Corley Brown and Zoe R. Cook.

Office manager is Kathy Lawler Merlette.

Photography supervisor is Paul Talbot. Photography editor is Scott Nemzek.

Digital photographic copy work was performed by Joseph M. Bruccoli.

The SGML staff includes Jaime All, Frank Graham, Linda Dalton Mullinax, Jason Paddock, and Alex Snead.

Systems manager is Marie L. Parker.

Typesetting supervisor is Kathleen M. Flanagan. The typesetting staff includes Jaime All, Patricia Marie Flanagan, Mark J. McEwan, and Pamela D. Norton. Freelance typesetter is Wanda Adams.

Walter W. Ross did library research. He was assisted by Jaime All and the following librarians at the Thomas Cooper Library of the University of South Carolina: circulation department head Tucker Taylor; reference department head Virginia W. Weathers; Brette Barclay, Marilee Birchfield, Paul Cammarata, Gary Geer, Michael Macan, Tom Marcil, Rose Marshall, and Sharon Verba; interlibrary loan department head John Brunswick; and interlibrary loan staff Robert Arndt, Hayden Battle, Barry Bull, Jo Cottingham, Marna Hostetler, Marieum McClary, Erika Peake, and Nelson Rivera.

Dictionary of Literary Biography® • Volume Two Hundred Fifty

Antebellum Writers in New York
Second Series

Dictionary of Literary Biography

Stephen Pearl Andrews

(22 March 1812 – 21 May 1886)

Peter Lamborn Wilson

BOOKS: *An Oration, Delivered on the Fourth of July, 1835, Before the East Feliciana Temperance Society* (New Orleans: East Feliciana Temperance Society, 1836);

The Complete Phonographic Class-Book, Containing a Strictly Inductive Exposition of Pitman's Phonography, Adapted as a System of Phonetic Short Hand to the English Language; Especially Intended as a School Book, and to Afford the Fullest Instruction to Those Who Have Not the Assistance of the Living Teacher, by Andrews and Augustus French Boyle (Boston: Phonographic Institution, 1845);

The Phonographic Reader; A Complete Course of Inductive Reading Lessons in Phonography, by Andrews and Boyle (Boston: Phonographic Institute, 1845);

A Lecture on Phonotypy and Phonography; or, Speech-Printing and Speech-Writing (Plymouth, Mass.?, 1846?);

The Phonographic Reporter's First-Book, 3 volumes, by Andrews and Boyle (New York: Andrews & Boyle, 1847);

The Primary Phonotypic Reader: For the Use of Schools and Families, by Andrews and Boyle (New York: Boyle, 1847);

Compendium of Phonography, by Andrews and Boyle (New York, 1848);

Christ's Sermon on the Mount, in Phonography, by Andrews & Boyle (New York: Andrews & Boyle, 1848);

Discoveries in Chinese. A Paper Prepared for the American Ethnological Society (New York, 1849); republished as *Discoveries in Chinese; or, The Symbolism of the Primitive Characters of the Chinese System of Writing* (New York: C. B. Norton, 1854);

The Phonographic Word-Book Number One . . . Intended Immediately to Succeed the Complete Phonographic Class-Book,

Stephen Pearl Andrews (Brentwood Public Library, Brentwood, New York)

and the *Phonographic Reader,* by Andrews and Boyle (New York: Andrews & Boyle, 1849);

The Phonographic Word-Book Number Two . . . Intended Immediately to Succeed the Phonographic Word-Book No. One, and the Phonographic Class-Book and Reader, by Andrews and Boyle (New York: Andrews & Boyle, 1849);

Memorial of Inhabitants of the United States, Praying for the Printing of the Proceeding of Congress in Phonotypy (Washington, D.C.: Office of Printers to the Senate, 1850);

The Science of Society.—no. 1. The True Constitution of Government in the Sovereignty of the Individual as the Final Development of Protestantism, Democracy, and Socialism (New York: W. J. Baner, 1851);

The Science of Society.—no. 2. Cost the Limit of Price: A Scientific Measure of Honesty in Trade, as One of the Fundamental Principles in the Solution of the Social Problem (New York: W. J. Baner, 1851);

A New and Comprehensive French Instructor, by Andrews and George Batchelor (New York: D. Appleton, 1855);

The Practical Pronouncer and Key to Andrews and Batchelor's New French Instructor, by Andrews and Batchelor (New York: D. Appleton, 1856);

The Primary Synopsis of Universology and Alwato, the New Scientific Universal Language (New York: Dion Thomas, 1871);

The Basic Outline of Universology. An Introduction to the Newly Discovered Science of the Universe; Its Elementary Principles; and the First Stages of Their Development in the Special Sciences. Together with Preliminary Notices of Alwato . . . (New York: Dion Thomas, 1872);

The Alphabet of Philosophy (N.p., 1876);

Primary View of the English Standard Phonetic Alphabet (New York, 1876);

The Primary Grammar of Alwato, the New Scientific Universal Language, Growing out of the Principles of Universology (Boston, 1877);

Elements of Universology, an Introduction to the Mastery of Philosophy and the Sciences (New York: S. P. Lathrop, 1881);

Ideological Etymology; or, A New Method in the Study of Words (New York: S. P. Lathrop, 1881);

The Labor Dollar (Boston: B. J. Tucker, 1881).

OTHER: Constitution, Leyes Jenerales, etc. de la Republica de Tejas, translated by Andrews (Houston, 1841);

Josiah Warren, Equitable Commerce: A New Development of Principles as Substitutes for Laws and Governments, edited by Andrews (New Harmony, Ind., 1846);

Love, Marriage, and Divorce, and the Sovereignty of the Individual. A Discussion by Henry James, Horace Greeley, and Stephen Pearl Andrews: Including the Final Replies of Mr. Andrews, Rejected by the Tribune (New York: Stringer & Townsend, 1853; enlarged, Boston: B. R. Tucker, 1889);

Josiah Warren, True Civilization, edited by Andrews (Princeton, Mass.: B. R. Tucker, 1875).

PERIODICALS EDITED: La Aurora, 1 (22 November 1845);

American Phonographic Journal, 1 (January–February 1846);

Anglo Saxon, 1 (5 December 1846); 2 (1 February 1850);

Propagandist, 1 (6 November 1850); 2 (17 November 1852);

American Phonographer, edited with John W. Leonard, 1 (June 1851); 1 (September 1851).

SELECTED PERIODICAL PUBLICATIONS–
UNCOLLECTED: "Phonotypy and Phonography, or Speech-Printing and Speech-Writing," Young American's Magazine, 1 (January 1847): 55–60;

"Principles of Nature, Original Physiocracy, The New Order of Government," Spiritual Age, 1 (20 September 1857);

"The Great American Crisis," Continental Monthly, 9 (December 1863): 658–670; 5 (January 1864): 87–99; 5 (March 1864): 300–317;

"A Universal Language: Its Possibility, Scientific Necessity, and Appropriate Characteristics," Continental Monthly, 5 (May 1864): 532–543;

Woodhull and Chaflin's Weekly, 1 (14 May 1870); 12 (10 June 1876);

"The Pantarchy," Season, New Series, 3 (16 September 1871): 186;

"Civilization a Failure," Golden Age, 1 (29 April 1873): 3;

"The Pantarchy Defined–the Word and the Thing," Banner of Light, 33 (21 June 1873): 3;

"The Introduction of Phonography into America," Browne's Phonographic Monthly, 2 (July 1877): 106–111.

Although Stephen Pearl Andrews's few admirers might well admit that the man is nearly forgotten, his influence remains real and abiding. Andrews was a passionate publicist for nearly every cause of the mid-nineteenth- century reform era–abolition, phonology, universal language, Fourierism, individualist anarchism, phrenology, spiritualism, women's rights, free love, hydrotherapy, communism, temperance, and Swedenborgianism–not to mention his own original contributions to the ferment, Pantarchy and Universology. With the anarchist Josiah Warren he founded Modern Times, one of the more notorious (and perhaps most colorful) of the nineteenth-century utopian communities. He managed the campaign of Victoria Woodhull, the first woman to run for president of the United States. He published the *Communist Manifesto* (1848) of Karl Marx and

Andrews with a specimen of his phonography, a system of shorthand invented by Swedenborgian mystic Isaac Pitman, which Andrews thought would be useful for teaching reading (from Browne's Phonographic Monthly, *July 1877)*

Friedrich Engels for the first time in the United States. Andrews wrote and published incessantly and voluminously. The ideas he supported (such as "Individual Sovereignty") filtered into the mix of American language and persisted when Andrews himself was forgotten. Through his disciple Benjamin R. Tucker, Andrews influenced a whole generation of American anarchists. During the reprint craze of the 1960s and 1970s, many of his works were republished in library editions, and finally he acquired a worthy biographer in Madeleine B. Stern (*The Pantarch: A Biography of Stephen Pearl Andrews,* 1968). If Andrews nevertheless remains "lost," it is not for want of being found again–and again.

Andrews was born in New England–Templeton, Massachusetts–on 22 March 1812 and was named after a maternal uncle, Colonel Stephen Pearl. Andrews's family and friends often called him Pearl. Like many nineteenth-century Reformers, he grew up in an atmosphere of Nonconformist piety. His father, Elisha Andrews, a Baptist minister, lost his Templeton pulpit on a matter of principle and moved to Hinsdale, New Hampshire, when Pearl (youngest of eight children) was only four. His mother, Wealthy Ann Lathrop Andrews, came from another religious New England family. From his father the boy first heard of temperance and pacifism, and he began to learn Latin and Greek with "a smattering of Hebrew, Syriac and Chaldaic"; later in life he claimed to have mastered more than fifty languages. The only source for Pearl's early childhood and youth remains his own unfinished "Autobiography" of about three hundred pages, which languishes in manuscript (some of it faded and stained to illegibility) in the Andrews archive at the Wisconsin Historical Society. But given his later achievements, one may well believe his own description of himself as a gravely serious and precocious child, bullied by "schoolmates and play-fellows" but bold enough to argue his mother into granting shelter to four runaway slaves. "These are my brothers," he told her.

Andrews remembered his two years (1828–1829) at the Amherst Academy's classics department as "one of the happiest" periods of his life. Besides Latin and Greek he immersed himself in French, natural sciences, and theology. He worked too hard, damaged his eyesight, and had to quit–much to his own disappointment. But his older brother Thomas lifted him out of his depression by finding him a job. Pearl's oldest brother, Elisha, had moved to Jackson, Louisiana, and there founded a "Female Seminary." When Elisha died, Thomas took it over and called upon Pearl (and their sister Ann) to come and teach there. In 1830, aged only eighteen, Pearl Andrews

began work as a "professor" of eighty girls only slightly younger than himself, including one–Mary Ann Gordon–who later became his wife. Born and raised an abolitionist, he began to take the step from theory to practice after a slave he had befriended was lynched by Regulators. Then his brother Thomas, who had moved to nearby Clinton to practice law, was attacked and wounded by a proslavery mob. Pearl rushed to help him and defend him, and ended by settling in Clinton to join his brother's law firm. In 1833 Stephen Pearl Andrews was admitted to the Louisiana Bar in New Orleans; two years later he moved there to practice law on his own.

Andrews's first published work–a 4 July 1835 oration delivered to the East Feliciana Temperance Society–appeared in New Orleans. In the same year he also married his first wife and former student, Mary Ann; the couple had three sons. Andrews later published a treatise on Spanish land-grant law, of which not a single copy survives. After four uneventful years he immigrated to the Republic of Texas, where he settled in Houston and found work translating the law code of the republic into Spanish. Meanwhile, however, in an unpublished essay on slavery, he mused, "If I do not believe in Slavery, I must believe in freedom." And belief alone was not enough. Something must be done.

His plan–which he shared with the eminent New Orleans abolitionist Lewis Tappan–had the charm of simplicity: Great Britain would be persuaded to loan Texas a great sum, "say of ten millions of pound sterling . . . if she will alter her constitution and take effectual steps to abolish slavery" in Texas. By 1842 Andrews was ready to launch the scheme at a mass meeting in Houston; despite proslavery heckling from the crowd, he carried the day with "a somewhat brilliant portraiture of the future destiny of Texas as a new and model nation" overflowing with British wealth. But, according to an unpublished manuscript, written years later, "A Private Chapter on the Origin of the [Civil] War," he was thrown out of Galveston and threatened with lynching. In 1843 his house in Houston was mobbed, and he was forced to escape by night with his wife and infant son across flooded prairies. Back in New Orleans he was hounded by the press as a "negrophilist" until he fled north to New York. Despite the violence, Andrews still held hope for his scheme; with the cautious blessings of John Quincy Adams, he and Lewis Tappan set out for England.

Oddly enough, the plan might well have worked. The British Anti-Slavery Society welcomed "the Tappan Committee" with ovations. George Hamilton-Gordon, Lord Aberdeen, the foreign secretary, declared himself in favor after hearing Andrews's plea. Even Henry John Temple, Lord Palmerston, was moved. Various liberal lords and ladies lionized the Americans, and they were cheered in the House of Lords. By the time Andrews returned to America, he had every expectation of success. But the great scheme was ruined by diplomatic machinations carried out in London by the Texas Chargé d'Affaires, Ashbel Smith—chiefly by blackening Andrews's reputation and denying his right to speak for the government of the Republic of Texas. In 1844 a treaty was signed whereby Texas would join the United States as a slave state. Andrews had failed completely, and he later came to feel that this failure constituted one of the true "origins" of the Civil War.

Andrews continued his antislavery agitation as an active member of the Liberty Party (along with Henry B. Stanton and poet John Greenleaf Whittier). While in England, however, he had acquired a new obsession—"phonography," invented by the Swedenborgian mystic Isaac Pitman. Convinced that English spelling was irrational, Andrews believed that freed slaves could make the leap to literacy via the new system of "shorthand." Settled now in Boston, Andrews mastered the art, founded a phonographic institute, and published works by Pitman and himself. (Andrews's *The Complete Phonographic Class-Book, Containing a Strictly Inductive Exposition of Pitman's Phonography, Adapted as a System of Phonetic Short Hand to the English Language; Especially Intended as a School Book, and to Afford the Fullest Instruction to Those Who Have Not the Assistance of the Living Teacher,* published in 1845, marks the first appearance of Pitman shorthand in America.) A few former slaves were taught to read in one month. Andrews acquired students and disciples. A national society was founded; his wife Mary Ann and William Lloyd Garrison both sat on the executive council. Educator Horace Mann was enthusiastic. Magazines were launched; a movement was born. But Andrews seemed unable to take advantage of this apparent success. In 1848 he moved back to New York and opened a phonographic depot. One by one his ventures failed until he was forced to seek other ways to survive. Introducing Pitman shorthand to America was his one great triumph—but instead of freeing minds from the slavery of ignorance, the shorthand was taken up by business secretaries and court stenographers—agents of oppression, in Andrews's opinion. Certainly shorthand became useful when Horace Greeley of the *New York Tribune* hired Andrews to cover senatorial news from Washington (he also reported for the Democratic Party paper *The Union*). But this position was small reward

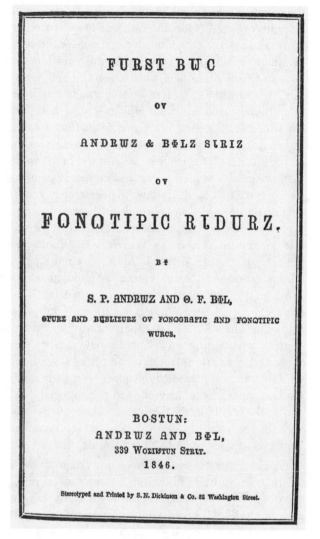

Title page for the first book in Andrews and Augustus French Boyle's series of readers in phonography (New York Public Library, Astor, Lenox and Tilden Foundations)

for "the father of American phonography." Luckily, Andrews had acquired yet another new cause for which to struggle, "Equitable Commerce."

In 1850 Andrews met Josiah Warren in Boston. Another descendant of New England Puritans, Warren was called "the first American anarchist," as E. M. Schuster remarks in her 1932 classic, *Native American Anarchism.* He was also a professional musician and a "Yankee inventor" of genius. A lard-burning lamp had made him a small fortune, which he had sunk in Robert Owen's experimental utopia of New Harmony, Indiana. Warren remained loyal to Owen's ideal community even through its catastrophic collapse; afterward, however, he abandoned philanthropic socialism and decided that the individual, not society, constituted the basic human unit. He coined the slogans "Individual Sovereigntyism," "Equitable Commerce," and "Cost the Limit of Price" to popularize his new and revolutionary system. He founded or attempted to found colonies (Equity and Utopia, both in Ohio), and opened his famous "Time Store" in Cincinnati in 1827. Here he sold goods at wholesale cost (figured in "labor dollars") plus handling (that is, a fee for the *time* needed to process a sale): the venture succeeded, but he was eventually forced out of business by capitalist competitors. In his spare time, Warren invented a new technique for printing stereotype plates, and Andrews at once recognized its usefulness in publishing phonological texts, hitherto a costly and time-consuming process. Andrews was also an instant convert to Warren's economic and political doctrines. Although Andrews continued to admire aspects of Charles Fourier's "Utopian Socialism," he now launched himself on a career as Warren's chief spokesman and publicist and embraced Individualism with all his usual enthusiasm. Using Warren's type fonts, he founded a new journal, *The Propagandist,* to promote libertarian philosophy along with the cause of phonology. Andrews's mature voice made its appearance; he eschewed the editorial "we" and spoke boldly in the first person. The journal survived only from 1850 to 1852, but it launched Andrews as a stylist and a propagandist.

The meeting with Warren proved a decisive moment in Andrews's life; but Andrews was already too old at thirty-eight and too experienced to serve as a mere disciple. He published or presented Warren's views as his own, but he also read the works of Fourier; Claude-Henri de Rouvroy, Comte de Saint-Simon; Emanuel Swedenborg; and Pierre-Joseph Proudhon, as well as Immanuel Kant and Georg Wilhelm Friedrich Hegel, Karl Marx, and Mikhail Aleksandrovich Bakunin. (In the Wisconsin archive a curious manuscript called "Swedenborg and Bakunin" survives as a testament to Andrews's belief in himself as a higher synthesis of these two apparently irreconcilable thinkers.) All these influences and more can be traced in the major work Andrews then produced, *The Science of Society* (1851). The title alone earns him a place among the pioneers of sociology (he also read the works of Auguste Comte), if not recognition as "the father of American Sociology." This book has proved his most enduring and was long kept in print by a mysterious group of Indian anarchists, the Libertarian Socialists of Bombay (who also published both the works of Benjamin Tucker and the ancient Indian Rationalist philosophers).

Andrews begins with a ringing defense of his basic—and still quite controversial—premise, a "science of society":

> The propriety of the use of the term Science, in such a connection, may be questioned by some whom habit has accustomed to apply that term to a much lower range of investigation. If researches into the habits of beetles and tadpoles, and their localities and conditions of existence, are entitled to the dignified appelation of Science, certainly similar researches into the Nature, the wants, the adaptation, and so to speak, into the true or requisite *moral and social habitat* of the spiritual animal called man, must be, if conducted *according to the rigid methods of scientific induction from observed facts, equally entitled to that distinction.*

He goes on to define Individuality as a cosmic principle: "It pervades universal nature. . . . There are no two objects in the universe which are precisely alike. . . . *Infinite diversity is the universal law.* . . . This indestructable and all-pervading Individuality furnishes itself the law, and the only true law, of order and harmony." This philosophy and the anarchist implications of it are clearly derived from Warren. But the use of the word "harmony"—the key term in Fourier, signifying utopian society perfected through Association—reveals that Andrews has not abandoned the possibility of social order for sheer chaos or for the predatory "individualism" of the emerging Capitalists. If Andrews befriended Warren and Tucker, he was also close with Albert Brisbane, the leading American Fourierist. Scholars who classify Andrews simply as a Warrenite Individualist have clearly never bothered to read anything by Andrews. He derived conclusions from his reading of Fourier, whom he—in the preface to *Love, Marriage and Divorce, and the Sovereignty of the Individual. A Discussion by Henry James, Horace Greeley, and Stephen Pearl Andrews: Including the Final Replies of Mr. Andrews, Rejected by the Tribune* (1853)—called "really about the most remarkable genius who has lived." Above all, the idea of "Passional Attraction" proved indispensable to the grand synthesis proposed in *Science of Society.* If every individual can realize his or her true passion in complete freedom, the result will be harmony, not discord—hence the notion of "Attractive Labor" and Fourier's marvelous vision of a world that will produce infinitely more than the present degraded "Civilization" because everyone will work at that which pleases most, rather than merely alienate labor to the highest bidder. (The Wisconsin archive includes a fragment of a utopian novel by Andrews, clearly based on Fourier, in which the hero awakens twenty thousand years in the future and finds himself in a world of Phalansteries.) A delightful passage in *Science of Society* reduces Fourier's grand vision of the gastrosophic orgy to the staid bourgeois bounds of an American dinner party–but the principle remains the same: social harmony at table is realized not through the coercion of law or morality, but voluntarily and spontaneously through attraction. Someone has said that Fourier believed the only true sin was to eat lunch alone. Warren would not have agreed. But Andrews found the via media, or rather the synthesis on a higher plane, between the seemingly opposite views of the Individual Sovereign and the Socialists. Already Andrews saw before him the vistas of a "Universology" that would comprehend and reconcile all contradictions and provide a philosophical basis for the real unity of all true Reform causes, and not merely a "united front."

In the spring of 1851, after a successful Spiritualist séance in which the advice and blessing of ascended souls were showered upon the seekers, Andrews and Warren plunged into plans for yet another American utopia–a village founded on the principles of Equitable Commerce and unfettered Individuality–to be called Modern Times. Sufficient land was purchased in the nearby yet bucolic Pine Barrens of Long Island, and lots were sold at cost to those who responded to the Prospectus. A later version of this text appeared in the *New York Tribune* in 1853:

> We take this method of informing our fellow-citizens, who are desirous of bettering their conditions in life by escaping from hostile competition, and obtaining and retaining for themselves the full results of their own labor, that an opportunity is presented . . . such as we believe exists nowhere else. . . . The object of the settlement *is to furnish an opportunity* to exchange labor equitably (bringing up the labor of women to the same prices as that of men) according to the plan expounded in "The Science of Society," by Andrews, and "Equitable Commerce" and "Practical Details in Equitable Commerce," by Warren.
>
> There is no combination or association, but certain cooperative advantages are offered, which, . . . persons are free to accept or reject. The settlers on the ground at the opening of this spring, all comfortably housed, and beginning to establish various trades and branches of business, are about 70. . . . There are great facilities for building here. . . . The climate is salubrious and delightful.

According to John Humphrey Noyes in his *History of American Socialisms* (1870), "Owen begat New Harmony; New Harmony (by reaction) begat Indi-

vidual Sovereignty; Individual Sovereignty begat Modern Times; Modern Times was the mother of free love, the Grand Pantarchy and the American branch of French Positivism." Noyes, himself the founder of the Perfectionist community at Oneida, one of the most successful and most controversial (for its practice of "complex marriage") of all the American utopias, spoke from intimate knowledge of the whole Reform scene. French Positivism was indeed represented at Modern Times by Henry Edger, Comte's chief American disciple. The Pantarchy was actually a somewhat later development. But Modern Times became most famous for its practice of free love; indeed, it became notorious. Nevertheless, most fads, social systems, radical diets, and styles of dress associated with reform (for example, bloomers) had an exponent at Modern Times. The doctrine of Individuality allowed for infinite eccentricity and endless experimentation. Andrews's colleague Orson S. Fowler (brother of Lorenzo, the other "father of American Phrenology") published plans in 1848 for an octagonal house, which played the same role in the Reform era as the geodesic dome in the 1960s. Two of these buildings survive at Modern Times (or Brentwood, its present name). Warren invented an inexpensive way to make bricks. Edward Newberry practiced both phrenology and dentistry. Moncure Daniel Conway visited and later wrote a novel with scenes set in Modern Times, *Pine and Palm* (1887). (He said the place was to be reached either "by railroad or rainbow" and gave it the Rabelaisian motto "Fay ce que voudras" [Do as thou wilt].) The English anarchist Ambrose Caston Cuddon visited, making a link with Bakunin. Thomas Low Nichols and his wife Mary Gove Nichols, hydrotherapists and mystics, proposed founding an institute at Modern Times and loudly proclaimed their adherence to Free-Love-ism. Marriage vanished and was replaced by a free-and-easy sexuality. Women who were sleeping with someone wore a red thread tied to a finger; its absence signaled readiness for a new affair. Andrews gave full support to these doctrines, so detestable to Anthony Comstock and other zealous crusaders against vice; in fact, Andrews engaged in public debate on the subject with Horace Greeley and Henry James Sr. (the Swedenborgian/ Fourierist father of the novelist) in the letters column of the *New York Tribune;* the letters–including several long Andrusian screeds that Greeley had refused to print–appeared as *Love, Marriage and Divorce,* edited by Andrews. New York newspapers sent reporters, who stirred up scandal over Modern Times. They found a blind German parading naked in the street; a woman who ate only beans until she died; astrolo-

Sketch of the utopian community created by Andrews and Josiah Warren on Long Island, New York
(A. J. Macdonald Papers, Yale University Library)

gers and alchemists; polygamists; and above all, "notorious" free lovers. Warren was in despair; he had no objection to such practices but saw no reason to dangle them like red rags before the bull of social prejudice and the envy of repressed puritans. He ceased to be a presence in the village he had founded. The Panic of 1857 put an end to Modern Times; its name was changed to Brentwood in 1864, and the community sank into obscurity. A diehard remnant immigrated to South America to start over again. But many colonists stayed on in Brentwood, quietly treasuring memories of freedoms and pleasures unknown to most poor humans. Like Oneida and Brook Farm, Modern Times had been a happy place to live.

As usual, Andrews was undaunted by failure. He began holding a salon at home, then moved it into rented quarters under the name "League Union of the Men of Progress." The growing group spun off various "Grand Orders" devoted to various causes, but the most successful proved to be the Grand Order of Recreation. The group for conversation and genteel fun was moved into its own quarters at 555 Broadway, over a saloon, and renamed "The Club"; it quickly became known as the Free Love Club. In fact, Greeley (now an enemy of Andrews) arranged for the *New York Tribune* to denounce the club under the rubrics of "Individual Sovereignty . . . in the sexual relations . . . free love . . . Passional Attraction." On 18 October 1855 the club was raided by the vice squad, and several members (including Albert Brisbane but not Andrews, who happened to be absent at the time) were carted off to the "Tombs," a notorious prison in New York, to languish overnight—an incident not recounted in Brisbane's *Mental Biography,* which he dictated to his wife in his dotage.

Andrews's wife Mary Ann died the same year, leaving him a widower with three young sons to care for. In his grief he undertook a drastic "hunger cure," a fast of epic proportions, which Stern believes brought him "closer to the 'lunatic fringe.'" A year later he married one of his disciples, Esther Hussey Bartlett Jones, a talented Spiritualist medium. Andrews loved her deeply; when she, too, predeceased him (in 1871) he published an obituary in which he wrote that "she excels Mary, 'the Mother of God.'" By this time Andrews believed himself to be a sort of messiah (or "demi-messiah," as Fourier was called by his adherents).

In 1855 Andrews began yet another project, a "Brownstone Utopia" or "Unitary Home," organized in some buildings on Fourteenth Street in New York. In effect, this home was a sort of communal hotel or boardinghouse for Individual Sovereigns—such as an apostate monk, a homeopathic physician, an opera baritone, and many authors, including Charles Wentworth Upham, Charles Robert Maturin (author of *Melmoth the Wanderer* [1821]), and the poet Edmund Clarence Stedman. Henry Harland, who later became an editor of the English periodical *The Yellow Book,* was born there in 1861, son of Andrews's disciple Thomas Harland and his stepdaughter Irene. The Unitary Home was a practical idea and lasted for years, but Andrews did not rest content. He launched his new obsessions there and made the home the headquarters of his Grand Pantarchy (a political system based on Andrews's blend of Warren and Fourier, in which he himself naturally occupied the position of Grand Pantarch—the title by which he is best remembered). To make clear the principles upon which Pantarchy was based—such as a universal religion, a universal code of law, and a universal language—he developed a new science, "Universology," and composed some of his most important works (at least in his own opinion), including *The Primary Synopsis of Universology and Alwato, the New Scientific Universal Language* (1871) and *Elements of Universology, an Introduction to the Mastery of Philosophy and the Sciences* (1881). The whole ensemble is reminiscent of Fourier: it has the same style of grandiose titles, the same obsession with numerology, the same impulse to explain everything through one vast and all-embracing system—and the same lack of success.

As an example of the scientific applications of Universology, Andrews was proudest of his breakthrough in language. He had always been obsessed with languages, claimed to have mastered most of them (he lectured on Chinese philology), and believed that all were imperfect reflections of a perfect and universal language, hitherto unknown to humanity. Andrews's techniques for establishing this language, which he called Alwato, were rather more Platonic than Aristotelian. Helped by a handful of fervent disciples at the Normal University of the Pantarchy, he *intuited* the real universal ur-sounds of consciousness itself and dictated them in a state of sheer inspiration. Alwato was probably Andrews's greatest failure; no more than two or three people ever learned it. The most approachable work on the subject is his *Primary Synopsis of Universology and Alwato.*

Victoria Woodhull ended her long and astonishing career in England—married to a rich aristocrat, sunk in religious fanaticism, and denouncing Stephen Pearl Andrews as a diabolical influence. But in 1870 she was thirty-two years old, beautiful, and highly successful. Raised in the Midwest by a confidence-trickster father, she and her sister Tennessee Claflin

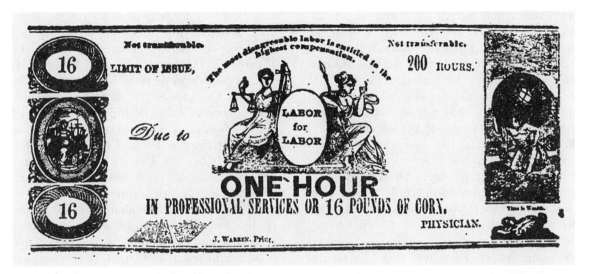

The Labor Dollar created by Andrews for use in bartering (East Hampton Library, East Hampton, New York)

spent their girlhood as itinerant Spiritualist mediums, giving public performances while "channeling" such dead luminaries as Demosthenes. The spirits directed them to New York. Somehow, the sisters earned the friendship and patronage of "Commodore" Cornelius Vanderbilt, who set them up on Wall Street as the first female stockbrokers in American history. Money poured in, and the "bewitching brokers" decided to launch a journal, *Woodhull & Claflin's Weekly*. Casting about for editorial assistance, they found Andrews, now barred from all the major papers and overjoyed at a chance to disseminate his teachings. The journal survived for six years and achieved notoriety as an organ for free love, feminism, Universology, anarchism, and a plethora of other causes. As *Woodhull & Claflin's Weekly* began to veer to the Left, Vanderbilt lost interest and dropped the sisters. Undismayed, they plunged into scandal and politics under the slogan "Progress! Free thought! Untrammeled Lives!" Thomas Nast caricatured Victoria Woodhull as "Mrs. Satan."

For a while Andrews even moved into the luxurious Woodhull mansion on Thirty-eighth Street as resident philosopher. Roused to enthusiasm by the Paris Commune, Andrews and the two sisters applied for membership in the International Workingman's Association and were granted a charter for a new "Section 12" in New York. *Woodhull & Claflin's Weekly* published *The Communist Manifesto* for the first time in America (30 December 1871). A huge parade in commemoration of the Paris Commune was organized and carried out with great publicity. But when Karl Marx in London heard about the Free-Love anarchist "pseudo-Communists," "sensation-loving

spirits," and "bourgeois intellectuals" who had wormed their way into the IWA, he arranged for Section 12 to be suppressed. Never at a loss, the group simply reformed as a political party and decided to nominate Victoria Woodhull as a candidate for president of the United States.

Since women were still forbidden to vote, the notion of electing a woman president seemed rather quixotic. But it was not simply a stunt. Victoria Woodhull was already president of the Spiritualist Association, and Spiritualists were already committed to reform; moreover, she appeared before a congressional hearing in Washington, where she delivered a rousing address (probably written by Andrews) in support of women's right to vote. This speech stirred great enthusiasm among the suffragists, especially the influential Susan B. Anthony. Only by a miracle could Woodhull hope to be elected, but for a short while she seemed a plausible leader of a potentially widespread and growing movement. Most Americans have forgotten that nineteenth-century feminism was in some ways even more radical than the modern version. As Andrews said at a Women's Rights Convention in May 1871, "it is no longer the suffrage question but the social question entire, and the complete social enfranchisement of the sexes, which are to be discussed and vindicated on this platform." But post–Civil War feminism was in the process of retreat from its radical premises. The suffragists had indeed reduced the struggle to one isolated issue–voting rights–in the belief that nothing could be done about "the social question entire" without political power. As for free love or economic reform, Susan B. Anthony and her

A letter to Theodora Freeman Spencer from Andrews, writing in Alwato, the universal language he invented
(from Madeleine B. Stern, The Pantarch: A Biography of Stephen Pearl Andrews, *1968)*

followers feared (probably correctly) that inherent American conservatism would reject suffrage if it were linked to such dangerous causes. Woodhull proclaimed at Steinway Hall, "Yes! I am a free lover! I have an inalienable, constitutional, and natural right to love whom I may, to love as long or as short a period as I can, to change that love every day if I please!" Anthony abandoned the Equal Rights Party after that speech. By the time of Woodhull's nomination in May 1872 (with Frederick Douglass as her running mate) the press was taking her hopeless cause as a joke. But to Anthony Comstock it was no laughing matter. By election time he had managed to have Woodhull arrested and jailed for sending obscene literature through the mail.

Woodhull's misfortune grew out of the once-famous but now forgotten "Beecher-Tilton Scandal." Henry Ward Beecher, famous for his eloquent liberal sermons at fashionable Plymouth Church in Brooklyn, had supposedly engaged in secret adultery with one of his own parishioners, Elizabeth Tilton, wife of Andrews's friend and fellow-phonographer, Theodore Tilton. In 1870 Elizabeth confessed her sin to her husband, who angrily revealed the story to feminist Elizabeth Cady Stanton, who told the story to Woodhull. Beecher's sister, Harriet Beecher Stowe, had attacked Woodhull under a thin veneer of caricature in her novel *My Wife and I* (1871). Beecher himself, however, had spoken in favor of free love. Woodhull was piqued by his hypocrisy, not his "sin." If Beecher loved Elizabeth Tilton, he should proclaim his love from the pulpit, not hide it in shame. In the 2 November 1872 issue of the *Woodhull & Claflin's Weekly* she accused Beecher. Never had the paper sold so many copies. One of them reached Comstock, the self-appointed censor of the American postal system; Woodhull went to jail; and the paper was briefly suppressed.

Three years later Theodore Tilton sued Beecher, and the case came to trial. Andrews was called as a witness. Great revelations of Free-Lovism were anticipated, but Andrews—always glad of a chance to talk—set the courtroom adoze with lengthy digressions on phonology, Chinese philology, the hidden causes of the Civil War, Universology, Alwato, and other set pieces. Beecher was exonerated and returned to his pulpit. Henry James Sr. and Andrews once again took up their cudgels in the columns of *Woodhull & Claflin's Weekly,* but the whole fiasco brought about a cooling of relations between the Pantarch and Woodhull. Victoria Woodhull's great American career was exhausted, and eventually she removed herself to Europe.

The Beecher-Tilton scandal marked the zenith of Andrews's fame, or rather "notoriety," as the papers always expressed it. In the last decades of his life he sank into obscurity. Tall, bearded, hawk-visaged, prophetic, he became one of the great American eccentrics. In fact, like Walt Whitman (another former Fourierist), Andrews might well be considered one of the pioneers of New York's "bohemia"; he even lived for a while on Waverly Place in Greenwich Village. A small coterie of admirers perhaps reinforced his own messianic self-image. He persevered with Alwato (publishing *The Primary Grammar* in 1877) and found a home for his interfaith New Catholic Church in a rented hall on Fourteenth Street at Fifth Avenue.

Among the loyal few the most valuable was "the youngest Pantarchist" (as Stern calls him), Benjamin R. Tucker, who launched a magazine, *The Radical Review* (1877), and offered Andrews an outlet for such works as his essay on "The Labor Dollar." Andrews and Tucker defended Ezra Heywood (the Free-Love anarchist) against the perverse persecution of Comstock, pushed Proudhonian critiques of property, and encouraged the flickering flames of utopianism. In 1876 Andrews published *The Alphabet of Philosophy:* "All the ideas we possess . . . are evolved from a primitive Single Pair of Ideas," Kant's Something and Nothing, or "Aughty and Naughty," a "*Somethingized* Nothing" and a "*Nothingized* Something."

Andrews lost one of his sons in the Civil War, but his son Charles, a successful dentist, provided Andrews not only with a home but also with respect, even going so far as to present a paper on dental terms in Alwato to the American Dental Association. The Manhattan Liberal Club on Fifteenth Street offered a podium and eventually a vice presidency to the venerable Pantarch. Ezra Heywood's Union Reform League invited Andrews to address its conventions in Princeton, Massachusetts, and adopted many of his planks into its radical platform of land and currency reform, free love and free speech, and labor unionism. In 1881 the league actually elected Andrews as its president. He published in fugitive journals such as *Popular Science News* and *The Truth Seeker*. With a relative of his mother, S. P. Lathrop, Andrews founded a publishing company and republished old works along with *The Elements of Universology*. In 1882 he helped start yet another club, the Colloquium, where liberal ministers and rabbis rubbed shoulders with outright freethinkers and mystics, and even the president of Rutgers College, G. W. Samson (who later delivered a eulogy at Andrews's funeral). In the "Colloquium Document

No. 1" Andrews summed up his entire philosophy: "In things proven, Unity; in whatsoever can be doubted, Free Diversity; in things not trenching upon others' rights, Liberty; in all things, Charity." The Colloquium dissolved a year before Andrews's death. Sick and bedridden as he was, he continued to pour out new essays, published by Lathrop as the Universal Tract Society Tracts with such titles as *Protestantism, Libertarianism, and Democracy, The Universal Church of the New Order,* and *The One Alphabet for the Whole World.* Charles Codman, an old Modern Timer still living in Brentwood, offered Andrews a country retreat, but he returned restlessly to New York. Theodore Spencer, a devotee (and possibly the only person ever to master Alwato) dissuaded Andrews from announcing himself as the reincarnation of Christ. On 21 May 1886, after adding a few last touches to his unfinished manuscript "Dictionary of Alwato," he closed his eyes "with a smile of recognition" (as reported in *The Truth Seeker*). Benjamin Tucker, now editor of his famous journal *Liberty,* offered the most moving eulogy: "More mental force went out with him than is left in any one person on the planet"; and he predicted that *The Science of Society* would be remembered when Alwato, Universology, and the Pantarchy were long forgotten.

But Andrews was forgotten almost at once. His grave at Woodlawn Cemetery was dug up for nonpayment of rent in 1890 and the body transferred to an unmarked plot. At his death one journalist wrote, "The world at large is unable to determine whether he was a crank or the founder of a great system of philosophy." The world at large soon made up its mind. Every once in a while a scholar or anarchist has tried to revive Stephen Pearl Andrews's memory as a great and forgotten ancestor of all lovers of liberty. But no niche has been found in American literature for the man who once proclaimed, "The moment that we put arbitrary limits upon freedom, there is no freedom."

Biography:

Madeleine B. Stern, *The Pantarch: A Biography of Stephen Pearl Andrews* (Austin: University of Texas Press, 1968).

References:

Mary Gabriel, *Notorious Victoria: The Life of Victoria Woodhull, Uncensored* (Chapel Hill, N.C.: Algonquin Books of Chapel Hill, 1998);

Carl J. Guarneri, *The Utopian Alternative: Fourierism in Nineteenth-Century America* (Ithaca, N.Y.: Cornell University Press, 1991);

Seymour R. Kesten, *Utopian Episodes: Daily Life in Experimental Colonies Dedicated to Changing the World* (Syracuse, N.Y.: Syracuse University Press, 1993);

John Humphrey Noyes, *History of American Socialisms* (Philadelphia, 1870).

Papers:

The papers of Stephen Pearl Andrews are held by the Wisconsin Historical Society in Madison. Some material is also found in the Benjamin R. Tucker Papers and the Rare Book Room at the New York Public Library, Forty-Second Street Branch. Other miscellaneous holdings may be found at the Public Library of Brentwood, Long Island, New York. The Brentwood Historical Society has extensive holdings on Modern Times.

T. S. Arthur

(6 June 1809 – 6 March 1885)

Joseph F. Goeke
University of South Carolina

See also the Arthur entries in *DLB 3: Antebellum Writers in New York and the South,* *DLB 42: American Writers for Children before 1900,* and *DLB 79: American Magazine Journalists, 1850–1900.*

BOOKS: *The Heiress,* 2 volumes, anonymous (New York: Harper, 1834);

The Young Wife's Book; A Manual of Moral, Religious, and Domestic Duties (Philadelphia: Carey, Lea & Blanchard, 1836);

Insubordination; A Story of Baltimore, anonymous (Baltimore: Knight & Colburn, 1841); also published as *Insubordination; An American Story of Real Life,* anonymous (New York: Colman / Baltimore: Knight & Colburn, 1841); republished as *Insubordination; or, The Shoemaker's Daughters, An American Story of Real Life* (Philadelphia: Berford, 1844);

The Widow Morrison: A Leaf from the Book of Human Life, anonymous (Baltimore: Knight & Colburn / New York: Giffing, 1841); republished in *Alice; or, the Victim of One Indiscretion* (1844);

The Ruined Gamester; or, Two Eras in My Life, anonymous (Philadelphia: Anners, 1842);

Six Nights with the Washingtonians: A Series of Original Temperance Tales (Philadelphia: Godey & M'Michael, 1842); *The Broken Merchant, and Other Tales,* 2 volumes (Boston: Colman, 1842); republished as *Temperance Tales, or, Six Nights with the Washingtonians,* 2 volumes (Philadelphia: H. F. Anners, 1849); revised and enlarged as *The Tavern-Keeper's Victims; or, Six Nights with the Washingtonians* (Philadelphia: Leary, Getz, 1860); enlarged again as *Six Nights with the Washingtonians; and Other Temperance Tales* (Philadelphia: Peterson, 1871);

Tired of Housekeeping (New York: Appleton, 1842);

The Story Book for Girls and Boys (Boston: Carter, 1842); republished as *The Story Book* (Philadelphia: Godey & M'Michael, 1843);

Bell Martin; or, The Heiress (Philadelphia: Burgess & Zieber, 1843); revised as *Bell Martin: An American Story of Real Life* (Philadelphia: Anners, 1843?);

Fanny Dale; or, The First Year After Marriage (Philadelphia: Burgess & Zieber, 1843); republished as *Fanny Dale; or, A Year After Marriage* (Philadelphia: Anners, 1847); republished as *A Year After Marriage* (Philadelphia: Peterson, 1854);

The Ladies' Fair, How to Be a Gentleman, and Other Tales (Philadelphia: Godey & M'Michael, 1843);

Madeline; or, A Daughter's Love and Other Tales (Philadelphia: Anners, 1843);

Making a Sensation, and Other Tales (Philadelphia: Godey & M'Michael, 1843);

Pride or Principle: Which Makes the Lady? anonymous (Philadelphia: Anners, 1843);

The Seamstress, a Tale of the Times, anonymous (Philadelphia: Berford, 1843);

The Stolen Wife; An American Romance, anonymous (Philadelphia: Berford, 1843);

Married and Single; or, Marriage and Celibacy Contrasted in a Series of Domestic Pictures (Philadelphia: Anners, 1843);

Lovers and Husbands: A Story of Married Life (Philadelphia: Anners, 1843);

Sweethearts and Wives; or, Before and After Marriage (New York: Harper, 1843);

The Ruined Family and Other Tales, bound with *Swearing Off and Other Tales* (Philadelphia: Godey & M'Michael, 1843);

The Tailor's Apprentice: A Story of Cruelty and Oppression, anonymous (Philadelphia: Godey & M'Michael, 1843);

The Little Pilgrims: A Sequel to The Tailor's Apprentice, anonymous (New York: Burgess & Stringer, 1843; Philadelphia: Godey & M'Michael, 1843);

The Two Merchants; or, Solvent and Insolvent (Philadelphia: Burgess & Zieber, 1843);

The Village Doctors, and Other Tales (Philadelphia: Godey & M'Michael, 1843);

Alice; or, The Victim of One Indiscretion, bound with *Mary Ellis; or, The Runaway Match* (New York: Allen, 1844; Philadelphia: Berford, 1844; Boston: Brainard, 1844); *Alice; or, The Victim of One Indiscretion* republished as *Alice Melville; or, The Indiscretion,* bound with *Mary Ellis; or, The Runaway Match* (Philadelphia: Anners, 1850);

Cecilia Howard; or, The Young Lady Who Had Finished Her Education (New York: Allen, 1844);

Family Pride, or, The Palace and the Poor House. A Romance of Real Life (Philadelphia: Lindsay & Blakiston, 1844);

Hints and Helps for the Home Circle; or, The Mother's Friend, as Mary Elmwood (New York: Allen, 1844);

Hiram Elmwood, the Banker; or, "Like Father, Like Son" (New York: Allen, 1844);

The Lady at Home; or, Leaves from the Every-Day Book of an American Woman, as Mrs. Mary Elmwood (New York: Allen, 1844); republished as *The Young Lady at Home: A Series of Home Stories for American Women* (Philadelphia: Evans, 1847); republished as *The Lady at Home; or, Happiness in the Household* (Philadelphia: Peterson, 1853);

The Martyr Wife: A Domestic Romance, anonymous (New York: Allen, 1844);

Prose Fictions. Written for the Illustration of True Principles, in Their Bearing upon Every-Day Life, 2 volumes (Philadelphia: Zieber, 1844);

The Two Sisters; or, Life's Changes, anonymous (Philadelphia: Zieber, 1844);

Anna Milnor, the Young Lady Who Was Not Punctual, and Other Tales (New York & Philadelphia: Ferrett, 1845);

The Club Room, and Other Temperance Tales (Philadelphia: Ferrett, 1845);

The Maiden; A Story for My Young Country-Women (Philadelphia: Ferrett, 1845); republished in *The Three Eras in a Woman's Life: The Maiden, Wife and Mother* (Boston: Crown / Philadelphia: Anners, 1848); republished again in *Anna Lee . . .* (London & New York: Nelson, 1871);

The Mother (Philadelphia: Anners, 1845); republished in *The Three Eras in a Woman's Life* (Philadelphia: Anners, 1848); republished again in *Anna Lee . . .* (London & New York: Nelson, 1871);

The Two Husbands and Other Tales (Philadelphia: Ferrett, 1845);

The Wife: A Story for My Young Countrywomen (Philadelphia: Ferrett, 1845); republished in *The Three Eras in a Woman's Life* (Philadelphia: Anners, 1848); republished again in *Anna Lee . . .* (London & New York: Nelson, 1871);

The Beautiful Widow (Philadelphia: Carey & Hart, 1847);

A Christmas Box for the Sons and Daughters of Temperance (Philadelphia: Sloanaker, 1847);

Debtor and Creditor; A Tale of the Times (New York: Young, 1847; New York: Collins, 1847);

Keeping Up Appearances; or, A Tale for the Rich and Poor (New York: Baker & Scribner, 1847);

Riches Have Wings; A Tale for the Rich and Poor (New York: Baker & Scribner, 1847);

Young Music Teacher and Other Tales (Philadelphia: Anners, 1847);

Retiring from Business; or, The Rich Man's Error (New York: Young, 1847);

Advice to Young Ladies on Their Duties and Conduct in Life (Boston: Phillips & Sampson, 1848);

Advice to Young Men on Their Duties and Conduct in Life (Boston: Howe, 1848);

Agnes; or, The Possessed: A Revelation of Mesmerism (Philadelphia: Peterson, 1848);

Love in a Cottage (Philadelphia: Peterson, 1848);

Lucy Sandford: A Story of the Heart (Philadelphia: Peterson, 1848);

Making Haste to Be Rich; or, The Temptation and Fall (New York: Baker & Scribner, 1848);

Rising in the World; A Tale for the Rich and Poor (New York: Baker & Scribner, 1848);

Temptations: A Story for the Reformed (New York: Oliver, 1848);

Love in High Life: A Story of the "Upper Ten" (Philadelphia: Peterson, 1849);

Mary Moreton; or, The Broken Promise (Philadelphia: Peterson, 1849);

Our Children: How Shall We Save Them? (New York: Oliver, 1849);

Sketches of Life and Character (Philadelphia: Bradley, 1849);

All for the Best; or, The Old Peppermint Man: A Moral Tale (Boston: Crosby & Nichols, 1850);

The Debtor's Daughter; or, Life and Its Changes (Philadelphia: Peterson, 1850);

The Divorced Wife (Philadelphia: Peterson, 1850);

Golden Grains from Life's Harvest Field (Philadelphia: Bradley; Lowell, Mass.: Crown, 1850);

Illustrated Temperance Tales, includes autobiographical sketch (Philadelphia: Bradley / Lowell, Mass.: Crown, 1850); revised and enlarged as *The Lights and Shadows of Real Life* (Philadelphia: Potter, 1850);

The Orphan Children; a Tale of Cruelty and Oppression (Philadelphia: Peterson, 1850);

Pride and Prudence; or, The Married Sisters (Philadelphia: Peterson, 1850);

True Riches and Other Tales (Philadelphia: Potter, 1850);

The Two Brides (Philadelphia: Peterson, 1850);

The Young Artist; or, The Dream of Italy (New York: Dodd, 1850);

The Banker's Wife; or, Like Father Like Son (Philadelphia: Peterson, 1851);

Confessions of a Housekeeper, as Mrs. John Smith (Philadelphia: Lippincott, Grambo, 1851); revised and enlarged as *Trials and Confessions of an American Housekeeper* (Philadelphia: Lippincott, Grambo, 1854); enlarged and republished as *Ups and Downs; or, Trials of a Housekeeper* (Philadelphia: Lippincott, 1857); and as *Trials and Confessions of a Housekeeper* (Philadelphia: Evans, 1859);

Home Scenes, and Home Influence: A Series of Tales and Sketches (Philadelphia: Lippincott, Grambo, 1851);

Lessons in Life, for All Who Will Read Them (Philadelphia: Lippincott, Grambo, 1851);

Off-Hand Sketches, a Little Dashed with Humour (Philadelphia: Lippincott, Grambo, 1851);

Seed-Time and Harvest; or, Whatsoever a Man Soweth, That Shall He Also Reap (Philadelphia: Lippincott, Grambo, 1851);

Stories for My Young Friends (Philadelphia: J. & J. L. Gibon, 1851);

Stories for Parents (Philadelphia: Lippincott, Grambo, 1851);

Stories for Young Housekeepers (Philadelphia: Lippincott, Grambo, 1851);

The Tried and the Tempted (Philadelphia: Lippincott, Grambo, 1851);

The Two Wives; or, Lost and Won (Philadelphia: Lippincott, Grambo, 1851);

The Way to Prosper; or, In Union There Is Strength, and Other Tales (Philadelphia: Bradley, 1851);

A Wheat-Sheaf Gathered from Our Own Fields, by Arthur and F. C. Woodworth (New York: Dodd, 1851);

Woman's Trials; or, Tales and Sketches from the Life around Us (Philadelphia: Lippincott, Grambo, 1851);

Words for the Wise (Philadelphia: Lippincott, Grambo, 1851);

The History of Georgia, from Its Earliest Settlement to the Present Time, by Arthur and W. H. Carpenter (Philadelphia: Lippincott, Grambo, 1852);

The History of Kentucky, from Its Earliest Settlement to the Present Time, by Arthur and Carpenter (Philadelphia: Lippincott, Grambo, 1852);

The History of Virginia, from Its Earliest Settlement to the Present Time, by Arthur and Carpenter (Philadelphia: Lippincott, Grambo, 1852);

Our Little Harry, and Other Poems and Stories (Philadelphia: Lippincott, Grambo, 1852);

Pierre, the Organ-Boy, and Other Stories (Philadelphia: Lippincott, Grambo, 1852);

The Poor Woodcutter, and Other Stories (Philadelphia: Lippincott, Grambo, 1852; Halifax, U.K.: Milner & Sowerby, 1855);

The Ways of Providence; or, "He Doeth All Things Well" (Philadelphia: Lippincott, Grambo, 1852);

Who Are Happiest? and Other Stories (Philadelphia: Lippincott, Grambo, 1852);

Who Is Greatest? and Other Stories (Philadelphia: Lippincott, Grambo, 1852);

Before and After the Election; or, The Political Experience of Mr. Patrick Murphy, as Patrick Murphy (Philadelphia: Bradley; Boston: Crown, 1853);

Cedardale; or, The Peacemakers (Philadelphia: Lippincott, Grambo, 1853);

Finger Posts on the Way of Life (Boston: Crown / Philadelphia: Bradley, 1853);

The Fireside Angel (Boston: Crown, 1853);

Haven't-Time and Don't-Be-in-a-Hurry and Other Stories (Philadelphia: Lippincott, Grambo, 1853);

Heart-Histories and Life-Pictures (New York: Scribner, 1853);

The History of New Jersey, from Its Earliest Settlement to the Present Time, by Arthur and Carpenter (Philadelphia: Lippincott, Grambo, 1853);

The History of New York, from Its Earliest Settlement to the Present Time, by Arthur and Carpenter (Philadelphia: Lippincott, Grambo, 1853);

The History of Vermont, from Its Earliest Settlement to the Present Time, by Arthur and Carpenter (Philadelphia: Lippincott, Grambo, 1853);

Home Lights and Shadows (New York: Scribner, 1853); republished as *Shadows and Sunbeams* (Boston: Crown, 1854; Philadelphia: Bradley, 1854);

The Home Mission (Boston: Crown; Philadelphia: Bradley, 1853);

Iron Rule; or, Tyranny in the Household (Philadelphia: Peterson, 1853);

The Last Penny and Other Stories (Philadelphia: Lippincott, Grambo, 1853);

The Lost Children and Other Stories (Philadelphia: Lippincott, Grambo, 1853);

Maggy's Baby and Other Stories (Philadelphia: Lippincott, Grambo, 1853);

Married Life; Its Shadows and Sunshine (Philadelphia: Lippincott, Grambo, 1853);

The Old Man's Bride (New York: Scribner, 1853);

Sparing to Spend; or, The Loftons and Pinkertons (New York: Scribner, 1853);

The String of Pearls, for Boys and Girls, by Arthur and Woodworth (Auburn, N.Y.: Derby & Miller, 1853; Buffalo: Derby, Orton & Milligan, 1853);

Trials of a Needlewoman (Philadelphia: Peterson, 1853);

Uncle Ben's New Year's Gift and Other Stories (Philadelphia: Lippincott, Grambo, 1853);

The Wounded Boy and Other Stories (Philadelphia: Lippincott, Grambo, 1853);

The Angel of the Household (Philadelphia: Bradley / Auburn, N.Y.: Yates, 1854; New Haven, Conn.: Bradley, 1854); revised and enlarged as *The Angel of the Household and Other Tales* (Philadelphia: Evans, 1858);

The History of Connecticut, from Its Earliest Settlement to the Present Time, by Arthur and Carpenter (Philadelphia: Lippincott, Grambo, 1854);

The History of Illinois, from Its Earliest Settlement to the Present Time, by Arthur and Carpenter (Philadelphia: Lippincott, Grambo, 1854);

The History of Ohio, from Its Earliest Settlement to the Present Time, by Arthur and Carpenter (Philadelphia: Lippincott, Grambo, 1854);

The History of Pennsylvania, from Its Earliest Settlement to the Present Time, by Arthur and Carpenter (Philadelphia: Lippincott, Grambo, 1854);

The History of Tennessee, from Its Earliest Settlement to the Present Time, by Arthur and Carpenter (Philadelphia: Lippincott, Grambo, 1854);

Ten Nights in a Bar-Room, and What I Saw There (Boston: Crown, 1854; Philadelphia: Lippincott, Grambo, 1854; Philadelphia: Bradley, 1854);

The Good Time Coming (Boston: Crown, 1855; Philadelphia: Bradley, 1855);

Trial and Triumph; or, Firmness in the Household (Philadelphia: Peterson, 1855);

What Can Woman Do? (Philadelphia: J. W. Bradley, 1856);

The Withered Heart (Boston: Crown, 1857; Philadelphia: Bradley, 1857);

The Angel and the Demon: A Tale of Modern Spiritualism (Philadelphia: Bradley, 1858);

The Hand But Not the Heart; or, The Life Trials of Jessie Loring (New York: Derby & Jackson, 1858);

The Little Bound-Boy (Philadelphia: Bradley, 1858);

Steps toward Heaven; or, Religion in Common Life: A Series of Lay Sermons for Converts in the Great Awakening (New York: Derby & Jackson, 1858);

Lizzy Glenn; or, The Trials of a Seamstress (Philadelphia: Peterson, 1859);

The Allen House; or, Twenty Years Ago and Now (Philadelphia: Potter, 1860);

Light on Shadowed Paths (Philadelphia: Potter, 1860);

Hidden Wings and Other Stories (New York: Sheldon, 1864);

Out in the World. A Novel (New York: Carleton, 1864);

Sowing the Wind and Other Stories (New York: Sheldon, 1864);

Sunshine at Home and Other Stories (New York: Sheldon, 1864);

Home-Heroes, Saints, and Martyrs (Philadelphia: Lippincott, 1865);

Nothing But Money, a Novel (New York: Carleton, 1865);

What Came Afterwards: A Novel, Being a Sequel to "Nothing But Money" (New York: Carleton, 1865; London: Hotten, 1865);

The Lost Bride; or, The Astrologer's Prophecy Fulfilled (Philadelphia: Peterson, 1866);

Our Neighbors, in the Corner House. A Novel (New York: Carleton / London: Hotten, 1866);

After the Storm (Philadelphia: Potter, 1868);

After a Shadow and Other Stories (New York: Sheldon, 1868);

The Peacemaker, and Other Stories (New York: Anderson, 1868);

Heroes of the Household (Philadelphia: Lippincott, 1869);

Not Anything for Peace and Other Stories (New York: Sheldon, 1869);

The Seen and the Unseen (Philadelphia: Lippincott, 1869);

Rainy Day at Home (Boston: Lothrop, 1870);

Talks with a Philosopher on the Ways of God with Man (Philadelphia: New Church Tract and Publication Society, 1870);

Tom Blinn's Temperance Society and Other Tales (New York: National Temperance Society, 1870);

Idle Hands and Other Stories (Philadelphia: Porter & Coates, 1871);

Orange Blossoms, Fresh and Faded (Philadelphia: Porter & Coates, 1871; Philadelphia: Stoddart / New York: Gibson, 1871);

Arthur as a young man (engraving by William G. Armstrong)

The Wonderful Story of Gentle Hand and Other Stories (Philadelphia: Stoddart, 1871);

Three Years in a Man-Trap, anonymous (Philadelphia: Stoddart, 1872);

Cast Adrift (Philadelphia: Stoddart / Cincinnati: Queen City / N.Y.: Gibson / Boston: Maclean / Chicago: Miller / New Castle, Pa.: Stewart / San Francisco: Dewing, 1873);

Comforted, anonymous (Philadelphia: Lippincott, 1873);

Woman to the Rescue; A Story of the New Crusade (Philadelphia: Stoddart / Chicago: Western Publishing / Boston: Smith / San Francisco: Bancroft, 1874);

Danger; or, Wounded in the House of a Friend (Philadelphia: Stoddart / Chicago: Western Publishing / Boston: Smith, 1875);

The Bar-Rooms at Brantley; or, The Great Hotel Speculation (Philadelphia: Porter & Coates, 1877);

Strong Drink; The Curse and the Cure (Philadelphia: Hubbard / St. Louis: Thompson / San Francisco: Bancroft, 1877); republished as *Grappling with the Monster; or, The Curse and the Cure of Strong Drink* (New York: Lovell, 1877);

The Latimer Family; or, The Bottle and the Pledge and Other Temperance Stories (Philadelphia: Peterson, 1877);

The Wife's Engagement Ring (New York: National Temperance Society, 1877);

The Mill and the Tavern (New York: National Temperance Society, 1878);

The Strike at Tivoli Mills and What Came of It (Philadelphia: Garrigues, 1879);

Feet and Wings; or, Among the Beasts and Birds with Uncle Herbert, as Uncle Herbert (Philadelphia: Lippincott, 1880);

Window Curtains (New York: Ogilvie, 1880);

Saved as by Fire; A Story Illustrating How One of Nature's Noblemen Was Saved from the Demon of Drink (New York: Lovell, 1881);

The Little Savoyard and Other Stories: A Collection of Instructive and Entertaining Sketches for Young Readers (New York: Worthington, 1891).

OTHER: *The Baltimore Book: A Christmas and New Year's Present,* edited by Arthur and W. H. Carpenter (Baltimore: Bayly & Burns, 1838);

The Snow Flake: A Gift for Innocence and Beauty, edited by Arthur (New York & Philadelphia: Ferrett, 1846);

Random Recollections of an Old Doctor, edited by Arthur (Baltimore: Taylor, 1846);

Wreaths of Friendship: A Gift for the Young, edited by Arthur and Woodworth (New York: Baker & Scribner, 1849);

The Brilliant: A Gift Book for 1850, edited by Arthur (New York: Baker & Scribner, 1850);

The Sons of Temperance Offering, edited by Arthur (New York: Nafis & Cornish, 1850, 1851);

Friends and Neighbours; or, Two Ways of Living in the World, edited by Arthur (Chicago: Keen & Lee, 1856; Cincinnati: Derby, 1856; Philadelphia: Peck & Bliss, 1856);

The Mother's Rule; or, The Right Way and the Wrong Way, edited by Arthur (Cincinnati: Derby, 1856; Philadelphia: Peck & Bliss, 1856; Rochester, N.Y.: Darrow, 1856);

Our Homes: Their Cares and Duties, Joys and Sorrows, edited by Arthur (Philadelphia: Peck & Bliss, 1856; Rochester, N.Y.: Darrow, 1856);

The Wedding Guest: A Friend of the Bride and Bridegroom, edited by Arthur (Chicago: Keen & Lee, 1856; Philadelphia: Peck & Bliss, 1856; Rochester, N.Y.: Darrow, 1856; St. Louis: Edwards & Bushnell, 1856);

Words of Cheer for the Tempted, the Toiling, and the Sorrowing, edited by Arthur (Chicago: Keen & Lee, 1856; Philadelphia: Peck & Bliss, 1856; Rochester, N.Y.: Darrow, 1856);

Little Gems from the Children's Hour, edited by Arthur as Uncle Herbert (Philadelphia: Lippincott, 1876);

The Prattler: A Picture and Story Book for Boys and Girls, edited by Arthur as Uncle Herbert (Philadelphia: Lippincott, 1876);

The Budget: A Picture and Story Book for Boys and Girls, edited by Arthur as Uncle Herbert (Philadelphia: Lippincott / New York: Lovell, 1877); excerpted in *Lucy Grey and Other Stories for Boys and Girls,* edited by Arthur as Uncle Herbert (Philadelphia: Lippincott, 1880);

The My Books, edited by Arthur as Uncle Herbert (Philadelphia: Lippincott, 1877)—includes *My Primer, My Pet Book,* and *My Own Book;*

The Playmate. A Picture and Story Book for Boys and Girls, edited by Arthur as Uncle Herbert (Philadelphia: Lippincott, 1878);

The Boys' and Girls' Treasury: A Picture and Story Book for Young People, edited by Arthur as Uncle Herbert (Philadelphia: Lippincott, 1879); excerpted in *Sophy and Prince and Other Stories for the Young,* edited by Arthur as Uncle Herbert (Philadelphia: Lippincott, 1881);

Uncle Herbert's Speaker and Autograph-Album Verses, edited by Arthur as Uncle Herbert (Philadelphia: Ruth, 1886).

PERIODICALS EDITED: *Baltimore Athenaeum and Young Man's Paper,* edited by Arthur & J. N. McJilton (1834–1836);

Baltimore Monument, continued as *Baltimore Literary Monument,* edited by Arthur & McJilton (1836–1839);

Baltimore Saturday Visiter, edited by Arthur (1837–1840);

The Ladies Magazine of Literature, Fashion and the Fine Arts, edited by Arthur (February 1844–July 1844);

Arthur's Magazine, edited by Arthur (1844–1846);

Arthur's Home Gazette, edited by Arthur (1850–1853);

Arthur's Home Magazine, edited by Arthur (1852–1885);

Children's Hour, edited by Arthur as Uncle Herbert (1867–1874);

The Workingman, edited by Arthur (1870–1872).

Cultural scholars often group T. S. Arthur with other didactic and reform writers as an author representative of those who fed the literary mainstream in the mid nineteenth century. Two popular works of temperance fiction, however, set his name somewhat apart. The first of these, *Six Nights with the Washingtonians: A Series of Original Temperance Tales* (1842), is a series of tales prompted by Arthur's attendance at early meetings of the Washington Temperance Society in Baltimore. The second, better-known work—*Ten Nights in a Bar-Room, and What I Saw There* (1854)—gives a graphic narration of the career of a small-town tavern and the devastation it causes in the lives of the townspeople. The latter of these two works has frequently been labeled the *Uncle Tom's Cabin* of the nineteenth-century temperance movement—a moral crusade that ultimately led to Prohibition in the United States. In conjunction with Arthur's many contributions to the temperance cause, his prolific output of mainly domestic novels and tales from the 1840s through the 1870s made his name a household word; one calculation suggests that he produced more than 5 percent of American fiction in the 1840s. The brand of didactic storytelling that appeared in Arthur's books and in his periodicals was trusted not to taint but to strengthen the home circle with an ever-present moral purpose. Nonetheless, although his fiction predominantly confirmed popular conceptions and urged proper behavior, Arthur's enthralling examples of the wrong path often gave his books their greatest popular appeal.

As a writer, journalist, publisher, and editor—first in Baltimore, then in Philadelphia—Arthur spent much of his life in connection with others of the same profession. Most notably, he moved within the same circle as Edgar Allan Poe, while Poe lived in Baltimore, and later published some of Poe's work. But Arthur's writings received more popular attention and earned more money during his own lifetime than did those of several of his contemporaries who are now considered major literary figures. His work was formulated for success, especially among women of the rising middle class, for whom a literary market had been determined by periodicals such as *Godey's Lady's Book* and Arthur's own *Arthur's Home Magazine,* which enjoyed a long run, from 1852 to 1898. The life of that magazine and the printing of at least a million copies of his books by 1860 indicate that Arthur prospered in supplying the wants of his audience.

Timothy Shay Arthur was born the second son to Anna Shay Arthur and William Arthur on 6 June 1809. The family then lived on a small farm near Newburgh, New York, and eventually grew to include at least two more sons and a daughter. Arthur's parents named him in honor of his maternal grandfather, Timothy Shay, who served as a volunteer militiaman under George Washington in the Revolutionary War. William Arthur worked as a miller, but his earnings provided only a limited education for his children. Therefore, as a young boy, Arthur was primarily schooled at home in Scripture, while unsteady health and natural shyness kept him most often in the company of his mother. In 1817 William and Anna Arthur moved their family from the Hudson valley to Baltimore, and there Arthur first attended formal school, at the age of nine. His teacher, however, considered him a dull boy as he struggled with the fundamentals of arithmetic and grammar. After Arthur spent about four years in school and worked with his father at the mill, his teacher advised

An issue of the popular monthly magazine Arthur founded to offer readers moral entertainment

William to find the boy a trade instead of further education. The death of William Arthur in the fall of 1822 resolved the matter, and Arthur at the age of fourteen was apprenticed to a tailor in order to relieve his widowed mother of the need to provide for him.

Several of Arthur's publications reflect the years he spent working for a master tailor. Some examples are *The Seamstress, a Tale of the Times* (1843), *The Tailor's Apprentice: A Story of Cruelty and Oppression* (1843), *Trials of a Needlewoman* (1853), and *Lizzy Glenn; or, The Trials of a Seamstress* (1859). These stories owe their subject matter to personal experience, but their style ordinarily conforms with other fiction of that time that urged social and labor reform through the exposé of urban strife. Accordingly, the influence of Charles Dickens frequently surfaces in these works, especially the earlier ones, in which character types and the occasional in-depth description seem patterned after those of the popular English author. *The Tailor's Apprentice,* which Arthur published anonymously, offers the story of Isaac, "a sickly-looking boy, whose large, thoughtful earnest eyes, frequently sought the face" of his widowed mother. Because of his mother's illness, Isaac is apprenticed at the age of eleven to "old Hard Paws" John Stoat, a tyrannical and physically abusive tailor whose mischievous apprentices—all older than Isaac—provide some comic relief. Published in the same year as Dickens's "A Christmas Carol," Arthur's story includes a brief subplot in which one of the boys, Tom Manly, plays a prank on an old miser named Jack Moneypenny. By disguising himself as a ghost, Tom extorts money from the terror-stricken landlord to pay for a cast-out tenant's funeral. Similar antics put on by a shoemaker's apprentices appear in one of Arthur's earliest published tales, *Insubordination; A Story of Baltimore* (1841). However, the majority of Arthur's later writing consists less of humor and more of the didactic, sentimental fiction characterized in Isaac, who eventually runs away from Stoat's shop.

Like Isaac, Arthur may have wished to escape from his own long indenture as a tailor's apprentice, for upon the threshold of his adult life he was unable to proceed to the level of journeyman. In a brief autobiography he reports, "Defective sight compelled me to give up the trade I had been acquiring for over seven years." During that time Arthur had read many books and studied on his own when not required at the shop, but his efforts had been spent "more to gratify a desire for knowledge than to gain information with the end of applying it to any particular use." Now that he could not see well enough to thread needles or sew fine stitches, Arthur accepted a friend's offer of employment at a counting room. There he worked for three years while continuing to improve his reading and writing in leisure hours. Then, in 1833, Arthur left his friends at the counting room after persuading the president of a banking company to hire him as a bookkeeper. The job required him to travel to New York on occasion, and his efficiency ultimately earned him a better position in Louisville, Kentucky, where he transferred in the summer of 1833. This brief stint as a man of the world provided material for many of the stories that Arthur went on to write, including *Hiram Elmwood, the Banker; or, "Like Father, Like Son"* (1844), *Debtor and Creditor; A Tale of the Times* (1847), and *Retiring from Business; or, The Rich Man's Error* (1847). Throughout Arthur's fiction, readers can find industrious, enterprising businessmen, whose actual work is often vague or unnamed and whose characters may be equally undistinguished. These men fill the roles of husband, father, lover, and even narrator, as is the case in *Ten Nights in a Bar-Room, and What I Saw There*. Thus, the badge of "businessman" often serves as an emblem of worth for other characters within a story and for the reading audience, although readers may also find merchants or traders in the same story who suffer great losses as a result of financial speculation. This flash of prestige, with its potentially treacherous undercurrent, parallels the time Arthur spent in Louisville. He had been working there ambitiously for only a few months when his employer's bank failed, and as a result of its collapse, Arthur returned to Baltimore jobless in the autumn of 1833.

By the winter of 1833–1834, however, an unexpected literary opportunity arose in Baltimore. "At this point in my life," Arthur explains, "I was induced, in association with a friend who was as fond of writing as myself, to assume the editorial charge of a literary paper." This weekly periodical, *The Baltimore Athenaeum and Young Men's Paper,* introduced Arthur and his friend, John McJilton, into the society of other striving and moderately successful writers, editors, and journalists in Baltimore. One coterie of such men converged regularly at the Seven Stars Tavern near Marsh Market Space in the warehouse district of Baltimore. This group–drawn together by their common connection as contributors to the *Baltimore Saturday Visiter*–called themselves the Seven Stars, after their favorite haunt. Among them were several notable and eccentric figures. John Lofland, the self-described "Milford Bard," was a man of some medical experience, a poet-for-hire, a deep drinker, and later a confessed opium addict. Branz Mayer, then a scholar from St. Mary's College and world traveler, later thrived as an historian. McJilton, Arthur's partner in editing, also wrote humorous pieces as "Giles McQuiggen" and drank with these men. Finally, there were Poe–then a bright but struggling writer who had recently distinguished himself by winning a contest in the *Saturday Visiter* with his story "MS. Found in a Bottle"–and Arthur, the future champion of temperance.

Years later, a critic marked the difference between Arthur and Poe in the 29 July 1843 edition of the Philadelphia *Saturday Courier* by making this claim: "Contrasted with that excellent and plain–yet eloquent and pathetic story teller, T. S. Arthur–Mr Poe loses in comparison, as far as the applicability of his Tales is concerned, for the very general reading of the extended multitude. But for learning, uniqueness and originality–we unhesitatingly say that Edgar A. Poe, in his own country, stands entirely alone." Poe himself offered a less forgiving appraisal of his Baltimore acquaintance in 1841 upon examining Arthur's signature as part of a popular series of articles on the autography of reputable figures. There, in the pages of *Graham's Magazine* below a woodcut reproduction of Arthur's autograph, Poe wrote, "Mr. Arthur is not without a rich talent for description in low life, but is uneducated, and too fond of mere vulgarities to please a refined taste. . . . His hand is a commonplace clerk's hand, such as we might expect him to write. The signature is much better than the general MS."

Although Poe's disdainful remarks on Arthur's education and mundane subject matter are generally accurate, Arthur later established a reputation for himself as a writer and editor in spite of his shortcomings. After Poe left Baltimore, Arthur continued as the editor of the *Athenaeum* until 1836, when he and McJilton assumed editorial control of another magazine–the *Baltimore Literary Monument*. In these early years of his literary career, Arthur read many articles that later fed his

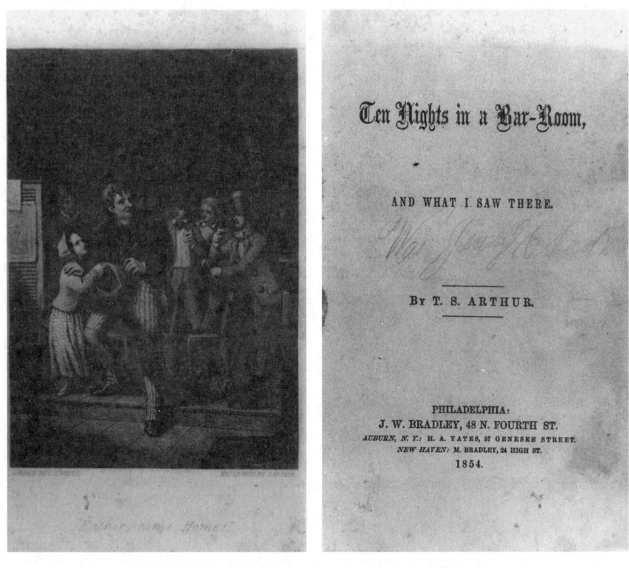

Frontispiece and title page for Arthur's 1854 temperance tale about a small-town tavern

fiction, including reports and excerpts on Swedenborgianism, temperance, and the new "science" of animal magnetism.

In the same year that he became editor of the *Baltimore Literary Monument*, Arthur married Eliza Alden, a woman seven years younger than himself and the daughter of an affluent Baltimore family. The role of husband drew Arthur further into the domestic sphere, and his first publication in *Godey's Lady's Book*–"The Soft Answer, A Domestic Tale" (1837)–reflected his new situation. The moral theme of this piece fit well in the pages of Louis Godey's magazine, and in that style, Arthur recognized the opportunity for success and advancement. He continued to build his commitment toward literature for the home by editing *The Baltimore*

Book: A Christmas and New Year's Present (1838) with his friend W. H. Carpenter. Gift books such as this one, which included Poe's tale "Siope," often gained more popularity for their ornate binding and illustrations than for their literary content, but their material success made them a regular product of Arthur's career.

Despite these steady advances, however, Arthur's family grew faster than his income, with two sons by 1840 and another child on the way. After his purchase of the *Baltimore Saturday Visiter* in 1837 and the termination of the *Baltimore Literary Monument* following McJilton's departure in 1839, Arthur's pockets were drained considerably. To mend the situation, he sold the waning *Saturday Visiter* and took employment as a writer for a political magazine, *The Baltimore Merchant*. Political journalism held little appeal for Arthur, but one assignment intrigued him. In recent months, talk about a new temperance group in Baltimore had grown remarkably. The Washington Temperance Society had been formed by six drinking buddies in need of a positive change, and their small group had burgeoned into a public association of reformed drunkards who stayed sober by recruiting others and telling their own stories at the society's meetings. Working for *The Baltimore Merchant,* Arthur observed several of the Washingtonians' early meetings and wondered at their popularity as well as the success of their approach to temperance as the movement quickly spread to other cities.

In 1841 Arthur and his family moved to Philadelphia, as Arthur's fiction had begun to gain popularity in the larger, nationwide periodicals. Philadelphia—home of Louis Godey and many other publishers—became Arthur's home, also, but he had not forgotten his experience in Baltimore among the Washingtonians. In this new town, which remained his home for the rest of his life, Arthur began earning money as a regular writer for *The Saturday Evening Post,* while also contributing pieces to various other magazines and assembling a collection of tales that eventually became *Six Nights with the Washingtonians.* Arthur's own visits to Washingtonian meetings serve as the thread for this series of first- and third-person accounts illustrating the evils of alcohol and the redemption of drunkards who signed the Washingtonian pledge of total abstinence. In these pages readers may find drunken revelry, bloated stupor, extreme cases of delirium tremens, broken families, and early death by intoxication. The repetition of the drunkard's steady downward spiral brings variation in the brand of drunken atrocity or the depth of inebriation. Released in 1842, the same year as Walt Whitman's *Franklin Evans,* another Washingtonian work, Arthur's collection of tales profited from the peak of Washingtonian enthusiasm. As he states in the preface, "Many of the very experiences to which the writer alludes have since been related by these pioneers, in almost every city in the Union, and the whole country can now attest their power to move the heart." Arthur's book helped to carry the temperance movement toward a fever pitch, and his tales continued to build temperance fiction as a genre, the imagery and devices of which appeared in now famous works by such writers as Herman Melville, Nathaniel Hawthorne, Poe, and Whitman.

Along with the success of *Six Nights with the Washingtonians,* Arthur's conversion to Swedenborgianism in 1842 exerted great influence on his future work. This form of Christianity, founded by Emanuel Swedenborg, the eighteenth-century Swedish mystic and scientist, had its broadest American following when Arthur became a part of it. Swedenborgian principles and moral beliefs give the foundation to most of Arthur's instructive tales after 1845, and *The Good Time Coming* (1855) stands as his strongest effort to disseminate Swedenborgian doctrine. In that novel Arthur plays on a familiar theme of failure in business followed by redemption in the home circle. Edward Markland, a businessman eager for fame and fortune, invests a large portion of his funds in a Central American mining expedition, which ends in ruin when a trusted representative fleeces the operation and disappears. While Markland neglects his family for business matters and even contemplates suicide after his financial loss, some curiously Swedenborgian neighbors offer friendly spiritual advice to his wife and eldest daughter. One of these people, Mr. Allison, delivers an abstract sermon to Fanny Markland, Edward's daughter, on corresponding natural and spiritual substances—a cornerstone of Swedenborgian thought. Such thinly veiled lectures in *The Good Time Coming* led one reviewer in the *New York Criterion* to profess: "Mr. Arthur's writings, though not of a high order, have yet generally had a certain genial character and domestic tone which have given them a wide circulation. The new volume before us, however, is calculated to be very mischievous. The author verges on Spiritualism, Swedenborgianism, and Reichenbachism, if not actually engulfed." While this "mischief" may have seemed uncharacteristic of Arthur's writing, speculation about the traditional rift between science and spirituality was not uncommon in literature of the time. Other works by Arthur, such as *Agnes; or, The Possessed: A Revelation of Mesmerism* (1848) and *The Angel and the Demon: A Tale of Modern Spiritualism* (1858) are evidence of his forays into the area of what might now be called paranormal phenomena.

Domestic, instructive fiction constituted the bulk of Arthur's work, though, and he gained prominence on the bookshelves and reading tables of American homes by writing and editing reams of stories to be read at the family hearth. By 1844, he had begun publishing *Arthur's Magazine,* in which many of his own tales and others like them first met the public. Notwithstanding the general domestic content, some variety did appear; for example, Arthur printed Poe's "The Sphinx," despite Poe's earlier harsh treatment of Arthur. After a two-year run, however, *Arthur's Magazine* was purchased in 1846 by Louis Godey, who then merged it with his own magazine. Not until 1850—after a period of confinement because of nervous exhaustion—did Arthur begin his next periodical, which he named *Arthur's Home Gazette,* ostensibly proclaiming his commitment to the domestic sphere. Within two more years, this weekly paper was also retired, in favor of a monthly called *Arthur's Home Magazine.*

Frontispiece and title page for a bound volume of the children's magazine Arthur founded (University of South Florida Library)

By this time, the name T. S. Arthur was well known, and it offered a guarantee of moral entertainment to readers. In fact, when posthumous attacks on Poe's reputation were circulating, Arthur used his position as a friend of the home circle to defend his former acquaintance in the December 1858 issue of his magazine. "In the name of decency," he declares, "if not humanity, let the outrage cease. We may trace to unbridled passion and depraved appetite and not to evil purpose, most of the sad errors of his existence." Arthur could make this demand for decency with considerable credibility, since his magazine appealed to so many readers by virtue of its moral content. To be sure, *Arthur's Home Magazine* continued to be published longer than almost any other nineteenth-century American periodical. Consequently, Arthur stood in reach of a vast audience, of whom the majority were women.

Since he was an author of neither great insight nor ingenuity, Arthur's message to these women tended to reinforce traditional feminine roles, except where moral duty might call them beyond the domestic sphere. An example of Arthur's ineffective reasoning on

the roles of women appears in his introduction to *What Can Woman Do?* (1856) when he asserts, "A large proportion of the wrong woman suffers in the present constitution of society may be fairly set down as the fault of women. Not so much to the women of this as of the preceding generation; for the men of the time are, *to a certain degree,* what their mothers have made them." He employs a similar logic in a story from *Orange Blossoms, Fresh and Faded* (1871)—a gift book intended to instruct newlywed couples so that they would not become jaded in marriage. After a maiden named Mary tells her married friend Bella that her husband has been riding about town with another woman, Mary convinces Bella that she should take better care of her physical appearance to guard against infidelity. Bella reacts by bathing, arranging her hair, and putting on a clean dress with "a small lace collar, scarcely whiter than her pure neck." When the husband comes home and is impressed by Bella's new look, Arthur takes the opportunity to instruct his readers: "And she thus saved him, in his younger and less stable years, from being drawn aside from the right way, and both herself and him from years of wretchedness." In this way, Arthur frequently assigns to women the duty of protecting their men from moral ruin.

Anna Lee Hartley, the heroine of *The Three Eras in a Woman's Life: The Maiden, Wife and Mother* (1848), represents Arthur's ideal moral woman. Anna makes no mistakes; her sons are not raised to be depraved men; and her husband remains faithful as well as sober. As a paragon for nineteenth-century women, Anna leads her own life, respecting "duty before pleasure." Meanwhile, a weaker friend elopes with a scheming drunkard; a proud neighbor squanders her husband's money; and another neighbor's daughter becomes a shameless coquette. This simple strategy of contrasting the good with the bad appears throughout Arthur's fiction as his most frequently employed literary technique, and although the characters are static and two-dimensional, the moral contrast proved successful with his readers. Because Arthur always strikes the comparison from the perspective of good characters, readers get the chance to indulge their curiosity about scandal or ruin while joining themselves with domestic heroes and heroines.

As for the place of women outside the home, Arthur seems to endorse only one purpose with any enthusiasm—that is, temperance reform. In *Woman to the Rescue; A Story of the New Crusade* (1874) and *The Bar-Rooms at Brantley; or, The Great Hotel Speculation* (1877) women are seen fighting publicly in their efforts at teetotalism. They leave their homes with the express purpose of drawing their sons and husbands back to them from the taverns. A pair of mothers in *The Bar-Rooms at Brantley* go so far as to become obsessed, attempting the assault and murder of local tavern keepers. One character justifies the action of a woman confined to an asylum, saying, "If she were my wife, I would bring her home, and give her liberty of the town. Desperate diseases, you know. A second aim might hit the mark." Although Arthur is careful not to voice such support for violent measures himself, he allows this bystander to speak without reproach. Such extreme action in the name of good would seem rather strange anywhere in Arthur's fiction, except regarding temperance. Arthur felt a sort of passion for this movement—originally founded on principles of moderation—which grew to demand the legal prohibition of alcohol.

Ten Nights in a Bar-Room, and What I Saw There remains Arthur's best-remembered attempt to draw the veils from the eyes of "the poor, ragged, emaciated drunkard" and the tavern keeper who provided his drinks. In this melodramatic novel, Simon Slade, a former miller who opens the Sickle and Sheaf Tavern, "sows the wind and reaps the whirlwind" in the small town of Cedarville. An anonymous businessman relates the ten-year decline of this once prosperous community as reflected in a series of his stays at the Sickle and Sheaf. Parallel with most of Arthur's temperance writings, a great deal of blame is pushed in the faces of tavern keepers and legislators, while working-class inebriates are often portrayed as victims. One Cedarville native—a fellow businessman of the narrator—assumes this perspective as he voices the growing demand for prohibition: "We are called fanatics, ultraists, designing, and all that, because we ask our law-makers to stay the fiery ruin. Oh, no! we must not touch the traffic. All the dearest and best interests of society may suffer; but the rum-seller must be protected."

Despite these political views that continually emerge in the text, Arthur's novel made its mark on American literary history more by its hyperbolic portrayals of delirium and drunken violence. A stage version of the book written in 1858 by William Pratt capitalized on these highly dramatic features, especially a lengthy segment involving the drunkard Joe Morgan and his daughter, little Mary. In a memorable scene from Arthur's book, Slade hurls a glass tumbler at Joe when Mary comes in search of her father, and she receives the blow intended for her father. The following, prolonged death of Mary at the Morgan home is rife with tears, delirious hallucinations for Joe, and curses for Simon Slade and his tavern. Over time, the plot became so familiar to readers that, in 1871, Bret Harte could portray a bottle-throwing tobacco lover to great humorous effect in his parody of Arthur, "John Jenkins; or, The Smoker Reformed."

Arthur tried to take advantage of this enduring popularity himself by writing two sequels to *Ten Nights in a Bar-Room* in the 1870s—the first, *Three Years in a Man-Trap* (1872), and the second, *The Bar-Rooms at Brantley*. Moreover, he remained active in the temperance movement by supporting and befriending activists, opening the Franklin Home for Inebriates in Philadelphia in the late 1870s and writing several other temperance works, including *Danger; or, Wounded in the House of a Friend* (1875), *Strong Drink; The Curse and the Cure* (1877), and *Saved as by Fire; A Story Illustrating How One of Nature's Noblemen Was Saved from the Demon of Drink* (1881).

As a father, Arthur continued to spend time with and provide for his family, which eventually included seven children. At least one of his sons joined him in editing *Arthur's Home Magazine*. A strong interest in his children motivated Arthur to write and edit many collections of children's tales and rhymes in his own name as well as under the pen name Uncle Herbert. In 1867 Arthur started the *Children's Hour*, a successful juvenile periodical, and in 1870 the *Workingman,* a magazine for working-class men and their families, was first printed. However, despite the significant activity of his later years, the time between 1840 and 1860 proved to be the most prolific for Arthur. During that time, he turned out a great number of the nearly two hundred novels, volumes of tales, and other instructional books that now constitute the bibliography of his works. The decades of mass productivity led him in later life to claim, "I never remember what I have written. My daughter read to me a book I had written many years ago. It all seemed new to me."

By 1881 Arthur was obliged to depend constantly on the assistance of others to read and write for him so that he could continue his work as editor of *Arthur's Home Magazine.* In his final years, Arthur's literary reputation had already begun to fade, while the reputations of others, such as Poe–who had seen little material success in his lifetime–gained prominence. Arthur himself sensed the relative modesty of his position among the rising literary giants of his age, and in 1882 he explained to his neighbor, Edward F. Palen, "I have had no educational advantages–no college course; I have always felt the lack of them. I had to work hard, to struggle to meet the wants of a large family, and do not wish to live my life over again, no, not even for one week, nor one month. And yet, all this has been divinely ordered." Arthur died in his home on 6 March 1885 at 11:00 P.M. from a combination of kidney disorder, anemia, and old age; he was nearly seventy-six years old.

Biographies:

T. S. Arthur: His Life and Works by One Who Knows Him (Philadelphia: Stoddart, 1873);

Donald A. Koch, "The Life and Times of Timothy Shay Arthur," dissertation, Western Reserve University, 1954.

References:

T. S. Arthur, "Brief Autobiography," *Illustrated Temperance Tales* (Philadelphia: J. W. Bradley, 1850); revised and enlarged as *The Lights and Shadows of Real Life* (Philadelphia: J. W. Bradley, 1851);

Carl Bode, *Anatomy of Popular Culture* (Berkeley: University of California Press, 1959), pp. 119–131;

Warren G. French, "T. S. Arthur's Divorce Fiction," *University of Texas Studies in English,* 33 (1954): 9–96;

French, "T. S. Arthur: Pioneer Business Novelist," *American Quarterly,* 10 (Spring 1958): 55–65;

French, "T. S. Arthur: An Unexpected Champion of Poe," *Tennessee Studies in Literature,* 5 (1960): 35–41;

"Godey's Portrait Gallery. No. I. T. S. Arthur," *Godey's Lady's Book,* 29 (November 1844): 193–194;

Donald A. Koch, Introduction in T. S. Arthur's *Ten Nights in a Bar-Room,* edited by Koch (Cambridge: Harvard University Press, 1964).

Papers:

Collections of T. S. Arthur's correspondence and manuscripts can be found at the University of North Carolina at Chapel Hill and the University of Virginia.

Henry Ward Beecher

(24 June 1813 – 8 March 1887)

Clifford E. Clark Jr.
Carleton College

See also the Beecher entries in *DLB 3: Antebellum Writers in New York and the South* and *DLB 43: American Newspaper Journalists, 1690–1872.*

BOOKS: *An Address, Delivered Before the Platonean Society of the Indiana Asbury University, September 15, 1840* (Indianapolis: Printed by W. Stacy, 1840);

The Means of Securing Good Rulers: A Sermon Delivered on the Occasion of the Death of Noah Noble, Late Governor of Indiana. By Henry Ward Beecher (Indianapolis: Printed by E. Chamberlain, 1844);

Seven Lectures to Young Men, on Various Important Subjects (Indianapolis: T. B. Cutler / Cincinnati: W. H. Moore, 1844); republished as *Lectures to Young Men on Various Important Subjects* (Salem: Jewett, 1845; London: Ward, 1851; enlarged edition, Boston: Ticknor & Fields, 1863); republished as *Twelve Lectures to Young Men on Various Important Subjects* (New York: G. H. Doran, 1870);

A Dissuasive from Moral Intolerance, Delivered at Bloomington, Ind., Before the Philomathean Society of the Indiana University (Indianapolis: S. V. B. Noel, 1845);

A Discourse Delivered at the Plymouth Church, Brooklyn, N.Y.: Upon Thanksgiving Day, November 25th, 1847 (New York: Cady & Burgess, 1848);

Industry and Idleness, with Causes of Dishonesty; to Which Are Appended Six Warnings (Philadelphia: W. S. Young, 1850);

Great Speech, Delivered in New York City, by Henry Ward Beecher, on the Conflict of Northern and Southern Theories of Man and Society, Jan. 14, 1855 (Rochester: A. Strong, 1855);

Star Papers; or, Experience of Art and Nature (New York: J. C. Derby / Boston: Phillips, Sampson / Cincinnati: H. W. Derby, 1855); enlarged as *New Star Papers; or, Views and Experiences of Religious Subjects* (New York: Derby & Jackson, 1859);

Defence of Kansas (Washington: Printed by Buell & Blanchard, 1856);

Henry Ward Beecher, 1835 (Beecher Family Papers, Yale University Library)

Man and His Institutions. An Address Before the Society for the Promotion of Collegiate and Theological Education at the West, Delivered in Tremont Temple, Boston, Mass., May 28, 1856. By Rev. Henry Ward Beecher (New York: Calkins & Stiles, 1856);

How to Become a Christian: An Address Delivered in Burton's Old Theatre (New York: Derby & Jackson, 1858); revised and enlarged as *How to Become a Christian* (Boston: American Tract Society, 1858);

Life Thoughts, Gathered from the Extemporaneous Discourses of Henry Ward Beecher, as by one of his congregation (Boston: Phillips, Sampson, 1858);

Notes from Plymouth Pulpit; A Collection of Memorable Passages from the Discourses of H. W. Beecher, with a Sketch of Mr. Beecher and the Lecture Room, as by Augusta Moore (New York: Derby & Jackson, 1858);

God's Seal and Testimony, a Sermon; Preached at Plymouth Church . . . with a List of Members Received at the Communions of May, June and July, 1858 (Brooklyn, N.Y., 1858);

Selected Sermons, as Delivered in Plymouth Church, Brooklyn (New York, Long & Farrelly, 1858);

Henry Ward Beecher and Theodore Parker: Mr. Beecher's Reasons for Lecturing in the "Fraternity Course": Being a Reply to Certain Criticisms Made upon Him for So Doing: Including His Opinion of Total Depravity (Boston: A. Williams, 1859);

Plain and Pleasant Talk about Fruits, Flowers and Farming (New York: Derby & Jackson, 1859); enlarged as *Pleasant Talk about Fruits, Flowers and Farming* (New York: J. B. Ford, 1874);

Summer in the Soul, or Views and Experiences (Edinburgh: A. Strahan, 1859);

Woman's Influence in Politics: An Address Delivered by Henry Ward Beecher, at the Cooper Institute, New York, Thursday Evening, Feb. 2d, 1860 (Boston: R. F. Wallcut, 1860);

Civil War: Its Causes, its Consequences, its Crimes, and its Compromises (New York: R. Vose, 1861);

Remarks at the Funeral . . . of Edward Corning, Held in Plymouth Church, Brooklyn, Thursday Afternoon, Jan. 31st 1861 (New York: Folger, 1861?);

War and Emancipation: A Thanksgiving Sermon, Preached in the Plymouth Church, Brooklyn, N.Y. on Thursday, November 21, 1861 (Philadelphia: T. B. Peterson, 1861?);

Eyes and Ears (Boston: Ticknor & Fields, 1862);

Royal Truths (Edinburgh: A. Strahan, 1862; Boston: Ticknor & Fields, 1866);

Freedom and War: Discourses on Topics Suggested by the Times (Boston: Ticknor & Fields, 1863);

American Rebellion. Speech of the Rev. Henry Ward Beecher, Delivered in the Free Trade Hall, Manchester, 9th October, 1863. With a Report of the Proceedings of the Meeting (Manchester, U.K.: Union and Emancipation Society, 1863); republished as *The American Cause in England! An Address on "The American War," Delivered at Free Trade Hall, Manchester, England* (New York: Coutant & Baker, 1863); also published as *England and America: Speech of Henry Ward Beecher at the Free-Trade Hall, Manchester, October 9, 1863* (Boston: J. Redpath, 1863); expanded as *American Rebellion: Report of the Speeches of the Rev. Henry Ward Beecher, Delivered at Public Meetings in Manchester, Glasgowe, Edinburgh, Liverpool, and London, and at the Farewell Breakfasts in London, Manchester, and Liverpool* (Manchester, U.K.: Union and Emancipation Society, 1864); revised as *Speeches of Rev. Henry Ward Beecher on the American Rebellion, Delivered in Great Britain in 1863* (New York: United States Book Co., 1887);

The National Bereavement. A Sermon (New York, 1865);

Oration at Raising the Old Flag over Fort Sumter, April 14, 1865 (New York: Schermerhorn, Bancroft, 1865); expanded as *Oration at Raising "The Old Flag" at Fort Sumter; and Sermon on the Death of Abraham Lincoln, President of the United States* (Manchester, U.K.: A. Ireland, 1865);

The Amendment to the Constitution. Beecher's Letters and Greeley's Reply (New York, 1866);

595 Pulpit Pungencies, edited by Homer L. Bartlett (New York: Carleton, 1866);

Familiar Talks on Themes of General Christian Experience, edited by Homer L. Barlett (New York: Carleton, 1866; London: Nelson, 1870);

Address on the Occasion of Laying the Corner Stone of the New Adelphi Academy. Delivered at the Clinton Avenue Congregational Church . . . (Brooklyn, N.Y.: Rome, 1867);

Norwood; or Village Life in New England (London: Sampson Low, Son & Marston, 1867; New York: Fords, Howard & Hulbert, 1867);

Prayers from Plymouth Pulpit (New York: Scribner, 1867);

Woman's Duty to Vote: Speech by Henry Ward Beecher, at the Eleventh National Woman's Rights Convention, Held in New York, May 10, 1866 (New York: American Equal Rights Association, 1867);

Sermons by Henry Ward Beecher, Plymouth Church, Brooklyn. Selected from Published and Unpublished Discourses, 2 volumes, compiled by Lyman Abbott (New York: Harper, 1868, 1869); republished as *Sermons. Selected from Published and Unpublished Discourses and Revised by Their Author* (London: Sampson Low, 1870);

Address of Rev. Henry Ward Beecher on Mission Sunday Schools, Delivered Before the National Sunday School Convention at Newark, N.J. April 29, 1869 (Newark, N.J., 1869);

Hindrances to Christian Development (New York, 1869);

The Name Above Every Name. A Sermon (New York, 1869);

Plymouth Pulpit: The Sermons of Henry Ward Beecher in Plymouth Church, Brooklyn, as from verbatim reports by T. J. Ellinwood (4 volumes, New York: Ford Press, 1869; 19 volumes, London: Dickinson, 1880);

Lecture-Room Talks; A Series of Familiar Discourses on Themes of General Christian Experience (New York: Ford Press, 1870);

The Overture of Angels (New York: Ford Press, 1870);

Christ the Deliverer: A Sermon (Boston: Boston Evening Traveller, 1871);

Common Sense for Young Men on the Subject of Temperance. A Sermon Preached by Henry Ward Beecher, in Plymouth Church, Brooklyn, on . . . February 5, 1871 (New York: National Temperance Society and Publication House, 1871);

Crime and its Remedy (London: Printed by R. Barrett, 1871);

The Life of Jesus, the Christ (New York: Ford Press, 1871 / Edinburgh & London: Thomas Nelson, 1871);

Morning and Evening Exercises: Selected from the Published and Unpublished Writings of the Rev. Henry Ward Beecher, edited by Lyman Abbott (New York: Harper, 1871);

Liberty and Love: An Appeal to the Conscience to Banish the Wine-Cup (New York: National Temperance Society and Publication House, 1872);

Yale Lectures on Preaching, 3 volumes (New York: Ford Press, 1872–1874); republished as *Lectures on Preaching* (London: Thomas Nelson, 1872);

Should the Public Libraries Be Opened on Sunday? An Address, by Henry Ward Beecher, Delivered at the Request of Members of the Mercantile Library Association of New York City, in the Cooper Union Hall. April 22d. 1872, phonographically reported by T. J. Ellinwood (New York: Ford Press, 1872);

The Discipline of Trouble: A Sermon (New York, 1873);

The Discipline of Sorrow . . . (New York, 1874);

A Summer Parish: Sabbath Discourses and Morning Service of Prayer at the Twin Mountain House, White Mountains, New Hampshire, During the Summer of 1874 (New York: Ford Press, 1875);

Oratory: An Oration by Henry Ward Beecher, Delivered Before the National School of Oratory, upon the Occasion of its Third Annual Commencement, Held in the American Academy of Music, Philadelphia, May 29, 1876, printed from the authorized report of Mr. T. J. Ellinwood (Philadelphia: Printed by Culbertson & Bache, 1876);

The Background of Mystery; A Sermon . . . 1877 (Brooklyn?, 1877);

Jew and Gentile: A Sermon (New York: Christian Union, 1877);

Past Perils and the Peril of To-Day (New York: Christian Union, 1877);

The Army of the Republic, Its Services and Destiny; An Oration Delivered at the Reunion of the Army of the Potomac at Springfield, Mass., Wednesday, June 5th (New York: Christian Union, 1878);

Christianity Unchanged by Changes. Two Addresses on the "Signs of the Times" (New York: Christian Union, 1878);

Why the Republican Party Should Be Trusted. The Key-note, by Henry Ward Beecher, at the Academy of Music, Brooklyn, Monday Evening, June 14, 1880 (Brooklyn, N.Y.: Union-Argus, 1880);

The Moral Uses of Luxury and Beauty: A Lecture (New York: Christian Union, 1882);

Statement Before the Congregational Association of New York and Brooklyn, in Which He Resigns His Membership and Gives His Doctrinal Beliefs and Unbeliefs (New York: Funk & Wagnalls, 1882);

A Circuit of the Continent: Account of a Tour through the West and South . . . Being His Thanksgiving Day Discourse at Plymouth Church, Brooklyn, Nov. 29th, 1883, Describing his Trip through Thirty States and Territories (New York: Fords, Howard & Hulbert, 1884);

Address of Rev. H. W. Beecher, at the Meeting of Independents, Brooklyn, Oct. 22, 1884 (New York: The Evening Post, 1884);

Beecher's "Cleveland letters." The Two Letters on Reconstruction of the Southern States. Written by Henry Ward Beecher, in 1866, upon Being Invited to Act as Chaplain of the "Soldiers' and Sailors' Convention," Held at Cleveland, Ohio, in the Summer of That Year (N. p., 1884);

Eulogy on General Grant . . . Delivered at Tremont Temple, Boston . . . Oct. 22, 1885 (New York: Jenkins & McCowan, 1885);

Rev. Henry Ward Beecher's Series of Important Sermons, on the Subject of Evolution and Religion. Published, as Delivered, for the Benefit of the Home for Consumptives, a . . . Charity of the City of Brooklyn (New York: Gallison & Hobron, 1885?);

Henry Ward Beecher in England, 1886; Addresses, Lectures, Sermons, Prayers, Biographical Sketch and Portrait (London: J. Clarke, 1886?);

Henry Ward Beecher in the Pulpit (London: Routledge, 1886);

Christian Philosopher, Pulpit Orator, Patriot and Philanthropist. A Volume of Representative Selections from the Sermons, Lectures, Prayers, and Letters of Henry Ward Beecher, with a Biographical Sketch by Thomas W. Handford, edited by Homer L. Bartlett (Chicago & New York: Belford, J. Clarke, 1887);

I Am Resolved What to Do; Last Sermon Preached by Rev. Henry Ward Beecher at Plymouth Church, Sunday Evening, February 17, 1887 (New York: Gallagher & Hoffer, 1887);

Last Sermons. Preached in Plymouth Church, Brooklyn, Since Beecher's Return from England, October, 1886 (London: J. Clarke, 1887);

Patriotic Addresses in America and England, from 1850 to 1885, on Slavery, the Civil War, and the Development of *Civil Liberty in the United States,* edited by John R. Howard (Boston: Pilgrim, 1887);

Proverbs from Plymouth Pulpit; Selected from the Writings and Sayings of Henry Ward Beecher by William Drysdale, revised in part by Beecher (New York: D. Appleton, 1887; London: Burnet, 1887);

A Summer in England with Henry Ward Beecher; Giving the Addresses, Lectures, and Sermons Delivered by Him in Great Britain During the Summer of 1886. Together with an Account of the Tour, Expressions of Public Opinion, Etc., edited by James B. Pond (New York: Fords, Howard, & Hulbert, 1887);

"Faith"; Last Morning Sermon Preached in Plymouth Church, Brooklyn, Sunday, Feb. 27, 1887 (Brooklyn, N.Y.: T. J. Ellinwood, 1891);

Best Thoughts of Henry Ward Beecher, edited by Lyman Abbott (New York: H. S. Goodspeed, 1893);

Gamblers and Gambling (Philadelphia: H. Altemus, 1896);

Autobiographical Reminiscences of Henry Ward Beecher, edited by T. J. Ellinwood (New York: Frederick A. Stokes, 1898);

Lectures and Orations, edited by Newel Dwight Hillis (New York & Chicago: Fleming H. Revell, 1913).

OTHER: *Plymouth Collection of Hymns and Tunes for the Use of Christian Congregations,* compiled by Beecher (New York: A. S. Barnes, 1855); enlarged as *The Baptist Hymn and Tune Book* (New York: Sheldon, Blakeman, 1857);

The Great Brooklyn Romance: All the Documents in the Famous Beecher-Tilton Case, unabridged, includes testimony by Beecher and others (New York: J. H. Paxon, 1874);

Herman Behr, ed., *The New Divinity: Lectures by Henry Ward Beecher, John Wycliffe, John Bunyan, Martin Luther, Mary Baker G. Eddy, Emmanuel Swedenborg, and Others* (New York: H. Beher, 1929; London: Kegan Paul, Trench, Trübner, 1929);

Herman Behr, ed., *The New Science. Lectures by Henry Ward Beecher, Henry James, Harriet Beecher Stowe, Hugh Latimer, William T. Stead, Luther Burbank, and Others* (New York: H. Behr, 1930; London: Kegan Paul, Trench, Trübner, 1930).

Writing to her brother Henry Ward Beecher in 1851, shortly after the passage of the Fugitive Slave Act, Harriet Beecher Stowe seethed with frustration. "Why I have felt almost choked sometimes with pent up wrath that does no good," she confessed. Stowe then urged her brother to intensify his attack on the wicked law. "Strive, pray, labor, Henry," she wrote. "Be the champion of the oppressed and my God defend and bless you." Although the fame that Stowe gained in the following year from the publication of *Uncle Tom's Cabin*

(1852) has somewhat eclipsed the visibility of her brother's stand on controversial social issues, the American public from the 1850s to the 1880s recognized Henry Ward Beecher as one of the leading preachers, essayists, newspaper editors, and popular orators of the day.

During his forty-year career at Plymouth Church in Brooklyn, New York, Beecher regularly held his 3,200 listeners spellbound. On the lyceum-lecture circuit, he commanded higher fees than either Ralph Waldo Emerson or Mark Twain. In addition to writing his sermons, which were published weekly in the newspapers and later collected and published separately, Beecher edited *The Independent,* a widely circulated religious newspaper, published one novel, *Norwood; or Village Life in New England* (1867), wrote *The Life of Jesus, the Christ* (1871), and delivered the highly respected *Yale Lectures on Preaching* (1872–1874). These extensive publications—together with his commitment to politics and political action, his crusades against slavery, his advocacy of women's rights, and his close connections with the leadership of the Republican Party—enabled him to influence public policies in ways that few preachers have ever matched, either before or after his time.

Beecher's eagerness to debate the heated political issues of his day represented a form of opportunism that often enmeshed him in controversy. Indeed, in later life, Beecher admitted that "the moment you tell me that a thing that should be done is unpopular, I am right there, every time." Beecher's enemies despised his stands in favor of abolitionism, temperance, women's rights, and the theory of evolution. In 1872 Victoria Woodhull, the radical advocate for free love and the editor of *Woodhull and Claflin's Weekly,* accused Beecher of having committed adultery with the wife of one of his parishioners. Exonerated in both the church trial and in the extended civil trial that later followed—it made the front page of *The New York Times* for six months running—Beecher regained his enormous popularity in the 1870s and kept it until his death in 1887. Nevertheless, significant numbers of the American public, both then and since, have considered him to have been guilty.

Born in Litchfield, Connecticut, on 24 June 1813, the eighth child of Roxana Foote Beecher and Lyman Beecher, a leading revivalist preacher, Henry Ward Beecher developed an early interest in religion. Like his five brothers who also became ministers, Beecher began his religious studies at Mt. Pleasant Academy in Massachusetts, continued them at Amherst College, from which he graduated in 1834, and earned his divinity degree at Lane Seminary in Cincinnati, Ohio. Shortly thereafter, he accepted a pastorate at the First Presbyterian Church in Lawrenceburg, Indiana, and on 3

August 1837 he married Eunice White Bullard, to whom he had become engaged while at Amherst. Two years later he was called to the Second Presbyterian Church in Indianapolis.

In Indianapolis the energetic Beecher, who preached daily at churches throughout the city, began to develop a national reputation. In 1844 he published *Seven Lectures to Young Men, on Various Important Subjects,* a melodramatic advice book that warned against prostitution and preached an ethic of self-discipline and self-control, an appeal that resonated with many Americans, who believed that the pall-mall expansion of the country westward threatened to undermine the nation's moral stability.

Beecher's growing skill as a preacher, as well as his commitment to the abolitionist and temperance crusades, brought him to the attention of a group of Congregationalist business leaders who invited him in 1847 to head the newly founded Plymouth Church in Brooklyn, New York. Eager to leave the malarial conditions in Indianapolis that in the previous year had killed his six-year-old son, George, and attracted by the array of religious papers printed in New York, Beecher accepted the call to the new pastorate.

At Plymouth Church, Beecher perfected a dramatic preaching style that drew on commonplace experiences to create powerful graphic images to which his audience might easily relate. Like his sister Harriet, who five years later wrote to him asking for ways "to make slavery a picture" (a request that she creatively fulfilled in the creation of Uncle Tom, a Christlike suffering slave) Beecher personalized his religious message by appealing to the everyday experiences of ordinary people. Speaking at a women's suffrage rally in 1860, for example, Beecher asserted that "this, then, is the sum of what I wished to say to you tonight. I have said it more in the expectation that it will work in you as a leaven than that it will bear immediate fruits. But, as the farmer sows seed in October that he does not expect to reap till July, so we must sow, and wait patiently for the harvest. I do not know that I shall see the day when woman will occupy her true position in society. My children may, if I do not; and I think that there will be some approach to it, even in my time; for thoughts move faster than they used to."

Much of Beecher's effectiveness, both as a preacher and as a public speaker, rested on the highly personal approach that he took to his audience. In order to create the sense of informality and direct personal contact, he designed Plymouth Church without a traditional pulpit. In place of it, he had a low, oval platform built, which reached out to the congregation and invited them to share his thoughts and musings. As the historian Thomas Bender has noted, Beecher described

Elizabeth Tilton, the member of Beecher's congregation whose husband sued Beecher for allegedly having an affair with her

his talks as "familiar conversations" and relied on his magnetic personality to overcome the diversity of American urban life at mid century. Playing upon people's emotions and appealing to everyday experiences, Beecher sought to create an informed public willing to wrestle with the ethical issues of the day.

By the 1850s Beecher had attracted national attention through his outspoken attacks on slavery. In addition to sermons, Beecher dramatized the ethical issues by holding mock slave auctions to save fair-complexioned young African American women from the terrors of the peculiar institution. When war broke out in 1861, he raised a new regiment in Brooklyn and supported the Northern war effort with encouraging articles in *The Independent,* which he edited from 1861 to 1864. He not only personally urged President Abraham Lincoln to issue the Emancipation Proclamation, but he also embarked on a public-speaking tour in Great Britain in 1863 to urge the English to remain neutral. Later published as *Patriotic Addresses in America and England, from 1850 to 1885, on Slavery, the Civil War, and the Development of Civil Liberty in the United States* (1887) and *Lectures and Orations* (1913), Beecher's political speeches identified the cause of the state with that of the church.

The Beecher family in 1859: (standing) Thomas, William, Edward, Charles, and Henry; (seated) Isabella Beecher Hooker, Catharine, Lyman, Mary Beecher Perkins, and Harriet Beecher Stowe (photograph by Mathew Brady; Stowe-Day Foundation, Hartford, Connecticut)

As the leading spokesman for popular Protestantism, Beecher combined an emphasis on moral duty and national destiny. Like many of his contemporaries, he thought that a belief in evangelical Protestantism should bring with it a commitment to social justice that would build a stronger nation. Fittingly, when the Civil War ended in 1865, Beecher was chosen to give the address upon the return of the U.S. flag to Fort Sumter in the harbor of Charleston, South Carolina.

After the Civil War, Beecher, his reputation enhanced by his work on behalf of the Northern cause, entered on the period of his greatest publishing successes. Robert Bonner, the flamboyant editor of the *New York Ledger,* paid him $24,400 to write a serialized novel, *Norwood*. Published as a book in 1867, the novel told the story of two pairs of young lovers, one from the North and the other from the South. The Northern romance resulted in marriage, while the secondary hero from the South died fighting at Gettysburg. As William Gerald McLoughlin has pointed out, the novel preached a gospel of love and forgiveness and brought Beecher's message to a far larger audience than he had previously reached in his other publications.

Beecher's successful novel was followed by the publication of ten volumes of sermons, a collection of informal church presentations titled *Lecture-Room Talks;*

A Series of Familiar Discourses on Themes of General Christian Experience (1870), and the editorship of a new religious periodical, the *Christian Union* (later called *The Outlook*). But he is perhaps best known for his *Yale Lectures on Preaching,* given at the Yale Divinity School, which set forth his ideas about the role of the minister in contemporary Christianity. A master of metaphor, Beecher transformed the doctrines of the Bible into everyday examples that his listeners could understand and identify with. Speaking in the third series of lectures about the question of whether God exists, for example, Beecher commented that he doubted the value of a preacher's trying to prove that God exists. "There is no use of demonstrating to men that there is music in one of Mozart's or Beethoven's symphonies," he asserted. "*Play it,* and I will defy them to get rid of saying that there is music in it. They recognize it at once."

In 1874, the same year that the last of the *Yale Lectures on Preaching* was published, Beecher was accused by Theodore Tilton, the radical editor of a competing religious paper, *The Independent,* of having committed adultery with Tilton's wife, Elizabeth. Tilton's suit confirmed the rumors that had been started two years earlier by free-love advocate Victoria Woodhull. The trial that followed resulted in a hung jury, nine to three in favor of his innocence. Not only did his church continue to support him, but also Beecher's success on the lecture circuit increased his popularity even further. Since Beecher was a popular national spokesman for middle-class Victorian values, many Americans refused to believe that he had been guilty.

In the 1880s Beecher turned his attention to the controversy over Darwinism. Seeking to reconcile religious beliefs with the growth of scientific knowledge, Beecher labeled himself "a cordial Christian Evolutionist" and argued that the continued spiritual and physical development of the nation was a confirmation of the validity of Charles Darwin's theory of evolution. While Darwin himself shied away from linking evolution to progress, Beecher saw the possibilities of combining the two theories.

Beecher continued his extensive lecturing schedule into the 1880s, speaking out on labor unrest, the tariff, and what he perceived to be a growing pattern of anti-Semitism in America. Then on 7 March 1887 he suffered a stroke and died in his sleep two days later.

Biographies:

W. C. Griswold, *Life of Henry Ward Beecher: A Comprehensive and Accurate History of the Great Divine from His Birth to His Grave* (Centerbrook, Conn.: W.C. Griswold, 1887);

Lyman Abbott, *Henry Ward Beecher: A Sketch of His Career* (Hartford, Conn.: American Publishing Co., 1887);

Thomas Wallace Knox, *Life and Work of Henry Ward Beecher: An Authentic, Impartial, and Complete History of His Public Career and Private Life from the Cradle to His Grave* (Hartford, Conn.: Hartford, 1887);

A. A. Willits, *"The Eloquent Orator": An Eloquent Tribute to the Life and Services of Henry Ward Beecher* (Louisville, Ky.: Courier-Journal, 1887);

William Constantine Beecher and Rev. Samuel Scoville, *A Biography of Rev. Henry Ward Beecher* (New York: C. L. Webster, 1888);

John R. Howard, *Henry Ward Beecher: A Study of His Personality, Career, and Influence in Public Affairs* (London: Brentano's, 1891);

John Henry Barrows, *Henry Ward Beecher: The Shakespeare of the Pulpit* (New York: Funk & Wagnalls, 1893);

Elbert Hubbard, *Beecher* (East Aurora, N.Y.: Roycrofters, 1903);

Hubbard, *Henry Ward Beecher as His Friends Saw Him* (Boston & New York: Pilgrim, 1904);

E. Haldeman-Julius, *Henry Ward Beecher, the Barnum of the Pulpit* (Girard, Kans.: Haldeman-Julius Publications, 1929);

Lyman Beecher Stowe, *Saints, Sinners, and Beechers* (New York: Blue Ribbon Books, 1934);

Lionel George Crocker, *Henry Ward Beecher's Speaking Art* (New York: Fleming H. Revell, 1937);

Paxton Hibben, *Henry Ward Beecher: An American Portrait* (New York: Press of the Readers Club, 1942);

Bessie G. Olson, *Henry Ward Beecher, a Great Pastor* (Chicago: Van Kampen Press, 1946);

Robert Shaplen, *Free Love and Heavenly Sinners: The Story of the Great Henry Ward Beecher Scandal* (London: Deutsch, 1954);

Jane Shaffer Elsemere, *Henry Ward Beecher; The Indiana Years, 1837–1847* (Indianapolis: Indiana Historical Society, 1973);

Altina L. Waller, *Reverend Beecher and Mrs. Tilton: Sex and Class in Victorian America* (Amherst: University of Massachusetts Press, 1982);

Halford Ross Ryan, *Henry Ward Beecher* (New York: Greenwood Press, 1990).

References:

Marie Caskey, *Chariot of Fire: Religion and the Beecher Family* (New Haven: Yale University Press, 1977);

Clifford Edward Clark, *Henry Ward Beecher: Spokesman for a Middle-Class America* (Urbana: University of Illinois, 1978);

Richard W. Fox, *Trials of Intimacy: Love and Loss in the Beecher–Tilton Scandal* (Chicago: University of Chicago Press, 1999);

William Gerald McLoughlin, *The Meaning of Henry Ward Beecher: An Essay on the Shifting Values of Mid-Victorian America, 1840–1870* (New York: Knopf, 1970);

Milton Rogoff, *The Beechers: An American Family in the Nineteenth Century* (New York: Harper & Row, 1981);

Altina L. Waller, *Reverend Beecher and Mrs. Tilton: Sex and Class in Victorian America* (Amherst: University of Massachusetts Press, 1982).

Papers:

The major collection of Henry Ward Beecher's letters is in the Beecher Papers in the Yale University Library. Smaller in size but also important are the Beecher letters in the Beecher-Stowe Collection in the Arthur and Elizabeth Schlesinger Library at Radcliffe College. Scattered letters may also be found in the Henry Ward Beecher Papers at the Library of Congress, in the Harriet Beecher Stowe Collection at the Stowe-Day Foundation in Hartford, Connecticut, and at the following libraries: Amherst College Library, Cornell University Library, Columbia University Library, Rutherford B. Hayes Library, Boston Public Library, Henry E. Huntington Library, University of Georgia Library, Fiske University Library, the Houghton Library of Harvard University, the Cincinnati Historical Society, and Historical and Philosophical Society of Ohio Library.

Park Benjamin

(14 August 1809 – 12 September 1864)

Bruce I. Weiner
St. Lawrence University

See also the Benjamin entries in *DLB 3: Antebellum Writers in New York and the South; DLB 59: American Literary Critics and Scholars, 1800–1850;* and *DLB 73: American Magazine Journalists, 1741–1850.*

BOOKS: *A Poem on the Meditation of Nature, Spoken September 26th, 1832, Before the Association of the Alumni of Washington College* (Hartford, Conn.: F. J. Huntington, 1832);

The Harbinger; A May-Gift, by Benjamin, Oliver Wendell Holmes, and John O. Sargent (Boston: Carter, Hendee, 1833);

Poetry: A Satire, Pronounced Before the Mercantile Library Association at Its Twenty Second Anniversary (New York: J. Winchester, 1842);

Infatuation: A Poem Spoken Before the Mercantile Library Association of Boston, October 9, 1844 (Boston: Ticknor, 1844);

True Patriotism. An Address Spoken at the Presbyterian Church, Geneva, N.Y. on the Fourth of July, 1851 (Geneva, N.Y.: I. & S. H. Parker, 1851);

Poems of Park Benjamin, edited, with an introduction and notes, by Merle M. Hoover (New York: Columbia University Press, 1948).

Despite new scholarly interests in the history of authorship, publishing, popular literatures, and uncanonized writers in the United States, Park Benjamin remains nearly forgotten. A prolific poet and influential editor of literary periodicals in Boston and New York in the 1840s, he failed to secure a place of lasting importance among his contemporaries. Perhaps this failure occurred because he never published a book of his own, devoting himself almost exclusively to editing and writing for periodicals. As some of his contemporaries feared, most notably Nathaniel Hawthorne and Edgar Allan Poe, ephemeral literary journals were no basis for lasting literary fame. Benjamin's career went virtually unnoticed after his death until 1948, when Merle M. Hoover published a biography and selected edition of Benjamin's poetry. Earlier, in *A History of American Magazines, 1741–*

Park Benjamin (portrait by Chester Harding; from Merle M. Hoover, Park Benjamin: Poet & Editor, 1948)

1850 (1930), Frank Luther Mott considered Benjamin's major editorial assignments in context, and in 1971 Lillian B. Gilkes published two lengthy essays, one on Benjamin's connections with Hawthorne and *The New-England Magazine* in the 1830s and the other on Benjamin's activities as an editor and as a literary agent in the 1840s. However, since 1971 there have been few scholarly treatments of his literary life. Despite this neglect, there is much in Benjamin's varied career to interest scholars of literary publishing and authorship in antebellum America.

Park Benjamin descended from an old New England family (leather workers who emigrated from

Sussex, England, in 1632), but he was born 14 August 1809 in Demerara, British Guiana. His father, Park Benjamin Sr., left shoemaking to follow the sea, eventually rising to captain a trading schooner, marry the daughter of a Barbados planter, Mary Judith Gall, and acquire interests in a Demerara plantation. In infancy young Park suffered from tropical fevers that left him partially crippled, a weakness some of his literary enemies later exploited, but otherwise he seems to have been unaffected by his exotic origins. His family's history of plantation commerce does not enter his work, perhaps because, for his health and education, he was sent at an early age to live with relatives in Connecticut. The tragic deaths at sea in 1824 of his father and older brother, who were returning to Demerara from New England, may also account for Benjamin's detachment from his place of birth. In any case, he enjoyed a relatively happy boyhood in Connecticut, attending school at Bacon Academy and preparing for college under the direction of James Savage, a Boston lawyer and editor to whom Benjamin's father entrusted his son's care before embarking on his fateful trip to Demerara in 1824. Young Benjamin matriculated at Harvard in 1825, where he began to form literary friendships with Oliver Wendell Holmes, George Hillard, and John O. Sargent, but Benjamin had to withdraw because of illness in his second year. When he was ready to continue in 1827, he entered the newly established Washington (now Trinity) College, to which his father originally intended him to go. At Washington College he joined the literary society and began to excel as a poet, attracting the notice especially of George D. Prentice, influential editor of the *New-England Weekly Review,* who published Benjamin's poetry and introduced him to the journalistic mode of caustic criticism.

Graduating at the head of his class in 1829, Benjamin became editor and part owner of the *Norwich Spectator,* but the paper was short-lived, and he was not ready to commit himself to a life of editorial labor. Like most of his contemporaries who wished to be authors, he had to face the facts of American literary life in the 1830s. "With the exception of those whom Fortune has placed beyond the necessity of exertion," he later commented in the December 1835 *New-England Magazine,* "there are no authors by profession. The efforts of American writers are, for the most part, made in hours of leisure, set aside from the time devoted to their regular business."

Benjamin returned to Harvard in 1830 to study law, finishing at Yale in 1832, and was admitted to the bars of both Connecticut and Massachusetts in 1833 and 1834, respectively. However, at Harvard he renewed acquaintances with Holmes, Sargent, and other Boston literati, and at Yale College, Benjamin met Nathaniel Parker Willis, a pretentious undergraduate whose literary ambition rekindled his own. Although Willis's interest in Benjamin's sister soon ended their friendship, Benjamin was encouraged by Willis to cultivate a literary salon in Boston and to contribute to *The American Monthly Magazine* (Boston), which Willis edited. Also, in 1833 Benjamin published with Holmes and Sargent a collection of poems, including nineteen of his own, titled *The Harbinger; A May-Gift,* and launched a plan to publish a library of fine books, only one of which, Thomas Carlyle's *The Life of Friedrich Schiller* (1833), appeared.

Largely unsuccessful in these literary pursuits and indifferent to the practice of law, Benjamin vacillated about what to do. Late in 1833 he traveled to Demerara, perhaps to assay his interests in the plantation and to see whether it might provide him with regular business. Apparently unable or unwilling to take an active role in the business, Benjamin returned to the United States in 1834 and accepted an offer from Sargent and Samuel G. Howe to join them in editing *The New-England Magazine.* From this point on, Benjamin devoted himself to literary editing and authorship. He soon found himself sole editor and proprietor of the magazine, publishing it until December 1835, when he moved to New York to join forces with Charles Fenno Hoffman and *The American Monthly Magazine* (New York).

Intending to publish a periodical with national scope, Benjamin and Hoffman employed Robert Montgomery Bird in Philadelphia as contributing editor for a short time and tried to cooperate with Robert M. Walsh, editor of the Philadelphia *American Quarterly Review,* which was foundering on the rocks of sectional rivalry with New York periodicals and finally capsized in 1836. Despite their national vision, Benjamin and Hoffman proceeded conservatively, following the successful formula of *The New-England Magazine.* They published original works by American writers, select reprints of well-known European authors, and biographical and critical notices of important public and literary figures. However, as he had done in *The New-England Magazine,* Benjamin injected a note of personal controversy, bantering with correspondents and slashing rival periodicals and authors, after the fashion of popular British periodicals.

During this period Benjamin helped to draw Hawthorne out of obscurity, publishing eighteen of his early tales and sketches in *The New-England* and *The American Monthly* magazines and favorably reviewing his fiction. Benjamin had little reputation as a literary critic, having followed the standard practice of reviewing anonymously, but he had written important essays in 1832 and 1833 for the *American Monthly Review* on the

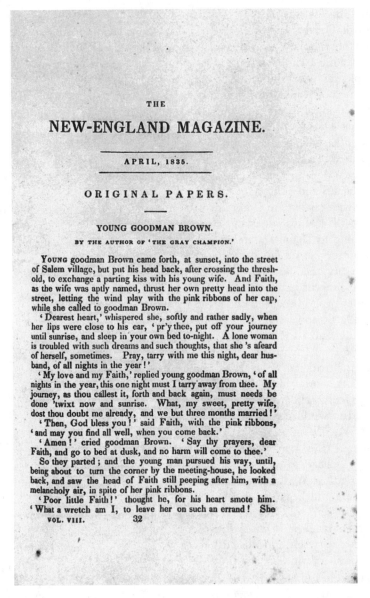

*First page from the issue of Benjamin's magazine that includes the first printing of a
well-known short story by Nathaniel Hawthorne*

poetics of Longinus and A. W. von Schlegel and the poetry of Richard Henry Dana Sr. and William Cullen Bryant, and in 1836 for Walsh's *American Quarterly Review* on Percy Bysshe Shelley's poetry and the English sonnets. In *The Origins of American Critical Thought, 1810–1830* (1961), William Charvat describes the essay on Bryant as "perhaps the period's only good analysis of the function of the lyric. . . . As a statement of the ground on which 'common sense' criticism and mystical poetry can meet, it is the most important critical document of the period." Unfortunately, Benjamin used his critical intelligence increasingly after 1836 to war with rival journalists, although his comments on many authors and literary issues are noteworthy.

Despite the high quality of *The American Monthly Magazine,* it could not withstand the political and economic uncertainties of the literary marketplace. Horace Greeley's association with the magazine in 1836 influenced Benjamin and Hoffman to affiliate more openly with Whig politics, putting off some subscribers. More damaging to the publication were a fire in 1836 and economic panic in 1837, which caused the publisher, George Dearborn, to fail. Reeling from personal financial losses and swayed by Greeley, Benjamin directed his energies toward newspaper journalism. Before *The American Monthly Magazine* went under in October 1838, he was editing Greeley's *The New-Yorker* so that Greeley could devote more time to politics. Benjamin was not content, however, to work in Greeley's shadow and joined Rufus W. Griswold in editing the *Evening Tattler* and *Brother Jonathan,* an oversized weekly edition of the *Evening Tattler.* A quarrel with the publisher soon ended that venture, and in October 1839 Benjamin and Griswold started a rival newspaper and a mammoth weekly, the *Signal* and *The New World.* Griswold lasted only six weeks, and his replacement, Epes Sargent, only a year with Benjamin. John Neal was hired as special contributor but soon withdrew over differences with the editor. These relationships and Benjamin's experience with Greeley confirm the opinion of some contemporaries that Benjamin was irascible, often embroiling others in controversy, and covetous of editorial control.

Nevertheless, under Benjamin's direction between 1839 and 1844, *The New World* eclipsed its rivals. Benjamin's literary and commercial vision was grandiose. "No pent-up Utica contracts our powers," the motto of *The New World* declared (borrowing from Samuel E. Sewall's "Epilogue to Addison's Cato"), "But the whole boundless Continent is ours!" To fit the whole continent, the pages of *The New World* sometimes reached four feet long and eleven columns wide. Benjamin advertised aggressively, organized newsboys to hawk the paper on New York streets, and contrived shrewdly with other publishers to beat his competitors, especially the *Brother Jonathan,* to be first in publishing new works. The whole venture smacked of P. T. Barnum, but Benjamin managed to combine sensational promotion and good editing. As before, he drew original contributions from the best writers in America—including Holmes, Poe, Neal, Henry Wadsworth Longfellow, Richard Henry Dana Sr., Washington Allston, Seba Smith, Catharine Maria Sedgwick, and Walt Whitman—and selectively mined British periodicals for their literary treasures. He also offered in a series of "Extras" between May 1842 and January 1844, in which he printed 105 complete novels and plays, including Whitman's *Franklin Evans, or the Inebriate* (which Benjamin published in 1842), Charles Dickens's *American Notes for General Circulation* (1842), Alexandre Dumas's *Pauline* (1842), Henri de Balzac's *Eugenia Grandet; or The Miser's Daughter,* translated by Edward S. Gould (1843), Frederika Bremer's *The Neighbors: A Tale of Every Day Life* (1842), and Eugene Sue's *The Mysteries of Paris* (1843). The European works were pirated—that is, in the absence of international copyright law, printed or reprinted without payment of royalties to authors—and sold on the streets by newsboys for 12 ½¢ or mailed to subscribers at newspaper rates. Anathema to book publishers, whose own pirated editions of foreign authors' works were being undersold, these "Extras" disseminated some of the best literature of the day and helped to create a market in America for cheap books.

By 1840 *The New World,* issued in folio and quarto versions, was the most popular weekly in America, selling as many as 15,000 copies per issue and as many as 100,000 copies of popular "Extras." Writing in January 1840 to George W. Greene, United States consul in Rome, Longfellow praised *The New World* as "by far the best paper I see, tho' [Benjamin] republishes from the English—whole books even."

Benjamin's piracy and literary squabbling have cast a shadow over his achievements. Hoover portrays him as a principled editor and champion of literary democracy, contending that his influence as an editor was largely salutary and that his fractiousness was "after all . . . only satisfying the demand of the day" for a "personal brand of journalism." Reviewing Hoover's biography in *The New England Quarterly* in 1948, Mott disagreed, suggesting that Benjamin "never showed any deep sincerity of purpose, and his ethics sometimes seem rather shabby." Poe offered a similar assessment of Benjamin in "A Chapter on Autography" in 1841. Poe acknowledged that Benjamin's influence as editor of *The American Monthly Magazine, The New-Yorker,* and *The New World* was "scarcely second to that of any editor in the country," owing to his "combined ability, activity, causticity, fearlessness and independence." However, in Poe's view, Benjamin's actions were not directed by independence of principle but by "unshaken resolution to follow the bent of one's own will, let the consequences be what they may." Benjamin thanked Poe for "his just notice—just as regards censure" in an October 1841 letter to George Graham, Poe's boss at *Graham's Magazine.* Reputedly thick-skinned, however, Benjamin seems to have had few qualms about his ethics.

Benjamin presumed to found *The New World* on moral principles, declaring in the prospectus in boldface print that his rule as editor "is never to publish a line which he would hesitate to read aloud in the hearing of virtuous and intelligent females. Thus the New World is made an unexceptional Family Newspaper." In 1840 Benjamin carried the standard in the so-called Moral War against James Gordon Bennett, whose irreverent reporting in *The New York Herald* about religious institutions and other subjects touched off a storm of controversy. Regardless of virtuous females, however, Benjamin's assault was vitriolic, inciting Bennett to refer to him as "Noah's Black Dwarf" and as "half Jew, half infidel, with a touch of the monster." Unruffled by the controversy, Benjamin seems to have been more interested in boosting the circulation of *The New World* than in defending family values or reforming the newspaper press. The example of Bennett's misconduct did not prevent Benjamin from attacking James Fenimore Cooper viciously that same year, calling him "the

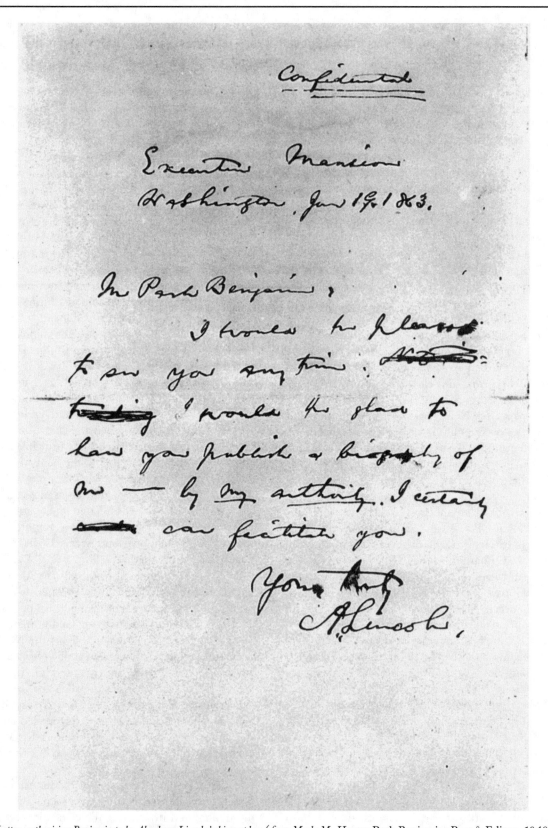

Letter authorizing Benjamin to be Abraham Lincoln's biographer (from Merle M. Hoover, Park Benjamin: Poet & Editor, *1948)*

craziest loon that ever was suffered to roam at large without whip and keeper." Although never fond of Cooper, Benjamin was mainly interested in attracting readers by exploiting the notoriety of Cooper's libel suits against several other editors for attacking him personally after the publication of *Home as Found* in 1838. Benjamin was named a defendant in one of the suits and ordered to pay Cooper $375.

The controversy over *Home as Found* sheds further light on Benjamin's principles and practices. In February 1842 he declined to attend a dinner in honor of Dickens, explaining in a letter to Washington Irving that he was finding more and more truth in Cooper's caricature in *Home as Found* of American sycophancy toward foreign authors. More likely, Benjamin was protesting Dickens's efforts to secure copyright protection for foreign authors in America, which would have put an end to the literary piracy that kept *The New World* and its competitors afloat. Benjamin told Irving that he would gladly attend a feast in Irving's honor, but the flattery was self-serving. Benjamin was always interested in promoting American writers but not at the expense of losing the opportunity to pirate the works of Dickens and other foreign authors. Chastised in 1842 for deflating the prices of books as a result of piracy, Benjamin stood on democratic principles. "The community . . . owes us a debt of gratitude for reducing the prices of works of literature to the means of the poorest classes. We have begun a great literary revolution, which will result in enlarging the understandings of the masses. It is truly democratic—utterly subversive of that intellectual aristocracy which has hitherto controlled the energies of the nation." However, his editorial policies appear to have been dictated largely by commercial interests and competition, and a strong inclination to have his own way, regardless of the consequences for fellow authors and publishers.

In the February 1845 *American Whig Review,* Evert A. Duyckinck assessed the period of cheap publications that Benjamin helped to usher in: "Native authors were neglected, despised, insulted; foreign authors were mutilated, pillaged, and insulted besides . . . the cupidity of the publishers overstocked the market and the traffic fell. . . . Doubtless a taste for reading was diffused." Perhaps cutthroat commercialism accomplished what democratic principles could not. In this regard Benjamin was no worse than many American publishers who were forced to compete in an expanding literary marketplace. In fact, he was better than most, managing business effectively while remaining committed to relatively high standards of literary quality. As Poe noted in "A Chapter on Autography," Benjamin's "judgment in literary matters" could be trusted, despite his questionable principles.

The New World declined when changes in postal regulations in 1843 made it more expensive to circulate and when English copyright laws restricted its sale in Canada. Even before resigning as editor in March 1844, Benjamin was pursuing other interests—writing a farce, *The Fiscal Agent,* which flopped on the New York stage in 1842, expanding his activity as a literary agent, and appearing more frequently in public to read his poems. However, he was not prepared to give up editing altogether and through the late 1840s took up several editorial posts, all short-lived. He moved to Baltimore in 1845 to edit *The Western Continent,* a new mammoth paper, but by July 1846 had sold his interest in the venture and moved back to New York. After the quick demise of the weekly *American Mail* in 1847, he tried to revive *The New World,* but it sank also when the publisher moved it to Philadelphia, where Benjamin could not control it and where it could not compete with rival weeklies.

These failures and marriage to Mary Brower Western in May 1848 redirected Benjamin's literary career once again. His wife suggested that he employ his skills as a public speaker and join the Lyceum lecture circuit. Benjamin lectured successfully from 1849 until his death in 1864, often sharing the podium with such notables as Greeley, Ralph Waldo Emerson, and Henry Ward Beecher. Most of Benjamin's lectures were in verse—mock heroic couplets on such topics as "Fashion," "The Age of Gold," "The Influence of Literature," and "True Patriotism." In this way he was able to support eight children and, when free from the tiring itinerary of the Lyceum tour, to live a life of relative leisure.

Late in life he returned to journalism, editing *The Churchman's Magazine* in 1858 and in 1859 *The Constellation,* which was even more colossal in size than *The New World.* Also in these final years, Benjamin became involved in Republican politics, seeking unsuccessfully to obtain a consular position. President Abraham Lincoln thought well enough of Benjamin to authorize him in 1863 to write a campaign biography, which he apparently never began.

Throughout a varied literary career, Benjamin wrote poetry for periodical publication, earning enough respect to be included in standard anthologies, such as Griswold's *Poets and Poetry of America* (1842) and Evert and George Duyckinck's *Cyclopaedia of American Literature* (1855). Hoover suggests that if Benjamin had had leisure, he "might have become a poet of distinction," but there is little in his poetry to support this opinion. He was, however, adept at a variety of verse forms, including songs, ballads, sonnets, and satiric verse lectures. Poe praised him in "A Chapter on Autography" as "skilful and passionate, as well as imaginative," noting

Walt Whitman's temperance novel, one of a series of works that Benjamin published as extras

especially the quality of his sonnets. Some of Benjamin's poems—such as "The Departed," "Song of the Stromkerl," and "The Old Sexton"—were set to music and remained popular until the end of the century. However, Benjamin's imaginative range was limited to conventional treatments of popular subjects. Sending several of his poems in January 1833 to Samuel G. Goodrich—author of the "Peter Parley" books for children and influential editor of the *Token,* an annual that featured the early writing of Hawthorne, Willis, and Longfellow—Benjamin wrote, "I recollect that you once told me that those pieces were apt to be the most popular which treated of love or religion." Benjamin strayed little from these subjects, providing readers with various expressions of sentimental love and piety. His poetry reads, therefore, like much of the magazine and newspaper verse of the day. Unlike Longfellow, Holmes, Bryant, Whitman, and John Greenleaf Whittier, Benjamin seldom addressed grittier issues such as slavery, poverty, commercialism, territorial expansion, or industrial and urban growth. This avoidance seems strange given his journalistic experience in New York and association with political activists such as Greeley, but it suggests how far removed popular literary sentiment was from social reality in antebellum America. Some further engagement as a poet with the issues of the day might have earned Benjamin more distinction. However, his poetry will still reward readers interested in popular literary expression in America in the 1840s and 1850s.

Although not a figure of major importance, Benjamin was an innovative and influential editor of literary periodicals, an astute literary critic (although too fond of critical invective), a pioneering literary agent, a successful lyceum lecturer, and a prolific poet. Willful and controversial, he was bound to make enemies, but he maintained cordial relationships with many authors and publishers, some of whom admired his literary talents and conviviality. Although drawn into several squabbles by Benjamin, Longfellow trusted him as an editor and literary agent and was entertained by his "oracular speech" at literary gatherings. In an August 1888 letter to Mary Ferris, Holmes remembered Benjamin as having a "sanguine disposition and eminently social nature," and as one who "could extemporize

verses with remarkable facility." Benjamin's literary career warrants further consideration, especially for what it reveals about developments in literary publishing, authorship, reading, and cultural values in antebellum America.

Biography:

Merle M. Hoover, *Park Benjamin: Poet & Editor* (New York: Columbia University Press, 1948).

References:

Alison Bulsterbaum, *"The New England Magazine,"* *American Literary Magazines: The Eighteenth and Nineteenth Centuries,* edited by Edward E. Chielens (New York: Greenwood Press, 1986), pp. 269–272;

Evert A. and George L. Duyckinck, "Park Benjamin," *Cyclopaedia of American Literature* (New York: Scribner, 1855), II: 344–345;

Lillian B. Gilkes, "Hawthorne, Park Benjamin, and S. G. Goodrich: A Three-Cornered Imbroglio," *The Nathaniel Hawthorne Journal,* 1 (1971): 83–112;

Gilkes, "Park Benjamin: Literary Agent, *Et Cetera,*" *Proof: The Yearbook of American Bibliographical and Textual Studies,* edited by Joseph Katz (Columbia: University of South Carolina Press, 1971), I: 35–89;

Rufus W. Griswold, "Park Benjamin," *The Poets and Poetry of America* (Philadelphia: Carey & Hart, 1842), pp. 358–365;

Frank Luther Mott, "The 'Mammoth' Papers," *"The New-England Magazine,"* and *"The American Monthly Magazine* (Benjamin's)," *A History of American Magazines, 1741–1850* (New York: Appleton, 1930), pp. 358–363, 599–603, and 618–621;

Edgar Allan Poe, "A Chapter on Autography," *Graham's Magazine,* 19 (November 1841): 226;

Kennedy Williams Jr., *"The American Monthly Magazine,"* *American Literary Magazines: The Eighteenth and Nineteenth Centuries,* pp. 15–19.

Papers:

The Park Benjamin Collection at the Columbia University Library in New York includes many of Benjamin's letters and other papers related to his literary career and personal affairs.

Anne C. Lynch Botta

(11 November 1815 – 23 March 1891)

George Egon Hatvary
St. John's University

See also the Botta entry in *DLB 3: Antebellum Writers in New York and the South.*

BOOKS: *Poems* (New York: G. P. Putnam, 1849);
Hand-Book of Universal Literature; From the Latest and Best Authorities; Designed for Popular Reading and as a Text-Book for Schools and Colleges (New York: Derby & Jackson, 1860; revised and enlarged, Boston & New York: Houghton, Mifflin, 1885).

OTHER: *The Rhode-Island Book: Selections in Prose and Verse, from the Writings of Rhode-Island Citizens* (Providence: H. Fuller, 1841);
Memoirs of Anne C. L. Botta, Written by her Friends. With Selections from her Writings in Prose and Poetry, edited by Vincenzo Botta (New York: J. Selwin Tait, 1894).

Anne C. Lynch Botta was a poet and prose writer of modest achievement; her talents were all the greater as the hostess of her literary salon. By her own admission, people were the main passion of her life and friendship was her mental sustenance. From 1845 on, her house at 116 Waverly Place in New York became the gathering place of the leading literary figures of the day, and she, as its guiding spirit, became a cultural force.

Anne Charlotte Lynch Botta was born 11 November 1815 in Bennington, Vermont, the daughter of Charlotte Gray Lynch of New England, granddaughter of Lieutenant Colonel Ebenezer Gray, who had fought in the American Revolution. Anne's father, Patrick Lynch, a friend of the poet Thomas Moore, had been imprisoned for taking part in the Irish Rebellion of 1798. Refusing allegiance to the British government, he was exiled, and he came to America and established a dry-goods business in Bennington. He and his wife had two children; Anne's brother died at eighteen. Anne was not quite four when her father was lost at sea.

She attended the Albany Female Academy, graduating in 1834. On returning to teach there, she met

Anne C. Lynch Botta

Augusta Melville, Herman Melville's sister, and the two women became lifelong friends. In subsequent years Augusta was probably the person who secured her, as yet unknown, brother's first invitation to Anne Lynch's salon. From Albany, Lynch moved to Shelter Island, where she tutored the Gardiner daughters, descendants of the seventeenth-century colonist Lion Gardiner, who gave his name to nearby Gardiner's Island. Here Lynch wrote "Leaves from the Diary of a Recluse," which appeared six years later in *The Gift* for 1845. It is an account of self-discovery that Edgar Allan Poe thought was perhaps the best specimen of her prose manner. By 1838 Lynch had settled in Providence, Rhode Island, where she tutored young women in her home, compiled *The Rhode-Island Book: Selections in Prose and Verse, from the Writings of Rhode-Island Citizens* (1841), an anthology of regional writing, and established her first literary salon.

After a brief stay in Philadelphia, where she formed a friendship with Fanny Kemble, the great actress and member of a famous theatrical family, Lynch proceeded to New York. Living with her elderly mother and also a former student, Sophie Congdon, sister of the journalist Charles Congdon, Lynch took the ferry each day to teach English at the Brooklyn Academy of Young Ladies. She was at this time a contributor of verse, prose, and anonymous reviews to *The New York Mirror, The Home Journal, The Democratic Review,* and *The Broadway Journal,* as well as annuals such as *The Gift, The Opal,* and *The Diadem.*

One of Lynch's salient characteristics as hostess was her tact. She liked to start discussions but tended not to take part in them; she had a sense of humor, and she could be witty, but she eschewed sarcasm. In person she was described as slender, attractive, with a round cherry face and dark hair, above medium height, dressed in simple good taste. On some she created a deep impression. Nathaniel Parker Willis, who affectionately called her Lynchie, wrote, "Her face is capable of the most illuminative beauty, always expressive, always frank and noble; her form is a perfection of female symmetry. She walks with perfect grace and freedom—her head admirably set on her." Bayard Taylor called her "a perfect jewel of a woman."

She received guests on Saturday evenings and on special occasions such as St. Valentine's Day. After being admitted to a dim hall, where they shed cloaks, shawls, and hats, her guests proceeded upstairs to two adjoining parlors with a coal fire at either end. Here Lynch received them, often dressed in white with a white flower in her dark hair.

The most frequently mentioned guests, apart from Willis and Poe, included Horace Greeley, Margaret Fuller, Catharine Maria Sedgwick, Ann Stephens, Elizabeth Oakes Smith, George Pope Morris, Richard Henry Stoddard, Bayard Taylor, Elizabeth F. Ellet, William Cullen Bryant, Fitz-Greene Halleck, Alice and Phoebe Cary, and Grace Greenwood; but others, such as Washington Irving, Ralph Waldo Emerson, and Herman Melville also made occasional appearances, as did some foreign visitors, such as Matthew Arnold, the Swedish novelist Fredrika Bremer, and the great Norwegian violinist Ole Bornemann Bull. There were painters, too, to be found there, such as Thomas Rossiter, Charlotte Saunders Cushman, Felix O. C. Darley, and Asher Durand.

Sometimes the invitations went out indirectly, as shown by Poe's note to Halleck: "Miss Lynch desires me to say to you that she would be *very* much pleased to see you to-night. . . ." There were sometimes so many people present that they had to find seats on the rug or the staircase. Tea and cookies were served; in the course of the evening someone might sit down at the piano, and the guests might dance the quadrille.

The star of these gatherings was undeniably Poe. His reading of "The Raven" (1845) became legendary. His quiet, compelling voice and his intense eyes staring forth from below his broad and high forehead held everyone spellbound. Among the admiring women, Fanny Osgood, wife of the painter Frances Sargent Osgood, has especially been remembered as one transported by Poe's recitations. One of the best-known poets of the period, she became childlike in her reactions—she would clap her hands or sit on a footstool, gaze up at Poe, and cry. "Do her infantile act," as acerbic Thomas Dunn English noted. Poe's reading of his eerie "The Case of M. Valdemar," a tale of mesmerism, *in articulo mortis* (in the grip of death) created another sensation. Mesmerism, or hypnosis, was a recently discovered phenomenon that excited the age, and the events described in this work of science fiction were accepted by many as possible.

Poe's "Literati of New York City," which began to appear in *Godey's Lady's Book* in 1846, included Anne Lynch. Of her work Poe writes, "In poetry she has done better than in prose, and given evidence of at least unusual talent." He refers to two "noble poems"—"The Ideal" and "The Ideal Found"—one a search, the other a discovery. The first begins,

> A sad, sweet dream; it fell upon my soul
>   When song and thought first woke their echoes there,
> Swaying my spirit to its wild control,
>   And with the shadow of a fond despair
> Darkening the fountain of my young life's stream—
>   It haunts me still, and yet I know 'tis but a dream.

The second begins,

> I've met thee, whom I dared not hope to meet,
>   Save in the enchanted land of my day-dreams:
> Yes, in this common world, this waking state,
>   Thy living presence on my vision beams—
> Life's dream embodied in reality,
> And in thy eyes I read indifference to me!

If Poe heard echoes in these poems of his own early verse, notably "A Dream" or "A Dream within a Dream," he raised no objection; perhaps he was flattered to think of Lynch as a disciple. The two poems are complementary; as Poe states, "They should be considered as one, for each by itself is imperfect." He

*Decorated title page for Botta's 1849 poetry collection
(Hamilton College Library)*

goes on to say, "In modulation and vigor of rhythm, in dignity and elevation of sentiment, in metaphorical appositeness and accuracy, and in energy of expression, I really do not know where to point out anything American much superior to them." Poe was formulating his poetic theory at this time, and he praises the poet for subordinating passion, which "delights in homeliness," to "ideality."

In a decade Walt Whitman burst upon the scene, followed by Emily Dickinson, both precursors of modernism that turned from the mid-nineteenth-century insistence on idealization and the hailing of abstract virtues—such as faith, love, and honor—in cliché-ridden, predictable rhyme. A hundred such poets fell by the wayside, and in some circles even the best, such as Poe, were suspect. No one any longer thinks of Anne Lynch's poetry as superior.

The possible biographical element in these two poems is a teasing question. "The Ideal Found" assumes the stance of the rejected lover. The fourth stanza begins,

But ah! If thou hadst loved me—had I been
All to thy dreams that to mine own thou art—

Does the Ideal, though found, reject, or does "thou" stand for a living person? Little is known about Lynch's inner life. To what extent did her passionate reaching out to friends and her celebrated charm and tact mask private unhappiness? In a letter to N. P. Willis in 1851 she complains of an empty heart. "I would love so, and I would rather have this power of loving, though it should, as it has 'run into waste, or watered but as the desert,' than to have all that I see others have. . . ." Earlier, in a letter to her, Willis speaks of "the intense passionateness of your nature."

More is revealed by contemporary sources about her mind. The leading biographical article in Botta's memorial volume was written by Sophie Congdon (now known as S. M. C. Ewer), who speaks of Botta's particular interest in the meditative philosophy of Epictetus, Marcus Aurelius, and Thomas à Kempis. William Ellery Channing Sr., Emerson, and the Transcendentalists in general appealed to her; she considered herself a Christian in a broad sense. On visiting Brook Farm, however, she was not won over, preferring to live in the midst of humanity. She was concerned with the rights of women; yet, surprisingly, she did not support the suffrage movement. She believed that women should be educated first. She was not an active abolitionist, but visiting a slave market in New Orleans on her wedding journey in 1855 and seeing human beings sold like cattle appalled her. She was interested in science, able to reconcile studying Charles Darwin and Herbert Spencer with her religious faith and her awareness of the ultimate mysteries of life and death.

In 1849 Lynch published her *Poems* in a handsome volume illustrated by Durand, Darley, and other artists. As might be expected, there were favorable notices.

In 1851 she spent some time in Washington, trying to obtain the delayed payment for her grandfather's military services. When she received the money due her, she invested a portion of it with Charles Butler, who had interests in railroads and western land. Apparently the venture was lucrative, enabling Lynch to travel. In 1853 she made the grand tour of Europe with the Butler family, meeting Thomas Carlyle on the way, a favorite with American tourists. In Italy she saw the great art Americans could not see in their own country and studied sculpture.

In 1855 she married Vincenzo Botta, three years younger than she. The couple may have met in Italy, for Botta had been a professor in Turin before coming to the United States and becoming a professor of Italian at the University of the City of New York (New York University). The Bottas resided at 25 West Thirty-seventh Street, where Anne Botta's hospitality and her conversaziones continued. This residence is the one that Emerson called "the house of the expanding doors."

The Bottas remained childless but were to all appearances happy. In a letter she wrote to him while he was in Italy for the 1865 celebration of the sixth century since Dante's birth, she says that she hopes to join him in the winter, addresses him as "my dearest one," and writes, "My desire is to live for your sake more than for my own."

In 1860 Anne Botta published *Hand-Book of Universal Literature; From the Latest and Best Authorities; Designed for Popular Reading and as a Text-Book for Schools and Colleges,* a survey of literatures both ancient and modern, both Western and Eastern. It is more derived than critically discerning, but it shows a vast interest and considerable knowledge. Her contemporaries thought of it as her major work, and the book went through several editions. She planned a similar hand-book of universal history, but it did not materialize.

Those who knew her commented on Anne Botta's youthfulness even into old age. During prepara- tions for her thirty-sixth wedding anniversary at the age of seventy-five, however, she caught a cold that devel- oped into pneumonia. She died on 23 March 1891. After her death, her husband gathered sketches and tributes by her friends for the *Memoirs of Anne C. L. Botta, Written by her Friends. With Selections from her Correspondence and from her Writings in Prose and Poetry* (1894). Largely eulogistic and no doubt censured in the editing, the book nevertheless provides valuable glimpses into Anne C. Lynch Botta's life, as well as a useful selection of her works.

References:

Vincenzo Botta, ed., *Memoirs of Anne C. L. Botta, Written by her Friends. With Selections from her Correspondence and from her Writings in Prose and Poetry* (New York: J. Selwin Tait, 1894);

Madeleine B. Stern, "The House of the Expanding Doors: Anne Lynch's Soirees, 1846," *New York History,* 23 (January 1942): 42–51.

Papers:

Some of Anne C. Lynch Botta's letters are in the Sarah Helen Whitman Papers in the John Hay Library, Brown University; in the John Henry Ingram Collec- tion in the Alderman Library, University of Virginia; and in the Special Collections of the Main Library, Uni- versity of Iowa.

Charles Frederick Briggs

(30 December 1804 – 20 June 1877)

Heyward Ehrlich
Rutgers University, Newark

See also the Briggs entry in *DLB 3: Antebellum Writers in New York and the South.*

BOOKS: *The Adventures of Harry Franco, A Tale of the Great Panic,* 2 volumes, anonymous (New York: F. Saunders, 1839);

Bankrupt Stories, as Harry Franco (New York: John Allen, 1843);

Working a Passage; or, Life in a Liner, as B. C. F. (New York: John Allen, 1844; second edition, enlarged, New York: Homans & Ellis, 1846);

The Trippings of Tom Pepper; or, The Results of Romancing. An Autobiography, 2 volumes, as Franco (volume 1, New York: Burgess, Stringer / W. H. Graham / Long & Brother / J. A. Tuttle / George Dexter, 1847; volume 2, New York: Mirror Office / W. H. Graham / Dewitt & Davenport / Long & Brother / George Dexter, 1850);

The Story of the Telegraph, and a History of the Great Atlantic Cable: A Complete Record of the Inception, Progress, and Final Success of That Undertaking, by Briggs and Augustus Maverick (New York: Rudd & Carleton, 1858).

Editions: *The Adventures of Harry Franco* (New York: Garrett, 1969);

Working a Passage (New York: Garrett, 1970).

OTHER: "Annual Report," in *Transactions of the Apollo Association, for the Promotion of the Fine Arts in the United States, for the Year 1843* (New York: Charles Vinton, 1844), pp. 3–10;

"Annual Report," in *Transactions of the American Art Union, for the Promotion of the Fine Arts in the United States, for the Year 1844* (New York: John Douglas, 1845), pp. 3–9;

"The Winds," in *The Missionary Memorial: A Literary and Religious Souvenir* (New York: E. Walker, 1846), pp. 52–60;

"A Commission of Lunacy" and "Channing," in *Voices of the True-Hearted* (Philadelphia: J. Miller M'Kim, 1846), pp. 102–104, 106;

"James Russell Lowell," in *Homes of American Authors,* edited by Briggs and G. P. Putnam (New York: Putnam, 1853); Briggs's contribution republished as *Little Journeys to the Homes of American Authors: Lowell* (New York & London: Putnam, 1896);

"The Harper" and "A Pair of Sonnets . . . Siaconset [and] Coatue," in *Seaweeds from the Shores of Nantucket,* edited by Lucy Coffin Starbuck (Boston: Crosby, Nichols / New York: C. S. Francis, 1853), pp. 52–56, 63–64;

Trow's New York City Directory, introduction by Briggs (New York, 1853–1877);

"A Literary Martyrdom," in *The Knickerbocker Gallery* (New York: Samuel Hueston, 1855), pp. 481–491;

"Peter Fink's Revenge," in *A Library of American Literature,* 11 volumes, edited by Edmund Clarence Stedman and Ellen Mackay Hutchinson (New York: Charles L. Webster, 1888–1890), VI: 219–222;

"The Pinto Letters of Charles Frederick Briggs," edited by Bette Weidman, in *Studies in the American Renaissance,* edited by Joel Myerson (Boston: Twayne, 1979), pp. 93–157—comprises Briggs's fictional letters to the *New York Mirror.*

PERIODICALS EDITED: *Broadway Journal* (4 January–22 February 1845), edited by Briggs; (1 March 1845–3 January 1846), edited by Briggs, Edgar Allan Poe, and H. C. Watson;

Holden's Dollar Magazine (January 1848–December 1851);

Putnam's Magazine (1853–1857), edited by Briggs and George William Curtis; (1868–1869), edited by Briggs;

Irving Magazine (1861);

Brooklyn Daily Union (1870–1873).

Charles Frederick Briggs—novelist, satirist, realist, critic, and journalist—wrote four novels set in New York City and at sea. He wrote three of them—*The Adventures of Harry Franco, A Tale of the Great Panic* (1839), *Working a Passage; or, Life in a Liner* (1844, 1846), and *The Trippings of Tom Pepper; or, The Results of Romancing. An Autobiography* (1847, 1850)—in his characteristic comic mode, and the fourth, *Bankrupt Stories* (1843), in an unexpected tragic vein. He was also a forerunner and champion of Herman Melville, first an editorial partner and then an opponent of Edgar Allan Poe, a literary confidant of James Russell Lowell, and an editor of *Putnam's Magazine, The New York Times,* and other periodicals. In an era of American nationalism and literary romanticism, he depicted contemporary social injustice in a startling manner by consciously modeling his work after Jonathan Swift, Henry Fielding, and Tobias Smollett. Perry Miller has described Briggs as the first American writer to make use of "the brutality of New York life—prostitution, murder, crime, competition, filth, [and] poverty." The best account of Briggs's cantankerous character is in Lowell's *A Fable for Critics* (1848), in which he appears as "half upright Quaker, half downright Come-outer," having uncommon "common sense," and, paradoxically, "quite artless himself . . . a lover of Art." In a world of social and literary ambition, Briggs remained modest and authentic; as Lowell remarked, "You are a great deal better than anything your write . . . and I always think of you without your pen. . . ." Briggs's career falls into five periods: his initial literary success with *The Adventures of Harry Franco* in 1839; his partnership with and later animosity toward Poe, starting with the founding of *The Broadway Journal* in 1845; his newspaper satires, starting in 1846, culminating in *The Trippings of Tom Pepper,* and his role as confidant for Lowell in the latter's composition of *A Fable for Critics;* his editorship of *Putnam's Magazine* and his encouragement of Melville after 1853; and his final journalism in the 1870s. Much of his work remains uncollected and even unidentified in newspapers and magazines, and the full assessment of his writing, career, and influence is not yet complete.

Born 30 December 1804 in Nantucket, Massachusetts, the son of Jonathan C. and Sally Coffin Barrett Briggs, Charles Frederick Briggs was raised in a seagoing merchant family. His strongest and most painful childhood memory was that of visiting his bankrupt father in debtor's prison after his father's China cargo was seized by the British in 1812. In 1831 Charles's oldest brother, William C. Briggs, captain of the *Phoebe,* was lost at sea, a reminder that the ocean was always dangerous. Charles himself went to sea at an early age, making voyages to London, Liverpool, and Argentina. Settling in New York City on Staten Island, across New York Bay from Manhattan, he retained ties to his birthplace by marrying Deborah Rowson of Nantucket in 1836 and by writing Nantucket verse from time to time. Little is known about his early life in New York City; he is listed in the city directory in 1838 as an employee of a Water Street wholesale grocer. Afterward he probably maintained a variety of business interests, few details of which survive. In 1846 Poe noted that Briggs had "a passion for being mysterious" about business affairs: "His most intimate friends seem to know nothing of his movements. . . . [He] has been engaged in an infinite variety of employments, and now, I believe, occupies a lawyer's office in Nassau street."

Briggs's literary apprentice work was published anonymously in New York newspapers and magazines of the 1830s and still remains unidentified. "I have always indulged 'on the sly,'" he admitted, "but as my early occupations were mercantile I carefully hid all my literary efforts so effectually under a bushel that I could not lay my hand on the half of them. . . ." Briggs was unknown and almost thirty-five when he burst upon the literary scene in 1839 with a highly successful first novel, *The Adventures of Harry Franco,* a quasi-autobiographical comic satire of social injustice in New York City with a report on the hazards of the sea. Afterward, taking "Harry Franco" as his nom de plume, Briggs contributed the "Gimcrackery" series and other humorous pieces to Lewis Gaylord Clark's *The Knickerbocker* magazine between 1839 and 1846. Some early Nantucket poems—including "The Harper," "Siasconset," and "Coatue"—were printed in *Seaweeds from the Shores of Nantucket* (1853). Briggs's initial success as a humorist made his acceptance

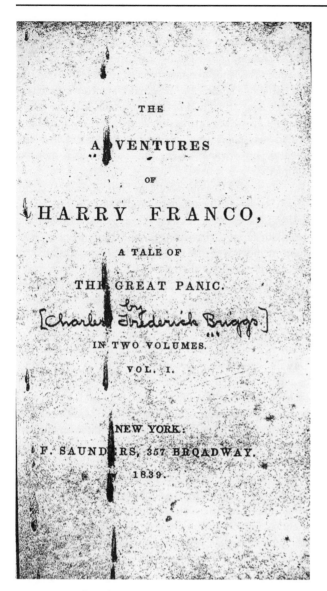

THE

ADVENTURES

OF

HARRY FRANCO,

A TALE OF

THE GREAT PANIC.

[Charles Frederick Briggs]

IN TWO VOLUMES.

VOL. I.

NEW YORK:

F. SAUNDERS, 357 BROADWAY.

1839.

Title page for Briggs's first novel, a partly autobiographical satire on life in New York City (Vanderbilt University Library)

bocker a novel called *Bankrupt Stories,* reflecting the economic depression after the panic of 1837. It was intended to be a *Canterbury Tales* for modern New York, in which ten failed merchants meet to exchange their personal narratives of financial ruin, Harry Franco pretending to be their editor. But the subject proved too distressing for *The Knickerbocker,* which terminated the serialization after two installments; only the first narrative of the projected series appeared in 1843.

In the early 1840s American authors were at a double disadvantage: publishers had a hard time paying contributors in bad times, and the market was flooded with freely pirated reprints of the works of famous British authors. The lack of an international copyright agreement became an acute problem in the new era of the steamship and the steam press. In 1843 Briggs took the initiative of proposing to a group of New York literary figures that they form the American Copyright Club to agitate in Congress for a bill on behalf of American authors. Briggs, a Whig, became annoyed at the "monkeyshines" of Cornelius Mathews, leader of the Jacksonian literary movement known as Young America. Briggs believed that Mathews tried to hijack the copyright movement into his campaign for radical cultural nationalism in American fiction, poetry, and criticism—all the literary prototypes to be written by him. The fracture lines between Briggs and Mathews, their allies, the magazines with which they were affiliated, and the ideologies represented by those magazines, determined the main divisions in the literary wars that followed.

Meanwhile, in 1844 Briggs published his third novel, *Working a Passage* (which required a second edition with an additional chapter in 1846). A short, unified moral tale of the enterprise and thrift of a young man who chooses to work his way home from Europe aboard ship rather than fall into debt, the novel exemplifies the virtues expounded by Benjamin Franklin, whose name is suggested by the initials of Briggs's pseudonym, "B.C.F." The death of Briggs's infant son, his firstborn, also in 1844, inspired Lowell's "On the Death of a Friend's Child" in *The Democratic Review.*

At the start of 1845 Briggs launched the *Broadway Journal* as a New York magazine with broad interests in literature, art, music, social developments, and politics, hoping to make the spirit of enterprise in New York speak for the nation more than the moral aura of Boston or the slave plantation ambience of South Carolina. Under Briggs, the *Broadway Journal* carried literary reviews and articles, extensive art and music criticism, commentary on the New York scene, columns in opposition to the U.S.–Mexican War, and articles by an impressive list of national contributors. Briggs had hoped to make the *Broadway Journal* the balance between Lowell and New England abolitionists and reformers on one side, and

as a writer of serious social criticism harder, whereas his initial success, following early literary activity that had long been concealed for fear of hampering his business career, coincided with his becoming a partner in the firm of Woods, Briggs, and Mather from 1840 to 1842.

While writing art criticism for *The New World,* Briggs formed a lifelong friendship with the painter William Page and through him with James Russell Lowell, becoming the latter's main literary confidant. Briggs wrote a poem on capital punishment for Lowell's magazine, *The Pioneer* (1843), but publication ceased after only three monthly issues, before Briggs's contribution could be printed. An ill-advised contract with the publishers had left Lowell with a personal debt of $750, a business lesson not lost on Briggs. Briggs began serializing in *The Knicker-*

Southern readers who remembered Poe as former editor of *The Southern Literary Messenger* on the other. Briggs hoped the *Broadway Journal* would be understood to be unsympathetic to slavery without becoming what he described to Page as a "radical reform paper." Always a maverick who found grounds for satire on both sides of a dispute, Briggs once told Page that he had "half a mind to turn reformer and try to reform the abolitionists" themselves, on one occasion using the argument that the local "harlots of Broadway" were as morally offensive as Southern slave owners.

To avoid catastrophic personal debt such as Lowell faced after the failure of *The Pioneer,* Briggs had begun the *Broadway Journal* as a limited liability venture capitalized out of petty cash with veto rights to the three partners—Briggs, his publisher, and his printer—each investing work or services in the expectation of shared profits. Briggs wished to publish only original material and to pay authors for it, and Lowell introduced Poe to Briggs as a contributor working for column rates. Although fearing at first that Poe would be "one of the Graham and Godey species," Briggs needed an experienced editor and lively reviewer, and since he was pleasantly surprised by Poe's independence, promoted him after several weeks to participating partner and co-editor with a place on the masthead. Briggs first printed Poe's name as the author of "The Raven," privately praising the poem as a "mere beautiful something entirely free from didacticism and sentiment." Lowell was leery of the sharing of editorial authority, but Briggs was sanguine. Poe discovered that his dream of owning his own magazine was becoming costly, for without the cash payments he had received at column rates, he was now out-of-pocket whenever he wrote for it as a partner.

To promote the magazine, Briggs encouraged Poe to expand the "Longfellow War," which he had begun in *Burton's Gentleman's Magazine* and continued in *The New York Mirror.* Poe's charges of plagiarism against Henry Wadsworth Longfellow, Briggs assured Lowell, were only intended to earn the magazine "a dozen or two of waspish foes" who would do it good. But the "Longfellow War" did not help the *Broadway Journal* in the way Briggs hoped; New England abolitionists stopped writing for the magazine, and Poe attracted few Southern subscribers.

At the end of the first volume, Briggs intended to reorganize the magazine; to dismiss Poe, who had begun drinking again; and to recapitalize it more conventionally by bringing in a proper investing publisher. Poe, hoping to retire to the country, tried to sell his share in the *Broadway Journal* or to get a $50 advance on his "American Parnassus" from Evert Duyckinck and Cornelius Mathews, editors of the short-lived magazine venture *Arcturus* (1840) and the principal voices in Young America. But at the last moment John Bisco, Briggs's sole remaining original part-

ner, refused to sell his share to J. Smith Homans, the new publisher, for the stipulated $50, or even for Homans's second offer of $100. Although probably never profitable, at least the magazine had succeeded in keeping its owners out of catastrophic debt. The mutual veto power in the original contract left the magazine at an impasse, and it suspended publication for one week.

Evidently Briggs did not encourage Homans to believe that Bisco's share was worth more than $100, but the editorial vacuum and inflated financial prospects of the magazine encouraged Poe to return to the magazine, convincing Bisco to resume publication of the magazine and to appoint him editor. Briggs was reluctant to continue, knowing that there would be better opportunities ahead; on the other hand, Poe was anxious to have a magazine connection, fearing that this opportunity might be his last; both were right. Briggs agreed to remain a silent partner in order to salvage what he could from Bisco and from Poe, who, Briggs reported, still "owes me now for money that I lent him to pay his board and keep him from being turned into the street." The affair left Briggs embarrassed and disappointed at the turn of events, which had as many reversals as one of his comic novels: "I lost my temper, I lost my good opinion of the public, and what was infinitely greater, my good opinion of myself." Soon, another round of complications arose that eventually involved Briggs again. Determined to own a magazine, Poe purchased Bisco's share by borrowing sums from Thomas Dunn English, Horace Greeley, and others, using Cornelius Mathews, a lawyer, as a witness for the *Broadway Journal* contract, suggesting a new alliance with Young America. Poe had no means of repaying his creditors, and he may have borrowed more than the purchase price of the magazine as a way to raise extra cash. But the magazine was barely Poe's before he liquidated it at the end of the year, leaving English aggrieved that he had unknowingly invested $30 in a moribund venture.

The praise of Briggs's "strong, manly satire" in an article by William A. Jones on "American Humor" in the September 1845 *Democratic Review,* which also described Poe as still an assistant to Briggs, produced a quick and vitriolic response from Poe. Previously, when Poe was on the Richmond *Southern Literary Messenger* and the Philadelphia *Burton's Gentleman's Magazine* and *Graham's Magazine,* he had produced a literary criticism that specialized in valiantly sticking to the text. But in the spring of 1846, Poe began a new series in *Godey's Lady's Book,* "The Literati of New York City," in which he promised to report what was being said about American authors in private conversations. Poe immediately attacked Briggs in the first installment, May 1846, as a vulgar follower of the school of "Flemish fidelity" and an uneducated imitator of Smollett, unable to write "three consecutive sentences of gram-

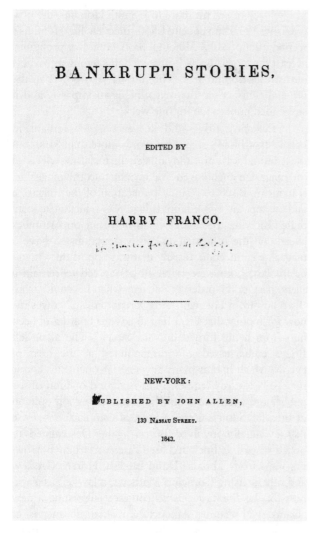

BANKRUPT STORIES,

EDITED BY

HARRY FRANCO.

NEW-YORK:
PUBLISHED BY JOHN ALLEN,
139 NASSAU STREET.
1843.

Title page for Briggs's tragic tales about life in New York during the depression that followed the panic of 1837 (Vanderbilt University Library)

matical English"; what was worse, Poe ridiculed Briggs's personal appearance. Briggs, following the manner of his "Thersitical Magazinist," replied in *The New York Evening Mirror*, depicting the 5' 8" Poe as though confined to the Bloomingdale asylum, standing "about 5 feet 1 or two inches, perhaps two inches and a half" in height, his phrenological bump of "ideality" large but his bump of moral sentiments "quite flat," resulting in his "balloonish appearance" and "lightheadedness" in behavior. For the moment the skirmish still vaguely observed the *Knickerbocker* rule that combat should be based on literary wit. Briggs confined to his private letters further details of Poe's "poltroonish character," keeping them in reserve as future ammunition.

Briggs could not keep out of the Poe-English affair that followed. In the third episode of "The Literati of New York City" Poe attacked English, his old Philadel-phia acquaintance, who was still grieved that he had somehow purchased a worthless share of the dying *Broadway Journal* from Poe. In his reply in *The New York Mirror*, English broke the fundamental rule of *Knickerbocker* literary warfare by divulging real personal information: he claimed that he had given Poe a physical beating, and he charged Poe with the detailed particulars of drunkenness, forgery, and fraud. Suddenly, literary New York, which had been only titillated or annoyed by "The Literati of New York City," was shocked. But when Poe threatened a libel suit, not against English but rather against the intellectually innocent but legally liable publisher of *The New York Mirror*, Hiram Fuller, public sympathy for Poe evaporated. William Gilmore Simms advised Poe to desist: "You are no longer a boy. 'At thirty wise or never.'" However, Poe persisted, and English, having overstated his case, did not appear at the trial, leaving Poe, his character still untested before the law, the winner of a substantial judgment against Fuller. Now *The New York Mirror* was thrown open to legally protected *Knickerbocker* literary satires on Poe. In English's own novel, *1844; or The Power of the Startled Falcon*, then being serialized in *The New York Mirror* (1846), Poe was introduced as "Marmaduke Hammerhead," drinker and wife beater. In Briggs's fictional Ferdinand Mendez Pinto letters, then running in *The New York Mirror*, the English poet R. H. Horne, whom Poe had actually praised in *Graham's Magazine*, seems to thank Poe for an article in "some wishy-washy Magazine," praising him as "a very good critic for a lady's magazine." In Briggs's *The Trippings of Tom Pepper*, also being serialized in *The New York Mirror* (beginning 14 November 1846), Briggs soon afterward introduced Poe as Austin Wicks, who becomes drunk in public and abuses the sympathy and confidence of women. The exchange permanently emboldened the nature of *Knickerbocker* literary satire and the role Briggs played in it.

Lowell had been considering several ideas for satires for several years. As early as 1845, Briggs had encouraged Lowell to contribute verse satires on Texas and some contemporary issues and to "mix a little bit of honey with yr. Mustard." Lowell had submitted abolitionist Matthew Trueman's letter to the *Broadway Journal*, but Briggs had rejected it as ineffective invective because "your satire bruises instead of cutting the flesh," reminding Briggs of the cry of a little girl who popped her head out of the cellar window when she saw her mother quarreling with another woman in the street: "Make haste mother and call Mrs Morelander a whore before she calls you one." The forces were gathering for literary warfare on a larger scale. The Lowell-Briggs alliance could count on the support of *The Knickerbocker* in New York, and Poe found himself connected with Young America, Cornelius Mathews, Evert Duyckinck, and, through them, the feminist Margaret Fuller, then the daily book reviewer of the

New York Tribune. The emerging literary issues were personal, critical, and theoretical. Previously Fuller had attacked Lowell on ideological grounds in the *New York Tribune,* and Briggs had countered in a short verse satire, "The Spirit of Criticism" in *The New York Mirror.* When Fuller carried her arguments against Lowell into more substantial book form in *Papers on Literature and Art* (1846), at the same time vigorously puffing Mathews as the great American playwright, Lowell found himself ready for "a little retaliatory satire." Briggs kept up the skirmish with a hostile article on Fuller in the *National Anti-Slavery Standard* and another satire on Mathews and Fuller in "The Great Editorial Dinner" in *The New York Mirror.* By the end of 1846, Mathews and Fuller were appearing regularly as targets of opportunity in Briggs's Ferdinand Mendez Pinto letters in *The New York Mirror.*

Late in 1847 Lowell sent to Briggs in manuscript the first installments of *A Fable for Critics,* already including a satire on Mathews. The draft sketch of Fuller followed in May 1848, by which time she had already been the target of nearly a dozen of Briggs's Pinto letters. Lowell thought that American authors had to work free of dependence on British literary models and had to choose between two ways of starting to do so: with radical theoretical manifestos or by doing their best creative work in traditional forms. Although *A Fable for Critics* is usually read today for its durable contemporary assessments of William Cullen Bryant, Washington Irving, James Fenimore Cooper, Ralph Waldo Emerson, Nathaniel Hawthorne, and Henry Wadsworth Longfellow, Lowell's real motive in writing the satire was to attack the two leading radical literary nationalists of the 1840s, Mathews and Fuller, for their excesses. The paranoid Mathews sees "'Gainst American letters a bloody conspiracy" aimed at him personally to punish him for his zeal in promoting the copyright question; Fuller plays a central role as Miranda, with her "I turn the universe" air; Poe appears, too, "with his raven, like Barnaby Rudge, / Three fifths of him genius and two fifths sheer fudge." By contrast, Briggs's enigmatic, paradoxical character was never better captured than in Lowell's appreciative portrait:

> There comes Harry Franco, and as he draws near,
> You find that's a smile which you took for a sneer . . .
> He's in joke half the time when he seems to be sternest,
> When he seems to be joking, be sure he's in earnest . . .
> Is half upright Quaker, half downright Come-outer,
> Loves Freedom too well to go stark mad about her,
> Quite artless himself, is a lover of Art,
> Shuts you out of his secrets and into his heart.

Lowell made a gift of the copyright to Briggs for his encouragement and guidance in the composition of *A Fable for Critics.* The proceeds went to purchase a small silver plate as an heirloom for Briggs's infant daughter,

Charlotte. In the long run Melville and Walt Whitman, who are not mentioned in *A Fable for Critics,* were to prove Lowell wrong in his attempt to check literary criticism and theory in the name of cultural nationalism. But at the same time *A Fable for Critics* served as an important precedent for the antiradicals to follow in Hawthorne's *The Blithedale Romance* (1852) and Melville's own *Pierre* (1852).

The growth of Briggs's family also marked his turn toward more regular literary employment. He became editor of *Holden's Dollar Magazine* from 1848 to 1851, and around this time he apparently took his first customhouse position. Briggs was especially amused by Felix O. C. Darley's illustrations for Augustine J. H. Duganne's "A Mirror For Authors," which appeared in *Holden's* under the pseudonym "Motley Manners, Esq.," the January 1849 issue including the couplet "With tomahawk upraised for deadly blow, / Behold our literary Mohawk, Poe!" But Briggs's most memorable contributions to *Holden's* are his insightful reviews of Melville's *Omoo* (1847), *Redburn* (1849), and *White Jacket* (1850). Pleased by *Omoo,* he hoped the accounts of missionaries were not true (Briggs had contributed to *The Missionary Memorial* in 1846 a sketch called "The Winds"). According to Briggs, Melville's *Mardi* (1849) possessed "a dreamy kind of voluptuousness" but was "flawed by an apparent want of motive." Briggs praised *Redburn* for the use of "a good many forecastle traditions familiar to every sailor" and for the accuracy of the Liverpool scenes, but he faulted the American reviewers:

> Many of the notices of Redburn that we have seen, speak of him [Melville] as a second De Foe, but there is hardly an English writer he so little resembles as the author of Robinson Crusoe. The charm of De Foe is his simplicity of style, and artistic accuracy of description; the author of Redburn on the contrary is, at times, ambitiously gorgeous in style, and at others coarse and abrupt in his simplicity. But his style is always copious, free and transparent. His chief defect is an ambitious desire to appear fine and learned that causes him to drag in by the head and shoulders remote images that ought not to be within a thousand miles of the reader's thoughts.

Briggs wrote that *White Jacket* was "the finest, most accurate and entertaining of any narrative of sea life that has ever been published."

The death of Poe in 1849 left Briggs allied with Poe's detractors. Rufus Griswold, Poe's literary executor, appointed by Poe's mother-in-law, had a negative view of Poe's character and a bizarre sense of his own importance in Poe's life, falsifying Poe's papers in order to aggrandize himself. Briggs and Lowell, who had their own experience of Poe, were among those who supported Griswold's view of Poe's character. Briggs, still stung by Poe's apparent "spirit of revenge" toward those who had helped him, noted in *Holden's* (December 1849) that Poe seemed destined "to malign those who had befriended him."

In January 1853 Briggs launched *Putnam's Monthly* with himself as editor and the close support of George William Curtis and Parke Godwin, drawing upon a circle of contributors consisting of veterans of Brook Farm and the *New York Tribune,* including Bayard Taylor, Charles A. Dana, George Ripley, and Horace Greeley. Building upon the subscription list of *The American Whig Review,* Briggs went on to attract original work by Melville, Longfellow, Lowell, and Henry David Thoreau. Benefiting from the backing of George Palmer Putnam, a longtime supporter of international copyright and the publisher of Wiley & Putnam's landmark Library of American Literature, *Putnam's Monthly* became the most distinguished American magazine of the nineteenth century and the first nationally successful American magazine to be based on original work by American authors, in sharp contrast to its chief rival in New York, *Harper's,* which still specialized in reprints of works by English authors.

Briggs wrote a great many articles in *Putnam's Monthly* himself, including reviews of Thoreau's *Walden* (1854) and Harriet Beecher Stowe's *Uncle Tom's Cabin* (1852). Melville was among the American writers solicited by *Putnam's Monthly* to contribute, and the second number in 1853 included Fitz-James O'Brien's "Our American Authors–Melville." Melville's contributions did much intellectually to set the sophisticated New York tone of *Putnam's Monthly.* Conversely, Briggs's encouragement did much to inspire Melville to start a second career as a writer of magazine tales after both New York and London publishers lost interest in his novels upon the critical failure of *Pierre.* Melville's first tale, "Bartleby the Scrivener," appeared in *Putnam's Monthly* during its first year, drawing on subjects and settings that had appeared in Briggs's own New York City fiction, although creatively transformed in hitherto unexplored ways.

After printing "The Encantatas" in 1854, *Putnam's Monthly* rejected Melville's "Two Temples" (written in 1854 but not published until 1924) because of its probable offense to the parishioners of Grace Church in New York. But Melville received a remarkable pair of personal letters of explanation from both Briggs the editor and Putnam the publisher, letters so appreciative and encouraging that Melville made no known effort to publish the work elsewhere, instead continuing as a contributor to *Putnam's Monthly.* Melville's contributions totaled eight works, including "The Bell Tower" (August 1855), "Benito Cereno" (October and November 1855), and the serialization of *Israel Potter* (from July 1854 to March 1855). Recent critical interest has turned to the question of Briggs's influence upon Melville after 1853. Melville's last two published novels appeared in a new environ-

ment; *Israel Potter* was written for serialization in *Putnam's Monthly,* and *The Confidence-Man* (1857), published by Dix and Edwards, the firm that had taken over *Putnam's* in its final years, has some of the features of a serialized magazine work although it never actually appeared in that form.

In 1854 Briggs contributed to *Homes of American Statesmen* an article on Benjamin Franklin, whose name had been fused with Briggs's own in his pen names, "Harry Franco" and "B.C.F." Our "Good Genius," Franklin, had shaped the "national character" in its infancy, and his *Autobiography* (parts published in America in 1818), at the head of American letters, was "the cornerstone of our literature," becoming the American model "in the great art of making the most of the world." In 1855 Briggs contributed "A Literary Martyrdom" to *The Knickerbocker Gallery,* printed with a lithograph of Briggs based on a Matthew Brady ambrotype. Marvin Smilak, once a quiet student of Greek and Latin, succumbs to public frenzy as a literary editor after his slight initial success, as Melville's Pierre Glendinning had done, but Marvin "sold out to somebody as deluded as he had been."

Briggs joined *The New York Times* from 1856 to 1862 as an assistant editor, acting as managing editor when Henry J. Raymond was away. Perhaps the last skirmish in the Briggs-Mathews feud came when Rufus Griswold reviewed Evert and George Duyckinck's long-awaited *Cyclopædia of American Literature* (1855), which had slighted Briggs and puffed Mathews, in *The New York Herald* of 13 February 1856, putting to rest the myth of the scholarly superiority of the Duyckincks and Young America to speak for the literature of the United States. Briggs regretted that Griswold's article, which Perry Miller has called "the most destructive review in American history," had not appeared in *The New York Times,* and he hoped it would be preserved in book form. During the same years Briggs was also a member of Frederick Law Olmsted's planning committee for Central Park. With the assistance of Augustus Maverick, he wrote a celebration of the "greatest event" of the nineteenth century, which would further "the transmission of thought," in *The Story of the Telegraph, and a History of the Great Atlantic Cable* (1858). From 1859 to 1870 Briggs was a clerk in the debenture room of the New York Custom House, a job said to have been procured for him by Raymond. In 1861 Briggs edited *The Irving Offering,* and afterward he contributed articles on Henry Fielding and William Page to the *New American Cyclopædia* (1860–1863).

Briggs tried to revive *Putnam's Monthly* in 1868, after the Civil War, calling for Melville, "that copious and imaginative author," to become a contributor. From 1870 to 1873 Briggs was editorial assistant and financial editor of *The Brooklyn Daily Union,* serving briefly as editor. His final post, as contributor to *The Independent* from 1874 to

1877, resulted in some interesting pieces, including his retrospective view of 1874, "The Good Old Times: New York Fifty Years Ago," which delineated the old city of the 1820s, before modern conveniences and the proliferation of newspapers and theaters.

Briggs's central contribution as a novelist was to write the three works in the Harry Franco series. In *The Adventures of Harry Franco, A Tale of the Great Panic* Briggs had displayed many literary conventions that are of renewed interest because of their apparent influence on Melville. Arriving in the city by night boat, Harry encounters a series of steamship drummers and city confidence men. Wrongly accused of abolitionist activity, he suffers the indignity of a false report of the incident in the press. His rival for Georgiana De Lancy, his beloved, proves to be his own "haughty cousin." A decade before Briggs himself became a regular literary contributor to *The New York Mirror,* Harry is surrounded by would-be writers whose highest aspiration is to publish a prize article there, and he is asked to make loans based on the assurance of one aspirant that he will win. Going to sea, he observes the wide gulf between the common seamen and the officers on a merchant ship, and afterward, aboard a U.S. warship, he observes an old seaman cruelly flogged with twenty-four lashes for a minor offense. Anticipating *Billy Budd* (written 1888–1891, published 1924), Harry remarks that his fellow sailors are of three character types, "a bully, a buffoon, and a butt," and he elects to strike the bully. The redemptive counterpart to the satire in the book is the disclosure of the depth of working-class solidarity among common seamen, reflected perhaps for the first time in American fiction. Protecting a fellow seaman by refusing to testify, Harry averts a severe flogging by climbing to the top of the rigging. There he observes below another loyal seaman refusing to testify despite his extended flogging of thirty-six lashes. Preferring death to flogging, Harry loses his hold when fired upon from below and falls into the sea, still hearing the unforgettable rush of air, crew, and water that haunts him, whether starting from a deep sleep or "in my ears even now as I write." Finally forgiven for his bravery and ordeal, Harry is rewarded for his loyalty by a subscription from the crew of the generous sum of $1,000, the showiest pledges remaining unpaid.

Returning to New York after two years at sea, Harry sees the New York world of speculation in lots, bonds, and money. Cheated of all his savings, he becomes homeless and sleeps on a bench at the Battery, where an impoverished poet sings the praises of Waverley Place in Washington Square as the finest neighborhood in the city for outdoor sleeping, a jab at the vogue of Walter Scott among even the lowliest. Harry works for a time as a copyist of mercantile letters, living in the building where he works. His beloved Georgiana proves to be

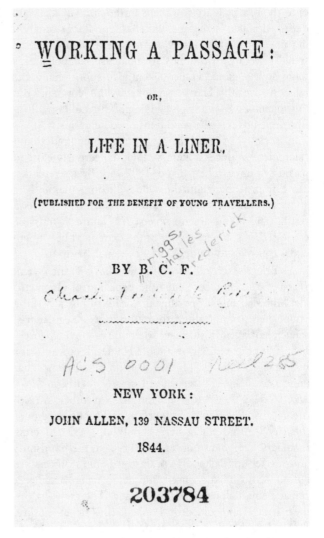

Title page for Briggs's comic novel about a young man who practices the virtues advocated by Benjamin Franklin (Ball State University Library)

the niece of his employer, Mr. Marisett. Suddenly proposing marriage to her, he is unexpectedly accepted on the condition that he first undergo a true religious conversion. Harry's employer dispatches him to New Orleans in an attempt to gain control of the cotton market. But Harry flagrantly disobeys orders to return to New York as the panic of 1837 widens, and he cannot resist entering a gambling house, where he promptly loses all the company funds. Upon walking into the garden to shoot himself, Harry blunders into a black church, where his first religious awakening blossoms. As the economic panic spreads, he returns to New York to find that Georgiana has gone to South Carolina to live on the rice plantation she has inherited. Following her, Harry is shipwrecked en route to Charleston, completing his religious conversion as the ship breaks up in the surf. Thrown unconscious onto the beach, Harry awakens in the arms of the wandering, desolate Georgiana, who has found her plantation in ruins. Meanwhile, Harry's father has suddenly become wealthy because of some "fortunate speculations," his town now renamed Francoville in his honor. Finally, the religious, wealthy Harry is reunited with Georgiana. But the adaptation of the happy ending of the traditional British comic novel to the conditions of contemporary American society, so fluid in alternating serendipities and calamities, produces a literary result dangerously close to parody or farce. The panic of 1837 was, Briggs remarks, more improbable than the wildest fiction, making the "honest historian" into an "outrageous romancer." As a result, nature and art are reversed: "Nature, it must be confessed, is sometimes *outré* in the extreme; but art generally contrives to render herself extremely natural."

Briggs's second novel in the Harry Franco vein, *Working a Passage,* continues the depiction of shipboard life. Stranded in Europe after the death of his father, the young hero cannot afford to sail home as a regular passenger, not even in steerage, where direst poverty forces people to prepare their own food. He decides to work for his passage, setting sail from Liverpool in a manner that anticipates Ishmael's departure from New York in *Moby-Dick* (1851): "It was the last day of November; a cold, dreary, drizzling day; a dirty yellowish vapour hung over the city." Amid the generous but impoverished crew members, Briggs introduces Jack Plaskett, the handsome and mysterious sailor. By contrast, the ship's officers are ignorant and inexperienced, the new captain actually a Philadelphia tailor on his first voyage. The crew, led by the narrator and joined by Plaskett, rises up in mutiny, demanding that the captain return to Liverpool for better sails and officers. Mocking all such literary confrontations, the inept captain unexpectedly agrees, but the narrator and Plaskett jump ship anyway.

Briggs exposes shipboard conditions, such as ships' officers' "pure carelessness and imprudence," which actually cause many shipwrecks falsely attributed to storms, and the obsolete class structure of the American navy, following the inflexible British system of separating officers, who have no concern for their men, from the seamen, who often are the better sailors. Anticipating *Billy Budd,* Briggs discusses the Somers affair of 1842, describes the execution of the mutineers as "horrible murders," and produces a character teased so cruelly as "leather-lips" that he eventually leaps into the sea. At the end, Briggs's young sailor proudly addresses the reader with the claim that he has preserved his independence and integrity by avoiding the moral abyss of debt: "Bear in mind, young traveler, when you pine after luxuries that do not happen to be within your reach, that it is possible to endure hard labor and be happy with no other refreshments than potatoes and salt, provided they are honestly earned."

The Trippings of Tom Pepper, Briggs's third and final novel in the Harry Franco series, was serialized irregularly in *The New York Mirror* starting in 1846, suffering from the wide spacing of its two gatherings in book form in 1847 and 1850. The first volume, which Melville owned, was offered as a premium to subscribers to *The New York Mirror.* Briggs wrote in the first person because only the "autobiographist" can provide a "moral daguerreotype of character," a view that disqualifies the writer of biographies and literary histories as inherently unreliable. One of the editors of the weekly edition of *The New York Mirror,* also called the *American Literary Gazette,* was Evert Duyckinck, the constant associate of Cornelius Mathews. Both appear in the portrait gallery of *The Trippings of Tom Pepper,* along with Hiram Fuller, editor of the daily edition of *The New York Mirror,* as Ferocious (Cornelius Mathews), Tibbings (Evert Duyckinck), and Wilton (Hiram Fuller); other identifications include Myrtle Phipps (William Gilmore Simms), Lizzy Gil (Anne Charlotte Lynch/Elizabeth Ellet), and Woolish (Henry Tuckerman).

The special target of the satire is Jasper Ferocious, Esq. (Mathews), the spokesman for Young America, who wants American literature to be "Individual, national, indigenous" as well as "National, idiosyncratic, and peculiar," and whose prize work is *Christopher Cockroach, Citizen.* Ferocious reads to Tom with such determination that he is unaware that Tom has fallen asleep: "Young America, sir, must keep his eyes open; he must study deep, dive down into the mysteries of his author; grapple with him; bring up the pearls and diamonds of his fancy, and play with his leviathan thoughts." Mathews's rhetoric seemed ridiculous in 1847, but a few years later, the satire was turned against Briggs when Melville began to create just such a literature.

But the star of Briggs's satire is Austin Wicks (Poe), the American Francis Jeffrey, "author of the 'Castle of Duntriewell,' a metaphysical romance, and a psychological essay on the sensations of shadows." Wicks, inebriated after one glass of wine, praises the poetical talent of Lizzy Gil (Lynch/Ellet) in order to ask her for the loan of $5. The character Lizzy seems to reflect Poe's connections both to Ms. Lynch and her salon and to Ms. Ellet, who corresponded with Poe. Replying compassionately to his claim to be a genius, Lizzy offers him not just $5 but a note for $50, reflecting a generous collection on his behalf. But Wicks is incapable of gratitude, "and with a baseness that only those can believe possible who have known him, he exhibited Lizzy's note to some of her acquaintances, as an evidence that she had made improper advances to him."

The funniest sequence in the book begins when Tom follows a street prostitute to her room and falls asleep, awaking to find himself naked and robbed of his clothes. To escape, he steals some of her clothes, which mark him as soon as he appears on the street, and a do-good Quaker family "rescue" him and take him home. Still dressed as a woman, Tom falls in love with the daughter, Desire Goodwill, but he dare not accept her invitation to share her bed, while he also struggles to evade the amorous advances of the son, Wilson Goodwill. Pressed to begin his "reform" by identifying his seducer, he names Ferocious (Mathews). Tom finally escapes by stealing the brother's clothes, assuming a name based on the initials he finds sewn into them. Throughout the novel, Tom does not know who he is, assuming identities based on what he learns or is told. Playing with Anglophilia, Briggs allows Tom at various times to be known as Bedford Horton and Eustace St. Hugh and, like Billy Budd, to believe himself to be the illegitimate son of a British gentleman, a naval officer. But Tom has so many different beliefs and illusions as to who he is and who his father may be that the more he attempts to speak the truth as he knows it, the more he is taken for a romancer. His adventures are "trippings," and the moralizing subtitle of the book is *The Results of Romancing*. Although Tom is an American Candide in pursuit of the truth about himself, he lives in a literary domain where comedy begins when the author changes the apparent identity of his hero; Briggs produces satire by inverting that convention, making the name Tom Pepper into a well-known byword for liar.

The sexual satire in *The Trippings of Tom Pepper* is unexpectedly tactile by 1840s standards. The young Tom, kissing the young Sylvia, suddenly stops when he becomes aware of his unexpected sexual awakening. Like Tom Jones, Tom Pepper loves several women at the same time. He would love to love Desire Goodwill, but he is determined to marry Pauline, who accompanies him unescorted into St. James Park, where he immediately offers her kisses and a marriage proposal, both of which she accepts. Tom's girls, unlike those of popular literary romances, are more likely to say "yes" than "no," whatever their social class. Tom's brave new world is one in which the young are easy about sex and marriage while everyone is anxious about money and property. By contrast, the world of adult men and women includes a realistic portrayal of domestic bickering.

Briggs's street descriptions provide an early view of the impact of American city life on the psyche of its inhabitants. Venturing around Wall Street, Tom senses that the metamorphosis of his identity will continue as long as he has "a character to establish, a fortune to make":

> . . . I went into that busy mart with a vague expectation that somebody might make me a present of a few hundred dollars, or invite me to accept a situation in an office where the duties were light and the pay large, or propose to take me into partnership in some profitable business. But all such wild expectations soon vanished when I saw how intensely interested every man seemed to be in his own affairs, and how little notice anybody bestowed on me. . . . But the bustle of the street was infectious, and I hurried along with the rushing crowd as though I too had a mission to discharge, a note at bank to pay, or a bill to collect, or a deposite [*sic*] to make, or differences to settle. I had enough to do in truth, or I had employment to find, a character to establish, a fortune to make.

By contrast, the price of economic failure in New York was the complete loss of identity for those who lived in a slum:

> The sun was up now, and the street, which looked so dismal by night, looked disgusting by day. The swine that had been sleeping in the gutters were now in motion, turning over the heaps of filth in the middle of the street; wretched looking creatures, of both sexes, were hobbling to the grocer for their morning dram; the stealthy dissipators of the night before were cautiously leaving the foul haunts where they had been overtaken by sleep; the mechanics who lived in the neighborhood, were going to their daily labors; the milkman and the baker were travelling their rounds, supplying the daily wants of miserable beings, who ate the bread of vicious idleness, and lived by the wages of infamy. The place was sickening and disgusting, and I was so confused by suddenly waking up in such a scene, that it was long before I could remember in what manner I got there, or why it was that I was out of my bed at such an hour. . . .

Enlisting in the U.S. Navy to escape his city fate, Tom finds he is the fifteenth William Brown to sign up on the same ship, and almost immediately he is flogged with twenty-four strokes for a minor offense: "Terrible as all these preparations were, the fear of the lash was nothing to compare to the degradation of the flogging." For Briggs, physical pain was a common fact of life, but the humiliation of flogging was not. (The punishment of flogging brought out the same emotions of disgrace as debtor's prison, which he recalled in a letter to Lowell. As a small child, he had been held up to peer through an opening in a building that had not a window but a small opening with iron bars; there he saw his father's face in such a state of agony that he was unable to respond to the child's cries with any sign of recognition.) Tom soon deserts the navy, but he strikes an officer while trying to avoid recapture, expecting afterward to be hanged and buried at sea for his crimes. Captain Willing warns him that he will be court-martialed and then punished severely because the captain must always maintain order at the start of a long voyage. Tom accepts his fate, as Billy Budd was to do half a century later:

I could easily understand how [*sic*] the necessity of preserving the most rigid discipline at all times on board of a ship, where there were so many men, even in comparatively trivial matters, to insure perfect obedience in time of difficulty and danger; and I could readily conceive of the feelings of Captain Willing when he refused to screen me from the decision of the court martial while he showed me a desire to do me a kindness." But the supposedly inflexible and impersonal law of military necessity suddenly becomes quite flexible and personal when the Captain learns he had an old tie to Tom's father.

In many ways, Briggs, a regular contributor to *The Knickerbocker* from 1839 to 1846, exemplified the "New York tone": he was a Whig, a merchant, and a civilized man with leisure for reading and composition; he displayed an unprudish taste for bawdiness, identified neither with Southern slavery nor Northern abolitionists, and had a horror of both German romanticism and New England transcendentalism. Moreover, he was definitely a novelist and not a romancer. He rejected Edward Bulwer-Lytton's idea that fiction should follow an a priori scheme, and he despised secondhand knowledge, such as Cooper's seamanship, seemingly based on "ideas from some naval spectacle at the 'Bowery,'" whereas to Briggs the sea was always "sublime and terrible."

Yet, in other ways, Briggs was not a typical Knickerbocker at all. The source of Briggs's strength is that he was both an insider, who had risen to a degree of success in both the New York business and literary worlds, and, at the same time, an outsider, a cantankerous "Ishmael," as his friends sometimes referred to him, one who preferred to follow his own path. He never lost his Quaker simplicity and come-outer enthusiasm, qualities not always in demand in the higher Episcopal circles of New York. His expectations of a comfortable life were deeply scarred by his fall from respectability into poverty, more traumatic for being wholly unexpected. He wrote in large part to correct social injustice, but *The Knickerbocker,* blunting the point of his satire in *Harry Franco,* saw it only as "an unpremeditated, natural sketch of the different phases which the career of an American boy sometimes assumes." To New York readers who lacked compassion, Briggs seemed the creator not of a world of literary realism demanding social justice but rather of a quirky domain that was simply funny.

Briggs left no literary manifestos. Yet, he was something of an eighteenth-century primitive who believed in natural rights and an innate moral sense that defied rational analysis; he satirized the Dribble children in *The Trippings of Tom Pepper* as "well regulated machines" without impulses of their own. Bassett in the same novel speaks for Briggs as an advocate of the full natural person: "Man is not a mere talking machine, but a thinking one, and speech was designed to express his thoughts, not to dis-

guise them, as has been thought by some. But thoughts cannot be disguised; they will show themselves without the thinker knowing it–there is a language of action, and of looks, as well as of words–and your thoughts will discover themselves in spite of all your endeavors to hide them." At home on Staten Island during the hot summer of 1843, Briggs shocked the sedate Duyckinck, who found him "as nearly in a state of nudity as decency permitted," without shoes, stockings, neckerchief, coat, suspenders. Briggs's literary style, which Duyckinck admired, was equally spare and natural: "he knows his words and never says too much."

Briggs's reputation has changed as rapidly as the prospects of a young hero in an eighteenth-century English comic novel. His death 20 June 1877 was marked by obituaries in many New York newspapers, including the *Times, Tribune, Herald, Sun, World,* and *Independent.* At the time of his death, he was remembered mainly as an editor and journalist, which is what he had been for close to thirty years and is how he is described in the obituary in *The New York Times* and in the entry in *The Cambridge History of American Literature* (1917–1921). At the turn of the century, James Russell Lowell's biographers, Charles Eliot Norton and Horace Scudder, used Briggs's letters to tell the story of his friend Lowell. Although Norton was a respected scholar, he perversely refused to return the Lowell letters he had borrowed from Briggs's heirs even after legal admonitions to do so, setting off a chain of events in which a large body of Briggs's letters disappeared from scholarly view during the first two-thirds of the twentieth century.

Meanwhile, George E. Woodberry, in his biography of Edgar Allan Poe, depicted Briggs as an editorial associate of Poe who had written unsympathetic biographic sketches of him. After Arthur Hobson Quinn disclosed Rufus Griswold's forgeries of Poe, the image of Poe as victim tended to tar all those who had been critical of him as though they all had been members of one gang, the enemies of Poe. Perry Miller in *The Raven and the Whale* (1956) established the context of the Briggs-Mathews satiric wars, authenticated the significance of Briggs as a novelist in his own right, and set the stage for the appreciation, still not yet complete, of Briggs's impact on Melville.

Although Melville's style reflects the new literary temperament of the mid 1840s, his subjects often follow conventions established by Briggs: the autobiography of the first voyage of a young man of good family going to sea with emotions of depression and desperation yet in hope of youthful adventure; the discovery of working-class solidarity among sailors; the two-class system of officers and men, which defies American republican and democratic beliefs; the problem of incompetent ships' officers and the imminent response of mutiny or jumping

THE BROADWAY JOURNAL.

VOL. I. NO. 10.

Three Dollars per Annum.
Single Copies, 6 1-4 Cents.

NEW YORK, SATURDAY, MARCH 8, 1845.

C. F. BRIGGS, EDGAR A. POE, H. C. WATSON, EDITORS.

Published at
153 BROADWAY, by
John Bisco.

Poe's name joins the masthead.
Berg Collection

Flag for the periodical Briggs edited with Edgar Allan Poe and H. C. Watson

ship; the emotional and physical horrors of undeserved flogging; the psyche-altering thrill of falling from the topmast into the sea; sailor character types, including the handsome sailor; the parallels between going to sea and going to New York City (where *Moby-Dick* begins); and, finally, the multiethnic ship's crew as a microcosm of American society. As a novelist of the emerging city, Briggs is again a forerunner of Melville in describing the confidence man and trickster, the perfidious complications of banking and the law, the moral lawlessness of the streets, and the New York of radical literary and social movements.

Briggs's main creation, Harry Franco, is an urban savage determined to succeed without quite knowing how. Briggs uses him to challenge the hortative tradition of well-intentioned maxims, sermons, and readings, suddenly made irrelevant by a rapidly changing world. The machinery of the traditional British novel, based on social rank as defined by birth—with plots of the discovered identity of foundlings, lost children, and illegitimate offspring—provided Briggs with rich opportunities for parody and satire. The pictures of pure goodness and pure evil in popular literary romances were to Briggs even more laughable. In American life in the 1830s and 1840s, birth as the measure of social rank was being supplanted by the possession of property, but the economy was too transient and too volatile to support any durable social establishment. Briggs discovered that American life, inserted into the older forms of the eighteenth-century British novel, seemed radically wild, wonderfully improbable, inherently fictional. The central American hypocrisy, which Briggs exploited in all his comedy and satire, was that despite declared ideologies of Jeffersonian and Jacksonian social egalitarianism and a commitment to the Puritan and Franklinesque ethics of work and thrift, Americans of middle station saw differences in class and race in moral terms, both despising the poor and blacks

beneath them and worshiping anyone above them, apparently above them, or just pretending to be above them.

But Harry in his constant pursuit to define his Byronic self-made self has no choice but to confront the city or the sea and the ordeals of fear, poverty, isolation, anomie, and aporia (logical problem with no solution). While driven by the need to rise in the new society, Harry remains emotionally connected to the lost pastoral of his childhood and looks at city civilization with the eyes of a first-generation immigrant. He is both picaro and critic: his adventures include real dangers and real entertainments, but he looks at society from slightly outside it, supporting comedy and satire. Harry Franco becomes an urban-nautical forerunner of that rural-nautical American hero Huck Finn, and the similarity of initials may not be coincidental, since Samuel Langhorne Clemens (Mark Twain) in his 1871 "burlesque autobiography" calls himself a Tom Pepper.

Briggs was still working as a writer and editor on the day he died in 1877. His obituary in *The Independent* appeared in the same issue as the last of his final series of fictional letters from Elder Brewster Jr. of Brewsterville, Massachusetts. Still writing satirically on his favorite subjects of social conformity and ethnic discrimination, Briggs found the news of the day more improbable than fiction: Frederick Douglass, once a fugitive slave, having become a federal marshal in the District of Columbia, was urging blacks to achieve political power by acquiring property, while the Grand Union Hotel of Saratoga was denying admission to Joseph Seligman, a Jewish banker from New York, because he might appear to be too wealthy.

Someone at *The Independent* found in Briggs's desk an undated article on Poe, whom Briggs had never forgiven: "He aimed at nothing, thought of nothing, and hoped for nothing but literary reputation." Briggs's final statement attempted to dissuade Poe's supporters from striving "to compel the world to award him a character which he never coveted and held in supreme contempt." Afterward, life seemed destined to continue to imitate art. A myth persists that Briggs wrote a hostile article on Poe for *The Encyclopedia Britannica,* a statement supported in the *Dictionary of American Biography,* which probably got it from an obituary in *The New York Sun.* The article is mentioned (and is even described) by several Poe critics. But the article does not exist. There is a *Britannica* article, however, signed by Robert Carter, Lowell's associate in 1843 on *The Pioneer.* After thirty years as a respected New York journalist, three mysteries survived Briggs: long ago he had once had a substantial literary career as a novelist; no one knew any longer the full extent of his writings; and he had not helped to clarify matters because, as stated in *The New York Times,* he had never had "the slightest particle of literary ambition."

Letters:

Garnett McCoy, "I Am Right and You Are Wrong: Letters of Advice to an Artist of the 1840s" [Briggs to William Page], *Archives of American Art Journal,* 28 (1988): 15–21.

Biography:

Bette S. Weidman, "Charles Frederick Briggs: A Critical Biography," dissertation, Columbia University, 1968.

References:

Thomas Bender, *New York Intellect: A History of Intellectual Life in New York City* (Baltimore: Johns Hopkins University Press, 1987), pp. 161–168;

John Bryant, "Melville and Charles Frederick Briggs: Working a Passage to *Billy Budd,*" *English Language Notes,* 22 (June 1985): 48–54;

Bryant, ed., *A Companion to Melville Studies* (Westport, Conn.: Greenwood Press, 1986);

John J. Cawelti, *Apostles of the Self-Made Man* (Chicago: University of Chicago Press, 1965);

Martin Duberman, *James Russell Lowell* (Boston: Houghton Mifflin, 1966), pp. 51–52;

Heyward Ehrlich, "The *Broadway Journal:* Briggs's Dilemma and Poe's Strategy," *Bulletin of the New York Public Library,* 73 (February 1969): 74–93;

Ehrlich, "Charles Frederick Briggs and Lowell's *Fable for Critics,*" *Modern Language Quarterly,* 28 (September 1967): 329–341;

Jay Leyda, *The Melville Log* (New York: Harcourt, Brace, 1951);

Perry Miller, *The Raven and the Whale* (New York: Harcourt, Brace, 1956), pp. 47–58;

Sidney P. Moss, *Poe's Literary Battles: The Critic in the Context of His Literary Milieu* (Durham, N.C.: Duke University Press, 1963);

Charles Eliot Norton, ed., *Letters of James Russell Lowell,* 2 volumes (New York: Harper, 1894);

Horace Scudder, *James Russell Lowell: A Biography,* 2 volumes (Boston: Houghton, Mifflin, 1901);

Joshua Taylor, *William Page: The American Titian* (Chicago: University of Chicago Press, 1967), pp. 55–57;

Dwight Thomas and David K. Jackson, *The Poe Log: A Documentary Life of Edgar Allan Poe (1809–1849)* (New York: G. K. Hall, 1987);

Bette S. Weidman, "The *Broadway Journal:* A Casualty of Abolition Politics," *Bulletin of the New York Public Library* (February 1969): 94–113;

Weidman, Foreword to *The Adventures of Harry Franco* (New York: Garrett, 1969);

Weidman, Foreword to *Working a Passage* (New York: Garrett, 1970);

George W. Woodberry, *The Life of Edgar Allan Poe,* 2 volumes (Boston: Houghton Mifflin, 1909).

Papers:

The most extensive collections of Charles Frederick Briggs's papers are at Cornell University, the New York Public Library, the Gay Library at Columbia University, and the Houghton Library at Harvard University, with additional holdings scattered elsewhere.

Albert Brisbane

(22 August 1809 – 1 May 1890)

Michael C. Mattek
Marquette University

See also the Brisbane entry in *DLB 3: Antebellum Writers in New York and the South.*

BOOKS: *Two Essays on the Social System of Charles Fourier, Being an Introduction to the Constitution of the Fourienne Society of New York* (New York, 1838);

Social Destiny of Man; or, Association and Reorganization of Industry (Philadelphia: C. F. Stollmeyer, 1840);

Association; or, A Concise Exposition of the Practical Part of Fourier's Social Science (New York: Greeley & McElrath, 1843); republished as *A Concise Exposition of the Doctrine of Association. Or, Plan for a Re-organization of Society, Which Will Secure to the Human Race, Individually and Collectively, Their Happiness and Elevation* (New York: J. S. Redfield, 1843);

Theory of the Functions of the Human Passions, Followed by an Outline View of the Fundamental Principles of Fourier's Theory of Social Science (New York: Miller, Orton & Mulligan, 1856);

Treatise on the Functions of Human Passions; An Outline of Fourier's System (New York: Dewitt, 1857);

Philosophy of Money (N.p., 1863);

General Introduction to Social Science. Part First—Introduction to Fourier's Theory of Social Organization, by Brisbane; *Part Second—Social Destinies*, by Charles Fourier (New York: C. P. Somerby, 1876).

OTHER: Redelia Brisbane, *Albert Brisbane: A Mental Biography with a Character Study by His Wife, Redelia Brisbane*, largely dictated by Albert Brisbane (Boston: Arena, 1893).

PERIODICAL PUBLISHED: *Phalanx* (5 October 1843 – 28 May 1845).

SELECTED PERIODICAL PUBLICATION–UNCOLLECTED: "The American Associationists," *United States Magazine and Democratic Review*, 18 (February 1846): 142–147.

During the 1840s, utopian communities sprang up throughout the United States. The largest utopian movement was that of the Associationists, whose com-

Albert Brisbane, circa 1839

munities, or "phalanxes," were based upon the teachings of the French social scientist Charles Fourier. The man responsible for bringing Fourier's theories to the United States for publication and dissemination was Albert Brisbane. Brisbane disapproved of the trial communities of the Associationists, however. Since they were far smaller than the prototype outlined by Fourier, Brisbane believed them incapable of achieving the social harmony of Fourier's model. In his lifelong interest in and support of Fourier's writings, Brisbane was attempting to carry out a search for mathematical laws, which he believed undergirded not only the hard sciences of astronomy and mechanics but also the social sciences of philosophy, sociology, and economics.

Albert Brisbane was born 22 August 1809 in Batavia, located in the western portion of New York State. His father, James Brisbane, was a large landowner who had moved to the region in 1789 when the Holland Land Company sent him and four others to survey and lay out for development its four million acres. Of Scottish descent, James Brisbane left the Scottish Presbyterian Church and remained a skeptic all his life. In similar fashion, Albert later also questioned and challenged the doctrines of established Christian religions. Albert's mother, Mary Stevens Brisbane, who was deeply interested in the sciences, gained some local renown for her knowledge of astronomy, a love of which she passed along to her son; Albert's study of astronomy formed the model for his inquiries into the humanities and social sciences later in life. He sought in the behavior of people and societies the same cosmic laws that governed the planets and stars. Other early influences on Albert included his close contact with nature—especially through his love of hunting, fishing, and horsemanship—and the development of his mechanical skills, which were fostered by his being welcomed in the workshops of the village.

Albert's formal education commenced in New York City. First placed in a boarding school in Flushing, Long Island, he begged his father to move him because of the rowdy students there. Albert boarded with a French family on Garden Street, but he was unable to learn the French language from tutors using the traditional rote method and so he was referred by his new schoolmaster, Mr. Ingersoll, to Jean Manesca, who had developed a new method—which Albert found effective—for learning the French language. After mastering, and also embracing, the Enlightenment philosophies of Manesca, Albert studied Spanish and Latin using the same method of conversation and composition. Impressed by Manesca's intellectual curiosity, Albert desired to study philosophy in Europe and quickly persuaded his father to allow him to do so.

Leaving for Europe in May 1828, Brisbane arrived at Le Havre and was impressed with the greater level of authority granted women in France. Arriving in Paris for his studies, he met a fellow American who introduced him to the aged Marquis de Lafayette, and thus Brisbane was inaugurated into French society. That summer, while eating ice cream, he suddenly realized the injustice of property ownership. His father owned land that produced an income derived from the labor of the farmers and the working classes. In reality, then, they were the ones paying for the ice cream. This epiphany, while awakening Brisbane to labor injustices, did not lead him to forsake the luxuries that personal property afforded him.

Brisbane began to learn German that same summer, and in the fall he began his studies at the Sorbonne, following les cours (the courses) of Victor Cousin, François-Pierre-Guillaume Guizot, and Abel François Villemain—the popular lectures on philosophy, history, and literature. Disappointed with Cousin's philosophic method of simply synthesizing previous theories, Brisbane decided to study Georg Wilhelm Friedrich Hegel and the Germans firsthand, since Cousin had spoken at length about them. Therefore, in May 1829 Brisbane set out for Berlin, the city of "absolute logic."

As "probably the only American in Berlin as a student and traveler of leisure," Brisbane was somewhat of a curiosity and thus was able to float among the upper levels of German society. He called on Johann Wolfgang von Goethe shortly before Goethe's death and was introduced to prominent Jewish bankers, through whom he met the Mendelssohns, including the composer, Felix. At the university, Brisbane was excited by the mechanical and mathematical complexity of the human body through his study of anatomy. However, Hegel's stodgy method of instruction and his theory of primitive energy left Brisbane in the "darkness of despair," once again disappointed with the European philosophers.

Disheartened by Christian civilization, Brisbane traveled east to Turkey to observe the "barbaric" civilization. While traveling through Asia Minor and Constantinople, he was struck by the poverty and lack of individual freedom caused by political despotism. The people's spirit of hospitality, however, was a stark contrast to the self-interests and rigid quid pro quo of Western capitalism. While in Turkey, Brisbane was once again impressed with the moral influence of women and realized how stultifying the isolated household and subordination to males had been to his mother's personal ambitions.

Having now observed social structures in wilderness America (those of both European settlers and Native Americans), urban America, Europe, and Asia Minor, Brisbane concluded that the particular form or system of government did not affect the fundamental constitution of society. All his travels, at home and abroad, had only served to reveal the gross inequalities in every social structure. Continuing his travels, Brisbane visited Greece, Malta, Syracuse, Sicily, Naples, and Rome, where he encountered Felix Mendelssohn, with whom he traveled to Florence.

Upon his return to Paris in the early summer of 1831, Brisbane studied the St. Simonians' doctrines, which included the elevation of the laboring classes to industrial equality, the elevation of women, and the reform of sexual relations. Brisbane shortly abandoned the St. Simonians because its two leaders, Prosper Enfantin and Saint-Amand Bazard, exercised dictatorial control and because the new religion they taught seemed too contrived. Fleeing the dissension within the St. Simonians, Brisbane traveled to England, Ireland, and Scotland, where he equally disdained the selfish individualism and struggle for personal survival that he witnessed there.

Later, while traveling in Germany, Brisbane received from his friend Jules Lechevalier, whom Brisbane had asked to keep him updated on new theories arising from France, a copy of Charles Fourier's *Traitée de l'association domestique agricole* (1822). Fourier advocated reorganizing society into self-contained agricultural/industrial cooperatives, or "phalanxes," comprised of approximately 1,600 persons. The cornerstone of Fourier's plans was the creation of social "harmony"—making labor attractive, rather than mundane or oppressive, by organizing workers into "series" and "groups" wherein individual workers rotated through various tasks. The configuration of these groups, Fourier thought, was in exact harmony with the laws of nature and thus with the spiritual forces behind those natural laws. By thus pooling and organizing the talents of skilled workers, a phalanx could enjoy such "guarantees" for its workers as education, housing, sustenance, and leisure. In time, such phalanxes supposedly would create universal wealth, education, refinement and elevation, and a practical unity in society, because the system, since it was in harmony with the laws of nature, would unleash the passions within naturally moral human beings.

Enthralled by Fourier's works, Brisbane in May 1832 departed Berlin for Paris, where he studied with Fourier himself for the next two years and met such disciples of Fourier as Victor-Prosper Considérant. Describing his tutoring sessions with Fourier, Brisbane states, "I took these lessons twice a week—in all twelve—at five francs a lesson. I would spend with him an hour at a time, sometimes asking questions, sometimes talking generally on problems of social science. . . . I discovered later that his Theory of Laws had to be carefully and profoundly studied in order to penetrate to the bottom and understand it clearly."

In the spring of 1834, Brisbane, having now studied in Europe for six years, left for the United States with the intention of propagating Fourier's theories in the New World. Reportedly in poor health for the next four years, Brisbane limited his writings to his theories on currency and banking, an especially relevant topic in light of President Andrew Jackson's Specie Circular of 11 July 1836 (which required that purchase of public lands be made only in gold or silver, an effort to curb land speculation) and Jackson's previous war with finan-

Charles Fourier, whose utopian ideas Brisbane propounded (lithograph by Cisneros, 1847; after a portrait by Jean-François Gigoux)

cier Nicholas Biddle over the Bank of the United States (formed by President James Monroe and opposed by Jackson), of which Biddle was president. In addition to his writings on currency issues, Brisbane also engaged in land speculation. He hoped to earn enough from his land dealings to finance the first trial phalanx; however, the Panic of 1837, itself the result of President Jackson's Specie Circular, put an end to Brisbane's dreams of quick and enormous profits.

By 1839 Brisbane began an earnest grassroots effort to spread the doctrines of "Associationism." He organized a Fourierist society of Associationists and began lecturing in New York and Philadelphia. Soon he had arranged to have a front-page column (for which the Associationists paid $500) published in Horace Greeley's recently founded daily newspaper, the *New York Tribune*. Through Greeley's publication, word of Associationism was spread throughout the country, gaining adherents, primarily among the working classes and especially among the farmers, as well as attracting a group of social reformers. Brisbane's two most significant works that explained and explicated Fourier's teachings were published during this same period—his *Social Destiny of Man; or, Association and Reorganization of Industry* (1840) and *Association; or, A Concise Exposition of the Practical Part of Fourier's Social Science* (1843).

Although Brisbane was enthralled by Fourier's scope of investigation and his adeptness at social organization, he nevertheless cautiously avoided Fourier's more speculative, almost fairy-tale visions of life in a harmonic universe. In his more-speculative writings, Fourier proclaimed his theories on planetary copulation, the future evolution of humans with tails, and a future world in which the oceans would be transformed into a lemonade-like substance. Brisbane, in his writings and proselytizing, presented only those parts of Fourier's writings that he deemed acceptable to an American audience, such as how labor could be made attractive and how Association could be financially and materially advantageous. Fourier's more-controversial theories—such as those on the benefits of sexual orgies and open marriage, and his attacks on organized religion—were excluded from the Associationists' platform. Even with these deletions, however, Associationism was not free from criticism. The clergy derided it because Fourier's underlying belief in the goodness of human passions undermined "their theology which looked upon man as a fallen and sinful creature. . . . The doctrines of Association were treated as atheistic, immoral, tending to break up the family; as communistic doctrines, destroying individual property; as doctrines sinking the individual in the mass, and establishing a system of prosaic monasticism."

Despite such criticisms of Associationism, grassroots support of Brisbane's message led to the springing up of about thirty undersized communities, or "Practical Phalanxes." Brisbane looked with disdain at these attempts: they included fewer acres and a smaller population of inhabitants than Fourier's prototype; they were nearly always grossly underfinanced and weighed down in debt; and their members lacked the spiritual maturity Brisbane thought critical for such an undertaking. Brisbane had envisioned a patient accumulation of funds to construct a single, full-scale phalanx. What he received instead was a myriad of autonomous associations spread out in the North, primarily in western New York State, Massachusetts, New Jersey, and the midwestern states. The North American Phalanx in Red Bank, New Jersey, lasted the longest of those phalanxes that arose during the heyday of the movement, the 1840s and 1850s; it existed from 1843 to 1855. The Clarkson Phalanx in New York State was the most populated, with 420 members; the Alphadelphia Association in Kalamazoo County, Michigan, was the largest, with 2,814 acres; and the Wisconsin Phalanx was the most successful financially, disbanding in 1850 in order to reap the benefits of rising land values.

The most famous phalanx, though, was Brook Farm, which lasted from 1841 to 1847, officially affiliating with Fourierism in 1845. From this location *The*

Harbinger, the official publication of the American Union of Associationists, was published, until a fire led to the disbanding of Brook Farm in 1847; thereafter, *The Harbinger* was published in New York City until 1849. *The Harbinger* enabled the operational phalanxes to stay informed of undertakings and successes of other associated communities. It also served as a vehicle to maintain some level of uniformity among these communities. The paper published extensive translations of Fourier's works, along with literary and music reviews, responses to current events, and calls for social reform. Brisbane contributed many and sundry articles to *The Harbinger* from 1845 through 1847—including "Movement in Favor of a Social Reformation," "The Question of Slavery," "Theory of the Human Passions," "Religious Movement in Germany," "Interest on Capital," "Government—The Church—Marriage," "Industrial Reform," "False Association Contrasted with True Association," and "The Famine in Ireland."

Brisbane traveled to Paris again in 1844, where he had copies made of Fourier's unpublished manuscripts and also undertook an extensive study of musicology and embryology. Returning to the United States in December, Brisbane reexamined all of Fourier's teachings through the lenses of his recently acquired knowledge of music and physiology, including not only Fourier's plans for agrarian communities based on his "Law of the Series" but also his theory of the "passions of the soul" (that is, psychology) and evolution of human societies. Brisbane attempted to synthesize Fourier's teachings with his own observations in order to discover the one universal law behind the evolution not only of Western civilizations but also of historical religions, philosophies, and social institutions.

Just as the economic panic of 1837, which lasted well into the first half of the 1840s, had made Associationism attractive to dispossessed Americans, the economic recovery of the latter part of the decade contributed to the demise of interest in communal living. In addition, the collapse of the small operational phalanxes tainted the public's view of the soundness of Fourier's doctrines. Brisbane felt that the small-scale operational phalanxes in no way adequately demonstrated the soundness of Fourier's theories; he continued to promote, according to Carl J. Guarneri, "plans for one huge experiment that would demonstrate conclusively the truth of Fourier's theory. For three decades he circulated innumerable proposals, as if one detail changed or another sponsor contacted could make the dream achieve reality."

After the demise of the Associationist movement in the 1850s, Brisbane continued his study of music, mechanics, philosophy, and astronomy. His inventions included a system of transportation by means of hollow

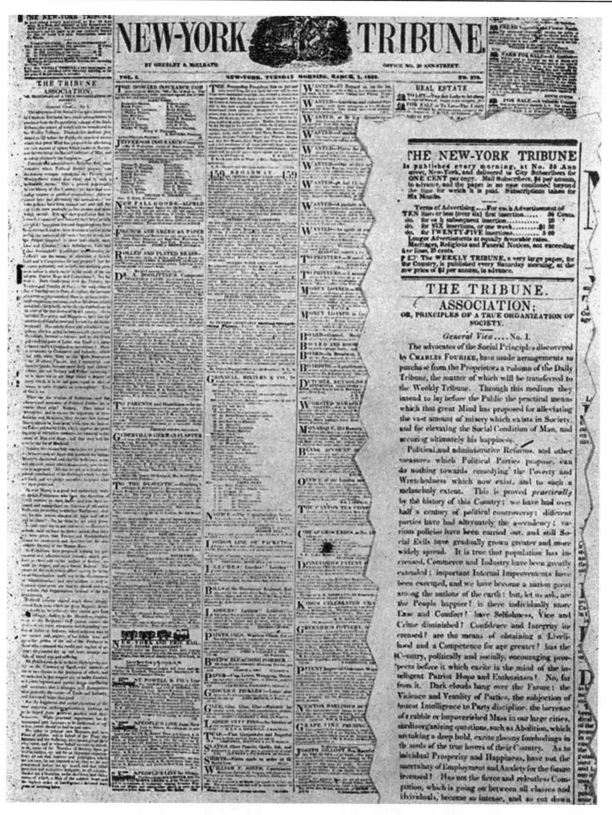

*Brisbane's first column on Fourierism (far left and far right), in the 1 March 1842 issue
of Horace Greeley's newspaper (Wisconsin Historical Society)*

THEORY

OF THE

FUNCTIONS

OF THE

HUMAN PASSIONS,

FOLLOWED BY AN OUTLINE VIEW OF

THE FUNDAMENTAL PRINCIPLES

OF

FOURIER'S THEORY OF SOCIAL SCIENCE.

BY

ALBERT BRISBANE.

NEW YORK:
MILLER, ORTON, & MULLIGAN.
25 PARK ROW.
1856.

Title page for Brisbane's book summarizing Fourier's views (Widener Library, Harvard University)

spheres in pneumatic tubes, a system of underground fertilization, a new form of steamship, a new type of propeller for the bow of a ship, compressed wood, and an oven designed to cook in a vacuum, thus dispensing with yeast and other artificial means of raising bread and pastry. Even Brisbane's inventions, however, were linked to his advocacy of Fourierism, for he pledged profits from his patents toward Fourierist propaganda or a new communal experiment.

Although Brisbane's domestic and sexual life was scandalous in relation to his times, little was publicly revealed about his conduct until an alimony trial in 1883. During his first European tour, he employed prostitutes and seduced a chambermaid. His first marriage was in 1833 to Adele le Brun, reportedly a Bavarian countess, whom he had met two years before. The two separated, and she returned to Europe in 1838. Although advocating increased importance for women in his model communities, Brisbane himself took many concubines throughout his life, then cast them off when bored with them. Guarneri says in his *The Utopian Alternative: Fourierism in Nineteenth-Century America* (1991) that "the most notable example was Brisbane's on-again-off-again relationship with Lodoiska Durand, Jean Manesca's daughter. When she sued for divorce in 1883, testimony at the sensational trial revealed that Brisbane had had an affair with her in 1839 or 1840, lived with her at three different times, and fathered three children by her before breaking off the relationship; he claimed that their marriage was invalid because he had never been divorced from his first wife, Adele le Brun. The court ordered him to pay alimony of $25 per week." With his wife Sarah White, he fathered three children, the most notable of whom was Arthur Brisbane, later editor of the *New York Evening Journal*. Brisbane's last wife, Redelia Bates Brisbane, recorded his conversations regarding his life, Fourier's theories, and his own intellectual speculations and included them in her biography of her husband, *Albert Brisbane: A Mental Biography with a Character Study by His Wife, Redelia Brisbane,* published in 1893. The work is designed to highlight Brisbane's intellectual gifts and drive, but it also reveals his ineptitude as a leader. Some historical details are errant because of Brisbane's faulty memory, since he dictated the contents while in his seventies; however, the work still ranks as a necessary and overall accurate portrayal of Brisbane's life. Understandably, no references are made to his sexual escapades; however, Guarneri includes in his book information he recovered from Brisbane's personal journals and correspondence, which are housed at Syracuse University.

Brisbane died 1 May 1890 in Richmond, Virginia. His lasting literary and political legacy exists not in what he himself wrote but in the influence that his activities had on reformist novelists, journalists, city designers, and feminists during the nineteenth century. Through his lifelong advocacy of Fourierism, Brisbane made available ideological alternatives to laissez-faire economic models in the United States. Much of his system of socialism was incorporated by Edward Bellamy in his best-seller, *Looking Backward, 2000–1887*. Published in 1888, Bellamy's book in turn spurred the creation of "Bellamy Clubs," stimulated utopian thinking to such an extent that forty-six other utopian novels were published in the United States between 1889 and 1900, and contributed to the rising influence of the Populist Party in American politics. Earlier in the century, Brisbane's advocacy contributed to the rise of worker cooperatives and impacted the work of the premier American landscape architect and park designer, Frederick Law Olmstead (who designed Central Park in New York City as a harmonious melding of city and country environments). Brisbane's advocacy for economic independence and sexual freedom for women, moreover, helped pave the way for the feminist movements of the 1850s, and Margaret Fuller gives an overall favorable account of Fourierism in her book, *Woman in the Nineteenth Century* (1845). Vituperative renunciation of Fourier and Brisbane also occurred in literary works. Nathaniel Hawthorne's egotistical reformer, Hollingsworth, in *The Blithedale Romance* (1852) is thought to be modeled on Brisbane himself, and James Fenimore Cooper's little-known work *The Crater* (1847) warns of the dystopia that emerges when a utopia is constructed upon the mistaken belief in the inherent goodness of human nature.

Albert Brisbane is little known today outside the realm of scholars who study American utopian movements. His importance in American history and literature was surprisingly widespread during the nineteenth century, however, despite the contradictions of his personal life, his ineptness at leadership, and the limiting of his abilities to proselytizing the works of others rather than creating original works of his own.

Biographies:

Redelia Brisbane, *Albert Brisbane: A Mental Biography with a Character Study by His Wife, Redelia Brisbane* (Boston: Arena, 1893);

Oliver Carlson, *Brisbane: A Candid Biography* (New York: Stackpole, 1937).

References:

Arthur Bestor, "Albert Brisbane–Propagandist for Socialism in the 1840s," *New York History,* 28 (April 1947): 153–158;

William Hall Brock, "Phalanx on a Hill: Responses to Fourierism in the Transcendentalist Circle," dissertation, Loyola University–Chicago, 1995;

Sterling F. Delano, The Harbinger *and New England Transcendentalism: A Portrait of Associationism in America* (Rutherford, N.J.: Fairleigh Dickinson University Press, 1983);

Michael Fellman, *The Unbounded Frame: Freedom and Community in Nineteenth-Century American Utopianism* (Westport, Conn.: Greenwood Press, 1973), pp. 3–19;

Carl J. Guarneri, *The Utopian Alternative: Fourierism in Nineteenth-Century America* (Ithaca, N.Y.: Cornell University Press, 1991);

Lloyd E. Rohler Jr., "The Utopian Persuasion of Albert Brisbane, First Apostle of Fourierism," dissertation, Indiana University, 1977.

Papers:

Much of Albert Brisbane's personal papers and correspondence is located in the George Arentis Research Library, Syracuse University, and in the Illinois Historical Survey, University of Illinois.

William Cullen Bryant

(3 November 1794 – 12 June 1878)

Frank Gado

See also the Bryant entries in *DLB 3: Antebellum Writers in New York and the South; DLB 43: American Newspaper Journalists, 1690–1872; DLB 59: American Literary Critics and Scholars, 1800–1850;* and *DLB 189: American Travel Writers, 1850–1915.*

BOOKS: *The Embargo, or Sketches of the Times; A Satire, by a youth of thirteen,* anonymous (Boston: Printed for the purchasers, 1808); second edition, corrected and enlarged as *The Embargo; or, Sketches of the Times. A Satire . . . Together with The Spanish Revolution and Other Poems,* as Bryant (Boston: Printed for the author by E. G. House, 1809);

An Oration, Delivered at Stockbridge. July 4th 1820 (Stockbridge: Printed by Charles Webster, 1820);

Poems (Cambridge, Mass.: Printed by Hilliard & Metcalf, 1821);

Poems, by William Cullen Bryant, An American (New York: E. Bliss, 1832; London: J. Andrews, 1832; enlarged edition, Boston: Russell, Odiorne & Metcalf, 1834; enlarged again, New York: Harper, 1836; enlarged again, New York: Harper, 1839); revised and enlarged again, with poems arranged by Bryant according to order of composition (Philadelphia: Carey & Hart, 1847; enlarged again, 2 volumes, New York: D. Appleton, 1855; London: Sampson Low, 1858);

Semi-Centennial Celebration of the Inauguration of Washington. Ode (New York, 30 April 1839);

Popular Considerations on Homoeopathia (New York: W. Radde, 1841);

The Fountain and Other Poems (New York & London: Wiley & Putnam, 1842);

The White-Footed Deer and Other Poems (New York: I. S. Pratt, 1844);

A Funeral Oration, Occasioned by the Death of Thomas Cole, Delivered before the National Academy of Design, New-York, May 4, 1848 (New York: D. Appleton / Philadelphia: George S. Appleton, 1848);

Letters of a Traveller; or, Notes of Things Seen in Europe and America (New York: Putnam, 1850);

William Cullen Bryant, circa 1845 (daguerreotype attributed to Mathew Brady)

Reminiscences of the Evening Post: Extracted from the Evening Post of November 15, 1851, with Additions and Corrections by the Writer (New York: William C. Bryant, Printers, 1851);

Letters of a Traveller, second series (New York: D. Appleton, 1859);

A Discourse on the Life, Character and Genius of Washington Irving, Delivered Before the New York Historical Society,

*at the Academy of Music in New York on the 3d of April,
1860* (New York: Putnam, 1860);

Thirty Poems (New York & London: D. Appleton, 1864);

Hymns (N.p., 1864);

Letters from the East (New York: Putnam, 1869);

*Some Notices of the Life and Writings of Fitz-Greene Halleck,
Read Before the New York Historical Society, on the 3d of
February, 1869* (New York, 1869);

*A Discourse on the Life, Character and Writings of Gulian
Crommelin Verplanck, Delivered Before the New-York
Historical Society, May 17th, 1870* (New York:
Printed for the Society, 1870);

Orations and Addresses (New York: Putnam, 1873);

Poems (New York: D. Appleton, 1876);

*A Popular History of the United States, from the First Discovery
of the Western Hemisphere by the Northmen, to the End of
the First Century of the Union of the States,* 4 volumes,
by Bryant and Sidney Howard Gay (New York:
Scribners, 1876–1881);

The Poetical Works of William Cullen Bryant, 2 volumes,
edited by Parke Godwin (New York: D. Apple-
ton, 1883, 1884).

OTHER: *Miscellaneous Poems Selected from the United States
Literary Gazette,* includes 26 poems by Bryant (Boston: Cummings, Hilliard/Harrison Gray, 1826);

The Talisman, 3 volumes, edited, with contributions by
Bryant, Robert Sands, and Gulian Verplanck, as
Francis Herbert (New York: Elam Bliss, 1827,
1828, 1829);

"The Skeleton's Cave" and "Medfield," in *Tales of
Glauber-Spa,* 2 volumes, by Bryant, William Leggett, Catharine Maria Sedgwick, and James Kirke
Paulding, as Francis Herbert (New York: Harper,
1832), I: 193–239, 243–276;

The Iliad of Homer, 2 volumes, translated by Bryant (Boston: Fields, Osgood, 1870);

The Odyssey of Homer, 2 volumes, translated by Bryant
(New York: James R. Osgood, 1871–1872);

Picturesque America, edited by Bryant (New York: D.
Appleton, 1872–1874).

No line of his poetry survives in the consciousness of his nation, and none of his editorial pronouncements still resonate from his five decades with
the *New-York Evening Post;* yet, no frieze interpreting
nineteenth-century intellectual America is thinkable
without William Cullen Bryant. The fame he won as a
poet while in his youth remained with him as he
entered his eighties; only Henry Wadsworth Longfellow and Ralph Waldo Emerson were his rivals in popularity over the course of his life. "Thanatopsis," if not
the American poem best known abroad before the mid

nineteenth century, certainly ranked near the top of
the list, and at home schoolchildren were commonly
required to recite it from memory. At Bryant's death,
all New York City went into mourning for its most
respected citizen, and eulogies poured forth as they
had for no man of letters since Washington Irving, its
native son, had died a generation earlier. That the loss
of the two writers produced comparable responses was
appropriate, for they had introduced the first flowering of a United States national literature and helped
establish New York as its capital. Just as publication of
Irving's *The Sketch Book* in 1819–1820 had brought
international legitimacy to American fiction, the publication of Bryant's *Poems* in 1821 had signaled the maturation of an American voice in poetry.

The shaping of Bryant's mind and personality
owed much to his family circumstances in Cummington, Massachusetts, a small village in the Berkshire
hills, carved from the forest scantly a generation
before his birth on 3 November 1794. His father,
Peter Bryant, a physician and surgeon, had evidently
chosen to settle in Cummington to pursue the affections of Sarah Snell, whose family had migrated from
the same town in eastern Massachusetts; he boarded
at the Snell house and in due course married Sarah.
Several years later he undertook a risky business
speculation and lost everything, including the humble, roughly hewn cabin in which he had installed his
wife and two infant children. Desperate—Cullen had
been born within the year—he sought to recoup
enough to stay out of debtor's prison by sailing as a
ship's surgeon. That plan was also ill-starred: the
French stopped the ship at sea, and Peter Bryant was
interned for almost a year in Mauritius. When he
returned, he was forced to depend on his father-in-
law's generosity to restore his place in the community.
The birth of a third child, another boy, further
squeezed financial prospects, and six months before
young Cullen's fifth birthday, the Bryants resumed
residence with Sarah's parents. Peter Bryant's letters
to his own father indicate correct yet chafed relations
with the patriarchal Squire Ebenezer Snell, despite the
reestablished physician's financial infusions into the
homestead as his fortunes improved. Adding a section
to the house provided accomodation for both Bryant's medical office and the four more children born
from 1802 through 1807. Although the arrangement
allowed for a measure of insulation, Cullen Bryant
lived in a coil of the two families until he departed
from the house to practice law at age twenty-two.

Years later, Bryant underscored that he was not
among those who look back upon childhood as a
happy period. The burden of farm chores, imposed as
much for their value as moral discipline as for neces-

sity, taxed his frail physique and delicate health, and although he was ever the prize pupil, eager to please by demonstrating his brightness, the district school imposed a strict regimen: lessons were taught under threat of the switch. Yet Cummington also offered bountiful compensations. An inquisitive child, Cullen learned to make a companion of thoughts stimulated by nature. The observations of plants and flowers, of birds and sky, and of brooks and rolling fields that occupy so much of his verse resulted from the boy's delight in investigating his surroundings. Social isolation fostered romantic sensibilities that would suit the evolving tastes of the new century.

A different worldview was pressed on him by his grandfather. Western Massachusetts in the late eighteenth and early nineteenth centuries generally eschewed the liberal religious ideas that fanned out from Boston; western Massachusetts looked, for example, to the more conservative Calvinism of New Haven and the Albany area of upstate New York. Ebenezer Snell, a deacon in the Congregationalist Church, studied theological writers and was as intractable in his interpretation of Scripture as in his rulings as a local magistrate. From prayer services he conducted for his family in the mornings and evenings, he made certain that religious precepts informed the Bryant children's upbringing. Young Cullen was introduced to meter and poetry through the hymns of Isaac Watts, and he found an outlet for a love of language by constructing a makeshift pulpit of the parlor furniture from which he delivered sermons in imitation of those he heard at church. Worship stressed death and the power of the devil, and perhaps because of the boy's vulnerability to illness and chronic severe headaches, he pondered mortality, even at his tender age, and saw God's image as cast in a mold of fear and gloom.

The more compelling influence on Cullen's mental development, however, came from his father, a man of curtailed ambitions who aspired to be a citizen of a society well beyond the horizons of Cummington. Peter Bryant, like his father before him, had chosen to pursue a medical career, but his passionate preference was for the arts—for music and, particularly, poetry. As an erudite American, he had immersed himself in the ancients, and his classical nurture was reflected in his admiration for Alexander Pope and the other eighteenth-century British paragons of the Augustan style in poetry. Cullen schooled his sense of poetry according to his father's tastes. "In the long winter evenings and the stormy winter days," he wrote in his aborted autobiography, "I read, with my elder brother, books from my father's library—not a large one, but well chosen." But Peter

Bryant furnished more than the means for a love of literature. He also wrote verse, and if his derivative efforts fell short of distinction, they were nonetheless well turned. When his precocious son began stringing couplets together, Peter Bryant took delighted notice. To be sure, he held the boy to a demanding standard and was quick to derogate his exercises as doggerel—one poem, he dismissed as "tinsel"; another, as a likely object for shame in later years—but Cullen found great satisfaction in being taken seriously, and he wholeheartedly accepted his father as a mentor. By the age of thirteen, he was something of a prodigy. The *Northampton Hampshire Gazette* had published several of his poems, including a fifty-four-line exhortation to his schoolmates that he had drafted three years earlier. Beginning with a patriotic invocation of the American Revolution and concluding with a charge to "Keep Heaven's bright mansions ever in our eyes, / Press tow'rds the mark and seize the glorious prize," it rapidly became a standard selection for school recitations in the region. If, given his age, the pose he struck in a poem composed in 1807 was patently absurd—"Ah me! neglected on the list of fame! / My works unnotic'ed, and unknown my name!"—it nonetheless indicated the height of the ambitions he entertained.

Amazingly, fame more immediate than he could have imagined awaited. In this early fame, too, his father was the instrument. He had been elected as a representative to the state legislature in 1806, and his letters and his trips home to Cummington imported the political excitement of Boston. Cullen absorbed it avidly, styling his juvenile understanding according to his father's Federalist partisanship. In 1807 the young nation was bitterly divided by party and region over issues that soon ignited the War of 1812; seeking to enforce American neutrality in the Napoleonic hostilities between Britain and France, President Thomas Jefferson led his followers in Congress to pass the Embargo Act, a bar to commerce with the belligerents that struck at the economy of New England and New York. At no time prior to the Civil War was the union of states so threatened with dissolution, and Peter Bryant shared in the alarm of his pro-British party that Jacobin mob rule would result from the impoverishment of the Northeast. Cullen saw an opportunity to ply his Augustan sensibilities. Addressing Jefferson as "the scorn of every patriot name, / The country's ruin, and her council's shame," he cited cowardice before "perfidious Gaul" and alluded to the rumors of Jefferson's dalliance with the "sable" Sally Hemings as reasons he should "resign the presidential chair" and "search, with curious eye, for horned frogs, / 'Mongst the wild wastes of Louisianian bogs." Peter Bryant, cheered by the satire, encouraged his son to write more, and when the legislator returned to Boston after the holiday recess, he passed the poem about among his Federalist friends—including a poet of minor reputation who joined the father in editing and polishing the work. In the spring of 1808, *The Embargo; or, Sketches of the Times; A Satire, by a youth of thirteen* appeared as a pamphlet of a dozen pages. It soon sold out, and a second edition—in which the 244 lines of the first had swollen to 420 and, with the addition of other poems, the number of its pages had tripled—was published at the start of 1809. The book remained the talk of Boston, not only as a political rallying cry but also, a reviewer for *The Monthly Anthology* noted, as the earnest of a talent that promised "to gain a respectable station on the Parnassus mount, and to reflect credit on the literature of his country."

Raised in a household governed by the severe code of parsimony and hard work, Peter Bryant keenly regretted that he had not been allowed to indulge his appetite for humanistic education during his early years. The enthusiastic public response to his son's *The Embargo,* coupled with his own lack of fulfillment, forged his determination to provide Cullen with the advantages he himself had been denied, despite nagging concerns about his financial resources and a desire to treat all his children even-handedly. Moreover, colleges had been erupting like a rash on the young republic, and Peter Bryant recognized that society would soon draw its leaders from this new, formally trained elite. But a second argument also affected his decision: although writing poetry might win respect, it provided no one with a livelihood; a profession, however, would ensure his son the economic stability to permit development of his literary interests. Accordingly, five days after his fourteenth birthday, Cullen traveled fifty miles to board with his uncle, who was to tutor him in Latin.

The Reverend Thomas Snell quickly perceived his kinsman's special talent for language and quickly leapfrogged to more-advanced texts. "Translation from Horace. Lib. I. Car. XXII," one of the supplementary poems in the second edition of *The Embargo,* apparently had barely been blotted before the printer set it in type during the first weeks of 1809. By the end of June, Cullen had translated Virgil's *Eclogues* and part of the *Georgics* in addition to the entire *Aeneid.* Then, in August—after a month on the family farm again "treading labor's round, / To guide slow oxen o'er the furrowed ground; / The sturdy hoe or slender rake to ply, / 'Midst dust and sweat, beneath a summer sky"—he proceeded to the Reverend Moses Hallock's school in Plainfield, a few miles directly north of Cummington. There Cullen immersed himself in Greek from his waking hour to bedtime and "dreamed of Greek" in between; at the end of the term, in October, he could read the New Testament "from end to end almost as if it had been in English." He spent most of the next year, except for a spring period with Hallock to learn mathematics, at home, expanding his reading in the classics, being tutored in French by his father, and acquainting himself with philosophical writers and post-Augustan British poets. Cullen obviously found a scholar's delight in acquiring knowledge, but the pace and range of his studies were not exclusively a function of his aptitude. Hallock's tuition fees, like Thomas Snell's, were minimal, and Peter Bryant, ever mindful of the cost of education, trusted that his son's diligence, coupled with sufficient private study, would enable him to enroll at nearby Williams College in October 1810 as a sophomore, thereby saving a year of tuition.

Although the tactic succeeded, Cullen's stay at Williams College did not survive the year. His most conspicuous achievement, the poem "Descriptio Gulielmopolis," satirically expressed discontent with Williamstown and living conditions at the college, but Cullen's greater disappointment probably resulted from an absence of intellectual zest among "pale-faced, moping students [who] crawl / Like spectral monuments of woe." The academic program offered little stimulation: only two tutors had the responsibility for instruction of all sophomores, and the courses were far afield from his interests. Obtaining an honorable withdrawal, he retreated to Cummington for another period of intense solitary study, this time aimed at admission to Yale College that fall as a junior. Besides his "more laborious academic studies," he delved into his father's medical library, "became a pretty good chemist" by reading the work of Antoine-Laurent Lavoisier and performing experiments, and perused the work of Carolus Linnaeus to gain a basic knowledge of botany. But then Peter Bryant, reassessing the family's financial prospects and possibly influenced by concern about his own health, reluctantly concluded that Cullen would have to abandon college. What funds he could devote to brightening his son's future Peter Bryant decided to apply directly toward launching him in a legal career.

Like Virgil, his favorite Roman poet, Cullen believed he lacked the eloquence and confident manner required for the practice of law; moreover, he felt inhibited in the presence of lawyers because of his youth. No Gaius Maecenas appeared to rescue him from the drudgery he foresaw, however, and a month after turning seventeen, he left for Worthington, six miles down the road from Cummington, to begin to study law. During the first weeks of 1812, he still

Bryant's childhood home in Cummington, Massachusetts

hoped he might find some way to go to Yale, and writing to a friend while obviously feeling sorry for himself, he considered farming or a trade, possibly even blacksmithing–a transparently implausible option, considering his bouts of pulmonary weakness and his recurrent headaches–as preferable to the law should he not realize his wish to resume undergraduate classes at Yale the next term. But he was too much the product of his social class to ignore practical exigency: before the school year was over, he had resigned himself to study law and strove to relegate literature to an ancillary role in his life.

This shift in attention was not altogether without benefit. In the four years since he had graduated from public school to begin collegiate preparation, Cullen had laid an impressive foundation of knowledge in diverse fields. The wunderkind who had combined intelligence with cleverness to win the applause of his elders still had much to master, however, as a young adult trying to determine his place in the world. If, during his two and a half years at Worthington, he only rarely excused himself from the rigor of poring over the black-letter pages of jurists Sir Thomas Littleton and Sir Edward Coke to write verse, he more freely closed his books to enjoy the company of his contemporaries. At seventeen and eighteen, he was discovering the pleasure of conversing with his fellows at the tavern, and, with rising enthusiasm, of assaying the young ladies in the genteel parlors of the neighborhood. Then, in mid 1814, his legal preparation entered a second phase. Leaving the Berkshires

for Bridgewater, the area of his family's origins, he joined the law office of Congressman William Baylies. It was a superb opportunity. Baylies's absences in Washington gave Bryant experience in running a practice; equally important, they required him to brief his employer on the politics of his district in regular written reports–an exercise that not only served as a drill for his later newspaper work but also led him to examine his political thinking instead of merely reflecting Peter Bryant's Federalist views. Those close to Cullen Bryant noted his maturation, and at least one of his friends believed he might soon move from Bridgewater to Boston for several months, frequenting the courts to overcome his shyness while, as he said, "engaging a little in the pleasures of the town to wear off a little of [my] rusticity." But whatever his reveries may have been, he was probably still too diffident to pit himself against the sophistication of the city; when his father declined to finance a Boston stay, Cullen quickly asserted that Bridgewater had offered a sufficiently lively contrast to Worthington. Upon concluding his training (having characteristically squeezed the usual five years to four), he was admitted to the bar in August 1815, then returned to his home in Cummington for three months. Significantly, though he gathered reassurances from his mentors as to his gifts and prospects for success as an attorney, he set up his office in decidedly rural Plainfield, within view of the front porch on which he had played as a child.

Bryant's frame of mind as he was about to enter a field for which he felt ill-suited is revealed in a poem that begins, "I cannot forget with what fervid devotion / I worshipped the visions of verse and of fame." Not the law, which presumably would occupy his future, but the blighted promise of poetic greatness in the past is the subject; moreover, he dwells on the loss of a natural ease in writing. Once: "Each gaze at the glories of earth, sky, and ocean, / To my kindled emotions, was wind over flame." Poetry was merely the expression of charged consciousness: "And the thoughts that awoke, in that rapture of feeling, / Were formed into verse as they rose to my tongue." But now the innocence of a rustic youth that could effortlessly speak in Nature's voice has been corrupted– whether by sin (as critics conventionally hold) or, more likely, by the simple need to traffic in society to earn a living. The poet-become-lawyer has thereby forfeited genius:

Bright visions! I mixed with the world, and ye faded,
  No longer your pure rural worshipper now;
In the haunts your continual presence pervaded,
  Ye shrink from the signet of care on my brow.

In the old mossy groves on the breast of the mountain,
　In the deep lonely glens where the waters complain,
By the shade of the rock, by the gush of the fountain,
　I seek your loved footsteps, but seek them in vain.

Oh, leave not forlorn and forever forsaken,
　Your pupil and victim to life and its tears!
But sometimes return, and in mercy awaken
　The glories ye showed to his earlier years.

He was all of twenty-one years old.

Despite lamenting the loss of a poetic voice, however, Bryant was using one that he finally made his own. The prodigy who had written *The Embargo* had skillfully mimicked Pope—as, indeed, most rhymesters of the day were doing. Subsequently, in imitating the classical writers who underlay the Augustan Age, he had begun to appreciate the greater spontaneity they manifested in what were, for them, original encounters with their subjects; to render Horace and Virgil, he realized with his father's tutoring, meant to produce a corresponding vitality. Even so, he had still been interpreting. Then, beginning in 1810–1811, a surge of wholly new influences transformed his understanding of poetry. One was William Wordsworth and Samuel Taylor Coleridge's *Lyrical Ballads,* the revolutionary primer first published in England a decade before. Peter Bryant brought a copy from Boston sometime in 1810. As a student of poetry, he probably felt obliged to acquaint himself with this boldly different address to its art and subject matter, but he evidently was not much impressed. To his son, however, Wordsworth's language immediately gushed like "a thousand springs"; Nature for the first time spoke with a dynamic authenticity, or so he said in later years. In fact, Wordsworth's full impact may not have registered until after Bryant had begun studying law in Worthington. There his mentor, catching him scrutinizing *Lyrical Ballads,* warned him against repetition of the offense; fearful of being sent away, Bryant steeled himself to obedience for a year before loosing his curbed enthusiasm. Although most of his poetry during this period cannot be dated with precision, the Wordsworthian influence, so unmistakable in "I Cannot Forget with What Fervid Devotion," appears to become dominant only at its end.

In the meantime, Bryant had fallen under the sway of the so-called Graveyard Poets. Henry Kirke White, virtually forgotten today, had attained a moment of great renown, though less for the merit of his lugubrious verse than for the controversy sparked by an attack on it in *The Monthly Review* (London) and its defense by Robert Southey; White presently achieved martyrdom by dying in 1809 at the age of twenty. Bryant no doubt felt an affinity with the ill-starred young Scotsman, who had managed to elude his doom as a lawyer only to perish, some said, from too assiduous dedication to study. An equally potent influence was Robert Blair, another Scotsman, whose enormously popular 1743 poem "The Grave" had marked a shift in taste and practice from the crisp wit and erudition of the neoclassic age to the brooding emotional indulgence that would fuse with subsequent elements of romanticism. Bryant briefly states his admiration for Blair as a poet in an autobiographical fragment, and the direct language Blair marshals into blank verse points the way of Bryant's development, but the true attraction unquestionably lies in the subject: the effort to accept the inevitability of death and overcome fear of extinction.

A siege of typhus, or a typhuslike illness, felled inhabitants of the Worthington area at a steady rate in 1813. Several of Bryant's friends were among those stricken, but the suffering and death of a particular young woman plunged him into a melancholy. In April 1813 he had broken his pledge not to write verse while studying law by composing a poem for the wedding of his best childhood friend; weeks later, the bride lay dying. The groom wrote to ask that "your lyre not be silent" in the anticipated event, and upon her death in July, Bryant composed the first of his cluster of funereal poetry. Then, one August morning, his vigorous grandfather Ebenezer Snell was found cold in his bed. Since the stern Calvinist had based his relationship with his grandson on obedience and respect rather than on love, the old man's death caused no emotional upheaval, but the sudden absence of such a commanding figure undermined the earthly justification of life and amplified the resonance of Kirke White's despairing question, "Who will hear of Henry?" Bryant had been encouraged to believe he would win the immortality of fame, but the tightening grip of the law on his fate seemed at times like strangulation. If his ambitions perished under the drudgery of small town litigation and deed registration, who would hear of Cullen?

These various dark strands almost certainly led to the composition of the approximately fifty middle lines of the poem that later, when published, raised him to the front rank of American poets. "Thanatopsis" simply and repeatedly represents death as awaiting the nothingness toward which all life ineluctably moves. Yet, the poem is not about the horror of death but, implicitly, about the philosophical challenge to the mind to accept its ultimate obliteration. Albert F. McLean, who has written the only book-length critical study of Bryant, maintains that the poem "avoids any confrontation with religious problems"; taking direct aim at Tremaine McDowell's earlier assertion that "Thanatopsis" manifests a readiness "to break with the orthodoxy of Cummington," McLean emphatically excludes the possibility of finding in it "any heretical denial of basic Christian doctrine." But if the resurrection of the body and the immortality of the soul are basic to Christian doctrine, Bryant was nothing if not heretical. In portraying death as the "surrendering up [of] thine individual being . . . to mix for ever with the elements," and in rejecting the possibility that one's "growth," or conduct, of life is of any consequence beyond the physical matter to which the body will reduce, the poem wholly negates the meaning of Christ as redeemer.

Bryant's belief in his grandfather's Calvinist God had been deteriorating since before he attended Williams, where the exertions of the school on behalf of a conservative creed were in reaction to forceful liberal currents. Far more cogent, however, was Peter Bryant's accelerating rejection of traditional theology. He had never enlisted in the narrow piety of the Snells; his devotion to the ancient writers reflected a much more humanistically inclined temperament, and evidently he passed on this general vision of life to his son, who was also his close intellectual companion. But the father's more basic rupture with religious convention dates from the legislative sessions in Boston, where he was fully persuaded by the writings of William Ellery Channing and other early Unitarians. Although Peter Bryant continued to attend the Congregational Church in Cummington, he was one of those who refused to give public assent to Trinitarian liturgy, and a few years later he joined the Unitarian Church. His son was not baptized in any church until 1858, when he, too, enrolled as a Unitarian, but there can be no doubt that, while still in his teens, Cullen Bryant was powerfully affected by his father's retreat from theism. For a young man at the end of adolescence, the notion of a universe without God as a moral arbiter or even without a meaning to life made manifest through creation was especially unsettling. "Thanatopsis," from its inception, has the mark of a daring effort to stare into the abyss.

Relying solely on Bryant's casual recollection across several decades, editors have frequently assigned 1811 as the date of composition of the poem, but better evidence, including his wife's note on the manuscript, points to 1813, when the stimulus of the Graveyard Poets was strongest. (An alternative possibility moves it to as late as 1815.) Whichever date is correct, however, that the poem lay unfinished for some years before publication should not be read as the sign of an unresolved religious crisis. Although that view is occasionally advanced, no independent record supports it; moreover, the theory that a poet would transcribe a philo-

sophical problem in carefully wrought meter only to suspend composition until he solved the problem is implausible on its face. Bryant may have been reexamining his religious beliefs, as those on the verge of adulthood tend to do, but there was nothing tentative about the perception his poem described.

The first version of "Thanatopsis"—patently a long fragment, since it begins and ends with metrically incomplete lines—greets the reader, alerting him to the ephemerality of life and to the common fate of all mankind, the disappearance of every trace of individual consciousness. The subsequent additions of an introduction (1821) and a conclusion (circa 1818), while leaving that view unchanged, present it in a dramatically new relationship in which the words of truth belong to "a still voice," addressing a communicant with Nature's "visible forms." Previously, Nature's language of gladness and eloquence of beauty have been suited to his "gayer hours," and her "healing sympathy" has infused his "darker musings"; now, "When thoughts / Of the last bitter hour" grip the communicant's spirit and cause him to shudder, he is urged to yield to Nature once again. Earth, he is told, is "one mighty sepulchre," receiving all who ever have lived or will live. Bryant regards this realization as liberating, for its lesson is not to make too much of death.

> The gay will laugh
> When thou art gone, the solemn brood of care
> Plod on, and each one as before will chase
> His favorite phantom; yet all these shall leave
> Their mirth and their employments, and shall come
> And make their bed with thee.

In closing, the still voice instructs the communicant to live, "not like the quarry-slave at night," but as a freed being, "sustained and soothed / By an unfaltering trust" that death's state holds no terrors. The end of consciousness is comparable to lying "down to pleasant dreams."

Tracing a chronological development of Bryant's ideas through his poems can be misleading, for he was not engaged in a systematic evolution of religious belief. Even so, if the substantial concept of "Thanatopsis" was set down in 1813, it clearly opened the way from a depressive pondering of death toward an affirmation of Nature as guide and moral teacher. All three of the most significant poems he wrote either just before or during 1815 reflect Wordsworth's impact. "The Yellow Violet" praises early spring's modest flower, which had caused him to stop in appreciation of its color and faint perfume; but "midst the gorgeous blooms of May," he paid the humble stalk no attention. Much like fellow New

Englander Robert Frost, who a century later, described the figure of a poem as "what begins in delight and ends in wisdom," Bryant turns these contrasting responses to the flower into a parable:

> So they, who climb to wealth, forget
>   The friends in darker fortunes tried.
> I copied them—but I regret
>   That I should ape the ways of pride.

"Inscription for the Entrance to a Wood"—like "Thanatopsis," written in blank verse—proclaims a romantic celebration of Nature as a refuge from a world of "guilt and misery." The wood is implicitly an alternative church, with the sun shedding "a blessing on the scene" through "a thick roof of green" while a choir of chirping creatures rejoice in what Bryant specifically characterizes as prelapsarian "abodes of gladness." Although citing "the primal curse" of Eden occasions a single mention of the biblical God, the reference is surely metaphoric; nothing in the meaning of the poem supports a particularly Christian reading—indeed, in proposing the wood as a respite from the misery of human history that "God yoked to guilt," the poem might even lend itself to an anti-Christian interpretation. Much more amenable to orthodox sensibilities—a fact that helps account for its great popularity in the nineteenth century—"To a Waterfowl" finds confirmation of a Power benevolently involved in earthly matters. As the bird in flight disappears into the "abyss of heaven" when sunset yields to night, the poet absorbs the lesson:

> He who, from zone to zone,
> Guides through the boundless sky thy certain flight,
> In the long way that I must tread alone,
>   Will lead my steps aright.

What is compatible with traditional Christianity, however, is not necessarily Christian. Obviously, the waterfowl's migration and its envelopment by the night constitute a metaphor for death, but in this poem, as in "Thanatopsis," the poem speaks of dispelling fear through acceptance of harmony with Nature, not through a God who consigns the soul to heaven or hell.

During the eight months he spent in Plainfield, Bryant, advised not to do anything that the local inhabitants might think hinted at loftiness, seems to have put poetry aside. But the recess from the muse was not simply a matter of appearances: determined to make a success at the law, he struggled to overcome his inhibitions about public speaking and to cultivate the trust of potential clients. His beginning there proved unhappy. "In Plainfield," he wrote to a

friend, "I found the people rather bigoted in their notions, and almost wholly governed by the influence of a few individuals who looked upon my coming among them, with a great deal of jealousy." By June of 1816, having despaired "of ever greatly enlarging the sphere of my business," he began investigating the prospect of joining an established practice in Great Barrington, and in October he moved to the Housatonic Valley town as the partner of George Ives. Letters written during this period reflect his resolution to defeat inclinations toward indolence and focus on his practice; the following May, Ives, recognizing his junior partner's keener industry, and perhaps his superior ability, sold him his share of the practice at a bargain price. Bryant was reconciled to what appeared to be his fate. Responding to an inquiry from Baylies, he confessed,

> Alas, Sir, the Muse was my first love and the *remains* of that passion which not *rooted out* yet chilled into extinction will always I fear cause me to look coldly on the severe beauties of Themis. Yet I tame myself to its labors as well as I can, and have endeavoured to discharge with punctuality and attention such of the duties of my profession as I was capable of performing. . . . Upon the whole I have every cause to be satisfied with my situation.

The next item on his agenda was marriage. After the dearth of opportunities in Plainfield, Bryant's social life revived in Great Barrington. While his letters to former fellow law students pumped them for news of the lovely young ladies he had left behind in Bridgewater, he was scouting local entertainments. At Christmas time, he met Frances Fairchild, a nineteen-year-old orphan with "a remarkably frank expression, an agreeable figure, a dainty foot, and pretty hands, and the sweetest smile I had ever seen." By March, in writing a message of congratulation to a recent groom, Bryant worried aloud about his "many unlucky reflections" and feelings "of secret horrour at the idea of connecting my future fortunes with those of any woman on earth," but those tremors also attested the intensity of his desire to wed Fanny. And to qualify as a husband, he knew, would require concentrated application to his law practice. Poetry seemed best forgotten.

Meanwhile, however, a curious happenstance in Boston was working to change Bryant's direction. Peter Bryant's associations with the city's intellectuals had spurred an enthusiasm for an ambitious two-year-old publication, the *North American Review,* which, he wrote his son in June of 1817, would nicely serve as "the means of introducing you to notice in the capital." When his son, fixed on defining himself as a law-

Frances Fairchild Bryant, the poet's wife (miniature by an unknown artist; New-York Historical Society)

a single poem about death—to which one of them, drawing on his Greek, affixed the descriptive title "Thanatopsis." The blunder was understandable. (Commentators have remarked that the four quatrains wrongly attached at the beginning, a separate poem, not only clash with the blank verse that follows but also, in stating that heaven has sentenced man forever to "view the grave with fear," present a directly opposite view of death. Yet the coupling is not so odd as it may first seem: to perceive the blank verse as a dialectical response to the quatrains is quite plausible.) So sutured, and misattributed, this version of "Thanatopsis" was evidently the editors' favorite. But the poems identified as the son's from the start—"A Fragment" (later revised and published as "Inscription for the Entrance to a Wood") and two Horatian odes, one an imitation and the other a translation—were also well regarded; in December, the editors invited more submissions. A month later, Bryant sent, via his father, a revised version of a fragment by Simonides, which he had translated while at Williams, and a "little poem which I wrote while at Bridgewater," presumably "To a Waterfowl." These poems, along with the poem written for his friend's wedding in 1813, appeared in the March issue.

That none of these poems was a new composition prompted by the encouragement from the *North American Review* indicates that publication brought no hurrahs as had been raised when *The Embargo* appeared; indeed, Bryant had stirred a greater public response with his debut in print at the age of thirteen in the *Hampshire Gazette*. But the approbation of the Boston literati mattered far more in the long run than a quickening of popular appeal. In February, Phillips, now engaged as Bryant's agent, suggested that Bryant review a book by Solyman Brown as an excuse to produce a critical history of American poets and poetry, thereby establishing himself as the preeminent authority on the subject. Greatly aided by both his father's collection and his counsel, the twenty-three-year-old superbly met Phillips's expectations. The essay served not only as a cornerstone of American literary history but also as a thoughtful, temperate exordium to the many arguments for American literary nationalism about to erupt. A second essay, "On the Use of Trisyllabic Feet in Iambic Verse," published in September 1819, reworked material possibly first drafted when he was sixteen or seventeen and trying to shake free of Pope's neoclassical cadence; even so, the essay did much to bolster his credentials as a scholar of metrical technique. That same month Williams College awarded Bryant an honorary master's degree.

yer, ignored this prodding, Peter Bryant seized the initiative. Taking some drafts his son had left behind in his desk and rewriting two others in his own hand, Peter Bryant submitted them to Willard Phillips, a friend of long standing from Cummington and an editor of the *North American Review*. Phillips in turn conveyed them to the staff of the journal, who immediately perceived a remarkably gifted new American voice—indeed, Richard Henry Dana is reputed to have declared, in astonishment, "Ah, Phillips, you have been imposed upon; no one on this side of the Atlantic is capable of writing such verses." The debut of this new voice, however, was clouded by confusion. Because the poems submitted were in two different handwritings, the editors assumed for many months following their September publication that they were the work of two different poets—father and son. Since the *North American Review,* like many journals of that time, did not identify its contributors, the readership was unaware of the error; but a second mistake, consequent of the first, muddled the poet's intentions. Seeing that one group of poems bore titles while the rest, in Peter Bryant's hand, bore none, the editors apparently believed that the latter constituted

Meanwhile, Bryant had almost suspended writing poetry of his own. Edward Channing, the chief editor of the *North American Review,* recognizing Bryant's importance to the aspirations of the journal, had solicited a commitment "to spend a little time from your profession and give it to us." But Bryant's major allegiance continued to be to his practice. When he had reached into his file and submitted "The Yellow Violet," Channing felt compelled to reject it because, without worthy companion pieces, it was too short to justify a poetry department. Apparently, the only poem Bryant completed during the year that followed was "Green River," a skillfully wrought hymn to Nature reminiscent of "Inscription for the Entrance to a Wood," which ends, ruefully, with the poet envying the stream, free to glide "in a trance of song," while he, bound to his office, is "forced to drudge for the dregs of men, / And scrawl strange words with the barbarous pen." A second poem, "The Burial-Place," contrasts the graves of England, adorned with symbolic plants of remembrance, with those of New England, neglected by the Pilgrims and left to vegetation. But this promising conceit remained a fragment, its development unresolved. Preoccupation with the conduct of Bryant's law office may not have been the only impediment. Death once again weighed heavily on his mind—perhaps because he was enduring another period of poor health and his father was fast losing ground to consumption. Bryant's most sustained new project during the year was an essay, "On the Happy Temperament," which, contrary to what the title might suggest, scorned unbroken cheerfulness as a manifestation of insensibility. Yet its motive was not saturnine: Bryant seems to have been trying to convince himself to accept death as an inevitable aspect of the mutability that lends "wild and strange delight to life."

In March 1820, Peter Bryant's lungs filled with blood as his son sat beside him, watching him die. More than a father, he had been his son's close companion and his most esteemed mentor; although Bryant had foreseen his father's death for more than a year, he felt the loss deeply. He had attempted to anticipate the event in "On the Happy Temperament," but "Hymn to Death," the poem he completed while mourning, transformed the probative speculation of the essay into a strange paean, launched by an intellectual attempt to celebrate Death's justice and equality. "True it is, that I have wept thy conquests," the poet admits,

> Yet while the spell
> Is on my spirit, and I talk with thee
> In sight of all thy trophies, face to face,

> Meet is it that my voice should utter forth
> Thy nobler triumphs; I will teach the world
> To thank thee.

He hails Death as "Deliverer! / God hath anointed thee to free the oppressed / And crush the oppressor." Once his father dies, however, Bryant is unable to maintain the intellectual argument, and it collapses under the experience of grief. His tender memories of the father who has been taken away are affronted by thoughts of the evildoers "left to cumber earth." This injustice causes him to shudder at the hymn he has written; yet, he refuses to erase the stanzas: "let them stand, / The record of an idle revery." Despite the enfeebling calculated ambiguity of its finale, "Hymn to Death" is more charged with passion than any verse Bryant would ever write again. Paradoxically, however, its anger cloaks a subtle movement away from the heresy of "Thanatopsis," particularly in postulating "a happier life" for his father after resurrection. (During the same months he was composing "Hymn to Death," Bryant wrote five contributions for a hymnal issued by the Unitarian Society of Massachusetts. Though still nominally a Congregationalist who continued to pay his tithe, he had rejected the core of Christian dogma, but these verses, while no more traditional than the Unitarian Church, show him edging toward accommodation with conventional belief.)

Marriage 11 January 1821 to Frances Fairchild, the girl for whom he had written "Oh! Fairest of the Rural Maids," lifted Bryant's sorrow. The next year, almost to the day, the couple had a daughter, who was given her mother's name. When a rift over succession to the editorship at the *North American Review* led Dana to resign, he started his own publication, *The Idle Man;* to solicit Bryant's participation seemed an obvious decision. Although the two had not yet met, Bryant held Dana in high esteem (the correspondence begun at this point initiated a close friendship that lasted for the rest of their lives). Bryant sent four poems to the short-lived *Idle Man.* "Green River," as yet unpublished though written the previous year, stands above the rest. The thoroughly Wordsworthian "Winter Scenes" (later retitled "A Winter Piece") suffers from comparison to its model in tilting much more toward recollection than toward emotion; that notwithstanding, it is good enough to be mistaken for portions of "The Prelude," which would not appear in print for another three decades. "The West Wind" advances a simple thought through seven undistinguished quatrains; in both reach and achievement, it is the least important of the group. "A Walk at Sunset" reveals the most in terms of Bryant's evolving interests. After beginning as a meditation on a natural event, it shifts to the process of history and the poet's role in relation to the "savage men" whose campfires once burned where he now stands. These two objectives, however, never truly join. The figure of sunset—coupled with sunrise in the last stanza—seems at first to be a metaphor concerning the displacement of one people by another, but failing to develop any extended meaning, it remains merely a simile. The relationship of the Indian past to white American identity had come to dominate Bryant's attention; yet, he had arrived at neither an understanding of its significance nor a means of treating it in his poetry.

In the spring, Bryant's supporters from the *North American Review* had persuaded the Phi Beta Kappa Society at Harvard to invite Bryant to read at the August commencement (incidentally informing him, to his surprise, of his election to membership four years earlier). Bryant accepted and, overcoming his usual trepidation about speaking in public, struggled to write a poem to match the honor. "The Ages," designed, he stated, "to justify and confirm the hopes of the philanthropist for the future destinies of the human race," has epic scope. A preamble of sorts at the head of its thirty-five Spenserian stanzas addresses Bryant's familiar questions about the meaning of mortality and seems to allude obliquely to his father's death—the echoes of "Hymn to Death" are quite distinct—but then, after a transitional recognition that change is the way of all Nature, the poem arrives at its real subject. Age by age, the stanzas review the development of civilization—from tribalism to the rise of Egypt, from Greece and Rome to the Christian Middle Ages, from the Renaissance and Reformation to the confrontation of Europe with a Mohammedan challenge—until the climactic discovery of the New World. The purpose of history now approaches fulfillment. Following horrible conflict between the natives and the colonists (which the poet describes with evenly divided sympathies), peace and prosperity reign: "wide the wood recedes, / And towns shoot up, and fertile fields are tilled; / The land is full of harvests and green meads." Surpassing its material achievement, finally, is the realization of the historic mission of America:

> Here the free spirit of mankind, at length,
> Throws its last fetters off; and who shall place
> A limit to the giant's unchained strength,
> Or curb his swiftness in the forward race?
> On like the comet's way through infinite space,
> Stretches the long untravelled path of light,
> Into the depths of ages; we may trace,
> Afar, the brightening glory of its flight,
> Till the receding rays are lost to human sight.

The twentieth century passed a hard judgment on "The Ages." Critics all but ignored it, and Tremaine McDowell even omitted it from his extensive collection for the Bryant volume in the American Writers Series. It fared considerably better in the nineteenth century, when the idea of the Manifest Destiny of America rallied much popular support. Bryant himself, despite his lessening regard for it in later years, continued to acknowledge the position of "The Ages" in his public's affection by always placing it first in the six collections of his poems issued in his lifetime. Its ideal moment, however, was 1821. Among the graduates in Bryant's Harvard audience sat Ralph Waldo Emerson, whose address "The American Scholar," delivered under exactly the same auspices 31 August 1837, has been called the cultural Declaration of Independence of the nation. But even as Bryant delivered his poem in carefully rehearsed, understated tones, American writers were engaged in answering Sidney Smith's famous taunt from Britain the year before, "Who, in the four corners of the globe, reads an American book?" Washington Irving had just conquered a British audience as well as an American one; his former collaborator, James Kirke Paulding, was marshaling the satiric counterattack of "new" England against the old; and James Fenimore Cooper that same year had published *The Spy* (1821) and was in the course of portraying a mythic America for Europe by creating his best-known character, frontiersman Natty Bumppo. Missing was an American poet whose work could stand comparison with British rivals—and that is precisely the role into which "The Ages" boosted Bryant. In proclaiming a messianic America, Bryant was implicitly building a case for literary nationalism as the means of realizing the separate identity of America. As "The Ages" was the necessary poem expressing America's recognition of its purposes in coming of age, Bryant was the necessary poet. The Boston coterie that had contrived Bryant's appearance at Harvard seized the moment. Before Bryant left Cambridge, Phillips, Dana, and Channing had arranged for the publication of Bryant's *Poems* with "The Ages" at the front, followed by "To a Waterfowl," "Translation of a Fragment by Simonides," "Inscription for the Entrance to a Wood," "The Yellow Violet," "Song" (subsequently retitled "The Hunter of the West"), "Green River," and "Thanatopsis" with its new beginning and ending. Sales were disappointing—a year later the printing costs of the book had not yet been recovered—but reviews were good, not only in Boston and New York but also in England, where Bryant in a short time became the best-known American poet. In May 1823, while commiserating over dashed financial hopes, his friend Phillips could nonetheless rejoice that "the book has finally given you an established reputation."

Reputation, however, could not provide for a wife and daughter or ease Bryant's sense of obligation toward his mother and younger siblings since his father's death. Bryant was glad to have been elected and appointed to several minor political offices, including a seven-year term as justice of the peace for Berkshire County, to supplement his income as an attorney, but his grudging concessions to his profession would not subside. When a letter from Channing in June 1821 offered an apology for "soliciting literary favours" that would interrupt his duties, Bryant replied that none was due "to one who does not follow the study of law very eagerly, because he likes other studies better; and yet devotes little of his time to them, for fear that they should give him a dislike to law." For the two years after he had completed "The Ages" and had seen *Poems* praised, no alternative to reluctant fealty to his practice appeared possible. Then, in December 1823, came a bolt from the blue: Theophilus Parsons, the founding editor of the *United States Literary Gazette,* sought to entice him to join "most of the best writers in Boston" in the new venture by contributing "ten or twenty pieces of poetry." As Parsons mentioned "pecuniary compensation" but indicated no amount, Bryant coyly trusted to Parsons's generosity in proportion to what Parsons would pay his most esteemed other contributors. Consistent with his opinion that Bryant was indispensable to the success of the periodical, Parsons, politely apologizing, offered $200 per year for a monthly average submission of one hundred lines of verse. Bryant happily accepted. Well above the usual rate, the sum equaled approximately 40 percent of his annual law earnings.

Within a twelve-month period, Bryant contributed twenty-three poems to the *Literary Gazette,* seventeen under the terms of his agreement with Parsons and six more in 1825, when Bryant shed his commitment after a new editor, trying to economize, offered half the salary for half the number of lines. As the necessity of keeping to a schedule would suggest, the output is highly uneven in quality. "The Rivulet," among the best of all his poetry, relates a small stream that flowed at the edge of his home in Cummington to the flow of his own life. The six stanzas of rhymed couplets divide thematically into pairs. The first pair, recalling Bryant's boyhood, ends with his dreams of fame that would give him immortality. The first stanza of the second pair begins, "Years change thee not," and proceeds to note the constant features of the stream; its second stanza begins "Thou changest not—but I am changed" and proceeds to note the transfor-

mations in himself and his vision of the world. The third pair looks to the future: the man—"trembling, weak, and gray"—may, before yielding his ashes to the mold, return to his "childhood's favorite brook" and have it sparkle in his eye before, in the final stanza, he lies dead, and the children of "ages after ages" repeat his cycle beside the "endless infancy" of the stream. Over the course of ninety lines, the simple rhymes and a simple idea provide a framework for the complex interlacing of the elements of the poem. But "The Rivulet" had already been written before his contract with Parsons. Too much of what he wrote to quota reflects an impulse to supply appropriate embellishment for the next issue—for example, "March," "November," "Autumn Woods," and "Summer Wind." Although here and there an arresting image or a felicitous line can be found, for the most part the statements are clichés and the rhymes convenient. Even "To –" (subsequently retitled "Consumption")—a sonnet composed in 1824 while his most beloved sibling, Sarah, lay dying—ruins a tender, personal expression of despair with a trite rhyme in a banal last line.

Also, Bryant may have begun catering to popular taste; despite having lamented a recent proliferation of Indian narratives, he fed the public's appetite with "An Indian Story" and "Monument Mountain," as well as another meditation on the displacement of one race by another in "An Indian at the Burial-Place of His Fathers." Boldness was evinced by only a few experiments with metrical irregularity, a salient concern. Two of these poems are in rhyme—"Rizpah," a Bible story in the vein of Greek tragedy, which Edgar Allan Poe criticized for "having a frisky or fidgetty rhythm, [that] is singularly ill-adapted to the lamentations of the bereaved mother," and "Mutation," a sonnet treating the need both to let agony pass and to accept it as a function of constant change. The third poem, written in blank verse, is Bryant's finest poetic achievement of the year, but "A Forest Hymn" represents more than skill; it also shows the poet's further shifting in the direction of religious orthodoxy. Beginning, "The groves were God's first temples," it argues that the forest is an appropriate place for communion with God—not, as Bryant had previously held, that God is immanent in Nature, or that the universe is the material manifestation of spirit. In a passage that anticipates Herman Melville, he recognizes God's power to destroy but chooses to base his worship on the sustaining principle in God's creation, "finished, yet renewed forever."

Oh, from these sterner aspects of thy face
Spare me and mine, nor let us need the wrath

Thanatopsis.

To him who, in the love of Nature, holds
Communion with her visible forms, she speaks
A various language. For his gayer hours
She has a voice of gladness and a smile
And eloquence of beauty, and she glides
Into his darker musings with a mild
And healing sympathy, that steals away
Their sharpness ere he is aware. When thoughts
Of the last bitter hour come, like a blight,
Over thy spirit, and sad images
Of the stern agony, and shroud, and pall,
And breathless darkness and the narrow house,
Make thee to shudder and grow sick at heart,
Go forth, under the open sky, and list
To Nature's teachings, while from all around—
Earth and her waters and the depths of air—
Comes a still voice. Yet a few days and thee
The all-beholding sun shall see no more
In all his course; nor yet within the ground,
Where thy pale form was laid with many tears,
Nor in the embrace of ocean shall exist
Thy image. Earth, that nourished thee, shall claim

Page from a fair copy, circa 1813, of Bryant's best-known poem (Manuscripts Division, New York Public Library, Astor, Lenox and Tilden Foundations)

Of the mad unchained elements to teach
Who rules them. Be it ours to meditate,
In these calm shades, thy milder majesty,
And to the beautiful order of thy works
Learn to conform the order of our lives.

In September 1824, a judgment Bryant had won for a client was reversed by an appellate court; that "a piece of pure chicane" should triumph over the merits of the case so outraged Bryant that he decided to leave the law. But this event was only the precipitating reason. Although, as he stated in "I Broke the Spell That Held Me Long," he thought he had finally been disenthralled of the "dear witchery of song," writing poetry at a steady pace for the *Literary Gazette* had proved otherwise. Also, the stipend paid by the *Literary Gazette,* though not, by itself, enough to live on, encouraged him to believe that he might at last be able to earn a living in the publications world. Great Barrington was an additional reason to leave the practice of law. The town that had seemed so pleasant after the misery of Plainfield now irritated him with its provincial isolation and the pinched lives of its inhabitants. Friendship with the Sedgwick family of nearby Stockbridge increased that disaffection. Through Charles Sedgwick, a fellow attorney whom he had known at Williams, Bryant had met the other three Sedgwick brothers and their sister Catharine Maria—all intellectuals with a devotion to literature. "The law is a hag," Charles wrote to his friend; "besides, there are tricks in practice which would perpetually provoke disgust." Two Sedgwick brothers lived in New York City and sought to persuade Bryant to relocate where "any description of talent may find not only occupation but diversity of application." Meanwhile, Dana was growing concerned that Bryant, enmeshed in his practice and local political life, would "let his talent sleep."

Almost a half year before the appellate court ruling that so embittered him, Bryant had visited Robert Sedgwick in New York and hobnobbed with the most important writers of the city, including James Fenimore Cooper. Bryant was intrigued. In February, he again visited the Sedgwick brothers, and in the spring they were lending assistance to complex negotiations that would make him the editor of a merged journal, *The New-York Review and Atheneum Magazine.* Bryant felt liberated. On returning home to close his office in Great Barrington, he saw Charles, who reported to his brother Henry in New York that "every muscle of his [Bryant's] face teemed with happiness. He kissed the children, talked much and smiled at every thing. He said more about your kindness to him than I have ever heard him express

before, in regard to any body." Leaving his family in the Berkshires, the newly appointed editor hurried to New York on the first of May to push the first number of his publication to press.

Though unconvinced that he was suited to "sitting in judgment on books," Bryant applied himself to the task most creditably; however, the second part—that is, the "magazine," with its store of original works—presented more of a problem. The first issue featured a poem by Fitz-Greene Halleck, a New Yorker of rising reputation, whose contribution, "Marco Bozaris" (about a Greek revolutionary hero), advanced a popular, emotional cause to which Bryant had pledged himself while in Great Barrington. But as little of comparable appeal was submitted for later numbers, Bryant had to draw down his own meager file of poems and then to try his hand at writing a tale in order to fill the magazine. Subscriptions, meanwhile, fell short of the publisher's hopes. Exactly a year after its start, publication was suspended, but for several anxious months Bryant had been making plans with a Boston editor to create an extension of the *Literary Gazette* and to merge it with a vestigial *New-York Review* to form *The United States Review and Literary Gazette.* Ambitiously intended as a national publication, to be issued simultaneously in Boston and New York, it lost its first co-editor almost at once, and his successor, a classics scholar working as a librarian at Harvard, soon showed that the relationship with his partner in New York would not run smoothly. The first number appeared in October 1826; a year later, despite infusions of Bryant's poems and another tale, this journal, too, collapsed.

In abandoning the law to go to New York, Bryant had said he was uncertain whether he was exchanging one "shabby business" for another, and after the failure of two journals, the second of which cost him an investment of almost half of his salary for a year, one might have expected regret over his choice. Instead, despite an onerous workload, the experience had proved a heady adventure. Upon his arrival, he boarded with a French family, the Evrards, so that he might polish the language he had first studied with his father. When Bryant's wife, Fanny, and their daughter moved to the city, they joined the crowded Evrard household for about a month. The renewal of his French had nearly immediate application: for the July issue of *The New-York Review,* Bryant not only wrote a long essay appreciating Jean de Nostredame's 1575 work on the troubadour poets but also translated Provençal poetry to accompany the critical evaluation. Acquaintance with the famed Cuban poet José Maria Hérédia encouraged Bryant to learn Spanish and to study Spanish literature, as well as to translate Hérédia's poems into English. Close ties with Lorenzo Da Ponte, Wolfgang Amadeus Mozart's great librettist, who had moved to New York from London and had made promotion of Italian opera his mission, introduced Bryant to this art during his first year in New York. Da Ponte published several works in Bryant's journal, including observations on Dante, and he went on to translate some of Bryant's poetry into Italian. James Fenimore Cooper, whom Bryant had met through the Sedgwicks on his first visit to New York, invited Bryant to join his Bread and Cheese Lunch Club, beginning an intimate relationship that lasted until Cooper's death in 1851. Installed as members at the same time were another poet, James Hillhouse, and the painter Samuel F. B. Morse (who later gained greater fame as an inventor). "The Lunch," as it was known, gathered most of the active writers and artists of the city, and it became the hub of Bryant's social life. He had discovered in early adolescence a strong attraction to sketching; now, in the presence of artists determined to create a new age of American painting, that interest revived. In Thomas Cole, whom he had also first encountered through the Sedgwicks, he found a kindred spirit, and he became friends with other artists at the Lunch—Asher Durand, Henry Inman, John Wesley Jarvis, and John Vanderlyn. In 1827 the National Academy of Design, newly formed by the group, elected Bryant its "Professor of Mythology and Antiquities." His literary friends at the Lunch and "the Den," a meeting room in Charles Wiley's bookstore where Cooper held forth, were equally prominent. Besides Hillhouse and Cooper, they included the brilliant conversationalist Robert C. Sands, whose long poem *Yamoyden* (1820), written with James Eastburn, had begun the vogue for Indian subjects; the favorite poet of the moment, Fitz-Greene Halleck; the estimable Knickerbocker and Congressman Gulian Verplanck; and James Kirke Paulding, who had recently published the satirical novel *Koningsmarke* (1823) and was the foremost advocate of a national literature. In addition, Bryant came to know William Dunlap, both a painter and an eminent figure in New York theater. Although, on the advice of the Sedgwicks, Bryant had aborted his one attempt at writing for the stage, a political farce undertaken while in Great Barrington, his interest in theater continued. Through Dunlap, he soon served on two juries: one, in 1829, awarded a prize to John Augustus Stone's *Metamora* (1829), performed with distinction by Edwin Forrest; the second, in 1830, chose Paulding's *The Lion of the West* (1830), which was the most successful American comedy up to that time.

As both an American poet with European recognition and an editor at the center of the cultural renaissance of New York City, Bryant found himself called upon to play the role of prophet. Immediately prior to his move to the city, the *North American Review* had published his review of Catharine Maria Sedgwick's *Redwood* (1824). Although initially intended to promote his good friend's novel, the article developed into a rallying cry for an indigenous American literature—a cause perfectly suited to the expansive mood of New York. The following spring, the man who had once worried about speaking in public was delivering four lectures on poetry at the New York Athenæum. Carefully reasoned and balanced, these lectures warrant comparison with Emerson's "The American Scholar" of a decade later as a charter for national literary achievement. Reflecting his sympathies with Wordsworth, the first lecture contends that poetry is "not merely a tissue of striking images" but language that commands feeling; its "magic" owes not to imitation but to suggestion in going past the imitative limits of words. The second lecture, building on the assertion at the close of the first, that all human beings have the capacity for poetry, maintains that the value of poetry rests in aligning the practice of virtue with emotion, and thus works for the social good. To illustrate his point, Bryant states that by paying homage to the emanations from God that constitute Nature, poetry necessarily excludes self-interest. Although neither of the first two lectures specifically addresses national questions, the third, which does, extends from the implications of their arguments. To those who complain that America is the captive of a scientific attitude and lacks the historical lore to inspire mystery, Bryant replies that because the imagination is stimulated by knowledge, the American writer's opportunities have actually multiplied. To those who maintain that the "quiet and commercial" genius of the United States will vanquish the demand for contemporary poetry, Bryant cites the universality of the poetic instinct. "Verses have always been, and always will be written, and will always find readers; but it is of some consequence that they should be good verses, that they should exert the healthful and beneficial influences. . . . " So oriented, the poets of America will find available all the material that has ever moved the poets of other times and places. If Cupid cannot be fitted to an American setting, what he represents is nonetheless present—and the poetry issuing from that direct encounter will be that much better. The fourth lecture moderates the independent course advocated by the third. The poet must never forget that he deals in an art to which many centuries of trial and error have contributed; to benefit from that process, he must school himself in the poets of the past. If America is to realize its destiny as a nation of poets, it cannot isolate itself from the poetry of England or from the poetry of all Europe. In 1826 Bryant was sounding cautionary advice similar to T. S. Eliot's a century later in "Tradition and the Individual Talent" (1919).

Only thirty-one when he presented his lectures, Bryant seemed the best candidate to realize the future he described, but a job he believed temporary and supplementary when he began it in July ordained a different course. Alexander Hamilton had founded the *New-York Evening Post* in 1801 as an organ for his Federalist Party, but as the party weakened, William Coleman, the original editor, slipped from Federalist principles. An injury to Coleman in mid June of 1826, following a previous stroke that had cost him the use of his legs, forced him to rely on a substitute to help run the paper. Bryant was an obvious choice. Worried about the possibility of financial ruin, he had just obtained a license to practice law in New York, but journalism posed a happier alternative. Moreover, his politics meshed with Coleman's, who had virtually become a Democrat. Bryant, as an associate in his father's Federalism in the days of "The Embargo," had ardently declared for protectionism; gradually, however, first while assisting Baylies, then more systematically in Great Barrington, he had studied political economy and come firmly to the side of free trade. Although no document records the moment Bryant took control of the editorial page of the paper, the moment is almost certainly marked by a sudden change to carefully reasoned briefs against high tariffs. Bryant had also been veering toward Democratic positions in other areas, and he admired Andrew Jackson and felt personally drawn to Paulding's friend Martin Van Buren; all of these inclinations helped to create comfortable relations between the notoriously fiery Coleman and his assistant editor.

In October, despite Bryant's commitment to lead *The United States Review,* the position at the *Evening Post* was made permanent, and Coleman's deterioration over the next three years led him to assume the title appropriate to the responsibilities he had been bearing—editor in chief. When Dana, Bryant's artistic conscience, had warned that journalistic meddling in politics would stifle his poetry, Bryant had answered that the paper would "get only my mornings, and you know politics and a belly-ful are better than poetry and starvation." But perhaps Bryant was being somewhat disingenuous. The financial prospect with the *Evening Post* was alluring: Bryant bought a share of the paper and later added to his portion of ownership, confident it would make his fortune—as indeed it eventually did. More important, for all his protestations about having to "drudge for

the Evening Post," politics fascinated him. In addition to liberal economic policies that included free trade, support for labor to organize, opposition to monopolies, pro-immigrant policies, and low interest rates, he consistently stood for resistance to the spread of slavery. In 1820, during a period when public speaking still frightened him, he had orated against the Missouri Compromise and denounced Daniel Webster for his role in bringing about such a morally repugnant law. As editor of the *Evening Post,* he remained true to that conviction, leading his readership in the direction of the Free-Soil Party, and when that movement joined the amalgam of the Republican Party, Bryant and the *Evening Post* were among the most energetic and outspoken adherents for its first presidential candidate, John Frémont. Four years later, in 1860, Bryant was a principal supporter of Abraham Lincoln, and after the Civil War began, Bryant became a forceful advocate of abolition. Clearly, by the time Bryant had reached old age, his roles as editor and political sage had eclipsed his importance as a poet in the mind of the public.

At the start of his newspaper career, that role would have seemed a most unlikely end. The lad with the Calvinist upbringing from the Berkshire backcountry swiftly adapted to the metropolitan ways of New York in becoming one of its most prestigious literati. If the *North American Review,* however briefly, had made Boston the center in the cultural life of the nation, Bryant, as much as any other single figure, shifted that focus to New York. His poetic accomplishments accounted for only a part of his influence; equally important was the conviviality that drew the writers and artists of the city to him. One manifestation of this quality was *The Talisman.*

At the end of 1827, after the demise of *The United States Review,* Bryant, in company with Robert Sands and Gulian Verplanck, promoted the idea of a Christmas gift book, similar to annuals in England and to *The Atlantic Souvenir* in Philadelphia. Unlike its models, which were miscellanies by many hands, *The Talisman* was entirely attributed to the work of a single author, Francis Herbert—who was, in fact, a construct combining the three friends. Each assumed responsibility for about a third of the pages of the annual, though all participated in the work of the others. Two of Bryant's three tales for the initial *Talisman* seem to have been suggested by his collaborators. Recounting a purported Indian legend supplied by Verplanck, "The Cascade of Melsingah" resembles many other specimens of the genre and is the weakest of the three. "The Legend of the Devil's Pulpit," probably suggested by Sands, has a rather flawed plot, but there is a sprightliness to the lampooning of local fig-

Bryant in 1873 (engraving by S. Hollyer after a photograph by Napoleon Sarony)

sively of tales. Bryant was receptive. The birth of another daughter the previous June and the subsequent move to a new house in Hoboken, New Jersey, made the Harpers' bid quite tempting, but there is also good reason to believe that Bryant accepted because he welcomed the opportunity to write more fiction and because he so thoroughly enjoyed working with his friends. To Verplanck (who withdrew at the last moment) and Sands, Bryant added his editorial associate on the *Evening Post,* William Leggett, and Catharine Maria Sedgwick and James Kirke Paulding. Supposedly stories told by visitors to the waters at Ballston, New York, *Tales of Glauber-Spa* (1832) includes two tales by Bryant—"The Skeleton's Cave," a long piece evidently influenced by Cooper, and "Medfield," a moral tale about a good man guilty of one shameful act when he had lost his temper.

That Bryant never wrote another tale is commonly attributed to lack of seriousness about the genre and to the poor quality of his efforts. But these explanations are misleading. He was primarily a poet, and the writing of the first annual did have something of the character of a lark. Even so, his fiction deserves more respect than it has received. His first two tales, inspired by Washington Irving, may have been conceived by an editor pressed for material to fill his *New-York Review;* nevertheless, they are prose expressions of his vision for American literature outlined in his poetry lectures. "A Pennsylvania Legend," about an avaricious humpback who finds a cache of gold, imports the effects of European Romantic tales into an American setting; "A Border Tradition," a ghost story rationally explained, seeks to exploit the rich variety of the ethnic enclaves of America—in this case, the Dutch in New York. Had he thought little of these efforts, he likely would not have embarked on *The Talisman,* given its major emphasis on fiction. Moreover, the contemporary response to his stories was encouraging: the three volumes of the annual were critically well received, largely because of their prose, and the complete run of *Tales of Glauber-Spa* sold so quickly that it was reprinted. Bryant's talent for fiction is nowhere more evident than in "The Indian Spring," published in *The Talisman* for 1830. A prose treatment of his abiding fascination with the imposition by white settlement on the home of a fading race, "The Indian Spring" shows skillful use of the double in portraying guilt within the American identity. Indeed, excepting only one or two pieces by Washington Irving, no previous American short story is its equal. "Medfield" provides further evidence that Bryant had a sober regard for tale writing. In April 1831, escalating insults between Bryant and a rival newspaper editor had ended with Bryant whipping his adver-

ures that appealed to readers. "Adventure in the East Indies," a complete fabrication by Bryant about a tiger hunt, almost redeems a poor story through imaginative writing.

Despite the haste in which it was produced, *The Talisman* for 1828 was pronounced a success, and the collaborators, who now formed the nucleus of the Sketch Club (or Twenty-One, for the number of members), developed a successor for 1829—this volume was to accommodate other club members and to feature artwork. Bryant contributed five poems, a translation of a Spanish ballad, and a travel account of Spain (which, of course, he had not visited), in addition to one tale of terrible cruelty and vengeance, "Story of the Island of Cuba." A final volume of the annual was compiled for 1830, despite duties elsewhere that taxed all three collaborators. Again, Bryant's share in "Francis Herbert" was both varied and weighty: in addition to half a dozen poems, he wrote three tales. But even though *The Talisman* had run its course, the success of the concept prompted a different publisher, Harper and Brothers, to ask for another, similar collection in 1832 consisting exclu-

sary, who, at about the same time, drew a knife from his cane. Mortified by his loss of self-control, Bryant published an apology, and even after the rival's death, he expressed regrets for the "scandalous affair" to the man's son. Bryant wrote "Medfield" the next year as an expression of his remorse.

The signal literary event of the decade for Bryant, however, was his publication of a new edition of *Poems* in January 1832, shepherded to press by Irving. At 240 pages, it added all poems published in the previous decade (plus five that he had set aside), and although relatively few of them were at the level of the best from the 1821 *Poems,* the greater number broadened the base of his achievement. The response made clear that Bryant was "his country's foremost poet," and a British edition, edited by Irving, brought recognition not only as the outstanding poet of the "primeval forest beyond the sea" but also as one worthy of inclusion among the ranks of the principal English Romantics. Also in 1832, Bryant traveled first to Washington, D.C., then, after swinging through the upper South, to Illinois. His experience of the great rivers of the nation, and then of the awesome sweep of prairie, profoundly touched him. The next year, he published his great blank verse poem "The Prairies," which in 1834 became the most notable addition to yet another edition of *Poems.* (Two years later, Harpers took Bryant as one of its writers and, with many reprintings at a generous royalty, spread his popularity still further, making him rich in the process.)

While Bryant's fortunes as a poet were rising, political strife and its effects on the conduct of the *Evening Post,* in addition to the shock of his close friend Robert Sands's sudden death in December 1832, were exacting a heavy psychic toll on the man. As 1833 was closing, he began arranging for his friend Leggett to substitute for him at the *Evening Post* so that he could leave for Europe with his family to enjoy a respite. But new problems arose: William Coleman's widow demanded immediate payment from him on the mortgage she held for the newspaper, and the Jackson administration failed to make good a promised appointment as diplomatic courier. When, amid raging abolition rioting, the ship finally sailed for Le Havre in mid 1834, Bryant felt enormous relief, and he settled into a lassitude that continued as he traveled from France to an eight-month stay in the cities of Italy and finally to Munich and Heidelberg. The family had fixed no limit to their European tour, but news that Leggett was physically and perhaps mentally ill drew Bryant home in early 1836. The premature departure may not have been altogether unwelcome. American scenes and subjects recurred in the few poems he wrote while abroad, and his perceptions of Europe seem to have been unexceptional confirmation of prejudices. His most pleasant days were those spent with Americans Henry Wadsworth Longfellow; Longfellow's companion, Clara Crowninshield; and the sculptor Horatio Greenough and his wife.

Before his departure for Europe, Bryant had considered selling his share of the newspaper, but Leggett had so mismanaged its finances and driven off so many advertisers with his "radical" expression of its political position that the returning editor had no choice but to immerse himself once again in its daily operation. National economic woes further hurt revenues, and the *Evening Post* did not regain its financial footing until 1839. But from that point on, the paper prospered, steadily increasing the value of Bryant's 60 percent ownership. Its reputation grew as Bryant etched the faults of his political opponents with his acid editorials. After having almost abandoned poetry, he began writing verses at an increasing rate, and in 1842 he signed an exclusive contract with *Graham's Magazine* to print his verses at $50 each. That same year *The Fountain and Other Poems* was published; it was composed entirely of poems written after his return from Europe. Then, at the end of 1844, a slim paperback edition of ten poems, most of which had been printed in *Graham's,* appeared as *The White-Footed Deer and Other Poems;* it was the first number of Home Library, a series conceived by Bryant and Evert Duyckinck to promote American writers. Other honors were also paid him during this period. A lifelong homeopath—he had been taught herbal medicine by his father—he published *Popular Considerations on Homoeopathia* in 1841 and was chosen to head the New York Homoeopathic Society at the conclusion of that year. Also in 1841, he was chosen for the governing committee of the Apollo Association (soon renamed the American Art Union); two years later, and twice thereafter, he was elected the president of the organization. Organizations for two causes for which he had crusaded also elected him to their presidencies—the American Copyright Club (which he addressed in 1843) and the New York Society for the Abolition of the Punishment of Death.

Yearning to resume the travels that had been interrupted a decade earlier, Bryant returned to Europe in 1845, this time leaving his family behind. The tour, financed by his companion Charles Leupp, began with two months in England and Scotland, where Bryant visited the elderly Wordsworth and virtually all the notable literati, then proceeded through most of the Continent for the next three months. (For New Yorkers, the trip would have special significance

William Cullen Bryant (standing at right) and his brothers, Austin, William, Peter Rush, and Arthur, 1864

since Bryant, who had previously urged the city to build a park, redoubled his campaign after admiring the magnificent parks of London.) As soon as he resumed his office at the *Evening Post* he had to confront Parke Godwin, who, having married Fanny Bryant in 1842, had presumptuously overstepped his bounds during his father-in-law's absence. Godwin left the paper the following year. Bryant, however, was seeking a trustworthy assistant to relieve his burdens so that he might indulge his appetite for travel. In 1846, John Bigelow filled that need, and in 1848 he was made a partner. The next spring, Bryant and Leupp sailed to Savannah, Georgia, then to Charleston, South Carolina, from where, after visiting Bryant's good friend, the novelist William Gilmore Simms, they embarked for Cuba. Ever since meeting Cubans soon after he had moved to New York, Bryant had entertained a romantic notion of that Caribbean island, but the practice of slavery that he observed there, made more terrible by the execution of a slave before his eyes, shattered his youthful illusions. When the two men returned to New York for seven weeks before sailing for Liverpool, the horror resumed. A rivalry between Edwin Forrest, a great American Shakespearean actor (and an intimate

friend of Bryant), and an equally celebrated English tragedian attracted a mob that was determined to drive the foreigner from his theater; this action was bad enough, but then police and a unit of militia fired their guns into the mob, creating a massacre. Within a week, another catastrophe began to swell with the first of more than a thousand deaths from a cholera epidemic in the city. Europe promised escape from human misery, and indeed Bryant and Leupp delighted in the weeks spent in remote areas of Scotland. But after they left England, they found a Europe everywhere menaced by militarism.

Shortly after Bryant returned to New York in the fall of 1849, his old friend Dana called upon him and urged that he collect for publication the many letters he had sent to the *Evening Post* from his travels of fifteen years. This suggestion produced *Letters of a Traveller; or, Notes of Things Seen in Europe and America* in May 1850. For all the reservations critics expressed, the book proved a popular success. Two years later, Bryant and Leupp were again off for Liverpool, then south through Paris, Genoa, and Naples before arriving in Egypt for a four-month exploration of the cities of the Ottoman Empire. These journeys, too, were reported to the *Evening Post,* and in 1869, after sixteen years had passed, the accounts were published as *Letters from the East*. One other travel book was set in motion by a penultimate trip to Europe, begun in 1857. Bryant had given all his strength to the Frémont presidential campaign and feared for the future of his nation when Democrat James Buchanan won the presidency. In addition, his wife's health gave him concern, and he thought the sun of southern Europe might prove beneficial. They were accompanied by their daughter Julia (who, thanks to her father's language drills, knew Italian) and a friend of hers. Again they traveled to major cities, this time including Madrid, but the focus of the trip was Italy. The trip that had been partly planned for Frances Bryant's health almost caused her death when she was stricken in Naples by a respiratory infection that lasted for four months. Her husband cared for her himself with homeopathic treatment and was convinced he had saved her life. When a friend, the Reverend Robert Waterston, came to call, Bryant disclosed that he had never been baptized. The Unitarian minister then baptized Bryant, Julia, and her friend, and the Waterston and Bryant families took communion together. The Bryants visited with the Hawthornes in Rome, where Nathaniel Hawthorne was writing *The Marble Faun* (1860), and then again in Florence, where they also spent time with Robert and Elizabeth Barrett Browning. The sojourn came to a bitter end, however, when news came that the Reverend Waterston's daughter had died of an illness contracted during the visit to Naples. *Letters of a Traveller, Second Series,* published in 1859, ends with a memorial to the dead young woman.

As Bryant had feared at his embarkation in 1857, he returned to a United States in grave danger of dissolution and war. Once again, he poured his energies into electing a Republican president. He had instantly recognized Lincoln as a man of greatness when they met in 1859, and Bryant introduced Lincoln to the crowd of 1,500 New Yorkers in the pivotal Cooper Union speech. But after Lincoln's election, Bryant was saddened by what he saw as timidity in Lincoln's not immediately emancipating all slaves and in not prosecuting the war vigorously enough. The dispute taxed the editor, as did the managerial problems inherent in the doubling of the circulation of the newspaper during the war years. Then, in 1866, Bryant's wife fell critically ill, and during her agony, Bryant spent as little time as possible in his office. After her death at the end of July, he made one final trip to Europe, taking Julia with him.

Although Bryant kept his title as editor on his return, the active running of the paper was left in other hands. In 1864 his last collection of new poems

had been published for his seventieth birthday. He had long since been regarded as a fireside poet, augustly unassailable; yet, no one mistook *Thirty Poems* for a display of genius. One critic had accurately summed up Bryant's career by comparing him disadvantageously to the great poets of the age—Wordsworth, Samuel Taylor Coleridge, John Keats, and Alfred Tennyson—in their idiosyncratic strengths, yet noting that "he is, nevertheless, the one among all our contemporaries who has written the fewest things carelessly, and the most things well." But as his translation of a selection from the *Iliad* in *Thirty Poems* hinted, Bryant was not quite finished. Translation, he explained, was the work for careful old men, and in February 1869, he wrote his brother that he had completed the translation of twelve books of the *Iliad,* which were published the subsequent year. The next twelve books, amazingly, were completed in less time than the first twelve had required, and the second volume of the epic appeared in June 1870.

In his last years, Bryant brought out two revised collections of his poems, in 1871 and 1876, each with some new additions, but his most forceful works lay far in the past. Even so, he remained active to the end. His last publisher, Appleton, aware that Bryant's name now guaranteed a handsome sale, asked him to write the text for *Picturesque America* (1872–1874), a folio of engravings that cost more than $100,000 to print–a gargantuan sum in those days. Bryant agreed, though he soon wearied of the task of furnishing "the most tedious of all reading." A second massive project, *A Popular History of the United States, from the First Discovery of the Western Hemisphere by the Northmen, to the End of the First Century of the Union of the States* (1876–1881), was almost entirely written by Sidney Howard Gay, who was then the managing editor of the *Evening Post,* but Bryant wrote the introduction laying out the scheme of history, with distinctive emphases on pre-Columbian peoples and on the deleterious effects of the politics of race on the idealistic principles of the nation.

To the end, Bryant believed in physical fitness as well as mental exercise. A great walker, he insisted on climbing ten flights of stairs to his office instead of taking the elevator, and he made daily use of the barbells he had had crafted for him. At the end of May 1878, he spoke at the dedication of a bust of the great European and Italian liberal revolutionary Giuseppe Mazzini in Central Park in New York. The sun beat on his head, leaving the old man a bit dizzy, but he characteristically insisted on walking home. At his door, he fell and suffered a concussion. A week later, a stroke paralyzed one side of his body, and he became comatose. Death came on 12 June 1878.

Letters:

The Letters of William Cullen Bryant, 6 volumes, edited by William Cullen Bryant III and Thomas G. Voss (New York: Fordham University Press, 1975–1992).

Bibliographies:

Henry C. Sturges, *Chronologies of the Life and Writings of William Cullen Bryant, with a Bibliography of His Works in Prose and Verse* (New York: D. Appleton, 1903);

Jacob Blanck, "William Cullen Bryant," *Bibliography of American Literature* (New Haven: Yale University Press, 1955);

Judith T. Phair, *A Bibliography of William Cullen Bryant and his Critics 1808–1972* (Troy, N.Y.: Whitston, 1975);

James Rocks, "William Cullen Bryant," *Fifteen American Authors Before 1900*, edited by Earl N. Harbert and Robert A. Rees (Madison: University of Wisconsin Press, 1984), pp. 55–79.

Biographies:

Parke Godwin, *A Biography of William Cullen Bryant,* 2 volumes (New York: D. Appleton, 1883);

John Bigelow, *William Cullen Bryant* (Boston: Houghton Mifflin, 1890);

Charles H. Brown, *William Cullen Bryant* (New York: Scribners, 1971).

References:

Michael P. Branch, "WCB: The Nature Poet As Environmental Journalist," *American Transcendental Quarterly,* 12 (September 1998);

Stanley Brodwin and Michael D'Innocento, eds., *William Cullen Bryant and His America* (New York: AMS Press, 1983);

William Cullen Bryant II, *Power for Sanity: Selected Editorials of William Cullen Bryant, 1829–1861,* compiled and annotated by Bryant II (New York: Fordham University Press, 1994);

James T. Callow, *Kindred Spirits: Knickerbocker Writers and American Artists 1807–1855* (Chapel Hill: University of North Carolina Press, 1967);

Bernard Duffey, "Romantic Coherence and Romantic Incoherence in American Poetry," *Centennial Review,* 7 (Spring 1963): 219–236; 8 (Fall 1964): 453–464;

Tremaine McDowell, ed., *William Cullen Bryant: Representative Selections, with Introduction, Bibliography, and Notes,* American Writers Series (New York: American Book, 1935);

Albert F. McLean, *William Cullen Bryant,* revised edition (Boston: Twayne, 1989);

Alan Nevins, *The Evening Post: A Century of Journalism* (New York: Boni & Liveright, 1922);

Donald A. Ringe, *The Pictorial Mode: Space and Time in the Art of Bryant, Irving and Cooper* (Lexington: University of Kentucky Press, 1971).

Papers:

The largest collection of William Cullen Bryant's papers is held by the New York Public Library; the Bryant Library in Roslyn, New York, also has holdings.

Lewis Gaylord Clark

(5 October 1808? – 3 November 1873)

Benjamin F. Fisher
University of Mississippi

See also the Clark entries in *DLB 3: Antebellum Writers in New York and the South; DLB 64: American Literary Critics and Scholars, 1850–1880;* and *DLB 73: American Magazine Journalists, 1741–1850.*

BOOK: *Knick-Knacks from an Editor's Table* (New York: D. Appleton, 1852).

PERIODICAL EDITED: *Knickerbocker* (1834–1859?; October–December 1863).

OTHER: *The Literary Remains of the Late Willis Gaylord Clark: Including the Ollapodiana Papers, the Spirit of Life, and a Selection from His Various Prose and Poetical Writings,* edited by Lewis Gaylord Clark (New York: Burgess, Stringer, 1844);

The Knickerbocker Sketch-Book: A Library of Select Literature, edited by Clark (New York: Burgess, Stringer, 1845);

Willis Gaylord Clark, *The Poetical Writings of the Late Willis Gaylord Clark,* edited by Clark (New York: J. S. Redfield, 1847);

The Lover's Gift; and Friendship's Token, edited by Clark (Auburn, N.Y.: J. C. Derby, 1848);

"Life of Daniel Webster," in *The Life, Eulogy, and Great Orations of Daniel Webster,* edited by Clark (New York: DeWitt & Davenport, 1854);

"John C. Colt," in *Remarkable Trials of All Countries,* compiled by Thomas Dunphy and Thomas J. Cummins (New York: Dossy & Cockcroft, 1867), pp. 226–310.

SELECTED PERIODICAL PUBLICATIONS—UNCOLLECTED:

FICTION

"Les Rivaux," *Philadelphia Album and Ladies' Literary Gazette,* 1 July 1829: 1–3;

"A Contrasted Picture," *Knickerbocker,* 3 (April 1834): 281–289.

Lewis Gaylord Clark (portrait by C. L. Elliott; from The Knickerbocker, July 1849)

NONFICTION

"Charles Dickens," *Harper's New Monthly Magazine,* 25 (August 1862): 376–380;

"Reminiscences of John Phoenix," *Round Table* (12 March 1864): 196–197; (12 April 1864): 244;

"Charles Loring Elliott," *Lippincott's Magazine,* 2 (December 1868): 652–657;

"Recollections of Washington Irving," *Lippincott's Magazine,* 3 (May 1869): 552–560;

"Noah Webster," *Lippincott's Magazine,* 5 (April 1870): 448–452.

Lewis Gaylord Clark's fame is inextricable from that of *The Knickerbocker,* a popular and respected American literary periodical that flourished between 1833 and 1860. More important, perhaps, Clark's name has been kept alive in the annals of Edgar Allan Poe. During Poe's last years, Clark lost no opportunity to vilify Poe as an immoral drunkard whose writing was inartistic. Although Clark turned out little original work himself, in comparison with many other American authors his editorial columns in *The Knickerbocker* each month from 1834 to 1860 total no mean bulk. They also evince an informed, if often prejudicial, outlook upon American culture as it developed during that era. British and American writers and writings, musical and dramatic concerns, and, most notably, humor occupied Clark's thinking, as borne out by the pages of his "Editor's Table." Thus, Clark ought not to be overlooked in chronicles of national letters, although he was far more significant as a magazine editor than as a creative writer. Little of a scholarly nature has been written about him.

Lewis Gaylord Clark and his twin brother Willis Gaylord were born in Otisco, New York, on 5 October 1808. The twins' father, Eliakim Clark, was descended from Lieutenant William Clark of Massachusetts, who moved, after his service in the Revolutionary War concluded, to Onondaga County, New York. Eliakim Clark married Lucy Gaylord, a daughter of Lemon Gaylord, who immigrated to New York from Connecticut. The Clark twins' childhood in rural New York was happy, contributing materially to their love of nature. The Clark brothers' formal schooling was enhanced at home because of their father's enthusiasm for literature and philosophy and additional instruction in classics by one of their mother's relatives, the Reverend George Colton. Two of Lewis's lifelong reading interests began during these early years–the works of Noah Webster and those of Washington Irving. Willis Gaylord, Lucy Clark's brother and editor of the *Gennessee Farmer and Albany Cultivator,* inspired his nephews' inclinations toward journalism. Willis Gaylord Clark established himself in that field in Philadelphia, beginning in 1829; with like intentions Lewis eventually entered the New York City literary world in 1832. Confusion over which twin was which often arose in the literary world of their day; one of the most glaring examples was the attribution to Lewis in the "Miscellaneous Selections" of the *Cincinnati Mirror* on 22 August 1835 of what was a segment of Willis's "Ollapodiana" papers from the August 1835 *The Knickerbocker.*

Before his career in New York commenced, Lewis contributed a short story to the 1 July 1829 issue of the *Philadelphia Album and Ladies' Literary Gazette,* a recently established weekly. "Les Rivaux" was one of the all-too-typical thin stories of thwarted love that appeared in the pages of American literary periodicals at that time. With an appropriate epigraph from William Shakespeare's *Twelfth Night* concerning a backfire caused when a coquettish pretense of loving one man in order to spur the ardor of another mushroomed beyond its intended effect, the chronicle of Egbert Glenville and Alice Grey seems a calculated appeal to the sentimental notions of love cherished by many magazine readers among contemporary audiences during the formative years of the national literature of the United States. Alice's apparent preference for a fop, Medwin, so emotionally wounds Glenville that he contemplates sailing to Europe to enjoy what, on account of his uncertain health, might be his few remaining years. Unexpectedly, he reappears to surprise Alice and the nameless storyteller, who is his friend, as they converse, and Alice owns up to creating unanticipated jealousy in Glenville. He and Alice marry, find great pleasure in their domestic life, and have a daughter; the narrator becomes a welcome member of this family circle; and Medwin exits the tale enveloped with the same pretentious Beau Brummel displays of foolish language and assumed superiority regarding the world of high society that he manifested when he appeared. Such a contrast between the virtues inherent in genuine rural simplicity, as revealed in Glenville and Alice, and those of the citified pretentiousness of Medwin (and as Glenville ultimately triumphs) place this tale with many of the tales by James Kirke Paulding, Frederick W. Thomas, and William Gilmore Simms, as well as with plays such as Royall Tyler's *The Contrast* (1787) and Paulding's *The Lion of the West* (1830), which highlighted what were deemed genuine American values to the disadvantage of those ideals originating in mere smatterings of European culture and which typically made their possessors ostentatious. The French title may suggest a teasing aspect underlying the story, though, along with sprinklings of French within the piece, it may hint that the author was "educated" and sophisticated. The situation was trite and the characters were cardboard, but the tale was evidently considered a catch by the *Philadelphia Album.* Along with some verse by John Greenleaf Whittier, Sumner Lincoln Fairfield, and Clark's twin, Willis, the story was complimented as exemplifying the "literary assistance of several gentleman who have acquired no inconsiderable reputation as American writers." All in all, "Les Rivaux" marks no great beginning for Lewis Gaylord Clark as a creative writer, but it does adumbrate certain features in his writing that remained with him until the end of his career forty years later.

In October 1834 Lewis Clark married Ella Maria Curtis; in the course of their long and happy marriage the Clarks had six children. The couple enjoyed their family life and entertaining. In early 1834 Clark and his friend Clement Edson purchased *The Knickerbocker,* established in 1833 by a New York physician, Samuel Langtree. When Clark became editor, he succeeded Langtree and two others, Charles Fenno Hoffman and Timothy Flint, who were then renowned literary men. Save for a few editorial ventures in book form, Clark worked chiefly as editor and writer for *The Knickerbocker* until 1859 or 1860 and again briefly during 1863; the magazine ceased publication in 1865.

As the editor for *The Knickerbocker,* Clark had to keep abreast of the contemporary cultural climate. He did so with amazing efficiency, and the periodical benefited from his labors. His own initial venture into the pages of *The Knickerbocker* occurred in April 1834 with a story, "A Contrasted Picture." This slight moralistic tale centers on the relocation of a young farmer, William Leonard, friend of the unnamed narrator, from Hudson Valley environs to New York City, where he engages in mercantile ventures. Leonard's urbanization involves the rejection of his rural sweetheart, Emily Williams, and his gravitating toward the wealthy, fashionable, but cold Miss B____. Emily languishes and dies from unrequited love. To impress his new love, Leonard resorts to embezzlement, is sent to prison, and there becomes an object of pity to all who behold him. The tale concludes with the narrator's remark that the story demonstrates the moral of pride preceding destruction. This piece rises to no artistic heights, as Clark himself must have realized; at one point his storyteller laments, "Had I but the pen of an IRVING" to enliven this portrait of the "London of America," it could be more than a "pencil sketch of the scene." But, he says, no "pen or pencil could depict the buoyant *newness* of feeling and excitement which [New York City] awakened within us." The "contrast," of course depicts the youthful, idealistic Leonard as against the demoralized, criminalized person he becomes—both "pictures" associated with love relationships.

In terms of what came to be the usual fare in *The Knickerbocker,* Clark attempted to secure contributions from the greatest writers in the United States, a practice that fostered his own conceptions of American literary nationalism. Naturally, given the associations with Washington Irving's renowned literary character, Diedrich Knickerbocker, Clark inclined toward "Knickerbocker" viewpoints and techniques—that is, he sought writers who could impart artistic and social enhancements to the overall respectability of the magazine. Knickerbocker principles embodied a conservative outlook as regards politics, culture, and cultivated sensibilities in the main; these beliefs led ultimately to attempts at maintaining reputations that eventually might fade with the passing of time. Irving, Paulding, Whittier,

Willis Gaylord Clark, Lewis Clark's twin brother (engraving by John Sartain; from The Casket, *January 1840)*

William Cullen Bryant, James Fenimore Cooper, Fitz-Greene Halleck, Austin Flint, Francis Parkman, Nathaniel Hawthorne, and Henry Wadsworth Longfellow were courted because of this editorial outlook. Although never a contributor, Ralph Waldo Emerson was accorded frequent reviews. Less well-known writers who seemed likely to rise to prominence—for example, Jeremiah N. Reynolds (whose name has been remembered in connection with Edgar Allan Poe and Herman Melville), Mary Gardiner, Henry Cary ("John Waters"), Richard B. Kimball, Mary Hewitt, Philip Pendleton Cooke, Frederick W. Shelton, Frederick S. Cozzens ("Richard Haywarde"), Thomas Bangs Thorpe, James Humphrey Morris ("K. N. Pepper"), Matthew C. Field ("Phazma"), Charles Frederick Briggs ("Harry Franco"), Charles Godfrey Leland, Richard Henry Stoddard, and, of course, Willis Gaylord Clark—won recurrent attention by means of publications and editorial endorsements in *The Knickerbocker*. Significantly, these figures were undoubtedly connected in Clark's mind with the principles that American writers should cease to imitate European antecedents, as advocated, for example, in the April 1835 article in the "American Literature" series in *The Knickerbocker*.

Western writing also held out notable charms for editor Clark; his greatest success in that area was the serialization of Francis Parkman's *The Oregon Trail* in

1847. Others, whose reputations have not endured so lastingly as Parkman's, such as Frederick W. and Lewis Foulk Thomas, brothers who were at the time living in or near Cincinnati, likewise gained favorable press and space. Lewis Thomas's volume of verse, *Inda, a Legend of the Lakes: With Other Poems* (1842), was acclaimed in April 1845 as the first book of poems "that ever emanated from the press west of the Mississippi"; Frederick Thomas's poems occasionally graced pages of *The Knickerbocker,* and Clark's reviews of his books were consistently sympathetic. James Hall, Caroline M. Kirkland, and Albert Pike were also heralded for notable uses of Western materials.

Much of the other material published in *The Knickerbocker,* no doubt reflecting Clark's own tastes, is characterized by sentimentality—for example, Longfellow's "Psalms" of life, moralistic tales by Paulding and moralistic verses by Bryant ("The Prairies" excepted), or the "Ollapodiana" articles by Willis Gaylord Clark, which ran in the mid 1830s. Although the familiar essays of "Ollapod" have long since lost any vitality they may have had, they were once sufficiently popular to furnish quarry for plagiarizing, according to the "Editor's Table" for March 1845. Then, too, although Clark obviously admired and willingly published the Gothic fictions of such writers as Irving, Kimball, and William Leete Stone—which constitute some interesting fare in the supernatural vein—he reserved greatest honors for "The Iron Foot-Step"; a specimen of febrile literary Gothicism, by Cary (as John Waters), published in *The Knickerbocker* of April 1840, was later much complimented by Clark in editorial remarks and included in his edited volume *The Knickerbocker Sketch-Book: A Library of Select Literature* (1845). In this work Clark touted "The Iron Foot-Step" as approved by Washington Irving and having foundations in strict truth. The chief interest in this blend of sentimentality and weak supernaturalism is a crippled man's ghost prompting a friend to reveal the documents essential for the financial security of the dead man's widow and children. Far more compelling are Stone's "The Skeleton Hand" and "The Spectre Fire-Ship," both published in *The Knickerbocker* during 1834. Clark's conception of valid supernatural fiction doubtless accounted for his condescending assessments in the "Editor's Table" (February 1840 and January 1843) of Ann Radcliffe's Gothicism. His predilections may have led him to dismiss harshly William Harrison Ainsworth's *Jack Sheppard* (1839)—one of the "Newgate" novels, which were descendants of earlier Gothic novels—juxtaposing it, to its disadvantage, with Charles Dickens's *Oliver Twist* (1837). Just so, an interest in German literature that was evident in several issues of *The Knickerbocker* during the 1830s soon disappeared, and the regard manifested toward Thomas Carlyle's works condoned their comic elements but slighted what seemed to be their Transcendental obfuscations, another trait repeatedly associated with "Germanism."

In addition to promoting an American literature, *The Knickerbocker* expressed admiration for and published imitations of British authors such as Dickens; Joseph Addison; Richard Steele; Oliver Goldsmith; Walter Scott; George Gordon, Lord Byron; Charles Lamb; Thomas De Quincey; Sir Henry Bulwer; William Makepeace Thackeray; Alfred Tennyson; Wilkie Collins; and George Alfred Lawrence. The humor of Lamb, Dickens, and Thackeray, in particular, Clark thought approximated that of Irving's Knickerbocker and Geoffrey Crayon, and therefore today one might well construct chapters in the history of those English writers' reputations, especially Lamb's, from the reviews, "Editor's Table" sections, and allusions elsewhere throughout *The Knickerbocker.* Willis Clark's "Ollapodiana" columns commenced with a paean to Lamb, and allusions to his "Elia" essays were commonplace in those papers. Years later, Lewis Clark was attentive enough to Lamb's texts to note omissions from an edition of his works. He thought other British writers were worthy of extended notice as their works came out—for example, complimentary notices of Thackeray's books, notably *Vanity Fair* (1847) and *Pendennis* (1848–1850), and recurrent allusions to and quotations from his *Yellowplush Papers,* which began to appear in *Frazier's Magazine* in 1837–1838 and in their substance seemed to devolve from Lamb's wit. Clark's review of the first part of Tennyson's *Idylls of the King* (1859) predicted that it would be remembered as its creator's greatest artistic achievement, and the validity of that comment has long since proved to match the opinions of Tennyson specialists.

The wares of American humorists were especially welcomed by Clark, and thus the comic works of Frederick S. Cozzens, whose once admired *Sparrowgrass Papers* (1856)—inspired by Frederick W. Shelton's "Letters from up the River" (serialized in *The Knickerbocker* and brought out in volume form in 1853 as *Up the River*)—commenced serial publication in *The Knickerbocker* before moving to *Putnam's.* Cozzens, too, was a devotee of Lamb's writings; therefore his own productions emulate, if faintly, the Englishman's much more substantial "Elia" essays, just as they resemble pallid imitations of Irving's writings. Charles Godfrey Leland's "Meister Karl" and "Mace Sloper" articles were also popular *Knickerbocker* features in the 1850s. The contributions of Thomas Bangs Thorpe, best remembered as a frontier or "Old Southwest" humorist, were not so many as Cozzens's and do not represent Thorpe's finest achievements. Irving's writings in the magazine during the 1840s—eventually published in one volume as *Wolfert's Roost* (1855)—were a miscellany to be sure, although they were repeatedly praised by such writers as Clark and Cozzens. Parodies of Longfellow, Poe, and Walt Whitman enlivened some of the columns by "Old Knick" (Clark's pseudonym). Melville's *Typee* (1846) and *White Jacket* (1850) were commended for their humorous passages, and Jeremiah N. Reynolds's article, "Mocha Dick: or, the White Whale of the Pacific: A Leaf from a Manuscript Journal," which inspired Melville's *Moby-Dick* (1851) in part, first appeared in *The Knickerbocker* in May 1839. Several articles concerning the nature of humor are likewise of more than passing interest. Cozzens's (Richard Haywarde's) "On Wit and Humor," December 1850, posited that humor typically aligns with pathos, while wit is more often caustic. Humor anticipates an immediate response of mirth; wit goes farther and is more perceptive: "It distorts, multiplies, and grotesquely colors like a prism." Companion reading may be found in "The Science of 'Diddling,'" August 1848; con-man tactics are analyzed and the linkages of fear and extortion are noted. Such elements of comedy were much in vogue among Poe and the frontier humorists—for example, George Washington Harris, Augustus Baldwin Longstreet, Johnson Jones Hooper, and Thorpe—and they gained firmer footholds in the creations of Melville, Samuel Langhorne Clemens ("Mark Twain"), William Faulkner, and Flannery O'Connor. The "Editor's Table" columns also repeatedly considered the nature of humor, and a review of Thorpe's collection of comic sketches, *The Hive of the Bee Hunter* (April 1854), highlighted that author's "certain dry humor of description, which is especially captivating" because he expresses his "close observation of nature and character" in a clear, simple manner.

Clark himself may be numbered as another *Knickerbocker* humorist. His takeoffs on country newspapers in a series of "Bunkumville" sketches, made distinctive by such flourishes as dialect spellings and different sizes of type, may enlighten present-day readers about the world of newspaper journalism during the second quarter of the nineteenth century. Likewise, Clark's reviews (he wrote most of the ones that appeared in the magazine during his editorial tenure) were informative, sometimes peppered with dashes of well-intentioned wit. His monthly "Editor's Table" abounded in witty and amusing observations concerning the arts, most notably literature. Typically, an "Editor's Table" opened with a review or several reviews, briefer than those in the "Literary Notices," which always preceded the pages of the "Editor's Table." Then followed commentaries on music and drama. A final section, "Gossip with Readers and Correspondents," often amplified issues addressed elsewhere in the "Editor's Table" or

the magazine articles in the current or earlier volumes. As time passed, the "Editor's Table" lengthened, just as it came increasingly to be compiled of snippets from writings by others. An editorial history of *The Knickerbocker* also ran for several years; its content was not confined to the magazine proper but often identified contributors who first published anonymously—for example, that "Phazma" was Matthew C. Field, that "John Waters" was Henry Cary, or that "Richard Haywarde" was Frederick S. Cozzens. Thus, the editorial history has been useful to researchers.

Two notable departures from Clark's customary geniality are arresting—his onslaughts on William Gilmore Simms and Edgar Allan Poe. Simms's early works met with approval in *Knickerbocker* reviews. *Guy Rivers* (1834) was praised in the August 1834 "Literary Notices": "In many respects this novel is superior to the general works of Mr. Cooper." Simms's female characters are more natural and his plotting better, because less strained, than Cooper's. The great promise manifested in *Guy Rivers* made "Old Knick" hope for more work from so accomplished a writer. A follow-up appeared in the "Editor's Table" for March 1835: Simms's *The Yemassee* (1835) successfully embodies "genuine materials of American Romance," with notable "poetical" passages. Clark's endorsements of Simms's art did not center solely on what have continued to be upheld as the Southerner's major achievements—that is, his novels (or, as he preferred, "Romances"). In January 1839 Clark applauded Simms's short-story collection *Carl Werner, an Imaginative Story; With Other Tales* (1838) and his *Southern Passages and Pictures* (1839), a volume of what Clark called Simms's "poetical 'fugitives,'" ranking the latter far above the general run of American poetry of the day. Moreover, Clark found Simms's treatment of "German school" (by which he meant "Gothic") fiction far above the typical horrifics associated with such writing by his contemporaries. A change in the attitude of *The Knickerbocker* became noticeable once Simms apparently identified during the 1840s with the "Young America" movement that, to Clark, seemed to impinge with trashy creations on provinces that had been occupied by writers he admired, such as Halleck, Irving, Bryant, Paulding, Robert C. Sands, and Theodore Sedgwick Fay. Simms also spoke out about the disadvantages of Southern authorship in comparison with the situations of Northern writers. Abolition issues intensified "Old Knick's" antagonism toward Simms, who, as a Southerner, advocated Southern slaveholders' causes. In the "Literary Notices" for April 1846, reviewing Simms's volume of short stories *The Wigwam and the Cabin* (1845), Clark lambasted the Southern writer's inclinations toward and his management of comedy: "But whoever looks

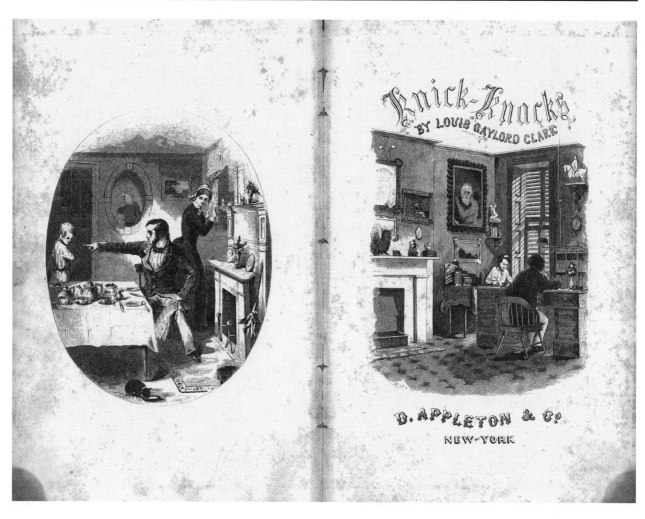

Frontispiece and decorated title page for the 1853 edition of Clark's columns from The Knickerbocker *magazine (Thomas Cooper Library, University of South Carolina)*

for humor in Mr. Simms might as well look for a smile in the jaws of an alligator; he is as incapable of humor as he is of perceiving that quality in others." The verdict of time has not upheld Clark's opinion; Simms is now recognized as a foremost nineteenth- century American humorist.

Clark's animosity toward Poe seems to have originated in what he construed as Poe's slighting remarks about both Clark brothers, as well as about William Leete Stone, a *Knickerbocker* favorite, and in Poe's success, during his editorial stint with *Graham's Magazine,* in turning that publication into a serious competitor for *The Knickerbocker.* The memory of Poe's savaging of Theodore Sedgwick Fay's egregious novel, *Norman Leslie* (1835), when Poe reviewed it in *The Southern Literary Messenger* in 1835, may have rankled in Clark's mind as an outrageous attack upon one of the darlings of the New York literary establishment. Whatever aroused Clark's ire, it developed into a determined scurrility

toward Poe the man, who was, of course, in many minds, inextricably connected with Poe the writer. Poe responded in his own trenchant manner to aspersions from Clark—for example, demeaning Clark's editorial abilities, a response that only further inflamed the powerful New York editor. Clark ultimately gained the upper hand because he controlled a prestigious literary organ and was a friend of many other powers in the contemporary literary establishment, while Poe's own employment as editor ceased in the mid 1840s, just as many of his professional-personal relationships turned sour. Clark variously evaluated "The Raven" during 1845 and 1846, initially praising it, but thereafter declaring that even this poem would not go far in upholding Poe's reputation as a poet. A bit of doggerel in the November 1846 *Knickerbocker,* "Epitaph on a Modern 'Critic.' 'P'oh' Pudor!" hit at Poe's literary abilities, hinting that gin accounted for his excrescences. Onslaughts of this venomous nature likewise came from other enemies of Poe. They typify the attempts of his detractors to get even with him, once he was no longer a periodical editor who could rebut such attacks. A series of scurrilities, for example, appeared during 1848 in the pages of *The John-Donkey,* a weekly into which went editorial comments by Thomas Dunn English, whose feelings toward Poe were particularly hostile. Even after Poe's death, Clark persisted. In an October 1850 review of the third volume of *The Works of the Late Edgar Allan Poe: With Notices of His Life and Genius* (1850–)–edited by Rufus W. Griswold, Nathaniel Parker Willis, and James Russell Lowell–Clark again attacked Poe's style and his caustic critical pronouncements, charging him with plagiarism, unwarranted attacks on Henry Wadsworth Longfellow and others, and scandalous irregularities in his personal life, especially in his relationship with Sarah Helen Whitman. In 1860 notices of Whitman's *Edgar Poe and His Critics* (1860), Clark continued to emphasize Poe's emotional instability. Along with his mean-spirited outpourings on Simms, those on Poe reveal a vicious streak in Clark, the repeated champion of kindly humor.

The articles Clark published after his years at *The Knickerbocker* consisted mainly of reminiscent biographical sketches of several persons whose influence or personal friendship he cherished. Typically, these essays placed their subjects in terms that link them with contributors to *The Knickerbocker* or Knickerbocker circles and, more pointedly, that depict their relationship with Clark. Charles Loring Elliott, a portrait painter whose work Clark admired, was one such subject. Washington Irving was another. Clark emphasized Irving's "inimitable personal humor . . . playful sallies of wit," and his unflaggingly "cheerful, genial mood." Clark's designation of this piece as a "desultory paper" characterizes all of his later writings. Since Clark's selections of humorous articles for publication in *The Knickerbocker* in the main bore a stamp of Irvingesque geniality, he understandably emphasized Dickens's whimsical humor in an essay on that author. Clark devoted even greater space to Dickens's visit to the United States in 1841, particularly to the gala dinner in New York City, which included many prominent figures connected with *The Knickerbocker.* Understandably, though, the cool reception of Dickens's less-than-favorable comments regarding American culture in some parts of *Martin Chuzzlewit* (1844) could not be overlooked. Greater value appeared in Clark's assessment of Dickens's literary method. Tersely, Clark quoted a letter to himself from Dickens wherein the latter's ideas concerning plot and characterization in *Martin Chuzzlewit* belied the charge leveled at him in the periodical press of his own day, that he wrote away at the parts of his novels heedless as to unity within the whole work. From such testimony,

Clark and any other reader may realize that Dickens was a far more attentive and careful writer than much negative criticism has implied. Just so, in his recollections of George Horatio Derby ("John Phoenix"), the American comic writer, Clark submitted that Derby was a fine humorist because he never descended to levels of ill nature that often sounded in the works of other literary comedians. Clark also complimented Derby for his ability to treat grave issues; readers often, thought Clark, too lightly assumed that a humorist was constitutionally incapable of expressing any depth of sobriety.

Like Herman Melville, Clark worked for a time in the New York City Custom House. In the latter part of his life, he relocated to Piermont, New York, where he lived in a cottage purchased in part with proceeds from *The Knickerbocker Gallery: A Testimonial to the Editor of the Knickerbocker Magazine from its Contributors* (1855), a memorial volume written by former *Knickerbocker* contributors for the purpose of purchasing the house. Clark wrote occasional articles for *Lippincott's Magazine* and *Harper's New Monthly Magazine* after *The Knickerbocker* failed. After a short illness from a stroke in 1873, he died on 3 November. Lewis Gaylord Clark admired and fostered a variety of literary nationalism that he personally could not achieve, as is borne out by the repeated praise in reviews and "Editor's Table" pages for much that was far rougher or bleaker in American humor than Clark himself effected, with the possible exception of his brutal editorial attacks upon Simms and Poe. Clark's lifelong penchant for the Irvingesque and his equal enthusiasm for Lamb's writings limited his outlook. In this respect, the selections Clark chose for *Knick-Knacks from an Editor's Table* (1852) might well suggest that he was as unmanly, sanctimonious, sentimental, and bloodless as Nathaniel Hawthorne, supported by his widow, Sophia, portrayed him to be. No wonder that what was intended to be a two-volume edition of *Knick-Knacks* stopped with just one. Similarly, despite his hagiographic memoir of his brother and his acclaim for Willis's literary art, both Lewis's introductory section and the primary works in *The Literary Remains of the Late Willis Gaylord Clark: Including the Ollapodiana Papers, the Spirit of Life, and a Selection from His Various Prose and Poetical Writings* (1844) are rather dreary fare. Clark did manage to conscript many of the foremost literary talents in his day as quondam contributors to *The Knickerbocker,* but most of the contributions from such eminent hands tended to fall somewhat below their creators' major art. *Knickerbocker* verse in particular, with a few notable exceptions, is now considered vapid. Moreover, Clark's own inflexible principles, evident in his ceaseless championing of Irving, Longfellow, and Lamb, prevented him from seeing any good in the "Young America" movement that brought new life to

American literature during the 1840s. Because he associated Simms and Poe with that movement, moreover, it occasioned offensives of the worst sort in his editorial columns. Long years in the editor's chair also crippled Clark's own abilities to write what would have lasting qualities, although arguments have been tendered for including some of his "Editor's Table" items in anthologies of American humor. Nevertheless, Clark's endeavor with *The Knickerbocker* did further the causes of many aspirant writers from the 1830s to 1860, and it simultaneously supplied reading that for several decades appealed to the growing numbers of the literate in the United States. Clark merits remembrance for those feats.

Letters:

Leslie W. Dunlap, ed., *The Letters of Willis Gaylord and Lewis Gaylord Clark* (New York: New York Public Library, 1940).

References:

Richard James Calhoun, "Literary Criticism in Southern Periodicals during the American Renaissance," *Critical Theory in the American Renaissance,* edited by Darrel Abel (Hartford: Transcendental Books, 1969), pp. 76–82;

"Finickings from Old Knick," *Boston Aurora Borealis,* 24 (February 1849): 38;

Benjamin F. Fisher, "The Knickerbocker," *American Literary Magazines: The Eighteenth and Nineteenth Centuries,* edited by Edward E. Chielens (New York, Westport, Conn. & London: Greenwood Press, 1987), pp. 189–194;

Fisher, *"The Knickerbocker," American Humor Magazines and Comic Periodicals,* edited by David E. E. Sloane (New York, Westport, Conn. & London: Greenwood Press, 1987), pp. 128–133;

Fisher, "Poe and the *John-Donkey:* A Nasty Piece of Work," *Essays in Arts and Sciences,* 29 (October 2000): 17–41;

The Knickerbocker Gallery: A Testimonial to the Editor of the Knickerbocker Magazine from its Contributors (New York: S. Hueston, 1855);

Perry Miller, *The Raven and the Whale: The War of Words and Wits in the Era of Poe and Melville* (New York: Harcourt, Brace, 1956);

"Miscellaneous Selections," *Cincinnati Mirror, and Chronicle; Devoted to Literature and Science,* 22 (August 1835): 1;

Sidney P. Moss, *Poe's Literary Battles: The Critic in the Context of His Literary Milieu* (Durham, N.C.: Duke University Press, 1963;

Moss, *Poe's Major Crisis: His Libel Suit and New York's Literary World* (Durham, N.C.: Duke University Press, 1970);

"Notices of Periodicals," *Orion,* 1 (August 1842): 323;

John Paul Pritchard, *Literary Wise Men of Gotham: Criticism in New York, 1815–1860* (Baton Rouge: Louisiana State University Press, 1963);

[William Gilmore Simms], "The Newspaper and Periodical Press," *Southern Quarterly Review,* 1 (January 1842): 5–66;

Herman E. Spivey, *"The Knickerbocker Magazine,* 1833–1865: A Study of Its Contents, History, and Significance," dissertation, University of North Carolina, 1935;

Kendall B. Taft, ed., *Minor Knickerbockers* (New York, Cincinnati, and others: American Book Company, 1947);

Thomas Bangs Thorpe, "Lewis Gaylord Clark," *Harper's New Monthly Magazine,* 48 (March 1874): 587–592.

Papers:

Lewis Gaylord Clark's papers, mostly letters, are scattered among many libraries in the United States. Chief repositories are the New York Public Library, Pierpont Morgan Library, Firestone Library at Princeton University, Massachusetts Historical Society, Historical Society of Pennsylvania, Haverford College, and University of Rochester.

James Fenimore Cooper

(15 September 1789 – 14 September 1851)

Stephen Railton
University of Virginia

See also the Cooper entries in *DLB 3: Antebellum Writers in New York and the South* and *DLB 183: American Travel Writers, 1776–1864.*

BOOKS: *Precaution,* anonymous, 2 volumes (New York: A. T. Goodrich, 1820; 3 volumes, London: Henry Colburn, 1821);

The Spy: A Tale of the Neutral Ground, anonymous, 2 volumes (New York: Wiley & Halsted, 1821; 3 volumes, London: G. & W. B. Whittaker, 1822);

The Pioneers; or, The Sources of the Susquehanna: A Descriptive Tale, 2 volumes (New York: Charles Wiley, 1823; 3 volumes, London: John Murray, 1823);

Tales for Fifteen; or, Imagination and Heart, as Jane Morgan (New York: Charles Wiley, 1823);

The Pilot: A Tale of the Sea, 2 volumes (New York: Charles Wiley, 1823; 3 volumes, London: John Miller, 1824);

Lionel Lincoln; or, The Leaguer of Boston, 2 volumes (New York: Charles Wiley, 1825; London: John Miller, 1825);

The Last of the Mohicans: A Narrative of 1757, 2 volumes (Philadelphia: H. C. Carey & I. Lea, 1826; 3 volumes, London: John Miller, 1826);

The Prairie, 3 volumes (London: Henry Colburn, 1827; 2 volumes, Philadelphia: Carey, Lea & Carey, 1827);

The Red Rover, 3 volumes (Paris: Hector Bossange, 1827 [unauthorized edition]; London: Henry Colburn, 1827; 2 volumes, Philadelphia: Carey, Lea & Carey, 1828);

Notions of the Americans: Picked up by a Travelling Bachelor, 2 volumes (London: Henry Colburn, 1828; 2 volumes, Philadelphia: Carey, Lea & Carey, 1828);

The Borderers, 3 volumes (London: Henry Colburn, 1829); also published as *The Wept of Wish Ton-Wish,* 2 volumes (Philadelphia: Carey, Lea & Carey, 1829);

The Water Witch; or, The Skimmer of the Seas, 3 volumes (Dresden: Printed for Walther, 1830; London:

James Fenimore Cooper (portrait by John W. Jarvis; Yale University Art Gallery)

Henry Colburn & Richard Bentley, 1830; 2 volumes, Philadelphia: Carey & Lea, 1830);

The Bravo. A Venetian Story, 3 volumes (London: Henry Colburn, 1831); also published as *The Bravo* (Philadelphia: Carey & Lea, 1831);

Letter of J. Fenimore Cooper to Gen. Lafayette, on the Expenditure of the United States of America (Paris: Baudry, 1831);

The Heidenmauer; or, The Benedictines, 3 volumes (London: Henry Colburn & Richard Bentley, 1832); also published as *The Heidenmauer; or, The Benedictines: A Legend of the Rhine,* 2 volumes (Philadelphia: Carey & Lea, 1832);

The Headsman; or, The Abbaye des Vignerons, 3 volumes (London: Richard Bentley, 1833; 2 volumes, Philadelphia: Carey, Lea & Blanchard, 1833);

A Letter to His Countrymen (New York: John Wiley, 1834; London: John Miller, 1834);

The Monikins, 3 volumes (London: Richard Bentley, 1835; 2 volumes, Philadelphia: Carey, Lea & Blanchard, 1835);

Hints on Manning the Navy (New York: West & Trow, 1836);

Sketches of Switzerland (Philadelphia: Carey, Lea & Blanchard, 1836); republished as *Excursions in Switzerland* (London: Richard Bentley, 1836);

A Residence in France; With an Excursion up the Rhine, and a Second Visit to Switzerland, 2 volumes (London: Richard Bentley, 1836); also published as *Sketches of Switzerland . . . Part Second,* 2 volumes (Philadelphia: Carey, Lea & Blanchard, 1836);

Recollections of Europe (London: Richard Bentley, 1837); also published as *Gleanings in Europe [France],* 2 volumes (Philadelphia: Carey, Lea & Blanchard, 1837);

England. With Sketches of Society in the Metropolis, 3 volumes (London: Richard Bentley, 1837); also published as *Gleanings in Europe. England,* 2 volumes (Philadelphia: Carey, Lea & Blanchard, 1837);

Excursions in Italy, 2 volumes (London: Richard Bentley, 1838); republished as *Gleanings in Europe. Italy,* 2 volumes (Philadelphia: Carey, Lea & Blanchard, 1838);

The American Democrat; or, Hints on the Social and Civic Relations of the United States of America (Cooperstown, N.Y.: H. & E. Phinney, 1838);

Homeward Bound; or, The Chase: A Tale of the Sea, 3 volumes (London: Richard Bentley, 1838; 2 volumes, Philadelphia: Carey, Lea & Blanchard, 1838);

Home As Found, 2 volumes (Philadelphia: Lea & Blanchard, 1838); republished as *Eve Effingham; or, Home As Found,* 3 volumes (London: Richard Bentley, 1838);

The Chronicles of Cooperstown (Cooperstown, N.Y.: H. & E. Phinney, 1838);

The History of the Navy of the United States of America, 2 volumes (Philadelphia: Lea & Blanchard, 1839; London: Richard Bentley, 1839);

The Pathfinder; or, The Inland Sea, 3 volumes (London: Richard Bentley, 1840; 2 volumes, Philadelphia: Lea & Blanchard, 1840);

Mercedes of Castille; or, The Voyage to Cathay, 2 volumes (Philadelphia: Lea & Blanchard, 1840; 3 volumes, London: Richard Bentley, 1841);

The Deerslayer: or, The First War-Path, 2 volumes (Philadelphia: Lea & Blanchard, 1841; 3 volumes, London: Richard Bentley, 1841);

The Two Admirals, 3 volumes (London: Richard Bentley, 1842; 2 volumes, Philadelphia: Lea & Blanchard, 1842);

The Jack O'Lantern (Le Feu Follet): or, The Privateer, 3 volumes (London: Richard Bentley, 1842); also published as *The Wing-and-Wing, or, Le Feu-Follet,* 2 volumes (Philadelphia: Lea & Blanchard, 1842);

Le Mouchoir: An Autobiographical Romance (New York: Wilson, 1843); republished as *The French Governess; or, The Embroidered Handkerchief* (London: Richard Bentley, 1843);

The Battle of Lake Erie, or Answers to Messrs. Burges, Duer, and Mackenzie (Cooperstown, N.Y.: H. & E. Phinney, 1843);

Wyandotté: or The Hutted Knoll, 3 volumes (London: Richard Bentley, 1843; 2 volumes, Philadelphia: Lea & Blanchard, 1843);

Ned Myers; or, A Life Before the Mast, 2 volumes (London: Richard Bentley, 1843; 1 volume, Philadelphia: Lea & Blanchard, 1843);

Afloat and Ashore: or, The Adventures of Miles Wallingford, 3 volumes (London: Richard Bentley, 1844; 2 volumes, Philadelphia: Published by the Author, 1844);

Lucy Hardinge, 3 volumes (London: Richard Bentley, 1844); also published as *Afloat and Ashore, or, The Adventures of Miles Wallingford . . . in Four Volumes, Volumes 3 and 4,* 2 volumes (Philadelphia: Published by the Author, 1844);

Satanstoe; or, The Family of Littlepage. A Tale of the Colony, 3 volumes (London: Richard Bentley, 1845); also published as *Satanstoe; or, The Littlepage Manuscripts. A Tale of the Colony,* 2 volumes (New York: Burgess, Stringer, 1845);

The Chainbearer; or, The Littlepage Manuscripts, 3 volumes (London: Richard Bentley, 1845; 2 volumes, New York: Burgess, Stringer, 1845);

Lives of Distinguished American Naval Officers, 2 volumes (Philadelphia: Carey & Hart, 1846);

Ravensnest; or, The Redskins, 3 volumes (London: Richard Bentley, 1846); also published as *The Redskins; or, Indian and Injin: Being the Conclusion of the Littlepage Manuscripts,* 2 volumes (New York: Burgess & Stringer, 1846);

Mark's Reef; or, The Crater. A Tale of the Pacific, 3 volumes (London: Richard Bentley, 1847); also published as *The Crater; or Vulcan's Peak. A Tale of the Pacific,* 2 volumes (New York: Burgess, Stringer, 1847);

Jack Tier; or, The Florida Reef, 2 volumes (New York: Burgess, Stringer, 1848); also published as *Captain*

Spike; or, The Islets of the Gulf, 3 volumes (London: Richard Bentley, 1848);

The Bee-Hunter; or, The Oak Openings, 3 volumes (London: Richard Bentley, 1848); also published as *The Oak Openings; or, The Bee-Hunter,* 2 volumes (New York: Burgess, Stringer, 1848);

The Sea Lions; or, The Lost Sealers, 3 volumes (London: Richard Bentley, 1849; 2 volumes, New York: Stringer & Townsend, 1849);

The Ways of the Hour (New York: George P. Putnam, 1850; 3 volumes, London: Richard Bentley, 1850);

New York . . . Being an Introduction to an Unpublished Manuscript . . . Entitled The Towns of Manhattan, edited by Dixon Ryan Fox (New York: William Farquhar Payson, 1930);

The Lake Gun, edited by Robert E. Spiller (New York: William Farquhar Payson, 1932);

Early Critical Essays, 1820–1822, edited by James F. Beard Jr. (Gainesville, Fla.: Scholars' Facsimiles & Reprints, 1955).

Collection: *Cooper's Novels,* 32 volumes (New York: W. A. Townsend, 1859–1861);

The Writings of James Fenimore Cooper, 16 volumes, edited by James F. Beard and others (Albany: The State University Press of New York, 1980–1991).

PLAY PRODUCTION: *Upside Down, or Philosophy in Petticoats,* New York, Burton's Theatre, 18 June 1850.

Throughout much of the nineteenth century James Fenimore Cooper was one of the most widely read novelists in the world and one of the most highly acclaimed. During his lifetime a series of well-publicized quarrels with his country caused his prestige to suffer, but at his death in 1851 he maintained his place as the foremost American novelist. Throughout much of the twentieth century a handful of his novels were still widely read, though mainly by adolescents. Today he is known chiefly by his reputation as a novelist rather than by his novels. The thirty-two novels he wrote, however, at least the majority of them, are considerably better than they are reputed to be. That he will ever again enjoy a vogue is inconceivable; his aesthetic assumptions, his prose style, and the conventions of character and narrative to which he subscribed are too irretrievably outdated. Cooper, in fact, is one of the few great nineteenth-century American authors who never seems "modern," as do such writers as Edgar Allan Poe, Herman Melville, Walt Whitman, and Emily Dickinson. Time has favored those writers: while readers in the twentieth century discovered the genius of those writers, however, they neglected Cooper's. Yet,

readers today, after some adjustment of their expectations and a little practice with Cooper's syntax, could still read eight or ten of his tales with real pleasure. And the student of American literature and history has many reasons to read him. As the first popularly successful novelist of America, Cooper contributed greatly to the literary and cultural life of this country. His single greatest achievement, as he himself recognized, was in creating the character of Natty Bumppo, the central figure of the five Leather-Stocking Tales. Backwoodsman, hunter, warrior, prophet of nature, and frontiersman at home with Native Americans, Natty has stepped from the pages of the tales to assume a permanent place in the national imagination. He has many descendants among the heroes of American fiction, movies, and television. The Leather-Stocking Tales gave millions of readers around the world their first introduction to the mythological realm of the pathless wilderness—a realm of nightmare, where silent Mingoes lurk in the depths of the gloomy forest; of dream, where a stately buck stoops to drink at the margin of an enchanted lake; and, above all, of freedom, where the human ego can find adventures commensurate with its narcissistic longings. Yet, not even Natty's commanding presence should overshadow the whole of Cooper's achievement, which was scattered throughout his novels—his romances of forest and sea, his tales of colonial and revolutionary history, and his novels of politics and society. In the pages of all these works Cooper helped his young nation, still struggling to attain its intellectual independence from Europe, to discover and take imaginative possession of itself.

Cooper was born in Burlington, New Jersey, on 15 September 1789, the same year that George Washington became the first president of the newborn republic. At his birth Cooper was named simply James Cooper. Fenimore, his mother's maiden name, he took for himself when he was thirty-seven and a famous writer. (He actually petitioned the New York state legislature for the right to call himself James Cooper Fenimore, but that request was denied.) From his mother, Elizabeth, he also acquired the taste for reading fiction that led to his eventual choice of a literary career. His father was a man of actions rather than words, though his influence on his son's books was at least as important as his deeds. William Cooper was a self-made man. Among other investments and speculations, he was the founder and patriarch of Cooperstown, the upstate New York village over which he presided as landlord, as first judge of Otsego County, and as the representative to Congress from the district. A leading spokesman for the Federalist Party, which reflected Alexander Hamilton's fears about the people and fought to keep political power in the hands of men of property, Judge

Cooper's birthplace (at left) in Burlington, New Jersey

Cooper was a major figure in the early history of New York state. By his energy and ambition, by what his friends called his tough-minded shrewdness and his enemies called his lack of scruples, he took advantage of the unsettled economic conditions of the American Revolution to rise from poverty and to make extensive purchases of undeveloped land. Judge Cooper was, in fact, the kind of man who made enemies: he was rugged, short-tempered, impatient with opposition, an enthusiastic wrestler who was not afraid of violence, and an authoritarian who was determined to impose his will upon the world. These traits were assets for a captain of pioneers. As a man William Cooper was a good match for the wilderness he wanted to civilize, and as a landlord he was conspicuously successful. In 1807 he could boast that he had been responsible for settling more acres of forest than any other individual in America.

These same traits, however, made him a formidable father. By no means a brutal man, William Cooper was nonetheless a demanding one, and family

tradition suggests that he reigned over his family as despotically as he ruled over his tenants in Cooperstown. He died in 1809, when James was twenty. The exact cause of his death remains unclear, but according to family tradition, it resulted from a head wound inflicted by a political opponent. He was survived by one daughter and five sons, of whom James was the youngest. Cooperstown remains today as a legacy to William Cooper's public achievement, but the personal fortune he had amassed was gone within a decade—in part because several of the land titles it rested on were shaky, but mainly because his children squandered it. William Cooper tried hard to found a dynasty and failed; yet, his son James's lifework, especially his literary career, can in some ways be understood as an attempt to come to terms with the meaning of his identity as Judge Cooper's son.

Thus, the novelist's early years, while not particularly crowded with incident, are extremely relevant to the fictions he wrote in the second half of his life. As an infant he was carried from his birthplace in New Jersey through the woods to Cooperstown, where his father was making the wilds habitable for his own family and for the settlers who were leaving their homes behind to try their fortunes in a newer land. Many of Cooper's novels are about the process of pioneering a new settlement. His third novel, *The Pioneers; or, The Sources of the Susquehanna: A Descriptive Tale* (1823), is based fairly closely on his memories of the village he grew up in. *The Pioneers* is the richest account in existence of the infancy of a frontier community. The point of contact between civilization and the wilderness makes a fascinating study. Almost outside the pale of society, the immigrants waged a kind of war on nature, struggling with the many trees that had to be cleared before the settlers could plant the crops that their economic survival depended on but were also needed to provide fires to protect them against the bitter cold of snowy winters. Houses were huddled together along the few streets, laid out in straight lines that promised a city but that remained littered with the stumps that could not be pulled. From Elizabeth Cooper's point of view, the scarcest commodity in the community was refinement. There were, however, pretensions to it. Judge Cooper's "Mansion-House," as it was grandly titled, was built to resemble a European manor house. Despite the campaign being fought with axes against the native trees, poplars were actually imported from Europe and carried into the depths of the American woods to adorn the judge's grounds. And every settler had one best dress or suit to wear to the services that were occasionally held in a makeshift church. Since everything had to be created, social distinctions were almost erased by the necessity for cooperation; yet, the settlers anxiously tried not merely to be but also to seem more prosperous than their neighbors.

William Cooper's town was put in a beautiful spot among the mountains on the shores of Lake Otsego. But life there was rude—from the "manners" of the domestic help in the Mansion-House to the "skill" of the one doctor in the village. Elizabeth Cooper, accustomed to the comforts of gentility, was miserable in the wilderness and often pleaded with her husband to let her move back to New Jersey. Winters in the woods of New York were her worst times, and three times during the 1790s she took her children to Burlington to escape the cold and snow. But according to family tradition, James's voice was always one of the loudest in urging her to return to Cooperstown. When he was ten, his older sister Hannah wrote a friend that her brothers were sufficiently wild to show that they had been bred in the woods; all the evidence indicates that James was less interested in the social ambitions of the village than in the excitements of the wilderness that lay around it. No doubt he, like most

American children, encountered "wild Indians" in his play—there may even have been pirates on Lake Otsego. Much of his success as a novelist he owed to his ability to get his readers to believe in imaginary Mingoes and rovers. But by the end of the eighteenth century, Cooperstown was a relatively tame place. Indian raids, like the Native Americans themselves, were part of the past of the region. What Cooper knew about Native Americans he learned later, from books, just as many of his contemporaries met their first aborigines in his books. Growing up beside a lake at the edge of the forest, though, clearly offered Cooper a base of experience for the stories he later told the world: as a child he played in the woods and on the water; as a novelist he wrote his best books when his imagination played in one of those two settings.

Considering his father's domineering disposition, James probably prized especially the freedom of outdoor play. Until William Cooper's death, most of James's actions were dictated by the orders of his father, who arranged first for his youngest son's schooling and then for his career. Although William Cooper had little formal education himself, he wanted his children to have the benefit of the right schools, and he determined that James should be trained in them for a career in law. James's education would have been the best that money could buy and better than anyone might have expected from the backwoods had James himself been a more willing student. After being tutored in Cooperstown and spending several winters in a private school in Burlington, in 1801 he was sent to Albany to learn Latin and the proper behavior for a Federalist gentleman from an Episcopal clergyman who kept an elite boarding school for the sons of men of property. Among James's classmates were a Van Rensselaer, a Livingston, and a Jay. In 1803, at the age of thirteen, James was enrolled in Yale College. Still learning how to dress and spend like a gentleman, he ran up large debts with tailors and bootmakers. The 250 or so Yale students at that time were known for rowdiness, often brawling in groups with sailors off the ships moored in New Haven, but James's conduct went beyond even those generous limits. In 1805, after an academic career that already included more than its share of scrapes, pranks, and minor rebellions, he was formally expelled from the college. The trouble began with a fight in which James was badly beaten by another student, John Boyle. Both young men were suspended, but only James was expelled. According to family tradition, that was because in retaliation for the beating, James used a charge of gunpowder to blow up Boyle's door. Three years earlier, one of James's older brothers, William Jr., had been expelled from Princeton for burning down Nassau Hall. Blowing up privies was

Judge William Cooper, Cooper's father (portrait by Gilbert Stuart; from James Franklin Beard, ed., Letters and Journals of James Fenimore Cooper, *volume 2, 1960)*

was not quite true for Cooper, of course, but if the schools left him an indifferent Latinist, his years as a sailor gave him a lifelong passion for the sea, one that he indulged enthusiastically in almost a third of his books.

Cooper was still in the navy at the end of 1809, when his father died. His father's death meant that he could make his own decisions about the direction of his future. To James's disappointment, he had seen no active duty at sea, so he left the navy with no regrets for an aborted military career. He put himself on furlough in 1810, partly to help his older brothers administer William Cooper's complicated estate, but mainly to court Susan De Lancey of Mamaroneck, New York. James Cooper and De Lancey were married 1 January 1811, and shortly afterward he formally resigned from the navy. Leaving the service left him entirely without a career, but at that point there was no need of one. With his father's death he had inherited $50,000; the property at Cooperstown promised to support him indefinitely; and his new wife was also wealthy.

Susan Cooper's father, John Peter De Lancey, was, like James's father, a successful New York Federalist. In marrying her Cooper confirmed a commitment to his class and was thought to have done well for himself socially. Emotionally, he did even better. For forty years Cooper's marriage was a fixed point of happiness in an otherwise often melodramatically uneven life. He and Susan had seven children. Two died in early childhood, but four daughters (Susan, Caroline, Anne, and Maria) and one son (Paul) survived. Susan became her father's literary executor. With his wife Cooper also shared both the triumphs and the defeats of his literary career, and in the warmth of his domestic life he consistently claimed to find a compensation for the misunderstandings he was subjected to in the larger world. The unreasonableness with which he quarreled with public adversaries indicates that he could not always have been easy to live with. Like Cooper's mother, who disliked the wilderness, his wife may have felt at times that her life was held hostage by her husband's willful ambitions. But he was a kind husband and a devoted father. There can be no doubt that Susan Cooper was a good wife.

Nearly a decade lies between Cooper's marriage and his decision, at age thirty, to become an author. That choice was absolutely unpremeditated: not even Cooper himself, as he reflected upon its antecedents from the middle of his literary career, could account for it. To him the decision always seemed "purely accidental." Perhaps if more were known about Cooper's life between 1811 and 1819, all the steps that eventually led to his becoming an author could be traced more easily.

a typical student prank at Yale, but the faculty (perhaps aware of what had happened at Princeton) took an explosion inside a college building more seriously.

From Yale, James Cooper returned to Cooperstown, where he stayed for a little more than a year, reading law with a lawyer in the village and no doubt presenting a challenge to his father about where to send him next. In 1806 Cooper went to sea. There is some evidence that he ran away from home to do so, though by the time he shipped out of Philadelphia on board a vessel owned and captained by a friend of his father, he had apparently reached an agreement with his family about his future. To prepare himself for a career as an officer in the United States Navy, Cooper sailed before the mast aboard the *Sterling,* a merchant vessel that traded between New York and London. This training as a sailor qualified him to join the navy as a midshipman at the beginning of 1808. More important was the way that Cooper's experiences on the North Atlantic served him as a novelist two decades later, when he created the genre of nautical romance. Melville, who proved that the genre could yield a masterpiece, said in *Moby-Dick* (published in 1851, the year Cooper died) that a whaling ship had been his Yale College. That

From the record available, the one pattern that emerges clearly is failure, not traumatic, but steady and persistent. During the first ten years of his marriage, Cooper tried to fill the role that his class defined for him. At the beginning and end of this period he resided in Westchester County, close to the De Lancey family estate; from 1814 to 1817 he lived in Cooperstown, close to his mother and his own family's estate. He adopted the duties of the Federalist gentleman, whose station was both to serve and to adorn society: he became an officer in the state militia, worked as secretary for several Bible and agricultural societies, and campaigned briefly for the Federalist Party. But in none of these roles did Cooper show any signs of distinguishing himself, and in any case the foundation on which this identity rested–his inherited wealth–was breaking up. His brothers' prodigality and various legal entanglements rapidly reduced Judge Cooper's grand estate to mortgaged ruins. When the last of his brothers died in 1819, James Cooper himself was seriously in debt. The De Lancey fortune was still sound, but he had used up his in-laws' good will. The tacit duty of the Federalist gentleman was to take good care of his own economic interests. Cooper tried hard to imitate his father's success at speculation, but during this period, as indeed throughout his entire life, he displayed little business talent; his investments almost inevitably wound up costing money instead of making it.

By the winter of 1819–1820 Cooper arrived at a moment of crisis, one that involved his identity as well as his finances. He himself would not have described the moment in these terms, but his sudden and surprising decision to write a novel shows that his future, which ten years earlier had seemed so well delineated, had grown indistinct enough to force him to make a serious effort to redefine it. Reading novels had been a favorite pastime of his mother, one of the ways she sustained herself amidst the cultural impoverishment of a frontier community. Judge Cooper, like most nineteenth-century American fathers and like the stern ancestors who rebuke Nathaniel Hawthorne in "The Custom-House" introduction to *The Scarlet Letter* (1850), would certainly have frowned on the impracticality and frivolity, perhaps even the effeminacy, of making a life out of writing stories. As the first novel Cooper wrote reveals, fiction provided him with a means to retreat from the present realities of his doubtful position in the community of gentlemen. Yet, if failure in life helped drive him into the imaginative world of art, at the same time, make-believe gave Cooper something else–a chance at age thirty to begin a new career, to find a new identity as the first professional novelist of America, and to achieve an international

stature that eventually made his father's achievement seem small and local.

How Cooper became an author is a story that has often been told. The details were first recorded by his oldest daughter, Susan Cooper, and seem to be true. One day, late in 1819 or early in 1820, he was reading a current British novel aloud to his wife. The book was so bad that, throwing it down, he declared he could write a better one himself. His wife is said to have laughed in disbelief: Cooper enjoyed reading, but disliked writing, even letters, and had never shown any symptoms of a creative temperament. Cooper's response to his wife's laughter suggests a lot about his defensiveness and foretells his characteristic reaction to criticism: to prove her wrong he sat down immediately to compose a tale. He probably also had something to prove to himself. The first ten years of his adult life had amounted to a series of social gestures that may have elegantly masked a ripening conviction of personal inadequacy. Cooper's was not an introspective personality; as in this instance, his tendency was always to assert rather than to examine himself, and he left no record of the motives behind his determination to begin writing a novel to prove how wrong his wife was about him, nor any account of the hopes and misgivings that kept him at the new task of writing week after week until the long book was done. Practically, at a time when his finances were in critical condition, spending his time writing was as frivolous as anything he could have done. Yet, if he wrote his first novel mainly to demonstrate that he was capable of accomplishing something of his own, his stubbornness led him to a career.

After swearing the man who printed it to secrecy about his identity, Cooper published his first novel anonymously in November 1820. *Precaution* is a bad book but a telling cultural document–a good guide to the many obstacles that stood in the path of an American literature in the early nineteenth century. In 1819 the British critic Sydney Smith sarcastically inquired who, anywhere in the world, had read an American book that was any good. Although Washington Irving drew some of the sting out of Smith's barb by beginning serial publication of *The Sketch Book* to wide acclaim that same year, America was still suffering from the cultural inferiority complex that was a legacy of its colonial dependency on England. Not only were pirated British novels sold in the United States more cheaply than domestic ones, on which royalties had to be paid, but also the widespread belief was that imported fictions were necessarily better. Irving's *The Sketch Book* was published in book form first in England in 1820, and its acceptance by British reviewers and readers added to its cachet with Americans. Cooper,

Elizabeth Fenimore Cooper, Cooper's mother, in the family home, Otsego Hall, Cooperstown (New York State Historical Association, Cooperstown)

who had to pay for publication of *Precaution* with his own money because no American printer would take the risk, found a different way to solve this marketing problem. His novel was a fiction in more ways than one. The first book by the author who can be called the founding father of American novels was set in England; its characters were exclusively English; and it deceived even its English reviewers into assuming that an English citizen had written it. Determined still to seem the gentleman of independent means, Cooper told his printer that he wrote *Precaution* merely to amuse himself, but his concern with making the book marketable is obvious enough. He decided how long the novel should be by estimating the number of words in one of Walter Scott's popular Waverley Novels. He patterned the story of his novel after the type of domestic comedy that was currently fashionable and out of which Jane Austen made enduring art. Cooper was interested in being fashionable, not in creating art. Although his original goal was to write a better book, there is nothing intrinsically wrong with his desire to write a marketable one. His contribution to American literature would have been much less significant if he had not found ways to match what he wanted to say as an artist with the popular expectations of his audience. Throughout his career his imagination was largely governed by contemporary literary conventions, and especially during the 1820s, while he was still in the process of proving

that an American writer could make a living by writing, he knew he had to cater to the tastes that his readers had acquired from abroad. Yet, if one were to subtract from *Precaution* all that it owed to its British models, absolutely nothing would be left to call Cooper's. It is difficult to say which is the more surprising–that he should ever have written a novel in the first place, or that, after this derivative beginning, he would go on to create great literature.

Cooper's novel made no grand entrance on the scene. Because of its disguise, *Precaution* received decent critical notices but did not sell enough copies to recover its cost. Before it appeared, though, Cooper had already started a second novel. Once he tapped his imagination he discovered creative energies that were not easily depleted: between 1820 and 1850 he produced thirty-two novels, more than a dozen volumes of nonfiction, an extensive collection of pamphlets, public letters and articles, and one play. Yet, this prolific career almost ended as abruptly as it had begun when the disappointing commercial performance of his first book caused him to break off work on the second. Friends, however, advised him to finish it. And Cooper had two compelling reasons of his own to do so, though he admitted only one of them. As an American, he said, he felt a need to atone for the British accent of *Precaution*. As a man he also may have wanted to reaffirm his masculinity, for reviewers and readers treated *Precaution* not only as a British book but also as a woman's one.

The "femininity" of Cooper's first book says something both about him and about the novel as a cultural form. For him novel reading was associated with his mother. Writing that first novel gave him a chance to withdraw from the social sphere, where he was failing in the role of gentleman bequeathed him by his father, into an imaginative feminine refuge. Novel reading was also gendered feminine by the culture. The first best-selling novels of the United States—*Charlotte Temple* (first American publication, 1794) and *The Coquette* (1797)—were by and about women. Like Charles Brockden Brown, who had tried a generation earlier to become the first professional novelist in America, Cooper might also have seen "femininity" as a marketing strategy, the best means of gaining access to the predominantly female novel-reading public. In 1823 he also published *Tales for Fifteen; or, Imagination and Heart,* two short tales for young readers, under the pseudonym Jane Morgan. But his second novel, published in 1821, though also published anonymously, left no room for doubt about its author's nationality or gender. In *The Spy: A Tale of the Neutral Ground,* he turned from domestic novels to the manlier model of Scott's historical romance, and this time the story is not only set in America but also is about a patriot during the Revolutionary War. Washington even appears several times.

Although the elements of plot and characterization that form *The Spy* are still basically conventional, this second novel is an immeasurably better tale. Cooper employed Scott's techniques as deftly as he handled the patriotic sentiments of the book—combining the proper amounts of action, suspense, love, heroism, and history. The story, about a man who serves General Washington, at the hazard of his own life and the cost of his reputation, by circulating as a peddler behind enemy lines, was based on a true account Cooper heard from his acquaintance John Jay, the Federalist statesman and first chief justice of the Supreme Court. Historical truth, however, subserves a legendary end. Cooper's familiarity as a reader with popular fiction as well as his shrewdness as a writer aware of his audience can be seen in the skill with which he feeds the appetite for the romantic. Giving his readers the formal elements they expected from a British fiction and a story they could be proud of as Americans was a brilliant strategy. The critical reception of *The Spy* left Cooper with a grudge against American reviewers, who hesitated to pronounce judgment on the book until they knew whether or not English critics approved. Yet, long before the favorable reviews from abroad arrived, the reading public in the United States welcomed the book warmly and bought it eagerly. With publication of *The Spy,* Cooper's career was firmly established. At age thirty-two he became the first professional novelist in the United States.

Success was not less sweet to Cooper for having been delayed or for being attained by such an unlikely means. His income from royalties began arriving just in time to save his household from bankruptcy. The acclaim that greeted *The Spy* gave him a new public identity as an eminent man of letters. In keeping with the practice of the day, all of Cooper's early novels were published anonymously, but the novelist's name was no secret, and when in 1821 he moved his family into New York City, he stepped directly into the role of celebrity, at least on the limited scale permitted by the local social conditions. During the five years that he lived in town, for example, he formed and regularly attended "The Bread and Cheese," a group of leading New Yorkers (merchants, professional men, journalists, and a few artists) who met weekly to discuss current affairs and to nurture American culture. These years were good for Cooper: he had finally found a way to make himself useful and recognized among his generation. His father had built a community in the wilderness, and Cooper could see himself as the leading pioneer in the new world of American literature.

Indeed, having succeeded in establishing his own identity, Cooper was ready to confront his father's achievement directly. In *The Pioneers* he chose to sacrifice some of his concern with public taste to a more personal desire: as he said in its preface, *The Pioneers* was written "exclusively to please myself; so it would be no wonder if it displeased every body else." There was no need for this apology; looking forward to the latest work by the author of *The Spy,* Americans bought 3,500 copies of *The Pioneers* before noon on the first day of its publication. That was an extraordinary number for the time; for example, *The Scarlet Letter,* the best-selling of all Hawthorne's novels, sold only about twice that many copies in its first *year* of publication. Yet, Cooper's point about pleasing himself was no mere ploy. Of the ten novels Cooper wrote during the first decade of his career, *The Pioneers* is the most autobiographical. In the estimation of most modern scholars, it is also the best of all his novels and something close to a legitimate masterpiece. As its subtitle says, the novel is "A Descriptive Tale," a loosely organized narrative of life in a frontier settlement. Set a dozen years after the close of the American Revolution, it is (like all Cooper's fiction between 1821 and 1838) an historical novel, but now the novelist had a large private investment in the history. In *The Pioneers* he returns imaginatively to the landscape of his childhood. Not only does *The Pioneers* re-create the Cooperstown he had grown up in, but its

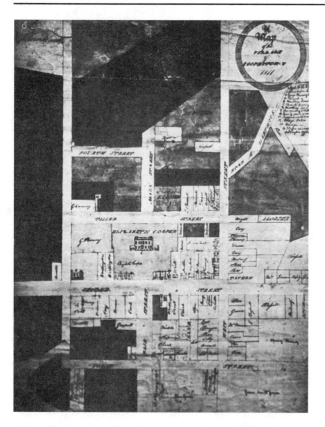

Map of Cooperstown, New York, in 1811, showing William Cooper's distribution of property among his heirs

characters also include representations of his father (in Judge Marmaduke Temple, founder and landlord of Templeton) and his sister Hannah (in Elizabeth Temple, the heroine of the story). Judge Temple is a widower, so the novelist's mother is conspicuously absent. And there are no children at all in the story, though James would have been around five years old at the period in which it is set. But the conflicts of the novel acquire even greater resonance when it is read as autobiography. At its center is a profound ambivalence toward the figure of the father and toward the enterprise of civilizing the continent, which the father personifies. In writing this book, Cooper is striving to come to terms at once with the psychic legacy of his own childhood and with the collective errand of America to move into the wilderness. Where did he come from? What is the country becoming? Trying to answer these two questions produced a novel whose moral and emotional urgencies can still be felt today.

A reader of today, however, starts outside the conventions of the historical romance and so is likely to be alienated by the same features that made earlier generations of readers feel at home in the text. Its hero and heroine, for instance, not only speak and pose in impossibly stylized ways, but they also are involved in a for-

mulaic love story destined to end, in the last chapter, with a marriage that is tasked with resolving the thematic conflict between the competing claims of civilization and the wilderness. As nineteenth-century readers would have expected, the heroine is identified with the values of civilization: in the scene where he proposes to her, Oliver, the hero of the romance, credits Elizabeth with having "tamed" him. Even during his lifetime, Cooper's handling of the love story that he and his audience agreed had to be a major part of all his novels and especially his depiction of the ladies who were almost invariably cast as his heroines were condemned as the weakest aspects of his work. Intelligent, independent, proud as well as compassionate, Elizabeth is better drawn than most Cooper "females," but to readers accustomed to the modern representation of women, she is bound to seem stifled by the behavioral conventions of both her social class and her literary role. The novel as a whole also suffers from Cooper's sense of allegiance to conventions of Romance as defined by British writers such as Scott.

Not by coincidence, the pioneers at Templeton are suffering from almost exactly the same problem as the novel–trying to impose a set of imported conventions onto the American landscape. The architecture of the "mansion-house" (as Judge Temple's imposing home is called) imitates the finest European models, but it is so poorly suited to the topography and climate of the place that the roof has to hold up the columns. In their haste to acquire the forms of civilization, the settlers are stripping the mountains of their trees, the lake of its fish, and the forest of its animals–not to mention the land of its aboriginal inhabitants. The novel shows the settlers chopping down trees and slaughtering bass and pigeons. The destruction of Native American culture has already happened before the story begins, but the cast of characters includes "Indian John," Christianized and alcoholic, the sole surviving remnant of the tribe that earlier lived on the land the pioneers are civilizing. Once he was a great warrior; now he is a threat only to the moral complacency of white society. As the narrative progresses through a year in the life of the settlement, the overt tone remains respectful both toward Judge Temple and toward his settlers' achievement in "taming the very forests," but the reader is given more and more reasons to wonder what kind of spirit inhabits the societal forms that the settlers serve as the god to which they sacrifice the order of nature in the new world.

This ambivalence is brought into focus by the growing prominence in the plot of the one white character who is most unmistakably aligned with nature and the new world and who is also the one most clearly without any precedent in European fiction. In the first chapter he materializes from behind a pine tree—a tall, lean old man, dressed in deerskin "after the manner of the Indians," carrying a long hunting rifle. He is identified by the narrator as Natty Bumppo, or the Leather-Stocking, and his first spoken words are "No–no—Judge." By the end of the first chapter he has disappeared back into the woods. Amazingly, much of Natty's character sprang into life in Cooper's imagination in this first scene, but Cooper seems to have conceived Natty at first as only a minor, and probably essentially comic, figure. An aging hunter, he is angry at the way the settlers are driving away the game from the woods he has lived in for forty years, but the other characters present in that scene ignore his mutterings.

Natty's presence grows steadily, however, throughout the novel. Living alone in a hut across the lake from the village, he comes to embody in his own person the spirit of the place. Temple is the man with the title of "Judge," but the more Natty speaks in his eloquent vernacular against the "wicked and wasty ways" of civilization, the more his judgments seem prophetic. He is illiterate, but his knowledge of nature and his prowess with the long rifle establish his authority amid the inauthenticities and incompetencies of the settlers. Natty moves to the narrative center at the climax of the novel, a trial scene that puts Natty and the ideal of justice into opposition against Temple and the institution of the law. Natty even begins to subvert the conventional structure of the novel, taking over from Oliver, the formal hero, the job of rescuing Elizabeth (twice). In fact, at the end Natty effectively empties the conventional structure of much of its meaning, for what commands the reader's attention in the last chapter is not the hero and heroine's marriage, though in that marriage Cooper intends to adumbrate the future of American civilization. Instead, the most memorable event at the end of The Pioneers is Natty's decision to disappear back into the woods. Although Elizabeth pleads with him to stay, he shoulders his rifle, whistles for his hound, and becomes the first imaginary American hero to disappear in the direction of the sunset.

Cooper had no thought of setting up a sequel. Throughout his career, despite the evidence of the popularity of the subsequent Leather-Stocking Tales, his American and English publishers were invariably wary about sequels and paid him less for them. By the end of The Pioneers, though, both he and his readers recognized in Natty a character in whose company they wanted to remain. Biographically, Natty may have served Cooper as a created, surrogate father figure, the heroic embodiment of his wish to rebel against his father's authority. The antagonism between Judge Temple and Natty is what gives the novel its dramatic shape, and both the novel and the character achieve their greatest power when Natty, after breaking out of Judge Temple's jail, exiles himself from Templeton. But if Natty was created as part of Cooper's project to please himself, there is no doubt about how powerfully he appealed to Cooper's contemporary readers. Someone wrote to the novelist that emotionally he "longed to go with Natty at the end." Even as readers busily devoted themselves to the labor of taming the continent for themselves, they sympathized with Natty's plight, oppressed by the sound of axes in the clearings and the new laws that governed in the woods.

Of course, the Leather-Stocking was not the first American to leave to escape the evils of society, and later he was joined there in spirit by such significant figures as Henry David Thoreau and the fictional Huck Finn. The conflicts dealt with in The Pioneers—the claims of the wilderness versus the pursuit of progress, the natural freedom of the solitary individual versus the inevitable obligations and compromises that come from membership in society, and Old World conventions versus American possibility—are cultural issues that remain alive to this day. Ralph Waldo Emerson called The Pioneers "our first national novel," perhaps because it gives expression to these central American antitheses. Pioneering was the great national enterprise for the first half of the nineteenth century: there were thirteen states at Cooper's birth, but before he died there were thirty-one, and California was the brightest star on the flag. A third of Cooper's novels evoke the process of settling the land, a preoccupation of both his conscious desire to treat representatively American themes and his unconscious need to keep returning to the figure of his father. What characterizes The Pioneers as the first of his novels about, in the last words of the text, "the march of the nation across the continent" is its extraordinary ambivalence, its refusal to resolve the great contradictions on which American civilization rests. Cooper's nostalgia for the frontier village of his childhood is a source of much of the achievement of the novel. But as he wrote it, he tapped into a deeper nostalgia, the longing for a world that neither he nor anyone else has ever lived in, though that this world was fictional hardly makes it seem less real as Natty describes the wilderness before the settlers brought in their secondhand civilization and destroyed it. Natty retreats at the end into that unfallen world, damning American society by his absence. Although Cooper intends to reassure the reader about the social future that Elizabeth and Oliver will preside over, they are actually standing in a cemetery as they watch Natty disappear into the wilderness. Natty is seventy years old, and going alone into the woods as winter comes on—but his action feels like life. Elizabeth and Oliver are young, rich, and in love—yet, somehow the cemetery

SIR,

We have in the press, and will publish early in February—

THE

LAST OF THE MOHICANS;

A NARRATIVE OF 1757.

In 2 vols. 12mo.

BY THE AUTHOR OF THE SPY, PIONEERS, &c.

For which we shall be happy to receive your orders on the terms annexed, which are the same as for the former works of this author.

Yours, respectfully,

H. C. CAREY & I. LEA.

Philadelphia, Jan. 10, 1826.

12 copies	-	-	-	20 per cent. cash.
25 copies	-	-	-	25 per cent. do.
50 copies	-	-	-	25 per cent. 3 months.
100 copies	-	-	-	25 per cent. 6 months.

Approved endorsed notes will be required for all purchases on credit.

Advertisement for Cooper's 1826 novel, set during the French and Indian War (Clifton Waller Barrett Library, Manuscript Department, University of Virginia Library)

seems like the appropriate setting for them, among all the corpses (trees, animals, Indians, and the idea of autonomy) that civilization has produced.

Cooper's sixth and seventh novels feature Natty again. A modern publisher would advertise *The Last of the Mohicans: A Narrative of 1757* (1826) as the "prequel" to *The Pioneers,* but the books are extremely different. As Cooper's most melodramatic adventure novel, *The Last of the Mohicans* uses colonial history–the French and Indian War and the 1757 massacre of the British garrison at Fort William Henry–as the backdrop for an implausible but compelling fantasy of sexual desire and physical violence. Out of the hackneyed conventions of Gothic romance–light and dark heroines, a satanic villain, and shrieks in the middle of the night–Cooper creates a tale that says as much about the conflicts within the European-American psyche as *The Pioneers* said about the conflicts in European-American society.

The adventure begins when two half sisters, Cora and Alice, stray into the depths of the wilderness in an ill-advised attempt to join their father, commander of Fort William Henry. General Montcalm's French army is moving down Lake Champlain to besiege the fort, and the woods are already full of hostile Indians. From this point of departure the story moves, at a pace that

nineteenth-century readers found almost too gripping, through scenes of suspense and violence. Twice the women are captured by the fierce and treacherous Magua and have to be pursued and rescued by Natty, accompanied by Chingachgook (Indian John from *The Pioneers*) and Chingachgook's son, Uncas. Cooper's readers were so anxious about the women's safety that they seemed to miss completely the moment at which Natty turns this story of "Indian savagery" back on its readers. As Natty and Duncan, the nominal hero and a Virginian serving in the British army and betrothed to Alice, plunge into the depths of the wilderness a second time to save the women, Natty tells Duncan that the lurid fear that the story uses to generate its suspense– the fear that the beautiful young women will be raped by savages–is all in the white imagination: "I know your thoughts, and shame be it to our color, that you have reason for them; but he who thinks that even a Mingo would ill treat a woman, unless it be to tomahawk her, knows nothing of Indian natur, or the laws of the woods." The story can really be said to begin within the pale of white civilization: at the end of the first chapter, before Magua looks at Cora with his malevolent leer, before the women have even entered the forest, Cora is gazing at his "swarthy lineaments," his almost naked body, with "an indescribable look of pity, admiration and horror." As a fantasy, *The Last of the Mohicans* dramatizes what the ideological constraints of Cooper's culture make "indescribable." Out of Cora's ambiguous gaze across racial lines the fantasy erupts. At the end of the second chapter, as the white characters enter the dark and unknown woods, the Other is looking back at Cora and her sister: "the branches of the bushes that formed the thicket were cautiously moved asunder, and a human visage, as fiercely wild as savage art and unbridled passions could make it, peered out" and looked at "the graceful forms of the females waving among the trees."

Cora is one of Cooper's greatest woman characters, but she is doomed by the elements that probably allowed Cooper to make her so impressive. There could be no hint of "admiration," for instance, in any look that the fairer Alice might bestow on Magua's body. The reader has already come to admire Cora's extraordinary courage and generosity of spirit when, halfway through the novel, the significance of the fact that she and Alice are *half* sisters is revealed. Their father is a British officer, but Cora's mother, his first wife, was "remotely descended" from an African slave; thus, Cora occupies a liminal territory between the races, which in a sense is the place where the whole story is set. She is in a fatal spot. Uncas, who is as noble as Magua is base, who would be a candidate for the role of hero were he not "red," is as attracted as Magua is to Cora, who would surely be the heroine of the novel if she were not "black." Cora and Uncas seem fully formed to live naturally in the new world, and their marriage would imaginatively represent the prospect of unity among the three great racial groups of the nation. Both Natty and the narrator, however, remain unalterably opposed to intermarriage. Consequently, the only possible resolution to all the passions the novel stirs up is violence: the first half of the novel climaxes with the massacre of white men, women, and children at Fort William Henry, and the second half, with the slaughter of Indian men, women, and children at a Mingo village in the woods. In this second massacre, Magua is killed, but so are Cora and Uncas; thus, Duncan and Alice are left to marry, and the future of America is left to the white race purged by the story itself not only of the possibility of racial mixing but also of its "unbridled" desires.

Before the act of genocide that is the climax of the story, Cora acknowledges her impurity and accepts her tragic fate. As the novel ends with the funeral of Cora and Uncas, the surviving Indians—the Mohicans who have fought to rescue Cora from Magua—also acquiesce in their inevitable extinction. If at the end of *The Pioneers* Cooper's narrative leaves the representatives of white civilization in a cemetery, the end of *The Last of the Mohicans* leaves an entire Indian tribe in what seems like a cemetery. The Mohicans win their fight against the Mingoes, but their loss of Uncas "seemed to have turned each dark and motionless figure into stone"; "even the inanimate Uncas appeared a being of life, compared with the humbled and submissive throng by whom he was surrounded." American readers of Cooper's day understood the Mohicans to be submitting to their racial fate. The triumph of European-American civilization has been inevitable from the title page: The title makes clear from the start that this story can only end with a funeral, not a wedding. This novel was Cooper's most popular, probably one of the most widely read of all nineteenth-century novels, and its breathless combination of sex and violence, capture and pursuit, enthralled audiences around the world. But it satisfied American readers in ways that were specifically determined by the exigencies of national culture. White Americans felt the same conflict between guilt and greed over the extermination of the Native American that they felt over the exploitation of the wilderness. In this novel Cooper established the influential literary image of the Indian that was part of his contribution to the national consciousness. Many contemporaries objected to Cooper's idealization of the Delawares; in fact—like Harriet Beecher Stowe's *Uncle Tom's Cabin* (1851–1852) a generation later—*The Last of the Mohicans*, though on a smaller scale, provoked counter-narratives,

novels such as Robert Montgomery Bird's popular *Nick of the Woods* (1837) and even the unfinished sequel to *Huckleberry Finn* (1884) that Samuel Langhorne Clemens (Mark Twain) began, attempting to discredit the iconography of the "noble savage." But Cooper's instinctive decision to create two separate versions of the "Indian" proved incredibly popular with the majority of readers. On the one hand, he portrays the Delawares, the tribe that adopts Natty, as heroic—chaste, brave, loyal, dignified, and graceful. On the other hand, he represents the Mingoes, or Iroquois, as demonic—ferocious, cunning, and rapacious. The two massacres in the novel are staged in a way that lets the conscience of white America completely off the hook. In the first massacre, armed Indians slaughter defenseless whites. Thus, the second one not only seems a legitimate act of retaliation, but also, when Indian women and children are slaughtered, other Indians are the culprits. In that battle Uncas is killed by Magua, leaving Natty to cry over a grave with his friend Chingachgook, "the last" of the Mohicans. Because the Delawares are tragic, noble but doomed by an act of fate, white readers can grieve over their passing. Because the Mingoes are monstrous, they must be destroyed. In 1826 when *The Last of the Mohicans* was published, most of the relocations and wars that came close to destroying Native American culture were still in the future. The novel, though, treats the extinction of "the red man" as an accomplished fact of the distant past, one that white readers could simultaneously mourn and celebrate.

Cooper repeated some of these formulae—such as the kidnapped lady and the competing Indian tribes—in *The Prairie* (1827), which in terms of Natty's story is a truer sequel to *The Pioneers*. *The Prairie* is set ten years after Natty fled Templeton to escape the sound of axes. Now almost eighty, he lives as a trapper among the solitary vacancies west of the Mississippi River. The improbable plot involves Natty in the rescue of another imperiled woman, but Cooper is more interested in using the story to explore the theme that gave *The Pioneers* so much power—the progress of civilization—represented in this book not by a village being built in the woods but by a Conestoga wagon full of squatters making its way across the Great Plains. The cast of characters that Cooper gathers around that wagon with the mysterious freight it carries spans the range of social classes, and, as is the case in most of Cooper's fictions, the characters are less individuals than social and moral types who serve to dramatize the thematic conflicts of the novel. The distinguished virtues of the leading lady and gentleman, both products of an advanced culture, suggest that the continent *should* be civilized. The energetic competence of its middle-class hero and heroine suggests how the vast country *will* be civilized. The

Page from Cooper's rough draft for his 1827 novel, The Prairie *(Beinecke Rare Book and Manuscript Library, Yale University)*

moral squalor of the lowest-class villain, an outlawed squatter named Ishmael Bush, seems unequivocally to suggest that it *must* be civilized, that without the restraints of society, men would degenerate into brutes. That had been Judge Temple's argument for the necessity of punishing Natty, the squatter and outlaw in *The Pioneers*. Like Natty, Bush hates settlements and feels at ease in the depths of the pathless, lawless prairie, but there is nothing sympathetic in his character until the end, when he himself recognizes the necessity for laws and, after convening his own ad hoc court in the middle of the prairie, sentences one member of his family to die for murdering another and then with great dignity sees the sentence carried out. A fierce, patriarchal, ultimately even tragic figure, Bush is one of Cooper's most impressive characterizations. Bush's commanding presence subverts the official class sentiments of the novel, but as a novelist Cooper invariably had trouble creating ladies and gentlemen who are as memorable and convincing as his humbler women and men. Bush's conversion at the end, from outlaw to self-appointed judge, is meant to reinforce the allegiance of the novel to the social order. The action of the story takes place at the moment that, further north, Meriwether Lewis and William Clark are mapping the prairie as the advance agents of the nation that will soon build homes, fences, and courthouses on the prairie. *The Prairie* can be read as an endorsement of that process.

Yet, the strength of this novel, like that of all five Leather-Stocking Tales, lies in its ambiguity on this point. Whenever Cooper's imagination returned to Natty, it sought to nourish itself with the idea of an unspoiled wilderness and with the character of the man who remains outside the bounds set by judges and the social order. If, on the one hand, law prevails in the novel, on the other hand, so does Natty's realm of freedom from restraint. From the start, when Natty's figure looms up against the setting sun right in the westward route of Bush's wagon, the real dramatic issue in the novel is not the virginity of its abducted lady, but that of the threatened prairie—and that is ultimately left intact. At the conclusion of the novel all the white characters retreat eastward, back across the Mississippi—all the white characters, that is, except Natty. In the last chapter Natty dies facing west, away from the society he despises, and is buried among the Indians with whom he had lived in preference to the members of his own race. Echoing the endings of both *The Pioneers* and *The Last of the Mohicans,* these final gestures define the meaning of Natty. As a warrior and scout and as a rescuer of ladies and heroines, he may temporarily serve the interests of society and play a recognizable role in conventional romance, but neither set of forms—the societal nor the literary—can finally contain him. By excluding himself from the various endings of the novel, especially from the party of reunited lovers who represent the future of civilization, Natty makes sure the readers' emotional sympathies remain invested in a place outside the conventional order, a place where Natty remains true to the possibility of some fundamental, natural self. Natty preserves his identity by rejecting society entirely. He does not need to marry, hold a job, or pay a mortgage. He does not even need money. He belongs to the wilderness, where alone he can remain uncompromised by emotional commitments to others. He is like the adolescent who runs away from home, except that Natty never has to return, never has to accept the responsibilities of adulthood. All these associations help to explain what generations of readers, regardless of the age at which they read the Leather-Stocking Tales, have found so appealing about Natty's character and way of life: he represents a believable fulfillment of the pervasive desire to escape the exactions of adult reality.

The other great scene of freedom in Cooper's work is the sea. Although other novelists used the sea as a setting earlier than Cooper, he is credited with creating the genre of sea fiction because of the way (as Joseph Conrad, a later master in the genre, observed) the ocean setting in Cooper's nautical novels "interpenetrates" the story being told and shapes the lives of the sailors it is about. Cooper's first sea novel was his fourth novel, *The Pilot: A Tale of the Sea* (1823), written immediately after *The Pioneers*. As with *Precaution,* this story originated in Cooper's reflex compulsion to prove himself. Apparently, one day a friend happened to praise the amount of nautical knowledge displayed in Walter Scott's latest novel, *The Pirate* (1821). Cooper sincerely admired the Waverley Novels, but as a former sailor he took exception to his friend's remark. Cooper thought that Scott was clearly a landlubber. In addition, Cooper knew he was already being identified as "the American Scott." Since the phrase was intended as an honorific, he could not overtly object; he did say, however, that any nickname is odious to a gentleman, and the comparison might have seemed to him to imply some reservations about his own originality and achievement. It also seemed to keep the United States in a dependent relationship to Great Britain. So, as with *Precaution, The Pilot* was written to surpass a British model—to show what he could do, to give readers a real taste of salt water, and literally to leave England behind. Set during the American Revolution, *The Pilot* begins with a breathtaking account of an American ship beating its way off the English coast into a growing storm, past an enemy cruiser, and through dangerous reefs. The pilot is John Paul Jones, fighting for both the open independence of the sea and for American free-

Susan De Lancey Cooper, circa 1830 (portrait by Susan Fenimore Cooper; from Mary E. Phillips, James Fenimore Cooper, *1913)*

dom. Contemporary readers may have wanted a glossary to follow all the pilot's masterful maneuvers, intricately described in the nautical terms Cooper had learned during his own service at sea, but safe in their armchairs they enjoyed the excitement and were enthralled by the romantic strangeness of the scene. Though Cooper wondered whether a book about the ocean would sell, *The Pilot* quickly achieved popularity. Its success did not stop critics from referring to him as "the American Scott," but it did give Cooper's imagination a vast new space in which to operate—the realm of the untamed ocean.

The Red Rover (1827) and *The Water Witch; or, The Skimmer of the Seas* (1830) are the other two nautical romances Cooper wrote during the first decade of his career. In all three of these narratives, the ocean is a place similar to Natty's forest—a realm of danger and adventure, of course, but more significantly of liberty and individuality. His Byronic heroes—Jones and the pirate Red Rover—are colonial American rebels against English tyranny and thus outlawed opponents of society. As a story about smuggling, *The Water Witch* focuses more on borders than on open spaces, but it is subversive in a new way. One of the boundaries it transgresses is the gender line. "Master Seadrift," for

most of the story believed to be the reckless leader of the smugglers, turns out to be a woman. The tale stops short of erasing the gender line: "he" turns out in fact to be a lady, and the revelation of "his" femininity actually redeems the virtue of the heroine of the novel, who is suspected of having eloped with daring "Master Seadrift." Yet, while the playful manipulation of the rules of law and gender in the novel does not permanently threaten the ideological status quo, it deepens the association of the sea with personal freedom. The sailors in these novels have the oversized, glamorous stature typical of the Romantic period. Their impressive seamanship, like Natty's skills as marksman and hunter, establishes their autonomy: though they respect its storms and currents, they seem almost superior to the ocean itself. When Tom Sawyer runs away from home in Clemens's novel about him, he and his friends play at being pirates on the model provided by Cooper's sea tales. As Cooper knew, his readers turned to fiction for vicarious release from quotidian cares and realities. Although set in the past, his most popular books were less about grappling with history than about escaping the present. The asocial hero and the tale of adventures in open spaces together made Cooper's reputation. By the time *The Water Witch* appeared, ten years after his improbable literary career began, his books were regularly translated into most continental languages, and he ranked only behind Scott in popularity with the novel readers around the world.

Not all of Cooper's novels from this decade were equally successful. He was daunted by the poor reception of *Lionel Lincoln; or, The Leaguer of Boston* (1825), a tale of the early months of the American Revolution in and around Boston, with a panoramic description of the Battle of Bunker Hill as its historical showpiece. The breadth of Cooper's ambitions and depth of his loyalty to the cause of American culture can be measured by his hope that *Lionel Lincoln* would be first of twelve more novels, each focusing on the events of the American Revolution in a different colony. He intended to call the series "Legends of the Thirteen Republics," but the poor showing of *Lionel Lincoln* at the booksellers convinced him to abandon the project. Despite this relative failure, however, and that of his attempt to portray the Puritan past of New England in *The Wept of Wish Ton-Wish* (1829), Cooper was thoroughly committed to the role of American novelist. In 1826 he and his family left New York to spend seven years in Europe, where they traveled extensively and resided for various periods in London, Naples, Venice, Vevey, and (for most of the time) in Paris. Going abroad was partly a career move. There was no international copyright law, but Cooper found out he could secure British rights to his books if their earliest publication was in England. Arranging for first publication of his books in England was one of his first priorities when he reached the Old World: *The Prairie,* set further into the American continent than any other of his books, was also the first of his books to be published in London before appearing in America. With only a few exceptions, throughout the rest of his career he took care to ensure that his British publisher could bring out each novel at least a week in advance of the American publication, and by that means he earned a steady income in pounds to complement his American royalties. He was frankly interested in that money but determined to show no hint of selling out to a British audience. "With me," he told his English publisher in 1831, "it is a point of honor to continue rigidly an American author." As he wrote a friend in 1831, "I was born and will live and die a Yankee." He took pride in being able to meet and associate with the great figures of the Old World as an equal but felt that his international stature reflected just as well on his country as on himself. Even abroad, Cooper counted on the support of his American reading public, emotionally as well as commercially. And for the time being, he and those readers were on the best possible terms.

As a Yankee, and particularly as the American friend of the Marquis de Lafayette, the hero of the American Revolution, who became an important person in Cooper's life while he lived in Paris, he decided to involve his writing overtly in politics. *Notions of the Americans: Picked up by a Travelling Bachelor* (1828) was written at Lafayette's suggestion to answer conservative European indictments of democracy in America. Although the novel rests on the narrative fiction of being a travel book written by a Belgian visiting the United States in 1824, the year Lafayette was feted as a returning Founding Father, the book is Cooper's first substantial work of nonfiction. It makes heavy use of statistics and analysis to prove the efficiency of a republican form of government and the virtues of an egalitarian form of society. Cooper designed it specifically to counteract the many English accounts of travel in the United States, which tended ritualistically to find only confirmations of the superiority of an aristocratic culture in the encounter with the young and raw democracy of America. Cooper's intentions are admirable; yet, the book he wrote protests too much about the greatness of all things American to have made many British converts, and it struck Yankee readers, who expected every book by Cooper to amuse them, as heavy going. A less stubborn writer than Cooper might have been warned by this experience about asking his audience to revise their expectations too drastically. Yet, knowing Lafayette, the preeminent republican of Europe, and living in Paris in the midst of the Euro-

pean revolutions of 1830 led Cooper to a growing interest in political questions. This preoccupation dominated the next phase of his career and led in turn to a traumatic rupture with his audience at home. Though he could not possibly have guessed it, by 1830 Cooper's happiest years as an author were already over.

The trouble had its roots both in his temperament, which gave even his patriotic loyalty a self-righteous cast, and in the provincialism of America, which was uncomfortable with any direct assault on the cultural hegemony of Europe. After 1828 journalists in the United States began more and more belligerently to condemn Cooper's involvement in foreign affairs. In particular they took him to task for writing his *Letter of J. Fenimore Cooper to Gen. Lafayette, on the Expenditure of the United States of America* (1831), a pamphlet published in Paris and written to support his friend's position on a matter of finances in the French parliament. At the same time, his American readers became restive with his use of fiction for politically didactic ends. Between 1831 and 1833 Cooper published his "European trilogy": *The Bravo. A Venetian Story* (1831), *The Heidenmauer; or, The Benedictines* (1832), and *The Headsman; or, The Abbaye des Vignerons* (1833). Set respectively in Italy, Germany, and Switzerland, these books attempt to be both historical romances and civics lessons about the vices of aristocratic governments. *The Bravo* is actually a first-rate story of political intrigue and corruption that takes full advantage of its Venetian setting to present its thesis in an exotic romance, but even this first third of the trilogy did not sell in the usual numbers, and in the next two novels Cooper displayed much less interest in being entertaining than in being politically correct as a spokesman for republican rule. From Cooper's perspective he was simply following out the thematic and artistic agenda inherent in his identity as an American novelist, but while he put the accent on *American,* his readers expected it to fall on *novelist.* The first American celebrity novelist, Cooper was also the first to become trapped inside the literary image he himself had created, the expectations he had conditioned his readers to bring to his books. His contemporary readers wanted adventure, not serious fiction. Nor did they want their national novelist to undertake to scrutinize European society. On his side, Cooper's own expectations were still more severely shocked. He was prepared to be criticized by the English for living up to his duty (as he perceived it) as an American writer, but he never anticipated being abused for it in the American press. Believing that this project represented the next step toward maturity for himself and American literature, he refused to consider how the novels themselves might have disappointed his readers. He construed his countrymen's not buying these books as an act of pure pro-

Susan Fenimore Cooper's portrait of herself and her siblings: Caroline, the artist, Paul, Anne, and Maria, circa 1833 (New York State Historical Association, Cooperstown, New York)

vincial cowardice, proof that the nation lacked the nerve to stand with him in his literary offensive against Europe. He felt deserted and betrayed by the popular audience on whose approval he depended; his letters from this period candidly express by turns his outrage and his mortification. By 1833 they start expressing something else—a determination to retire, to quit writing novels for the country that had deserted him while he was serving it.

The vehemence of his reaction, which confused his contemporaries further, was not entirely rational. Cooper had bound up too much of his private identity in his public role, and that role, he realized as much in shame as in anger, rested on the unstable ground of popular opinion. Fully aware that he himself was in the process of creating American fiction, he should not have expected that everyone else would automatically agree upon definitions. As historians have noted, during the Jacksonian era of the 1830s, the nation was going through an identity crisis of its own. What Cooper took for a malicious personal assault upon him was actually only one of the many zealous partisan disputes with which the era abounded: his most vituperative critics all wrote for Whig publications and attacked the prominent novelist as a means to further their own political agenda. Had Cooper been living at home he might have recognized this cause—though his personality was always overly vulnerable to criticism—but trying to be a good American abroad, trying to

extend the influence of American letters and principles in the Old World, he saw these partisan attacks and the drop in sales as evidence that the whole nation had turned against him. In 1833 he decided to return to the United States—to see, he said, if he still had a country. Seven years after leaving his native land in triumph, he returned to New York disgruntled and dispirited, in many ways more an expatriate than he had ever been abroad. He was in no mood to seek reconciliation with his compatriots. He went out of his way to avoid former acquaintances but stuck to the resolution about his career that he had formed the previous year in Switzerland. In June 1834 he printed *A Letter to His Countrymen,* a remarkable farewell address in which the forty-four-year-old novelist tells Americans that, since they are too culturally enslaved to foreign ideas to support a literature of their own, he was going to "lay aside the pen."

As matters turned out, he meant rather that he would abandon fiction. He kept writing, publishing seven books in the next four years—a plodding satire in the mold of Jonathan Swift's *Gulliver's Travels* (1726) titled *The Monikins* (1835); five travel books about the European countries he had lived in and visited; a sharply pointed and at times penetrating treatise on politics and society in America, *The American Democrat; or, Hints on the Social and Civic Relations of the United States of America* (1838); while also working on the research for his definitive *The History of the Navy of the United States of*

America (1839). He kept writing in part because he was determined not to let his critics have the last word and in part because no other means of making a living offered itself; he apparently quieted his scruples by drawing a distinction between writing fiction (which would have provided the entertainment he felt his readers no longer deserved) and writing the kind of nonfiction that would provide the instruction he felt they sorely needed. Cooper's publishers, growing weary of this mounting pile of serious prose, regularly expressed their hopes that he would submit a new novel, but Cooper avowed his intention to maintain himself in the roles of critic and historian. In any case, he probably would have reversed himself eventually. There was a much smaller market for his nonfiction—*The American Democrat,* for example, was not published in England—and between 1833 and 1838 his income diminished considerably. But an event that Cooper construed as another challenge to his honor forced him out of his self-imposed retirement. In 1837 he decided to return to writing fiction in order to defend the new notions of America that he had bitterly learned over the preceding seven years and to attack a group of enemies that he had acquired that summer.

After sailing home from Europe in 1833, Cooper spent seven months in New York City, but his intention all along had been to relocate his family to Cooperstown. He had been away for seventeen years, but now the idea of going home to find refuge from his quarrel with America appealed strongly to him. He went all the way home, back to Mansion-House, the home his father had built and that the novelist bought and restored in 1834. Cooper lived there for the rest of his life. Indeed, between 1834 and his death in 1851 he left the village so seldom, particularly in view of his prominence as the leading novelist of the nation, that people began to think of him as a recluse. He still had many good friends, was involved in a wide range of enterprises, and with his writing sought to play an active role in national affairs. Yet, to a degree he did become reclusive. Unable to forgive the American public for what he felt was an act of betrayal, he remained distrustful of their power, even of their favor. At times, in fact, he succumbed to a mild form of paranoia, believing that there was a secret journalistic conspiracy that schemed to embarrass and annoy him. Most of the happiness that Cooper enjoyed during the last third of his life he found at home, within his family. Whenever he journeyed outside the gates of his house, he put on a thick coating of reserve. Even the books he wrote often bristle with points of contention; he was always willing to seize the slightest narrative occasion for an authorial intrusion, and his narratives often limp along under a load of ill-tempered digressions about American provin-

cialism and other cultural follies. Many of the novels Cooper wrote in the second, chastened half of his career are as well conceived, as aesthetically resonant as the ones he wrote at its bright beginning, when he sought his contemporaries' approval with fewer misgivings; but beyond question these novels would uniformly have been better, more aesthetically satisfying, had Cooper and his country never quarreled. Cooper's career gives the lie to the cliché that there are no second acts in American lives, but its darkened second act does offer an early and graphic example of the kind of drama that American writers frequently enact. The work of many of the greatest American writers— Charles Brockden Brown, Melville, Henry James, Kate Chopin, Charles Waddell Chesnutt, and F. Scott Fitzgerald, for instance—was profoundly affected by their readers' responses. For his part, Cooper felt his sense of rejection as a wound that nothing could heal and that many occurrences could reopen.

One of these events took place in Cooperstown in 1837 and drove him back to writing novels. The story seems petty—as if Captain Ahab had been nibbled into rage by minnows instead of maimed by a great whale— but to Cooper the occurrence was symptomatic of the most serious social ills of his culture. An argument arose between him and some of his neighbors over the possession of a piece of property called the Three Mile Point on Lake Otsego. For two generations the Cooper family had allowed the public to use this site for picnics and fishing, and the villagers began mistakenly to assume that Judge Cooper had bequeathed it to the public. When a group of them injured some of the trees on the point, Cooper decided to reassert the family's property rights and printed a notice against trespass in the local newspaper. Both sides badly handled the controversy that followed. A group of villagers, feeling that the people's rights were being threatened, lashed out at the novelist's character—there was even some talk of removing his novels from the town library and burning them. Their half of the story, full of errors and distortions, was reported in three upstate Whig newspapers, which caricatured the novelist as a would-be aristocrat who would have been happier domineering over serfs than living among freemen.

At exactly this time abolitionists were beginning to move slavery to the center of public attention; Cooper had much of moment to say about American society but remained convinced that slavery was essentially a local problem for the South to handle. That throughout the late 1830s and 1840s he defines the greatest social problems facing America in terms of various property disputes in the state of New York is both a symptom of his reclusiveness and a sign of real moral blindness. Cooper, finding himself again

The Leather-Stocking Monument at Cooper Park, Cooperstown

attacked by the people and abused by the press, had convictions of his own about whose freedom was at stake. Finding himself again beset by American democracy, Cooper responded along several lines. First, he sued the three Whig newspapers that had attacked him for libel. Next, he added to *The American Democrat* a few strongly spiced conclusions about the tyranny of the majority in a democracy. Cooper was among the earliest social critics to point out the enormous power exerted in America by numbers and by public opinion, and the threat that this power poses to the freedom of individual thought and expression. Alexis de Tocqueville's *Democracy in America* (1835) makes this point more dispassionately, but that Cooper pointed by shaking a fist does not detract from his insight. By comparison with Tocqueville, or even with his earlier novels, Cooper's social criticism suffers from his inability to imagine and articulate more than one side of an issue, but his observations about the relationship between democracy and conformity, earned firsthand in the melodramatic course of his own career as popular and unpopular figure, are still

worth consideration. Finally, convinced that the incident required yet a stronger response, Cooper seized the most powerful of his weapons, the pen of the novelist. By writing a novel, he could address the international constituency of his readers. A tale about the Three Mile Point dispute and the various social issues involved would, he decided, enable him to present his side of the case to the world.

Actually, in a complex series of returns, he wound up writing two tales, *Homeward Bound; or, The Chase: A Tale of the Sea* and *Home As Found,* both published in 1838. The first is set on board a transatlantic packet and includes just enough nautical adventure to suggest that Cooper is trying to connect his return to novel writing with his earlier, popular romances. But now his ultimate focus is not on life at sea. It is on society, on the cultural confrontation between the two castes of passengers on the ship. The first group marks another point of connection. The Effinghams, returning to Templeton after twelve years in Europe, are descended from the hero and heroine of *The Pioneers.* By asking readers to think about Oliver and Elizabeth's future rather than the past Natty stepped back into, Cooper is in effect revising the ending of the earlier novel, but contemporary readers focused on something else in *Homeward Bound.* As far as they were concerned, Edward Effingham and his daughter Eve—Americans of taste, elegance, wealth, discernment, and a host of additional unfailing virtues—were transparently disguised versions of Cooper and his daughter Susan. Cooper vehemently, and ineffectually, disclaimed these identities in a series of public statements. He did, however, explicitly intend the Effinghams to model moral and social virtues. Heroism in this novel consists of resisting vulgarity, not of shooting a rifle or sailing a ship, but the need for such heroism is acute. Like a party of settlers besieged in the woods by "savages" on the warpath, the Effinghams are affronted on shipboard by Steadfast Dodge, a Yankee newspaper editor who embodies all the evils—inquisitiveness, acquisitiveness, demagoguery, crassness, and above all, an inability to know his place (as defined by the Effinghams' superiority)—that Cooper associated with the rabidly democratic tendencies of America. Cooper stages the confrontation between Effingham and Dodge as starkly as that between virtue and vice in a medieval morality play, but the antagonists are unevenly matched; vulgarity always has refinement at a disadvantage, and short of throwing Dodge overboard—a solution that is not even thinkable to persons with the Effinghams' sense of decorum—they cannot defeat him. Among the adventures of the novel is a firefight with hostile Arabs on the coast of Africa in defense of the ship as property, but defending Effingham land against a hostile public on the shores of Lake Otsego requires a much less violent and less satisfying strategy.

That strategy is the focus of *Home As Found*. After a series of satiric encounters with upstart society in New York City, the Effinghams get back to Templeton, where the spirit of Natty Bumppo still lingers, but the type that Dodge represents has become legion. Eventually, Edward's genteel and patient desire to believe the best of his compatriots smashes against his neighbors' greedy attack on Fishing Point (as Three Mile Point is called in the novel). In what is clearly a fantasy version of his own actions in Cooperstown, Cooper's hero behaves with dignified nobility throughout the crisis. Both of these novels are vitiated by Cooper's failure to treat Edward, the Cooper figure in the novel, with even the slightest irony, and his enemies, the townspeople and newspapermen, with any sympathetic abatement of contempt. *The Pioneers* is also about who really has a moral right to the land at Templeton; the greatness of *The Pioneers* as a novel derives from the way Cooper refuses to resolve the conflicts he is dramatizing. In *Home As Found,* however, he is not so much writing fiction as using it. Yet, *Home As Found* is worth reading—not only as the first legitimate attempt at an American *roman de société* but also as genuinely perceptive social criticism. Its most memorable character is Aristabulus Bragg, Cooper's version of the self-made man as social-climbing parvenu, prototype of such later literary figures as Hawthorne's Jaffrey Pyncheon, William Dean Howells's Silas Lapham, and Sinclair Lewis's Babbit. Despite the acerbic way Cooper develops them, the chief complaints of the novel about American culture—that it venerates dollars instead of tradition, that its relentless deference to the mass encourages a mediocre conformity, and that politicians flatter and follow rather than lead the public—cannot glibly be dismissed.

Nor did his contemporaries find them easy to accept. The Effingham novels were widely disliked and attacked by reviewers with a vehemence that was probably without precedent in American literary culture. But because to attack the author rather than the ideas of the novels was simpler, Cooper was accused of turning against the readers who had made him famous, of aristocratically claiming to be too good for the people whose popular support had made him great. His contemporaries thought that to indict his country in books he knew the whole world would read was an act of treason. He did feel that the United States had grown too bad for any right-minded person to approve; on the other hand, he insisted that his own motives were patriotic, that he wrote these novels to recall to a nation that had been overrun with falsely democratic innovations its true republican principles. Most gravely threatened, he felt, were the rights of the

individual—by which he meant the gentleman—in the face of the people's grasping ambitions. Similarly, his several libel suits against the press, which dragged on through the mid 1840s, were to him an effort to compel the editors to respect the individual's character and privacy. The majority, it seemed to him, wanted everything—from his family's property to his own good name. The frankness with which Cooper resisted them shows a kind of courage, though a self-destructive kind. How much, one has to wonder, can an author hope to gain by setting himself violently at odds with the press that reviews his books and the public that buys them? What Cooper needed most was the self-respect that had been threatened when he realized how much of his achievement as a writer was held captive by popular approval. At least that would explain his apparently perverse determination in the Effingham novels to be unpopular. While these two books made him a novelist again, they further widened the gap between him and his audience. For the rest of his career, though many of his subsequent novels sold well, though many of his readers were ready to forgive him for *Home As Found,* Cooper felt unpopular and unappreciated. But he was never willing to acknowledge his own responsibility for this estrangement.

On the other hand, his next novel may in part have been Cooper's attempt to ask for his audience's forgiveness. In some ways, at least, this novel was even more an act of returning than was *Home As Found*. His next novel is an adventure story that leaves behind the contemporary social scene and escapes into the cool shadows of the forest with Natty Bumppo, the most popular of his heroes. *The Pathfinder; or, The Inland Sea* (1840) was the fourth Leather-Stocking Tale, and a year later Cooper published *The Deerslayer; or, The First War-Path* (1841), the fifth and last novel in the series. Although Natty Bumppo had died in *The Prairie,* in these final two tales Cooper brought him back to life as a young man. *The Pathfinder* and *The Deerslayer* deal with the earliest years of Natty's backwoods career as a warrior. Once again he and Chingachgook are on the trail of painted Mingoes, a much more popular source of villainy than American democracy. By turning back to a youthful Natty, Cooper perhaps signals the wish to restore his own career to its earliest years and invites his audience to forget the quarrels that had divided them in the pleasures of the kind of tale that had formerly delighted them. Natty allows Cooper to find the path that had once led to imaginative power and popular success. Natty, though, has to confront a new risk in both these novels. In the tales from the 1820s, Natty gets close to a young woman only when he is rescuing her for the

Cooper, 1850 (portrait by A. Bigelow; after a daguerreotype by Mathew Brady; New York State Historical Association, Cooperstown)

conventional hero. In fact, amidst the powerful sexual passions that drive the narrative in *The Last of the Mohicans,* Natty says explicitly that he knows nothing about "the feeling in youth, which binds man to woman." In *The Pathfinder* and *The Deerslayer,* although the emphasis remains on woodcraft and action, Cooper changes the structure of his romances and flirts with changing the essence of Natty's character by involving him directly in the romance plot. In the first of these two books, Natty loves; in the second, he is beloved. Neither book, however, ends with his wedding. When he disappears into the woods, he is accompanied by his Indian friend instead of a bride. Love may befit Natty's renewed youth, but marriage would certainly mean an end to his way of life as a "warrior of the wilderness." Throughout the series Natty chooses to remain true to himself.

Of these two final tales, *The Deerslayer* is the more resonant. It can also be read as the third book in a trilogy that begins with *The Pioneers* and includes *Home As Found:* all three of these books are set on the shores of Lake Otsego, the place where Cooper spent the first thirteen and the last fifteen years of his life. The first of these books is the most realistic—a deeply conflicted, and thus thematically balanced, representation of what is gained and lost in the process by which American society "civilizes" the wilderness. By the time the Effinghams return from Europe to Templeton in the second book, all the stumps are gone, but so is Cooper's sense of hope for the future of society. Nor can he imagine a sympathetic alternative; at the end of *Home As Found* the Effinghams talk of going back to Europe. Alienation from the present and anxiety about the foreseeable future led Cooper's imagination back into a kind of prehistoric past; the last of his Cooperstown novels is the most mythic. Lake Otsego itself is known only as the Glimmerglass. There is a family living on the lake, but no trees have yet been cut down. The world Cooper imagines in *The Deerslayer* is the heroic kingdom he played in as a child himself; it only exists in the human imagination. Though the Leather-Stocking Tales have often been arranged according to the chronology of Natty's life (*The Deerslayer, The Pathfinder, The Last of the Mohicans, The Pioneers, The Prairie*), they are best read in the order of their composition. This arrangement brings most clearly into relief Natty's identity as a figure to whom Cooper and the readers who find the same deep pleasure in Natty's company can attach their estrangement from life as it must be lived. His progression backward from *The Pioneers,* in which an old hunter vainly struggles against the onset of progress, to *The Deerslayer,* in which he is reborn on the same spot as a young warrior posing heroically against an almost pristine environment, gives the shape of his life its most moving resonance. Natty has to retreat before the momentum of American history, but he somehow manages to defeat time itself. Altogether the five Leather-Stocking Tales create an American mythos.

In between *The Pathfinder* and *The Deerslayer* Cooper wrote a romance about Christopher Columbus's discovery of the "New World," but *Mercedes of Castille; or, The Voyage to Cathay* (1840) deals with this potentially mythic material in a flatly conventional fashion. Although in this period literary tastes were changing as the popularity of Scott's historical romances gave way to the success of Charles Dickens's contemporary urban melodramas, Cooper stuck with the fictional subjects he was familiar with. In the next three years he published three nautical tales—*The Two Admirals* (1842), *The Wing-and-Wing, or, Le Feu-Follet* (1842), *Afloat and Ashore; or, The Adventures of Miles Wallingford* (1844)—and one more story about a frontier settlement, *Wyandotté; or, The Hutted Knoll* (1843). Despite the disruptions of the 1830s, he had not lost his touch as a storyteller; although these books include occasional eruptions of his anger, his concern in each of them was primarily to tell a good story. Even after the quarrel with his audience, Cooper was still able to support himself as a novelist throughout the 1840s, though he had to work harder to do so. Mainly because of increased competition from pirated foreign novels, his income per novel dropped sharply. In 1826, for example, *The Last of the Mohicans* sold for $2.00. In the first year of its publication sales were 5,750, and Cooper's return was $5,000. When *The Wing-and-Wing* was published in 1842, on the other hand, readers could buy it for 50¢. Thus, though it sold more than twelve thousand copies in its first year, Cooper's return was less than $1,200. In the first decade of his career he wrote about one novel every year; he referred to each as his "annual novel." In the 1840s he averaged two novels a year and felt underappreciated at the same time. He remained at odds with the forces at work in his society. He had never promised to resign his role as a critic of his times, and in 1844 he saw a new and alarming reason to resume it.

Living in Cooperstown, he was emotionally isolated from most of the major political crises of the decade: the Mexican War, for example, like slavery, was an issue that he never seriously addressed. But the "anti-rent war" of the mid 1840s seemed to Cooper, as he wrote a friend, "the great American question of the day." The battlefields of this war were the parts of upstate New York that had originally been settled and organized according to the patroonship system. A vestigial remnant of the beginning of the state as a Dutch colony, the system gave proprietors such as the Van Rensselaers and the Schuylers some basically feudal privileges over the farmers who lived as tenants on their estates. The patroon system survived the American Revolution, but when the agricultural economy of the region weakened, tenants became increasingly resentful about the demands of the old ways. In the early 1840s the farmers rose up against their landlords. They staged a militant rent strike, dressing as mock Indians and banding into rowdy groups to intimidate owners and sheriffs, and they demanded titles to the farms they had worked for years. Violence broke out several times, and the state militia had to be mobilized. Many Americans sympathized with the tenants' argument that the system itself was un-American, that the patroons' aristocratic privileges were incompatible with democratic principles. Cooper's sympathies were entirely with the patroons. To him the principle that mattered was the same one that had been at stake in the Three Mile Point controversy: once again "the people"

were trying to take something that did not belong to them.

Cooper had planned a novel to present his side of that earlier controversy (and wound up writing two novels when the "homeward" part of the story took on its own narrative momentum). To present the patroons' side of the anti-rent conflict, he plotted out the longest, most elaborate work of fiction he ever undertook. The Littlepage Manuscripts is a trilogy of novels designed to settle authoritatively the moral and social questions unsettled by the anti-rent strife. Cooper set out to defend the patroons—first, by showing the risks and sacrifices originally involved in creating their estates out of the wilderness, actions that gave the owners an historical as well as a legal right to their profits; and second, by showing how the upper class that the patroons represented, as men of wealth and culture, was crucial to the health of American culture. The three novels recount the growth of an estate—Mooseridge—from colonial times, when the land had to be wrested from savage Indians and wild beasts, to the present, when men who dressed like Indians and acted like beasts sought to steal the fruits of the landlords' labors. To bond his readers to the patroons' point of view, Cooper decided that each novel would be narrated in the first person by successive generations of the Littlepage family. Their stories would bear witness both to their services to social progress and to their merits as gentlemen. The Littlepage Manuscripts form an interesting antithesis to the Leather-Stocking Tales: the two series cover much the same portions of American history, but while Natty was the democratic adversary of landlords who scorned the idea of owning the wilderness, Cooper's heroes the Littlepages are the landlords themselves.

The three books that resulted from this intention vary enormously in their literary and rhetorical success. The first, *Satanstoe; or, The Littlepage Manuscripts. A Tale of the Colony* (1845), in which Cornelius Littlepage describes his adventures in exploring and defending the family's patent at Mooseridge, is one of Cooper's most charming and best-made novels. Although its Dutch characters owe something to Washington Irving and something to conventional stereotypes, the book deserves to be better known today, especially for its marvelous pictures of colonial life in Manhattan and Albany. But the closer the series gets to the present that Cooper shared so uneasily with his readers, the more unpleasant, even hostile, the narratives become. *The Chainbearer; or, The Littlepage Manuscripts* (1845), set during the American Revolution and narrated by Cornelius's son Mordaunt, reminds the reader of *The Pioneers,* except that all the moral conflicts that the earlier novel had examined so powerfully have apparently been

The Byronic Pirate in Cooper's The Red Rover *(illustration by F. O. C.
Darley for* Cooper's Novels, *1859–1861)*

decided once and for all on behalf of the rich. The title, for example, refers to the surveyor whom Mordaunt hires to divide the estate up into rentable lots; the image of binding the wilderness with chains would have made the Leather-Stocking shudder, but in this series it is seen as unequivocally heroic, while the property and class lines that are being laid down by those chains are treated as permanent. Cooper's first narrator, Corny, puts a humanly sympathetic face on the figure of the owner, but the narrative technique of the trilogy winds up working against Cooper's purpose in the end. At the end of *The Redskins; or, Indian and Injin: Being the Conclusion of the Littlepage Manuscripts* (1846), which deals with the anti-rent war and the American scene then, Cooper in fact felt he must add a postscript in his own name apologizing for the tone of the narrator of his novel. The only useful place for such an apology would have been at the head of the narrative, but even there it could not have solved the problem Cooper created for himself by making the voice that is supposed to epitomize culture and breeding so shrill and impolitic. Hugh Littlepage, Mordaunt's grandson, repeatedly becomes almost hysterical with rage and contempt as he describes the behavior of his rebellious tenants. Although in its larger design Cooper's trilogy recalls the shape of the Puritans' Jeremiads, in which the greatness

of the past is held over the heads of those present as a kind of sword to drive them back to the promised land, *The Redskins* is less a work of social criticism than an outburst of class prejudice. It is hard to read and completely alienates readers from the point of view they are meant to identify with. To anyone interested in Cooper's emotional life, however, it is a fascinating document; through the persona of Hugh Littlepage, the novelist reveals more than he meant to about his deepest feelings toward the majority of his fellow Americans, "the people" for whom as a professional writer he had to perform. Whenever Cooper wrote about the present—without, that is, any historical distance between the story he was telling and the audience he was telling it to—he tended to lose rhetorical and aesthetic control of his work. In the real world the anti-rent agitation had subsided by the time the last installment in the trilogy appeared: the patroons had, by 1846, been stripped of most of their privileges. But even if it had appeared in time, *The Redskins* was poorly calculated to help their cause.

Cooper was fifty-seven years old in 1846. His nostalgia is a source of the achievement of *Satanstoe,* but after that novel Cooper could no longer make his preference for an earlier America serve his powers as an imaginative writer. On the other hand, the extent of his estrangement from contemporary society is made palpable in the next novel he wrote, *The Crater; or Vulcan's Peak. A Tale of the Pacific* (1847). This fable, about a man shipwrecked on a volcanic atoll in the Pacific, combines Daniel Defoe's *Robinson Crusoe* (1719) and the last part of *Gulliver's Travels* with Cooper's compatriots cast as the Yahoos. *The Crater* begins as an idyll, a solipsistic fantasy. With no neighbors, majorities, or newspaper editors to besiege him, Mark Woolston can arrange life on his uninhabited island entirely to suit himself. One can readily comprehend Cooper's pleasure in this part of the story. As a child he played in the woods to escape what he could not reconcile himself to at home. Alone on his island, Mark is part child at play, part author creating his own vision of what reality should be, even part developer—like William Cooper, shaping a wilderness into the expression of his own will to imperial dominion. Mark's edenic life depends, however, upon others' eyes not noticing his kingdom. Just as the novelist must ultimately publish the work of his imagination, so the day comes when the crater is discovered by others. This day does not bring Mark's deliverance but rather the beginning of the end. His island is soon invaded by Yankee settlers arguing about rights and clamoring for innovations, making the place as unbearable to Mark as America often was to Cooper. He leaves—just in time. In the first great apocalyptic ending in American fiction, the story climaxes when the vol-

The graves of Cooper and his wife at Cooperstown

cano erupts so violently that the entire island sinks into the ocean. The ending is Cooper's wrathful judgment on American society and also a parable of the way, for an artist at odds with his audience, the joy of creation can give way to a self-destructive rage against the conditions of literary performance: rather than share Mark's creation with others, the narrative erases it completely. (Melville enacted much the same dynamic when, five years after *The Crater* appeared, the *Pequod* sinks into the same ocean at the end of *Moby-Dick*.)

The Crater is an act of fantasy, or more properly, two fantasies—having the world to oneself and destroying whatever and whoever thwarts one's will. More realistically, Cooper talked often in the last years of his life about moving back to Europe. Instead he remained in Cooperstown, though he felt antagonized even by his neighbors in the village. He also kept writing novels, though he engaged in many second thoughts about his literary career. Despite all the controversies, he was still to most of his contemporaries the leading novelist of the nation. While he repeatedly told others that the only motive he still had for writing was financial, the 1840s were in fact the most prolific period of his career. The range and number of his fictions testify to the unabated vigor of his imagination. The canon of his thirty-two novels reveals how, if he often returned to a

few subjects, such as the sea or the forest, he seldom repeated a technique or a theme. He remained attached to romantic conventions as structural devices, but at any given point in his career the next novel was likely to be a new departure, an experiment with a different kind of story. Involving Natty in the romantic subplot is one example. Another is that after *The Crater*, he wrote *Jack Tier; or, The Florida Reef* (1848), another nautical tale centered on the life of a pirate, but realistically written, in place of the picturesque treatment he had given this subject in *The Red Rover*. He emphasizes the sordidness and brutality of Captain Spike's character. This kind of change can be plotted on the map of nineteenth-century literary history; the rover can be located in the aesthetic context defined by the popularity in the 1820s of the Romantic corsairs of George Gordon, Lord Byron, just as the increased realism of *Jack Tier* appears at the same time as Richard Henry Dana's and Melville's deromanticized depictions of life at sea. Although Cooper found the means (often professionally suicidal ones) to express himself in his art, from the beginning to the end of his career he also remained alert to the broad and evolving patterns of novelistic types and readers' expectations. Cooper's was not the kind of imagination—like Scott's, Dickens's, Melville's, or Gustave Flaubert's—that brings new forms of art into existence. But neither was he a formula writer. That he was ready in a work such as *Jack Tier* to revise the portrait of piracy he had himself largely created is typical of the many changes he went through as an artist.

In 1848 Cooper began one final change; he started actively and searchingly reading the Bible. All his life he had been a nominal Episcopalian; no matter how high he advanced the claims of the self in his earlier novels, he never, unlike many of the other Romantics, disparaged the authority of the God of Christianity. But at the end of his life what had been merely a cultural identification with Christianity was converted into a deeply personal piety. To be sure, Cooper's personality still pushed through his faith. At no point, for instance, did he seem to feel that being a devout Christian required him to forgive his enemies. Yet, religion became an important part of his daily life and of his literary career. His next two books—*The Oak Openings; or, The Bee-Hunter* (1848) and *The Sea Lions; or, The Lost Sealers* (1849)—are narratives of religious conversion. At this period Victorian America was in general becoming more outspokenly Christian and the most popular fictions of the next decade—books such as *The Wide, Wide World* (1850) or *Uncle Tom's Cabin*—are unctuously pious. Also, although generally young men are impatient for adventure and old men turn to God, to call Cooper's late discovery of faith merely another instance of his conventionality is unfair. There were obvious reasons why Cooper, who had once felt reborn by his popular success (in 1826 he desired to become James *Fenimore* Cooper) but who later suffered so much abuse and misunderstanding from the world, felt the need to look elsewhere for judgment and reward. His faith in God's providential purposes may have helped to compensate him for the faiths he had lost.

Still, he was not quite prepared to renounce his interest in the matters of this life. His last novel, *The Ways of the Hour* (1850), tries once again, as did *Home As Found* and *The Redskins,* to examine contemporary society. Like those earlier works, *The Ways of the Hour* is often more a harangue than a narrative. The story revolves around a murder mystery and a woman on trial for her life, but as Cooper makes insistently clear throughout, the real crimes are the offenses that the American public keeps committing against legal principles, sound politics, and individual rights. *Home As Found,* his first imaginative effort to chastise and reform his contemporaries, had provoked a storm of hostile reactions, but by this point his contemporaries simply shrugged off his complaints. They had heard most of them before, though one of the issues troubling Cooper in this novel is new. During the 1840s, the Women's Rights movement emerged out of the Abolitionist movement to agitate for radical changes in the legal and social standing of women. Seneca Falls, where the first Women's Rights convention was organized by Elizabeth Cady Stanton in 1848, is not far from Cooperstown. The specific contemporary event that seems to have precipitated Cooper's last novel was the passage of the Married Women's Property Act by the New York state legislature; it gave wives the right to control their own property. The mystery in *The Ways of the Hour* concerns Mary Monson. She turns out to be innocent of the murder she is convicted of by a jury that is prejudiced against her wealth and aristocratic demeanor and influenced more by gossip than by facts; but the narrative treats her decision to leave her husband and use her money her own way as wrong, as much the cause of the problem as the stupidity of the jury. Indeed, one of the running issues of the novel is the way Mary first transforms her jail cell into the surreal equivalent of a domestic interior and then insists on leaving it for long walks through the city at night and other errands; her determination to be free is not treated as exemplary, but as mad. At the same time that her character allows Cooper to rebuke contemporary women's rights advocates, however, he also projects his own story onto Mary, who keeps wanting to be loved, understood, and forgiven by the people who condemn her.

For the past several years he had been in ill health, suffering from bad circulation and a debilitating coldness in his extremities. With these symptoms in mind, to consider the setting of his penultimate novel is illuminating. *The Sea Lions* is about a group of sealers who voyage to an unknown, uninhabited island near Antarctica, further south than any explorer had penetrated. Polar exploration was a popular subject at the time. Edgar Allan Poe's one novel, *The Narrative of A. Gordon Pym* (1838), is also about a voyage toward the South Pole. But the most compelling context in which to read *The Sea Lions* is the biographical one. The novel achieves its greatest power in the chapters in which Cooper describes the long, dark, sterile, terrifying winter that the men, trapped by the ice, are forced to spend on the island. When the mercury disappears into the ball of the thermometer, showing that the temperature has dropped under forty degrees below zero, readers may begin to feel the cold seeping into their extremities. The polar winter is a blank vision on nothingness, a white negation of life. In this long and frozen dark night of the soul, Roswell Gardiner, the hero of the tale, becomes a Christian; staring into the icy void, he becomes certain that God's immortal grace presides over it. Aesthetically, Cooper renders the terror of dying with more effectiveness than the consolations of an afterlife, but (perhaps with the help of telling Gardiner's story) he appears personally to have made his peace with his own approaching death. In July 1851, he was formally confirmed in the Episcopalian Church in Cooperstown. In September, one day before his sixty-second birthday, he died.

His death revived his standing among his contemporaries. Remembering the contribution he made to American letters, the country tended to forget the many contentions. Collected editions of his novels began appearing in the 1850s and sold by the thousands until the beginning of the twentieth century. At the end of his life Cooper expressed the wish that no biography would be written. Since at that time in the young history of American literature no biography had ever been written of an American writer, his wish is both a salutary sign of how much his career accomplished and a sad reminder of his own ambivalence about it. The first full-length biography of his life was published in 1882, and a new one has been written at least once every generation since; one of the best is *James Fenimore Cooper* (1949) by James Grossman. An outrageously funny and notoriously unfair essay by Clemens, titled "Fenimore Cooper's Literary Offenses" (1895), helped to destroy Cooper's reputation as an artist. Yet, even when literary critics stopped ranking Cooper among the best American writers, he remained a major figure. His work has long been of interest to social historians, who have read his complicated and conflicted career, in the words of Vernon Louis Parrington in *Main Currents in American Thought* (1927), as "a testimony to the confusions of a generation in the midst of epic changes." As the study of literature becomes increasingly a means of access to the study of culture, Cooper's novels should continue to command attention. Perhaps not even the academic world of today wants Cooper's books to represent the idea of an "American classic," but they have many stories to tell besides their often conventional plots—the creation of a past for the new republic, the roles into which white society cast Native Americans (none of which included a place in its future), and the anxieties of identity, class, and literary performance produced by a democracy. But probably at the center of critical and popular attention will always be the Leather-Stocking Tales. Beginning with D. H. Lawrence's provocative discussion of them in *Studies in Classic American Literature* (1923), the tales have been viewed with increasing scrutiny as a dramatization of the ideological forces summoned into being by the determination of nineteenth-century America to settle (or, as a more recent strain of thought would put it, colonize) the continent. Adolescents hardly ever read the Leather-Stocking Tales now (though they do see versions of them at the movies and on television), but that the hero of James Fenimore Cooper's tales remains one of the most original, revealing, and significant figures in U.S.

literary history means that Natty Bumppo probably will never die.

Letters:

Correspondence of James Fenimore Cooper, 2 volumes, edited by his grandson, James Fenimore Cooper (New Haven: Yale University Press, 1922);

Letters and Journals of James Fenimore Cooper, 6 volumes, edited by James Franklin Beard (Cambridge, Mass.: Harvard University Press, 1960–1968).

Bibliographies:

Robert E. Spiller and Philip C. Blackburn, *A Descriptive Bibliography of the Writings of James Fenimore Cooper* (New York: R. R. Bowker, 1934);

Jacob Blanck, *Bibliography of American Literature* (New Haven: Yale University Press, 1957), 2: 276–310;

Alan Frank Dyer, *James Fenimore Cooper: An Annotated Bibliography of Criticism* (1991).

Biographies:

Susan Fenimore Cooper, *Pages and Pictures from the Writings of James Fenimore Cooper* (New York: Townsend, 1861);

Thomas R. Lounsbury, *James Fenimore Cooper* (Boston: Houghton Mifflin, 1882);

W. B. Shubrick Clymer, *James Fenimore Cooper* (Boston: Small, Maynard, 1900);

Mary E. Phillips, *James Fenimore Cooper* (New York: John Lane, 1913);

Ethel Outland, *The "Effingham" Libels on Cooper* (Madison: University of Wisconsin Press, 1929);

Henry Walcott Boynton, *James Fenimore Cooper* (New York: Century, 1931);

Marcel Clavel, *Fenimore Cooper: Sa vie et son oeuvre: La jeunesse (1789–1826)* (Aix-en-Provence: Imprimerie Universitaire de Provence, 1938);

Dorothy Waples, *The Whig Myth of James Fenimore Cooper* (New Haven: Yale University Press, 1938);

James Grossman, *James Fenimore Cooper* (Stanford, Cal.: Stanford University Press, 1949);

Donald A. Ringe, *James Fenimore Cooper* (New York: Twayne, 1962);

Warren S. Walker, *James Fenimore Cooper: An Introduction and Interpretation* (New York: Barnes & Noble, 1962);

Stephen Railton, *Fenimore Cooper: A Study of His Life and Imagination* (Princeton: Princeton University Press, 1978);

Robert Emmet Long, *James Fenimore Cooper* (New York: Continuum, 1990).

References:

Charles Hansford Adams, *The Guardian of the Law: Authority and Identity in James Fenimore Cooper* (University Park: Pennsylvania State University Press, 1990);

Martin Baker and Roger Sabin, *The Lasting of the Mohicans: History of an American Myth* (Jackson: University Press of Mississippi, 1995);

W. C. Brownell, *American Prose Masters* (New York: Scribners, 1909);

Robert Clark, ed., *James Fenimore Cooper: New Critical Essays* (London: Vision, 1985);

Marcel Clavel, ed., *Fenimore Cooper and His Critics: American, British and French Criticisms of the Novelist's Early Work* (Aix-en-Provence: Imprimerie Universitaire de Provence, 1938);

Joseph Conrad, "Tales of the Sea," *Outlook,* 4 (June 1898): 74–78;

Mary E. Cunningham, ed., *James Fenimore Cooper: A Re-Appraisal* (Cooperstown: New York State Historical Association, 1954);

Donald Darnell, *James Fenimore Cooper: Novelist of Manners* (Newark: University of Delaware Press, 1993);

George Dekker, *James Fenimore Cooper the Novelist* (London: Routledge & Kegan Paul, 1967);

Dekker and John P. McWilliams, eds., *James Fenimore Cooper: The Critical Heritage* (London: Routledge & Kegan Paul, 1973);

Leslie Fiedler, *Love and Death in the American Novel* (New York: Criterion, 1960);

Wayne Franklin, *The New World of James Fenimore Cooper* (Chicago: University of Chicago Press, 1982);

Kay House, *Cooper's Americans* (Columbus: Ohio State University Press, 1966);

William P. Kelly, *Plotting America's Past: Fenimore Cooper and the Leatherstocking Tales* (Carbondale: Southern Illinois University Press, 1983);

D. H. Lawrence, *Studies in Classic American Literature* (New York: Seltzer, 1923);

R. W. B. Lewis, *The American Adam: Innocence, Tragedy, and Tradition in the Nineteenth Century* (Chicago: University of Chicago Press, 1955);

John McWilliams, *The Last of the Mohicans: Civil Savagery & Savage Civility* (New York: Twayne, 1995);

McWilliams, *Political Justice in a Republic: James Fenimore Cooper's America* (Berkeley: University of California Press, 1972);

Marvin Meyers, *The Jacksonian Persuasion* (Stanford, Cal.: Stanford University Press, 1957);

Warren Motley, *The America Abraham: James Fenimore Cooper and the Frontier Patriarch* (New York: Cambridge University Press, 1987);

Blake Nevius, *Cooper's Landscapes: An Essay on the Picturesque Vision* (Berkeley: University of California Press, 1976);

Francis Parkman, "Review of *The Works of James Fenimore Cooper,*" *North American Review,* 74 (January 1852): 147–161;

Vernon Louis Parrington, *Main Currents in American Thought* (New York: Harcourt, Brace, 1927);

H. Daniel Peck, *A World By Itself: The Pastoral Moment in Cooper's Fiction* (New Haven: Yale University Press, 1977);

Thomas Philbrick, *James Fenimore Cooper and the Development of American Sea Fiction* (Cambridge, Mass.: Harvard University Press, 1961);

Geoffrey Rans, *Cooper's Leather-Stocking Novels* (Chapel Hill: University of North Carolina Press, 1991);

John F. Ross, *The Social Criticism of Fenimore Cooper* (Berkeley: University of California Press, 1933);

Henry Nash Smith, *Virgin Land: The American West as Symbol and Myth* (Cambridge, Mass.: Harvard University Press, 1950);

Robert E. Spiller, *Fenimore Cooper: Critic of His Times* (New York: Minton, Balch, 1931);

Alan Taylor, *William Cooper's Town: Power and Persuasion on the Frontier* (New York: Knopf, 1995);

Samuel Langhorne Clemens (Mark Twain), "Fenimore Cooper's Literary Offenses," *North American Review,* 161 (July 1895): 1–12;

W. M. Verhoeven, ed., *James Fenimore Cooper: New Historical and Literary Contexts* (Amsterdam: Rodopi, 1993);

Warren S. Walker, *James Fenimore Cooper: An Introduction and Interpretation* (New York: Barnes & Noble, 1962);

Walker, *Plots and Characters in the Fiction of James Fenimore Cooper* (Hamden: Archon, 1978);

James D. Wallace, *Early Cooper and His Audience* (New York: Columbia University Press, 1986);

Yvor Winters, *Maule's Curse* (New York: New Directions, 1938).

Papers:

The largest collection of James Fenimore Cooper's papers is in the Beinecke Rare Book Room and Manuscript Library, Yale University. The New York State Historical Association, at Cooperstown, has many items relating to the Cooper family.

Charles A. Dana

(8 August 1819 – 17 October 1897)

Karen S. H. Roggenkamp
University of Minnesota, Twin Cities

See also the Dana entries in *DLB 3: Antebellum Writers in New York and the South* and *DLB 23: American Newspaper Journalists, 1873–1900.*

BOOKS: *A Lecture on Association, in Its Connection with Religion* (Boston: Benjamin H. Greene, 1844);

The Life of Ulysses S. Grant, General of the Armies of the United States, by Dana and James Harrison Wilson (Springfield, Mass.: Gurdon Bill / Cincinnati: H. C. Johnson / Chicago, Ill.: Charles Bill, 1868);

The Art of Newspaper Making. Three Lectures (New York: D. Appleton, 1895; London: Unwin, 1895);

Lincoln and His Cabinet (Cleveland & New York: Printed by DeVinne Press, 1896);

Proudhoun and His "Bank of the People" (New York: B. R. Tucker, 1896);

Eastern Journeys: Some Notes of Travel in Russia, in the Caucasus, and to Jerusalem (New York: D. Appleton, 1898);

Recollections of the Civil War (New York: D. Appleton, 1898).

OTHER: Johann Wolfgang von Goethe, *The Autobiography of Goethe,* 2 volumes, edited by Parke Godwin, part three of volume 2, translated by Dana (New York: Wiley & Putnam, 1846, 1847; 3 volumes, London: Wiley & Putnam, 1847);

Clara Fechner, *The Black Aunt. Stories and Legends for Children,* translated by Dana (New York: R. Garrigue, 1848);

Fechner, *Nut-Cracker and Sugar-Dolly, and Other Stories and Legends,* translated by Dana (London: Joseph Cundall, 1849); republished as *Nutcracker and Sugardolly: A Fairy Tale* (New York: C. G. Henderson, 1852);

Christmas Eve and Other Stories, translated by Dana (Boston: Crosby & Nichols, 1852);

The Princess Unca and Other Stories, translated by Dana (Boston: Crosby & Nichols, 1852);

Annie and the Elves and Other Stories, translated by Dana (Boston: Crosby & Nichols, 1852);

Charles A. Dana during the Civil War, when he served as assistant secretary of war (Massachusetts Commandery, Military Order of the Loyal Legion and the U.S. Army Military History Institute)

Johnny and Maggie and Other Stories, translated by Dana (Boston: Crosby & Nichols, 1852);

Meyer's Universum; or, Views of the Most Remarkable Places and Objects of All Countries, edited by Dana, 2 volumes (New York: Herrmann J. Meyer, 1852, 1853);

The United States Illustrated in Views of City and Country, edited by Dana, 2 volumes (New York: Herrmann J. Meyer, 1855);

The Household Book of Poetry, selected and edited by Dana (New York: D. Appleton, 1857; revised and enlarged, New York: D. Appleton, 1869; revised edition, New York: D. Appleton, 1873);

The New American Cyclopædia: A Popular Dictionary of General Knowledge, edited by Dana and George Ripley, 16 volumes (New York & London: D. Appleton, 1858–1863);

German Fairy Tales, translated by Dana (New York: International Book, 1865);

Household Book of Songs: For Four Voices, edited by Dana and Francis C. Bowman (New York: D. Appleton, 1871);

Fifty Perfect Poems, selected and edited by Dana (New York: D. Appleton, 1883);

Laurence Oliphant, *Haifa, or Life in Modern Palestine,* edited by Dana (New York: Harper, 1887; London: W. Blackwood, 1887).

PERIODICAL EDITED: *New York Sun* (1868–1897).

SELECTED PERIODICAL PUBLICATIONS—
UNCOLLECTED:

NONFICTION

"Commerce," *Harbinger,* 1 (21 June 1845): 31–32;

"Social and Political Science," *Harbinger,* 1 (14 July 1845): 109–110;

"Civilization: The Isolated Family," *Harbinger,* 1 (27 September 1845): 251–253;

"Labor for Wages," *Harbinger,* 2 (25 April 1846): 318–319;

"The Social and Religious Movements," *Harbinger,* 2 (23 May 1846): 378–381;

"Doings in Paris," *New York Tribune,* 30 June 1848, p. 1;

"Balance Sheet of the Revolution," *New York Tribune,* 13 February 1849, p. 1.

POETRY

"Via Sacra," *Dial,* 4 (October 1843): 210;

"Auf Weidersehen!" *Harbinger,* 1 (14 June 1845): 8;

"Erotis," *Harbinger,* 2 (7 February 1846): 139.

Charles A. Dana is best known as the independent editor of *The New York Sun* from 1868 through 1897, but his principal philosophies and interests were formed during the antebellum period. Dana was a man of contradictions: he was an idealist who insisted on practicality, a humble person whose ego led to damaging encounters with employers, an advocate of education who respected the uneducated masses, and a Republican who edited the most successful Democratic-based newspaper of the 1870s and 1880s. While this periodical—often termed "the newspaperman's newspaper"—is what formed Dana's reputation, according to Janet E. Steele in *The Sun Shines for All: Journalism and Ideology in the Life of Charles A. Dana* (1993), the key "to understanding Dana as an intellectual lies in the ideas that he developed at

Brook Farm" in the 1840s and "that evolved into the Free Soil crusade of the 1850s."

Charles Anderson Dana was born 8 August 1819 in Hinsdale, New Hampshire, to Anderson and Ann Dennison Dana. When Charles was young, his father's business failed, forcing the family to move to Gaines, New York. Tragedy followed the family, however, for Ann Dana died in 1828, leaving Charles and three younger children motherless. Anderson Dana moved his family again, to Vermont, where he had been raised, and Charles was sent to live with an uncle. Always a bright child, Charles thrived at the neighborhood school, pursuing what became a lifelong interest in language and literature. At twelve, he left Vermont to clerk at another uncle's store in Buffalo, New York. While in Buffalo he continued his self-education: he acquired more languages (even learning the local Seneca dialect) and attempted to become thoroughly versed in world literature and history. He also helped form the "Coffee Club," a literary coterie whose members included influential members of the Buffalo community and to whom Dana presented papers on such topics as early English poetry.

In 1837 Dana was uprooted once again when financial panic ruined his uncle's business. Perhaps aided by his mentors in the Coffee Club, Dana gathered the funds necessary to continue his formal education, and in 1839 he entered Harvard University, where he placed seventh out of seventy-four students at the end of his first year. As much as Dana enjoyed the challenging academic environment, his attendance was spotty, for he frequently requested leaves of absence to earn money for his own support. The strain of academic work, financial hardship, and schoolteaching led to his almost losing his eyesight, and ultimately he completed only two full years at Harvard.

While attending lectures by Ralph Waldo Emerson and George Ripley at Harvard, Dana grew interested in Transcendentalism, taking to it, as he wrote one friend, "rather kindly, though I stumble at some notions." As early as 1840, Dana was considering Ripley's vision of an associative farming community; and when Dana's eyes finally demanded rest in the fall of 1841, he joined Ripley at Brook Farm in West Roxbury, Massachusetts, and purchased three shares of stock. A pragmatist at heart, Dana never professed complete confidence in the most idealistic goals of Brook Farm, but his residence there from 1841 through 1846 allowed him to explore his ideas about social reform. The farm association presented to Dana an environment of blended idealism and pragmatism that influenced his thinking during the rest of his career. While his chief occupations included teaching German, Greek, and Spanish at the Brook Farm school (where

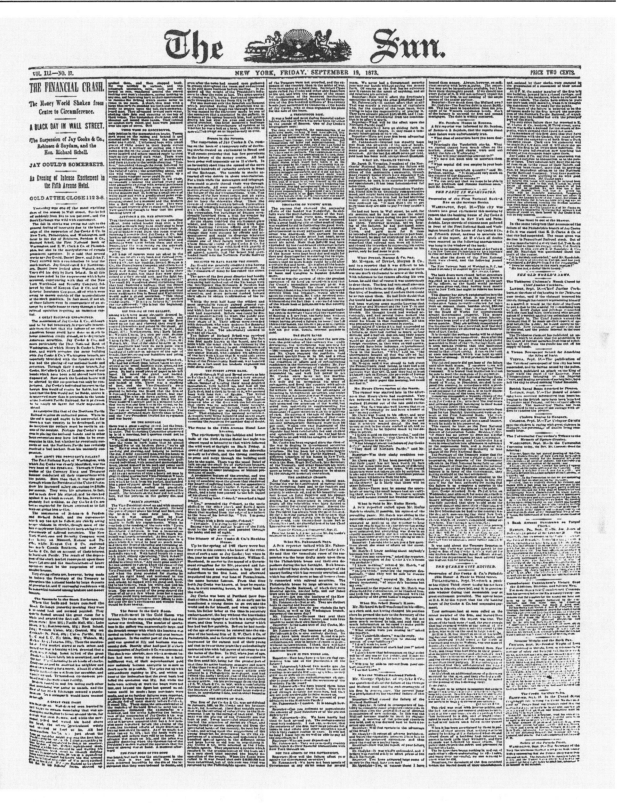

The new seven-column format that Dana introduced during his tenure as editor

he was nicknamed "The Professor") and doing hard farmwork, Dana also served as recording secretary for the community as well as a trustee and a member of the finance and education committees.

Dana produced his first notable literary work while he resided at Brook Farm. Having occasionally written for *The Dial,* he became principal assistant and chief contributor to Ripley's newspaper *The Harbinger* in 1845. During the next two years, Dana frequently published essays, editorials, reviews, and poems in the periodical—contributions that underscore his enthusiasm for change. For instance, in a 27 September 1845 article titled "Civilization: The Isolated Family," Dana asserts that society is moving toward mass reformation: "The squalid rags of the beggar, the pomp of wealth, the prison, the church, the reformer's conventicle, and the conservative's counting-room, all variously betoken the coming revolution." Nevertheless, the article argues, changes in society must assure that selfish individuality does not stifle cooperation. Association thus is the answer to make the human family "what God designed it should be, a source of unmixed good and happiness to Man." Similarly, in "Social and Political Science," published 14 July 1845, Dana calls for readers to change their perspectives; for "the great majority of human beings" are "plunged in degradation and misery" while "those who are at the head of affairs, either overlook the facts entirely, or at best know no palliative for these evils." Dana spotlighted urban rather than rural conditions in this and other articles, as he later did in his career as newspaper editor, asking his readers to "look at manufactories and mechanics' shops, where labor is cheated of its rights, and man made into a machine; look at your cities overflowing with vice and wretchedness."

At Brook Farm, Dana met his future wife, Eunice MacDaniel, who had settled there with her widowed mother and two siblings. They married in New York City on 2 March 1846, one day before the new Phalanstery at Brook Farm burned down, essentially ending the experiment. Within months, Dana and his bride moved to Boston, where he found work as an exchange reader and editor at *The Daily Chronotype.*

The intellectual contacts Dana had made at Brook Farm paid off quickly when Horace Greeley invited him to serve as city editor of the *New York Tribune,* beginning in February 1847. Just a month later Zoe, the first of the Danas' four children, was born. During this post–Brook Farm period Dana also continued his nonjournalistic literary work and furthered his interest in foreign languages by translating a portion of Johann Wolfgang von Goethe's autobiography as *The Auto-biography of Goethe* (1846, 1847) and Clara Fechner's *Die Schwarze Tante* (1847) as *The Black Aunt. Stories and*

Legends for Children (1848). Biographer James Harrison Wilson suggests the translation proved popular with American children and stands as an early example of foreign works translated specifically for children.

Dana's writing became known among American adult readers only after he traveled to Europe in 1848 and 1849. Long interested in foreign nations and life-styles, Dana was spurred by revolution in France and the social and economic conditions of workers across Europe to spend nine months overseas and return correspondence for publication in the *Tribune* and four other newspapers. Greeley begrudgingly agreed to a syndicated correspondence contract; and Dana, deeply affected by the revolutionary temper he witnessed in the streets of Paris, published his first letter in the *Tribune* on 30 June 1848. In this letter, as in many of the letters that followed, Dana presents information gathered from direct observation of proceedings in government buildings and of workers protesting in the streets. Dana trekked across Europe, graphically describing in his correspondence the framing of a new French constitution, scenes among workers in Berlin, and street fighting in Germany and Prussia. Overall, Dana's letters from Europe support individual rights and especially the rights of workers, proposing that aggression is sometimes necessary to bring about economic justice. His letter of 13 February 1849, for example, asserts that violent revolution in this case opens "wide the way of progress" and puts "society face to face with the questions on which its fate depends." Dana's experiences in Europe forced him to revise somewhat the idealistic (and ultimately conservative) ideas about social change he had expressed in *The Harbinger.* Though still confident in the capability of nonaggressive reform, Dana was growing more militant in his letters than he had been in his earlier writings, calling for full-scale insurrections when necessary, rather than expressing faith in a nonviolent, evolutionary path toward social and economic change.

When he returned to New York in March 1849, Dana brought with him strong opinions about the continuing strife in Europe—views that, as Steele suggests, gave him "a renewed appreciation of the republican institutions that flourished on American soil." Dana threw that appreciation into his work at the *Tribune,* where he had been promoted to managing editor, second in command (a somewhat misleading title since Dana essentially ran the paper during Greeley's frequent absences from New York). Although biographers cannot determine absolutely which *Tribune* items Dana wrote himself, he obviously supported the general Free-Soil policies of the paper, advocating economic independence and civil liberties for white American workers and writing against the further spread of slavery, which threatened those economic and civil ideals. Dana also obtained original literary works for the *Tribune* from such authors as Nathaniel Hawthorne, Charles Dickens, and Charlotte, Emily, and Anne Brontë, as well as regular columns from Karl Marx, whom Dana had befriended in Europe.

From 1849 through the 1850s Dana was completing many literary projects of his own. In addition to translating more German children's stories, including *Christmas Eve and Other Stories* (1852), *Nut-Cracker and Sugar-Dolly, and Other Stories and Legends* (London, 1849; American publication as *Nutcracker and Sugardolly: A Fairy Tale,* 1852), *The Princess Unca and Other Stories* (1852), and *Annie and the Elves and Other Stories* (1852), he edited two illustrated texts, including *Meyer's Universum; or, Views of the Most Remarkable Places and Objects of All Countries* (1852, 1853), a compendium of fascinating spaces across the world, for which he commissioned steel engravings and contributed an essay on the "General Post-office at Washington." Dana also edited *The United States Illustrated in Views of City and Country* (1855), which pairs descriptive essays written by himself, Greeley, Ripley, and others with detailed etchings of public buildings and natural wonders. The volumes "aim to lay before the American people faithful and spirited illustrations of what is characteristic and beautiful in the scenery and memorable in the public buildings of all portions of the country."

But Dana's two major projects of the 1850s were *The Household Book of Poetry,* first published in 1857, and *The New American Cyclopædia: A Popular Dictionary of General Knowledge,* begun in 1858 and continued through 1863. *The Household Book of Poetry,* a collection that he subsequently revised and republished, proved, in Dana's words, "a fair pecuniary success." Northern critics praised the compilation, but critics from the South, who associated Dana's *Tribune* status with regional prejudice, complained of bias, citing Dana's exclusion of Edgar Allan Poe's verse as evidence. Dana's work with Ripley on the sixteen-volume *New American Cyclopædia*—a premier omnibus of history, science, art, and literature—also brought him financial security. Indeed, according to Steele, the work earned Dana and Ripley more than $180,000 by 1880. *The New American Cyclopædia* also gave Dana contacts with the leading intellectuals who contributed articles to the volumes. A work "primarily intended for popular instruction and entertainment," the encyclopedia attempts "to furnish a condensed exhibition of the present state of human knowledge."

Dana's family grew in the 1850s along with his list of publications. Three more children—Paul, Ruth, and Eunice—were born to the Danas, and Dana expressed deep joy in his family. A doting father, he

The New York Sun *building, 1868*

wrote to one friend that "There's no delight like that in a pack of young children. . . . The man who hasn't half a dozen young children about him must have a very mean conception of life."

As the 1850s progressed and Dana gained more power at the *Tribune,* tensions grew between him and Greeley because their opinions differed over the possible secession of Southern states and because the strong-willed Dana disliked serving in a position subordinate to Greeley's. More politically radical than Greeley, Dana did not hesitate to write columns that might alienate Southern sympathizers. Moreover, his insistence on independent opinions led him to print occasional editorials that were at odds with Greeley's personal views and with the agenda of the newly formed Republican Party. The final break between the two men came on 27 March 1862, when Dana bitterly resigned at the request of *Tribune* stockholders.

The Civil War, however, brought Dana into a different kind of national spotlight. After a brief career arranging cotton trades between Union and Confederate states, he began work under Secretary of War Edwin Stanton, first investigating Ulysses S. Grant's conduct in the field (Grant was suspected of alcoholic intemperance while on duty), and then as assistant secretary of war, beginning in July 1863. For the remainder of the war, Dana traveled with primary Union generals into battle and witnessed many military campaigns.

After the war Dana immediately returned to journalism, a career he never again left. For ten months, beginning in May 1865, he edited *The Chicago Republican,* a new partisan paper, but he left after a disagreement with stockholders, initiated largely by Dana's continuing thirst for public and political power. Cast adrift once more, Dana soon found his true calling and the position that made his name memorable. Back in New York, he seized a chance late in 1867 to purchase *The New York Sun,* one of the oldest newspapers in the city, from editor Moses Beach for $175,000. The readership of *The Sun* was composed almost entirely of Democratic, working-class readers; but Dana, relying on the capital of Republican stockholders, transformed *The Sun* into the most successful New York newspaper of the 1870s and early 1880s without alienating either his readers or his stockholders. Always insistent on his own political independence, and now in a position to practice it as chief editor, Dana divorced his paper from strict party affiliations, blending the convictions about workers' rights he had nurtured during his experiences at Brook Farm and in Europe with his permeating senses of humor, literary quality, and pragmatic politics.

Dana pursued some smaller literary projects after he purchased *The Sun,* including a campaign biography of Grant, some travel narratives, and a memoir of his own Civil War experiences. But Dana's central literary project was the newspaper itself. Although *The Sun* catered to poorly educated working-class and immigrant populations, Dana refused to lower the writing standards of the paper or to condescend to his readers. Rather, he insisted on high literary style from his reporters, and he published daily an array of topics, from crime to politics and from literature to "sensationalistic" pieces. Dana is credited with creating the modern newspaper "human interest" story, and his one golden rule for reporters was to "be interesting," or to animate the dry facts of any story for his readers.

Although Dana's *Sun* maintained a respectable circulation through the last decades of the nineteenth century, the popularity of the paper waned during the late 1880s and 1890s under the pressure of unprecedented commercial competition from Joseph Pulitzer's *New York World* and William Randolph Hearst's *New York Journal.* Dana, who had never accepted the neces-

sity of advertising and publicity, found it impossible to keep pace with the self-promotion of the *World* and the *Journal.* Simultaneously, his editorial views grew more conservative. He began supporting non-Democratic political candidates in his editorials, essentially alienating himself and the traditions of the paper and from the working-class readership he had pursued throughout most of his career. After losing scores of readers to new competitors, Dana began to support publicly the interests of capital and the higher social class to which he belonged. The 1890s became for him a decade of defensive reminiscence, and he published works recounting his travel experiences, his years at Brook Farm, and his philosophies on the newspaper industry.

When Dana died on 17 October 1897, leaving his newspaper to his son Paul, *The New York Sun* remembered him in the simple way he had requested, with a short announcement: "CHARLES ANDERSON DANA, Editor of THE SUN, died yesterday afternoon." With his death, the conservatism of Charles A. Dana's final years as editor of *The Sun* cemented his lasting reputation. But in reality most of his life both in and out of journalism was informed by the much-less-conservative ideals he had discovered during the antebellum years, first at Brook Farm and with *The Harbinger,* and then as an editor for the *New York Tribune.*

Biographies:

James Harrison Wilson, *The Life of Charles A. Dana* (New York: Harper, 1907);

Charles J. Rosebault, *When Dana Was* The Sun: *A Story of Personal Journalism* (New York: R. M. McBride, 1931);

Candace Stone, *Dana and* The Sun (New York: Dodd, Mead, 1938);

Alfred H. Fenton, *Dana of* The Sun (New York: Farrar & Rinehart, 1941).

References:

Frank M. O'Brien, *The Story of* The Sun (New York: Doran, 1918), pp. 202–425;

Janet E. Steele, The Sun *Shines for All: Journalism and Ideology in the Life of Charles A. Dana* (Syracuse, N.Y.: Syracuse University Press, 1993).

Papers:

The major collections of Charles A. Dana's papers are held at the Library of Congress, the New York Public Library, and the New York Historical Society. Other Dana materials are held at Columbia University, the Massachusetts Historical Society, and the Boston Public Library.

Evert A. Duyckinck
(23 November 1816 – 13 August 1878)

and

George L. Duyckinck
(17 October 1823 – 30 March 1863)

Donald Yannella
Barat College

See also the Evert A. Duyckinck entry and the George L. Duyckinck entry in *DLB 3: Antebellum Writers in New York and the South* and the Evert A. Duyckinck entry in *DLB 64: American Literary Critics and Scholars, 1850–1880.*

BOOKS: *The Literary: A Miscellany for the Town,* by Evert A. Duyckinck (New York: Henderson Greene, 1836);

The Life of George Herbert, by George L. Duyckinck (New York: General Protestant Episcopal Sunday School Union and Church Book Society, 1859);

The Life of Thomas Ken: Bishop of Bath and Wells, by George L. Duyckinck (New York: General Protestant Episcopal Sunday School Union and Church Book Society, 1859);

The Life of Jeremy Taylor: Bishop of Down, Connor, and Dromore, by George L. Duyckinck (New York: General Protestant Episcopal and Sunday School Union and Church Book Society, 1860);

The Life of Hugh Latimer, by George L. Duyckinck (New York: General Protestant Episcopal Sunday School Union and Church Book Society, 1861);

National History of the War for the Union: Civil, Military, and Naval: Founded on the Official and Other Authentic Documents, 3 volumes, by Evert A. Duyckinck (New York: Johnson, Fry, 1861–1865);

National Portrait Gallery of Eminent Americans: Including Orators, Statesmen, Naval and Military Heroes, Jurists, Authors . . . , 2 volumes, by Evert A. Duyckinck (New York: Johnson, Fry, 1862);

Memorial of John Allan, by Evert A. Duyckinck (New York: Printed for the Bradford Club, 1864);

Fitz-Greene Halleck, by Evert A. Duyckinck (New York: Privately printed by W. L. Andrews, 1868);

Evert A. Duyckinck

A Memorial of Francis L. Hawks, D.D., LL.D.: Read Before the New-York Historical Society, May 7th, 1867; With an Appendix of Proceedings . . . , by Evert A. Duyckinck (New York: The New-York Historical Society, 1871);

A Memorial of Henry Theodore Tuckerman: Read Before the New-York Historical Society, Jan. 2, 1872: With An Appendix of Proceedings, by Evert A. Duyckinck (New York: Printed for the Society, 1872);

A Memorial of John David Wolfe: Read Before the New-York Historical Society, June 4, 1872. With a Notice of Proceedings, by Evert A. Duyckinck (New York: Printed for the Society, 1872);

Lives and Portraits of the Presidents of the United States from Washington to Grant, by Evert A. Duyckinck (New York: Johnson, Wilson, 1873);

Portrait Gallery of Eminent Men and Women of Europe and America: Embracing History, Statesmanship, Naval and Military Life, Philosophy, the Drama, Science, Literature and Art, with Biographies, 2 volumes, by Evert A. Duyckinck (New York: Johnson, Wilson, 1873);

A Brief Catalogue of Books Illustrated with Engravings by Dr. Alexander Alderson, with a Biographical Sketch of the Artist, by Evert A. Duyckinck (New York: Printed by Thompson & Moreau, 1885).

OTHER: William Makepeace Thackeray, *The Confessions of Fitz-Boodle; and Some Passages in the Life of Major Gahagan,* edited by Evert A. Duyckinck (New York: D. Appleton, 1852);

Thackeray, *The Yellowplush Papers,* edited by Evert A. Duyckinck (New York: D. Appleton, 1852);

Cyclopædia of American Literature: Embracing Personal and Critical Notices of Authors, and Selections from Their Writings. From the Earliest Period to the Present Day, 2 volumes, edited by Evert A. and George L. Duyckinck (New York: Scribner, 1855; revised edition, with supplement, 1866; updated by M. Laird Simons (Philadelphia, New York & London: T. E. Zell, 1875);

Wit and Wisdom of the Rev. Sydney Smith: Being Selections from his Writings and Passages of his Letters and Table Talk, edited by Evert A. Duyckinck (New York: Redfield, 1856);

The Poets of the Nineteenth Century: Selected and Edited by the Rev. Robert Aris Willmott, with English and American Additions Arranged by Evert A. Duyckinck, edited by Robert Aris Willmott and Evert A. Duyckinck (New York: Harper, 1858);

William Irving, James Kirke Paulding, and Washington Irving, *Salmagundi; or, The Whim-whams and Opinions of Launcelot Langstaff, Esq. [pseud.] and Others,* with a preface and notes by Evert A. Duyckinck (New York: G. P. Putnam, 1860);

Philip Freneau, *Poems Relating to the American Revolution,* memoir and notes by Evert A. Duyckinck (New York: W. J. Widdleton, 1865);

History of the World: From the Earliest Period to the Present Time, 4 volumes, compiled by Evert A. Duyckinck (New York: Johnson, Fry, 1869–1871);

Alexander Alderson, *Illustrations of Mother Goose's Melodies: Designed and Engraved on Wood by Alexander Alderson, M.D.,* with an introduction by Evert A. Duyckinck (New York: Privately printed by Charles L. Moreau, 1873);

Francis L. Hawks, *Poems Hitherto Uncollected, by the Rev. Francis L. Hawks,* edited with a preface by Evert A. Duyckinck (New York: Privately printed by Charles L. Moreau, 1873);

A Memorial of Fitz-Greene Halleck: A Description of the Dedication of the Monument Erected to his Memory at Guilford, Connecticut; And of the Proceedings Connected with the Unveiling of the Poet's Statue in the Central Park, New York, edited by Evert A. Duyckinck (New York: Privately printed by Amerman & Wilson, 1877);

Early American Wood Engravings by Alexander Anderson and Others, introduction by Evert A. Duyckinck (New York: Burr & Boyd, 1877);

The Complete Works of William Shakespeare, edited by George L. Duyckinck (Philadelphia: Porter & Coates, 1879);

The Complete Works of Shakespeare, edited by William Cullen Bryant, with the assistance of Evert A. Duyckinck (New York: Amies Publishing, 1888).

PERIODICALS EDITED: *Arcturus: A Journal of Books and Opinions,* edited by Evert A. Duyckinck (December 1840–May 1842);

Literary World, edited by Evert A. and George L. Duyckinck (6 February 1847–31 December 1853).

Evert A. Duyckinck is probably best remembered by modern literary and cultural historians as a key figure in the New York literary world from the late 1830s to the 1850s. He is especially prominent for scholars of major literary figures such as Edgar Allan Poe, Herman Melville, and Washington Irving, with whom Duyckinck had important relationships; he served them and a host of others as an editor, an associate, and a friend. He was one of the figures at the center of New York culture, particularly in the 1840s and 1850s. The wealth of manuscript diaries he kept and letters he wrote and received are a virtual treasure trove for the historian, and when published, they might well prove to be the major portion of his legacy to literary history. These pages and more than seventeen thousand volumes from the personal library collected by him and his brother, George, were donated to the Lenox Library in New York City; when the New York Public Library was established in the 1890s, the books were moved to the main building, and the invaluable papers—which include correspondence from such major American authors as Melville, Poe, Ralph Waldo Emerson, and William Cullen Bryant—were deposited in the Manuscripts Division, where they are housed at present. Evert Duyckinck as he emerges from these manuscripts is much warmer, more sophisticated, and more aware than the figure one encounters in the assessments of his memorialists and more recent literary historians; he is also much less retiring than he was pictured by William A. Butler, his memorialist before the New York Historical Society, whose description was used in part by another eulogist, Samuel Osgood.

Chroniclers such as Sidney P. Moss and Perry Miller have emphasized Evert Duyckinck's participation in the rivalries and battles among the literati of New York in the 1840s and 1850s. But his involvement in such journalistic backbiting accounts for only a small portion of his career and his contribution to literature. More important, he was a skilled editor of books and periodicals, an adept cultivator of others' talents, a man of scholarly and retiring bent who nevertheless was deeply engaged in observing and responding to the culture of the period, and, finally, a collector of books, periodicals, and art who was more than generous in making his extensive library available to his friends. The informal salon he conducted in the basement of his home at 20 Clinton Place was a hospitable and congenial gathering place for writers, artists, and editors, as well as amateurs and enthusiasts. In his social and professional life Duyckinck managed what few if any modern men of letters are capable of: while he pursued a life of serious literary and scholarly labors, he also was deeply involved in the lives and works of contemporary creative writers. For him no wall separated the worlds of academe and creativity. Had Duyckinck not left his rich written record in manuscript and if literary historians did not understand how central he was in the cultural life of the period, he would nevertheless enjoy a solid position in American literary historical annals because of his major contribution to American literary scholarship, the *Cyclopædia of American Literature: Embracing Personal and Critical Notices of Authors, and Selections from Their Writings. From the Earliest Period to the Present Day* (1855). Compiled, edited, and composed in collaboration with his brother, George, this reference work survives as a remarkably comprehensive historical survey of its subject from the beginnings of the early seventeenth century to the mid nineteenth century. Both Evert and George Duyckinck also enjoy a place in nineteenth-century American culture as a result of their labors on *The Literary World,* one of the most tasteful

George L. Duyckinck

and important journals published in the mid nineteenth century.

The Duyckincks shared in a culturally rich and stimulating household. Evert Augustus Duyckinck was born on 23 November 1816 and lived his entire life on the island of Manhattan, New York City. The older of two boys born to Evert and Harriet June Duyckinck, he grew up in a reasonably prosperous, though not wealthy, home in which scholarship, the arts, and the life of the mind were cultivated. The Dutch roots of the family reached far back into seventeenth-century New Amsterdam, and Evert counted among his forebears the prominent group of painters who bear the same surname as well as a paternal grandfather who had been actively engaged in the American Revolutionary War. George Long Duyckinck was born on 17 October 1823, seven years after his more prominent brother. The father of Evert and George enjoyed a long and successful career as a bookseller and publisher; his store, located on Water Street in what was then the small town of New York City, provided the boys with an environment that obviously shaped their abiding interest in letters and the arts. The father has the distinction of having given the Harper brothers their first order for a

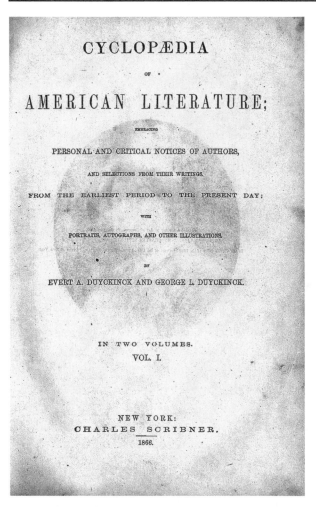

Title page for the comprehensive historical survey in which the Duyckincks sought "to exhibit and illustrate the products of the pen on American soil" (Collection of Matthew J. Bruccoli)

book under their own imprint, an edition of *Seneca's Morals,* published in 1817.

The Duyckinck brothers' lives spanned an exciting, though potentially disturbing, period of growth and change in the city, a time of developments that paralleled those that were taking place across American society and culture. Born and bred in a "walking city," they, like their contemporaries, witnessed the spread of the city northward, its burgeoning into a modern metropolis. In brief, they lived through events that dramatically changed the styles, patterns, and values of American society, politics, and institutions as well as the tastes of the culture in the arts and literature. Evert, in particular, not only observed these developments but also participated in them and helped shape the events, at least in the literary world in which he moved.

Graduated from Columbia College in 1835, Evert Duyckinck, who was later to serve his alma mater as a trustee, read law for two years and was

admitted to the bar in 1837 although he did not enter the practice of law. He had already begun to live out his commitment to literary life. One of the key figures in a group of young men with literary ambitions, the Tetractys Club, Duyckinck was evidently the sole or principal author of a satirical pamphlet published late in 1836, *The Literary: A Miscellany for the Town.* (The pamphlet, which was the first issue of a periodical that did not materialize, has been identified as Evert Duyckinck's by Osgood, his memorialist, and—more recently—by Eugene Exman, the historian of the Harper Brothers publishing firm.) Modeled in some degree upon the *Salmagundi* papers (1807–1808) of William and Washington Irving, and James Kirke Paulding thirty years earlier, one of the papers in *The Literary* was judged as libelous by its prospective publisher, Harper, but only after they had manufactured stereotyped plates. Duyckinck found another publisher for the forty-eight pages of satirical verse and prose, which is most valuable and interesting for its lead essay, "The Club," a lightly veiled description of the Tetractys and its members—Duyckinck, William A. Jones, Jedediah B. Auld, Russell Trevett, and Cornelius Mathews. After contributing short essays and articles to several magazines, such as the *American Monthly* and the *New-York Review,* Duyckinck traveled to Europe in 1838 and 1839, where he visited Holland, France, and the British Isles. He returned to the United States and married Margaret Wolfe Panton in the spring of 1840. George, a lifelong bachelor, moved into 20 Clinton Place, where he resided with his brother's family until his death.

Evert Duyckinck soon embarked on his first important literary venture as co-editor (with Mathews) of the short-lived, high-quality monthly *Arcturus: A Journal of Books and Opinion.* The wide reading he had done during his twenty-four years served him well; his tastes were discriminating and eclectic, and his sensitivity to the economic necessities imposed by the marketplace was nicely balanced by a rather clear understanding of the cultural needs of his countrymen. In an industry that was experiencing the first euphoria—even madness—brought on by the prospects of a growing mass market for books, magazines, and newspapers, Duyckinck and Mathews managed to produce a periodical of some distinction. The two editors attracted contributions by such authors as Henry Wadsworth Longfellow, James Russell Lowell, and even Nathaniel Hawthorne. During the year and a half it was published (December 1840–May 1842), they served up a regular fare of poetry, fiction, essays, and articles on a wide range of topics, not all literary. What editor, for instance, could ignore the politics of this volatile period? The quality of *Arcturus* is perhaps best illustrated by a few comments offered by Poe, one of the more demanding critics of the period; in "An Appendix for Autographs" (1842) he notes that *Arcturus* is "a monthly journal which has attained much reputation" and praises Mathews for his "well-written retrospective criticisms." Poe again mentioned *Arcturus* in his sketch of Duyckinck in "The Literati of New York City" (1846), in which he judged it "decidedly the very best magazine in many respects ever published in the United States . . . upon the whole, a little too good to enjoy extensive popularity."

When Evert Duyckinck and his contemporaries began their literary activities in the 1830s and early 1840s, George Duyckinck was scarcely a teenager. Following the deaths of his father and mother, he lived under the watchful and affectionate guidance of his brother. George had attended the academy at Geneva, New York (today Hobart College), and in 1843 was graduated from the University of the City of New York (New York University). As had been the case with his brother and Mathews, George Duyckinck was admitted to the bar but did not practice law. Although the brothers' age difference separated them less as they grew older in the 1840s, George remained on the periphery of Evert's circle before his first trip to Europe, a grand tour in 1846 and 1847, a period when political and social changes were sweeping the Continent. (George traveled with William Allen Butler, one of his brother's memorialists more than thirty years later.) George was an observer of Evert's friends' militant nationalist period, not a participant.

After his time at *Arcturus,* Evert Duyckinck's next major venture as an editor was the two series, Library of American Books and the Library of Choice Reading, published by Wiley and Putnam. Duyckinck took command in 1845 and began to offer the American reading public a tempting selection of high-quality literature in inexpensive editions. The Library of Choice Reading, a sustained series that might well be compared to the Modern Library in the twentieth century, offered its audience, among its almost one hundred volumes, titles such as William Makepeace Thackeray's *Journey from Cornhill to Cairo;* Charles Dickens's *Pictures from Italy* and *Dombey and Son;* Johann Wolfgang von Goethe's *Autobiography* and *Wilhelm Meister;* the *Autobiography of Benvenuto Cellini;* William Hazlitt's *Literature of the Age of Elizabeth* and *Characters in Shakespeare's Plays;* Charles Lamb's *Essays of Elia* and *Dramatic Poets;* John Keats's *Poetical Works;* Thomas Carlyle's *Heroes and Hero-Worship, Sartor Resartus,* and *History of the French Revolution;* and Oliver Goldsmith's *The Vicar of Wakefield.* The Library of American Books, which in the light of American literary history and Duyckinck's stature is infinitely more important, boasted titles such as Hawthorne's *Mosses from an Old Manse;* Poe's *The Raven and Other Poems* and a

selection of his tales; Melville's first book, *Typee;* William Gilmore Simms's *The Wigwam and the Cabin;* Margaret Fuller's *Papers on Literature and Art;* and John Greenleaf Whittier's *Supernaturalism in New England.* Most of the volumes in these series sold for only fifty cents, a bargain even in the mid 1840s.

While he was engaged in these projects from 1845 to 1847, Evert Duyckinck also kept his hand in the world of periodicals. The industry was in a boom period. In 1845 he served as interim editor of the radical monthly, the *United States Magazine and Democratic Review,* while the regular editor, John L. O'Sullivan, was absent in Europe. For a short period in the autumn of 1846 Duyckinck offered his moral support and even some contributions to the satirical weekly *Yankee Doodle.* Patterned after the highly successful British magazine *Punch, Yankee Doodle* got off to a fairly successful start in October 1846; its quality soon began to diminish, however, and it limped along under the guidance of George G. Foster until Mathews took the editorial reins in July 1847. For the next three months Evert Duyckinck was part of the inner sanctum that controlled the small weekly. The greatest claim to fame of *Yankee Doodle* remains the series of satires by Melville on General Zachary Taylor.

But the Duyckincks' major editorial effort was *The Literary World,* begun in 1847. Sponsored and published by Wiley and Putnam, its first editor was Evert Duyckinck, who was joined by his brother, George, in 1848. Evert Duyckinck's initial tenure as sole editor was short, lasting from 6 February to 24 April 1847. But in twelve weekly issues he established his credentials as a solid and dependable editor with a genuine sense of taste and remarkable integrity. He also revealed a youthful zeal for which he paid with his job. George Duyckinck wrote many articles for *The Literary World,* which will probably remain unidentified because of their having been unsigned, a common practice in the period. In the next five years he helped guide the development of the significant editorial policies of the journal.

Evert Duyckinck had been on the liberal—indeed, the radical—side of the two major, intimately related issues that confronted the American literary world in the 1840s—literary nationalism and international copyright. The central questions that underlay these problems had been debated for decades before and continued to entertain American intellectuals, including writers, well into the twentieth century. To what degree should American culture, specifically American literature, be influenced by the parent culture of Europe, particularly that of England? Or, from another angle, how autonomous, how free of the European heritage, must American culture be in order

Decorated title page for Evert A. Duyckinck's 1873 book, biographies intended for the popular market (Thomas Cooper Library, University of South Carolina)

to establish its own integrity and articulate itself? There were, and are, no simple, generally accepted answers to such queries. In Duyckinck's day there were relatively conservative spokesmen, on the one hand, such as Irving and Hawthorne, and, on the other hand, there were radicals, such as Emerson and Walt Whitman. The issues were complex, multilayered, and knotty; they were packed with political, sociological, and artistic implications. As is always the case when a culture engages in a dialogue that is crucial to its values and future, some spokesmen must take extreme positions, if only to clarify the questions.

From the late 1830s Evert Duyckinck had been one of the key figures in the Young America group of literary nationalists, centered in New York City. Committed to encouraging and establishing a vital, indigenous literature of high quality, they participated in an ongoing discussion with their less liberal opponents—a discussion that frequently degenerated into polemic, personal animosity, and downright nastiness. Duyckinck, his close friend Mathews, and the whole circle in which they moved were intent on establishing conditions that would better cultivate American writing.

Their stridency must be understood in light of the frustration they and their fellow American literati experienced as a result of there being no international copyright law. The most obvious disadvantage they suffered was that English publishers, particularly, could pirate their work unless they had established foreign copyright prior to American publication. For this reason, Melville, for example, published his earlier works abroad before bringing them out through an American press. English authors, as well as many American publishers, treated European writers in a fashion that was equally shoddy and immoral. Dickens's works were pirated with impunity by American firms, which made fortunes on his and others' writings and never had to pay royalty fees. In this way, the issues of American literary nationalism and international copyright were wed. Why print the work of an unknown American author and pay royalties to him for minimal sales when a publisher could offer the American reading public the work of a Dickens or a Thackeray, surefire sellers, and not be required to pay royalties? For many American publishers the question was virtually rhetorical. Under such discouraging circumstances, the nationalists asked, "How can we establish a genuine American literature?" To reduce literary nationalism to a form of counterculture or to dismiss Duyckinck and his circle as ill-educated, narcissistic chauvinists would be to ignore the circumstances that fired the nationalist movement and to forget that these men were widely read, steeped as a matter of fact in the European literary tradition, particularly that of England.

During his short tenure as founding editor of *The Literary World,* Duyckinck gave vent to his convictions by challenging his conservative adversaries and, equally vigorously, broadcasting the nationalists' credos. To get a sense of his commitment to the cause, one need only read the essays on the subject that appeared in *The Literary World* during the late winter and spring of 1847, many of which Duyckinck evidently wrote, while others were probably composed by the arch-spokesman for the cause, Mathews. As might have been expected, the tone and substance of the sheet increasingly upset the publishers of the weekly journal, and they fired Duyckinck in late April. For the next year and a half the journal fell into the hands of Charles Fenno Hoffman, who virtually ignored Duyckinck's editorial mission in which he demanded and promoted high standards of criticism and taste in order to encourage a vigorous, democratic literature.

Evert Duyckinck and George, who had been abroad on his grand tour in 1847, bought the journal a year and a half later, in October 1848, and during the next five years brought American criticism to new thresholds. Originally, *The Literary World* had been subtitled "A Gazette for Authors, Readers, and Publishers," but the more sophisticated, low-key, eclectic, and comprehensive purposes of the Duyckincks were presaged in the new subtitle, "A Journal of American and Foreign Literature, Science, and Art," which the journal bore beginning in February 1848, under Hoffman. In its third incarnation, *The Literary World* offered regular columns and reviews of fiction, poetry, drama, and nonfiction, including criticism, as well as notices on music and art. A sense of the range of authors covered, or at least mentioned, is easily obtained by glancing at Daniel A. Wells's index to the journal. In addition to penetrating and honest discussions of the writings of authors such as Irving, James Fenimore Cooper, Hawthorne, Simms, Melville, and Poe, the Duyckincks published the monumental piece of criticism by Melville, "Hawthorne and his Mosses," and other essays that have been of great value to historians of the period. *The Literary World* of 1848–1853 was a quieter, more balanced weekly than it had been during Duyckinck's first period as editor. Clearly, he had matured, and, while he may have become more conservative, he was wisely asserting his convictions by journalistic actions rather than through the words of manifestos. If the strategies were different, the purposes were similar.

A student of American cultural history will find few if any better records of literary activity and taste, especially of the New York variety, than in *The Literary World*. Spawned by a vital, even frenetic, period of growth and change in publishing, the magazine bridged the fluidity of the 1840s and the later, more controlled, larger circulation efforts by major publishing houses—*Harper's Monthly Magazine* (1850) and *Putnam's Monthly Magazine* (1853)—which probably contributed to the demise of *The Literary World*.

As heavy as the responsibility of producing a weekly might have been, the Duyckinck brothers bought the monthly *Holden's Dollar Magazine* early in 1851 and published it until August 1851. Although there was hardly enough time for them to improve its quality, they did enliven it somewhat. Most of the material was printed anonymously—in keeping with the conventions of the period observed by Evert in his earlier ventures in magazine editing, including *The Literary World*—but Evert penciled in the initials of contributors in his own copy of *Holden's* (now owned by the New York Public Library) as he had for the early numbers of *Yankee Doodle*. While engaged in these activities, Duyckinck found time in 1852 to edit two volumes by Thackeray for the series Appletons' Popular Library of the Best Authors—*The Confessions of Fitz-Boodle; and Some Passages in the Life of Major Gahagan* and *The Yellowplush Papers*.

Shortly after *The Literary World* closed at the very end of 1853, Evert Duyckinck–assisted once again by George–launched into the work that became their magnum opus, the *Cyclopædia of American Literature*. Composed of two hefty royal octavo volumes totaling almost 1,500 double-column pages, three editions of the *Cyclopædia of American Literature* were published by Charles Scribner (1855, 1856, 1866); the 1866 edition included a 157-page "Supplement" of obituaries of authors who had died in the intervening decade, continuations of earlier articles, and new pieces on recently published authors, including George Duyckinck, who had died in 1863 while the third edition was in progress. In the early 1870s M. Laird Simons revised the two volumes, integrating the "Supplement"; T. E. Zell published the fourth edition in 1875, after its having been circulated in fifty-two parts from 1873 to 1874.

The Duyckincks reported in their "Preface" that in constructing the more than five hundred author entries, chronologically arranged according to dates of birth, they had attempted to present "memorials and records" of American writers, "to exhibit and illustrate the products of the pen on American soil." They attempted to be as inclusive and comprehensive as time and production costs permitted and were fully aware that they by no means were offering an authoritative bibliographical work. The *Cyclopædia of American Literature* is a descriptive historical record rather than a judgmental critical compendium. It was silently divided into three sections–Colonial, Revolutionary, and what modern historians have labeled the Early National and Renaissance periods–and successfully attempted to be above sectional rivalries; the authors were evidently right in their claim that in no prior work were the contributions of the South as generously recognized.

In addition to biographical essays, the *Cyclopædia of American Literature* offers extracts of authors' works as well as useful bibliographical information. As a matter of fact, the modern literary historian must with some embarrassment admit that many of the paths the Duyckincks opened or suggested have been bypassed by subsequent generations of scholars. This is not to say that subsequent reference works have not supplanted the *Cyclopædia of American Literature*. The point is that the *Cyclopædia of American Literature* is a landmark work in American literary history, a demonstration of remarkable energy and sophistication, which might still prove quite useful to the modern scholar. As they note in their preface, the Duyckincks consulted the standard references of the day on the subject, as well as knowledgeable figures such as Washington Irving, the omnipresent New Yorker and physician John W. Francis, the Unitarian minister Samuel Osgood, Henry T. Tuckerman, William Gilmore Simms, and John Esten

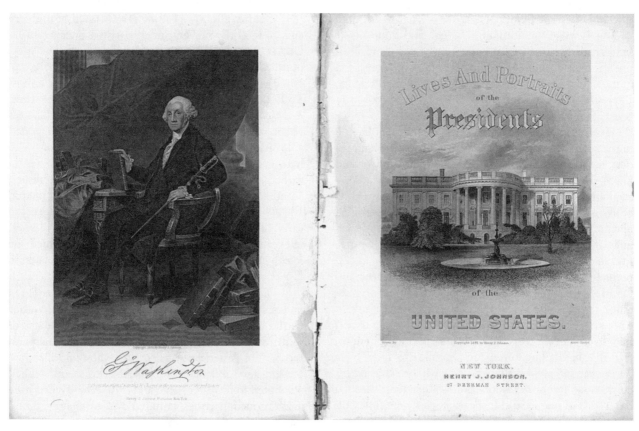

Frontispiece and decorated title page for the 1881 edition of Evert A. Duyckinck's biographies of the first eighteen chief executives (Thomas Cooper Library, University of South Carolina)

Cooke and worked with materials from a host of institutional and private libraries and archives. In its scope the *Cyclopædia of American Literature* is noteworthy; in its erudition and scholarly tenacity, it is remarkable—considering the state of American literary scholarship at the time. It is all the more so when one realizes that the vast bulk of it was gathered, compiled, and composed in fewer than two years.

In 1856, the year following the first edition of the *Cyclopædia of American Literature,* Evert wrote a biographical/critical introduction of 104 pages to a generous selection of the work of the Englishman Sydney Smith, who is probably best remembered in the annals of American literary history for his query, posed shortly before the 1819 publication of Irving's *The Sketch Book,* "Who reads an American book?" Once again Duyckinck demonstrated his skills as a scholar, as well as the breadth and catholicity of his judgment and taste. The essay stands as one of his better performances in criticism, the literary genre he was dedicated to improving.

George Duyckinck, an intense and devout Episcopalian, was a communicant in St. Thomas Church and in 1855 was elected to the executive committee of the General Protestant Episcopal Sunday School Union and

Church Book Society. (He had attended Grace Church in his youth.) He undertook the composition of a series of biographies for the organization and spent a great deal of time and energy on these projects. Following a second trip to Europe, in 1857, where he gathered some of his research material, he wrote and published within a few years four biographies, which averaged some 225 pages. These works reflected his interest in Renaissance literature and culture, an enthusiasm that his brother, Evert, shared. These were also serious and reflective works aimed at an audience that shared the Duyckincks' Anglican piety: *The Life of George Herbert* and *The Life of Thomas Ken: Bishop of Bath and Wells,* in 1859; *The Life of Jeremy Taylor: Bishop of Down, Connor, and Dromor,* in 1860 (Taylor had long been a favorite of the Duyckincks and their friends); and *The Life of Hugh Latimer,* in 1861. According to George Duyckinck's memorialist William F. Morgan, the rector of St. Thomas Church, when Duyckinck died in 1863, he was at work on a fifth biography, one on Archbishop Leighton.

After George Duyckinck's death, personal tragedy continued to overtake Evert. His son Evert had died in 1857, and his son George died in 1873. A third son, Henry, an Episcopal clergyman, died in 1870.

Osgood commented on the suffering of Evert Duyckinck's professional life as a result of the rapidly accelerating changes that took place in the New York literary world beginning in the 1840s; he remarked that Duyckinck possessed "little of the dash and muscle that came with the coming push and progress" and observed that from the time he first met him in 1849, Duyckinck was astonished by the remarkable growth and change taking place in the city. Indeed, by the time he was in his late thirties, certainly by his early forties, Duyckinck increasingly identified with an older Knickerbocker world that was being overrun, a late Knickerbocker literary scene that was fast dissolving. This response does not suggest that he stopped functioning, but it does indicate that he became increasingly uncomfortable amid the new developments. Tenaciously, and perhaps symbolically, he continued to reside at 20 Clinton Place as the area deteriorated from a once-pleasant "walking city" neighborhood into a district of boardinghouses and businesses. Osgood may have exaggerated the reclusive quality of Duyckinck's character—perhaps having taken his cue from Butler's memorial from which he quotes—but there does emerge a middle-aged Duyckinck bearing a striking resemblance to those New Yorkers in the fiction of Melville and Henry James, for example, who cling to a simpler past as the congested, urban-industrial world rolls forward and as the mass literature of post–Knickerbocker New York gluts the marketplace.

In the 1860s and 1870s Duyckinck was occupied with a series of memorials for old friends and associates. The most enduring is *Irvingiana: A Memorial of Washington Irving*, published in 1860. Duyckinck's seventeen-page literary biography, drawn in part from the essay he had composed for the *Cyclopaedia of American Literature* entry, headed the collection and is a scholarly and moving tribute to the man who had presided for so long over literary New York. The volume brought together another thirty items, including addresses by George Bancroft, Edward Everett, Longfellow, Osgood, and Francis, a poem by Tuckerman, a *New York Evening Post* editorial, a verse by Lowell, prose pieces by Nathaniel Parker Willis, George William Curtis, and James Grant Wilson, and a small selection of Irving's own writings. In the preface to his edition of *Salmagundi*, republished in 1860, Duyckinck revealed the depth of his feelings for Irving. Having commented on "formidable incursion" of *Salmagundi* "into the realm of taste" more than half a century earlier, he reflected on an old New York that, like Irving, had passed on: "How distant it all seems. There is nothing of New York of the present time in its [*Salmagundi*'s] pages—of our bustling, driving, busy era. . . . The demon of ceaseless work had not then taken such full possession of the world." It is as if the

Age had been won by Irving's own "lean, bilious-looking fellow," the disputatious man whose pockets are full of handbills in "Rip Van Winkle."

As old friends died—Duyckinck himself was not yet fifty—there were other memorials to be written: for the collector of art and literature, John Allan, in 1864; for his clergyman at St. Thomas, Francis L. Hawks, in 1867; for his old friend Fitz-Greene Halleck in 1868; for John David Wolfe, the wealthy hardware merchant and staunch fellow Episcopalian; and for Henry T. Tuckerman, the literary man, in 1872.

In 1858 Harpers brought out Duyckinck's American edition of Robert Aris Willmott's successful anthology, *The Poets of the Nineteenth Century*. Duyckinck added some 200 pages of new English and American works to Willmott's original 400 pages. And in 1861 Duyckinck began a mutually advantageous connection with another New York publisher, Johnson, Fry and Company (later Johnson, Wilson and Company). Between 1861 and 1865 Duyckinck composed a *National History of the War for the Union: Civil, Military, and Naval: Founded on the Official and Other Authentic Documents,* which was published in three handsome, royal octavo, double-column volumes, as were all the books in the Johnson, Fry and Johnson, Wilson series. Totaling more than 1,900 pages, the *National History of the War for the Union* is a chronologically arranged account of the Civil War that offers detailed accounts of battles and political maneuvers and is handsomely and effectively decorated with steel engravings from original paintings by Alonzo Chappel and Thomas Nast. While these three volumes were in progress, Duyckinck completed another two volumes, *National Portrait Gallery of Eminent Americans: Including Orators, Statesmen, Naval and Military Heroes, Jurists, Authors . . .* (1862), totaling more than 900 pages. The focus in this work is on statesmen and politicians from the Revolution to the period of his lifetime. Perhaps because he personally shared the patriotism that was sweeping the North, his biographical sketches are remarkably optimistic and uncritical. The student of the Young America group's radical assessment of the Mexican War and of the activities of public figures such as James K. Polk, Zachary Taylor, and Winfield Scott would do well to consider Duyckinck's almost fulsome praise for it and them here and in the *Lives and Portraits of the Presidents,* published a decade later.

In 1865 he edited and wrote a twenty-one-page introduction (in part quoted from the *Cyclopædia of American Literature* essay) for *Poems Relating to the American Revolution* by Philip Freneau. A handsome volume, it employs old-fashioned typefaces even in its introduction. From 1869 to 1871 the four-volume *History of the World: From the Earliest Period to the Present Time* appeared. Composed of more than 2,500 pages, it is based on the *Encyclopaedia*

Britannica and the work of J. A. Spencer; Duyckinck collected and arranged the materials, and the volumes boast another series of high-quality steel engravings. Alonzo Chappel and others supplied designs; Chappel also worked on *Lives and Portraits of the Presidents of the United States from Washington to Grant* (1873), which included biographies of all eighteen presidents to that time, as well as the texts of the U.S. Constitution and George Washington's "Farewell Address," and a facsimile of the Declaration of Independence. Complementing this volume in the same year, and completing this series of books designed for a popular market, was the *Portrait Gallery of Eminent Men and Women of Europe and America: Embracing History, Statesmanship, Naval and Military Life, Philosophy, the Drama, Science, Literature and Art, with Biographies* (1873), which in its two volumes offered a wide range of biographical sketches. Like the others in the series these volumes offered exquisite engravings.

Duyckinck was a knowledgeable and discriminating judge and collector of graphics. He had early in his youth cultivated artistic taste and so was comfortable in the expanding world of book illustration. In 1873, shortly before he became incapacitated by his final, lingering illness, he wrote a witty, appreciative introduction to a limited edition of fifty copies of *Illustrations of Mother Goose's Melodies: Designed and Engraved on Wood by Alexander Alderson, M.D.;* Alderson was one of the most skilled craftsmen of the period. In the posthumously published *Brief Catalogue of Books Illustrated with Engravings by Dr. Alexander Alderson* (1885), printed in an edition of one hundred copies, there is an enthusiastic biographical sketch, probably written by Duyckinck, accompanying an authoritative listing of the work of this Alderson, which, according to a note by Benson Lossing, Duyckinck compiled. The last book published in Duyckinck's lifetime in which he had a hand was another limited edition (sixty copies), privately printed in 1873 by master craftsman Charles L. Moreau—*Poems Hitherto Uncollected by the Rev. Francis Hawks.* Duyckinck wrote a two-page preface for the small volume.

In the year following his death in 1878, there appeared one hundred copies of *Fitz-Greene Halleck: A Description of the Dedication of the Monument Erected to his Memory at Guilford, Connecticut; And of the Proceedings Connected with the Unveiling of the Poet's Statue in the Central Park, New York* (1877). It includes twenty-four illustrations, including portraits of Duyckinck, Whittier, Bryant, William Allen Butler (Duyckinck's memorialist), and Halleck.

Evert and George Duyckinck shared a lifelong interest in the literature of the English Renaissance, which culminated in respective editions of the works of William Shakespeare. George Duyckinck's one-volume edition was the most important literary labor he undertook on his own. For modern readers, it provides the best evidence of his abilities as a scholar; it shows the depth and range of his taste and judgment. Published sixteen years after his death by the Philadelphia firm of Porter and Coates, George Duyckinck's one-volume *The Complete Works of William Shakespeare* (1879) is based on the Collier Folio of 1632. (Evert Duyckinck used the 1623 Folio for the edition that he helped Bryant to develop.) The handsome royal octavo, double-column book includes a 10-page "History of the English Drama and Stage to the Time of Shakespeare"; twenty-one short chapters, totaling 50 pages, titled "The Life of William Shakespeare"; a transcription of Shakespeare's will; and introductory notes, covering 37 pages, on the plays as well as the poems. In addition, George Duyckinck prepared textual notes that are sprinkled throughout the 968 pages of the volume. Based principally on the work in J. Payne Collier's eight-volume edition of 1853, George Duyckinck's *The Complete Works of William Shakespeare* has not survived the test of time among Renaissance scholars. However, this fact does not diminish its value as a major document for the literary historian interested in its editor.

Almost a decade later, in 1888, when Evert Duyckinck prepared his three volumes of *The Complete Works of Shakespeare,* Bryant acknowledged his dependence on Duyckinck's expert knowledge in preparing the copy-text. Another set of royal octavo volumes with double columns, the first of the volumes offers a nine-page "Life of William Shakespeare" by Evert Duyckinck, as well as one hundred photogravure illustrations from "original designs" by Alonzo Chappel and by Felix O. C. Darley, whose connection with the Duyckincks went back at least to the days of *Yankee Doodle* under Foster.

If the latter twenty years of Evert Duyckinck's career were less creative, eventful, and productive of enduring work than the first twenty had been, they were no less industrious. He was not a creative writer, as the phrase is understood in the modern world; he published no fiction, no poetry, and no plays. He was an author of nonfiction prose, most of it critical, biographical, and historical, and an expert editor of books and periodicals. He will continue to enjoy a significant place in American literary history alongside his associates and friends such as Melville, Hawthorne, Bryant, Simms, and Poe. His manuscript diaries and letters assure him of such a position. And for those readers of Duyckinck who are willing to admit the importance of the critic and literary historian in the cultural heritage, he will endure as an even more important figure.

Biographies:

Obituary of the Late George L. Duyckinck (New York: General Protestant Episcopal Sunday School Union and Church Book Society, 1863);

William Allen Butler, *Evert Augustus Duyckinck: A Memorial Sketch* (New York: Trow's, 1879);

Samuel Osgood, *Evert Augustus Duyckinck, His Life, Writings, and Influence: A Memoir* (Boston: David Clapp, 1879);

Whitehead Cornell Duyckinck and John Cornell, *The Duyckinck and Allied Families* (New York: Tobias A. Wright, 1908).

References:

Charlene Avallone, "*Holden's Dollar Magazine*," in *American Literary Magazines: The Eighteenth and Nineteenth Centuries*, edited by Edward E. Chielens (New York: Greenwood Press, 1986), pp. 175–183;

Debra Brown, "*Arcturus*," in *American Literary Magazines*, edited by Chielens (New York: Greenwood Press, 1986), pp. 43–46;

Lorne Feinberg, "*Yankee Doodle*," in *American Humor Magazines and Comic Newspapers*, edited by David E. E. Sloane (New York: Greenwood Press, 1987), pp. 319–322;

Ezra Greenspan, "Evert Duyckinck and the History of Wiley and Putnam's Library of American Books," *American Literature*, 64 (December 1992): 677–693;

Robin Grey, *The Complicity of Imagination: The American Renaissance, Contests of Authority, and Seventeenth-Century English Culture* (Cambridge: Cambridge University Press, 1994), pp. 34–37;

George Edwin Mize, "The Contributions of Evert A. Duyckinck to the Cultural Development of Nineteenth-Century America," dissertation, New York University, 1954;

Larry Reynolds, *European Revolutions and the American Renaissance* (New Haven: Yale University Press, 1988);

Benjamin T. Spencer, *The Quest for Nationality: An American Literary Campaign* (Syracuse, N.Y.: Syracuse University Press, 1957);

John Stafford, *The Literary Criticism of "Young America": A Study in the Relationship of Politics and Literature, 1837–1850* (Berkeley: University of California Press, 1952);

Daniel A. Wells, "'Bartleby the Scrivener,' Poe, and the Duyckinck Circle," *ESQ: A Journal of the American Renaissance*, 21 (First Quarter 1975): 35–39;

Wells, "Evert Duyckinck's *Literary World*, 1847–1853: Its Views and Reviews of American Literature," dissertation, Duke University, 1972;

Wells, "An Index to American Writers and Selected British Writers in Duyckinck's *Literary World*, 1847–1853," *Studies in the American Renaissance 1978*, edited by Joel Myerson (Boston: Twayne, 1978), pp. 259–278;

Edward L. Widmer, *Young America: The Flowering of Democracy in New York City* (New York: Oxford University Press, 1999);

Donald Yannella, "*The Literary World*," in *American Literary Magazines*, edited by Chielens (New York: Greenwood Press, 1986), pp. 224–230;

Donald and Kathleen Malone Yannella, "Evert A. Duyckinck's Diary: May 29–November 8, 1847," in *Studies in the American Renaissance 1978*, edited by Myerson (Boston: Twayne, 1978), pp. 207–258.

Papers:

The letters, journals, and other papers of Evert A. Duyckinck and George L. Duyckinck are located in the Manuscripts Division of the New York Public Library.

Parke Godwin

(25 February 1816 – 7 January 1904)

Jonathan A. Cook
Northern Virginia Community College, Alexandria

See the Godwin entries in *DLB 3: Antebellum Writers in New York and the South* and *DLB 64: American Literary Critics and Scholars, 1850–1880.*

BOOKS: *Democracy, Constructive and Pacific* (New York: J. Winchester, 1844);

A Popular View of the Doctrines of Charles Fourier (New York: J. S. Redfield, 1844);

Vala: A Mythological Tale (New York: G. P. Putnam, 1851);

Political Essays (New York: Dix, Edwards, 1856);

A History of France (New York: Harper, 1860);

Out of the Past (New York: G. P. Putnam, 1870);

A Biography of William Cullen Bryant: With Extracts from his Private Correspondence, 2 volumes (New York: D. Appleton, 1883);

Commemorative Addresses: George William Curtis, Edwin Booth, Louis Kossuth, John James Audubon, William Cullen Bryant (New York: Harper, 1895);

A New Study of the Sonnets of Shakespeare (New York: G. P. Putnam, 1900).

OTHER: *Tales from the German of Heinrich Zschokke,* translated by Godwin, Fanny Godwin, Christopher P. Cranch, and Gustave C. Hebbe, edited by Godwin (New York: Wiley & Putnam, 1845);

The Autobiography of Goethe. Truth and Poetry: From My Life, 2 volumes, translated by Godwin, John H. Hopkins, Charles A. Dana, and John S. Dwight, edited by Godwin (New York: Wiley & Putnam, 1846, 1847);

Hand-Book of Universal Biography (New York: G. P. Putnam, 1852); republished as *Cyclopedia of Universal Biography: A Record of the Names of the Most Eminent Men of the World* (New York: A. S. Barnes, 1855); republished as *The Cyclopaedia of Biography: A Record of the Lives of Eminent Persons,* with a supplement, brought down to August 1877 (New York: G. P. Putnam, 1878);

Parke Godwin

The Poetical Works of William Cullen Bryant, 2 volumes, edited by Godwin (New York: D. Appleton, 1883);

The Prose Works of William Cullen Bryant, 2 volumes, edited by Godwin (New York: D. Appleton, 1884).

PERIODICALS EDITED: *Pathfinder* (25 February 1843 – 3 June 1843);

Harbinger (November 1847 – February 1849);

142

Putnam's Monthly Magazine (January 1853 – October 1857);

Putnam's Magazine (April–November 1870);

New York Evening Post (1878–1881).

Journalist, editor, and man of letters, Parke Godwin played a key role in many economic, social, and political reform movements in nineteenth-century America, from the Age of Andrew Jackson to Reconstruction. As a contributor or editor affiliated with such influential publications as *The New York Evening Post,* the *United States Magazine and Democratic Review,* and *Putnam's Monthly Magazine,* Godwin sought to formulate a new social compact for the nation amid the dramatic socio-economic changes of the antebellum era. In the 1840s, in response to the severe depression following the Panic of 1837, he was one of the leading advocates of "utopian" socialism based on the writings of the French theorist Charles Fourier. In the 1850s, like many Northern intellectuals, Godwin allied himself with the antislavery cause, eventually playing a significant role in the creation of the Republican Party and the election of Abraham Lincoln. During the Civil War, Godwin served as an influential editor at *The New York Evening Post* and in that capacity continued as a critic of Reconstruction. Throughout his life Godwin played the role of engaged intellectual while seeking to influence the shaping of opinion on both the regional and national levels. Finally, Godwin was also an accomplished man of letters and student of European Romanticism, who eventually produced several volumes of literary, historical, and biographical studies, including a translation of Johann Wolfgang von Goethe's autobiography and a standard life of his famous father-in-law, poet and newspaper editor William Cullen Bryant.

Parke Godwin was born 25 February 1816 in Paterson, New Jersey, the son of Abraham Godwin, a dry goods merchant and small-scale manufacturer who had served as an officer in the War of 1812 and filled a seat in the state assembly, and Martha Parke Godwin, who was of Dutch descent. After attending an academy in Kinderhook, New York, Godwin entered Princeton College in the early 1830s, where he was strongly influenced by his study of French and American Enlightenment writers, whose belief in progress and social justice he made his own; he was also a devoted student of European, and especially German, Romanticism. A sincere Christian, though without denominational affiliation, Godwin, after graduating in 1834 from Princeton, vacillated between the ministry and the law as a profession. He read law in Paterson and went to Kentucky, where he passed the bar and intended to practice law. Before he began his practice, however, he left Kentucky and returned to Princeton, where he studied divinity

for a few months in late 1835 and early 1836. He arrived in New York City the latter part of 1836 with the intention of starting a law practice. Encountering William Cullen Bryant at the boardinghouse where he was lodging, Godwin was invited by the well-known Democratic editor to take a position on *The New York Evening Post.* Thus began a long-term, occasionally turbulent, professional relationship—the two were not personally close—that was consolidated by Godwin's marriage to Bryant's daughter Fanny on 12 May 1842. (The couple eventually had a total of eight children.) The other key event of Godwin's early New York years was the Panic of 1837, which threw thousands out of work and initiated a severe national depression for the next six years—a socio-economic debacle that shaped Godwin's thought for some time to come.

At *The Post,* Godwin showed his Locofoco Democratic credentials by attacking the Whigs as the party of privilege while decrying the operation of machine politics within both parties; he thus continued a role on the paper earlier assumed by the late Jacksonian radical William Leggett. After Godwin served a stint in Washington, D.C., Bryant offered him a partnership in *The Post* in 1840 and put him in charge of foreign correspondence. During this period Godwin was also immersing himself in various contemporary intellectual currents and causes, such as Chartism, Utilitarianism, Swedenborgianism, and legal reform. Uniting his interests was an attempt to develop a new "science of society" based on secularized Christian norms of cooperation in industry and government. Such a radical program was designed to correct the recent breakdown of the economy, which had put a third of New York workingmen out of jobs and a third on reduced wages. (The search for a new socio-economic system in the 1830s and 1840s that preoccupied Godwin and other reformers was comparable to a similar quest among intellectuals a century later during the Great Depression.) As a promising young New York journalist, Godwin started writing for John L. O'Sullivan's *United States Magazine and Democratic Review* in 1839, contributing half a dozen articles on various subjects, including legal reform (for example, "Jeremy Bentham and Law Reform") and contemporary literature (for example, "Percy Bysshe Shelley"). His articles on legal reform in that publication and elsewhere were credited with aiding the movement to modernize the legal code of the state of New York, ridding it of some of the archaisms of the common law. In the early 1840s, Godwin also befriended other prominent reformers and men of letters, such as George Ripley, Charles A. Dana, and William Henry Channing (nephew of the great Boston Unitarian, William Ellery Channing), all of whom were currently immersed in the new theories of "association" pio-

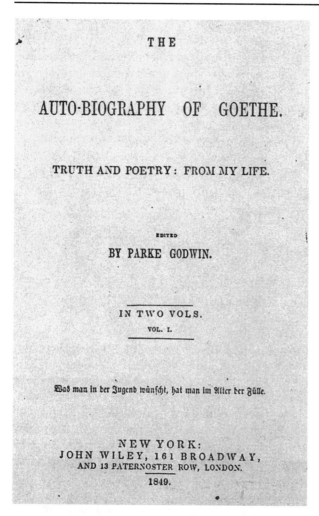

THE

AUTO-BIOGRAPHY OF GOETHE.

TRUTH AND POETRY: FROM MY LIFE.

EDITED

BY PARKE GODWIN.

IN TWO VOLS.

VOL. I.

Was man in der Jugend wünscht, hat man im Alter der Fülle.

NEW YORK:
JOHN WILEY, 161 BROADWAY,
AND 13 PATERNOSTER ROW, LONDON.
1849.

Title page for the edition of the German work that Godwin translated with John H. Hopkins, Charles A. Dana, and John S. Dwight (Thomas Cooper Library, University of South Carolina)

neered by Charles Fourier. Ripley and Dana were engaged in running the new Brook Farm community in West Roxbury, Massachusetts, the "transcendental" utopia started in 1841 that switched to a Fourierist plan of operation three years later before expiring in 1847. (Godwin wanted to join the Brook Farm experiment but domestic obligations kept him from doing so.) Channing was a Unitarian minister of Christian socialist persuasion and editor of the reformist journal *The Present,* to which Godwin contributed.

By 1843 Godwin was an enthusiastic convert to the ideas of Fourier, which had first been introduced to America by Albert Brisbane in *The Social Destiny of Man* (1840). One of the leading socialist thinkers of his era, Fourier had developed the concept of a "phalanx," or small township, of about 1,600 individuals or 400 families living in a large communal residence or "phalanstery" and engaged in "attractive industry." He planned that members would voluntarily join various "groups and series" and be assigned to labor at several tasks for differing lengths of time, with varying degrees of compensation–depending on their capital investment, the nature of their work, and their native talent–but with the guarantee of a basic subsistence for all. The system was, in effect, a form of cooperative capitalism intended to meet the needs of all classes. According to Fourier, individuals had a complex array of temperamental qualities and "passions"–there were exactly a dozen passions and 810 personality types in Fourier's complex system–that required expression in both constantly varied work and in a restructured social life. The ultimate goal was a condition of universal "harmony" based on social cooperation and individual enjoyment. The more sexually daring, "free love" aspect of Fourier's thought was downplayed in American expositions of his work, which emphasized the socio-economic benefits of his system.

Godwin started his own Fourierist journal, *The Pathfinder,* in February 1843, borrowing the title from James Fenimore Cooper's recent novel of the same name; the magazine lasted for only three months. The culmination of Godwin's intellectual engagement with Fourier was the two short books he published in 1844, *Democracy, Constructive and Pacific* and *A Popular View of the Doctrines of Charles Fourier.* The former was an attack on the economic inequality of contemporary America, while the latter offered a progressive "utopian" solution to this inequality. In *Democracy, Constructive and Pacific* Godwin argued that the great revolutions of the previous century that had ushered in an age of *political* equality had so far failed to bring about the necessary *economic* equality; indeed, the advent of free trade (laissez-faire) and unbridled competition had only resulted in growing income disparities between rich and poor. "Theoretically, constitutionally, legally," Godwin noted, "there are no privileged classes in this nation; the odious laws of caste are annulled. But, practically, positively, really, we still live under a regime of caste, we are still governed by classes, all our social helps and appliances are still distinguishing, partial and confined to the few." The remedy, as outlined in *A Popular View of the Doctrines of Charles Fourier,* was Fourier's detailed plan of association, in which class differences would be overcome and the organization of labor regulated by individual preference. Godwin's exposition of Fourier's ideas gave a concise overview of the Frenchman's scheme of reform, which was ultimately grounded in Enlightenment rationalism and optimism: "In the society to be discovered, Reason and Passion will be in perfect accord; duty and pleasure will have the same meaning; without inconvenience or calculation, man will follow his bent; hearing only of Attraction, he will never act from necessity and never curb himself by restraints; and, consequently, he will find a charm in all his functions."

Unlike Horace Greeley's openness to Brisbane's promotion of Fourierism in the *New York Tribune,* in which Brisbane had a regular column starting in 1842, Bryant closed *The Post* to Godwin's campaign for Fourier, an action that led to Godwin's selling his share in the newspaper in 1844. Godwin wrote tracts for the Polk campaign of that year and was rewarded after the Democratic victory with a position as collector in the New York Custom House, a sinecure he held until the change of administration four years later. The mid 1840s represented the peak era of Godwin's agitation on behalf of Fourierism, involving a concerted attempt to enlist the working classes in the cause of Association. In 1844 he gave the keynote address at a general convention of socialists at Clinton Hall in New York, and the next year he was involved in founding a new organization, the American Union of Associationists, along with Brisbane (whom he personally disliked). Godwin was actively engaged in lecturing to various trade union groups at this time while promoting the reputation of Brook Farm and other contemporary experimental phalanxes. The Fourierist cause was also being popularized by the official journal of the movement, *The Phalanx,* started by Brisbane in New York in 1843; renamed *The Harbinger* two years later (the French noun *fourrier* means, among other things, "harbinger"), the weekly journal moved to Brook Farm, with Godwin serving as a contributing editor along with Ripley, Dana, and John S. Dwight.

Yet, despite the efflorescence of ultimately short-lived Fourierist communities across the country in the mid 1840s, Godwin was increasingly disappointed by the failure of the working classes in general to support the cause of Association, in part because the movement advocated gender equality, which in turn was a potential challenge to the traditional family structure. (Evangelicals, too, such as Henry Ward Beecher, attacked the movement for this reason.) In November 1847 *The Harbinger* was moved back to New York under Godwin's editorship, assisted by Ripley and Dana, but it folded two years later just as he lost his customhouse appointment. By this time the campaign for social and industrial reform in the North was being overtaken by the slavery crisis, while the return of national prosperity in the later 1840s, however unequal in its benefits, favored the acceptance of the economic status quo. In the meantime, the working-class movement promoted cheap western lands for homesteading and largely ignored Associationism.

Along with his varied political writings and activities in the 1840s, Godwin also functioned as a man of letters, chiefly in connection with his interest

THE

HISTORY OF FRANCE.

BY

PARKE GODWIN.

VOL. I.

(ANCIENT GAUL.)

NEW YORK:
HARPER & BROTHERS, PUBLISHERS,
FRANKLIN SQUARE.
1860.

Title page for the only volume of work Godwin published in the 1860s

in German literature, which he shared with his Brook Farm friends. He prepared an English edition of the tales of the popular Swiss-German writer Heinrich Zschokke, which appeared in 1845, with translations by Godwin, his wife, Christopher P. Cranch, and Gustave C. Hebbe. The next year Godwin served as the editor and one of four translators (along with John H. Hopkins, Dana, and Dwight) of *The Autobiography of Goethe. Truth and Poetry: From My Life* (1846, 1847). A projected book on Emanuel Swedenborg, Fourier, and Goethe, on the other hand, to be called "Teachers of the Nineteenth Century," was never finished. A lover of vocal music and opera, Godwin also produced a one-hundred-page illustrated "fairy tale" version of the life of Jenny Lind, the "Swedish nightingale," titled *Vala: A Mythological Tale* (1851).

Unlike the New England reformers with whom he was affiliated, Godwin was an advocate of "manifest destiny" and so supported the Mexican War of

OUT OF THE PAST:

(CRITICAL AND LITERARY PAPERS.)

BY

PARKE GODWIN.

NEW YORK:
G. P. PUTNAM & SONS.
1870.

Title page for the collection of essays Godwin wrote for Putnam's Monthly *and the* Democratic Review

1846–1848; he saw the acquisition of Texas and other western territory as a safety valve for white workers. Indeed, like other contemporary Democratic liberals, such as O'Sullivan and Walt Whitman, he favored peaceful American expansion, thereby spreading republican institutions throughout North America and possibly the rest of the hemisphere. As the advocate of the working classes in the North, moreover, Godwin opposed the abolitionism of New Englanders such as William Lloyd Garrison, considering it a diversion from the task of improving the lot of white workers. In his view, abolitionists were guilty of simplistic moralism that lacked any practical vision of how to free the slaves. Frustrated by the growing shift of interest among his fellow reformers, Godwin by the later 1840s was turning his attention to political developments in Europe, especially in the wake of the revolutions of 1848 that temporarily displaced various monarchical regimes across the Continent.

As part of his interest in European political developments in the late 1840s and early 1850s, Godwin supported the "national workshops" of Louis Blanc in France, as well as the cause of Hungarian independence promoted by the charismatic Louis Kossuth, whom Godwin met in New York during Kossuth's visit to the United States in search of political support. In 1852 Godwin made an extended trip to Europe, his first visit to the Old World. Among his experiences abroad, he noted the evidence of class division in England, discussed the volatile political situation in France with Pierre-Joseph Proudhon (who predicted another pan-European revolution), and was harassed by the police in Vienna. In general, he found Europe to be marked by political autocracy and cultural decadence, but he discovered a kindred spirit in Proudhon.

On his return to New York from Europe, Godwin was named political editor of the new *Putnam's Monthly* along with Charles F. Briggs and George William Curtis as editors; the new journal promised to publish the best in current American essay writing and fiction. Godwin produced many articles for *Putnam's Monthly* on various subjects but was best known for the Free-Soil Party political commentary he contributed to the magazine. By the early 1850s Godwin had become an advocate of Northern antislavery, attacking Presidents Zachary Taylor and Millard Fillmore as puppets of the South in *The Post,* for which he had resumed writing by 1850. Like many other Northern liberals, however, Godwin's full-scale commitment to antislavery occurred with the passage of the Kansas-Nebraska Act in 1854, which stimulated him to produce several outspoken attacks in *Putnam's Monthly* on the retrograde politics of the era, with its intolerable threat to Western free soil. For Godwin, as for many others at this point, the overriding issue was the containment, not the abolition, of slavery. He also criticized the current Know-Nothing Party, which arose in opposition to the dramatic increase in foreign immigration, especially from Ireland and Germany. Active in founding the new Republican Party in 1856, Godwin contributed to the party platform at its first convention, helping to identify the new party with the cause of reform. (He also probably gave its unsuccessful candidate, John Charles Frémont, his moniker of "pathfinder.") That same year a selection of Godwin's essays from *Putnam's Monthly* was published under the title *Political Essays,* but the magazine itself folded in 1857, and Godwin was subsequently asked to be a contributing editor to the new *Atlantic Monthly,* a position he soon relinquished because of editorial conflicts with James Russell Lowell.

Among Godwin's contributions to *Putnam's Monthly* during its five-year life were several substantial essays—"American Authorship," "Comte's Philosophy," "Strauss's *Life of Jesus*," "Thackeray the Novelist," "Goethe," "Ruskin's Writings," "Causes of the French Revolution," "Motley's Rise of the Dutch Republic," and "Emerson on England"—all of which demonstrated the writer's broad range and versatility as a critic, on a par with the best of contemporary English reviewers. These and several earlier articles for the *Democratic Review* later appeared in another collection of reprinted magazine pieces, *Out of the Past* (1870). Godwin was also busy in the later 1850s composing a history of France, but he published only one volume—on ancient Gaul, ending in the tenth century—in 1860. At this time, too, Godwin unsuccessfully sought a professorship of history and political economy at Columbia College. By the end of the decade he returned to working full-time for *The Post,* becoming a one-third owner in 1860 and thereafter making a substantial profit from this large-circulation daily.

Actively promoting the election of Lincoln, Godwin hoped for a government job from the new administration but was opposed by the old-Whig faction in the Republican Party, led by William Henry Seward. During the Civil War, Godwin was a stalwart supporter of the Union, using *The Post* to rally Northerners to the cause and attacking copperhead sentiment and organizations. He also criticized Lincoln's failure to declare the slaves free during the early stages of the war; now fully committed to abolition, Godwin advocated the use of black troops in the Union army. In February 1862 he met personally with the president to promote emancipation and was assured that as soon as the Union army controlled more territory, Lincoln would declare the slaves free. (After the Battle of Antietam in September 1862, Lincoln set January 1863 as the date for his official Emancipation Proclamation.) Although Godwin supported the Union, he criticized administration policy and published details of the Northern war effort; he in turn was criticized by the government for the disclosure of data on Union army activities.

Following the Civil War and with the advent of the Gilded Age, Godwin entered a new phase of reform activity, attacking the machinations of the "Tweed Ring" in New York City and developing into a strong critic of the Republican Party. In the latter role he formed the Independent Republican Association in 1872 in opposition to Ulysses S. Grant, and opposed the election of Rutherford Hayes four years later. With the death of William Cullen Bryant in 1878, Godwin became managing editor of *The Post,* but he sold the

paper three years later to the German-born financier and former journalist, Henry Villard, who installed a new set of editors, including Carl Schurz and E. L. Godkin. In a dedicated act of filial piety, Godwin went on to produce complete editions of his father-in-law's prose and poetry, along with a two-volume biography that remains a comprehensive, gracefully written "life and letters" of the poet-journalist. In 1895 Godwin also issued a volume of *Commemorative Addresses* on notable friends and contemporaries—Curtis, Edwin Booth, Kossuth, Audubon, and Bryant—and in 1900, the year of his final retirement, a study of William Shakespeare's sonnets. Parke Godwin died in New York City in 1904, a lone survivor from a distinguished generation of antebellum reformers. Little known today, Godwin deserves a further study highlighting the significant part he played in several phases of nineteenth-century progressive politics and culture.

Biographies:

Carlos Baker, "Parke Godwin, Pathfinder in Politics and Journalism," in *The Lives of Eighteen from Princeton,* edited by Willard Thorp (Princeton: Princeton University Press, 1946);

John R. Wennersten, "A Reformer's Odyssey: The Public Career of Parke Godwin of the New York *Evening Post,*" dissertation, University of Maryland, 1969.

References:

Carl Guarneri, *The Utopian Alternative: Fourierism in Nineteenth-Century America* (Ithaca, N.Y.: Cornell University Press, 1991);

John P. Hoskins, "Parke Godwin and the Translation of Zschokke's Tales," *PMLA,* 20 (1905): 265–295;

Edward K. Spann, *Ideals and Politics: New York Intellectuals and Liberal Democracy, 1820–1880* (Albany: State University of New York Press, 1972);

John R. Wennersten, "Parke Godwin, Utopian Socialism, and the Politics of Antislavery," *New York Historical Society Quarterly,* 60 (July/October 1976): 107–127.

Papers:

Parke Godwin's papers are in the Goddard-Roslyn Collection (microfilm); the Bryant-Godwin Papers, New York Public Library; and the Parke Godwin Papers, Princeton University.

Horace Greeley

(3 February 1811 – 29 November 1872)

Jo Ann Manfra
Worcester Polytechnic Institute

See also the Greeley entries in *DLB 3: Antebellum Writers in New York and the South; DLB 43: American Newspaper Journalists, 1690–1872;* and *DLB 189: American Travel Writers, 1850–1915.*

BOOKS: *An Address before the Literary Societies of Hamilton College, July 23, 1844* (Boston: Andrews Prentiss & Studley, 1844);

Protection and Free Trade: The Question Stated and Considered (New York: Greeley & McElrath, 1844);

The Tariff as It Is, Compared with the Substitute Proposed by Its Adversaries in the Bill Reported to the U.S. House of Representatives by Gen. McKay of N. C. from the Committee of Ways and Means (New York: Greeley & McElrath, 1844);

Association Discussed; or, The Socialism of the Tribune Examined. Being a Controversy between the New York Tribune and the Courier and Enquirer, by Greeley and H. J. Raymond (New York: Harper, 1847);

Alcoholic Liquors: Their Essential Nature and Necessary Effects on the Human Constitution (New York: Brognard, 1849);

Hints toward Reforms: in Lectures, Addresses, and Other Writings (New York: Harper, 1850; enlarged edition, New York & London: Fowlers & Wells, 1853)– includes "Alcoholic Liquors" and "The Crystal Palace and Its Lessons";

Glances at Europe: In a Series of Letters from Great Britain, France, Italy, Switzerland, &c., during the Summer of 1851. Including Notices of the Great Exhibition, or World's Fair (New York: Dewitt & Davenport, 1851);

The Crystal Palace and Its Lessons: A Lecture by Horace Greeley (New York: Tribune Office, 1852);

Why I Am a Whig: Reply to an Inquiring Friend (New York: Tribune Office, 1852);

What the Sister Arts Teach as to Farming. An Address before the Indiana State Agricultural Society, at Its Annual Fair, Lafayette, October 13th, 1853 (New York: Fowlers & Wells, 1853);

Horace Greeley

A History of the Struggle for Slavery Extension or Restriction in the United States, from the Declaration of Independence to the Present Day. Mainly Compiled and Condensed from the Journals of Congress and Other Official Records, and Showing the Vote by Yeas and Nays on the Most Important Divisions in Either House (New York: Dix, Edwards, 1856);

The Tariff Question (New York, 1856);

Aunt Sally, Come Up! or, The Nigger Sale (London: Ward & Lock, 1859);

Divorce: Being a Correspondence between Horace Greeley and Robert Dale Owen (New York: R. M. Dewitt, 1860);

An Overland Journey, from New York to San Francisco, in the Summer of 1859 (New York: Saxton, Barker / San Francisco: Bancroft, 1860);

The American Conflict: A History of the Great Rebellion 1860–65; Its Causes, Incidents, and Results: Intended to Exhibit Especially Its Moral and Political Phases, with the Drift and Progress of American Opinion Respecting Human Slavery from 1776 to the Close of the War for the Union, 2 volumes (Hartford: O. D. Case / Chicago: G. & C. W. Sherwood, 1864, 1866);

An Address on Success in Business, Delivered before the Students of Packard's Bryant & Stratton New York Business College, by Hon. Horace Greeley, at the Large Hall of the Cooper Union, November 11, 1867 (New York: S. S. Packard, 1867);

Recollections of a Busy Life: Including Reminiscences of American Politics and Politicians, from the Opening of the Missouri Contest to the Downfall of Slavery; To Which Are Added Miscellanies: "Literature as a Vocation," "Poets and Poetry," "Reforms and Reformers," "A Defense of Protection," etc., etc., Also, A Discussion with Robert Dale Owen of the Law of Divorce (New York: J. B. Ford, 1868);

Essays Designed to Elucidate the Science of Political Economy, while Serving to Explain and Defend the Policy of Protection to Home Industry, as a System of National Cooperation for the Elevation of Labor (Philadelphia: Porter & Coates, 1869);

What I Know of Farming: A Series of Brief and Plain Expositions of Practical Agriculture as an Art Based upon Science (New York: C. W. Carleton, 1871);

Mr. Greeley's Letters from Texas and the Lower Mississippi: To Which Are Added His Address to the Farmers of Texas, and His Speech on His Return to New York, June 12, 1871 (New York: Tribune Office, 1871);

The True Issues of the Presidential Campaign. Speeches of Horace Greeley during His Western Trip and at Portland, Maine (New York: Tribune Office, 1872).

OTHER: William Atkinson, *Principles of Political Economy; or, The Laws of the Formation of National Wealth,* with an introduction by Greeley (New York: Greeley & McElrath, 1843);

The American Laborer, edited by Greeley (New York: Greeley & McElrath, 1843);

The Writings of Cassius Marcellus Clay, edited by Greeley (New York: Harper, 1848);

Epes Sargent, *The Life and Public Services of Henry Clay,* edited and completed by Greeley (Auburn, N.Y.: Derby & Miller, 1852);

Margaret Fuller, *Literature and Art,* introduction by Greeley (Philadelphia: Porter & Coates, 1852);

Art and Industry as Represented in the Exhibition at the Crystal Palace, New York–1853–4, edited by Greeley (New York: Redfield, 1853);

Margaret Fuller Ossoli, *Woman in the Nineteenth Century,* and *Kindred Papers,* edited by Arthur B. Fuller, with an introduction by Greeley (Boston: John P. Jewett, 1855);

A History of the Struggle for Slavery Extension or Restriction in the United States, compiled and edited by Greeley (New York: Dix, Edwards, 1856);

A Political Text-Book for 1860: Comprising a Brief View of Presidential Nominations and Elections, compiled and edited by Greeley and John F. Cleveland (New York: Tribune Association, 1860);

The Tribune Almanac for the Years 1838 to 1868, Inclusive, edited by Greeley (New York: New York Tribune, 1868);

Charles T. Congdon, ed., *Tribune Essays: Leading Articles Contributed to the New York Tribune, 1857–63,* introduction by Greeley (New York: Redfield, 1869).

SELECTED PERIODICAL PUBLICATIONS–UNCOLLECTED: "Our Country," *New-Yorker,* 15 October 1836, p. 57;

"Education," *Jeffersonian,* 10 November 1838;

"The Law of Organic Changes in Popular Governments," *New-York Weekly Tribune,* 28 May 1842, pp. 305–306;

"The Suffrage Question," *New-York Daily Tribune,* 2 June 1846, p. [2];

"River and Harbor Improvements," *DeBow's Review,* 4 (November 1847): 291–296;

"A Lesson for Young Poets," *New-York Daily Tribune,* 25 May 1848, p. [2];

"Concession–Compromise," *New-York Daily Tribune,* 20 February 1850, p. [2];

"Why Have a Tariff?" *New-York Daily Tribune,* 23 June 1851, p. 4;

"Is It a Fraud?" *New-York Daily Tribune,* 15 February 1854, p. 4;

"Commissioner Loring and the Fugitive Law," *New-York Daily Tribune,* 6 June 1854, p. 4;

"After the Battle," *New-York Daily Tribune,* 9 November 1854, p. 4;

[Dred Scott Case], *New-York Daily Tribune,* 7 March 1857, p. 4;

"Going to Go," *New-York Daily Tribune,* 9 November 1860, p. 4;

"Secession in Practice," *New-York Daily Tribune,* 16 November 1860, p. 4;

"The American Experiment," *New-York Daily Tribune,* 27 November 1860, p. 4;

Greeley's birthplace in Amherst, New Hampshire

"The Southern Grievance," *New-York Daily Tribune,* 28 November 1860, p. 4;

"Christianity and Color," *Douglass' Monthly,* 3 (November 1860): 366;

"The Question of the Day," *New-York Daily Tribune,* 11 December 1861, p. 4;

"The Proclamation of Freedom," *New-York Daily Tribune,* 24 September 1862, p. 4;

"Will There be Peace?" *New-York Daily Tribune,* 6 December 1862, p. 4;

"The Day," *New-York Daily Tribune,* 4 July 1863, p. 4;

"Opening the Presidential Canvass for 1864," *New-York Daily Tribune,* 23 February 1864, p. 4;

"Magnanimity in Triumph," *New-York Daily Tribune,* 11 April 1865, p. 4;

"The True Bases of Reconstruction," *New-York Daily Tribune,* 27 November 1866, p. 4;

"The Latest Phase of Reconstruction," *New-York Daily Tribune,* 14 January 1867, p. 4;

"The Fruits of the War," *Galaxy,* 4 (July 1867): 364–366;

"Journalism and Justice," *New-York Daily Tribune,* 6 May 1871, p. 4;

"Official Notice to Mr. Greeley of the Liberal Republican Nomination," *New-York Daily Tribune,* 22 May 1872, p. 4.

PERIODICALS EDITED: *New-Yorker* (26 March 1836–11 September 1841);
Jeffersonian (17 February 1838–9 February 1839);
Log Cabin (2 May 1840–20 November 1841);
New-York Tribune (10 April 1841–29 November 1872);
Clay Tribune (4 May 1844–2 November 1844).

From the Jacksonian Era to Reconstruction, Horace Greeley was the most famous journalist in the United States—the first newspaperman nominated for president of the United States by a major political party. For more than three decades Greeley managed the *New-York Daily Tribune.* Under his direction the weekly edition of the newspaper attracted a national readership, becoming the most widely influential periodical in the United States in the mid nineteenth century. While not the originator of modern urban journalism, Greeley was among its most brilliant practitioners. For example, his two-hour interrogation of Brigham Young in 1859 is considered to have been the first important "media interview" in history. More significantly, Greeley's hundreds of lectures, editorials, articles, essays, pamphlets, and published letters, together with his several books, made him a powerful and prestigious mid-nineteenth-century opinion leader. Although his ill-fated campaign for the White House late in life tarnished his legacy to some extent, Greeley remains an important historical and literary figure. Even those who may not recognize his name will remember the legendary advice he popularized: "Go West, young man, go West," though it was originally said by John Soule, an Indiana editor.

The dedication to "Our American Boys" that prefaces Greeley's autobiography seems designed in part as a summary description of his own early life: "born in poverty, cradled in obscurity, and early called from school to rugged labor." But that is rags-to-riches romanticism. Born on the family farm near Amherst, New Hampshire, on 3 February 1811, Horace was the eldest of five surviving children of Zaccheus and Mary Woodburn Greeley. The feckless Zaccheus Greeley, at the time of Horace's birth, was poor only in the sense that he had a farm mortgage to pay off. Although the family was obscure, it was hardly anonymous: it enjoyed strong kinship ties within the Scots-Irish community of south-central New Hampshire. Mary Greeley, a vigorous reader, imparted a love of books to her precocious son, whose maternal grandfather entered him in school at the age of four. In 1820, when Horace was nine, the local sheriff seized the farm to satisfy financial obligations unwisely incurred by Zaccheus Greeley, who fled the neighborhood to escape debtor's prison. The family reassembled on a hardscrabble tract in western Vermont. "We had been farmers of the poorer class in New Hampshire; we took rank with day-laborers in Vermont," Greeley recalled in *Recollections of a Busy Life: Including Reminiscences of American Politics and Politicians, from the Opening of the Missouri Contest to the Downfall of Slavery; To Which Are Added Miscellanies: "Literature as a Vocation," "Poets and Poetry," "Reforms and Reformers," "A Defense of Protection," etc., etc., Also, A Discussion with Robert Dale Owen of the Law of Divorce* (1868). In 1826, when the discouraged Greeleys moved once again, this time to northwestern Pennsylvania, young Horace stayed behind, apprenticed to a newspaper editor in the village of East Poultney.

When the newspaper failed in 1830, Greeley rejoined his family and worked briefly for another newspaper in Erie before that job, too, petered out. By then, however, Greeley was a seasoned journeyman printer with editorial ambitions, as well as a monumental confidence in his own genius and erudition that sustained him the rest of his life. In August 1831, with $25 in his pocket, he set out to seek his fortune in New York City. There he found work as a compositor, and in early 1833 he formed a partnership in a printing business that prospered after the partners secured a portion of the New York State lottery printing contract. Greeley and his partner also collaborated with a would-be editor in innovating a cheap, for-cash daily newspaper, the *New-York Morning Post,* the first "in New York," Greeley remembered proudly in *Recollections of a Busy Life,* "–perhaps in the world." But, seriously undercapitalized, it quickly died.

Others, however, had the same idea. Later in 1833, editor Benjamin H. Day brought out *The New York Sun,* which featured two innovations. First, unsatisfied with subscription sales, Day sent newsboys into the streets to hawk daily editions of *The Sun* for a penny, in contrast to the usual higher price. Second, Day shifted the content of the paper from the typical emphasis on "commercial intelligence" to coverage of everyday life in the city. Within a few years *The New York Sun* had become the "penny press" model for urban newspapers everywhere.

Meanwhile, Greeley had convinced his partner that with the lottery contract as a backup they should reenter the crowded field of Manhattan journalism, this time less ambitiously, by publishing a weekly with Greeley as manager. *The New-Yorker,* billing itself as a journal of literature and news, made its appearance as a four-page (later sixteen-page) weekly in 1836. Its editor, seeking readers among the literate urban artisan class, priced it cheaply at $2.00 a year for a subscription. Poetry, essays, and book reviews occupied its front and back pages, with advertisements and nonpartisan political news filling its inside sheets. The newspaper, although not a moneymaker, enjoyed a successful circulation almost from the start.

James Gordon Bennett's *New York Herald,* founded as a daily in 1835, took Day's editorial reformation a step further by inaugurating what is today known as tabloid journalism, a forthright sensationalism in which violent death and scandal proved to be daily staples. Day's *Sun* and Bennett's *Herald* were edited with a pronounced, if unacknowledged, Democratic Party bias. Soon Greeley, a deeply committed Whig, whose self-imposed nonpartisan stance in *The New-Yorker* was proving to be ideologically unbearable, was talking of countering Day and Bennett with a penny Whig paper. Three circumstances collaborated in pushing him toward that goal.

Greeley as a young man

The foremost impetus for Greeley in starting a Whig paper was the need to support his family. On 5 July 1836 he married Mary Youngs "Molly" Cheney, aged twenty-two, a transplanted schoolteacher from Connecticut. The couple eventually had five children—Arthur Youngs, born in 1844; Mary Inez, 1846; Ida Lillian, 1848; Ralph Uhland, 1851; and Gabrielle, 1857. (Only Ida and Gabrielle survived into adulthood.) The Panic of 1837 was another stimulus to Greeley's journalistic redirection; the panic caused *The New-Yorker* subscription list to drop by a third. Having dissolved his printing partnership, Greeley had no state lottery contract to fall back on. Finally, he was spurred by a great stroke of luck. In 1838 Thurlow Weed, the powerful political boss of the Whig Party in New York State, invited Greeley to manage a special campaign paper, *The Jeffersonian,* in aid of William H. Seward's gubernatorial bid. Seward won office, and Greeley was recruited to oversee another Whig organ, *The Log-Cabin,* devoted to promoting the presidential ambitions of William Henry Harrison.

The 1840 presidential contest, with its use of media images and candidate merchandising, is considered the first modern political campaign in the United States. Greeley participated enthusiastically. "I tried to make The Log-Cabin as effective as I could . . . and to render it a model of its kind," he remembered in *Recollections of a Busy Life*. "The times were so changed that it was more lively and less sedately argumentative than The Jeffersonian." The name *The Log-Cabin* was itself a campaign symbol, alluding to Harrison's supposed birth in a backwoods cottage. The subscribers to the paper eventually reached eighty thousand; its success prompted Greeley to realize the dramatic readership potential for political journalism when coupled with the new mode in electioneering.

On 10 April 1841 Greeley brought out the first number of the *New-York Daily Tribune*. "My leading idea was the establishment of a journal removed alike from servile partisanship on the one hand and from gagged, mincing neutrality on the other," he recalled in *Recollections of a Busy Life*. ". . . I believed there was a happy medium." With this entrepreneurial act, Greeley secured his position as the Manhattan-based equal of the upstaters Weed and Seward in a political triumvirate ("the political firm of Seward, Weed, and Greeley," as he called it) that dominated the Whig Party of the state of New York for the next fifteen years.

Greeley's essentially reportorial "writing to deadline" is what defined the vernacular, to-the-point style found in his books as well as his editorials. In the prefaces to his longer works, he characteristically attributes his lack of rhetorical polish to the need for haste. But the results are still a pleasure to read. As Erik S. Lunde observes in *Horace Greeley* (1981), Greeley "could take complex issues and treat them with the felicity and simplicity of expression found in forefathers like Paine, Jefferson, and Franklin, with whom he was most often compared."

Association Discussed; or, The Socialism of the Tribune Examined. Being a Controversy between the New York Tribune and the Courier and Enquirer (1847), one of Greeley's most important pamphlets, stemmed from his lifelong commitment to social reform. During one of the most intensely reformist eras of the nation, he crusaded for almost every major proposal of the antebellum decades. Early issues of the *Tribune* supported antislavery and liquor prohibition, the two most dynamic reforms of the period, as well as sexual purity and international pacifism ("there never was a good war or a bad peace," wrote Greeley in reference to the conflict between Texas and Mexico), and the paper opposed smoking, prostitution, and gambling. Of all major propositions of the time, only female suffrage failed to win his enthusiasm. Soon Greeley's reform editorials and lectures had spread his reputation well beyond New York City. As early as 1846, according to David Donald in *Charles Sumner* (1996), Harvard law professor William Kent complained that Charles Sumner of Boston, a fledgling reform politician, "is Utopian as Horace Greele[y]."

Fourierism, a utopian design for harmonious communitarian living conceived by the French intellectual Charles Fourier, fascinated Greeley. A customized version by an American disciple, Arthur Brisbane, was known as "association." In the early 1840s the *Tribune* carried a regular column by Brisbane, and Greeley himself was for several years president of the American Union of Associationists. Greeley also helped organize several Fourierist "phalanxes" (or communes) and was a heavy financial investor in three, one of them a converted Transcendentalist venture, Brook Farm, in Massachusetts.

In August 1846 Henry J. Raymond, a former Greeley protégé then editing for the *New-York Courier and Enquirer,* initiated an exchange of views on association, which that winter became a formal debate of twelve Greeley letters and Raymond's rebuttals. Aside from some sparring over a proper interpretation of Thomas Paine and Edmund Burke and about the standard of living in late medieval and contemporary England, the exchange is a remarkable disputation. Along with high-order sophistry, it anticipates some of the later arguments of Henry George, Karl Marx, Washington Gladden, Walter Rauschenbusch, John Dewey, and even Sigmund Freud.

In his letters about association, Greeley seeks to explicate a system that will nonviolently abolish poverty and economic bondage and to preserve the sacred rights of private property. He insists that the current competitive economy is inhumane and getting worse, that the paramount problem is land monopoly, and that the only solution lies in the organization of local, largely self-sufficient phalanxes. Each commune would be a kind of free-market collective farm organized as a joint-stock company, in which "a number of families [collaborate] in the ownership and occupancy of a single Domain of Five or Six Thousand Acres, the occupants inhabiting a single edifice . . . located on its most eligible site, and cultivated by the labor of all or nearly all the male members of suitable age, while a portion of them, larger or smaller according to the season and the weather, with most of the women and children, will be employed in the various Manufactures prosecuted by the Phalanx." Members would profit according to how much money they had initially invested in the endeavor, how much income their individual skills were worth, or how productively they worked—"a *proportional* distribution of products to Labor, Capital and Talent, according to the just claims of each." In time, these township-sized phalanxes

might spread by moral example, eventually recasting the entire socioeconomic structure of the nation.

Raymond's task is easier. He argues that as bad as things might be, they are getting better, and he contends that a widespread conversion to radical Christian social morality would have to precede, rather than follow, any successful large-scale communitarian program. Raymond's clinching arguments, however, are those that expose some of the more socially advanced details of Fourier's thought—such as women's economic liberation from men, communal child care, and adult sexual freedom—that Greeley rejects. By insisting that the American version of Fourierism embraces only the reorganization of economic relationships, Greeley is essentially reduced to a theoretical justification for industrial and agricultural cooperatives.

In the winter of 1848–1849 Greeley was in Washington to serve out an unexpired term in the U.S. House of Representatives. His crusade against certain House practices, especially his relentless exposé of abuses in the mileage expense system, infuriated his colleagues. According to Glyndon G. Van Deusen in *Horace Greeley: Nineteenth-Century Crusader* (1953), by the close of the session Greeley was easily "the most unpopular man on Capitol Hill." Even Seward and Weed, Van Deusen adds, were convinced that the congressman's "zeal, unregulated by prudence, was a serious limitation to his usefulness."

Greeley's first full-fledged book, *Hints toward Reforms: in Lectures, Addresses, and Other Writings* (1850), consists of ten long and twenty short essays. He later described it in *Recollections of a Busy Life* as mainly "Lectures and Addresses prepared for delivery before village lyceums and other literary associations from time to time throughout the preceding six or eight years." Harper agreed to publish it, Greeley said, "on condition that I paid the cost of stereotyping (about $400), when they would give me (as I recollect) ten cents per copy on all they sold. . . . I believe the sales nearly reimbursed my outlay for stereotyping; so that I attained the dignity of authorship at a very moderate cost." An essay titled "The Emancipation of Labor" recapitulates Greeley's central arguments in *Association Discussed,* and four of the other long pieces, including one on Fourier and his predecessors, echo those themes. "Life—the Ideal and the Actual" argues (as Raymond had) that social and economic conditions are rapidly improving, and that modern civilization stands on the threshold of a golden age. In "The Formation of Character" Greeley praises Ralph Waldo Emerson and other Transcendentalists "for the perception and expression of moral truth generally." Two other long essays largely deal with education, and

An issue of the newspaper Greeley founded in 1841

"Alcoholic Liquors" urges Americans to abandon drinking alcohol.

Of the short essays, six oppose capital punishment, easy credit, Free Trade, flogging in the U.S. Navy, tobacco, and labor militancy. Of special note, in view of Greeley's later outspoken advocacy of emancipation, is "Slavery at Home: Answer to an Invitation to Attend an Anti-Slavery Meeting." In this version of an open letter Greeley wrote to a Cincinnati antislavery convention (originally published in the *Tribune* on 20 June 1845) he declines the invitation and offers readers three recommendations: each should insure that he or she is not a "slaveholder" respecting children, wives, tenants, and employees; each should give priority to such localized "slavery" over that existing in the distant South; and each should endeavor to improve the condition of *free* African Americans residing in the North. Invoking the theme of association, Greeley ends by urging free blacks to resettle in their own self-governing communities.

In the 1855 enlarged edition of *Hints toward Reforms,* Greeley included as an appendix a speech he had published separately in 1852, "The Crystal Palace and Its Lessons." After summarizing his observations

about the 1851 London World's Fair that appeared in *Glances at Europe: In a Series of Letters from Great Britain, France, Italy, Switzerland, &c., during the Summer of 1851. Including Notices of the Great Exhibition, or World's Fair* (1851), Greeley concludes with three truths that he thinks the exhibition conveyed: "the practicability and ultimate certainty of Universal Peace," the liberating effect of new technologies, and the inevitability of an associationist solution to the problems of labor.

By the 1850s Greeley and Bennett had become the two most celebrated journalists of New York. Their renown derived from rival styles and dissimilar constituencies. Bennett's *Herald* featured sex scandals, police-blotter reports, editorial flippancy, and dubious medicinal advertisements. Greeley's *Tribune,* while imitating Bennett's energetic news gathering, distanced itself from its rival by emphasizing good taste, morality, and serious intellectual appeal. Bennett's daily maintained an unbeatable metropolitan circulation. Greeley's weekly, designed for a readership outside the city, had made its editor a household name throughout New England, the Middle Atlantic States, and the Midwest. On the eve of the Civil War, *The Herald* boasted the highest daily sales (seventy-seven thousand) in the world, while the *New-York Weekly Tribune* enjoyed a nationwide circulation of approximately two hundred thousand.

By then Greeley presided over about five hundred employees, including a circle of talented writers and subeditors. At one time or another he commanded the services of Charles A. Dana, Margaret Fuller (the first woman journalist on the staff of a major newspaper), Whitelaw Reid, George Ripley, Bayard Taylor, Samuel Langhorne Clemens, and, as a major European correspondent for nearly a decade, Karl Marx.

Greeley's personal style as an open-door manager endeared him to employees and visitors alike. James Parton, in *Greeley* (1882) describes the *Tribune* office as "a very cheerful place. . . . Foreman and editor, officeboy and head clerk . . . converse as friends and equals." According to Lunde, John G. Shortall (in an essay included in the Greeley papers in the Library of Congress) affectionately pictured Greeley the editor as

> sitting at a desk as high as his chin, . . . his long flaxen hair, curling a little at the ends very thinly covering his large shapely head, . . . his gold framed spectacles well upon his forehead, and his chin almost touching the large, white, well-formed hand with which he wrote his almost undecipherable "Copy." . . . When he turned toward you, however, the curiously shrewd, yet child-like face, cleanshaven, with its sweet smile, and the combination of directness, earnestness, honesty, visible in it, when once well seen, could never be forgotten.

Greeley's appeal was eclectic. His personal friendships ranged from P. T. Barnum, with whom he regularly dined, to Henry David Thoreau, whom he served for several years as an unpaid literary agent. Greeley was admired by industrialists and industrial workers alike, and his country roots and rustic eccentricities made this big-city editor popular with rural folk everywhere. Yet Greeley was no angel: he silently nourished long-standing resentments that could erupt unpleasantly at chosen moments; he could be nonchalant about Molly's health and household concerns; he liberally sprinkled his talk at the office with the expletives "hell" and "damn"; and he could be difficult to work for.

In 1851 Greeley crossed the Atlantic to report firsthand on the World's Fair, then toured the Continent, spending in all four months overseas. During this trip he sent reports to the *Tribune* that subsequently appeared as his second book, *Glances at Europe*. "I was surprised by an offer to publish in a volume the letters I had written," Greeley says in *Rec-*

ollections of a Busy Life. ". . . I consented, and revised them. . . . I recollect my share of the proceeds was about $500."

In his letters Greeley expresses great interest in the progress of reform in Great Britain as compared to reform in the United States. Political reform moves more slowly in England, he thinks, with prohibition lagging twenty years behind. According to a letter dated 23 May 1851, he again expressed his lack of commitment to abolition at a meeting of the British Anti-Slavery Society. In a fifteen-minute speech, Greeley suggested that Britons might better focus on the imperfections of their own institutions than on the labor system of the American South. Scant applause greeted these remarks. In a later dispatch on 6 August 1851 he describes the English as "horror-stricken at the toleration of Slavery in the United States, in seeming ignorance that our Congress has no power to abolish it." He chides Parliament, "which *had* ample power," for waiting until 1834 to abolish West Indian slavery.

In a letter from Paris dated 12 June 1851 he disapproves of the pervasive hedonism. He claims that "Nowhere is Amusement more systematically, sedulously sought than in Paris; nowhere is it more abundant or accessible. . . . Paris is the Paradise of the Senses; a focus of Enjoyment, not of Happiness."

He finds much in Italy to admire, especially its lush agriculture, but he cautions in a 6 July 1851 letter that "such a thing as Enterprise is utterly unknown south of Genoa." According to a 29 June 1851 letter its unimaginable wealth of art and architecture (St. Peter's Cathedral is "the Niagara of edifices") proves to be the only redeeming feature of Rome. Venice, from a 9 July 1851 letter, overwhelms him with its sad, decaying beauty, and "two or three larger gondolas marked 'Omnibus' this or that," identifying them as group-operated, only briefly uplift his spirits. He writes in the same letter, "The Omnibus typifies Association—the simple but grandly fruitful idea which is destined to renovate the world of Industry and Production, substituting Abundance and Comfort for Penury and Misery. For Man, I trust, this quickening word is yet seasonable," he concludes; "for Venice it is too late."

Greeley's political views toward Italy obviously had been influenced by Margaret Fuller of the *Tribune*, who in 1848 became involved in the Roman insurgents' losing effort to make the Papal States a republic; she became an outspoken Italian revolutionary before dying with her Italian husband in a shipwreck. What the various Italian states so desperately need, Greeley reasons, is political unity, a necessary precursor to the emergence of the peninsula as a liberal democracy. Change will have to come through violence, he accurately predicts, his pacifism abandoned. "Farewell, trampled, soul-crushed Italy!" he writes on 10 July 1851 on crossing into Switzerland. He had failed to foresee that Italian unification would occur within the next decade. Weeks later Greeley was back in London to sit in on a Universal Peace Congress, with which, especially given the Italian case, he no longer sympathized. The effect of pacifism, he says in a letter dated 25 July 1851, is simply "to break the spirit of downtrodden nations, and, by thus postponing the inevitable struggle, protract to an indefinite period the advent of that Reign of Universal Justice which alone can usher in the glorious era of Universal Peace."

Touring Ireland before returning home, Greeley was appalled by the post-famine conditions there. Its economy in shambles, unemployment epidemic, public education a disgrace, industrial training nonexistent, and rural housing unbelievably dreadful, Ireland in all its desolation, he says on 31 July 1851, has to be witnessed to be believed. For these horrifying conditions the British, he later notes in letters from August 1851, refuse to take any moral responsibility.

Eight years later Greeley embarked on a second monumental excursion, which again he documented through dispatches to the *Tribune* that were later assembled into a book—*An Overland Journey, from New York to San Francisco, in the Summer of 1859* (1860). He recalled in *Recollections of a Busy Life* that "its publishers failed, however, very soon after its appearance; so that my returns from it . . . were inconsiderable." Charles T. Duncan, in the introduction to his 1964 edition of the book, terms Greeley's junket, with perhaps only a little overstatement, "one of the most famous trips in the annals of journalism." Including the return to New York by sea, it consumed the better part of five months.

In *Recollections of a Busy Life* Greeley describes this trip as an effort to create public support for a transcontinental railroad that would open the trans–Missouri West to rapid commercial exploitation and settlement. But, as during his European tour, agriculture and natural resources constantly preoccupy him: he gives close attention also to geography, politics, religion and ethnicity, manners and morals, food and clothing, housing, and education.

On this trip Greeley was treated as a celebrity virtually everywhere he went. He first proceeded by rail to the end of the tracks at St. Joseph, Missouri; he then set out by stagecoach more or less on the route to be followed a decade later by the Kansas Pacific, the Union Pacific, and the Central Pacific Railroads. Reaching Denver, he paused two weeks and in his book describes the famous Pike's Peak gold rush in some detail. In *An Overland Journey* he judges that "the

hardest (though sometimes the quickest) way to obtain gold is to mine for it—that a good farmer or mechanic will usually make money faster—and of course immeasurably easier—by sticking to his own business than by deserting it for gold-digging."

Greeley paused again, this time in Salt Lake City, where he conducted an historic interview with Young, the president of the Mormon Church, and in general praises a population that is industriously creating an agricultural oasis in the empty wilderness. (He does not, interestingly enough, comment on the communitarianism that so strongly undergirded the Mormons' economic system.) Far from expressing any prurient interest in multiple marriage, the religiously sanctioned custom that so outraged most Americans, Greeley calmly and correctly predicts that a revisionist revelation will one day prohibit the practice.

After a harrowing trip over the Sierra Nevada Mountains, Greeley spent a month in northern California, venturing out from Sacramento to the gold-mining regions and to the breathtakingly beautiful Yosemite Valley. He meditates at length in his account on the future of crop agriculture on the West Coast, predicting that fruit "is destined to be the ultimate glory of California," although he is less certain about the potential of California as a world-class wine region. He finds the greatest lacks in California to be women and public schools.

Before boarding ship at San Francisco, Greeley mustered several impressions of that budding metropolis. All the city needs, he writes, is a rail connection with the East to "make her the New York of this mighty ocean—the focus of the trade of all America west of the Andes and Rocky Mountains, and of Polynesia as well, with an active and increasing Australian commerce." If a protective tariff were added, he says, "San Francisco would become, what she ought now to be, a great manufacturing center—the united Manchester and Birmingham of the South Seas." His concluding report, written after returning to New York via Panama, summarizes the case for a coast-to-coast railroad.

In 1856 Greeley took part in the founding of the Republican Party; assembled a lengthy pamphlet on the slavery issue for the first Republican presidential campaign, *A History of the Struggle for Slavery Extension or Restriction in the United States from the Declaration of Independence to the Present Day. Mainly Compiled and Condensed from the Journals of Congress and Other Official Records, and Showing the Vote by Yeas and Nays on the Most Important Divisions in Either House* (1856); and five years later was an unsuccessful Republican candidate for the U.S. Senate. The slavery pamphlet proved useful preparation for Greeley's fourth book, a two-volume history of the origins and course of the Civil War. Predicting brisk sales, its publishers met with Greeley only days after the infamous New York City Draft Riots had subjected him to great personal danger. They persuaded the initially reluctant Greeley to write the book and to agree to a subscription-sale speculation. In *Recollections of a Busy Life* Greeley recalls, "The compensation offered would be liberal, in case the work should attain a very large sale, but otherwise quite moderate." With the aid of a research assistant, he completed the first volume of *The American Conflict: A History of the Great Rebellion 1860–65; Its Causes, Incidents, and Results: Intended to Exhibit Especially Its Moral and Political Phases, with the Drift and Progress of American Opinion Respecting Human Slavery from 1776 to the Close of the War for the Union* (1864) while the war still raged. Then occurred one of Greeley's most notorious exploits, his unrealistic attempt in July 1864, with Abraham Lincoln's approval, to negotiate a peace. His rendezvous with Confederate representatives in Canada proved fruitless.

The sale of the first volume of his history, said Greeley in *Recollections of a Busy Life*, "was very large and steady," amounting to nearly 125,000 copies sold in three years. But volume two of the history appeared in 1866, after Appomattox, just as Greeley was urging, in line with his appeal for sectional reconciliation, the release from prison of Jefferson Davis, controversial former president of the Confederacy. Nearly 50,000 copies of volume two had been sold by the time Greeley helped organize Davis's bail. Then sales nearly ceased for a time as thousands of subscribers refused to accept their copies.

Biographer Van Deusen's concise assessment of *The American Conflict* remains valid: "Hastily written, based on insufficient and often unsatisfactory data, [sectionally] biased, oracular in its military judgments, sometimes inaccurate in detail, it was nevertheless the best thing that had been done on the war." But Greeley's history is not just about the fighting: the first 327 pages are devoted to slavery. In these pages Greeley traces the beginnings of the African slave trade, the establishment of slavery in the colonies, the accommodation to slavery by the founding fathers of the country, and the sequential political crises generated by slavery between 1820 and 1860.

Greeley also spends approximately fifty pages on a still-useful précis of the wartime experience of blacks, discussing the issues of fugitive slaves, emancipation, black military enlistment and equal pay, and Confederate treatment of black prisoners of war. Included in this section is "The Prayer of Twenty Millions," originally published in the *Tribune* on 20 August 1862. Considered to be Greeley's most famous editorial, it has been reprinted in the many editions of

Henry Steele Commager's *Documents of American History* (1934). As a delegate to the 1860 Republican national convention, Greeley had been essential in bringing about the nomination of Lincoln. But by 1862 Greeley had become impatient with the president's hesitant stance on emancipation. An open letter to Lincoln, "The Prayer" powerfully excoriates the president's reluctance to use his wartime powers to free the slaves of all owners loyal to the Confederate cause. It also considers African American recruitment—another touchy issue for Lincoln—as absolutely crucial to victory. In volume two of the history Greeley says that he is convinced that "we shall be baffled and repelled" by the Confederacy without "scouts, guides, spies, cooks, teamsters, diggers, and choppers, from the Blacks of the South—whether we allow them to fight for us or not." (In judging the quality of black soldiers later in the book, Greeley maintains that they are equal to white soldiers in deportment, obedience, and physical stamina, if not always in "intelligence and tenacity.") In time, Lincoln strongly agreed with Greeley's views on both emancipation and black recruitment, assessments that did not go unnoticed in the *Tribune*. In short, Greeley, like present-day American historians (who have discarded economic conflicts of interest, cultural sectionalism, and opportunistic politics to account for the war), emphasizes slavery as the cause of the Civil War and places the black experience at the center of wartime developments.

Greeley's fifth book, *Recollections of a Busy Life,* has received mixed reviews. Lunde considers it one of the outstanding autobiographies in American letters, of the same quality perhaps as Benjamin Franklin's self-portrait. Biographers William Harlan Hale and Van Deusen, judging by less purely literary criteria, are not as enthusiastic. "The work is a prime source for the history of his early years and family background," notes Hale in *Horace Greeley: Voice of the People* (1950), "but in approaching the chronicle of his maturity Greeley became either so distracted or inhibited that there his narrative loses all but incidental value." According to Van Deusen in *Horace Greeley,* "Greeley's *Recollections* are useful . . . but it has to be kept constantly in mind that he was a most persuasive pleader in his own defense, one who had no hesitation in suppressing facts that were to his disadvantage."

Like most of Greeley's books, the autobiography is an edited collection—in this case, of installments written for *The New-York Ledger.* "I wrote my Recollections because Mr. Bonner [the editor] urged and paid me to do so," says Greeley in *Recollections of a Busy Life,* "and because I hoped thus to make clear to many of our younger generation several points in our country's internal history which have been

THE OLD ROOKERY

Courtesy of Herald Tribune

The original office building for Greeley's newspaper

widely misunderstood." Apparently he meant no more than that he would tell his side of the story with respect to various controversial issues, such as his wartime criticism of Lincoln and support of Jefferson Davis's release from prison.

The book is half chronological—beginning with his parental genealogy and going down through the end of the Civil War—and half topical. The latter part includes his religion (Unitarian), his personal regimen (no tobacco or alcohol), his politics, his thoughts on leisure, his adoration of Henry Clay, his assessment of Margaret Fuller ("the most remarkable, and in some respects the greatest, woman whom America has yet known"), his views against lending money (which his own behavior notoriously contradicted), as well as those on spiritualism, the libel laws, farming, and death.

Greeley recalls that his schooling ended at age fourteen when his parents rejected an offer "made by the leading men of our neighborhood" to enroll him free of charge at Phillips Exeter Academy, with the expectation of college to follow. His curtailed education was not a source of bitterness, or so he says; he thanks his parents for their decision and elsewhere fre-

quently ridicules the supposed virtues of the higher education of his time, with its heavy emphasis on Latin and Greek. The best college "yet established in our country," he says, is West Point.

Sometimes Greeley blurred biographical facts in *Recollections of a Busy Life* to suit a later view of himself. An example is his passage on abolitionism. His slight regard for the movement had been implicit in his open letter to the Cincinnati antislavery convention in 1845 *(Hints toward Reforms)* and in his remarks to the British antislavery convention in 1851 *(Glances at Europe).* In *Recollections of a Busy Life* this kind of blurring is also reflected in Greeley's disdain for antislavery speechmaking during his brief term in Congress. The author admits to holding such an attitude early on: "Granted (most heartily) that Slavery ought to be abolished, how was that consummation to be effected by societies and meetings of men, women, and children, who owned no slaves, and had no sort of control over . . . those who did?"

Then, says Greeley, "two events, of nearly simultaneous occurrence, materially modified these preconceptions." The first was the Texas Revolution, which seemed to many Northerners an attempt to add another slave state to the Union; the second was the assassination of the abolitionist editor Elijah Lovejoy in Illinois. Both events occurred in the mid 1830s, however, and hardly explain Greeley's lukewarm attitudes of the 1840s and 1850s. The best that can be said is that by the time he founded the *Tribune,* he had become an "antiextension" Whig, opposing the spread of slavery into the West but, like most political intellectuals, unwilling to agitate against its legal existence in the South. Not until the Civil War began did Greeley champion outright abolition, although his lifelong concern for the civil equality of free African Americans always marked him as an outspoken racial progressive.

Greeley's occasional flashes of psychological insight in *Recollections of a Busy Life* are startling—for example, "The most *conservative* of mankind . . . are those who have nothing to lose" and "Men always hate those they have wronged." Implicit in his comparison of Seward, Weed, and himself on racial attitudes is an insightful model of racism: "Seward, born in comfortable circumstances, and educated a gentleman, had none of the 'Poor White' prejudice against Blacks; while it was otherwise with Weed, whose origin and training had been different. *My* New England birth and Federal[ist] antecedents saved me from sharing this infirmity, to which the poverty and obscurity of my boyhood might else have exposed me." Two of the most interesting of the topical chapters of the autobiography are "Socialism" and

"Socialistic Efforts." They continue Greeley's discussion of association where his debate with Raymond had left off. Association is not nineteenth-century communism, which Greeley rejects because that philosophy mandates absolute equality of income, which he believes goes against human nature. Neither is it exemplified by producers' and consumers' cooperatives, which, while advantageous, are only "one-sided, fragmentary Association."

The benefits of association, Greeley says in *Recollections of a Busy Life,* are both economic and social. The great economic gain is agricultural efficiency, especially since the size of the enterprise would permit it to take advantage of new labor-saving technologies. Socially, the advantage is a greatly enhanced sense of togetherness. Greeley dreamily imagines "the edifice which shall yet lodge commodiously and agreeably two thousand persons, giving each the requisite privacy and independence," and "the prosecution of agricultural and other labor by large bands, rendered picturesque by uniforms, and inspired by music." Moreover, "such recreations as dramas, concerts, readings, &c.,–now utterly beyond the reach of rural workers,–would give a new zest to life."

The autobiography ends on page 429 and is followed by nearly two hundred pages of "Miscellanies." These works offer a mixture of formal essays and addresses on literature, poetry, reform, incidents of the lecture circuit, and a lengthy debate with reformer Robert Dale Owen about divorce (which Greeley flatly opposes except on grounds of adultery) that originally appeared in the *Tribune.* Of these addenda, a lecture dating from the 1850s titled "Reforms and Reformers" is most remarkable for its psychological portrait of "the earnest, true Reformer" whose "life is indeed no holiday. . . . Not merely that his bread is apt to be coarse and his couch somewhat rugged,–he was prepared for this,–but the intractability of ignorance, the stubbornness of prejudice, the thanklessness of those [aided], are indeed appalling." The occupational hazard of trying to uplift the masses, Greeley muses, "is coming gradually to dislike and despise them." One wonders how closely, if at all, this opinion reflects his own experience. Certainly, he acknowledges no such belief anywhere else.

A speech appended to Greeley's recollections, which urges a protective tariff, dates from 1843. Thus, his sixth book, published in 1869, *Essays Designed to Elucidate the Science of Political Economy, while Serving to Explain and Defend the Policy of Protection to Home Industry, as a System of National Cooperation for the Elevation of Labor,* represents at least twenty-six years of research and reflection on an intellectually difficult issue. Protectionism has stirred Americans dating from Alexander Hamilton's *Report on Manufactures* (a report made to Congress on 5 December 1791 and published in 1792) down to congressional ratification of the North American Free Trade Agreement in the 1990s. The post–Civil War period was a high-tariff era, but the policy was under relentless attack by Free Trade partisans. Greeley's aim was to counter this criticism through a series of articles in the *Tribune,* subsequently compiled as a book. His resulting explication is perhaps the best full-length protectionist argument ever designed for the general public; a century after its writing, in 1972 it was reprinted as a volume in the Arno Press series on "The Evolution of Capitalism."

Greeley's book includes two chapters on "Coöperation" that bring the author's long romance with association to a conclusion of sorts. In these essays he abandons Fourierism in favor of cooperation, which some fifteen years earlier he had described as merely a primitive starting point for social and economic reorganization. By formally collaborating to become their own employers and retailers, American "producers" (that is, manufacturers, workers, and farmers) would raise their incomes and lower their expenditures. Thus, cooperation became Greeley's postwar prescription for emancipation from "wage slavery" and commercial profiteering. His optimism about the future of cooperation soared with the upsurge in industrial and agricultural cooperative enterprises that characterized the late 1860s, a trend that extended–especially through the Knights of Labor and Patrons of Husbandry (or the Grange)–well into the 1870s and 1880s.

In *Essays Designed to Elucidate the Science of Political Economy* local cooperation becomes a metaphor for national protectionism–the effort to establish, through substantially obstructive tariff duties on manufactured imports, the kind of self-contained national economy, with its regional and entrepreneurial interdependence, championed by Hamilton, by Clay, and most recently by economic nationalists such as Patrick Buchanan. Greeley's main argument is that protecting American industry from foreign competition causes it to expand, diversify, and compete domestically, thereby creating jobs and a larger home market for agriculture without materially injuring consumers. Subsidiary benefits, set forth in successive chapters, include reducing the immense number of retailers (*"useless exchangers or traffickers"*) and also of import-export merchants, thereby turning them to "productive" work; minimizing the net loss of gold currency, the medium of international commerce, by wiping out the trade deficit of the United States; adhering to the allegedly protectionist wisdom of George Washington, Thomas Jefferson, James Madison, and other venerated founders of the

CINCINNATUS.

H. G. THE FARMER RECEIVING THE NOMINATION FROM H. G. THE EDITOR.

Political cartoon suggesting that Greeley used the New-York Tribune *to "nominate" himself as a candidate for the presidency (from* Harper's Weekly, *10 February 1872)*

United States; inducing industrialization of the South and the West, thus reducing farmers' transportation costs by shortening market distances; accelerating the movement of surplus farmers into industrial employment; keeping manufacturing wages higher than abroad; aiding "specie resumption" (the Treasury plan to redeem depreciated wartime greenbacks for gold dollars) through higher tariffs payable in gold; reducing the tax burden on Americans by increasing tariff revenues; and stimulating immigration through the promise of industrial jobs. Other chapters examine protective tariffs with respect to the sugar beet industry in France and sheep raising in the United States.

Greeley's treatise is vulnerable at several points. His essay on immigration is one of his weakest arguments. In attributing the abrupt rise in post-1820 immigration rates to the new manufacturing jobs created by protection, Greeley conveniently slights the positive impediments to pre-1820 immigration—the trade embargoes, the Napoleonic Wars, and the War of 1812—all of which seriously disrupted trans-Atlantic shipping. Greeley's assertion that protectionism does not foster higher prices is plausibly contradicted by

evidence that a two-price system prevailed for protected industrial products at the turn of the century. Thus, in 1905 the U.S. Steel Corporation sold 90 percent of its output within the United States for an average of about $40 per ton, "dumping" the remainder overseas for about $30 per ton—presumably its actual market value. Meanwhile, an eight-horsepower traction engine selling domestically for $1,225 could be purchased abroad for the equivalent of $917, a $400 grain thresher for $300, a $100 potato digger for $90, a $16 gross of kitchen knives for $12, and so on. As intellectually independent as Greeley was, he could never escape the protectionist embrace of his old political hero, Clay.

In his *Recollections of a Busy Life* Greeley offers a surprising confession. This universally celebrated founder and manager of what might well have been called "America's newspaper," this dazzling success story, this exemplar of the nineteenth-century entrepreneurial instinct, declares, "I should have been a farmer." That Greeley had escaped from the farm at the earliest feasible age is something he attributes to the lack of intellectual challenge in traditional agriculture. "I *would* have been a farmer," he insists, "had any science of farming been known to those among whom my earlier boyhood was passed."

To help remedy this deficiency Greeley produced his seventh book, *What I Know of Farming: A Series of Brief and Plain Expositions of Practical Agriculture as an Art Based upon Science* (1871), a collection of fifty-two brief essays. In the preface he reiterates his remarks on vocational choice. Had he read such a book as he has just written, he says, "my subsequent career would have been less anxious and my labors less exhausting." Creatively responding to "problems which require and reward the amplest knowledge of Nature's laws, the fullest command of science, the noblest efforts of the human intellect, I should have since pursued the peaceful, unobtrusive round of an enthusiastic and devoted . . . tiller of the soil." There are now many how-to books on farming, he concedes. But he offers his own in the hope that "there may be some who will read this treatise for its writer's sake—will read it when they could not be persuaded to do like honor to a more elaborate and erudite work." Couched, he says, in language any fifteen-year-old should understand, the book targets the younger generation of farmers and would-be farmers.

Read today, in an era of growing suspicion of modern agribusiness, with its chemical dependency on antibiotics, pesticides, and herbicides, Greeley's book often resembles a brief for organic farming. Based primarily on his experience in resuscitating the Westchester County acreage he had purchased in 1853, but also drawing on firsthand knowledge of European, Western, and Southern agriculture, the essays argue that if correctly pursued, farming is a profitable business. Greeley enumerates the "dos and don'ts" of success: never till more acres than can be managed properly; an adult-lifetime tenure on a given farm is necessary to learning how best to use and to care for that farm; never undertake farming without some sort of apprenticeship; never purchase too much land; feed rather than pasture livestock; keep some acreage in commercially valuable timber; install tile drainage under regularly cultivated fields; irrigate; minimize purchases of commercial fertilizer; plow deeply; and devote ten hours per week to professional reading.

Greeley also discusses the protection of birds as a method of insect control, fruit trees and viticulture, haying, grain and root crops, sycophancy in the public praise of farmers, sheep raising, keeping proper records, rocks as assets, the tendency to over-fence, the ineffectiveness of agricultural fairs, soil science, the coming invention of the farm tractor, urban sewage as fertilizer, rural depopulation, small versus large farms, railroad companies as potential retailers

of perishable products, and the fallacy of laying off farmworkers in winter.

Two things, however, are oddly missing. First, in writing of the "need for more thought, more study, more intellect, infused into our Agriculture," Greeley fails to mention the most important institutional developments of the period for the diffusion of technical information to farmers—establishment of the U.S. Department of Agriculture and of a system for federal funding of agricultural colleges in every state. By his silence, Greeley may have been deferring to farmers' habitual scorn of "book farming" and also may have seen the early agricultural schools (with their penchant for curricula that included Latin and Greek) as designed for the education of a rural elite.

Second, in his discussion of the need for farmers' clubs, Greeley disregards the formation and incipient growth of the Patrons of Husbandry. This national association, amounting to a federation of hundreds—later thousands—of neighborhood Granges, had been created specifically to improve the educational, cultural, and social environment of farmers and their families. That the *Tribune* editor knew nothing of this development seems hard to credit.

A chapter on "Co-operation in Farming" returns readers to a persistent theme. Greeley recommends that those moving west to take up lands on the frontier should not go as individuals: they will face many a year without roads, schools, churches, or stores. Migrants should instead proceed according to the tenets of cooperation, buying into a joint-stock company that can then make a massive purchase of contiguous wild lands, ultimately to be deeded to the individual stockholders. Upon settlement, the members of the collective enterprise can immediately form a civic community and assemble the morale-building amenities of civilization without delay. Cooperative farming also might inspire such efficiencies as collaborative fencing of "several square miles into one grand enclosure for cultivation" from which the colony's free-ranging cattle would be usefully excluded. Greeley views agricultural cooperation as an especially valuable option for African Americans "now precariously subsisting by servile labor in the cities."

Another chapter, "Western Irrigation," describes how cooperation is playing out on twelve thousand acres of northern Colorado. The so-called Union Colony had been the brainchild of the agricultural editor of the *Tribune,* but Greeley enthusiastically endorsed it. He purchased his own $1,000 share in the company, chaired its organizational meeting, served as its first treasurer, granted it liberal newspaper publicity, and allowed the village in the settlement to carry his name. In 1870, its first year,

Greeley's house in Chappaqua, New York

Greeley, Colorado, and its hinterland already harbored about two thousand residents.

To outsiders, the principal distinction of the Union Colony was its ban on liquor. But the pride of its cooperative enterprise, as described in *What I Know of Farming,* was its extensive irrigation system, fed by a canal linking the Cache la Poudre River with the South Platte River, from which feeder ditches conveyed water through the village and to the surrounding farms. Two other canals are being dug, notes Greeley, to irrigate approximately forty thousand acres in all.

A few months after publication of the farming treatise, another well-publicized trip, occasioned by an invitation to give the keynote address—"Suggestions to Farmers"—at the Texas State Fair in Houston, resulted in Greeley's final work of importance, *Mr. Greeley's Letters from Texas and the Lower Mississippi: To Which Are Added His Address to the Farmers of Texas, and His Speech on His Return to New York, June 12, 1871* (1871). Once again, reports sent back to the *Tribune* were collected on his return and, together with the text of his speech to Texas farmers and his speech at a reception following the trip, were published in pamphlet form. The reception speech summarizes Greeley's thinking on Southern Reconstruction, a policy concern that helped prompt his entry into presidential politics in 1872.

Greeley's state fair address assures Texans that agriculture is the hallmark of civilization, that it is gradually demanding more intelligence, that not just steam power but also electricity will soon be harnessed in its service, that cotton monoculture will give way in the South when a crop of equal value is discovered, that the region should develop its own textile mills, that the current availability of good literature could arrest the exodus of farm boys to the city, and that the heedless clear-cutting of trees must end. Ten specific maxims follow these remarks—beginning with some general principles of progressive agriculture and ending with a few trademark homilies; farmers should spend some part of each day in study, should plant flowers, should have a good home library, and should remember that wealth from farming is slow but sure.

Since heavy rains prevented Greeley's planned circuit of Texas beyond the Houston and Galveston areas, his observations derive primarily from southeast Texas. He advises would-be agricultural colonists that good land is cheap when purchased in large tracts. Since the countryside is so bountiful, he is surprised that southeast Texans seem to be living "almost entirely on Meat, Bread, and Coffee." He deplores their importation of flour and pork when they could so easily supply themselves but predicts that as they are weaned from their overemphasis on cotton they will produce more food.

On his way home, two letters summarize Greeley's thoughts on race relations in the lower South. The former slaveholders of the region, he says, "have uniformly assured me that their ex-slaves are working better than they expected, and better this year than ever before." Most are renting or sharecropping. "I judge that the Freedmen of the Cotton States are this day in as good circumstances as the Hired Workers who till the soil of any European country," Greeley says, and he discounts white testimony that "when this generation of field-hands, trained to steady work as slaves, shall have died off, matters will have changed for the worse."

Although whites universally insisted that the freed people spend their earnings unwisely, blacks themselves told Greeley that such was not the general pattern. "They assure me that many are buying lands; others accumulating money in the Freedmen's Savings Bank with intent to own homes at no distant day; and that nearly all are doing better from year to year. . . . I have conversed with no Black who was not hopeful and confident as to the future of his race."

All whites tell Greeley that they accept the demise of slavery. But the vast majority of former slaveholders, he speculates, would have it back if it were possible. "They sigh for the good old times when every 'nigger' obeyed orders without dreaming of resistance or demur, and without expecting any pay." Politically, he has no illusions about Southern whites. They are now committed to working within the two-party system, but "expect to regain as Democrats through elections the power they lost as Rebels through war. . . . They persist in a clamor against what they call 'nigger equality' (but which means Negro Enfranchisement, Negro Education), which precludes their swaying the Negro Vote as they otherwise might and would."

Everywhere Greeley sees material progress, and he expects that Southern attitudes will eventually follow suit. "It were irrational to expect that all the bitterness engendered by twenty years of sectional collision, including four of bloody war, should be effaced in a day, and of course it is not; but the tendency is right, and Time will exert its healing influence. . . . The re-cementing of the union will be thorough and enduring."

Greeley's Union Square speech at his post-trip reception in New York in June is perhaps the only extempore talk included in all the author's writings. Greeley the potential presidential candidate speaks to a crowd of several thousand. As a brief political talk, it exemplifies yet another mode of public discourse so impressively mastered by this talented communicator.

In contrast to his letters, Greeley abruptly recasts sectional reconciliation in the rather simplistic terms that later characterized his presidential campaign. He begins by asserting that while the South had certainly touched off the Civil War, in a larger sense the conflict resulted from a colossal breakdown in communication: "the North and South failed to understand each other." (His own history of the war had posited an irrepressible conflict between freedom and slavery dating back to 1619.) He goes on to suggest that the failure of the Andrew Johnson and Ulysses S. Grant administrations to allow "the leading men of the South" to resume immediate political control of the former Confederate states had been "a very great mistake." There are two relatively small groups of Southern troublemakers seriously impeding sectional reconciliation, he says. The Ku Klux Klan is one; it must be eradicated by firm federal action. A predatory minority of Northern carpetbaggers is an "equally pernicious" presence, responsible for many fiscal misdeeds by Southern legislatures. That group, too, must be overcome.

Greeley closes with a few words on the "New Departure" pledge of the national Democratic Party to drop race as a political issue. He thinks most Democrats are sincere, which is all to the good. "I am weary of fighting over issues that ought to be dead—that logically *were* dead years ago," he says. "When Slavery died, I thought that we ought speedily to have ended all that grew out of it by Universal Amnesty and Impartial Suffrage." In other words, the former Confederate states should have been returned to the Union as self-governing political entities; the only change that should have been demanded of them was to guarantee voting rights to adult male former slaves. He thinks that this step is being achieved, and he closes by summoning all who hear him, Republicans and Democrats alike, to forget the past and to prepare themselves for new issues (such as "industrial policy") that lie ahead.

Clearly Greeley was maneuvering himself into a potential challenge of Grant. Greeley's coming break with the administration was motivated partly by pique at President Grant's backing of an anti-Greeley faction of the New York Republican Party, partly by the corruption scandals that plagued the Grant White House, and partly by a conviction that Grant lacked the skills needed to bring Reconstruction to a successful resolution.

In March 1872 Greeley formally cut his ties to the Republican Party by resigning from its national central committee. In May he accepted a nomination by the rump "Liberal Republican" party to run for president of the United States. In July the Democratic

Party also named him as its candidate, and he spent the next four months traveling, speech making, and handshaking. Toward the end of this exhausting political campaign, on 30 October 1872, Molly Greeley died. A week later, on 5 November, Americans voted by a landslide to give Grant another term; Greeley won less than 44 percent of the popular vote.

Physically debilitated and psychologically crushed by the death of his wife and the loss of his political hopes, Horace Greeley suffered a mental collapse and died on 29 November 1872. His funeral occasioned a day of public mourning in New York City, with huge crowds thronging the streets and scores of dignitaries, including President Grant, attending the service.

Letters:

Greeley on Lincoln with Mr. Greeley's Letters to Charles A. Dana and a Lady Friend, edited by Joel Benton (New York: Baker & Taylor, 1893);

"Letters of Horace Greeley to Nathan C. Meeker," edited by Oliver M. Dickerson, *Colorado Magazine,* 19 (March 1942): 50–62; 19 (May 1942): 102–110.

Bibliography:

Suzanne Schulze, *Horace Greeley: A Bio-Bibliography* (New York: Greenwood Press, 1992).

Biographies:

J. Parton, *The Life of Horace Greeley, Editor of the New York Tribune* (New York: Mason, 1855);

L. U. Reavis, *A Representative Life of Horace Greeley* (New York: Carleton, 1872);

L. D. Ingersoll, *The Life of Horace Greeley* (Philadelphia: Potter, 1874);

Francis Nicoll Zabriskie, *Horace Greeley, the Editor* (New York: Funk & Wagnalls, 1890);

William Alexander Linn, *Horace Greeley, Founder and Editor of the New York Tribune* (New York: Appleton, 1903);

Don C. Seitz, *Horace Greeley: Founder of the New York Tribune* (Indianapolis: Bobbs-Merrill, 1926);

Henry Luther Stoddard, *Horace Greeley: Printer, Editor, Crusader* (New York: Putnam, 1946);

William Harlan Hale, *Horace Greeley: Voice of the People* (New York: Harper, 1950);

Glyndon G. Van Deusen, *Horace Greeley: Nineteenth-Century Crusader* (Philadelphia: University of Pennsylvania Press, 1953).

References:

Charles T. Duncan, "Editor's Introduction," in Horace Greeley, *An Overland Journey from New York to San Francisco in the Summer of 1859* (New York: Knopf, 1964), pp. xi–xxxii;

"Horace Greeley," *Making of America* <http://www.umich.edu/moa>;

Erik S. Lunde, *Horace Greeley* (Boston: Twayne, 1981);

Jo Ann Manfra, "Introduction," *Horace Greeley, An Overland Journey from New York to San Francisco in the Summer of 1859* (Lincoln: University of Nebraska Press, 1999), pp. v–xiv;

Charles Sotheran, *Horace Greeley and Other Pioneers of American Socialism* (New York: New York Press Club, 1889).

Papers:

Many of Horace Greeley's letters, private papers, and manuscripts can be found in the New York Public Library; the Library of Congress; the New-York Historical Society; the New Castle Historical Society, Chappaqua, N.Y.; the Cornell University Library; the Huntington Library; and the Denver Public Library.

Rufus W. Griswold

(13 February 1815 – 27 August 1857)

Angela Courtney
Fairfield University

See also the Griswold entries in *DLB 3: Antebellum Writers in New York and the South* and *DLB 59: American Literary Critics and Scholars, 1800–1850.*

BOOKS: *Washington and the Generals of the American Revolution,* written and edited by Griswold, William Gilmore Simms, E. D. Ingraham, and others (Philadelphia: Carey & Hart, 1847; revised, 1848);

The Republican Court; or, American Society in the Days of Washington (New York & London: D. Appleton, 1855; revised, 1859);

Washington, a Biography, 45 parts, completed by Benson J. Lossing (New York: Virtue, Emmins, 1856–1860).

OTHER: *The Biographical Annual: Containing Memoirs of Eminent Persons, Recently Deceased,* edited by Griswold (New York: Linen & Fennell, 1841);

The Poets and Poetry of America, with an Historical Introduction, edited by Griswold (Philadelphia, Carey & Hart, 1842; London: Wiley & Putnam, 1842; revised edition, Philadelphia: Carey & Hart, 1845; revised again, 1850; revised again and enlarged, Philadelphia: Parry & McMillan, 1856);

Gems from American Female Poets, edited by Griswold (Philadelphia: Hooker, 1842);

Readings in American Poetry, edited by Griswold (New York: Riker, 1843); also published as *Readings in American Poetry for the Use of Schools* (New York: Riker, 1843);

"Curiosities of American Literature," in *Curiosities of Literature, and the Literary Character Illustrated,* by Isaac D'Israeli (New York: D. Appleton, 1844), pp. 1–63;

Gems from the American Poets, edited by Griswold (Philadelphia: Hooker, 1844);

The Poets and Poetry of England, in the Nineteenth Century, edited by Griswold (Philadelphia: Carey & Hart, 1844);

The Poetry of Love, edited by Griswold (Boston: L. Tompkins, 1844);

Rufus W. Griswold, circa 1855 (portrait by Kellogg; from Joy Bayless, Rufus Wilmot Griswold, *1943)*

The Cypress Wreath: A Book of Consolation for Those Who Mourn, edited by Griswold (Boston: Gould, Kendall & Lincoln, 1844);

Poems by *Felicia Hemans,* edited by Griswold (Philadelphia: Sorin & Ball, 1845);

The Prose Works of John Milton: With a Biographical Introduction by Rufus Wilmot Griswold in Two Volumes, edited by Griswold (Philadelphia: Hooker, 1845; London: Wiley & Putnam, 1847);

Scenes in the Life of the Saviour, edited by Griswold (Philadelphia: Lindsay & Blakiston, 1846);

The Prose Writers of America, edited by Griswold (Philadelphia: Carey & Hart, 1847; London: Bentley, 1847);

The Female Poets of America, edited by Griswold (Philadelphia: Carey & Hart, 1849);

The Works of the Late Edgar Allan Poe, 4 volumes; volumes 1–2, *The Works of the Late Edgar Allan Poe: With Notices of His Life and Genius,* edited by Griswold, with contributions by Griswold, N. P. Willis, and J. R. Lowell (New York: J. S. Redfield, 1850); volume 3, *The Literati: Some Honest Opinions about Authorial Merits and Demerits, with Occasional Words of Personality. Together with Marginalia, Suggestions, and Essays. By Edgar A. Poe . . . with a Sketch of the Author,* edited, with contribution, by Griswold (New York: J. S. Redfield, 1850); volume 4, *The Works of Edgar Allan Poe with a Memoir,* edited, with contributions, by Griswold (New York: J. S. Redfield, 1856);

"Love Supreme. A Fragment from an Unpublished Story," in *the Knickerbocker Gallery: A Testimonial to the Editor of the Knickerbocker Magazine from Its Contributors* (New York: Samuel Hueston, 1855).

PERIODICALS EDITED: *Porcupine* (1835);

Western Democrat and Literary Inquirer (5 May 1835 – 26 May 1835);

Olean Advocate (8 August 1836 – 12 August 1837);

Vergennes Vermonter (8 February 1838 – 28 April 1839);

Evening Tattler (8 July 1839 – 15 February 1840);

Brother Jonathan (13 July 1839–Autumn 1839);

Evening Signal (12 October 1839–December 1839);

New World (26 October 1839–December 1839);

Daily Standard (1840 – 21 April 1841);

Graham's Magazine (May 1842–October 1843);

Quarterly Review of the American Protestant Association (January 1844–October 1845);

International Monthly Magazine (1850–1852);

Illustrated News (1 January 1853 – 26 November 1853).

Rufus Wilmot Griswold, in his day, was an influential critic, editor, and compiler of literary anthologies. Although his historical importance is rarely questioned, his critical abilities and supposed unbiased judgment are often suspect. While Griswold's own creative potential was average, his forte was his ability to influence the popular canon of his time. This truth aside, throughout his life Griswold wandered from compiling to writing on several occasions. Possibly his most famous, and most convincing, work of "fiction" is the obituary and subsequent memoir of his colleague, Edgar Allan Poe; Griswold is rarely mentioned today if not in reference to Poe's legacy. Otherwise, Griswold's writing was lim-

ited to editorials, often unsigned occasional poetry, and two historical works.

Griswold, the twelfth child in a family of fourteen, was born on 13 February 1815 to Rufus and Deborah Wass Griswold in Benson, Vermont. His father, a shoemaker and tanner, was descended from early New England settlers in Connecticut, while his mother's ancestors were prominent citizens of Martha's Vineyard. Though little else is known of Griswold's childhood, he was raised by an extraordinarily devout Congregationalist mother. When he was seven, his father sold the family farm and they moved to another Vermont village, Hubbardton.

In spite of his mother's influence, Griswold was apparently a difficult child and was sent from the family home to Rutland County, Vermont, as a newspaper apprentice. Soon afterward, he moved to Troy to live with one of his brothers with the supposed intention of enrolling in the Rensselaer School. Because of an attempted prank, the nature of which is unknown, directed at a professor, Griswold was expelled before ever fully enrolling and instead began working at his brother's store.

After a disagreement with his brother, Griswold relocated to Albany and soon became friends with George G. Foster; a relationship began that was based on mutual admiration and fascination. Under Foster's influence Griswold was introduced to the love of books, and the two young men spent much time in discussions of literature. Griswold eventually grew tired of this friendship and abandoned Foster. Easily bored with people and places, Griswold soon moved again, traveling for the next couple of years. In 1834 he began working at *The Constitutionalist* in Syracuse, where he remained for a year. Griswold, using the transparent pen name Toby Trinculo, soon began his own paper, *The Porcupine,* which he used to rile the residents of Syracuse. Never intending the paper to last, Griswold moved to Fredonia a few months after its inception to edit *The Western Democrat and Literary Inquirer,* a position he held for only three weeks as a result of printing an article offensive to many of the Protestant residents of Fredonia.

In 1836 Griswold moved to New York City, where he was introduced by a friend to Caroline Searles, then nineteen. He soon moved to Olean as editor of the *Olean Advocate,* where he busied himself with the paper and promoting the Whig platform. He wrote and published his own poetry under the name of Toby Trinculo, protesting debtors' prisons, a cause close to him that he took up on several other occasions in his life. His interest in politics brought him to make a failed attempt for the Whig nomination to run for state senator. In spite of his active life in Olean, Griswold

Frontispiece and decorated title page for one of the anthologies of works by American authors that Griswold
compiled in the 1840s, through which he earned a reputation as a staunch literary nationalist
(Thomas Cooper Library, University of South Carolina)

returned to New York City and Caroline Searles, leaving the doomed paper in the hands of an assistant. He and Caroline were married 20 March 1837, the same year in which he met Horace Greeley, publisher of *The New-Yorker.* Griswold and Caroline lived for most of their marriage with her family.

In 1837 Griswold had designs on publishing a magazine called "The American Anthology: A Magazine of Poetry, Biography, and Criticism," but he was as yet too poor and too obscure to be successful with such an endeavor. Instead, he turned to the ministry, but soon after becoming a preacher, he took control of *The Vergennes Vermonter,* a paper designed to promote the Whig presidential candidate, Henry Clay. Griswold moved to Vermont, leaving behind his new wife, now pregnant with their first daughter, Emily. Throughout his marriage, his wife and children stayed in New York while he moved to other cities, and there is disagreement among biographers on whether or not

he liked being away from them. Although the family missed the life in New York, the Griswolds stayed in Vermont for more than a year, with Rufus writing and publishing his own poetry as well as his opinionated political editorials.

Moving back to New York after the paper changed management, Griswold began to work on Greeley's daily *Whig.* On 8 July 1839 Griswold and Park Benjamin began the *Evening Tattler,* which was at once followed by a weekly companion, *Brother Jonathan.* These publications served as forums for gossip, poetry, novels from England (of questionable copyright), and editorials. In these papers Griswold attacked Edgar Allan Poe and James Fenimore Cooper for the first time, setting the groundwork for his later tumultuous relationship with these authors. After separating from their publisher and beginning two new similar papers—the *Evening Signal* and *The New World*—Benjamin pushed Griswold out of this venture. As a result of this rift,

Greeley introduced Griswold to Thomas W. White, who published the *Southern Literary Messenger,* for whom Griswold wrote anonymously but did not edit.

In 1840, the year Griswold's second daughter, Caroline, was born, Greeley made him assistant editor of *The New-Yorker,* where he once again acted as a Whig supporter of William Henry Harrison's candidacy for president. At this time Griswold met Charles Fenno Hoffman, a former editor of *The New-Yorker.* While working for *The New-Yorker* Griswold decided to compile a gift book titled *The Biographical Annual: Containing Memoirs of Eminent Persons, Recently Deceased* (1841), comprising writings of authors, artists, political figures, and other people of note who had died during the year. He left the project before it was completed and moved to Philadelphia to take a job at *The Daily Standard.* Greeley was unhappily left to finish Griswold's first compilation.

In Philadelphia, Griswold finally reached agreement with a publisher, Carey and Hart, who agreed to produce his long-planned anthology, *The Poets and Poetry of America, with an Historical Introduction* (1842). The announcement of his plans, coupled with his upward social movement, made him popular company with the literary circles in Philadelphia. Poe was among those eager writers who decided that building a relationship with Griswold would prove beneficial. Griswold continued his newspaper work even with the contract, moving to Boston with work at the *Boston Daily Times* and *The Boston Notion.* He was in Boston when Transcendentalism was in vogue; he tolerated its existence but found it quite contrary to the morals reflected in his strict Christian upbringing. He expanded his literary circle of friends and acquaintances to include such writers as Henry Wadsworth Longfellow and Oliver Wendell Holmes. As his old friend and proponent Greeley was taken in by the transcendental teachings, Griswold allowed Greeley some space in *The Quarto Boston Notion,* a monthly compendium of *The Boston Notion,* even while in his editorials he was taking strong moral stances against drinking and dancing.

Never one to remain static for long, Griswold was back in Philadelphia by August of 1841 to complete the book he was working on for Carey and Hart. During his return to Philadelphia, he was forced back to New York and his wife and children in order to recuperate from an illness later diagnosed as tuberculosis. He quickly returned to Philadelphia, and in spite of his illness was soon making the rounds of literary salons where he was a sought after guest. He met Poe in 1842, a relationship that apparently began amicably, though it soon turned to a quarrelsome banter that ultimately led to more serious mudslinging.

Quarrels aside, Griswold included Poe in his first anthology. To compile *The Poets and Poetry of America,* Griswold read much published poetry and made his choices from the volumes he read. The anthology included biographical sketches and occasional criticism, and for that Griswold relied heavily on his writer friends and often the poets themselves. The volume was criticized for sticking to the accepted "good" poets and neglecting, or at best relegating to an appendix, some authors whose work was much stronger and more deserving of recognition. The first edition of the anthology was published 18 April 1842 and included works by ninety-one poets. Although generally favorably accepted and strong in its nationalism, the book came under fire for being too laudatory toward New England writers at the cost of other, more worthy, Southern poets. Many critics considered Griswold's introductions to be hyperbole.

Poe apparently took offense at Griswold's anthology and voiced his displeasure in published reviews. His criticism seemed to reflect other general complaints about the work—uneven inclusion and harping nationalism. This review seems to have been the start of Poe's personal attacks on Griswold. The ensuing attacks appeared as anonymous opinion pieces in the Philadelphia *Saturday Museum.* The book remained popular, however, and went into a second edition within a year. It continued to be republished over the next fourteen years, with only a few major changes between editions. Poe's opinions regarding Griswold's anthology, perhaps prophetically, anticipated the present critical reception of the book. Poe suggested that Griswold would be remembered only by those whom he had wronged and that any lasting fame would necessarily fall to one whom he had wronged.

In January 1842 Griswold, who had become an ordained minister in the Baptist Church in 1837, went to Washington, D.C., where he campaigned, apparently unsuccessfully, to become a navy chaplain in order to secure himself a cruise to help his tuberculosis. Griswold became an editor at *Graham's Magazine* in 1842 and remained there until October 1843, filling a position vacated by Poe. This job was in Philadelphia, again requiring him to leave his now pregnant wife and his daughters.

In November 1843 Caroline Griswold gave birth to a son and died suddenly only days later, followed shortly by her infant son. Griswold was devastated by her death, returning immediately to New York, where he sat with the dead Caroline for thirty hours, often kissing her. The funeral was punctuated by Griswold throwing himself on his wife's casket inside the tomb. He stayed for hours, having frustrated his friends' attempts to draw him away. More than a month after returning to work in Philadelphia, Griswold went back to Greenwood Cemetery in New York and entered the tomb. He opened the casket and kissed his decaying wife, took locks of hair, and stayed until a friend forced him to leave. Ultimately resigning himself to Caroline's death, he returned to work at *Graham's Magazine,* where he cultivated problems with his coworkers–personality clashes and battling wills. Conditions under which he left *Graham's Magazine* are unclear, though rumors suggest he offended Graham by writing for rival papers under another name.

Realizing that his true talent did not lie in creative writing, Griswold in the early 1840s had begun in earnest to compile and edit anthologies. In 1841 he finished the compilation of *Gems from American Female Poets,* which was published in 1842. It was followed in 1843 by *Readings in American Poetry* and *Readings in American Poetry for the Use of Schools,* both born of the already widely received *Poets and Poetry of America.* Although Griswold fell under attack from critics for his staunch nationalism, that characteristic also came to his rescue. Foreign attacks from such periodicals as the English *Foreign Quarterly Review* sent the American critics scurrying to defend him.

Griswold wrote "Curiosities of American Literature" to appear as an appendix to the 1844 Appleton edition of Isaac D'Israeli's *Curiosities of Literature, and the Literary Character Illustrated* (first published, 1791–1834). Similar to much of Griswold's other original writing, "Curiosities of American Literature" often comprises strings of quotations from other writers and from his earlier essays. Griswold hurriedly compiled several gift books–including *The Poetry of Love* (1844) and *The Cypress Wreath: A Book of Consolation for Those Who Mourn* (1844). These books were hastily created from previously published material and reprinted often.

While campaigning for copyright laws to protect American writers, Griswold acted as unscrupulously as the publishers from whom he was trying to protect the writers. He reprinted and compiled poems from English poets, among them John Milton and Walter Scott, contradicting both his ardent nationalism and his pro-writer copyright stance. He became active in 1844–1845 in the American Protestant Association–an anti-Catholic, anti-Irish organization–and acted as editor for the *Quarterly Review of the American Protestant Association* for two years. While serving as editor for the *Quarterly Review,* Griswold edited the first American edition of Milton's prose works. The biographical sketch included had its roots in an essay he had written for the *Quarterly Review.* This book is important in that it is a first American edition; yet the introduction, while factual, suffers from Griswold's habit of overuse of long strings of quotations. In 1844 Griswold's anthology, *The Poets and*

Title page for the anthology in which Griswold promoted the verse of Elizabeth Oakes Smith, Frances Sargent Osgood, and other women he had met in New York literary circles (Thomas Cooper Library, University of South Carolina)

Poetry of England, in the Nineteenth Century, was published. The entries were accompanied by biographical sketches and often excessive praise. Generally, his critical abilities seem to be questionable at best.

In 1845 Griswold set his romantic sights on Charlotte Myers, a wealthy older woman (forty-two years old to Griswold's twenty-nine) from Charleston, South Carolina, who was visiting her aunts for the summer. His decision to marry her was motivated by the lure of money and comfort, in addition to any feelings he may have felt for her. The upcoming marriage put him in a strange position–the editor of the *Quarterly Review of the American Protestant Association* engaged to a Jewish spinster. Apparently he tried unsuccessfully to end the engagement, but Charlotte and her aunts refused to let him escape. The couple was married hastily, and because of an undefined though often alluded to physical condition, the marriage was never consummated. In late 1845 he and his youngest daughter, Caroline, traveled to Charleston to continue the pretense of marriage. Although he enjoyed the social opportunities in Charleston, Griswold soon became disenchanted with farcical married life. The couple agreed to a separation but not a divorce, and Griswold's daughter stayed with the Charleston sisters while he returned to Philadelphia. They remained married for six years, during which Griswold was quite unhappy.

In 1847 his *Prose Writers of America,* which included several of Poe's stories, was published, and he was commissioned to create a multivolume biographical dictionary and to write a history titled *Washington and the Generals of the American Revolution.* The biographical dictionary never reached completion. Griswold moved to New York near the end of 1847, where he quickly took up the cause of women poets, of whom he became an ardent fan and proponent. He became good friends with Elizabeth Oakes Smith and Frances Sargent Osgood and was a regular at the literary salons. He found himself a popular man among the literary women, his mysterious marital status proving quite attractive. In 1848 Griswold increased his popularity with the ladies when he decided to create a collection of poetry by women, published in December 1848. It followed much the same pattern and reception as many of his other works—those poets whom he praised were happy; those criticized were angry; and those left out were misunderstood. Nevertheless, as did most of his compilations, the book sold well.

At about this time, however, Griswold and Poe began to pursue with vigor their contrariety. They moved in the same circles, and both wanted to keep their friends among the female literati happy. Both were good friends with Osgood and caught up in feuds among the women and attempts by many, including Poe, to convince Griswold to modify biographical information or criticism about some of the women.

After Poe died on 7 October 1849, Greeley requested that Griswold write the obituary, "The Death of Edgar A. Poe," for the *New-York Tribune.* The biographical information was taken from the sketch Poe provided Griswold for *The Poets and Poetry of America,* but Griswold's elaboration on Poe's character—suggesting that though Poe's death would leave a void in the literary world, he would not be missed as a person—was what caused unrest among his contemporaries and tainted Poe's reputation. The obituary was printed in the *New-York Tribune* and in several other contemporary journals.

Soon after Poe's death, Maria Clemm, Poe's aunt, asked Griswold to edit and compile his works. Whether or not she knew that Griswold had written the uncomplimentary tribute, which he signed with his transparent pseudonym, Ludwig, she maintained that Poe had asked that Griswold edit his works. No evidence to support her claim exists, and her story changed years later after she fell out with Griswold.

J. S. Redfield agreed to publish two volumes of Poe's works for Griswold. The January 1850 publications included Clemm's claim that Poe had asked in writing that Griswold be left in charge of the compilation. Griswold documents his apparently volatile relationship with Poe by letters of uncertain authenticity, the originals seen only by Griswold. A letter from Poe implying his indebtedness to Griswold both monetarily and otherwise exists only in Griswold's *The Works of the Late Edgar Allan Poe* (1850). The collection aroused emotion regarding Poe's memory and elicited several responses in defense of the dead writer.

Griswold undertook the third volume in 1850, soon after the publication of the first two and as he was beginning editorial work for *The International Monthly Magazine.* The third volume of Poe's works offered Griswold an opportunity to vindicate himself in reaction to responses elicited by his obituary as Ludwig. In defense of the infamous obituary and the first two Poe volumes, Griswold produced letters supposedly exchanged between him and Poe making their relationship appear quite amiable. Many of these letters have no corresponding original, and many of those that do have existing originals have been changed by Griswold. He changed dates, moved around excerpts, and created new text. Griswold intimated Poe misused the sundry advantages that were handed to him and not to Griswold—talent, intelligence, and money. He included, in addition to falsified letters, stories that were either untrue or greatly exaggerated, accusing Poe of plagiarism and inherent lack of originality. Griswold published a fourth volume in 1856, and the set was in its seventeenth edition in 1858. He met with little support in his criticism of Poe's character and with derision for how he chose to represent Poe's greater body of work. Although many of the entries representing Poe's criticism spoke harshly about other authors, none is included that show Griswold in a bad light; thus, their authenticity is suspect.

Between 1850 and 1852 Griswold was in charge of *The International Monthly Magazine,* which comprised reprints from European magazines as well as original works from Americans, many of whom were his friends. In this magazine Griswold first published his "Memoir" of Poe (October 1850) and his sketch in honor of their friend Osgood. He also used this publication as an outlet for much of his biographical work.

In 1852 Griswold, having fallen in love with Harriet McCrillis, became frustrated with his marriage to Charlotte and decided the time had come for him to pursue a divorce. Charlotte was uncooperative with such a move and fought Griswold, appointing herself guardian to Griswold's youngest daughter. Griswold abducted his daughter, using her as a pawn to force Charlotte to concede to the divorce. After finalization he never saw either his former wife or his youngest daughter again.

Griswold and Harriet McCrillis were married on 26 December 1852, soon after Griswold accepted a position as editor of P. T. Barnum's *The Illustrated News*. The following spring Harriet and Emily, Griswold's oldest daughter, were involved in a train wreck on their way to Maine. Although both survived, they spent months in Maine recuperating while Griswold again lived alone in New York. On his way to see them, he fell victim to the recurring tuberculosis that had plagued him years earlier. He soon joined his family in Maine, fathered a son, William McCrillis, and returned to New York by the fall. There he began making preparations for his family to join him. However, he encountered problems from several angles. Charlotte decided to contest the divorce. More seriously, he and a neighbor child were involved in an explosion in Griswold's home while searching for a gas leak using a lit candle. Griswold was burned on his face and hands. He soon recovered and was joined by his family, only to take ill again in the spring of 1854.

During his courtship and marriage, Griswold had been accumulating materials for his work *The Republican Court; or, American Society in the Days of Washington,* published in 1855. He was able to speak with many descendants of the founding fathers and collected a great deal of primary material for his book. The text comprises, characteristically, quotations from many letters of the founding fathers and their wives and daughters. It was well received by the American public, republished several times, and even serialized. Today it is most interesting as evidence of popular sentiment during the time. He also revised *The Poets and Poetry of America* one last

time, for its sixteenth edition, and began work on *Washington, a Biography* (1856–1860), control of which was ultimately relinquished to Benson J. Lossing as a result of Griswold's failing health.

In 1856 the *Cyclopaedia of American Literature* was published by Evert A. and George L. Duyckinck. Angry at being usurped as the foremost anthologist in America, Griswold undertook an extensive and critically scathing review. He left nothing untouched—from grammar to history. Meanwhile, Charlotte's divorce contention was found to be valid, as the divorce decree had been misplaced by the courts. Harriet moved to Maine, and Griswold lived alone again in New York. Harriet returned to New York for Griswold's last days. Rufus W. Griswold died on 27 August 1857 and was buried in Greenwood Cemetery in Brooklyn, New York.

Letters:

Passages from the Correspondence and Other Papers of Rufus W. Griswold, edited by William H. Griswold (Cambridge, Mass.: W. M. Griswold, 1898).

References:

Joy Bayless, *Rufus Wilmot Griswold, Poe's Literary Executor* (Nashville: Vanderbilt University Press, 1943);

Jacob Neu, "Rufus Wilmot Griswold," *University of Texas Studies in English,* special Griswold issue, 5 (1925);

Peter Stitt, "Edgar Allan Poe's Secret Sharer, part I," *Gettysburg Review,* 10, no. 2 (1997): 183–188; "Edgar Allan Poe's Secret Sharer, part II," *Gettysburg Review,* 10, no. 3 (1997): 359–370.

Papers:

The Rufus W. Griswold papers are housed in the Boston Public Library. Other materials are in the J. T. Fields Papers at the Henry E. Huntington Library and in the Rufus W. Griswold papers, 1838–1853, at the Clifton Waller Barrett Library, University of Virginia Library.

Fitz-Greene Halleck

(8 July 1790 – 19 November 1867)

Michael Cody
East Tennessee State University

See also the Halleck entry in *DLB 3: Antebellum Writers in New York and the South.*

BOOKS: *Poems,* by Halleck and Joseph Rodman Drake as Croaker, Croaker & Co., and Croaker, Jun. (New York: N.p., 1819);

Fanny, anonymous (New York: C. Wiley, 1819); republished as *Fanny: A Poem* (London: T. Tickler, 1837); enlarged as *Fanny, with Other Poems,* anonymous (New York: Harper, 1839);

Alnwick Castle, with Other Poems, anonymous (New York: G. & C. Carvill, 1827; enlarged edition, New York: George Dearborn, 1836);

The Recorder: With Other Poems (New York: Henry Ludwig, 1833);

The Poetical Works of Fitz-Greene Halleck (New York: Appleton, 1847);

The Croakers, by Halleck and Drake (New York: N.p., 1860);

Young America: A Poem (New York: D. Appleton, 1865);

Lines to the Recorder (New York [Printed by Alvord], 1866);

The Poetical Writings of Fitz-Greene Halleck; With Extracts from Those of Joseph Rodman Drake, edited by James Grant Wilson (New York: D. Appleton, 1869);

Poems (New York: Hurst, n.d.).

OTHER: *The Works of Lord Byron, in Verse and Prose . . . with a Sketch of His Life,* edited by Halleck (New York: George Dearborn, 1833);

Selections from the British Poets, 2 volumes, edited by Halleck (New York: Harper, 1840).

Fitz-Greene Halleck was one of the most popular and important American poets during the first half of the nineteenth century. A member of the Knickerbocker Group of New York, he was known as the American Byron because of his romantic and satirical (though often imitative) verse. Halleck's business was banking, but as a literary amateur he won such fame that on 15 May 1877, almost ten years after his death,

Fitz-Greene Halleck, 1828 (portrait by Henry Inman; New-York Historical Society)

a statue of him was unveiled in New York's Central Park during a ceremony attended by such luminaries as President Rutherford B. Hayes, William Tecumseh Sherman, and William Cullen Bryant.

Born on 8 July 1790, Fitz-Greene Halleck was one of three children of Israel Halleck and Mary Eliot Halleck of Guilford, Connecticut. The poet's paternal lineage stretches back through various Puritan, Royalist, and Quaker ancestors to Peter Hallock, who in 1640, tradition says, was one of the first Englishmen to settle the north shore of Long Island. Halleck's maternal great-great-great-grandfather was John Eliot, the Apostle to the Indians and one of the translators of the *Bay Psalm Book*. Although little is known of Fitz-Greene's early home life, his mother, Mary, apparently retained more of the New England Puritan background than did her husband. Still, she was a lover of poetry and probably helped develop a similar love in young Fitz-Greene. Israel Halleck was a Royalist and, during the American Revolution, often in the company of Colonel Banastre Tarleton both on campaigns and at table. In the small Puritan town of Guilford, he lived life in the spirit of an English cavalier, a character his son Fitz-Greene later also assumed to some extent.

James Grant Wilson, Halleck's first biographer, in *The Life and Letters of Fitz-Greene Halleck* (1869) describes the young poet as a precocious child. Halleck took advantage of what formal education Guilford offered; he began reading early and once claimed to have read every book in the Guilford public library. His first attempts at poetry–"A View of the United States," "The History of New England," and "The Fortunate Family"–were probably written when he was eleven or twelve years old. At fifteen, Halleck began work, keeping the accounts at a relative's store in Guilford. He joined the state militia in the summer of 1808 and soon achieved the rank of sergeant. The following winter he began an evening school in which he taught bookkeeping, along with arithmetic and writing. All the while, Halleck continued to compose verse, and in 1810 two of his poems were published in a New York newspaper, *The Columbian*–"Paraphrase of an Extract from the Italian by Mrs. Radcliffe" (22 August 1810) and "The Indian Warrior" (28 September 1810).

In May 1811 Halleck moved to New York, where after two months he found work in the offices of a Quaker banker, Jacob Barker. New York was morally and intellectually freer than Guilford, and Halleck evolved from a narrow village boy to a young man broadened by experience in the world. But being reserved and sensitive, he lived some time in New York before forming any friendships. One of the first of these friendships, and by far the most important for Halleck's early career in letters, was with Joseph Rodman Drake, a young physician and poet. After establishing this successful relationship, Halleck began widening his social connections in the city by joining the Ugly Club, of which he was elected poet laureate in 1814. That same year, as the War of 1812 wore on, Halleck wrote several successful war lyrics. Part of a volunteer troop organized for the defense of New York, the poet wrote an ode named for this military company, "The Iron Grays." The verses inspired the entire camp and were subsequently published in *The Columbian* (29 October

1814). After the war ended, Halleck broadened his social circle in New York, took two trips into the Southern states in 1816, and continued to develop his friendship with Drake.

Halleck's apprenticeship as a poet ended when he and Drake published what has come to be known as the Croaker Papers. These thirty-five satirical poems appeared in the *New-York Evening Post* and the *National Advertiser* between March and July 1819. As Croaker, Drake wrote fourteen of the poems in the series; Halleck wrote another thirteen, under the pseudonym Croaker, Junior; and the two poets collaborated on another eight as Croaker & Co. The poems addressed current topics of either local or national interest, and they and their mysterious authors quickly became the talk of the town. Light and playful rather than dark and scathing, the tone and detail of the Croakers' satires delighted New Yorkers and inspired many imitators.

The majority of the later Croaker poems were written by Halleck. Drake, who had contracted tuberculosis during the winter of 1816–1817, was growing worse, and in the autumn and winter of 1819, he made a desperate visit to New Orleans in the hope of improving his health. Because of the success of the Croaker Papers, Halleck began to feel that he had come into his own as a poet, and he wrote throughout the solitary time left him by Drake's absence. The result was the long poem *Fanny,* published in New York on 27 December 1819.

Fanny sold well, in part because of its connection with the successful Croaker Papers; the poem extends the satire of the earlier works as it rambles through New York scenes and society. Similar in form and tone to *Beppo* (1818) and *Don Juan* (1819) by George Gordon, Lord Byron, Halleck's poem tells more of Fanny's father's story than that of the young woman for whom the work is named. Having begun as a merchant with "A retail dry-goods store in Chatham Street," Fanny's father rises to the ranks of the nouveau riche, and,

> having mustered wherewithal to meet
> The gaze of the great world, he breathed the air
> Of Pearl Street–and "set up" in Hanover Square.

After rambling through bits of narrative interrupted by the speaker's "tea-table chat" about the life and personalities of New York, as well as the lyrics of songs the merchant writes, the poem reaches its conclusion. In the midst of the party of which Fanny has always dreamed, "When she in turn should be a *belle*," a great chandelier crashes to the floor, ruining the party and foreshadowing the following evening when

with a most important face
And dreadful knock, and tidings still more dreadful,
A notary came—sad things had taken place. . . .

Soon the house is for rent, and Fanny and her father disappear to some unknown place where they "live . . . upon air / And hope, and such cold, unsubstantial dishes. . . ." The poem is an early example of Halleck's thematic concentration on the conflict between dreams and reality.

Critical reactions to *Fanny* were mixed. A reviewer in the 6 January 1820 issue of the *New-York Evening Post* wrote that, although similarities existed between *Fanny* and *Beppo,* "the imitation will be found in most respects superior to the original." But many readers outside New York had difficulty reading the poem because of its many local allusions. Much later, in the July 1846 issue of *Godey's Lady's Book,* Edgar Allan Poe wrote, "If we except a certain gentlemanly ease and *insouciance,* with some fancy of illustration, there is really very little about this poem to be admired." Poe did not approve of the lack of formality in Halleck's verses, but at times the colloquial quality in *Fanny* points toward the more natural poetics of Walt Whitman.

Drake returned from his journey to New Orleans in the spring of 1820. The trip had done little, however, to prolong his life, and he died in September. In "On the Death of Joseph Rodman Drake," Halleck begins with a memorial epitaph that praises Drake's public character:

Green be the turf above thee,
    Friend of my better days!
None knew thee but to love thee,
    Nor named thee but to praise.

But the poem ends with Halleck's private grief:

While memory bids me weep thee,
    Nor thoughts nor words are free,
The grief is fixed too deeply
    That mourns a man like thee.

Drake's death stunned Halleck, and in the summer of 1822, troubled by depression, he booked passage to England, apparently in an effort to restore his health.

At the end of September—after seeing London and its environs and making a brief journey into France—Halleck headed north for a visit to Scotland. Along the way he stopped by Percy Castle at Alnwick. There, in early October, he wrote one of his most noted poems, "Alnwick Castle." The poet tells of his visit to the "Home of Percy's high-born race." In the beginning the poem reveals a romantic preoccupation with the castle's glorious past, its vine-covered ruins, and its lush natural surroundings:

A gentle hill its side inclines,
    Lovely in England's fadeless green,
To meet the quiet stream which winds
    Through this romantic scene
As silently and sweetly still,
As when, at evening, on that hill,
    While summer's wind blew soft and low,
Seated by gallant Hotspur's side,
His Katherine was a happy bride,
    A thousand years ago.

But as the poet reads "upon the chapel walls / Each high, heroic name" in the Percy history, he sees the family's prestige slowly dwindling, from the one member who fought in the Crusades to the one who "Fought for King George at Lexington, / A major of dragoons." At this point, the poem takes on a marked sense of disillusionment as those "romantic times" of Hotspur's England have given way to "this bank-note world" in which "Alnwick's but a market town." The world the poet inhabits is in decline. Although "Nature's aristocracy" still exists at Percy's Castle in the beauty of the current chambermaid, the old home and its history have become a commodity that the traveler can experience "For ten-and-sixpence sterling." This sense of being unable to reconcile the ideal and the real is characteristic of Halleck's poetry.

Halleck returned to the United States in 1823, where "Alnwick Castle" was published in the 6 December issue of the *New-York Evening Post.* Throughout the middle years of the 1820s, his literary reputation continued to increase, and his social circle broadened to include the Sedgwicks, James Fenimore Cooper, Samuel F. B. Morse, Gulian Verplanck, James Kirke Paulding, Richard Henry Dana, and Bryant. In a 20 January 1825 letter Catharine Maria Sedgwick describes to her brother Charles her impression on first meeting Halleck at a party:

He had a reddish, brown complexion, and a heavy jaw, but an eye so full of the fire and sweetness of poetry that you at once own him for one of the privileged order. He does not act as if he had spent his life in groves and temples, but he has the courtesy of a man of society. He dances with grace, and talks freely and without parade.

During this period Halleck wrote "Lines on the Death of Lieut. Allen," "Magdalen," "Woman," "Marco Bozzaris," and "Connecticut." Bryant published "Marco Bozzaris" in the first issue of *The New-York Review, and Athenaeum Magazine* (June 1825). The poem tells the story of Greek patriot Marco Bozzaris's August 1823 death in battle during the Greek war for independence. It was a popular subject, and "Marco Bozzaris" was reprinted in several American and British publications over the next year and a half. Halleck's "Connecticut" also appeared in *The New-York Review* (March 1826). A longer lyric than either "Alnwick Castle" or "Marco Bozzaris," "Connecticut" includes more substantial American materials than the earlier poems–stanzas on such subjects as Connecticut's geography and the character of its people, the last witch trial in the state, Cotton Mather, and "Yankee Doodle."

The first collected edition of Halleck's poetry, *Alnwick Castle, with Other Poems,* appeared in 1827. In addition to the title poem, Halleck included sixteen of his more serious works, some of which were "Marco Bozzaris," "Connecticut," "Woman," "Magdalen," "On the Death of Joseph Rodman Drake," "Burns," and "Wyoming." "Burns"–inspired by Halleck's 1822 trip to Scotland, where he visited Robert Burns's birthplace and grave–had been published in the *United States Review and Literary Gazette* (January 1827), and after its inclusion in *Alnwick Castle, with Other Poems,* it became one of Halleck's most enduring lyrics. Critics in general voiced overwhelming approval of Halleck's talents displayed in the new book; their only regret was that the poet had not written more. The slender volume sold out quickly.

As Halleck's reputation as a poet and man of letters increased, his literary production began slowly to decrease. Although he wrote what was for him an unusual number of poems in the years between leaving Barker's employ late in 1828 and becoming the private secretary of John Jacob Astor in 1832, Halleck published relatively little new poetry for the remainder of his life. He began contributing his work to annuals and seeing it selected for anthologies such as Samuel Kettel's *Specimens of American Poetry* (1829) and George Barrell Cheever's *American Common-Place Book of Poetry* (1831). In addition to editing the 1832 publication of the poetic and prose works of Byron, Halleck wrote a few poems–including "The Field of the Grounded Arms," "Red Jacket," and "A Poet's Daughter"–that later appeared in George Dearborn's 1836 enlarged edition of *Alnwick Castle, with Other Poems.* In 1833 Halleck published *The Recorder: With Other Poems,* a short pamphlet; the title piece had been written in 1828 at the height of Barker's legal battle against Richard Riker, recorder of New York City, and it had already appeared in both the *New-York Evening Post* (20 December 1828) and the *New-York American* (24 December 1828). Despite his no longer being as creatively active as he had been in the 1820s, Halleck was increasingly sought after as a

Joseph Rodman Drake, Halleck's literary collaborator, circa 1820 (engraving by Thomas Kelly)

judge of literary contests and as a favorite guest at balls and parties.

Although a good poet, Halleck was never truly original. He was largely influenced by his reading, which, although limited by his relative lack of any deep knowledge of the classics, was broadened somewhat by his familiarity with European languages, especially French. His primary influences were the Bible and English poets such as William Shakespeare, Alexander Pope, Thomas Gray, Robert Southey, William Wordsworth, Byron, and Thomas Campbell. Halleck's theory of poetry, according to Nelson Frederick Adkins in *Fitz-Greene Halleck: An Early Knickerbocker Wit and Poet* (1930), was based on "a poet's ability to emotionalize the fact–to transform events by the subtle power of the imagination." Halleck's strength lay in his lyricism, and the strength of this quality, in turn, lay in his power of expression, his "ability," Adkins says, "to compress meaning into a single line or phrase." But what ultimately prohibited Halleck from becoming a great poet was that his facility of expression outstripped his feeling. Thus, in his lighter verse his technique and sensibilities are most evenly matched.

Another element in Halleck's character that hindered his development as a poet was his belief that a life solely devoted to belles lettres was impractical. In this notion can be seen both the balance and conflict between character elements that were the legacy of his parents: from his father, he gained a love of beauty; from his mother, a Puritan practicality. This juxtaposition of character elements naturally found its way into his poetry. In many of his best poems Halleck struggles without success to reconcile the differences between the world of the romantic ideal and that of quotidian reality.

Halleck never committed himself wholly to poetry, but he maintained a literary reputation, assuring both himself and his poetry a place in the literary life of the United States of the nineteenth century. New editions of his work continued to appear throughout his lifetime, and in 1837 Columbia College awarded him—along with fellow poets Bryant and Charles Fenno Hoffman—an honorary Master of Arts. In 1840 Halleck edited *Selections from the British Poets,* published by Harper and Brothers. Two years later, in February 1842, he met Charles Dickens during the novelist's famous visit to America. But throughout the 1840s Halleck's life was largely a social one, and he seems to have written little, if any, poetry, despite great encouragement from the literary world.

Early in 1849 Halleck left New York and retired to his native Guilford, but he made frequent trips—almost annually for the Fourth of July—to the city in which he had lived so long, keeping in touch with the literary culture of which he had so long been a part. He published one more piece of poetry during his retirement; "Young America" appeared in the *Ledger* (23 January 1864), but it is a weak satire of America as a fifteen-year-old boy and shows only occasional sparks of Halleck's former satirical vigor. After one last visit to New York in October 1867, Fitz-Greene Halleck died peacefully in Guilford the following month. On 8 July 1869 a monument was erected over his grave, during the dedication of which, a poem by Oliver Wendell Holmes was read. Eight years later the Halleck statue was dedicated in New York's Central Park.

References:

Nelson Frederick Adkins, *Fitz-Greene Halleck: An Early Knickerbocker Wit and Poet* (New Haven: Yale University Press, 1930);

Joseph Slater, "The Case of Drake and Halleck," *Early American Literature,* 8 (Winter 1974): 285–297;

James Grant Wilson, *The Life and Letters of Fitz-Greene Halleck* (New York: Appleton, 1869).

Papers:

The major collection of Fitz-Greene Halleck manuscripts and correspondence constitutes part of the Clifton Waller Barrett Library of American Literature at the University of Virginia.

Alice B. Neal Haven

(13 September 1827 – 23 August 1863)

Valerie DeBrava

BOOKS: *Helen Morton's Trial,* as "Cousin Alice" (New York: General Protestant Episcopal Sunday School Union, 1849);

The Gossips of Rivertown; With Sketches in Prose and Verse, as Alice B. Neal (Philadelphia: Hazard & Mitchell, 1850);

Pictures from the Bible, as Neal (Philadelphia: W. P. Hazard, 1851);

The Child's Fancy; or, Stories for Grave and Gay, as edited by "Cousin Alice" (Philadelphia: W. P. Hazard, 1852);

Watch and Pray; or, Helen's Confirmation, as "Cousin Alice" (New York: General Protestant Episcopal Sunday School Union, 1852);

"No Such Word as Fail"; or, The Children's Journey, as Neal (New York: D. Appleton, 1852);

"All's Not Gold that Glitters"; or, The Young Californian, as "Cousin Alice" (New York: D. Appleton, 1853);

Contentment Better Than Wealth, as Neal ("Cousin Alice") (New York: D. Appleton, 1853);

In the World, but Not of the World (New York: General Protestant Episcopal Sunday School Union, 1853);

Patient Waiting No Loss; or, The Two Christmas Days, as Neal ("Cousin Alice") (New York: D. Appleton, 1853);

The Pet Bird and Other Stories, as "Cousin Alice" (New York: D. Appleton, 1853);

First Lessons in Gentleness and Truth (Boston, 1854);

Nothing Venture, Nothing Have, as "Cousin Alice" (New York: D. Appleton, 1855);

Out of Debt, Out of Danger, as "Cousin Alice" (New York: D. Appleton, 1855);

The Church Bell (New York: General Protestant Episcopal Sunday School Union, 1856);

Charlie Hope: A Christmas Token (New York: General Protestant Episcopal Sunday School Union, 1857);

A Place for Everything, and Every Thing in Its Place (New York: D. Appleton, 1857);

The Coopers; or, Getting Under Way (New York: D. Appleton, 1858);

Loss and Gain; or, Margaret's Home (New York & London: D. Appleton, 1860);

Where There's a Will There's a Way (New York: D. Appleton, 1861);

The Good Report: Morning and Evening Lessons for Lent (New York: D. Appleton, 1867);

Home Stories (New York: D. Appleton, 1869).

OTHER: Joseph C. Neal, *Charcoal Sketches,* edited by Mrs. Joseph C. Neal (New York: Burgess, Stringer, 1848);

Whitcher, Frances M., *The Widow Bedott Papers,* with an introduction by Neal (New York: Mason, Baker & Pratt, 1856);

Mary E. Bradley, *Douglass Farm; A Juvenile Story of Life in Virginia,* edited by "Cousin Alice" (New York: D. Appleton, 1858).

Born Emily Bradley on 13 September 1827, the writer who later become known as Clara Cushman, Alice G. Lee, "Cousin Alice," Alice B. Neal, and Alice B. Haven lived a mosaic life as inventive and self-examining as her pseudonyms suggest. What often in the thirty-five years of her life proved to be a manifold, if not divided, existence can be traced back to her third birthday. When Emily's father, George Bradley, died on 13 September 1830, he left his three-year-old daughter the legacy of his temperament without the affirmations of his example. This temperament—which was proud, ambitious, and resolutely secular—was frequently at odds with the pious and unworldly temperament bestowed by his widow, Sarah Brown Bradley. Emily, therefore, was destined from the time of her father's death to struggle within the context of her maternal family against her father's spirit of brash confidence—a struggle that later came to fruition in school, marriage, and career.

A tangible, fragmenting consequence of her father's death came when, at the age of six, Emily was adopted by her maternal uncle. The Reverend J. Newton Brown and his wife were a childless couple living in Massachusetts when they agreed to bring Emily into their home. This adoption meant the first of several important moves for her as she moved from her native Hudson, New York, to Boston, where her uncle was editing *Fessenden and Company's Encyclopedia of Religious Knowledge* (1835). This move was followed a short time later by a move to Exeter, New Hampshire, where the Browns had lived before settling in Boston and where Brown was installed as a Baptist minister.

Emily attended school in Boston and Exeter. Her schooling in Exeter was cut short by a serious eye affliction that recurred for years with incapacitating bouts of blindness. The onset of weak health had, in fact, begun before her move to Boston, separating her from her siblings in what developed into a trying sense of separation from her peers. Now the social experience of school ended abruptly with Emily's withdrawal into a solitary, darkened room. The intellectual rigors persisted as Emily cultivated her imagination and her memory in the absence of books, parodying familiar poems and composing stories. She once astonished visitors by memorizing half of Tennyson's "In Memoriam" after one reading. Companionship, however, grew increasingly rare as the young invalid became acquainted with a solitude that haunted her into her adult years, driving her to an almost reckless dependence on the distractions of society.

At the age of nine, Emily returned to New York and to her remarried mother. In New York, while attending a Hudson girls' school, Emily developed what became the lifelong habit of journal writing. The discipline of introspection that this habit fostered later served as the basis for one of her juvenile stories, "Keeping a Journal," which appeared in *The Pet Bird and Other Stories* (1853). Emily's youthful journal documents a continuity of identity that contrasts with the upheaval of her circumstances, even as it records personal conflicts derived from her often divided outer life. Thus, as she bounced back and forth between households, leaving her mother a second time and returning to her uncle in her early teens, Emily cultivated a focus for her identity through her private writings.

Her introduction into yet another academic environment—this time at New Hampton, New Hampshire—found its compensatory (yet also conflicted) focus in journal entries that fixated on health and duty. While in Hudson, Emily had experienced a recurrence of blindness. On the eve of a trip to the Catskill Mountains with her brother and sister, she had been stricken with another temporary but debilitating bout of eye trouble. The generous self-control she had exercised on that occasion in urging her brother and sister to make the trip without her became, in the midst of academic plenty, a keen and aggravated feeling of entitlement that channeled into her personal writing a nagging sense of her potential and her limitations. Blind amid her uncle's library and compelled to absorb her lessons by listening to her classmates study aloud, Emily chafed against the limitations of her poor health. Her journal shows that she considered herself to have a calling paradoxically thwarted by the God-given circumstances of her health—what she often thought of as pronounced if frustrated talents. "What is the use of my good resolutions about system and time, and doing my best?" she asked herself in one journal entry. "I feel the sting of an incurable malady," she wrote, pronouncing in despair, "I am without God and without hope." Yet, no sooner does she articulate this dismal state of affairs than she flies in the face of her own hopelessness. "This bitterness must be overcome. It will poison my life."

Catalyzed by illness and the heightened awareness of mortality, Emily used this refined sense of her own intellectual and artistic potential as a unifying aspect of her existence. She struggled between the secular and ambitious spirit of her father and the otherworldly, dutiful spirit of her mother. "I sometimes feel that I am not born for a common destiny," she wrote in her journal during her schoolgirl years, "that I have talents which might elevate me above those with whom I now associate. . . ." The next paragraph of this journal entry concludes with the brash apostrophe, "henceforth, ambition, be thou my angel!" Almost as soon as Emily expresses this desire for individual, public distinction, though, she effaces the personal glory with words about duty and holy labor. "I would that it might be a holy ambition," she writes of her new "affirmation," "that I might have the love of the good as well as the worldly; that I might have the thanks of my fellowcreatures, as well as their praises." A moment after expressing her desire to rise above those around her, Emily casts her envisioned distinction as the dutiful surrender of talent for the good of others. "I will begin my work by improving my time, and by being ambitious in small things. I will strive to perform my *duty,* and when I come to the great struggle, I shall not be fainthearted." A competitive, worldly spirit, thus, is deflected into the self-effacing appreciation of the collective good emphasized by her mother.

This tension—potentially a "great struggle" in its own right—is, of course, not solely the consequence of parental influence. The tension points to the nineteenth-century gender ideology that censured a woman's tendencies toward competition and self-promoting public display. During the antebellum period in which Haven lived and wrote, young women were not encouraged to make public spectacles of themselves, particularly when such visibility presumed an aggressive ego. Thus, one of Emily's teachers, in a letter to her sister, expressed dismay and concern over her student's noncompliant, if gifted, nature. "Emily gives me many anxious hours," the teacher wrote. "She lacks heart; she lacks the power to rise above herself, and to forget herself in the happiness and good of others." Yet, where there is insensitivity and egocentrism, the watchful teacher concedes, there is also enormous talent. "She has an extraordinary mind; she is mentally fascinating, and will be so externally. She is proudly ambitious; and should she continue so, and ever have good health and the untrammelled use of her eyes, she will not rest till she has achieved a reputation as a writer." Such suspicious approval, always poised on the edge of equivocation, was characteristic even of Haven's first biographer. Cornelia Holroyd Bradley Richards ("Mrs. Manners"), the author of the 1865 biography, *Cousin Alice: A Memoir of Alice B. Haven,* exhibits the same ambivalence toward female accomplishment and propriety as the teacher at New Hampton. Commenting on the confidence of Haven's friends that she was headed toward "a brilliant literary career," Richards ventures her own opinion, printed in italics, that the proper fulfillment of a young woman's ambition must ultimately be self-sacrifice. These friends "did not foresee that this strong, personal ambition, would merge, as her heart expanded and her life developed, into nobler purposes and loftier aims, to whose accomplishment she would sacrifice every per-

sonal advantage and every thought of self." The predictions of success, this observation implies, overlooked the highest claim to recognition for a woman, which was the immersion of self in the roles of wife and mother. Of course, this observation by Richards is contradictory, given its expression in a narrative that would not have been written had Haven never adhered to her "personal ambition."

These divisions had immediate effect on Haven as an emerging writer. During her early years as a student, she contributed often to magazines and newspapers. The practice concerned her friends, who would have preferred that she publish, if publish she must, only after she had attained the height of her literary powers. Unable to wait, Haven satisfied her friends' desire for discretion by sending out material under assumed names. The earliest pseudonyms were "Clara Cushman" and "Alice G. Lee." This latter name is the one that the budding writer used when she sent a story, "The First Declaration," to *Neal's Saturday Gazette.* Joseph C. Neal, editor of the Philadelphia newspaper, responded enthusiastically, saying that the tale was "like moonlight on the flowers when the weary day is done, or like music on the water. . . ." Not surprisingly, other submissions followed, most of which were published or mentioned in the *Gazette.* On at least one occasion, however, Neal withheld a story from print because he felt it demonstrated a brash disregard for the conventions of small-town life, a disregard that might alienate some readers and that certainly called into question the feminine politeness of its author. In this manner, Neal took upon himself a power of censorship that passed from the literary to the personal as he eventually pursued an intimate correspondence with "Alice G. Lee." Within a year Neal managed to peer beneath the pseudonymous veil enough to feel comfortable proposing marriage. Thus, the editor and the young writer in December 1846 embarked on a shared existence in which love was balanced against redefining negotiations of identity and power. While the worldly Neal sought to improve his wife by introducing her into cultivated circles and teaching her the virtues of restraint, she responded by alternately embracing that benign, ladylike identity and hiding behind it. In choosing no longer to respond to the name "Emily," but only to the name "Alice," the young wife and emerging author embraced the identity supported by her editor-husband while asserting the inaccessibility of a prior self.

In July 1847, less than a year after her wedding, Neal found herself a widow. A sudden, peculiar illness—what his contemporaries called brain fever—struck Joseph Neal only a few months into the marriage, leaving him bedridden and frequently incoherent. Increasing periods of lucidity proved deceptively encouraging, for he died suddenly a few months after he was stricken. Alice, baffled by the unexpected loss of her husband, turned to Neal's elderly mother for support in what turned out to be the beginning of a prolonged, symbiotic intimacy. Realizing that they were essentially alone in the world, the two women decided to live together and provide for one another. Her former mother-in-law had a home to share, and Alice Neal could offer the affection and assistance of a daughter.

While relying on her mother-in-law for support on the domestic end, Alice Neal ventured boldly into the publicly competitive realm of newspaper publishing. At the age of twenty she confidently assumed her husband's responsibilities as editor of the *Gazette*–enlisting the contributions of various authors, writing editorials, and overseeing the juvenile department, "The Bird's Nest." To the surprise of many observers, neither Alice Neal's youth nor her sex prevented her from succeeding in her new editorial role. One of Joseph Neal's partners is quoted in Richards's biography as commenting on how worldly and capable Alice showed herself to be in handling her new responsibilities: "Alice Neal was the most remarkable woman I ever met. Young girl as she was at that time, she comprehended the business details laid before her, and showed a judgment in regard to them which no other woman I ever knew could have shown. . . ." Occasionally, Alice Neal was envied or distrusted for her competence, an experience that she registered with a defiant resilience in her poem "Unmasking." Addressing the watchful presence of her departed husband, she states, "And I go forth *alone,* to brave / Life's falsehood and its scorn; / Remembering that its cold deceit / Thou, too, hast nobly borne, / And with a pure humility, / Its offered honors worn." This guarded willingness to "go forth alone," to confront head-on the suspicious scrutiny of a world unaccustomed to independent women, eventually developed into a playful and deft appreciation of business affairs. According to Richards, years after her stint with the *Gazette,* Emily Neal Haven responded to a fellow writer who claimed to "detest business interviews and arrangements":

What a foolish thing for a sensible woman to say. *I enjoy them,* especially when I can have things my own way! I like to unravel a tangle or open a clear skein; it is as fine as getting out a problem in Algebra, and much more in my line! I like to use what little knowledge of business I have, and exercise my tact if necessary and I have always very pleasant business interviews.

Her propensity for self-effacement had evidently yielded to her assertive spirit of independence. The difficult balance she had maintained for years between humility and self-promotion now resolved itself into the confident negotiation of a problematic public realm.

After the death of her husband, she began making frequent visits to New York City, where her brother lived. There she met Anne Lynch, Ann S. Stephens, Elizabeth Oakes Smith, and other literati. There, too, she met the man who was to become her second husband, Samuel L. Haven. A New York broker who hoped to make a fortune out West, Samuel Haven was departing for California indefinitely when he obtained an informal promise from the young widow that she would marry him on his return East. Meanwhile, the years between 1848, the date of Samuel Haven's departure from New York, and 1 January 1853, when the couple married, were filled with activity for Alice Neal. She continued living with her former mother-in-law, while the publication of several literary works brought the young editor unprecedented recognition and financial independence.

The largely autobiographical story of a child's struggle with temporary blindness, *Helen Morton's Trial,* was published in 1849 by the Sunday School Union as the first in a series of books for Sunday school use. *The Gossips of Rivertown; With Sketches in Prose and Verse,* a work similar to the pieces Joseph Neal had censored for their cutting and sagacious (that is, unladylike) wit, appeared in 1850. *"No Such Word as Fail"; or, The Children's Journey,* the first in a series of children's books published by D. Appleton and Company, appeared in 1852, helping to secure Neal's reputation as "Cousin Alice," the mistress of didactic uplift. She also became a regular contributor to *Godey's Lady's Book* during this period, writing a range of stories and managing her own editorial department. One tale in particular, "Marrying a Planter" (printed in the June 1856 issue of *Godey's Lady's Book,* three and a half years after her second marriage) offers a revealing and complicated glimpse into Alice B. Haven's psyche, with her history of personal struggle with gender-inflected notions of duty and self-sacrifice.

"Marrying a Planter" gives the story of a pampered bride who leaves New York behind to settle with a Virginia planter. Rather than a roseate depiction of the marital "ever after," this tale offers an honest picture of the challenges that await a young woman who exchanges a privileged life of urban amusement for a modest, often monotonous life of rural production. The tale, in fact, presents the challenges as those not only of the disappointed bride, but also of the frustrated husband and the anxious mother-in-law. Having lived a life in which she "never did anything" (by which the mother-in-law, Mrs. Ridgely, means "sewing or housekeeping"), Ellen Washington is now faced with the responsibilities of cooking for her husband and knitting for the "servants." Insofar as she fails as a wife to embrace "the mysteries of ham-carving and sausage making, . . . pickling and packing," she fails to the censorious eye of her husband, Henry, and to the more charitably discerning eye of Mrs. Ridgely. "Poor child!" the mother-in-law sighs in sympathy after Ellen describes the life of amusement she led in New York, "But what have you found to do here [when] there are no lessons, and visitors, and not even a piano to keep you company? What a change for you!" Both regional and socioeconomic, the change to which Ellen must adjust is a surprising corrective to her urbane and detached notions of marriage as the simultaneous pursuit of separate pleasures, as well as to her narrow conception of the Southern matron's life as a pampered, passive existence. In answer to Ellen's recollection that a former schoolmate from the South "never . . . dressed her own hair until she came North . . . and . . . would not even learn fancy-work, it was such trouble," Mrs. Ridgely offers the vision of a rural, labor-intensive domesticity predicated on cooperation and self-sacrifice, a paternalistic domesticity that presents "housewifery" as the plantation mistress's redemption from solitude and boredom.

> . . . we are plain farm people. Further south, on rice and sugar plantations, where the heat is greater, and wealth is in proportion to the number of hands and acres, you might have realized this paradise of indolence; but, as far as society goes, you would still be worse off. Just think of miles of cotton and corn fields, with one solitary home in the middle of it, surrounded by negro cabins, the cotton press and its belongings, and the only white woman on the place besides yourself the overseer's wife, in nine cases out of ten a woman of no education or refinement, not half so companionable as a well-trained servant at the North. Think of the monotony of such an existence. . . . The gentlemen can ride . . . on horseback without a thought of the road, and often meet for drives, clubs, and political purposes; but carriage roads are by no means turnpikes, so, in sheer necessity, the ladies of the household are domestic, in the generally accepted sense of the term. Housewifery is their great resource, and, whatever they do as young girls, as wives, and mothers, they are busy enough.

Only when Ellen sheds her Northern, upper-class notions of marriage does she find harmony in her new home. Mrs. Ridgely's guidance helps the young bride to see the limitations of her "worldliness," offering an alternative horizon of industry and skill. Through such instruction, Ellen's urbanity becomes the ornamental chapter in a larger moral and spiritual calculus of self-sacrifice. Suddenly made dispensable as the by-products of a particular region and class, Ellen's expectations and

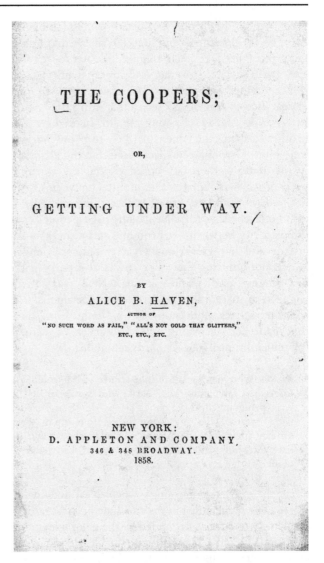

THE COOPERS;

OR,

GETTING UNDER WAY.

BY

ALICE B. HAVEN,

AUTHOR OF

"NO SUCH WORD AS FAIL," "ALL'S NOT GOLD THAT GLITTERS,"
ETC., ETC., ETC.

NEW YORK:
D. APPLETON AND COMPANY,
346 & 348 BROADWAY.
1858.

Title page for Haven's novel for which she drew on her own experiences during the early years of marriage (courtesy of Special Collections, Thomas Cooper Library, University of South Carolina)

attachments are swallowed up in a universalizing catechism of compliance. " . . . what is real happiness?" Mrs. Ridgely asks before supplying her own answer. " . . . I have always found the catechism answers it very well for us, when it tells us 'to do our duty in that state of life to which it has pleased God to call us,' instead of forgetting that there is such a thing as duty, or sitting down helplessly and fretting over it if seen."

The lessons in submission and sacrifice that "Marrying a Planter" offers its reader parallel Haven's own struggles as a daughter, a student, a writer, a wife, and a businesswoman. The expectations for self-effacement that made these struggles so difficult merely lurked during the interim years of her engagement to Samuel Haven. Between 1848 and

1853, when the broker returned from California, Alice Neal aggressively pursued the career that made her a recognized, respected figure. She wrote steadily and with success, forging a distinct identity as a clever, competent author. She also made a bold appearance on the social scene that contrasted with her retiring years as a young invalid. Invited by her brother to spend the winter of 1851–1852 in Charleston, South Carolina, she discovered that the hospitality of that Southern city could exceed the warmth even of its own climate. The months between October and February were filled with activity and gaiety as "the fascinating Mrs. Neal" surprised people with the disparity between her brooding seriousness as an author and her gregarious vivacity among friends. When not amusing the other guests at a party with her singing and piano playing, Neal was often engaged in memorable repartee. Her afternoons she spent horseback riding, often in a "Jenny Lind" hat that made her, according to one observer, "a picture for remembrance!" As Richards maintains,

> No one who met her during the winter of '51 [could] forget 'the fascinating Mrs. Neal,' whose movements were paragraphed in the public prints, whose *bon mots* were repeated, who was always the centre of the most brilliant circle in the room, who seemed too bright and happy to know any thing of the serious and shady side of life.

Even these winter mornings when Neal habitually wrote were spent sitting in the sunshine or in front of a crackling wood fire, surrounded by the natural levity of light and warmth. These months in Charleston were eager, exuberant months, quite different from the time that the young bride in "Marrying a Planter" spends in the South. Solemn and laborious self-sacrifice were absent from her milieu.

The return of Samuel Haven from California in 1852 soon changed the young widow's self-satisfied existence, however. While there is little personal record of Alice Haven's matrimonial mind-set, her journal—the 1 January 1853 entry for which notes her wedding in a factual tone—registers an overwhelming resignation. To the perception that "our marriage seemed hasty and unwise" Haven adds, "In the tangle of circumstances which surrounded me, I do not see how it would have been better to wait. I certainly believe our Father overruled all." On the day of her wedding Haven announced her marriage to her mother-in-law, Mrs. Neal, as though it were the result of arduous reflection. "Mamma, I have decided," she said with a portentous sense of her separation from the elderly woman, "I am Mr. Haven's wife." Tellingly, the language in Haven's journal becomes

increasingly pietistic after 1853, in part because Haven was struggling against her new husband's lack of faith by immersing herself in the tenets of her religion, but also because she was looking for a way to cope with the personal sacrifices of remarriage. Less than two weeks after her wedding, Haven wrote a private plea to her Creator: "Help me to pray constantly for my husband's best good, to look forward with cheerfulness and resignation to the events of the future." Day after day, Haven copied prayers into her journal: "Beware lest any man spoil you through philosophy and vain deceit, after the traditions of men, after the rudiments of the world, and not after Christ"; "Forbearing one another, and forgiving one another, even as Christ forgave you"; "And above all things, put on Charity, which is the bond of perfectness." Although it was not plainly visible to the friends she had made in Charleston, Haven had cultivated her religious impulses in recent years and sought now to preserve them in the face of a purely secular existence. Haven saw her religious tendencies, furthermore, as a way of dealing with the compromises inherent in her transition from a strong-minded widow to a compliant wife. Charity and forbearance could only ease the surrender of her independence.

Haven's fiction was another way for her to work through the contrary pulls of gratified individualism and domestic duty, a process evidenced by the publication of "Marrying a Planter" three years into her marriage. One of Haven's most popular works was *The Coopers*. Like "Marrying a Planter," *The Coopers* first appeared in *Godey's Lady's Book* between January and December of 1857. Published in book form by D. Appleton and Company in 1858, *The Coopers* illustrates the perils that await every newly married couple. As Haven's biographer Richards observes, "this volume is full of unobstrusive wisdom, sometimes dearly purchased by its writer, and therefore the more valuable to all making the experiment which now occupied her." This "experiment," marriage, emerges from *The Coopers*—as it does from "Marrying a Planter"—as the overriding good in a scenario of conflicts and disappointments. "Many a young couple," Richards remarks, "has learned, from the experiences of 'The Coopers,' to avoid quicksands, to 'find the leak,' and to sail safely into smooth water, where the voyage of life can be made pleasantly and profitably."

Between her marriage in 1853 and her death ten years later, Haven had five children. She continued to write, however, maintaining a literary reputation significant enough to precede her when she traveled with her husband. In 1859 Haven and her family moved to "The Willows," a New York estate that in its former identity as "Closet Hall" had been home to James Fenimore Cooper. In symbolic terms the move signified the convergence of Haven's literary and domestic ambitions and pointed toward a unity of identity that had escaped her for many years. Haven expressed this convergence and its liberating possibilities in a phrase that points ahead to Virginia Woolf. Writing to her sister, Haven describes "The Willows" as "a home of our own," a place where she can "take nature back to my heart" in a spiritual and familial openness as key to her creativity as the independence and privacy of Woolf's "room."

With the tensions between domestic duty and personal freedom apparently neutralized, the conflicts that always threatened to fragment Haven's life soon found expression in the Civil War. Haven felt the effects of the war not as a distant tragedy but as a set of intensely personal struggles and losses. In one letter she wrote, "I lie down and rise up with the desolation of the widow and the childless encompassing me. I pray always that God will give wisdom to our rulers, and bring peace to this poor land." During her final years, Haven wrote several poems about the war, including "Bull Run, Sunday, July 21st" (1862), "In the Fires" (composed 1861), and "Our Alas!", published in *Cousin Alice*. This last poem, written in response to the burning of Charleston and published only after Haven's death, reads, indeed, like a fiery expurgation of the author's personal history, as well as of the city's past–a "sister city" that chose to "bare her proud head to storms." Looking back now from the conservative perspective of Alice Haven–author, wife, and mother–and with the consolidating sense of rectitude that is the invention of both personal and political hindsight, the poet acknowledges the destruction of an alternative future with the burning of the Southern city: "Compelled, we 'stand afar to watch thy burning,' / With our alas! alas! for thy disdain. . . ."

In 1862 Haven suffered a hemorrhage that confined her to bed for the remaining year of her life. Advised by her doctors to "lay aside her pen," Haven fought against a feeling of ruin that attests to the smoldering consciousness of "Mrs. Neal." "After sixteen years of constant professional occupation," she wrote, "it was a struggle no human friend can appreciate to give up my business engagements." The sacrifice of all activity was unavoidable, however, as Haven's health continued to falter. The birth in 1863 of her fifth child hastened the decline, and by August this well-loved, prolific writer was dead at the age of thirty-five.

Biography:

Cornelia Holroyd Bradley Richards, *Cousin Alice: A Memoir of Alice B. Haven* (New York: D. Appleton, 1865).

References:

Evert A. Duyckinck and George L. Duyckinck, *Cyclopaedia of American Literature* (New York: Scribner, 1856), pp. 682–683;

Sara Josepha Buell Hale and Carrie Chapman Catt, *Woman's Record; or Sketches of All Distinguished Women, from "The Beginning" till A.D. 1850* (New York: Harper, 1853), pp. 755–756;

John S. Hart, *The Female Prose Writers of America* (Philadelphia: E. H. Butler, 1857), pp. 363–365;

Elizabeth F. Hoxie, "Haven, Emily Bradley Neal" in *Notable American Women* (Cambridge, Mass.: Belknap Press of Harvard University Press, 1971), pp. 158–159;

Stanley J. Kunitz and Howard Haycraft, eds., *American Authors, 1600–1900: A Biographical Dictionary of American Literature* (New York: Wilson, 1938), pp. 346–347;

Cornelia Holroyd Bradley Richards, "Alice B. Haven," in *Godey's Lady's Book* (January 1864): 50–58.

Charles Fenno Hoffman

(7 February 1806 – 7 June 1884)

Emily A. Bernhard Jackson
Brandeis University

See also the Hoffman entry in *DLB 3: Antebellum Writers in New York and the South.*

BOOKS: *A Winter in the West, by A New Yorker,* 2 volumes (New York: Harper, 1835; revised, 1835; London: Richard Bentley, 1835);

Wild Scenes in the Forest and the Prairie, 2 volumes (London: Richard Bentley, 1839); republished as *Wild Scenes in the Forest and the Prairie. With Sketches of American Life,* 2 volumes (New York: William H. Colyer, 1843);

Greyslaer: A Romance of the Mohawk, by the Author of "A Winter in the West," 3 volumes (London: Richard Bentley, 1840; New York: Harpers, 1840; revised edition, Philadelphia: Lea & Blanchard, 1841);

The Vigil of Faith, and Other Poems (New York: S. Colman, 1842; London: H. G. Clarke, 1844; enlarged, New York: Harper, 1845);

The Echo, or, Borrowed Notes for Home Circulation (Philadelphia: Lindsay & Blakiston, 1844);

Love's Calendar, Lays of the Hudson, and Other Poems (New York: D. Appleton, 1847);

The Pioneers of New-York. An Anniversary Discourse Delivered Before the St. Nicholas Society of Manhattan, December 6, 1847 (New York: Stanford & Swords, 1848);

The Poems of Charles Fenno Hoffman, collected and edited by Edward Fenno Hoffman (Philadelphia: Porter & Coates, 1873).

OTHER: *The New-York Book of Poetry,* edited with contributions by Hoffman (New York: George Dearborn, 1837).

PERIODICALS EDITED: *Knickerbacker* (1 January 1833–April 1833);

American Monthly Magazine (March 1835–December 1837);

Hewet's Excelsior and New York Illustrated Times (1845–February 1846);

New York Literary World (May 1847–November 1848).

Editor, poet, and novelist, Charles Fenno Hoffman was an active member of the literati in antebellum New York. His first great popular success came with a series of travel "letters" later collected into the book *A Winter in the West, by A New Yorker* (1835); after this publication his literary life was broad and varied, until a decline was caused by his later mental illness. Although the bulk of his work consists of often anonymous sketches, reviews, and short pieces in journals and newspapers, he also published volumes of travel writing, fiction, and poetry. In addition, he edited a number of influential periodicals, including *The New York Literary World.*

Hoffman was born 7 February 1806 in New York City. He was the son of Josiah Ogden Hoffman, a noted jurist, and Maria Barnes Hoffman, esteemed by her contemporaries as a "highly intellectual lady." Both sides of his family were socially distinguished old New Yorkers; his Barnes forebears included soldiers, judges, and a newspaper editor. In 1817, at age eleven, Hoffman was severely injured when he attempted to jump from a dock to a nearby ferryboat and mistimed the action. The ferryboat cut closer to the pier than he had expected and crushed one of his legs, which as a result had to be amputated above the knee. His recovery was swift, and the injury apparently left him with a determination to excel at outdoor pursuits: he became an avid horseback rider, swimmer, and rower. Horseback riding in particular served him well in his future career.

Hoffman was educated in schools in New York and New Jersey and entered Columbia University in 1821, placing thirty-fifth out of thirty-eight candidates for admission. This early, undistinguished academic notation was a harbinger of lackluster performances to come; Hoffman was interested in intellectual activities other than academic study. He left at the end of his sophomore year to study law with Harmanus Bleeker in Albany. Although the date of his admission to the New York bar is unknown, in 1827 he returned to New York City to practice law with his ailing father. At this time Hoffman began to be distracted by literature, submitting articles anonymously to Albany and New York City gazettes and magazines. At this time Hoffman began to be distracted by literature, submitting articles anonymously to Albany and New York City gazettes and magazines such as the *Corsair* and the *New-Yorker.*

In 1829 Hoffman began contributing to the *New-York American,* and in September of that year he assumed temporary editorship during an absence by the regular editor, Charles King. This leadership, though temporary, marked a turning point in Hoffman's career: he was now a man of literature rather than a man of law. Hoffman was responsible for the reviews published in the magazine, and his work was popular and well received. He chose to sign his pieces with an asterisk or the initial "H," declining to sign his name because he felt that the quality of the writing did not reflect well on him. Nonetheless, he was soon one of the literary lions of New York City, frequently present at literary clubs and dinners with other members of the literati.

In 1832, when Hoffman was only twenty-six years old, he accepted the position of editor at what was to become one of the most important American magazines of the next quarter century. The first issue of *The Knickerbacker* appeared on 1 January 1833 and under Hoffman's editorship featured contributions from such luminaries as William Cullen Bryant and James Kirke Paulding. Hoffman continued to write for the *New-York American* even as he fulfilled his editorial duties at *The Knickerbacker;* the attendant stress led to debilitating bouts of dyspepsia, and he was forced to resign his editorship after three months. *The Knickerbacker* passed into the hands of Timothy Flint, who changed the name to *The Knickerbocker.*

Hoffman, for his part, decided to cure his dyspepsia by undertaking a horseback tour of the West. To finance the trip he wrote a series of letters back to the *New-York American* as his travels progressed. In an America obsessed with wilderness and pioneering, both he and the magazine were virtually guaranteed high readership. Setting off in the winter of 1833, he traveled through portions of the Midwest, working his way through Pennsylvania to Cleveland and Chicago before finishing up in St. Louis. His descriptive letters include many tales of accidents and mishaps—a trip on horseback was necessarily somewhat treacherous for a man with one leg. His mind-set on the journey seems to have been somewhat counterintuitive to his role as guide: in one of his later letters, 2 June 1834, he remarks that "the majority of mankind have no innate sense of beauty and majesty." He described both admirably, and the letters still make pleasant and interesting reading today. Hoffman returned to New York in 1834, and in 1835 the letters, along with others that detailed experiences after his return, were published in the collection *A Winter in the West, by A New-Yorker.* The book was well received in America and in England, capturing the interest of the critics as well as the reading public.

Although the letters in *A Winter in the West, by A New-Yorker* are characteristic of their time, reflecting contemporaneous interest in the expanding frontiers of America and travel along those frontiers by ordinary, observant individuals, they still appeal to the modern reader. Hoffman's language is by turns poetic and factual, lyric and terse. The "letters" are in fact short essays—he begins by including the salutation "Dear," but soon leaves off that conceit, allowing his language and keen reporting to form a stronger bond with the reader. Each essay is roughly ten pages long. Hoffman fills these pages with descriptions of the countryside, geography and topography lessons, personal anecdotes, history lessons, biographical sketches, and even forays into satire. In Letter VII, for example, he describes his party's approach to Braddock's Field:

WILD SCENES

IN THE

FOREST AND PRAIRIE.

BY C. F. HOFFMAN, Esq.

AUTHOR OF "A WINTER IN THE FAR WEST."

IN TWO VOLUMES.

VOL. I.

LONDON:

RICHARD BENTLEY, NEW BURLINGTON STREET,
Publisher in Ordinary to Her Majesty.
Price Sixteen Shillings.

1839.

Title page for volume one of the collection in which Hoffman included essays drawing on his 1837 tour of the Hudson River valley (courtesy of Special Collections, Thomas Cooper Library, University of South Carolina)

Winding now through a deep dingle, where the path-side was festooned with vines, we crossed a small brook, and reached the shore Monongahela opposite to a broad alluvial flat, whose high cultivation and sunny aspect contrasted vividly with the wild and secluded dell from the mouth of which we beheld it. The road next led for some distance through a wood on the immediate back of the river, and then gaining a more public highway, we found ourselves, after passing several comfortable farmhouses, immediately in front of the battle-ground.

He follows this description with one of the battle and a brief biography of General Braddock himself. Hoffman's devotion to the American military man and his role as literary patriot are delightfully to the fore in his comments on Braddock. He is careful to include the general's reported remark to George Washington, at that time an officer serving under him and attempting to offer helpful advice: "By G-d, sir, these are high times, when a British General is to take counsel from a Virginia buckskin!"

Indeed, Hoffman's position as an American writer—that is, both a writer from America and a writer describing and cataloguing the emerging American nation—is intrinsic to *A Winter in the West, by A New-Yorker*. From his descriptions of the land before him to his comments on citizens of other nations, immigrants to America and the emerging urban underclass, his writing works to give a picture of America that helps to define it as a nation in its own right, with a national character, national hopes, and, as the story of Braddock and Washington shows, national myths. In these regards, *A Winter in the West, by A New-Yorker* is reminiscent of J. Hector St. John de Crèvecoeur's *Letters from an American Farmer* (1782).

In March of 1835 Hoffman became connected with *The American Monthly Magazine,* contributing articles and stories on New York history and the outdoors; as before, these articles were signed only with the initial "H," if at all. After a short while he assumed the editorship of the magazine, which he retained after it merged with *The New-England Magazine* in January of 1836. In December of 1836 Hoffman edited *The New-York Book of Poetry,* a work specifically defined to showcase the talents of native New York authors. The book was a critical and popular success, running to two editions in nine months.

Beginning in 1837 this new *American Monthly Magazine* began publishing Hoffman's serial novel, *Vanderlyn*. Chapters appeared sporadically, and publication also ended in 1837. More notable for excitement than pithiness, *Vanderlyn* is the meandering tale of a young man's adventures and misfortunes in the New York City of the early nineteenth century as he seeks to reunite himself with his lost love. Serial publication ended abruptly with chapter 20, and the novel was never published in book form. Early that same year Hoffman unsuccessfully attempted to expand the *American Monthly Magazine* into a national publication. Shortly after the failure of this venture he resigned his editorship, perhaps because of disagreements with the Philadelphia editor of the magazine, Robert Montgomery Bird, but more likely because of strains attendant on Hoffman as a result of the death of his father earlier in the year.

Even while he was with the *American Monthly Magazine* Hoffman had been contributing to *The New-York Mirror;* his unsigned but recognizable contributions date from April to December of 1837. Late in that same year he undertook a journey through the Hudson River valley, which served as material for "Scenes and Sources of the Hudson" and other stories. Many of these first appeared as contributions to the *New-York Mirror,* and Hoffman later included them in his 1839 collection, *Wild Scenes in the Forest and the Prairie.* For the next two years, 1838 and 1839, he concentrated on writing his novel *Greyslaer: A Romance of the Mohawk, by the Author of "A Winter in the West"* (1840).

Greyslaer, Hoffman's only published novel, is freely based on the Beauchamp-Sharpe murder case of 1825–1826, which was also the subject of two novels by William Gilmore Simms. The facts of the case are these: Congressman Solomon P. Sharpe, a major

figure in Kentucky politics and a man with several irascible enemies, was stabbed to death in his home in November of 1825. Jereboam O. Beauchamp, a young lawyer from a nearby town, was arrested for the crime. Another of those on whom suspicion fell gathered evidence against Beauchamp. Beauchamp then confessed to the murder, giving as his motive his belief that Sharpe had spread a rumor that he had committed adultery with Beauchamp's wife, Ann Cook Beauchamp. This rumor actually had been put about by another of Sharpe's enemies. After Beauchamp was convicted, his wife joined him in prison. On the morning of his execution, the pair attempted suicide by stabbing themselves. Discovered still alive by the guards, Beauchamp was taken to the gallows where, weak from loss of blood, he had to be held up as the noose was placed around his neck. His wife died from her wounds, and the two were buried in the same grave.

Although the facts of the case would seem lurid enough to defy sensationalization, Hoffman's fictional version of them is both exciting and interesting, albeit somewhat hackneyed by contemporary standards. The seduction—which, in reality, never occurred—and murder take second place, however, to the history of the valley of the Mohawk during the Revolutionary War, thus demonstrating yet again Hoffman's overwhelming interest in defining the nation of America. The book was extremely successful, its popularity aided by a dramatized version that appeared at New York's Bowery Theatre in 1840.

Although *Greyslaer* is seldom read today, it merits further study. Through the text Hoffman not only examines interactions between Anglo-Americans and American Indians during and after the Revolutionary War but also explores the rigidly structured male/female relations of the period and, in a wider sense, early Americans' relationship with their newfound land. Daniel Wells in his introduction to *Greyslaer* has argued that Hoffman's Joseph Brant is the first fully realized American Indian character in American literature, full of complex thought and expression with which previous such characters were not endowed by their authors. The novel itself is rich in complexities of insight; as Wells writes, "Beneath the surface lies the specters of psychological horror, madness, carnal knowledge, and genocide." These underlying themes put the novel above much contemporary literature. Before *Greyslaer* was published, Hoffman returned to editing, working as assistant editor of Horace Greeley's *The New-Yorker.* Hoffman left after three months, evidently amicably. In order to ensure that he would be free to write without outside limitations or demands, he accepted a position as a clerk in the office of the New York Surveyor of Customs, working there from May 1841 to July 1844. Since such appointments were usually political and changeover was high, Hoffman's three-year tenure was remarkable. During his time there he continued his writing, producing two collections of poetry, *The Vigil of Faith, and Other Poems* (1842) and *The Echo, or, Borrowed Notes for Home Circulation* (1844). Although his poetry was unfavorably received in Britain, he remained popular with the American critics and public.

Hoffman contributed to *Graham's Magazine* from 1842 to 1848, and in 1845 he joined the staff of the *Boston Evening Gazette,* contributing poems and articles. He also edited *Hewet's Excelsior and New York Illustrated Times* newspaper from its inception in 1845 until February 1846, when it folded. *Hewet's* sporadically published chapters of his serial novel, *Vondel: A Tale of Old Manhattan,* left unfinished because of the abrupt demise of the paper. In May of 1846 Hoffman began his final substantial literary job when he succeeded Evert Duyckinck as the editor of *The Literary World.* During the year and a half that Hoffman was editor the magazine prospered, maintaining the high standards set under Duyckinck.

In 1847 Hoffman published his last book, the poetry collection *Love's Calendar, Lays of the Hudson and Other Poems.* In the midst of his writing and editing he still had time to undertake lecturing, and in December of 1847 he presented the address "Pioneers of New York" to the St. Nicholas Society of Manhattan. The talk stressed New Yorkers' contributions to American life and letters protested New Englanders' claims to preeminence in those areas. It was published in 1848. Hoffman also continued work on another historical romance, "The Red Spur of Ramopo." This work never appeared in print, for Hoffman's maid mistook the finished manuscript for paper set aside as kindling and burned all but six pages before Hoffman discovered her error.

This incident, along with dwindling financial and literary prospects, took a toll on his mental and physical health, and in January 1849 he placed himself in Dr. Thomas Story Kirkbride's Pennsylvania Hospital for the Insane in Philadelphia. Hoffman was discharged as cured in April 1849. He took up a post with the U.S. State Department, Harrisburg, but the strains of this job led to another collapse. He re-entered the Philadelphia hospital, recovered again,

relapsed yet again, and entered the Harrisburg State Hospital. His illness would probably now be termed chronic manic depression; the constant ill health crippled Hoffman's ability to write.

As a novelist Hoffman was of his time. His travelogues and novels continue to make exciting, if not inspired, reading for a modern audience. As a critic, he was almost always positive, encouraging and aiding young writers whenever possible. As a literary personage, he was a supporter of copyright law, campaigning vociferously on its behalf, in keeping with his encouragement of American authors. As a man, he was gracious and charismatic; his contemporaries spoke often and positively of his personal charm and literary acumen. His chances for further literary and social contributions were cut short by his mental instability: Hoffman remained confined at the Harrisburg hospital for the rest of his life and died on 7 June 1884.

Biography:

Homer F. Barnes, *Charles Fenno Hoffman* (New York: Columbia University Press, 1930).

References:

John C. Hepler, "A Letter from Charles Fenno Hoffman to Whittier," *Bulletin of the New York Public Library,* 79 (Autumn 1975): 96–98;

Melissa McFarland Pennell, "Dark Lady Triumphant: Innovations in American Romance in Charles Fenno Hoffman's *Greyslaer," Mid-Hudson Language Studies,* 11 (1988): 41–49;

Edgar Allen Poe, "The Literati," in *The Complete Works of Edgar Allen Poe,* volume 15, edited by James A. Harrison (New York: AMS Press, 1965);

Kendall B. Taft, ed., *Minor Knickerbockers* (New York & Cincinnati: American Book, 1947), pp. 315–333;

Daniel Wells, "Introduction," in *Greyslaer, A Romance of the Mohawk,* by Charles Fenno Hoffman (Albany, N.Y.: New York University Press, 1990);

James Grant Wilson, *Bryant and His Friends: Some Reminiscences of the Knickerbocker Writers* (New York: Fords, Howard & Hulbert, 1886), pp. 409–413.

Papers:

The Hoffman family papers are held at the University of Michigan (William L. Clements Library). Some of Charles Fenno Hoffman's letters are held at the New York Public Library.

Washington Irving

(3 April 1783 – 28 November 1859)

Richard Dilworth Rust
University of North Carolina–Chapel Hill

See also the Irving entries in *DLB 3: Antebellum Writers in New York and the South; DLB 11: American Humorists, 1800–1950; DLB 30: American Historians, 1607–1865; DLB 59: American Literary Critics and Scholars, 1800–1850; DLB 73: American Magazine Journalists, 1741–1850; DLB 74: American Short-Story Writers Before 1880; DLB 183: American Travel Writers, 1776–1864;* and *DLB 186: Nineteenth-Century American Western Writers.*

BOOKS: *Salmagundi; or, the Whim-Whams and Opinions of Launcelot Langstaff, Esq. & Others,* 20 parts, republished in 2 volumes, by Irving, William Irving, and James Kirke Paulding (New York: D. Longworth, 1807–1808; London: Printed for J. M. Richardson, 1811; revised edition, New York: D. Longworth, 1814; revised by Irving, Paris: Galignani, 1824; Paris: Baudry, 1824);

A History of New-York, from the Beginning of the World to the End of the Dutch Dynasty. Containing Among Many Surprising and Curious Matters, the Unutterable Ponderings of Walter the Doubter, the Disastrous Projects of William the Testy, and the Chivalric Achievements of Peter the Headstrong, the Three Dutch Governors of New Amsterdam; Being the Only Authentic History of the Times that Ever Hath Been, or Ever Will Be Published, 2 volumes, as Diedrich Knickerbocker (New York & Philadelphia: Inskeep & Bradford / Boston: M'Ilhenny / Baltimore: Coale & Thomas / Charleston: Morford, Willington, 1809; revised edition, New York & Philadelphia: Inskeep & Bradford, 1812; London: John Murray, 1820; revised edition, 2 volumes, New York: Printed for the Grolier Club, 1886);

The Sketch Book of Geoffrey Crayon, Gent., 7 parts, as Geoffrey Crayon (New York: Printed by C. S. Van Winkle, 1819–1820; revised edition, 2 volumes: volume 1, London: John Miller, 1820; volume 2, London: John Murray, 1820; revised edition, Paris: Baudry & Didot, 1823);

Bracebridge Hall; or, The Humourists. A Medley, 2 volumes, as Crayon (New York: Printed by C. S. Van Winkle, 1822; London: John Murray, 1822);

Washington Irving, 1820 (engraving by M. I. Danforth, after a portrait by C. R. Leslie)

Letters of Jonathan Oldstyle, Gent., as The Author of *The Sketch Book* (New York: Clayton, 1824; London: Wilson, 1824);

Tales of a Traveller, 2 volumes, as Crayon (London: John Murray, 1824; abridged edition, Philadelphia: Carey & Lea, 1824; unabridged edition, New York: Printed by C. S. Van Winkle, 1825);

The Miscellaneous Works of Oliver Goldsmith, with an Account of His Life and Writings, 4 volumes (Paris: Galignani / Didot, 1825); biography revised in *The Life of Oliver Goldsmith, with Selections from His Writings,* 2 volumes (New York: Harper, 1840); biography revised and enlarged as *Oliver Goldsmith: A Biography,* as volume 11 of *The Works of Washington Irving* (New York: Putnam / London: John Murray, 1849);

A History of the Life and Voyages of Christopher Columbus, 4 volumes (London: John Murray, 1828; 3 volumes, New York: G & C. Carvill, 1828; revised, 2 volumes, 1831);

A Chronicle of the Conquest of Granada, 2 volumes, as Fray Antonio Agapida (Philadelphia: Carey, Lea & Carey, 1829; London: John Murray, 1829);

Voyages and Discoveries of the Companions of Columbus (London: John Murray, 1831; Philadelphia: Carey & Lea, 1831);

The Alhambra, 2 volumes, as Crayon (London: Colburn & Bentley, 1832); as The Author of *The Sketch Book,* 2 volumes (Philadelphia: Carey & Lea, 1832); revised as *The Alhambra: A Series of Sketches of the Moors and Spaniards by the Author of "The Sketch Book"* (Philadelphia: Carey, Lea & Blanchard, 1836); revised as volume 15 of *The Works of Washington Irving* (New York: Putnam, 1851);

A Tour on the Prairies, number 1 of *Miscellanies,* as The Author of *The Sketch Book* (London: John Murray, 1835); republished as number 1 of *The Crayon Miscellany* (Philadelphia: Carey, Lea & Blanchard, 1835);

Abbotsford and Newstead Abbey, number 2 of *Miscellanies,* as The Author of *The Sketch Book* (London: John Murray, 1835); republished as number 2 of *The Crayon Miscellany* (Philadelphia: Carey, Lea & Blanchard, 1835);

Legends of the Conquest of Spain, number 3 of *Miscellanies,* as The Author of *The Sketch Book* (London: John Murray, 1835); republished as number 3 of *The Crayon Miscellany* (Philadelphia: Carey, Lea & Blanchard, 1835);

Astoria; or, Enterprise beyond the Rocky Mountains, 3 volumes (London: Bentley, 1836); republished as *Astoria; or, Anecdotes of an Enterprise beyond the Rocky Mountains,* 2 volumes (Philadelphia: Carey, Lea & Blanchard, 1836); revised as volume 8 of *The Works of Washington Irving* (New York: Putnam, 1849);

Adventures of Captain Bonneville, or Scenes beyond the Rocky Mountains of the Far West, 3 volumes (London: Bentley, 1837); republished as *The Rocky Mountains; or, Scenes, Incidents, and Adventures in the Far West; Digested from the Journal of Captain B. L. E. Bonneville, of the Army of the United States, and Illustrated from Various Other Sources,* 2 volumes (Philadelphia: Carey, Lea & Blanchard, 1837);

Biography and Poetical Remains of the Late Margaret Miller Davidson (Philadelphia: Lea & Blanchard, 1841; London: Tilt & Bogue, 1843);

Mahomet and His Successors, volumes 12 and 13 of *The Works of Washington Irving* (New York: Putnam, 1849–1850); republished as *Lives of Mahomet and His Successors,* 2 volumes (London: John Murray, 1850);

Chronicles of Wolfert's Roost and Other Papers (Edinburgh: Constable, Low / London: Hamilton, Adams / Dublin: M'Glashan, 1855); republished as *Wolfert's Roost and Other Papers,* volume 16 of *The Works of Washington Irving* (New York: Putnam, 1855);

Life of George Washington, 5 volumes (New York: Putnam, 1855–1859; London: Bohn, 1855–1859);

Spanish Papers and Other Miscellanies, Hitherto Unpublished or Uncollected, edited by Pierre M. Irving, 2 volumes (New York: Putnam / Hurd & Houghton, 1866; London: Low, 1866); republished as *Biographies and Miscellaneous Papers by Washington Irving* (London: Bell & Daldy, 1867);

Journals and Notebooks, 5 volumes, edited by Nathalia Wright, Walter A. Reichart, Lillian Schlissel, Wayne R. Kime, Andrew B. Myers, and Sue Fields Ross (Madison: University of Wisconsin Press / Boston: Twayne, 1969–1986).

Collection: *The Complete Works of Washington Irving,* edited by Richard Dilworth Rust and others, 30 volumes (Madison: University of Wisconsin Press / Boston: Twayne, 1969–1989)—comprises volume 1: *Journals and Notebooks, Volume I, 1803–1806,* edited by Nathalia Wright (1969); volume 2: *Journals and Notebooks, Volume II, 1807–1822,* edited by Walter A. Reichart and Lillian Schlissel (1981); volume 3: *Journals and Notebooks, Volume III, 1819–1827,* edited by Reichart (1970); volume 4: *Journals and Notebooks, Volume IV, 1826–1829,* edited by Wayne R. Kime and Andrew B. Myers (1984); volume 5: *Journals and Notebooks, Volume V, 1832–1842,* edited by Sue Fields Ross (1986); volume 6: *Letters of Jonathan Oldstyle, Gent. and Salmagundi; or, The Whim-Whams and Opinions of Launcelot Langstaff, Esq. & Others,* edited by Bruce I. Granger and Martha Hartzog Stocker (1977); volume 7: *A History of New-York,* edited by Michael L. Black and Nancy B. Black (1984); volume 8: *The Sketch Book of Geoffrey Crayon, Esq.,* edited by Haskell S. Springer (1978); volume 9: *Bracebridge Hall; or, The Humourists,* edited by Herbert F. Smith (1977); volume 10: *Tales of a Traveller,* edited by Judith Giblin Haig (1987); volume 11: *The Life and Voyages of Christopher Columbus,* edited by John H. McElroy (1981); volume 12: *Voyages and Discoveries of the Companions of Columbus,* edited by James W. Tuttleton (1986); volume 13: *A Chronicle of the Conquest of Granada,* edited by Earl N. Harbert and Miriam J. Shillingsburg (1988); volume 14: *The*

Alhambra, edited by William T. Lenehan and Andrew B. Myers (1983); volume 15: *Astoria; or, Anecdotes of an Enterprize beyond the Rocky Mountains,* edited by Rust (1976); volume 16: *The Adventures of Captain Bonneville,* edited by Robert A. Rees and Alan Sandy (1977); volume 17: *Oliver Goldsmith: A Biography and Biography of the Late Margaret Miller Davidson,* edited by Elsie Lee West (1978); volume 18: *Mahomet and His Successors,* edited by Henry A. Pochmann and E. N. Feltskog (1970); volumes 19, 20, 21: *Life of George Washington* (I and II, III, IV, and V), edited by Allen Guttmann and James A. Sappenfield (1982); volume 22: *The Crayon Miscellany,* edited by Dahlia Kirby Terrell (1979); volumes 23, 24, 25, 26: *Letters, Volume I, 1802–1823* (1978), *Letters, Volume II, 1832–1838* (1979), *Letters, Volume III, 1839–1845* (1982), *Letters, Volume IV, 1846–1859* (1982), edited by Ralph M. Aderman, Herbert L. Kleinfield, and Jenifer S. Banks; volume 27: *Wolfert's Roost,* edited by Roberta Rosenberg (1979); volumes 28 and 29: *Miscellaneous Writings, 1803–1859,* Volumes I and II, edited by Kime (1981); volume 30: *Bibliography,* compiled by Edwin T. Bowden (1989).

OTHER: "The Catskill Mountains," in the *Home Book of the Picturesque* (New York: Putnam, 1852), pp. 71–78.

"I seek only to blow a flute accompaniment in the national concert, and leave others to play the fiddle & frenchhorn," Washington Irving said in an 1819 letter. While his flute music for a time was a dominant strain, it still remains discernible in the national concert. Rip Van Winkle is part of American mythology, and Irving's legend of Sleepy Hollow is still read. There continues to be an audience, too, for the rest of *The Sketch Book of Geoffrey Crayon, Gent.* (1819–1820), Diedrich Knickerbocker's *A History of New-York* (1809), *The Alhambra* (1832), and Irving's *Life of George Washington* (1855–1859). Other works such as *Tales of a Traveller* (1824), with its memorable story of "The Devil and Tom Walker," *Astoria* (1836), and *The Life and Voyages of Christopher Columbus* (1828) remain appealing.

In his time, as Eugene Current-García notes in his 1973 essay in *Studies in Short Fiction,* Irving set "the pattern for the artistic re-creation of common experience in short fictional form." Irving properly has been called the Father of the American Short Story as well as, according to William Makepeace Thackeray in "Nil Nisi Bonum," "the first Ambassador whom the New World of Letters sent to the Old." "For a long time," according to Charles Dudley Warner in *Washington Irving* (1881), "he was the chief representative of the American name in the world of letters." Irving was praised by Walter Scott; George Gordon, Lord Byron; Samuel Taylor Coleridge; and Thomas Moore; read repeatedly by Charles Dickens; admired by Fanny Kemble, Henry Wadsworth Longfellow, and Nathaniel Hawthorne; and considered by William Cullen Bryant to be the fountainhead of American fiction and history. Now, however, Irving is considered by some to be old-fashioned, a fate he anticipated in his essays in *The Sketch Book:* "Westminster Abbey" and "The Mutability of Literature." In the former he says: "Time is ever silently turning over his pages; we are too much engrossed by the story of the present, to think of the characters and anecdotes that gave interest to the past." Yet Irving acknowledges that imagination of a Shakespearean quality defies mutability–an opinion that may well apply to Irving's best work.

Washington Irving's connection to "the national concert" began auspiciously with his birth on 3 April 1783, just five days before the proclamation of peace between Great Britain and the new nation. Named after George Washington, who later, Stanley T. Williams reports in his 1935 biography, *The Life of Washington Irving,* Irving said, "laid his hand upon my head and gave me his blessing," the baby boy was the eleventh and last child of William and Sarah Sanders Irving. He was pampered and encouraged by his four living brothers–William Jr., Peter, Ebenezer, and John Treat–and by his three sisters–Ann Sarah, Catharine Rodgers, and Sarah Sanders. With the exception of being distanced from the strict orthodoxy of his father, Irving enjoyed close family connections throughout his life. He celebrated connections with his country in a variety of works, from the early humorous *A History of New-York* through his evocations of the Hudson River valley in *The Sketch Book* and *Tales of a Traveller,* his narratives of Western exploration and fur trapping, and his biographies of Christopher Columbus and George Washington.

The flute is an appropriate symbol for Irving, associated as it is with the imagination and idle pleasure. (Irving was actually quite skilled at playing the flute, as was Henry David Thoreau.) While he was given educational opportunities, Irving preferred the exercise of imagination that came outside the confines of a schoolroom. "The Author's Account of Himself" by Geoffrey Crayon in *The Sketch Book* applies quite closely to Irving himself: "I neglected the regular exercises of the school," he said, watching departing ships and wafting himself "in imagination to the ends of the earth." In his preface to the revised edition of that work, he quotes from his 20 November 1819 letter to Walter Scott, in which he says, "My whole course of life has been desultory, and I am unfitted for any periodically

Saturday, ~~August~~ July 31st 1803.

I sailed from New York for Albany in company with Mr & Mrs Hoffman. Mr & Mrs Ludlow Ogden Miss Eliza Ogden, Miss Ann Hoffman Mr Brandram & Mr Reedy & Stephen & Rupiau. We set off about 3 oclock in the afternoon and came to anchor in the evening at the entrance of the highlands.

Sunday, Aug 1.

~~We~~ went ashore with Mr Ogden & Mr Brandram for milk. we found a mean house with a lazy looking fellow seated in the fireplace.

While the woman of the house was ~~getting the~~ milking the cows we were entertaind by some curious enquiries & speculation of Brandram /who was lately from england/ He declared the man lived in "luxury & disipation" having nothing to do except to work a little on his farm. That he had good milk to drink and rye bread to eat – at the same time Brandram wished he had a bottle of wine from on board the sloop that he might cool it in a neighboring spring.

Page from a journal Irving kept when he was twenty (from Stanley T. Williams, The Life of Washington Irving, *1935)*

recurring task, or any stipulated labor of body or mind. . . . I shall occasionally shift my residence and write whatever is suggested by objects before me, or whatever rises in my imagination."

"When I was very young," Irving wrote in an April–May 1823 autobiographical letter to Amelia Foster, "I had an irrepressible flow of spirits that often went beyond my strength. Everything was fairy land to me." In an undated anecdote from his journals revealing his gullibility, Irving told how he was a "lively boy, full of curiosity, of easy faith, and prone to relish a story the more it partook of the marvellous." He could identify with his fictional old Dutch inhabitants, who credited to Hendrick Hudson and his crew the sounds of thunderstorms and with Diedrich Knickerbocker, who considered Sleepy Hollow an ideal retreat where one might "steal from the world and its distractions, and dream quietly away the remnant of a troubled life."

The study of law, in which Irving engaged starting in 1799, was almost diametrically opposed to exercise of artistic inclinations. "I could study any thing else rather than Law, and had a fatal propensity to Belles lettres," he said in an 1823 letter. In 1802–1803, that propensity found a public outlet in contributions of "Letters of Jonathan Oldstyle, Gent." to the New York *Morning Chronicle,* edited by Irving's brother Peter. There were nine of these letter-essays published in the *Morning Chronicle,* eight of which were published in 1824 without authorization, and to Irving's regret, by the New York printer William H. Clayton as *Letters of Jonathan Oldstyle, Gent.* (1824). With some wit and good humor, the nineteen-year-old Irving satirizes current New York actors and critics, and in his ninth letter lampoons contemporary dueling as "blunt unceremonious affairs." For a month in 1804 his satire found an outlet also in the Burrite newspaper *The Corrector,* edited by his brother Peter.

Relief from what Irving (in a 3 August 1805 letter to Alexander Beebee) called "the musty authors of the Law" and an opportunity to expand his horizons came in the form of an extended tour of Europe from June 1804 to January 1806. The *Wanderjahr* (year of wandering) was paid for by his brothers, who, in an undated letter written by William Irving, said, "It is with delight we share the world with you; and one of our greatest sources of happiness is that fortune is daily putting it in our power thus to add to the comfort and enjoyment of one so very near to us all." By means of letters Washington Irving would write regularly, the brothers intended to experience Europe vicariously through their talented sibling. Irving's grand tour took him primarily to Italy, Greece, Switzerland, France, the Netherlands, and England. His four European journals plus traveling notes reveal this American innocent abroad as

confident, curious, observant, and easily directed by chance occurrences or influences. "I am highly amused with the gay whimsical inhabitants of this country," he wrote his friend Beebee from Paris on 3 August 1805, telling how his "imagination has been on the full stretch vainly striving to grasp the accumulating wonders." The tour improved Irving's health, and he had an opportunity to meet prominent people such as the author Madame de Staël and the artist and poet Washington Allston. Yet, eventually he wearied of it, writing from London to his brother Peter on 20 October 1805, "I shift from city to city and lay countries aside like books, after giving them a hasty perusal. . . . In a short time one gets tired of travelling even in the gay & polished countries of Europe. . . . Curiosity cannot be kept ever on the stretch; like the sensual appetites, it in time becomes sated."

Upon his return to New York, Irving continued his law studies in the office of Judge Josiah Ogden Hoffman, passing the bar examination in November 1806. During this time he again joined with the "Lads of Kilkenny"—his brothers William, Peter, and Ebenezer, and friends Gouverneur and Peter Kemble, James Kirke Paulding, Henry Brevoort, Henry Ogden, David Porter, and Richard McCall. Often they enjoyed conviviality at Gouverneur Kemble's country place, Mount Pleasant, which became the model for a place they called Cockloft Hall in twenty numbers of social satire published as *Salmagundi; or, the Whim-Whams and Opinions of Launcelot Langstaff, Esq. & Others* (1807–1808). Paulding and Irving were the primary instigators, with William Irving also involved. This salmagundi, or medley of pieces, starts with Launcelot Langstaff apportioning satire on fashion to Anthony Evergreen and criticism to Will Wizard. Other dominant characters in the series are Mustapha Rub-A-Dub Keli Khan (reminiscent of Oliver Goldsmith's "Citizen of the World"), who writes to friends in Tripoli, and Jeremy Cockloft, who tells of his travels in the mid-Atlantic states. The high-spirited essays and letters wittily satirize the follies and foibles of the Gothamites, fulfilling the essayists' intent "simply to instruct the young, reform the old, correct the town and castigate the age." All in good humor, of course, they will "go on merrily" and "be more solicitous to make our readers laugh than cry; for we are laughing philosophers, and clearly of opinion, that wisdom, true wisdom, is a plump, jolly dame, who sits in her arm chair, laughs right merrily at the farce of life—and takes the world as it goes."

While assignments of authorship are not always clear, it is certain that Irving wrote pieces on the New York Assembly, fashions, theatrics, the character of Launcelot Langstaff, Cockloft Hall, and "The Little Man in Black." Since it moves beyond a simple character sketch to include plot and revelation of character, Launcelot Langstaff's narration of "The Little Man in Black" can be considered Irving's first short story. And the little antiquarian who on his deathbed bequeaths his volumes of Linkum Fidelius anticipates the antiquarian Diedrich Knickerbocker.

Knickerbocker is the fusty historian and collector of old wives' tales who serves as Irving's persona in writing *A History of New-York, from the Beginning of the World to the End of the Dutch Dynasty. Containing Among Many Surprising and Curious Matters, the Unutterable Ponderings of Walter the Doubter, the Disastrous Projects of William the Testy, and the Chivalric Achievements of Peter the Headstrong, the Three Dutch Governors of New Amsterdam; Being the Only Authentic History of the Times that Ever Hath Been, or Ever Will Be Published* (1809). Begun as a joint project with Peter Irving, Knickerbocker's *History of New-York* was first intended as a parody of Samuel Latham Mitchill's *A Picture of New-York; or The Traveller's Guide through the Commercial Metropolis of the United States* (1807). Peter Irving dropped out of the project in the spring of 1808, and Washington became the sole author of a literary work that became widely read abroad as well as in the United States and has continued to entertain audiences down to the present day. In *Washington Irving: An American Study, 1802–1832* (1965) William L. Hedges affirms that *A History of New-York* is Irving's masterpiece, his best book.

Although Irving first published *A History of New-York* in December 1809, he revised and rewrote parts of the book in 1812, 1819, 1824, 1829, and 1848. The 1812 edition includes about ten thousand words of new material, such as Oloffe's dream and the history of the Long Pipes and the Short Pipes, but cuts out about the same amount of material from the earlier edition—mainly monologues dealing with Knickerbocker as historian. The 1848 edition also includes extensive changes and forms the basis for the edition of *A History of New-York* in *The Complete Works of Washington Irving* (1969–1989).

The extended title of *A History of New-York* suggests the mock-heroic character of the book. The pompous claim fits Diedrich Knickerbocker, the obtuse narrator through whom Irving fulfills his purpose stated in "The Author's Apology" to the 1848 edition to "burlesque the pedantic lore displayed in certain American works" through "mock erudition." Irving explains that the book was "written in a serio-comic vein" and treats "local errors, follies and abuses with good-humored satire." Thus, the "unutterable ponderings" of Walter the Doubter turn out to be his snoring, and Peter the Headstrong's greatest chivalric achievement in "the most horrible battle ever recorded in poetry or prose," at Fort Christina, is to

recover from a fall into "a cushion softer than velvet, which Providence, or Minerva, or St. Nicholas, or some kindly cow had benevolently prepared for his reception" and knock out the Swedish leader—"without the loss of a single man on either side."

The "good-humored satire" Irving mentions was directed at a score of people, the most prominent of whom was Thomas Jefferson, caricatured in William Kieft, or William the Testy. Mary Weatherspoon Bowden, in *Washington Irving* (1981), details Irving's satire, showing how Kieft comes forth with Jeffersonian "proclamations, more proclamations when the first did not work, Non-Intercourse Acts, and philosophy." She reveals how DeWitt Clinton, mayor of New York in 1808–1809, is satirized as well, along with various other political figures. Their main fault is inaction in the face of bellicose British activities, to which Irving responds directly with what Bowden calls the whole point of Irving's book as expressed by his narrator: "to render a country respected abroad, it was necessary to make it formidable at home."

Irving published his unofficial history of New York during the bicentennial year of Hendrick Hudson's discovery of New York. While unhistorical in many places (for instance, the battle at Fort Christina never occurred), the work moves beyond contemporary satire to become a work solidly grounded in the history of New Netherlands. The fun was that it was both a history of early New York (New Amsterdam) and a response to contemporary life mediated by wit, imagination, and a lively sense of irony. That irony begins with Knickerbocker's confident belief he must start with "divers ingenious theories and philosophic speculations, concerning the creation and population of the world" and move through the history of humanity and then the peopling of America in order to have a suitable foundation for treating the settlement of Nieuw Nederlandts. What Knickerbocker takes seriously, readers recognize as Irving's good humor. Oloffe Van Kortlandt, with his talent, dreaming, was pronounced "a most useful citizen and a right good man—when he was asleep." Wouter Van Twiller is called "the Doubter" both from his surname (Twijfler in the original) and his habit of never making up his mind on a subject. A "model of majesty and lordly grandeur," Knickerbocker says, with Irving winking to let the reader in on the joke, Van Twiller "was exactly five feet six inches in height, and six feet five inches in circumference." And a fine lady in those days "waddled under more clothes . . . than would have clad the whole bevy of a modern ballroom."

Humor, however, in itself can be deceptive. Mark Twain wrote in *Following the Equator* (1897), "Everything human is pathetic. The secret source of Humor itself is not joy but sorrow." Twain also says, "Every one is a moon and has a dark side which he never shows to anybody." The dark side of Irving's moon was the death on 26 April 1809 of Matilda Hoffman, the young woman he had intended to marry. After her death, Irving assuaged his grief by completing *A History of New-York* at a friend's country estate.

Although Irving never mentioned her name to his closest friends, Matilda Hoffman had a great impact on his life, and throughout his life he carried her in his memory. The strongest evidence of her effect is an autobiographical fragment discovered posthumously. Pierre M. Irving, Washington Irving's nephew and authorized biographer, tells of a package he found in a locked cabinet after Irving's death. In it was a miniature of Matilda, a braid of her hair, a note with her name on it, and a private manuscript lacking opening and closing pages. The manuscript appears to be part of a letter to Amelia Foster, a woman whose family Irving enjoyed visiting in Dresden in 1822–1823, in response to her question as to why he had never married. In it, Irving reveals his deep love for Matilda. He tells how her father, Judge Hoffman, offered to take Irving into partnership with him and give Irving his daughter once this potential son-in-law was "capable of undertaking legal concerns." But Matilda died of tuberculosis, with Irving at her bedside. "I was the last one she looked upon," he said, and added that he related briefly "what if I were to tell with all the incidents & feelings that accompanied it would fill volumes." His heart, he said, "would continually recur to what it had lost. . . . Her image was continually before me, and I dreamt of her incessantly." In a notebook of 1822 he wrote, "She died in the beauty of her youth, and in my memory she will ever be young and beautiful." His 1810 notebook tells of his apathy and loneliness, of "past scenes of happiness & objects of affection—scenes that have passed away forever and objects of affection whose memories have been hallowed by the grave."

After the publication of *A History of New-York* in 1809, Irving tried and failed to get a clerkship in a New York court, took on modest responsibilities as a partner in the P. & E. Irving Company—which included lobbying in Washington for legislation favorable to an import firm like his, and then in 1812 revised his *History of New-York*. Following its publication he took on the editorship of *The Analectic Magazine,* a monthly periodical filled mainly with reviews of European and American writers. Irving wrote "Traits of Indian Character" and "Philip of Pokanoket" for the *Analectic,* essays he later included in *The Sketch Book.* He also wrote biographies of naval officers such as Commodore Oliver Perry and Captain David Porter. Then in August 1814, following the British burning of Washington, D.C., Irving

Irving at age twenty-two (portrait by John Vanderlyn; from Stanley T. Williams, The Life of Washington Irving, *1935)*

enlisted for a few months as aide-de-camp to New York governor Daniel Tompkins and accompanied him to Albany; Irving then went on assignment to Sackett's Harbor on Lake Ontario and to Lake Champlain.

With peace restored in 1815, Irving at first intended to go with his naval friend Stephen Decatur to fight the Dey of Algiers in the Mediterranean area, but with delay in the expedition, Irving determined instead to go to Europe on his own. He did not know he was about to begin seventeen years as an expatriate.

Irving's semi-autobiographical account of this experience is filtered through his persona Geoffrey Crayon in "The Author's Account of Himself" and "The Voyage," the essays that open *The Sketch Book.* Europe for him "held forth the charms of storied and poetical association." "Rich in the accumulated treasures of age," the Old World allowed him, he said, to escape "from the commonplace realities of the present, and lose myself among the shadowy grandeurs of the past." His trip allowed him to exercise his imagination bountifully—to fancy clouds, for example, "some fairy realms and people them with a creation of my own." Yet, this "solitary and idle" man (presuming Irving behind the mask of his persona) would find himself "a stranger in the land."

Irving unexpectedly was needed by his ailing brother Peter to help attend to the Irving business establishment at Liverpool. "It was my lot," he said in a 17 October 1815 letter, "almost on landing in Europe, to experience a reverse of fortune, which cast me down in spirit, and altered the whole tenor of my life." He little cared for "the sordid cares of the counting-house," and found increasingly that there was little he could do, despite great effort, to keep the Irving firm in England from plunging into bankruptcy. This step was finalized in March 1818, leaving Irving to muse in his notebook: "Commerce is a game where the merchant is one party & ruin the other." Yet, this commercial ruin paradoxically was a boon to Irving in that it contributed to the creation of his highly applauded artistic accomplishment, *The Sketch Book*. As James Ogilvie wrote him on 22 July 1817, "This seemingly unfortunate incident will supply this stimulus–you will return with renovated ardor to the arena you have for a season abandoned." Irving wrote in an April–May 1823 letter to Foster that he had determined to "raise myself from the degradation into which I considered myself fallen. I took my resolution–threw myself a stranger into London, shut myself up and went to work." As he said to his brother Ebenezer in a 3 March 1819 letter, "If I indeed have the means within me of establishing a legitimate literary reputation, this is the very period of life most auspicious for it, and I am resolved to devote a few years exclusively to the attempt."

Ten notebooks from this period from 1815 through 1818 show the workshop out of which Irving wrote *The Sketch Book*. They include references to transitoriness of literary fame, a fashionable bookseller, Stratford-on-Avon, the Boar's Head Tavern in East Cheap, old Christmas customs, an anecdote about a woman's dying of a broken heart, a destitute widow, Little Britain, William Roscoe's tranquility, the faithfulness of a wife toward her husband reduced almost to penury, English country churches, and decaying buildings with characteristics similar to those of Westminster Abbey. The undated notebooks also refer to the sorrow a son experiences at the death of his mother (Irving's mother died in 1817) and Irving's broken heart over Matilda Hoffman's death ("I feel like one withered up & blighted–broken heart is like a desert wherein can flourish no green thing–The romance of life is past"). The notebooks are also sketchbooks, including a variety of pen and pencil sketches, one of which supposedly was of William Shakespeare's chair and another of which was of the house of Sir Thomas Lucy–who figures as Justice Shallow in Shakespeare's *The Merry Wives of Windsor* (circa 1602).

Personal and financial losses had something to do with the production of "Rip Van Winkle," as did Irving's study of German language and literature. Unsuccessful in other ventures, Irving determined to delay his return to the United States until he had succeeded in establishing himself through his writing. While visiting with his sister Sarah and her husband Henry Van Wart in Birmingham in June 1818, Irving engaged with Van Wart in exchanging memories of Sleepy Hollow on the Hudson River. Retiring to his bedroom, Irving stayed up through the night writing about a ne'er-do-well old Rip who slept through two decades of his adult life. At breakfast the next morning, he read to the Van Warts what he had written. It became one of six sketches forming the first number of seven installments of *The Sketch Book* published during 1819 and 1820 by the New York printer C. S. Van Winkle. English publication of the book was offered first to "the Prince of Booksellers," John Murray II, who turned it down. A volume of the first four numbers was then published 1820 by John Miller in London. With the failure of Miller's firm, however, and with promotion of the book by Scott, Murray was persuaded to take over publication of the first volume and then to bring out the second volume. With this book, as Irving wrote Brevoort on 3 March 1819, "I have attempted no lofty theme, nor sought to look wise and learned. . . . I have preferred addressing myself to the feeling and fancy of the reader more than to his judgment. . . . [If my writings] possess merit in the class of literature to which they belong, it is all to which I aspire in the work."

With a nod to Geoffrey Chaucer, and figuratively with an artist's sketch pad in hand, Irving through Geoffrey Crayon provides in *The Sketch Book* word portraits of people such as William Roscoe, a faithful wife, James the First, a widow and her son, and Philip of Pokanoket. Irving delineates scenes such as an English country church, the tavern formerly called the Boar's Head Tavern, Westminster Abbey, and Little Britain in the center of London. Sketches on Christmas formed the fifth number of the first edition. Irving's tales of "Rip Van Winkle," "The Spectre Bridegroom," and "The Legend of Sleepy Hollow" are found early, midway, and late in the work.

Rip Van Winkle, whom Lewis Leary in his 1963 biography of Irving calls a boy with a dog, enters a mythic world of slumbering or ghostlike heroes and gods, from which he emerges twenty years later. Allowed in his old age to tell his tale repeatedly, Rip may reflect something of Irving's ambivalence about what was expected of himself in the world in conflict with the role of an imaginative storyteller. As Terence Martin points out in "Rip, Ichabod, and the American Imagination," *American Literature* (May 1959), Irving "worked in the context of a pervading mistrust of the

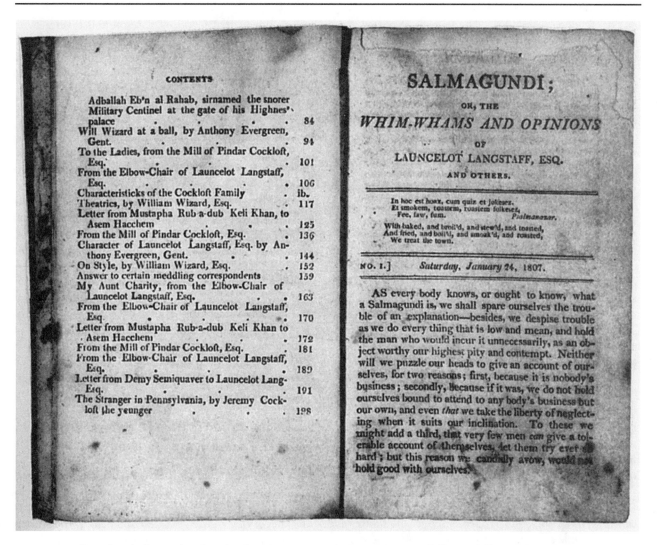

Pages from the first number of a series of social satires written by Irving, his brother William, and James Kirke Paulding
(from Stanley T. Williams, The Life of Washington Irving, *1935)*

imagination" and at once confronted and shared this suspicion. Writing behind the mask of Diedrich Knickerbocker and lamenting the desultory course of his life, Irving imagines an escape in which an older man "can be idle with impunity." A connection between Rip's awakening and Irving's can also be seen. "He said it had all come back to him," reported Irving's brother-in-law, Henry Van Wart. "Sleepy Hollow had awakened him from his long dull, desponding slumber; and then he read the first chapters of 'Rip Van Winkle.'"

Herman Von Starkenfaust in "The Spectre Bridegroom" takes advantage of others' propensities to superstition to act the part of a dead lover in order to win the hand of the Baron's lovely daughter. "The Legend of Sleepy Hollow" evokes a place that "still continues under the sway of some witching power," where superstition and an overactive imagination contribute to

Ichabod Crane's being routed by Brom Bones. As Daniel G. Hoffman shows in "Irving's Use of American Folklore in 'The Legend of Sleepy Hollow'" (1953), the conflict between the Yankee schoolmaster and the Dutch roisterer can also be seen as that between a Catskill Mike Fink, a type of frontier braggart, and a Connecticut Yankee.

The whole of *The Sketch Book* is colored by Irving's geniality, warmth, antiquarian curiosity, and feelings of mutability. The work was widely praised in both the United States and Great Britain; a typical response is that of Scottish critic John Gibson Lockhart, who wrote in "On the Writings of Charles Brockden Brown and Washington Irving" (*Blackwood's Edinburgh Magazine,* February 1820) that he considered Irving's style to be "very graceful–infinitely more so than any piece of American writing that ever came from any other hand, and well entitled to be classed with the best English writings of our day." John Neal added, "The touches of poetry are everywhere" (*Blackwood's Edinburgh Magazine,* 1825). In an address delivered after Irving's death, Longfellow remembered reading *The Sketch Book* "with ever increasing wonder and delight, spellbound by its pleasant humor, its melancholy tenderness, its atmosphere of revery, . . . and [its] fair, clear . . . style."

With the publication of *The Sketch Book,* Irving became a professional storyteller, the first American to earn his living wholly through his literary art. He was, Henry A. Pochmann says in "Irving's German Tour and Its Influence on His Tales" (*PMLA,* 1930), "less the amateur toying with esoteric aspirations beyond his reach than the canny professional gauging his grasp by his reach." Assessing his contribution, twentieth-century critic Fred Lewis Pattee in *The Development of the American Short Story* (1923) affirms that a study of the short story in its American phases begins with Irving, the first conscious literary artist in the new mode later called the short story. Ralph M. Aderman, in "Washington Irving as a Purveyor of Old and New World Romanticism" (1986) considers that in *The Sketch Book* Irving displayed many facets of the romantic temperament, such as "humor, sentiment, strong appeals to the emotions, Gothic elements, reverent appreciation of the past, admiration of the beauties of nature, New World elements like the Indian, topographical descriptions of both Old and New World settings, and sensitive reactions to local customs and folklore." Jeffrey Rubin-Dorsky, in *Adrift in the Old World: The Psychological Pilgrimage of Washington Irving* (1988), sees Irving responding in the book to an American crisis of identity, an apprehension over the future of the democratic experiment, with Irving's portrayal of the Old World providing an imaginative location of order and continuity to those feeling adrift.

The Old World is at the center of Irving's next work, *Bracebridge Hall; or, The Humourists. A Medley* (1822), again putatively written by Geoffrey Crayon, a persona who shares many of Irving's experiences but is less able to look at them realistically. In this book, Irving refers to his description in *The Sketch Book* of Christmas experiences at a country estate named Bracebridge Hall and sketches English manners and customs. Various locations have been posited as the model for Bracebridge Hall, especially the Van Wart estate, Aston Hall in Birmingham. But Irving apparently took some characteristics of the squire and his retinue from his observations of Scott when he visited him at Abbotsford in 1817. A great admirer of Scott, Irving nevertheless has Geoffrey Crayon criticize some elements of an old English society that was passing away.

The work, Irving told his brother Ebenezer in a 29 January 1822 letter, "is not like a novel, but rather a connected series of tales and essays." The overarching connection is that Geoffrey Crayon and several other people are brought together at the Bracebridge estate for an upcoming wedding. The occasion allows Crayon to explore Bracebridge Hall and environs; comment on people such as Simon Bracebridge, Lady Lillycraft, General Harbottle, and Ready Money Jack Tibbets; and describe customs such as horsemanship, falconry, fortune-telling, May Day, and village politics. As the various people gather together in the evening, storytelling is a natural entertainment. This custom allows Irving to have introduced the story of "The Stout Gentleman," a metafiction about how to tell a story. The nervous gentleman tells of a rainy day at a country inn relieved of its boredom by romantic hypotheses regarding a stout gentleman who becomes in the narrator's mind a "mysterious being" with "guttural breathings" and "creaking footsteps." The only romance, however, turns out to be that created in the mind of the narrator; the stagecoach of the subtitle is barely referred to in the last two paragraphs, and the only glimpse the narrator gets of the Stout Gentleman is "a full view of the broad disk of a pair of drab breeches"—which is close to what Irving in *Astoria* calls "vulgar jocularity" when a thieving Indian in departure claps his hand "on the most insulting part of his body."

"The Student of Salamanca" is a story written by a soldier recuperating at Salamanca and read to an attentive audience. This long story of a student, an alchemist, and the alchemist's daughter anticipates Irving's researches in Granada and the stories he later included in *The Alhambra.* The student, Antonio, like the later Irving, "paced the deserted halls of the Alhambra, the paradise of the Moorish kings," and his imagination "kindled as he wandered among these scenes." Antonio's relationship with the beautiful Inez compares with Irving's relationship with Matilda: "Their hearts mingled together, and understood each other without the aid of language." Unlike Irving, who could not rescue Matilda, Antonio rescues Inez from a seducer and her father from the auto-da-fé. The next story could also have a connection with Irving's feelings for Matilda. Furnished by Lady Lillycraft, "Annette Delarbre" is a melancholy story of love, loss, and restoration with Annette maddened by news that her lover, Eugene, was swept overboard on his return home. Eugene returns to find Annette deranged; he faithfully stays by her side, and, in time, her mental health is restored.

A fourth engaging story in *Bracebridge Hall* is "Dolph Heyliger," read by Geoffrey Crayon from the papers of Diedrich Knickerbocker. The story is prefaced by the description of a "crazy old mansion" reputed to be a haunted house. The story itself traces the escapades of Dolph Heyliger, son of the widow of a Dutch sea captain, who stays overnight in the haunted house, impulsively joins a half-blind commander on a sloop going up the Hudson River, is thrown overboard, joins a hunting party, hears a legend of a ghostly storm ship, and eventually finds hidden ancestral wealth at the bottom of the well near the haunted house. Like Rip Van Winkle, Dolph Heyliger later in life tells his story, although like Rip's story, the truth of Dolph's is in doubt, since he is noted "for being the ablest drawer of the long-bow [teller of tall tales] in the whole province."

While still working on *Bracebridge Hall* in 1821, Irving spoke of his "mass of writings" as being "rather desultory." The first American edition included some of this desultory character, although the much-revised English edition was a considerable improvement both in accuracy and form. Edward Everett in the *North American Review* for July 1822 pronounced the book "quite equal to any thing, which the present age of British literature has produced in this department." The British reviewers generally praised the book as well, although the reviewer for the *Gentleman's Magazine* in July 1822 thought that no family currently residing in Great Britain resembled the people in Irving's sketches. Bowden, however, sees this matter in another light. She shows that while Irving has Crayon present his characters through "historical and poetical associations," the Irving who is behind Crayon has realistic assessments of both the past and the present. Rubin-Dorsky sees Irving as echoing Jefferson and anticipating Andrew Jackson in ultimately repudiating the privileged elite and honoring the incorruptible yeoman farmer—reminding the American readers "of the vitality and energy of *American* ideals."

Despite feeling, as he said in an 11 June 1822 letter to Brevoort, "nearly killed with kindness" by the warm response in the United States to his writings, Irving the expatriate was not ready to return home. He wanted to confirm his reputation further by a collection of German-based tales and sketches, and thus he decided to go to the German-speaking area of Europe. First he went to Aix-la-Chapelle (Aachen), where he could take a water cure for a recurring lameness and skin irritation. He went on through Munich and Vienna, and then stopped for a time in Dresden, which he considered, as he wrote to Sarah Van Wart on 10 November 1822, "a place of taste, intellect, and literary feeling; and is the best place to acquire the German language." In Dresden he was feted by local royalty and was welcomed especially by an English family, Mrs. John Foster and her children. "The many evenings of homefelt enjoyment I have passed among you," Irving wrote to Mrs. Foster from Prague on 13 June 1823, "are the sweetest moments I have passed in Dresden." Irving was attracted romantically to the eighteen-year-old

Emily Foster, and presumably he unsuccessfully proposed marriage to the girl. In retrospection, he wrote in the same letter, "Oh, Dresden, Dresden! With what a mixture of pain, pleasure, fondness, and impatience I look back upon it!"

During the winter and spring of 1822–1823 Irving regularly visited the theater and the opera. Together with the Fosters, he participated in amateur theatricals, and in collaboration with Barham Livius, he translated and adapted Carl Maria von Weber's operas *Der Freischütz* (The Wild Huntsman) and *Abu Hassan* for the theater. Later, with the help of actor and dramatist John Howard Payne, he adapted popular dramas (for example, *Richelieu* by Alexandre Duval and Jacques-Marie Boutet de Monvel) for British audiences, hoping, as he wrote in a 4 September 1823 letter to his brother Peter, to "put some money in my pocket without costing much time or trouble, or committing my name." During this time he also became "tolerably well supplied with German localities, manners, characters, &c.," with the thought of developing tales and sketches to form a second sequel to *The Sketch Book*.

This second sequel ultimately became *Tales of a Traveller*. Although he was suffering spells of depression, during 1823–1824 he strove to piece together a disparate collection of a book already being advertised by his publishers. In a 14 August 1824 letter to his friend Thomas Moore he lamented, "I never have had such fagging in altering, adding, and correcting." The final version of *Tales of a Traveller* includes four dissimilar parts: "Strange Stories by a Nervous Gentleman," "Buckthorne and His Friends," "The Italian Banditti," and "The Money Diggers." The "strange stories" are primarily ghost stories told by the same nervous gentleman who related the story of "The Stout Gentleman," published in *Bracebridge Hall*. The connected stories related to Buckthorne—what Irving called his "history of an author"—were originally intended to be part of *Bracebridge Hall*, but at the suggestion of his artist friend Charles R. Leslie, Irving had held on to the manuscript with the intent (never fulfilled) of expanding it into a novel. "The Italian Banditti" section includes the tales most obviously appropriate to be called travelers' tales. Using the device of a group of travelers brought together at an inn in Terracina, Italy, Irving has the travelers tell a series of stories connected with robbers; afterward the travelers themselves are confronted by robbers. The fourth section, "The Money Diggers," focuses on stories of buried treasure, with the stories attributed to "the papers of the late Diedrich Knickerbocker."

In an essay included in *The Old World and New World Romanticism of Washington Irving* (1986), Judith G. Haig has asked, "Is there an itinerary in *Tales of a*

Irving delights in exercise of the fictive imagination, yet satirizes excesses of it and demonstrates some ambivalence toward it. For instance, in "The Adventure of My Uncle," the opening story of "Strange Stories," a fairly straightforward ghost story shows the play of the imagination. The story is somewhat undercut, though, by Crayon's being in doubt whether the storyteller "were in drollery or earnest." "The Adventure of My Aunt," the story that follows, starts as a ghost story but is fully explained with discovery of an intruder behind a picture. The subsequent story, "The Bold Dragoon, or The Adventure of My Grandfather," with the dragoon's presumed witness of furniture dancing in a haunted room, is a humorous instance of what Donald A. Ringe in *American Gothic: Imagination and Reason in Nineteenth-Century Fiction* (1982) calls Irving's sportive Gothic. A dark, delusional Gothic tale follows. "The Adventure of the German Student," frequently reprinted, tells how Gottfried Wolfgang pledges marriage to and spends the night with a woman who turns out to have been guillotined the day before. The narrator affirms the story is a fact, having learned it from Wolfgang himself in a Paris madhouse.

In "Buckthorne and His Friends," Irving through Geoffrey Crayon presents the problems of choosing poetry as a vocation and becoming a "poor devil author." Buckthorne, "or the young man of great expectations," confesses that he is "an incorrigible laggard" with "the poetical feeling" and "prone to play the vagabond." He writes sentimental poetry, and in his wanderings away from his father he acts with a traveling theatrical company. After many adventures and having been disappointed in love and inheritance, he becomes a hack writer—only at the end to inherit his cousin's estate. There are significant parallels between Buckthorne and Oliver Goldsmith, in whom Irving had a lifelong interest and whose biography he later wrote (published in 1849). Especially, both have poetical natures, scapegrace adventures, and disappointments with "great expectations."

"The Italian Banditti" section of *Tales of a Traveller* presents a darker picture. Although interlaced with humor, as in characterizations of the dour Englishman and the excitable innkeeper, these stories of Italian robbers portray fear and violence. The most poignant of these is "The Story of the Young Robber," in which a robber tells a captured painter about how he became an outlaw and the cause of his "ulcerated heart." Having fallen in love with a beautiful girl, Rosetta, in a jealous rage he murders her intended bridegroom and then joins a robber troop. He returns surreptitiously to Rosetta, but her screams bring the rest of the robber gang, who take her to the mountains as a prize and to claim a ran-

The title character in Irving's first short story, "The Little Man in Black" (frontispiece for the second volume of Salmagundi; *from Stanley T. Williams,* The Life of Washington Irving, *1935)*

Traveller?" While she does not find one, she discloses the connection in Irving's writings between travel and imagination to show how Irving is developing throughout the book the relationship between fact and fiction. After all, Geoffrey Crayon, the putative author of *Tales of a Traveller* and an "old traveller," tells the reader, "I have read somewhat, heard and seen more, and dreamt more than all. . . . When I attempt to draw forth a fact, I cannot determine whether I have read, heard, or dreamt it; and I am always at a loss to know how much to believe of my own stories." Travelers abound in the book, as do questions of truth telling. The epigraph to part 1, from John Fletcher's *Wife for a Month* (1624), sets up this questioning: "Do you think I'd tell you truths?"

som; she is gang-raped, and after the father denies the ransom, the young robber kills Rosetta according to the laws of the band. The robber's story is horrifying to the painter who hears it, just as the Venetian lady subsequently listening to the painter is "violently affected." After the travelers continue their journey the next day, this lady is herself carried off by bandits, but then rescued by the Englishman and his servant.

Part 4, "The Money Diggers," includes tales of pirates and their buried money. Crayon begins with reports about Captain Kidd and then moves to stories about Kidd's buried money. The first of these, "The Devil and Tom Walker," recounts a New England tale of a shrewish wife and her grasping husband. Tom Walker encounters the devil in the form of the Black Woodsman and learns of Kidd's hidden money. Unable to persuade her husband to accede to her demands that he sell his soul to the devil in order to obtain the treasure, the wife tries to bribe the devil in order to get the treasure, only for her to be presumably destroyed. Then Tom Walker makes a bargain with the devil, becomes a usurer, and eventually is taken away on a large black horse.

"Wolfert Webber, or Golden Dreams," the last tale in this section, is, like many of the other stories in *Tales of a Traveller,* framed in a series of narrative Chinese boxes. John Josse Vandermoere relates a tale he had heard, which in turn is recorded by Diedrich Knickerbocker and then by Geoffrey Crayon. Vandermoere's account of Wolfert Webber includes a story narrated by Peechy Prauw, "The Adventure of the Black Fisherman." Wolfert Webber tries his hand at money digging, uncovers a chest, but then is driven away. Despairing of life, he recovers when he learns his cabbage patch will be subdivided and will bring him a fortune.

Washington Irving initially thought that *Tales of a Traveller* would be well accepted. In a 25 March 1824 letter to John Murray II, his publisher, he said, "Those who have seen various parts of what I have prepared think the work will be the best thing I have written and that it will be very successful with the public." The reception was contrary to Irving's expectations. Several American reviewers condemned the stories, one calling it "a light kind of literature" (*United States Literary Gazette,* 15 November 1824) and another calling it "a mere shadow of the previous works of the same writer, without their spirit, humour, or interest" (*New-York Mirror, and Ladies Literary Gazette,* 25 September 1824). Some British reviewers disparaged the book, one referring to it as "second-rate manufactures" (*Blackwood's Edinburgh Magazine,* September 1824), another as lacking "originality of conception" (*London Examiner,* 5 September

1824), and still another as "feeble" (*Westminster Review,* October 1824). In response, John Neal, writing in *Blackwood's Edinburgh Magazine* in January 1825, said that while Irving had previously been "foolishly praised," he now was being wickedly dishonored. Writing about *Tales of a Traveller* in an 11 December 1824 letter to Henry Brevoort, Irving said, "As I do not read criticism good or bad, I am out of the reach of attack–If my writings are worth any thing they will out live temporary criticism; if not they are not worth caring about." Privately in his journal, however, he wrote, "It is hard to be stabbed in the back by one's own kin when attacked in front by strangers" (29 April 1825). Despite these attacks, Irving maintained his faith in what he had produced, saying to Brevoort:

> There was more of an artist like touch about it–though this is not a thing to be appreciated by the many. . . . For my part I consider a story merely as a frame on which to stretch my materials. It is the play of thought, and sentiment and language; the weaving in of characters, lightly yet expressively delineated; the familiar and faithful exhibition of scenes in common life; and the half concealed vein of humour that is often playing through the whole–these are among what I aim at, and upon which I felicitate myself in proportion as I think I succeed.

Weak public reception of *Tales of a Traveller* helped bring about what Irving called, in a 23 August 1825 letter to Emily Foster, "one of those long fits of literary inaction that sometimes get possession of me and dismantle all my mind." In December 1824 he warned his nephew Pierre P. Irving about "the pernicious effects of early publishing," which produces too often "a restless craving after popular applause." Irving hoped that none of those persons dear to him would be "induced to follow my footsteps and wander into the seductive but treacherous paths of literature." Those footsteps, he went on to say, were on a path that "has too often lain among thorns & brambles & been darkend by care and despondency." This unproductive time in Irving's life was made even more difficult by financial losses from a steamboat venture with his brother Peter, failure of the London banking firm of Welles and Williams, and losses from speculative investment in Bolivian copper mines.

Toward the end of 1825 and into 1826, Irving attempted to write a book of "American Essays," including topics such as "American Scenery," "National Prejudices," "Union," "American Character," and "Public Prosperity." Initially, he recorded in his journal, "Mind excited. Thinking over project of an American Work" (5 February 1825). His essays may in part have been intended as a response to criticism in American

Matilda Hoffman, Irving's fiancée, who died in 1809 (portrait by Edward G. Malbone; New-York Historical Society)

Hispanic bibliographer Obadiah Rich, and other archives to write his own life of the discoverer of America. A few months later, he acknowledged to Brevoort in a 4 April 1827 letter that in preparing this biography, "I have studied and laboured with a patience and assiduity for which I shall never get the credit." While anticipating "cold scrutiny & stern criticism" by his countrymen, he expressed delight in "study and in the creative exercise of the pen" and in discovering "a line of writing in which I have not hitherto ascertained my own powers." Writing the biography was also hard work; it was, as he said in his journal, "the hardest application and toil of the pen I have ever passed" (31 December 1827).

A History of the Life and Voyages of Christopher Columbus appeared in 1828, and for the remainder of the century was the standard life of Columbus. Claudia L. Bushman in *America Discovers Columbus: How an Italian Explorer Became an American Hero* (1992) asserts that "If Columbus had wanted to become an American hero and had mounted a campaign for the position, he could not have chosen a better biographer than Washington Irving." While performing impeccable research for his biography, Irving responded to what he called "a certain meddlesome spirit" in some historians to cast down the monuments of history. "Care should be taken," he said in *A History of the Life and Voyages of Christopher Columbus,* "to vindicate great names from such pernicious erudition. It defeats one of the most salutary purposes of history, that of furnishing examples of what human genius and laudable enterprize may accomplish." Irving planned, he said in the opening of book 1, to "relate the deeds and fortunes of the mariner who first had the judgement to divine, and the intrepidity to brave the mysteries of this perilous deep; and who, by his hardy genius, his inflexible constancy, and his heroic courage, brought the ends of the earth into communication with each other." Perhaps responding to American critics who criticized Irving for lacking sufficient nationality in his last-published book, *Tales of a Traveller,* he goes on to affirm a national purpose in his treatment of Columbus: "The narrative of his troubled life is the link which connects the history of the old world with that of the new."

Irving's *A History of the Life and Voyages of Christopher Columbus* contrasts in tone and approach markedly with *Tales of a Traveller.* The earlier book, putatively authored by Geoffrey Crayon, is prefaced by questions regarding truth, has many narrative frames, includes four disconnected main parts, and spoofs authenticity in its title (a traveler's tale is by definition one including exaggerations) and contents (for example, "The Adventure of the German Student"). Irving attached his own name as author to *A History of the Life and Voyages of Christopher Columbus,* a factual narrative, not a tale, of one of the

newspapers that he did not have "more independence—more nationality" (*Cincinnati Literary Gazette,* 5 March 1825). (In an undated entry in his notebook, Irving affirmed, "I never sacrificed my independence.") Yet, while he developed a plan and some ideas in his journal, "Notes Extracts &c, 1825," the book itself never materialized. Several essays designed for it, however, later made their way into print, including "National Nomenclature" (August 1839) and "A Time of Unexampled Prosperity" (April 1840), published a decade and a half later in *Knickerbocker Magazine.*

A major change in direction came in 1826 with an invitation from Alexander H. Everett, minister to Spain from 1825 to 1829, for Irving to come to Spain and be attached to the embassy. The first two volumes of Martín Fernández de Navarrete's history of the voyages of Columbus, compiled from papers by Bartolomé de las Casas, had just appeared, and Everett proposed that Irving translate them into English. Irving eagerly accepted the proposition, and by December 1826 he could report to John Murray II that he had a work "nearly ready for the press, 'The Life and Voyages of Columbus.'" Rather than composing a translation, though, he used Navarette's materials, the library of

world's greatest travelers. Irving in his preface affirmed his diligent efforts to collate "all the works that I could find relative to my subject, in print and manuscript, comparing them, as far as in my power, with original documents, those sure lights of historic research, endeavouring to ascertain the truth amid those contradictions which will inevitably occur." His third-person narrative is consistent throughout, and it follows a chronological plan from the early life of Columbus through his voyages of discovery and troubles in both the New World and the Old World to his death. Given historiographical practices of the time, the history is carefully documented—with a footnote on nearly every page.

Columbus, according to Irving, was magnanimous of spirit, pious, enterprising, nobly ambitious, courageous, persevering, and moved by "lofty and solemn enthusiasm." Irving applauds Columbus's genius and "the strong workings of his vigorous mind," noting in his discovery of the New World and his plan for a crusade to liberate the Holy Sepulcher how Columbus "considered himself selected by heaven as an agent" and how "his mind was elevated above selfish and mercenary views." Irving is aware as well of flaws in Columbus's plans and actions, that "his piety was mingled with superstition, and darkened by the bigotry of the age," as in the matter of greed and enslavement of Indians. Yet, Irving concludes his biography with praise for Columbus's "ardent and enthusiastic imagination," which "lent wings to his judgement." Further, he postulates how Columbus's magnanimous spirit would have been consoled amid penury and neglect "could he have anticipated the splendid empires which were to spread over the beautiful world he had discovered."

Rubin-Dorsky and Claudia L. Bushman find that Irving created a Columbus who was much like himself. Rubin-Dorsky in *Adrift in the Old World: The Psychological Pilgrimage of Washington Irving* (1988) sees Irving as a displaced person in a changeable world. Anticipating the nonfiction narrative, Irving embellished his sources to idealize Columbus and create "a romantic quest for the unattainable." Bushman in *America Discovers Columbus* sees Irving's Columbus as having "suffered American-style angst. Columbus's voyages to the New World paralleled Irving's quests in the Old." Both critics see Irving's romantic identification in ornamented style with an explorer who, in Bushman's words, "yearned to journey to magical places" as limiting the book as a work of history. And other twentieth-century historians have judged it similarly. In its time, though, Irving's *A History of the Life and Voyages of Christopher Columbus* was enthusiastically hailed as a major achievement.

Writing on 4 April 1827 to Brevoort, Irving said, "Since my arrival in Spain I have been completely immersed in old Spanish literature." Irving's biography of Columbus in four volumes was the first fruit of this immersion. Afterward, he continued to explore the manuscript and printed riches available to him in Madrid and Seville. He planned a second edition of *A History of the Life and Voyages of Christopher Columbus* and a related book, *Voyages and Discoveries of the Companions of Columbus* (1831). Out of his Spanish researches also came *A Chronicle of the Conquest of Granada* (1829); *The Alhambra* (1832); *Legends of the Conquest of Spain* (1835); *Mahomet and His Successors* (1849–1850); and miscellaneous additional Spanish writings such as those in Pierre M. Irving's edition of *Spanish Papers* (1866).

Voyages and Discoveries of the Companions of Columbus was intended to follow soon after *A History of the Life and Voyages of Christopher Columbus* but was delayed as Irving waited for volume three of Fernández de Navarrete's *Colección de los viages y descubrimientos* (Collection of Sea Voyages and Discoveries, 1825–1837) and repeatedly sought access to the Archives of the Indias in Seville—for which the king's permission was required. He worked a year in Seville, primarily in the archives at the Biblioteca Colombina. He also paid a visit to Palos, the place from which Columbus set sail for the New World. There he met with the leading descendant of the Pinzons and visited churches associated with Columbus's departure and return. His account of that visit, initially written as a letter to a friend, is appended to *Voyages and Discoveries of the Companions of Columbus*. In it he tells how moved he was to see the location from which Columbus embarked. His thirty-ninth and concluding appendix is the manifesto of Alonzo de Ojeda, adopted by the Spanish discoverers in general, which was read to the natives and which threatened them that if they did not convert to Catholicism, they would be subject to war and slavery. As presented in the body of *Voyages and Discoveries of the Companions of Columbus,* the Spanish cavaliers are both gallant and reckless, both generous and brave, and both bloodthirsty and implacable. The natives whom they subjugated are typically described as gentle and kind, exhibiting "a humanity that would have done honour to the most professing Christians."

With the publishing of *A Chronicle of the Conquest of Granada* in 1829, Irving wished to be freer with his fictive powers and not bound by accuracy in his narrative, so he created the persona of Fray Antonio Agapida as the narrator, a counterpart to the earlier Geoffrey Crayon. This nom de guerre allowed Irving, as he told his publisher on 9 May 1829, "to mingle a tinge of romance and satire with the grave historical details." In his introduction, Irving explains that with his glowing zeal in the cause of the Catholic faith, the previously unpublished friar, Agapida, is a "model of the good old orthodox chroniclers, who recorded . . . the united triumphs of the cross and the sword." Interspersed throughout Agapida's recovered narrative are Irving's comments, such as his celebration in the book's first chapter of the ruined present-day Alhambra with its "brilliancy and beauty in defiance of the ravages of time." Earl N. Harbert makes the distinction that *A Chronicle of the Conquest of Granada* is "romantic history," not "historical romance," with Irving's entertaining the reader without losing in the process "the intrinsic truth of history."

In his note to the revised edition of *A Chronicle of the Conquest of Granada* (1850), Irving tells how the idea for the book began when he found much about the war of Granada in his researches concerning Columbus's early life. He became "so exited by the stirring events and romantic achievements of this war" that he threw off a rough draft of *A Chronicle of the Conquest of Granada* and then put it aside to be finished later. Then after finishing the books on Columbus, Irving toured Andalusia, visited the ruins of the Moorish towns and castles, and passed some time in the palace of the Alhambra. He took many notes, he said, "to give local verity and graphic effect to the scenes described." The completed work bears Irving's enthusiastic response to it.

A Chronicle of the Conquest of Granada is an energetic work. From Agapida's perspective, this story of "desperate and bloody wars" that have "determined the fate of mighty empires" is a theme "worthy of the pen of the philosopher and the study of the sage." Irving's narrative, via Agapida, is a piecing together of various chronicles in a coherent form. Irving masterfully weaves together the various strands of his story, keeping the historical characters straight for the reader and showing the relationships of the various battles. He enlivens his narrative with fictive dialogue such as the Moorish king's response when surrounded by common Christian warriors: "'Slaves!' exclaimed King Boabdil, 'you have not taken me. I surrender to this cavalier.'" Irving also reminds the reader from time to time of the biases of his putative narrator with such comments as: "'Such,' says the pious Fray Antonio Agapida, 'was the diabolical hatred and stiffnecked opposition of this infidel to our holy cause.'" The sad climax of the story, in which, despite Fray Agapida's role, Irving's sympathies are strongly with the Moors, is Boabdil el Chico's surrender of Granada and his departure from his beloved city, "that delicious abode."

Irving's coloration came from his own romantic delight in Granada. As he said in a 17 April 1829 letter to Madame Pierre D'Oubril regarding an impending return to that city, "I wish to see Granada in all its glory; with its gardens and groves covered with flowers and foliage, and the Alhambra fragrant with orange & citron blossoms, and resounding with the song of the nightingale." In the spring of 1829 he not only had this opportunity, but he also was permitted to reside in part of the Alhambra. Visitors today can see the room designated by a plaque as the one in which Washington Irving lived. In a 16 June 1829 letter to his sister Catharine, Irving describes his experience of being able

> to wander about at perfect leisure and convenience among these beautiful and interesting remains of Arabian Magnificence, and the delightful tranquility and beauty of the place have combined to fix me here as with a Spell. . . . I feel as if living in one of the enchanted palaces that we used to read of in the arabian nights. I wander by day and night through great halls, all decorated with beautiful reliefs and with Arabic inscriptions, that have stood for centuries; through open courts, with fountains and flowers, where there is every thing assembled to delight the senses, yet where there is not a living being to be seen.

While living at the Alhambra from mid May through July 1829, Irving gathered legends of the place that found their way into his Spanish sketchbook, *The Alhambra*. His guide at the Alhambra, Mateo Ximínez, provided many of what Irving in the preface to the 1851 revised edition calls "whimsical and superstitious legends." These became the center of Irving's efforts to depict the Alhambra's "half Spanish half Oriental character; its mixture of the heroic, the poetic, and the grotesque; [and] to revive the traces of grace and beauty fast fading from its walls." Irving actually began writing his tales of the Alhambra in January 1829 and continued after he went in September to England, where he had been appointed secretary to the Court of St. James. His work on *The Alhambra* was especially intense in the fall of 1830, continuing, despite his embassy duties, through 1831 and into early spring of 1832.

The Alhambra is framed by Irving's account of his 1829 journey to Granada and his farewell to the place later in the year. "The Journey" portrays much of Spain as "a stern, melancholy country, . . . and indescribably silent and lonesome." By contrast, Granada, and especially its crown, the royal palace of the Alhambra, is a beautifully glistening place in which "the ear is lulled by the rustling of groves, and the murmur of running streams." As Irving writes in "The Author's Farewell to Granada," his feelings upon departure are similar to those of Boabdil, the last Moorish king, who shed tears on bidding "adieu to the paradise he was leaving behind." Coming to the end of what he called "one of the pleasantest dreams of a life," Irving with tender and sad feelings observes how the setting sun richly gilds the "bosky groves and gardens."

The first third of *The Alhambra* is a detailed description of the palace and grounds and of the cur-

"Rip Van Winkle's Return" and "Ichabod Crane and the Headless Horse Man," illustrations by F. O. C. Darley for the 1848 edition of The Sketch Book of Geoffrey Crayon, Gent. *(from Stanley T. Williams,* The Life of Washington Irving, *1935)*

rent inhabitants. It could serve then–indeed, still does–as a guide to a romantic appreciation of the Alhambra palace complex. In the remaining two-thirds of the book, Irving intersperses descriptive chapters (for example, "Public Fetes of Granada," "Relics and Genealogies," and "A Ramble among the Hills") with tales connected to the Alhambra. The first story, "The Adventure of the Mason," is related as an anecdote by Irving's "humble historiographer Mateo" as the two look out from a balcony into an obscure street below. Subsequent stories follow this pattern: curiosity about a place leads to inquiry about traditions and legends associated with it. Interest in the House of the Weathercock with its figure of a bronze warrior on horseback leads to researches that produce the "Legend of the Arabian Astrologer" that follows. In the legend, a Moorish king named Aben Habuz receives a magical bronze horseman as a talisman from an Arabian astrologer. Eventually affronting the astrologer, Aben Habuz loses both the effect of the talisman and a beautiful Christian princess–taken by the astrologer into an underground chamber. A visit to the Generalife, a "fairy palace" near the Alhambra, leads to the "Legend of Prince Ahmed Al Kamel"–a story, like the "Legend of the Arabian Astrologer," that has an enchanted cavern. Learning from an owl and a parrot, Prince Ahmed wins the daughter of the Christian king and departs with her on a flying carpet. Other legends that Irving enjoys retelling are of the Moor's legacy (enchanted treasure obtained by a water carrier), of the three beautiful princesses (who fall in love with three Christian cavaliers), of the Rose of the Alhambra (fair Jacinta with her enchanted lute), of the two discreet statues (which watch over hidden Moorish treasure), of Don Munio Sancho De Hinojosa (who became a phantom knight), and of the enchanted soldier (buried alive to guard Moorish treasure and freed temporarily by a student and a maiden with the seal of Solomon, but entombed again because a hungry priest broke his fast too soon).

Andrew B. Myers in his introduction to the 1983 Twayne edition of *The Alhambra* calls the work the crown of Irving's labors on Spain. In England the work was favorably reviewed by the *Literary Guardian* for May 1832 as the product of "decidedly the first English prose-writer of the day." (In April 1830, two years previous to the publication of *The Alhambra,* Irving had been awarded a gold medal by the Royal Society of Literature, and in 1831 he had received an honorary Doctor in Civil Law from Oxford University.) In the *North American Review* (October 1832) the work was considered as "equal in value to any of the others of the same class, with the exception of the Sketch Book." Stanley T. Williams in *The Spanish Background of American Literature* (1955) says, "No American . . . has ever been so

accepted, so interwoven as Irving into the texture of Spanish thought," and considered that apart from "Rip Van Winkle" and "The Legend of Sleepy Hollow," *The Alhambra* "is the peer of *The Sketch Book.*"

In April of 1832 Irving finally returned to the United States after an absence of seventeen years. His letters reflect his feelings that this return to his native land was "the happiest moment of my life," as he expressed in a 24 May 1832 letter to James Renwick. On 30 May 1832 to his brother Peter he wrote, "I have been in a tumult of enjoyment ever since my arrival; am pleased with everything and everybody, and as happy as mortal being can be." And his countrymen were happy with him, feting him at a public dinner on 30 May at the City Hotel in New York. While generally averse to such public distinctions, Irving was pleased with this one. He declined, however, invitations to public dinners in Philadelphia and Baltimore.

The author of *Tales of a Traveller* was a traveler himself, and during the summer of 1832 he visited Washington, D.C., Philadelphia, Boston, and various parts of New England. With Charles Joseph Latrobe and Count Albert-Alexandre de Portalès, acquaintances solidified during the voyage from Le Havre to New York, Irving toured Boston and the White Mountains of New Hampshire, then later traveled in western New York and into Ohio. An accidental meeting with Henry Ellsworth opened up further travel. As Irving wrote on 18 December 1832 to his brother Peter, Ellsworth was "one of the commissioners appointed by government to superintend the settlement of emigrant Indian tribes, to the west of the Mississippi. He was on his way to the place of rendezvous, and on his invitation, we agreed to accompany him in expedition."

Irving's account of this expedition is found in six surviving journals, three notebooks titled "Notes Concerning the Far West," and *A Tour on the Prairies,* part 1 of *The Crayon Miscellany* (1835). The tour took Irving and his companions from Fort Gibson near the confluence of the Neosho and Arkansas Rivers nearly to present-day Oklahoma City. This month-long excursion out and back from Fort Gibson was a memorable adventure. It included meeting several different tribes of Native Americans–Osages, Pawnees, and Creeks; hunting bees; and participating in hunts for turkeys, deer, elk, and buffalo. While in his introduction to the 1835 American edition of *The Crayon Miscellany* Irving confessed to having "no wonders to describe, nor any moving accidents by flood or field to narrate," his party did have the false fear of being attacked by three hundred Pawnees. Just being on the prairie was an excitement for Irving, breaking, as he says in a journal entry dated 16 October 1832, "thro a country hitherto untrodden by whiteman, except perchance the solitary trapper. A glorious world spread around us without an inhabitant." *A Tour on the Prairies* is full of vibrant sketches of Irving's companions, Indians, hunters, feasts and hunger, gallops on the prairie, humorous scenes and stories, and alarms—in all of which the narrator from the East appears to revel.

Irving's experiences in the West and his desire to write about his own country led to his accepting a request in 1834 by John Jacob Astor to write about Astor's fur-trading enterprise—a request that led in turn to Irving's writing the adventures in the Rocky Mountains of Captain B. L. E. Bonneville. Despite rumors to the contrary, Irving expected no remuneration from the wealthy Astor; rather, he intended to rely on returns from the sale of the book. Astor did, however, pay Irving's nephew Pierre M. Irving to sort through Astor's materials about his attempts to open a vast fur-trading empire in the Columbia River basin, to draw anecdotes from persons involved in the enterprise, and to forage among works in French and English relative to the regions involved.

Irving's motives for ultimately accepting the project were undoubtedly many: his attraction to the remote and adventurous aspects of Astor's enterprise, his long-held interest in the American frontier and its inhabitants, his present awareness of America and concern to write about American themes (stimulated by *A Tour on the Prairies* and the call for a national literature), his seeing in Astor's experiment how business enterprise can work hand in hand with national interest, his friendship with John Jacob Astor dating back to at least 1821, and his recognizing an opportunity to earn money with which to purchase a home on the Hudson River.

In February 1835 Irving purchased a "neglected cottage" and ten acres near Tarrytown, New York. He first named it Wolfert's Roost and then settled on its current name, Sunnyside. He described it as a "little, old-fashioned, stone mansion, all made up of gabled ends, as full of angles and corners as an old cocked hat." Today it is owned and maintained by Historic Hudson Valley, formerly Sleepy Hollow Restorations. The aura of Irving's presence is still felt in this charming home on the Hudson that Irving in *Chronicles of Wolfert's Roost and Other Papers* (1855) called his "snuggery."

During 1835 Irving published three numbers of the *Crayon Miscellany: A Tour on the Prairies, Abbotsford and Newstead Abbey,* and *Legends of the Conquest of Spain. Abbotsford* derived primarily from Irving's happy memories of a visit in the late summer of 1817 to Scott at his home and from his lifelong appreciation of him as a writer and friend. In commenting in a 1 September 1817 letter to his brother Peter on his visit to Scott at Abbotsford, Irving said, "As to Scott, I cannot express

my delight at his character & manners—He is a sterling golden hearted old worthy—Full of the joyousness of youth, with an imagination continually furnishing forth pictures—and a charming simplicity of manner that puts you to ease with him in a moment." *Abbotsford* is in the form of a letter, giving an account of Irving's four days in Abbotsford interspersed with pieces of Scott's poetry. In a charming manner, comparable to that found in Irving's letters to his closest family members and friends, Irving pays tribute to the Scottish laird whose friendship meant so much to him and who "cheered and gladdened" Irving by "the outpourings of his genius."

Newstead Abbey is based on Irving's "three weeks sojourn in the ancestral mansion of the late Lord Byron" in 1831. Irving took extensive notes concerning the history and architecture of the mansion together with anecdotes about the people—and ghosts—associated with the place. These notes lay "dormant" in his trunks until he arranged and polished them for inclusion with *Abbotsford* as part of the *Crayon Miscellany*. Besides the intrinsic interest of its sketches similar to those found in *The Sketch Book* and *Bracebridge Hall, Newstead Abbey,* with its many references to and quotations from the poet, is Irving's means of honoring Byron.

Legends of the Conquest of Spain is a compilation of materials developed while Irving was writing his Spanish works on Columbus, Granada, and the Alhambra. "The Legend of Don Roderick" was begun in 1827 and continued in 1829. Fray Antonio Agapida, narrator of *The Conquest of Granada,* is alluded to several times as the source of a couple of the legends concerning the overthrow of King Roderick and his army, and the subjugation of Spain by the Moors. The third legend in the book is that of the traitorous Count Julian and his family, a story of "human pride and the vanity of human ambition, and shewing the futility of all greatness that is not strongly based on virtue."

Irving completed *Astoria* in early 1836, publishing it in the fall of that year in England as *Astoria; or, Enterprise beyond the Rocky Mountains* and then later the same year in the United States as *Astoria; or, Anecdotes of an Enterprise beyond the Rocky Mountains*. While written in a romantic style and criticized by the nineteenth-century historian Hubert Howe Bancroft in his *History of the Northwest Coast* (1884) as being more fictional than historical, in the twentieth century the work has received high praise for its accuracy and objectivity from Hiram Martin Chittenden, author of the authoritative *History of the American Fur Trade of the Far West* (1902); Andrew B. Myers, in "Washington Irving, Fur Trade Chronicler: An Analysis of *Astoria* with Notes for a Corrected Edition" (1964); Edgeley W. Todd in his Editor's Foreword to *Astoria* (1964); and Wayne R. Kime in his "Alfred

Sunnyside, Irving's house near Tarrytown, New York

Seton's Journal: A Source for Irving's *Tonquin* Disaster Account" (1970). The initial critical reception of the book was favorable. A reviewer in the *Western Monthly Magazine* said that with all Irving's "power of humor and pathos, he is conscientious, and does not permit him imagination to *make* facts, to be passed off as real occurrences" (November 1836). The *North American Review* critic considered that Irving's account "adds all the dramatic interest of romance to the intrinsic value of authentic history, and the graces of his peculiarly graphic and beautiful style" (1840).

The book is a gripping romantic history with several narrative threads. *Astoria* provides an account of the voyage of the *Tonquin* under Captain Thorn's dictatorial direction with the intention of taking Astorians to the mouth of the Columbia River. In that same year, 1810, an expedition by land was begun under the leadership of Wilson Price Hunt, primarily following the route of Meriwether Lewis and George Rogers Clark from just a few years earlier. The Astorians on the *Tonquin* arrived at the mouth of the Columbia River in the spring of 1811 and set to work establishing a fur factory and a fort. Sailing further north to trade for sea otter skins, Captain Thorn affronted the natives there and incited a massacre of

the whites on board the *Tonquin*. Four surviving seamen temporarily made their escape, but the mortally wounded ship's clerk stayed on board and set up a revenge in which he blew up the ship when it was again occupied by the natives. Edgar Allan Poe drew on this event for a similar revenge explosion in his novel *The Narrative of Arthur Gordon Pym* (1838). The other Astorian party, under Hunt's direction, endured great trials from hostile Indian tribes, grizzly bears, difficult terrains—such as Hell's Canyon of the Snake River, and hunger and thirst. They eventually made it to the fort on the Columbia River in February 1812. A third major narrative thread is that of the journey of a small party under the direction of Robert Stuart, which made its way from Astoria back to Astor's headquarters in New York. Unhorsed by Indian marauders, the party struggled to get through the Rocky Mountains. For a time, the Astorians in the West set up fur-trading posts on various rivers, but Astor's overall plan was frustrated by equivocal sale of the goods to the North West Company and arrival in the winter of 1813 of British warships, confirming the takeover of the operation by the British.

Irving followed up *The Rocky Mountains; or, Scenes, Incidents, and Adventures in the Far West* (1837), called

Adventures of Captain Bonneville, or Scenes beyond the Rocky Mountains of the Far West in the first English edition (1837); it then became known by its English short title, *The Adventures of Captain Bonneville*. Irving first met Captain B. L. E. Bonneville in September 1835 at Astor's home at Hellgate in New York. Bonneville had just returned from his second trip to the Rocky Mountains, explorations that began in the spring of 1832. Busy with *Astoria* at the time, Irving was particularly interested in the maps in Bonneville's journal. Bonneville tried to write a book out of his travels, but on returning to the West in the spring of 1836, he sold his manuscript to Irving. This manuscript formed the staple of Irving's work, with Irving interweaving details from "the conversations and journals of some of the captain's contemporaries," as he says in the introduction, and giving it "a tone and coloring drawn from my own observation, during an excursion into the Indian country beyond the bounds of civilization." Despite the carping of a few critics, Irving's work is accurate overall. Irving had done his homework well, says Bernard De Voto in *Across the Wide Missouri* (1947).

The Adventures of Captain Bonneville continues Irving's interest in the American West and complements his exposition of the fur trade in *Astoria* and Western exploration in both *A Tour on the Prairies* and *Astoria*. It also culminates Irving's sympathy for the Indians, expressed two decades earlier in "Traits of Indian Character." Common to both works, as Alan Sandy points out in his introduction to the 1977 Twayne edition of *The Adventures of Captain Bonneville,* "are instances of Indian heroism, castigation of the white man for maltreatment of Indians, disagreement with the common idea of Indian stoicism, admiration for Indian oratory, comparison of the Indians to classical heroes, anecdotes of colorful Indians, and depictions of their picturesque encampments." Through treating Captain Bonneville's adventures, Irving tells the reader much about the fur trade when it reached its greatest height in its romantic rendezvous period. Too, Irving presents in a picturesque manner the magnificent scenery of the Rocky Mountain West. For example, he says,

We can imagine the enthusiasm of the worthy captain, when he beheld the vast and mountainous scene of his adventurous enterprise thus suddenly unveiled before him. We can imagine with what feelings of awe and admiration he must have contemplated the Wind River Sierra, or bed of mountains; that great fountain head, from whose springs, and lakes, and melted snows, some of those mighty rivers take their rise, which wander over hundreds of miles of varied country and clime, and find their way to the opposite waves of the Atlantic and the Pacific.

Looking at the three western works, Richard H. Cracroft in *Washington Irving, The Western Works* (1974) sees Irving's craft as his foremost concern, sometimes shaping the work with European analogies in mind. Coming at the works from a different angle, Peter Antelyes in *Tales of Adventurous Enterprise: Washington Irving and the Poetics of Western Expansion* (1990) finds a merger of literature (adventure) and market capitalism (enterprise) in Irving's three Western works. Engaged with Jacksonian culture, Irving was deeply divided, according to Antelyes, endorsing "expansionism while noting the dangers posed to American society by that expansion," celebrating enterprise in *Astoria* and criticizing its excesses in *The Adventures of Captain Bonneville.*

Letters of the latter 1830s show Irving making financial investments in Midwestern lands but primarily failing in them. On close terms with the current administration, Irving wrote Benjamin Butler, acting secretary of war, and President Martin Van Buren in behalf of John James Audubon. On 28 January 1837 Irving responded to a charge in the *Plaindealer* by its editor, William Leggett, that he altered a line in one of Bryant's poems to suit a British public. He was offered, and declined, the Democratic nomination for mayor of New York City. Then, in April 1838, he turned down President Van Buren's offer to be secretary of the navy. The death of Irving's brother Peter brought on deep depression. In this year Irving also magnanimously turned over the topic of the conquest of Mexico, on which he had been engaged, to William Prescott. Irving's nephew Pierre quotes the older writer as saying, "I doubt whether Mr. Prescott was aware of the extent of the sacrifice I made. This was a favorite subject, which had delighted my imagination ever since I was a boy. . . . When I gave it up to him, I in a manner gave him up my bread, for I depended upon the profit of it to recruit my waning finances."

Help for his waning finances came in 1839 by way of a contract with *The Knickerbocker, or New-York Monthly Magazine*. While his nephew says Irving felt he had "bound himself to the irksome obligations of periodical labor," the offer of $2,000 a year was more than Irving could turn down. In the next three years he contributed nearly three dozen pieces to the magazine, most of which were reprinted in *Chronicles of Wolfert's Roost and Other Papers* and in the posthumous volume of *Spanish Papers and Other Miscellanies, Hitherto Unpublished or Uncollected* (1866). Kime has others in his edition of *Miscellaneous Writings, I and II* (1981) in *The Complete Works of Washington Irving*.

Irving introduces *Chronicles of Wolfert's Roost and Other Papers* with an historical account of his home,

"The Roost," with its Dutch motto over the door, "Lust in Rust" (pleasure in quiet). "The Birds of Spring," presented by Geoffrey Crayon, is followed by a sketch from a steamboat, "The Creole Village." "Mountjoy" is a lengthy story about a young man caught up in his fancy and philosophy. It connects with the novel "Rosalie" that Irving worked on but never finished, and in the character of the narrator there are resemblances to the young Washington Irving, just as the girl the narrator is attracted to, Julia Somerville, bears some resemblance to Matilda Hoffman. In this potpourri, Irving has a ghost story derived from an old Knight of Malta; a story of the Great Mississippi Bubble; sketches of Paris in 1825; observations on the paradisiacal Dutch town of Broek; "Guests from Gibbet Island," a legend of pirates and ghosts from the Knickerbocker papers; "The Early Experiences of Ralph Ringwood," a story of frontier Kentucky based on the real experiences of William P. Duval; "The Seminoles," based on conversations with William Pope DuVal, governor of Florida; the death of the French Count Antoine Joseph Van Horn; "Don Juan: A Spectral Research"; the story of the Phantom Island, the Island of St. Brandan in the Canaries; and "Recollections of the Alhambra," with the story of one of the descendants of the Abencerrages.

Other *Knickerbocker Magazine* pieces, "Sleepy Hollow," "Communipaw," and "Conspiracy of the Cocked Hats," revisit the world of Diedrich Knickerbocker. The first is in Washington Irving's own voice, but the Communipaw and Cocked Hats pieces are presented as by Hermanus Vander Donk and Roloff Van Ripper. Essays on "National Nomenclature" and "Desultory Thoughts on Criticism" have been shown by Richard Dilworth Rust to be related to the intended "American Essays," which Irving worked on in the mid 1820s. A couple of the miscellaneous pieces reprinted in *Spanish Papers* are "Legend of Don Munio Sancho de Hinjosa" and "Pelayo and the Merchant's Daughter," later enlarged and retitled "The Legend of Pelayo," with Pelayo as the deliverer of Spain.

In the fall of 1840 Irving edited *The Life of Oliver Goldsmith, with Selections from His Writings* in two volumes for the Harper's Family Library. The extensive biographical essay Irving wrote as a preface, together with an earlier essay published in 1825, formed the basis of Irving's full-length treatment, *Oliver Goldsmith: A Biography,* published in 1849. Irving had a lifelong interest in Goldsmith, employing irony as a chief means of satire as had Goldsmith, just as he employed satire through exaggeration, as had Joseph Addison. Goldsmith's writings, Irving says in his preface to *The*

Life of Oliver Goldsmith, "were the delight of my childhood, and have been a source of enjoyment to me throughout life." Irving summarizes his portrait of Goldsmith by saying, "It is evident that his faults, at the worst, were but negative, while his merits were great and decided. He was no one's enemy but his own; his errors, in the main, inflicted evil on none but himself, and were so blended with humorous, and even affecting circumstances, as to disarm anger and conciliate kindness." The volume was, in the main, well received. In the opinion of the reviewer for *The Critic* it was "an almost perfect example of a well-written biography" (1 December 1849), and George Ripley wrote in the *New-York Tribune:* "Everything combines to make this one of the most fascinating pieces of biography in the English language" (1849). The volume that includes the biography of Goldsmith in the Twayne edition also includes the *Biography and Poetical Remains of the Late Margaret Miller Davidson,* apparently undertaken at the request of Davidson's mother and first published in 1841.

Earlier considered America's literary ambassador to the Old World, Irving in 1842 become Envoy Extraordinary and Minister Plenipotentiary to Spain. He served there four years, joining with the British legation to protect the young Queen Isabella II during the Carlist revolution and immersing himself thoroughly in the diplomatic world. His letters from this period reveal a vibrant and capable minister, serving his country well and endearing himself to the Spanish leadership and people. Most touching are his letters to Sarah Parris Storrow, a favorite niece living with her husband, Thomas W. Storrow Jr., and their children in Paris. Irving's long letters to her and other family members often provide what he called the "romance of the palace"—events pertaining to the young queen and her entourage. Writing to Sarah Storrow in October 1842, Irving revealed his feelings about Spain, his realistic assessment of his role as a writer exercising his imagination, and his worldview. Spain, he writes,

is rather a melancholy country in aspect as well as fortunes. A great part of the interior of the peninsula is naked and dreary, and looks like a desert. . . . The whole country must be regarded historically and poetically. It is clothed with romantic associations and the people are peculiar in all their habitudes as well as in their costumes. But a stranger from the gayer, more polished and luxurious countries of Europe has much to tolerate in coming to Spain. I see it much more in its positive light than I did sixteen or seventeen years since, when my imagination still tinted and wrought up every scene. I am at times affraid that these involuntary tintings of my imagination may have awakened expectations in others with respect to this country, which the reality will disappoint; and they will concur with an English traveller in the South of Spain in pronouncing me "the easily pleased Washington Irving." Would to God I could continue to be "easily pleased" to the end of my carreer. How much of a life chequered by vicissitudes, and clouded at times by sordid cares, has been lighted up and embellished by this unbought trickery of the mind. "Surely" says the bible "a man walketh in a vain shadow and disquieteth himself in vain—" but this has not been the case with me— Shadows have proved my substance; and from them I have derived many of my most exquisite enjoyments; while the Substantial realities of life have turned to shadows in my grasp. When I think what revelry of the mind I have enjoyed; what fairy air castles I have built—*and inhabited*—when I was poor in purse; and destitute of all the worldly gear on which others build their happiness; when I reccollect how cheap have been my most highly relished pleasures; how independent of fortune and of the world; how easily conjured up under the most adverse and sterile circumstances; I feel as if, were I once more on the threshold of existence, and the choice were given me I would say, give me the gilding of the imagination and let others have the sold gold—let me be the "easily pleased Washington Irving," and heap positive blessings on others, until they groan under them—

Returned from Spain in September 1846, after having helped settle the Oregon question in London, Irving remodeled his beloved Sunnyside and began a revision of his complete works for George Palmer Putnam. Fifteen volumes were published from September 1848 until August 1850. The edition eventually grew to twenty-seven volumes. While some works, such as *Astoria* and the four titles within *The Crayon Miscellany,* were lightly revised, other works, such as *A History of New-York* and *A Chronicle of the Conquest of Granada,* were extensively changed. In *A History of New-York,* Irving removed some dated allusions as well as, according to Michael L. and Nancy B. Black, editors for the Twayne edition, many of its fiercely antidemocratic passages. Harbert notes that the 1850 Author's Revised Edition of *The Conquest of Granada* allowed Irving in his "Note To The Revised Edition" to set forth the motives governing his alterations and revisions. As Irving says at the end of his introduction to the 1850 text: "Though I still retain the fiction of the monkish author Agapida, I have brought my narrative more strictly within historical bounds, have corrected and enriched it in various parts with facts recently brought to light by the researches of Alcantara and others; and have sought to render it a faithful and characteristic picture of the romantic portion of history to which it relates."

Irving added three volumes to his revised works: *Oliver Goldsmith: A Biography* (1849), derived

Irving, circa 1855 (from Brady's National Portrait Gallery, New York City)

from earlier writings about Goldsmith, and two volumes of *Mahomet and His Successors* (1850). The latter two volumes came out of what Irving called "a mass of matter that has been lying like lumber in my trunks for years." In 1847 he worked on, but did not publish, works that he considered complete but not thoroughly finished off: "The Chronicle of Pelayo"; the "Chronicle of Count Fernan Gonzales"; the "Chronicle of the Dynasty of the Ommiades in Spain . . ."; and the "Chronicle of Fernando the Saint, with the Reconquest of Seville." Then, while revising his other works, he turned to a topic that had first interested him in the 1820s, that of Mahomet and his successors. His notes toward "The Legendary Life of Mahomet" date to the period between 1826 and 1828 when Irving researched and wrote the life of Columbus. The first volume of *Mahomet and His Successors* was published in December 1849, the second in April 1850.

The capstone work of Irving's last years was the life of George Washington. It was, he said in an 18 December 1829 letter to Peter Irving, to be his "great and crowning labor." Named after the father of his country, Washington Irving long had dreamed of writing of George Washington. In 1825 Irving was approached by Archibald Constable, the Edinburgh publisher, about writing a life of Washington. Irving declined, saying he stood in too great awe of the subject and also that a satisfactory work would require a great deal of reading and research. The biographer should also be in the United States, he continued in a 19 August 1825 letter, "where he could have access to all kinds of official papers and public records and where he could have familiar & personal communication with the surviving companions & contemporaries of Washington." In 1841, nearly a decade after returning to America, Irving sought out biographies of Washington by Paulding and Mason Locke Weems. He also had information by Jared Sparks, likely the first volume of the twelve-volume edition of *The Writings of George Washington* (1834–1837), and the five-volume biography of Washington by John Marshall. During the decade of the 1840s Irving continued to gather information about Washington and his times. In a letter of 21 October 1851, he told his niece Sarah Storrow that he was "now fully engaged on the life of Washington. . . . At my time of life [he was sixty-eight years old], and with the liability to attacks of ill health, I cannot afford to risk any more interruptions."

Irving's subsequent letters reveal that he worked ambitiously on the life of Washington, visiting sites associated with Washington and his contemporaries, scouring libraries and private holdings for documents and pictures, and, as he writes in a 6 February 1853 letter to Pierre Irving, visiting persons such as "old Mr Custis at Arlington who has many personal recollections of Washington which he is fond of relating." His first two volumes of the *Life of George Washington* were published by Putnam in 1855. As Allen Guttmann and James A. Sappenfield point out in the introduction to their 1982 Twayne edition of the *Life of George Washington,* Irving's narrative sense served him well when he divided the long drama of Washington's life into five volumes. "The first volume ends with the Virginian's arrival at Cambridge, in the summer of 1775, for the siege of Boston. Subsequent volumes end climactically with the Battle of Princeton (Volume II), and the inauguration of Washington as the first president (Volume IV), and the death of the hero (Volume V). Only the third volume, which was hurried to the press, can be said to conclude in a relatively indecisive manner." The third volume came out in 1856, the fourth in 1857, and the fifth in 1859. Irving's portrait of Washington, Guttmann and Sappenfield say, is remarkably lifelike, even though at times Irving smooths away rough spots. Irving's labor, he said in an 8 January 1856 letter to Henry Tuckerman, was to arrange

"facts in the most lucid order and place them in the most favorable light; without exaggeration or embellishment; trusting to their own characteristic value for effect." Today, Bowden says, "the virtue of Irving's Washington is that it is magnificently readable."

Irving's creative life ended with the *Life of George Washington.* In a letter to Robert C. Winthrop on 4 April 1853, he had said regarding his concerns over finishing the life of Washington: "The shadows of departed years are gathering over me." But, he had said in an October 1848 letter to Pierre Irving, "I must get through with the work which I have cut out for myself. I must weave my web, and then die." With the completion of the fifth volume he laid down his pen. In mid September 1859, two and a half months before Washington Irving's death on 28 November 1859, a piece by N. P. Willis appeared in the *Home Journal,* which said, "Mr. Irving, by far the most honored man in our country, is, curiously enough, even less honored than loved." That honor continued through that century and much of the next. While not fully appreciated by the end of the twentieth century, Irving's overall accomplishment is significant. As James W. Tuttleton writes in *Washington Irving: The Critical Reaction* (1993), with the exception of the novel, Irving "is a significant innovator in nearly every prose genre of his time. And his range—English town and country life, Moorish Spain, Dutch colonial history, the discovery of the Americas, Revolutionary era politics, and the American West—is voluminous. Yet it is all composed with such a charm of personality and a winsomeness of style that it makes for continued pleasure." In "Rip Van Winkle's Lilac," Herman Melville says in tribute to Irving that he is now "sharing Fame's Indian Summer with those mellowing Immortals who as men were not only excellent in their works, but pleasant and love-worthy in their lives."

Letters:

Washington Irving: Letters, 4 volumes, edited by Ralph M. Aderman, Herbert L. Kleinfield, and Jenifer S. Banks (Boston: Twayne, 1978–1982).

Bibliographies:

William R. Langfeld and Philip C. Blackburn, *Washington Irving: A Bibliography* (New York: New York Public Library, 1933);

Stanley T. Williams and Mary A. Edge, *A Bibliography of the Writings of Washington Irving* (New York: Oxford University Press, 1936);

Haskell S. Springer, *Washington Irving: A Reference Guide* (Boston: G. K. Hall, 1976);

Springer and Raylene Penner, "Washington Irving: A Reference Guide Updated," *Resources for American Literary Study,* 11 (1981): 257–279;

James W. Tuttleton, "Washington Irving," in *Fifteen American Authors before 1900: Bibliographical Essays on Research and Criticism,* edited by Earl N. Harbert and Robert A. Rees (Madison: University of Wisconsin Press, 1984), pp. 330–356;

Edwin T. Bowden, *Washington Irving: Bibliography* (Boston: Twayne, 1989).

Biographies:

Pierre M. Irving, *The Life and Letters of Washington Irving,* 4 volumes (New York: Putnam, 1862–1864);

Stanley T. Williams, *The Life of Washington Irving,* 2 volumes (New York: Oxford University Press, 1935);

Claude G. Bowers, *The Spanish Adventures of Washington Irving* (Boston: Houghton Mifflin, 1940);

Philip McFarland, *Sojourners* (New York: Atheneum, 1979).

References:

Ralph M. Aderman, "Washington Irving as a Purveyor of Old and New World Romanticism," in *The Old World and New World Romanticism of Washington Irving,* edited by Stanley Brodwin (Westport, Conn.: Greenwood Press, 1986), pp. 13–25;

Aderman, ed., *Critical Essays on Washington Irving* (Boston: G. K. Hall, 1990);

Aderman, ed., *Washington Irving Reconsidered* (Hartford, Conn.: Transcendental Books, 1969);

Peter Antelyes, *Tales of Adventurous Enterprise: Washington Irving and the Poetics of Western Expansion* (New York: Columbia University Press, 1990);

Michael Davitt Bell, "Feelings and Effects: Washington Irving," in his *The Development of American Romance* (Chicago & London: University of Chicago Press, 1980), pp. 63–85;

Mary Weatherspoon Bowden, *Washington Irving* (Boston: Twayne, 1981);

Malcolm Bradbury, "Storied Associations: Washington Irving Goes to Europe," in his *Dangerous Pilgrimages: Transatlantic Mythologies and the Novel* (New York: Viking, 1996), pp. 53–83;

Stanley Brodwin, ed., *The Old World and New World Romanticism of Washington Irving* (Westport, Conn.: Greenwood Press, 1986);

Van Wyck Brooks, *The World of Washington Irving* (New York: Dutton, 1944);

William Cullen Bryant, *Washington Irving* (New York: G. P. Putnam, 1860);

Heiner Bus, *Studien zur Reiseprosa Washington Irvings* (Frankfurt Am Main: Verlag Peter Lang, 1982);

Claudia L. Bushman, *America Discovers Columbus: How an Italian Explorer Became an American Hero* (Hanover, N.H.: University Press of New England, 1992);

James T. Callow, *Kindred Spirits: Knickerbocker Writers and American Artists, 1807–1974* (Chapel Hill: University of North Carolina Press, 1967);

Richard H. Cracroft, *Washington Irving, The Western Works* (Boise, Idaho: Boise State University, 1974);

Eugene Current-García, "Irving Sets the Pattern: Notes on Professionalism and the Art of the Short Story," *Studies in Short Fiction,* 10 (Fall 1973): 327–341;

Allen Guttmann, "Washington Irving and the Conservative Imagination," *American Literature,* 26 (1964): 165–173;

Judith G. Haig, "Washington Irving and the Romance of Travel: Is There an Itinerary in *Tales of a Traveller?*" in *The Old World and New World Romanticism of Washington Irving,* edited by Brodwin (Westport, Conn.: Greenwood Press, 1986), pp. 61–66;

William L. Hedges, *Washington Irving: An American Study, 1802–1832* (Baltimore: Johns Hopkins University Press, 1965);

Hedges, "Washington Irving: Nonsense, the Fat of the Land and the Dream of Indolence," in *The Chief Glory of Every People,* edited by Matthew J. Bruccoli (Carbondale: Southern Illinois University Press, 1973), pp. 141–160;

George S. Hellman, *Washington Irving Esquire: Ambassador at Large from the New World to the Old* (New York: Knopf, 1925);

Daniel G. Hoffman, "Irving's Use of American Folklore in 'The Legend of Sleepy Hollow,'" *PMLA,* 68 (June 1953): 425–435;

Joy S. Kasson, "Washington Irving: The Citadel Within," in her *Artistic Voyagers: Europe and the American Imagination in the Works of Irving, Allston, Cole, Cooper, and Hawthorne* (Westport, Conn.: Greenwood Press, 1982), pp. 6–42;

Lewis Leary, *Washington Irving* (Minneapolis: University of Minnesota Press, 1963);

Terence Martin, "Rip, Ichabod, and the American Imagination," *American Literature,* 31 (May 1959): 137–149;

Ben Harris McClary, *Washington Irving and the House of Murray* (Knoxville: University of Tennessee Press, 1964);

Andrew B. Myers, ed., *A Century of Commentary on the Works of Washington Irving,* 1860–1974 (Tarrytown, N.Y.: Sleepy Hollow Restorations, 1976);

Myers, ed., *Washington Irving: A Tribute* (Tarrytown, N.Y.: Sleepy Hollow Restorations, 1972);

Myers, ed., *The Worlds of Washington Irving* (New York: New York Public Library and Sleepy Hollow Restoration, 1974);

Henry A. Pochmann, "Irving's German Tour and Its Influence on His Tales," *PMLA, 45* (1930): 1150–1187;

Pochmann, "Washington Irving: Amateur or Professional?" in *Essays on American Literature in Honor of Jay B. Hubbell,* edited by Clarence Gohdes (Durham, N.C.: Duke University Press, 1967), pp. 63–76;

Walter A. Reichart, *Washington Irving and Germany* (Ann Arbor: University of Michigan Press, 1957);

Donald A. Ringe, *American Gothic: Imagination and Reason in Nineteenth-Century Fiction* (Lexington: University Press of Kentucky, 1982);

Ringe, *The Pictorial Mode: Space and Time in the Art of Bryant, Irving and Cooper* (Lexington: University of Kentucky Press, 1971);

Martin Roth, *Comedy in America: The Lost World of Washington Irving* (Port Washington, N.Y.: Kennikat Press, 1976);

Jeffrey Rubin-Dorsky, *Adrift in the Old World: The Psychological Pilgrimage of Washington Irving* (Chicago & London: University of Chicago Press, 1988);

Rubin-Dorsky, "*The Alhambra:* Washington Irving's House of Fiction," *Studies in American Fiction,* 11 (1983): 171–188;

Rubin-Dorsky, "Washington Irving and the Genesis of the Fictional Sketch," *Early American Literature,* 21 (1986–1987): 226–247;

Richard Dilworth Rust, "Washington Irving's 'American Essays,'" *Resources for American Literary Study,* 10 (Spring 1980): 3–27;

William C. Spengemann, *The Adventurous Muse: The Poetics of American Fiction, 1789–1900* (New Haven: Yale University Press, 1977);

Robert E. Spiller, *The American in England in the First Half Century of Independence* (New York: Henry Holt, 1926);

Cushing Strout, *The American Image of the Old World* (New York: Harper & Row, 1963);

Edgeley W. Todd, "Washington Irving Discovers the Frontier," *Western Humanities Review,* 11 (1957): 29–39;

James W. Tuttleton, ed., *Washington Irving: The Critical Reaction* (New York: AMS Press, 1993);

Edward Charles Wagenknecht, *Washington Irving: Moderation Displayed* (New York: Oxford University Press, 1962);

Charles Dudley Warner, *Washington Irving* (Boston: Houghton, Mifflin, 1881);

Stanley T. Williams, *The Spanish Background of American Literature,* 2 volumes (New Haven: Yale University Press, 1955);

Philip Young, "Fallen from Time: Rip Van Winkle," *Kenyon Review,* 22 (1960): 547–573.

Papers:

Washington Irving's papers are to be found primarily at the New York Public Library. Other collections include Historic Hudson Valley, the Carl H. Pforzheimer Library, the Huntington Library, and the libraries of the University of Virginia, Columbia University, Yale University, Harvard University, and the University of Pennsylvania. See H. L. Kleinfield, "A Census of Washington Irving Manuscripts," *Bulletin of the New York Public Library,* 68 (1964): 1332.

Caroline M. Kirkland

(12 January 1801 – 6 April 1864)

Camille A. Langston
Northwest Vista College

See also the Kirkland entries in *DLB 3: Antebellum Writers in New York and the South; DLB 73: American Magazine Journalists, 1741–1850;* and *DLB 74: American Short-Story Writers Before 1880.*

BOOKS: *A New Home–Who'll Follow? or, Glimpses of Western Life,* as Mrs. Mary Clavers (New York: C. S. Francis / Boston: J. H. Francis, 1839); republished as *Montacute; or, A New Home–Who'll Follow?* 2 volumes (London: E. Churton, 1840); republished as *The Settler's Home; or, Glimpses of Western Life* (London: Allman, 1845); republished as *Our New Home in the West; or, Glimpses of Life among Early Settlers* (New York: James Miller, 1872);

Forest Life, as the Author of "A New Home," 2 volumes (New York: C. S. Francis / Boston: J. H. Francis, 1842; London: Longman, 1842);

Western Clearings, as Mrs. Mary Clavers (New York: Wiley & Putnam, 1845; London: Wiley & Putnam, 1846);

Holidays Abroad; or, Europe from the West, 2 volumes (New York: Baker & Scribner, 1849);

The Evening Book; or, Fireside Talk on Morals and Manners, with Sketches of Western Life (New York: Scribner, 1852);

The Book of Home Beauty (New York: Putnam, 1852);

A Book for the Home Circle, or, Familiar Thoughts on Various Topics, Literary, Moral, and Social. A Companion for the Evening Book (New York: Scribner, 1853);

The Helping Hand, Comprising an Account of the Home for Discharged Female Convicts and an Appeal in Behalf of That Institution (New York: Scribner, 1853);

Autumn Hours, and Fireside Reading (New York: Scribner, 1854);

Western Border Life; or, What Fanny Hunter Saw and Heard in Kanzas and Missouri (New York: Derby & Jackson / Cincinnati: H. W. Derby: 1856);

Memoirs of Washington (New York & London: Appleton, 1857).

Caroline M. Kirkland, circa 1852

OTHER: Jonathan Dymond, *The Principles of Morality and the Private and Political Rights and Obligations of Mankind: Abridged and Provided with Questions, for the Use of Schools and for Young Persons Generally,* adapted by Kirkland (New York: C. S. Francis / Boston: J. H. Francis, 1842);

Marion Reid, *A Plea for Women,* edited by Kirkland (New York: Farmer & Daggers, 1845); republished as *Woman, Her Education and Influence,* introduction by Kirkland (New York: Fowlers & Wells, 1848);

Spenser and the Faëry Queen, edited, with an introduction, by Kirkland (New York & London: Wiley & Putnam, 1847; London: Wiley & Putnam, 1847);

Mary H. Eastman, *Dahcotah, or, Life and Legends of the Sioux around Fort Snelling,* preface by Kirkland (New York: John Wiley, 1849);

Garden Walks with the Poets, edited by Kirkland (New York: Putnam, 1852);

A Few Words in Behalf of the Loyal Women of the United States, by One of Themselves (New York: Printed by W. Bryant, 1863);

The School-Girl's Garland, A Selection of Poetry, in Four Parts, edited by Kirkland (New York: Scribner, 1864); republished as *The Garland of Poetry for the Young: A Selection in Four Parts,* 2 volumes (New York: Scribner, 1868);

Patriotic Eloquence: Being Selections from One Hundred Years of National Literature, edited by Kirkland (New York: Scribner / Cleveland: Ingham & Bragg, 1866);

Poetry of the Flowers, edited, with an introduction, by Kirkland (New York: Crowell, n.d.).

SELECTED PERIODICAL PUBLICATIONS– UNCOLLECTED:

FICTION

"The Blighted Heart," *Graham's Lady's and Gentleman's Magazine,* 23 (July 1843): 1–7;

"The Hard Winter," *Union Magazine of Literature and Art,* 2 (January 1848): 43.

NONFICTION

"An Apology for Authors," *Knickerbocker Magazine,* 19 (February 1842): 97–102;

"Goethe," *Union Magazine of Literature and Art,* 1 (September 1847): 127–129;

"George Sand and the Journeyman Joiner," *Union Magazine of Literature and Art,* 1 (November 1847): 221–223;

"Forest Literature," *Union Magazine of Literature and Art,* 2 (May 1848): 201–212;

"Sightseeing in Europe," 8 parts, *Union Magazine of Literature and Art,* 3 (July 1848): 1–5; 3 (August 1848): 49–54; 3 (October 1848): 145–151; 3 (November 1848): 193–199; 3 (December 1848): 241–246; *Sartain's Union Magazine of Literature and Art,* 4 (January 1849): 57–62; 4 (February 1849): 127–132; 4 (March 1849): 181–185; 4 (April 1849): 232–235;

"Thoughts on Education," 2 parts, *Sartain's Union Magazine of Literature and Art,* 5 (July 1849): 40–43; 5 (October 1849): 236–239;

"Literary Women," *Sartain's Union Magazine of Literature and Art,* 6 (February 1850): 150–154;

"The American Ideal Woman," *Putnam's Magazine,* 2 (November 1853): 527–531;

"Reading for Amusement," *Sartain's Union Magazine of Literature and Art,* 6 (March 1860): 192–196.

Caroline M. Kirkland, most famous for her novel *A New Home–Who'll Follow? or, Glimpses of Western Life* (1839), edited the *Union Magazine of Literature and Art,* founded and taught in several girls' schools, and wrote articles on female education, slavery, and literary writing. Although many nineteenth-century women wrote both fiction and nonfiction, Kirkland's works differ from most; realism, satire, and feminism–three modes considered "inappropriate" for nineteenth-century women authors–make her writings distinctive.

Caroline Matilda Stansbury, eldest of Eliza Alexander and Samuel Stansbury's eleven children, was born on 12 January 1801 in New York City. Unlike most nineteenth-century girls, Caroline received a relatively sophisticated education; at the age of eight, she was sent to her aunt Lydia Mott's school. Later, Stansbury taught in Utica, New York, at another of her aunt's schools. While teaching, Caroline met William Kirkland, who was also an educator, and married him in 1828. Caroline and William Kirkland opened a seminary in Geneva, New York. They had seven children, four of whom survived into adulthood.

In 1835 William Kirkland moved Caroline and their children to Detroit in order to fulfill his dream of founding a city on the Michigan frontier. The couple worked at the Detroit Female Seminary for two years, William serving as principal and Caroline as a teacher. After acquiring eight hundred acres of woodland and swamp and a substantial capital in 1837, the Kirklands moved to the remote frontier and developed a village they named Pinckney.

While living on the frontier, Kirkland wrote her first novel, *A New Home–Who'll Follow?* under the pseudonym "Mrs. Mary Clavers." In a series of episodes, she chronicles the difficulties that women from eastern America experienced as they moved to and attempted to adapt to the overly romanticized West. In the novel a well-educated, middle-class, white woman named Mary Clavers struggles to establish a community with her neighbors. Much of the novel describes the hardships frontier women faced as they attempted housekeeping in the wilderness.

Kirkland's novel is unusual in several ways. She satirizes conventional masculine stereotypes of the romantic woman writer. Kirkland's use of satire to build a community of women in both the West and in literature, rather than to advocate women's superiority to men, distinguished her from her feminist contemporaries. Kirkland's use of realism in her description of the West is also atypical. Unlike most nineteenth-century stories about the West, such as those by James Fenimore

Cooper, Kirkland does not romanticize the West; instead, she portrays a harsh reality. The construction of Kirkland's novel also deviates from the nineteenth-century norm in that the work has a communal plot. Through a series of sketches, Kirkland traces the formation of the community. In addition, the genre of *A New Home–Who'll Follow?* defies definition. The work may be analyzed as domestic fiction, travel literature, a precursor to realism, regional writing of the Western frontier, or autobiography.

A New Home–Who'll Follow? was an immediate success. Edgar Allan Poe, in "The Literati of New York City," refers to the book as "an undoubted sensation" filled with "*truth* and novelty." Margaret Fuller, in her essay "American Literature; Its Position in the Present Time, and Prospects for the Future" for her *Papers on Literature and Art* (1846), considers *A New Home–Who'll Follow?* an "amusing book" that portrays the charm of simple life in its "rude and all but brutal forms." Rufus W. Griswold and John S. Hart, two nineteenth-century editors, also point out Kirkland's writing skill. Hart claims that "these sketches of western life were entirely without a parallel in American literature."

Although Kirkland probably used a pseudonym to keep her identity from her neighbors, the Pinckney citizens quickly identified themselves once the book became a success. Sandra A. Zagarell and other critics attribute the family's 1843 decision to move from Michigan to the outrage of the Pinckney neighbors at Kirkland's vulgar portrayal of them in *A New Home–Who'll Follow?* After five years of frontier life, during which they were cheated by a land agent and lost much of their money, the Kirklands returned to New York City.

In New York City the Kirklands taught school and contributed to periodicals, which continued to grow in popularity. During this time, Caroline Kirkland wrote for money. In a letter to her daughter, Elizabeth, Kirkland wrote, "I am busy penning some very dull stories for several publications. . . . I know not what we should do without this resource." On 18 October 1846, William Kirkland drowned in the Hudson River near Fishkill, New York, leaving his wife alone to support herself and her children by opening a school, teaching, and continuing to write for magazines.

Because of the literary connections Kirkland had in New York City, Israel Post, owner of the *Union Magazine of Literature and Art,* asked Kirkland to edit his publication. Kirkland's name added credibility to the periodical and, as a result, several popular nineteenth-century authors–such as William Cullen Bryant, Lydia Maria Child, Robert Lowell, Edgar Allan Poe, Catharine Maria Sedgwick, Lydia H. Sigourney, Henry David Thoreau, and Walt Whitman–submitted their works for publication.

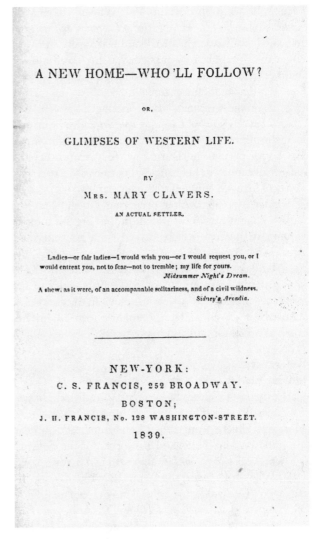

Title page for Kirkland's first novel, based on her experiences in the remote frontier town of Pinckney, Michigan (courtesy of Special Collections, Thomas Cooper Library, University of South Carolina)

During the one and a half years she was editor, Kirkland contributed editorials, Western sketches, and essays to the *Union Magazine of Literature and Art.* She wrote articles on a variety of literary personalities, including Johann Wolfgang von Goethe, Susan Warner, and George Sand; Western sketches; and editorials on topics such as female education, reading, and slavery. In her later years, Kirkland increasingly focused on reform literature. In 1845 she wrote a women's rights essay, which served as the introduction to Marian Reid's *A Plea for Women.* She also wrote on behalf of Native Americans and female convicts.

In 1848 Kirkland went to Europe after agreeing with her publisher, Post, to send back a series of travel impressions. When she returned from Europe in the fall of that same year, she found that the periodical had been sold to John Sartain and William Sloanaker, renamed *Sartain's Union Magazine of Literature and Art,* and relocated to Philadelphia. Kirkland was surprised to discover that John Hart was assigned as her co-editor and that her editorial duties were reduced to simply making contributions to the magazine.

Kirkland continued contributing essays to *Sartain's Union Magazine of Literature and Art* and writing articles; during her lifetime, she wrote at least eighty-three articles for periodicals. During her final years, she published collections of her articles, became associated with *Putnam's Monthly,* continued to teach, and wrote *Memoirs of Washington* (1857). After preparing a benefit for the Sanitary Commission, a philanthropic organization in support of soldiers, Kirkland died from a stroke on 6 April 1864.

Today, critics acknowledge Caroline M. Kirkland's writing as a precursor to realism and cite her work as an example of local color. In recent years, scholarly research and criticism has focused on her work as an editor and as a prose writer.

References:

Judith Fetterley, ed., *Provisions: A Reader from 19th-Century American Women* (Bloomington: Indiana University Press, 1985);

Margaret Fuller, "American Literature; Its Position in the Present Time, and Prospects for the Future," in her *Papers on Literature and Art* (New York: Wiley & Putnam, 1846), pp. 122–150;

Rufus W. Griswold, *The Prose Writers of America: With a Survey of the Intellectual History, Condition, and Prospects of the Country* (Philadelphia: Carey & Hart, 1849);

John S. Hart, *The Female Prose Writers of America: With Portraits, Biographical Notices, and Specimens of Their Writings* (Philadelphia: Butler, 1852);

Annette Kolodny, *The Land before Her: Fantasy and Experience of the American Frontiers, 1630–1860* (Chapel Hill & London: University of North Carolina Press, 1984);

Frank Luther Mott, *A History of American Magazines,* 5 volumes (Cambridge, Mass.: Belknap Press of Harvard University Press, 1938–1968), I: 769–770;

William S. Osborne, *Caroline M. Kirkland* (New York: Twayne, 1972);

Edgar Allan Poe, "The Literati of New York City," *Godey's Lady's Book,* 4 (August 1846): 75–76;

Audrey Roberts, "The Letters of Caroline M. Kirkland," dissertation, University of Wisconsin, 1976;

Stacy L. Spencer, "*Legacy* Profile: Caroline Kirkland (1801–1864)," *Legacy,* 8 (Fall 1992): 133–140;

Sandra A. Zagarell, Introduction, in Kirkland's *A New Home–Who'll Follow? or, Glimpses of Western Life,* edited by Zagarell (New Brunswick, N.J. & London: Rutgers University Press, 1990).

Papers:

Small collections of Caroline M. Kirkland's letters are held by the Alderman Library, University of Virginia; the John M. Olin Library, Cornell University; the Bentley Historical Library, University of Michigan; the Historical Society of Pennsylvania; the Massachusetts Historical Society; the Houghton Library, Harvard University; the Newberry Library, Chicago; and the Milton S. Eisenhower Library, Johns Hopkins University. The Cincinnati Historical Society; the Harry Ransom Humanities Research Center, University of Texas at Austin; and the Newberry Library, Chicago, hold Kirkland's manuscripts.

William Leggett

(30 April 1801 – 29 May 1839)

Boyd Childress
Auburn University

BOOKS: *Poems* (Edwardsville, Ill.: Published by the author, 1822);

Leisure Hours at Sea: Being a Few Miscellaneous Poems, by a Midshipman of the United States Navy (New York: G. C. Morgan & E. Bliss & E. White, 1825);

Tales and Sketches, by a Country Schoolmaster (New York: Harper, 1829);

Naval Stories (New York: G. & C. Carvill, 1834; revised and enlarged, 1835);

The Squatter: A Tale of Illinois (Chillicothe, Ohio: S. W. Ely, 1835);

A Collection of the Political Writings of William Leggett, Selected and Arranged, with a Preface, by Theodore Sedgwick Jr., 2 volumes, edited by Theodore Sedgwick (New York: Taylor & Dodd, 1840).

Edition: *Democratick Editorials: Essays in Jacksonian Political Economy by William Leggett,* edited by Lawrence H. White (Indianapolis: Liberty Press, 1984).

OTHER: "The Block-House," in *Tales of Glauber Spa. By Several American Authors* (New York: Harper, 1832), pp. 5–101.

SELECTED PERIODICAL PUBLICATIONS–
UNCOLLECTED: "Recollections of a Revolutionary Soldier," *Critic,* 1 (22 November 1828): 55–60;

"The Capture of Fort Montgomery," *Critic,* 1 (17 January 1829): 189–192;

"St. Martin's Cave," *Critic,* 1 (21 February 1829): 272;

"Running the Mail," *Critic,* 1 (24 February 1829): 254–255;

"Tom Wilson, and His Burnt Portfolio," *Critic,* 1 (21 March 1829): 320–322;

"Ignatius Loyola," *Critic,* 2 (9 May 1829): 10–14;

"Running the Mail: Returning on Board," *Critic* (9 May 1829 / 16 May 1829): 16–19;

"The Two Graves," *New-York Mirror,* 10 July 1830, pp. 2–3; 24 July 1830, pp. 21–22; 31 July 1830, pp. 29–30;

"A Scene off the Cape of Good Hope," *New-York Mirror,* 22 December 1832, p. 193.

PERIODICALS EDITED: *Critic* (1 November 1828 – 13 June 1829);

New-York Evening Post, for the Country (1834–1835);

Plaindealer. Equal Rights (1836–1837);

Examiner (22 May 1837–September 1837).

Few newspaper editors enjoyed more influence in the Jacksonian era than William Leggett of the *New-York Evening Post.* Leggett's reputation as a fiery editor often drew the ire even of his own party members–indeed, President Martin Van Buren once offered Leggett a post in the diplomatic corps just to keep him out of the political arena. Yet for all of his support of equal rights, abolitionism, and free trade and his unqualified opposition to the Bank of the United States and slavery, Leggett also wrote poetry and short fiction, although his efforts at verse were never as well received as his works of fiction, *Tales and Sketches* (1829) and *Naval Stories* (1834). Self-educated, a naval officer, and well known in literary circles, Leggett was one of that well-rounded breed of nineteenth-century journalists that included his boss William Cullen Bryant, William Leete Stone, and George Pope Morris, who used editorials to influence local, regional, and national issues but still found time to display considerable literary talents.

Leggett was born in Savannah, Georgia, on 30 April 1801. His father, Abraham Leggett, was a Revolutionary War veteran who had fought at Harlem Heights and White Plains and was taken prisoner at Fort Montgomery in 1777. The elder Leggett was paroled in 1781 and by 1784 had opened a crockery shop in New York City. Seeking a better financial opportunity, Abraham Leggett moved his family south, first to Charleston, South Carolina, and later to Savannah. But by 1805 the family had returned to New York, and William entered Georgetown College in 1815, but, as family fortunes once again failed, he was forced to withdraw from school. William turned to acting and was in a handful of productions before the fall of 1819 when his father moved the family once more, again hoping to improve on his economic standing. This time the Leggetts moved west to Edwardsville, Illinois, a small but growing town in the southern part of the state. In Edwardsville, William first encountered slavery, despite Illinois being a free state. In the *Edwardsville Spectator,* the aspiring writer published his first work—about ten poems—from 1820 until the time he left Illinois in 1822, but none of his verse was especially memorable. He became ill during the summer of 1820 with a fever that he never completely escaped, even during his adult life. With no sign of reversal of the family monetary struggles, the Leggetts returned to New York late in 1822, and William Leggett began a career in earnest—in the U.S. Navy. Nominated by Illinois senator Ninian Edwards, Leggett received an appointment as a midshipman on 4 December 1822, although confirmation did not reach him until early the next year, and he did not begin active service until June. His first post was aboard the USS *John Adams* out of Norfolk, assigned to search out pirates in the West Indies, but by September, Leggett was back in New York, a victim of yellow fever.

In May 1824 Leggett was assigned to the *Cayne,* headed to the Mediterranean area as part of a show of force by the United States. Foreign relations with Britain were strained, and a naval presence in the area was warranted. The Mediterranean was the scene of Leggett's short career as an officer, and stops at Gibraltar, Minorca, and Carthage provided him with a setting for some of his short fiction. Leggett, only twenty-two, was under the command of Captain John Orde Creighton, never known as a benevolent or tolerant officer. Leggett's temper got the best of him when he dueled with another midshipman during a stop at the port of Mahon. Leggett was restricted to the deck (not an uncommon punishment in the navy at that time), but he cried, complained, and attempted suicide (by a self-inflicted stab wound). These acts simply ensured he would remain bound to the deck, where, in early 1825, he had to endure all types of bad weather and became quite ill from a recurrence of the fever he had suffered earlier. Removed to the protection of the cockpit, he found conditions no better. In late January he wrote Commodore Thomas MacDonough concerning his situation and forced the hand of Creighton, who until that time had not brought charges against Leggett. Captain Creighton then charged Leggett with disobedience, ungentlemanly and unofficerlike behavior, leaving his station, and poor moral conduct (related to the suicide attempt). In April 1825 Creighton added disrespectful behavior and threatening an officer to the charges, and Leggett was brought to court-martial on 21 June. Speaking in his own defense in a verbose five-thousand-word statement, Leggett said that he considered his already imposed restrictions as enough punishment and attempted to put Creighton on trial. Leggett was found guilty of disobedience of orders, leaving his post, and attempting suicide, and on 5 July he was dismissed from the navy. The tribunal left him an out, however, as it recommended his case be heard by the Navy Department, which remitted his dismissal in September. Realizing his career in the navy was at an end, Leggett resigned in April 1826.

Although Leggett's years as a naval officer were less than distinguished, his experiences and travels did provide him with background and an historical setting for what proved to be his most successful fiction, *Naval Stories,* published almost a decade later. The years in the navy also brought out many of the qualities characteristic of the mature Leggett—a firm belief in individual freedom and dignity, a lack of fear of authority and, in many instances, of respect for authority, and the ability to express and support his convictions. His court-martial defense is a document with no small interest to anyone attempting to understand what motivated him as an editorialist.

With his military career at an end, Leggett turned his energies elsewhere. In 1822, while still living on the Illinois frontier, he had published a volume of poems. Notable only as the first literary volume published in the state, *Poems* includes little of value. Leggett's handful of verse published in the *Edwardsville Spectator* from 1820 to 1822 was mostly rhythmic doggerel satirizing slavery. But in *Poems,* a collection of forty poems, he attempted to borrow from poets such as George Gordon, Lord Byron; Thomas Campbell; and Thomas Moore, even imitating Byron in "Fare thee Well," a verse about leaving home for service in the navy. Leggett had no poetic style other than emulation, and his initial efforts at verse drew no attention. His poems were either sentimental or included a moral tone, and he used themes of sorrow, hope, beauty, and nationalism—all in accord with current trends in American verse. His only American influence was a poet whose work was best known after his death, Joseph Rodman Drake, whom Leggett had actually met. Although Leggett showed a willingness to experiment with stanzas and meters in his poems, they are generally monotonous. Leggett's second and last major attempt at verse, *Leisure Hours at Sea: Being a Few Miscellaneous Poems* (1825), drew faint praise. Using the sea as a setting and his naval experiences as a theme, Leggett produced a collection of greater worth than *Poems.* Reviews in *The New-York Statesman, The New York Review,* and the *North American Review* all had positive comments about *Leisure Hours,* as did the one in the *New York Commercial Advertiser,* which concluded that Leggett showed promise. In stark contrast was the review in the *United States Literary Gazette* on 1 February 1826, which suggested that the aspiring poet was better off studying "Bowditch's Navigator, than in the writing of bad verse." Whatever conclusion reviewers drew, Leggett published a mere handful of poems after his two collections and then only in newspapers and magazines—nineteen in *The New-York Mirror* during 1826 and 1827 and three in the *Commercial Advertiser* between August and October 1826. Leggett also published his own verse in *The Critic,* and a few of his selections were printed in *The Atlantic Souvenir.* He did win an award for poetry, the $50 Bowery Theatre Prize in 1828, for the best poem in celebration of New York's new Bowery, rebuilt after a fire. The *Dictionary of American Biography* and other standard biographical sources erroneously credit Leggett as the author of another collection of poems, *Journals of the Ocean* (1826). This small volume, however, was written by William Augustus Weaver.

The years following his naval service were uncertain for Leggett. He was in New York, where he wanted to be, but he was not blessed with many opportunities. He briefly attempted acting again but gave it up completely after a miserable performance at the Bowery Theatre. George Pope Morris hired Leggett as a theater critic for *The New-York Mirror* in November 1827, and he soon began writing literary criticism for the magazine as well. He followed this success with editorials for *The*

New-York Mirror and worked as an assistant editor for the *Merchant's Telegraph* before its six-month life span ended in June of 1828. On 28 February 1828, the then twenty-six-year-old Leggett married Elmira Waring of New Rochelle. The couple never had children. During the summer of 1828 Leggett resigned from *The New-York Mirror* and founded *The Critic.* He also produced his first significant work of fiction, writing "The Rifle" for *The Atlantic Souvenir* for 1828. Although Leggett had published a few selections of short fiction before in *The New-York Mirror,* "The Rifle" proved to be his first noteworthy piece.

For most of his adult life after 1825, Leggett's fortunes were tied to highly successful New York stage actor Edwin Forrest. In Leggett's acting debut, which was his last theatrical attempt, he was trying to follow in Forrest's footprints. After the *New York Gazette and General Advertiser* termed Leggett "rather unsuccessful" on stage, he borrowed money from Forrest to start *The Critic.* Forrest was Leggett's benefactor several other times, and Leggett attempted to repay Forrest with a favorable and laudatory biography of the actor, although the draft manuscript was never found after Leggett's death. Forrest supported Leggett and his wife during one entire year of their marriage and even purchased their New Rochelle home, which Leggett named Aylemere. Leggett went further into Forrest's debt in 1832 when he and William Cullen Bryant purchased control of the *New York Evening Post;* a $2,000 loan from Forrest was Leggett's share of the purchase price. Forrest was undoubtedly behind Leggett's publication of *The Plaindealer,* a weekly he began in late 1836, and *The Examiner,* a daily two-penny paper Leggett published briefly in 1837. In the summer of 1837 David Hale, editor of *The New York Journal of Commerce,* wrote that Leggett had written a Fourth of July speech for Forrest. Leggett took offense and was charged with assault and battery for attacking Hale.

From his start in journalism in 1826 until his premature death in 1839, Leggett wrote for newspapers, literary journals, and the mass public. He used several pseudonyms during the early stages of his career, including "Imogene," the single-letter "E," and "Zoe." The vast majority of his career was as a newspaper editor and editorial writer. His two collections of short fiction, *Tales and Sketches* and *Naval Stories,* received some serious attention among New York's literary circles, but Leggett's political editorials in support of the Jacksonians drew most of his readership. After the failure of *The Critic* in June of 1829, Leggett was rescued by Bryant at the *New-York Evening Post.* William Coleman had been senior editor at the *Evening Post,* but his death in 1829 led Bryant to hire Leggett to write book and drama reviews for the literary department. The failure of *The Critic,* the publication of *Tales and Sketches,* and Leggett's hiring at the *New-York Evening Post* all occurred during the early summer of 1829. Before Leggett had even settled in at the newspaper, he entered the arena of political journalism. The *Evening Post* was a Jacksonian organ, advocating free trade and opposing Henry Clay's American System and the Second Bank of the United States (with an especially strong stand against Nicholas Biddle) while supporting President Andrew Jackson's removal of deputy postmasters for abuses related to elections. Bryant also opposed nullification. Soon after Leggett assumed some editorial responsibility, his writing was difficult to distinguish from Bryant's.

Oddly enough, Leggett had accepted the position at the *Evening Post* on the condition that he not be asked to write on politics. This condition obviously underwent considerable transformation, and Leggett wrote with a sharp radical spirit. He attacked opponents so severely that he angered various heads of government agencies. His targets included banking, the exclusive rich, and conservatives, but he championed equal rights, the rights of abolitionists, free trade, and the protection of literary property. His admiration of English utilitarian Jeremy Bentham is obvious, so much so that the masthead of his short-lived newspaper, *The Plaindealer,* borrowed a quote from Bentham: "The immediate cause of all the mischief of misrule is, that the men acting as the representatives of the people have a private and sinister interest, producing a constant sacrifice of the interest of the people." Leggett's allegiance to equal rights stems directly from his naval service and subsequent court martial, when he felt his actions were justified and his superior officer in violation of his personal freedoms. Leggett also borrowed from Thomas Jefferson's belief that the role of government was to protect men from one another. Leggett believed he labored in economic obscurity, that he would never achieve widespread respectability by advocating a reform path, but that honor was more important than success measured by wealth.

Theodore Sedgwick–Leggett's friend, colleague, and successor at the *Evening Post*–admired Leggett as a lover of freedom and liberty, a man of courage and boldness, and a defender of truth. Sedgwick, who edited a collection of Leggett's political writings shortly after his death, also thought Leggett had little tolerance of his opponents and was not as intelligent as he was moral. Sedgwick paid Leggett this backhanded compliment in the introduction to the 1840 publication of political writings: "But the intellectual character of Mr. Leggett, marked as it was, was far inferior in excellence to his moral attributes." Like Sedgwick, John Greenleaf Whittier felt Leggett's legacy went well beyond his

death. Whittier wrote "No one has labored more perseveringly or, in the end, more successfully, to bring the practice of American democracy into conformity with its professions." A young Walt Whitman viewed Leggett as Jefferson's intellectual successor. Indeed, another edition of Leggett's democratic writings was published by the Liberty Press as late as 1984.

Leggett remains obscure as a poet and was a minor writer of fiction, but when these writings are coupled with his editorials and other miscellaneous writings, he emerges as a considerable nineteenth-century man of letters. His creative writing, a series of forty-six essays published in newspapers and magazines of his day, was dull and heavy. Leggett relied on Dr. Samuel Johnson (the English essayist) as a model, but Leggett was a poor essayist, bordering on plagiarism for many of his essays. His two books of published verse have little of merit to discuss, but his short fiction shows a well-developed writer who uses both his frontier Illinois experiences and his brief career in the navy as settings for interesting tales and stories. Just as Walt Whitman once compared Leggett's political philosophy to Jefferson's, others have compared Leggett's fiction to James Fenimore Cooper's and Walter Scott's. Leggett's first serious fiction was "The Rifle," published in *The Atlantic Souvenir* in 1828, although he had published short pieces in serial form in *The New-York Mirror* in 1827 and 1828 and in his own *The Critic* in 1828. His early prose fiction "The Trial" and "The Mistake" were published in both. But with the publication of "The Rifle," Leggett received serious attention from literary critics as well as $8 for the fifteen-thousand-word short story. He soon followed up on this success with *Tales and Sketches,* published by Harper in 1829. The collection of ten tales included his earlier published works "The Rifle" and "The Mistake." At least four of the ten tales were published in *The Critic* virtually simultaneously with *Tales and Sketches.* The volume was published anonymously but was unmistakably Leggett's work. Two of the entries in *Tales and Sketches,* "A Burial at Sea" and "A Watch in the Main-Top," were stories based on his years in the navy. "A Watch in the Main-Top" was also included in the second edition of his other collection of short fiction, *Naval Stories.* Like many writers of his day, Leggett received ample compensation for most of what he wrote.

For Leggett, the tale represented a short story. Only two of his "tales" are of considerable length–"The Squatter" from *Tales and Sketches* and "The Block-House," his contribution to *Tales of Glauber Spa. By Several American Authors* (1832), a collection of short fiction by some of New York's more prominent writers that Bryant published in 1832. Leggett returned to his Illinois years for the setting of these stories. *Tales and*

Sketches drew some attention for "The Rifle" (also published in *The Atlantic Souvenir* three years later). "The Rifle" is the story of a newly arrived doctor on the Illinois frontier who falls in love with a beautiful but poor young woman. The doctor is falsely accused of murder but is saved from a hanging by a wiley old hunter. Leggett borrows liberally from Scott and Cooper in "The Rifle." Scott used the unjustly accused in much of his work, and many of Cooper's tales used the killer with a hidden identity. Both writers utilized the poor girl as an integral figure in solving the crime, a pattern that Leggett also followed. Despite turning to the work of others for much of his plot, Leggett is often cited as a forerunner of the American detective story. He undoubtedly influenced others such as Morgan Neville, the author of "Last of the Boatmen" (*Western Souvenir,* 1829) and creator of the character Mike Fink, and the unfortunate Boston author William Joseph Snelling. Likewise, James Kirke Paulding, the highly successful author of *Westward Ho!* (1832) and a great many frontier tales, owed Leggett a literary debt. Leggett's story, however, fails to treat some of the issues a more mature Leggett utilized–self-reliance and equal rights. "The Rifle" is still unusual frontier realism. It is one of his best two or three stories. Leggett returns to the same setting and story development for "The Trial," which was first published serially in *The New-York Mirror* in 1827 and republished in *The Critic* in 1828, where it was titled "The Steel Clasp," its title in *Tales and Sketches.* "The Squatter" and "The Block-House" also follow the theme Leggett used in "The Rifle."

Leggett drew praise for *Tales and Sketches* primarily for the two sea tales included. *The New-York Mirror,* the same newspaper for which he had once labored, was more effusive, reporting that Leggett rivaled Cooper in sea fiction. "A Watch in the Main-Top," the story from which this most favorable comparison is derived, was among the best of Leggett's fiction, but his literary style and volume hardly approached that of Cooper. Reviews of *Naval Stories* were even more favorable to Leggett. Scholars have agreed, one concluding he, as quoted in Thomas Philbrick's *James Fenimore Cooper and the Development of American Sea Fiction* (1961), "may be compared to advantage even with Cooper" when evaluating his stories of the sea.

In January 1831 Leggett became a partner in Michael Burnham and Company, the firm that owned the *Evening Post.* Just short of two years later, in November of 1832, he and Bryant purchased the paper (Leggett's contribution was the $2,000 loan from Forrest), and the two became owners. Leggett decided to handle any editorials dealing with naval issues, but they were few in number. Instead, he mostly used his editorial energies to attack and counterattack the opposition

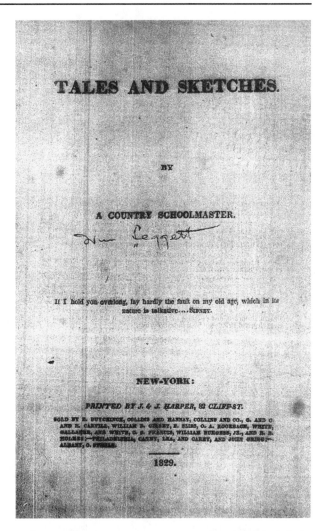

Title page for Leggett's collection of ten tales, including "The Rifle," "The Steel Clasp," and "A Watch in the Main-Top" (courtesy of Special Collections, Thomas Cooper Library, University of South Carolina)

press–in this case, the conservative press. Leggett's editorials reflect his stance in support of equal rights and the other causes he advocated. When William Leete Stone of the *Commercial Advertiser* used that paper to criticize Bryant, Leggett convinced Bryant a horsewhip was the only measure suitable for Stone. Bryant obliged, but Stone, the larger man, simply took the whip from Bryant. In his own behalf, Leggett, in the spring of 1833, had a street fight with James Watson Webb of the *Morning Courier and New-York Enquirer.* Leggett declared himself the victor.

Among Leggett's circle of friends were several notables, including Bryant, Forrest, poet Prosper M. Wetmore, Scottish-born New York businessman and author James Lawson, dramatist William Dunlap, actor Henry Placide, fellow newspaperman and writer George Pope Morris, and Fitz-Greene Hallack, a leading member of the Knickerbocker group of writers. Leggett also knew others, such as Paulding, Robert C. Sands, and Gulian C. Verplanck. At best, Leggett was at the far periphery of the Knickerbockers, although "The Encounter" was published in *The Knickerbocker*. Leggett also announced in *The New-York Mirror* (19 June 1830) the forthcoming publication of a novel, "Ralph Marvyn, or the Manic's Prophecy." It never appeared, however, nor does any other reference to it survive.

Of all of Leggett's writings, the longest (ninety-five pages) is "The Block-House," his contribution to the highly successful *Tales of Glauber Spa*. The collection—originally the idea of Bryant, Verplanck, and Sands at the request of publisher J. and J. Harper—was intended to be anonymous tales narrated by visitors to a healing springs who told their stories much in the same vein as the travelers in Geoffrey Chaucer's *Canterbury Tales*. Verplanck withdrew from the venture, but Bryant, Sands, and Paulding each contributed two stories, while Catharine Maria Sedgwick and Leggett each wrote one. The two-volume work was published in November 1832 and proved to be so popular that a second printing followed in December. "The Block-House" was Leggett's most complex tale and follows the form of his frontier accounts.

Leggett's tales of life at sea and in the navy were popular among a contemporary audience. All ten of his maritime tales were initially published in *Tales and Sketches, The New-York Mirror, The Knickerbocker,* and his own magazine, *The Critic*. In 1834 he published eight of them as *Naval Stories*. In a prefatory note, Leggett advised the reader that the stories had been published before but said that "the author has given them such revision as he thought might render them more worthy of the favour they have received." The next year "A Watch in the Main-Top" was added in a new edition. *Naval Stories,* his most lasting literary achievement, is exceptional for vivid descriptions of life at sea, with selections that range from the rather simple "A Night at Gibraltar" to the complex and autobiographical "Brought to the Gangway." Leggett replaces Cooper's romanticism with realism of an often cruel life in the navy, unjust and inhumane. Indeed, in most of his tales, Leggett provides some perspective of his own attitude toward naval officers, especially his own Captain Creighton. In "Brought to the Gangway," arguably his best tale, he tells the reader about the lieutenant who "was one of a class of officers happily not numerous." In "A Watch in the Main-Top" the narrator says that he sailed under "the hardest horse in the Navy." The constant theme of resentment of authority even shows in Leggett's less action-filled stories, such as "A Night at Gibraltar," in which a young officer, Mr. Transom, is assigned what he considers a rather wasteful watch.

In the comical "The Main-Truck," the captain is a man who often took to his bed and was irritable. This type of captain is a common thread through his tales of life at sea. This view was not new to the former naval officer, as it runs through the entirety of the five-thousand-word statement he read in his own defense at his court-martial in 1825. In that document he told the court, "I did not expect to find, among those who have so nobly and so effectually defended our country from foreign aggressions, a domestick tyranny, more hateful in its operation and more baneful in its effect." He refers to Creighton as a monster. In a 31 January 1825 letter to Commodore MacDonough written after Leggett's arrest, Leggett questioned the captain's authority. He also questioned Creighton's right to command, boldly writing "he should forfeit all claim to it as a man." These are but a few examples of Leggett's using his experience as an officer in his fiction. In "The Main-Truck" he introduces the reader to the commanding officer's son, a reference clearly pulled from his court-martial document in which he told the court that he was aware Creighton had a fine son and trusted the son would escape similar treatment. Although at times passionate beyond reason, far too effusive in denying any responsibility for his guilt, and void of the realistic portrayal of life in the navy as found in his fiction, Leggett's court-martial statement and letters to both Creighton and Commander MacDonough are still valuable for the insights they give into his later ardent defense of equal rights and to the plot development of his short fiction.

In several of his tales, Leggett introduces the expert sailor as storyteller. Never the accomplished officer, this narrator is, however, as sound a hand as could be found aboard, "with few equals as a sailor." In "The Main-Truck" this sailor is Tom Scupper. Leggett uses a junior officer who falls asleep as narrator in "A Night at Gibraltar." Undoubtedly, Leggett incorporates all of his sea and navy devices in "Brought to the Gangway," in which a young officer is accused of falling asleep on his late-night watch. The accusing officer ignores regard for the navy's dictates against whipping, replying "Flog first, and report afterwards, is my rule," when reminded of naval law. Leggett's obvious disdain for authority, his belief in the life in the navy as often cruel, and an heroic yet tragic end are all evident in this his best tale.

Whereas *Tales and Sketches* had received at best a mixed reaction, *Naval Stories* was met with widespread approval. Although opposition papers such as the *Commercial Advertiser* and the *Courier and Enquirer* did not mention Leggett's latest fictional output, *The New-York Mirror* said the work was among the best of recent fiction. *The Knickerbocker* was also extensive in its praise, as was the *New York American*. The reviewer in *The American Monthly Magazine* was not as kind; although he praised the work, he concluded that Leggett was second rank among maritime writers. There can be no doubt *Naval Stories*, Leggett's last effort at short fiction, was the zenith of his literary career. Leggett had, though, earlier published briefer selections surrounding his career in the navy in *The Critic*–including "A Burial at Sea," "Running the Mail," and "Tom Wilson, and His Burnt Portfolio." "A Burial at Sea" shows Leggett's softer side in a tale about a seaman who dies despondent over the loss of his beloved wife. The other two tales are typical of his questioning of authority. In "Running the Mail" Leggett uses the term that is the title to denote going ashore without permission. The captain, "like all mean men," forbids an officer shore leave, but the order is thwarted when the young officer's shipmates assist him in "running the mail." Even more autobiographical is "Tom Wilson," a story about a poet and daydreamer (as Leggett was as an officer) whose mood swings tie into sunny and cloudy days. In these earlier tales just as in the later ones, the cruel system, represented by a new commander, is ever present, as are Leggett's vivid and historically accurate scenes of life at sea and ashore.

Literary historians have also been complimentary of Leggett, especially Thomas Philbrick in his monograph, *James Fenimore Cooper and the Development of American Sea Fiction* (1961). Philbrick compares Leggett favorably with Cooper and concludes that the newspaperman's sea fiction exceeded that of two other noted writers of early nautical fiction, Nathaniel Ames and John Gould. Philbrick considers Ames and Gould inept. Although Ames possessed "thorough knowledge of nautical matters," he suffered from an inability to develop a plot. Gould's "improbable characters and situation" were not realistic or believable. But "Leggett's work, on the other hand, evinces in its growing strength and originality the talent and seriousness of a genuine artist," a writer who might be better than Cooper in fictional sea literature. Three threads are steady throughout Leggett's sea stories: the realism of the shipboard experience, emphasis on description and moderation in dialogue, and siding with the underdog against the naval system. This last feature sets Leggett apart from Cooper, who sided with officers. "Brought to the Gangway" almost certainly influenced Herman Melville's *White Jacket* (1850), although Melville scholars may disagree.

When Bryant left for extensive travel in Europe in 1834, Leggett had free run of the editorial page of the *Evening Post*. He attacked monopolies, the banking structure, and the navy's court-martial system. But he waved the biggest banner in support of the abolitionists, and Leggett was himself attacked in the opposition press. In the heat of the abolition riots in New York in the summer of 1834, Leggett was at his sharpest, and Webb suggested that the rioters turn their attention to the offices of the *Evening Post,* even going so far as to write they should tar and feather Leggett. In October 1835 Leggett collapsed under the strain of managing the paper and his running feud with other newspapermen, especially Webb. Yet Webb was not Leggett's only target. In his still classic history of the *Evening Post,* historian Allen Nevins briefly recounts Leggett's lack of scruples when it came to the opposition press. Nevins writes, "In one brief paragraph he managed to call the editor of the *Star* a wretch, liar, coward, and a vile purchased tool who would do anything for money." Leggett labeled Stone's *Commercial Advertiser* as "venomous drivel" but saved his harshest words for Stone, a true "non-entity." He called the editor of the *New-York American* a "detestable caitiff" and "a craven wretch, spotted with all kinds of vices." To Leggett, the *Courier and Enquirer* (Webb's paper) was "a blustering, bullying sheet, reeking with falsehood, pandering to the vulgar, profligate, impudent, inane, and inciting men to riot and bloodshed."

The two published collections of Leggett's editorials (Sedgwick's and the more recent Liberty Press edition) include ample material from which to assess his editorial style and often venomous attacks. He was intolerant of others' opinions and strongly believed in what he wrote. Sedgwick wrote of Leggett that "The vehemence of his temperament and the force of his original impressions often had an obscuring tendency upon his mind." Yet Sedgwick also found that "Truth was his [Leggett's] first love and his last–the affection of his life." Sedgwick thought Leggett bold and courageous: "He had no conception what fear was; physically, morally and intellectually, he had no idea of the meaning of the term." Yet these were the same traits that often made Leggett unappreciated in the public eye, and, for Leggett, his truth was the only truth, without qualification or question.

Leggett was the spokesman for the radical wing of the Jacksonians, the so-called Loco Focos. Writing on the elite nature of the Bank of the United States, which he opposed, Leggett, as quoted from an *Evening Post* piece reprinted in *Democratick Editorials: Essays in Jacksonian Political Economy by William Leggett* (1984), said, "but it is a poor argument to say that a bad system should be persevered in, lest a small minority of the community should suffer through future inconvenience." Here he is also stating his philosophy of equal rights. Along these same lines and in his best Jeffersonian tone, he criticized the influential *Journal of Commerce* for its stance on compensating property owners following the 1837 flour riots, sarcastically writing "We cannot think the *Journal*

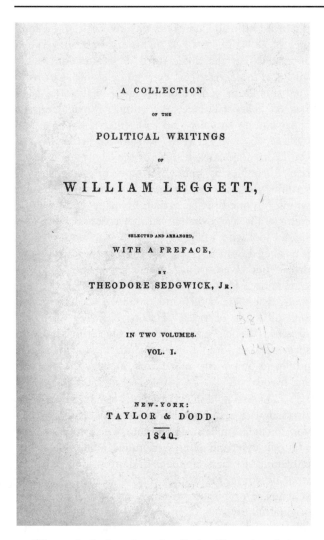

Title page for the first volume of a collection of Leggett's nonfiction writings, published the year after his death

of Commerce has given its usual attention to this subject; though this is not the first time it has shown a willingness to strengthen government at the expense of men's equal and inalienable rights." On slavery, which he abhorred, Leggett mentioned lessons of history: "It is not those who labour and have an interest in keeping up its [slavery's] price, but those who employ labour and have an interest in depressing it." Again on the issue of slavery, and at his heartfelt best, Leggett writes, "Slavery no evil! Has it come to this, that the foulest stigma on our national escutcheon, which no true-hearted freeman could ever contemplate without sorrow in his heart and a blush on his cheek, has got to be viewed by the people of the south as no stain on the American character?"

Although Leggett still wrote and was the voice of the working class, during parts of 1835 and 1836 he became ill (a recurrence of the fever he contracted in Illinois and was never fully free from), and his friend Sedgwick assumed responsibility for the paper since Bryant was still abroad. Leggett recovered briefly, but the *Evening Post* went without editorials during the late fall of 1835 and early 1836. Leggett's recovery was slow and never complete, but the Loco Foco Party wanted to nominate him for mayor of New York City in March 1836. He refused. Bryant returned in late March to find the finances of the *Evening Post* in total disarray because Leggett's editorials had cost the newspaper influential advertisers. In addition, Leggett had reprinted William Gouge's *A Short History of Paper Money and Banking in the United States,* a venture that lost more than $500. Former editor William Coleman's widow, now part owner, was in the process of foreclosing on the paper when Bryant returned from Europe, and she, too, opposed Leggett's hardline stance supporting the abolitionist cause. Yet Bryant wrote on 1 April 1836 to his wife, "Mr. Leggett's reputation and standing in the community are much raised." By agreement, Leggett lost his part ownership but kept a salary of $1,000 annually. Coleman's widow also had the power to restrain Leggett's editorials. For his part, Bryant wrote in a 4 July 1836 letter to his wife, "I had no objection to this, because Leggett sometimes needs a curb." Bryant nevertheless maintained a solid friendship with Leggett for the remaining few years of Leggett's life. Citing the need for independence in his writing, Leggett soon left the *Evening Post* to found *The Plaindealer,* a weekly first published in December 1836. By February of the next year, Leggett boasted of a circulation of thirteen thousand to fifteen thousand, but these are exaggerated figures. Some kind but anonymous reviewers in the *Examiner* (22 May 1837) wrote, "Mr. Leggett has no superior in the editorial chair of the public press" and "Whatever Mr. Leggett touches, he touches with power." Opposition reaction was not so kind, but by early 1837 *The Plaindealer* had a more realistic subscription base of 1,100 and a weekly sale of from 200 to 400 papers. Many in the opposition press subscribed just to see what Leggett wrote, and even President Martin Van Buren asked to be included as a subscriber. Bryant remarked in an 1860 speech on Washington Irving that the paper was "remarkable both for its ability and its love of disputation." On 22 May 1837 Leggett launched the *Examiner,* a source of political and economic editorials, but by the end of September both papers had ceased. Bad finances and bad health caught up with Leggett. Yet his standing in the political and journalistic community was not at an end. Gideon Wells suggested Leggett for the position of editor of *The Washington Globe,* and S. D. Langtree, editor of the Washington-based *U.S. Magazine and Democratic Review,* offered Leggett $1,000 to $1,200 as an annual payment for three to four editorial pieces a month.

Leggett's experience with *The Critic* was not all bad. Twenty years after the eight-month experiment in literature had failed, *The Literary World* ran a comment on Leggett and the magazine. The review from 20 February 1847 said that *The Critic* included Leggett's tales and essays as well as his "forcible dramatic criticism and reviews." The publication was admirable, and Leggett "did all this for the *Critic* and repeated the task weekly, and what is more, published the whole thing himself,– and was rewarded by the discontinuance of his work." Leggett himself did not think as highly of his magazine, remarking "it had better never been written." Leggett would never have been able to launch the weekly without financial assistance from his friend Forrest. Fully titled *The Critic, a Weekly Review of Literature, Fine Arts, and the Drama,* the publication featured sixteen double-columned pages per issue. Most of the content was written by Leggett himself, although he did include the verse of some minor poets, such as his friend Wetmore. For the most part, each issue consisted of nine or ten book reviews, verse, tales, and essays by Leggett. Fourteen of his own short stories appeared in *The Critic;* at least six of them had never been published before. "The Trial" and "The Mistake" had been published in *The New-York Mirror* first, and "The Rifle" was originally printed in *The Atlantic Souvenir* for 1828. All were printed in *The Critic.* In all, Leggett wrote approximately twenty-two thousand words per week for *The Critic,* but the task soon proved to be too daunting. It ceased publication on 13 June 1829. Announcing the cessation to his readers, Leggett said he had lost too much money and found "a paper written exclusively by myself" was too much for him. He had lost $1,000 in the venture but promised subscribers that his obligation to them would be filled by George Pope Morris with copies of *The New-York Mirror.*

Personally, Leggett was certainly courageous and a man loyal to his own convictions. He possessed a hot temper, and physically he was a sturdy man with a compact frame; yet he was prone to illness throughout his life. After Bryant returned from Europe in March 1836, he told his wife that Leggett was "much changed in his personal appearance, sallow, dark, emaciated with an expression of pain and anxiety in his countenance."

Leggett's last years were not pleasant for him. His health still failing, he spent most of his time at the family home in New Rochelle, attended by his wife. Feeling the climate would help Leggett's declining health, Bryant, influential in the Democratic Party, convinced Van Buren to appoint Leggett as a special agent to the Central American Republic. Leggett was greatly encouraged when he received a letter of appointment on 25 May 1839, but before mailing his letter of acceptance, he died in New Rochelle on May 29.

Upon his death, Leggett's estate was a modest $20 bill in his pocket, his home, and his library. Forrest purchased the library from Leggett's wife for $7,000, and the profits from Sedgwick's published collection of Leggett's political editorials went to the widow. The library was not worth what his old benefactor paid– Leggett was still indebted to Forrest from the grave. Following Leggett's death, eulogies of high praise ran in most New York newspapers, and a handful appeared in the literary magazines of the city. Perhaps his friend Sedgwick summarized Leggett's life and legacy best, calling him stubborn and impractical, impetuous and dogmatic, proud and obstinate, and often reckless. Leggett's *Naval Stories* certainly bear out Sedgwick's estimation, and Leggett would undoubtedly have been proud of such an epitaph. Bryant's tribute, "In Memory of William Leggett," published in the *Democratic Review,* read more kindly:

> His love of Truth–too warm, too strong,
> For hope or fear to chain or chill–
> His hate of tyranny and wrong
> Burn in the breasts he kindled still!

As an historical figure, Leggett was "Spokesman of Jacksonian Democracy," an appellation from noted American historian Richard Hofstadter. Hofstadter, in his "William Leggett, Spokesman of Jacksonian Democracy" (1943), points to the neglect of Leggett by historians but calls him "one of the most prominent and forceful spokesmen of the radical wing" of the Jacksonian Democrats. Leggett's constant agitation for equality eventually resulted in New York state legislation reforming banking law and an incorporation law in the 1846 state constitution. Hofstadter concludes, "Probably few men in America preached the bourgeois ideals of personal and property rights, freedom of contract, laissez faire, individualism, and private enterprise with as fine a sense for the needs and desires of the common man." Princeton historian Sean Wilentz argues Leggett was an ardent abolitionist whose staunch opposition was the foundation for antislavery Democrats years after his death, although history has overlooked his stand against slavery. In *The Jacksonian Persuasion: Politics and Belief* (1960) Marvin Myers views Leggett as a major proponent of anticapitalist political economy, or "economic liberty strictly on its own terms." Myers believes the basis for Leggett and the Loco Focos was a combination of "Jeffersonian liberalism and free-trade economics." All historians do not agree on Leggett's legacy, but the consensus is, as an original thinker and editorialist, his influence was greater after his death than during his lifetime.

Biographies:

Harry Ammon, "William Leggett, Equal Rights Editor," M.A. thesis, Georgetown University, 1940;

Page S. Proctor, "The Life and Works of William Leggett, 1801–1839," dissertation, Yale University, 1949;

Stanley N. Worton, "William Leggett, Political Journalist (1801–1839)," dissertation, Columbia University, 1954.

References:

John Bigelow, *William Cullen Bryant* (Boston: Houghton, Mifflin, 1893);

William Cullen Bryant, *Letters of William Cullen Bryant,* edited by William Cullen Bryant II and Thomas G. Voss (New York: Fordham University Press, 1975–);

Paul Goodman, *Of One Blood: Abolitionism and the Origins of Racial Equality* (Berkeley: University of California Press, 1998), pp. 167–172;

Richard Hofstadter, "William Leggett, Spokesman of Jacksonian Democracy," *Political Science Quarterly,* 58 (1943): 581–594;

Marvin Myers, *The Jacksonian Persuasion: Politics and Belief* (Stanford: Stanford University Press, 1960);

Allan Nevins, *The Evening Post: A Century of Journalism* (New York: Boni & Liveright, 1922);

Thomas Philbrick, *James Fenimore Cooper and the Development of American Sea Fiction* (Cambridge, Mass.: Harvard University Press, 1961);

John Seelye, "Buckskin and Ballistics: William Leggett and the American Detective Story," *Journal of Popular Culture,* 1 (Summer 1967): 52–57;

Seelye, "'Spontaneous Impress of Truth': Melville's Jack Chase: A Source, an Analogue, a Conjecture," *Nineteenth-Century Fiction,* 20 (March 1966): 367–376;

Sean Wilentz, "Jacksonian Abolitionist: The Conversion of William Leggett," in *The Liberal Persuasion: Arthur Schlesinger, Jr., and the Challenge of the American Past,* edited by John P. Diggins (Princeton: Princeton University Press, 1997), pp. 84–106.

Papers:

William Leggett's papers are held in the Leggett Family Papers, New York Genealogical and Biographical Society, New York. Papers dealing with Leggett's court-martial are based in the Naval Records Collection, National Archives, Washington, D.C. There is also some Leggett material in William Cullen Bryant's papers located in the Bryant-Godwin Collection, New York Public Library, New York, and the Alderman Library, Special Collections, at the University of Virginia.

Cornelius Mathews

(28 October 1817 – 25 March 1889)

Donald Yannella
Barat College

See also the Mathews entries in *DLB 3: Antebellum Writers in New York and the South* and *DLB 64: American Literary Critics and Scholars, 1850–1880.*

BOOKS: *The Motley Book: A Series of Tales and Sketches. By the Late Ben Smith* (New York: J. & H. G. Langley, 1838);

Behemoth: A Legend of the Mound-Builders, anonymous (New York: J. & H. G. Langley, 1839);

The True Aim of Life: An Address Delivered Before the Alumni of New-York University . . . July 16, 1839 (New York: Wiley & Putnam / Langley, 1839);

The Politicians: A Comedy in Five Acts (New York: Trevett, Bartlett & Wefford, Turner & Fisher, 1840);

Wakondah; The Master of Life. A Poem, anonymous (New York: George L. Curry, 1841);

An Appeal to American Authors and the American Press, in Behalf of International Copy-right (New York & London: Wiley & Putnam, 1842);

The Career of Puffer Hopkins (New York: Appleton, 1842);

Poems on Man in His Various Aspects Under the American Republic (New York: Wiley & Putnam, 1843); revised as *Man in the Republic: A Series of Poems* (New York: Paine & Burgess, 1846);

The Better Interests of the Country, in Connexion with International Copy-right (New York & London: Wiley & Putnam, 1843);

Big Abel, and the Little Manhattan (New York: Wiley & Putnam, 1845);

Americanism: An Address Delivered Before the Eucleian Society of New-York University, 30th June, 1845 (New York: Paine & Burgess, 1845);

Moneypenny; or, The Heart of the World: A Romance of the Present Day, anonymous (New York: Dewitt & Davenport, 1849); and *Moneypenny; or, The Heart of the World: A Romance of the Present Day Embracing . . . With Various Other Characters From the Upper and Lower Walks of Life. In Two Parts–Part II* (New York: Dewitt & Davenport, 1850);

Chanticleer: A Thanksgiving Story of the Peabody Family, anonymous (Boston: Mussey / New York: Redfield, 1850);

Witchcraft: A Tragedy in Five Acts (New York: S. French, 1852);

Calmstorm, the Reformer: A Dramatic Comment, anonymous (New York: Tinson, 1853);

A Pen-and-Ink Panorama of New-York City (New York: Taylor, 1853);

False Pretences; or, Both Sides of Good Society. A Comedy in Five Acts (New York: N.p., 1856).

PLAY PRODUCTIONS: *Witchcraft,* Philadelphia, Walnut Street Theater, 1846; New York City, Bowery Theatre, 1847;

Seeing the Elephant, New York City, Burton's Theatre, 1848;

Jacob Leisler, the Patriot Hero, or, New York in 1690, New York City, Bowery Theatre, 8 May 1848;

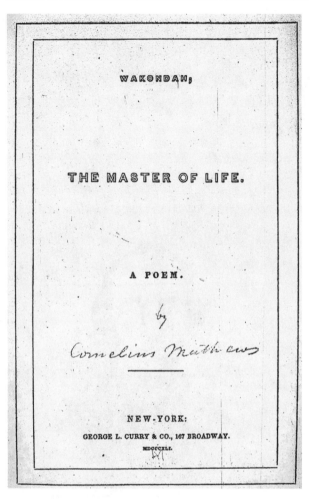

WAKONDAH;

THE MASTER OF LIFE.

A POEM.

by

Cornelius Mathews

NEW-YORK:
GEORGE L. CURRY & CO., 167 BROADWAY.
MDCCCXLI.

Title page for Mathews's narrative poem about prehistoric American Indians (Harris Collection, John Hay Library, Brown University)

False Pretences; or, Both Sides of Good Society, New York City, Burton's Theatre, 3 December 1855;

Broadway and the Bowery, or, the Young Mechanic and the Merchant's Daughter, New York City, Brougham Bowery Theatre, 10 November 1856.

OTHER: *Modern Standard Drama,* volumes 80–85, edited by Mathews (New York: Taylor, 1850);

Henry Schoolcraft, *The Indian Fairy Book. From the Original Legends,* edited anonymously by Mathews (New York: Mason Brothers, 1856);

Hiawatha and Other Legends of the Wigwams of the Red American Indians, edited anonymously by Mathews (London: Sonnenschein, 1882).

PERIODICALS EDITED: *Yankee Doodle* (10 October 1846 – 2 October 1847);

Elephant (22 January 1848 – 19 February 1848).

Cornelius Mathews, an ardent literary nationalist and social critic and a central figure in the group of young nationalistic writers known as "Young America," is remembered today less for any of his works than for the striking, if not to say unfortunate, impression he made in contemporary literary circles. From the late 1830s through the early 1850s, the period of his most significant literary activity, Mathews, as Perry Miller notes in *The Raven and the Whale: The War of Words and Wits in the Era of Poe and Melville* (1956), "excited among his contemporaries a frenzy of loathing beyond the limits of rationality." Characterized by James Russell Lowell in *A Fable for Critics* (1848) as "a small man in glasses . . . dodging about, muttering 'Murderers! Asses!'" and as repeatedly "accusing of slavish respect to John Bull / All American authors who have more or less / Of that anti-American humbug–success," Mathews did not push his causes with either patience or tact. Worse, his own body of work, which he envisioned as both a stirring proclamation of the ideals of literary nationalism and a compelling example of what a national literature should be–an encomium to the heroic American past and a vital criticism of present-day failures to measure up to the standard of that past–was often too clumsy, pompous, and superficial to do his countrymen or his reputation any good. However, despite his inability to exert a strong influence on the direction of American literature and life in his own day or to seem today much more than a curious reminder of long-dead literary issues, Mathews ought not to be neglected. Whatever his defects of presentation, his ideas were neither silly nor inconsequential ones. A national literature, as greater writers such as Ralph Waldo Emerson and Walt Whitman knew, was a necessity if the still young country was to be spiritually and intellectually vital. Moreover, as both of these writers taught, and as such others as Mark Twain and William Dean Howells later taught, a literature that ignores its own country to imitate slavishly the writers of another cannot help but promulgate doctrines that have the effect of removing readers from all that is best in their national heritage and daily way of life. Such ideas as these Mathews promoted, with a singular lack of success to be sure, but with an admirable if awkward sincerity. Finally, though other writers captured far better than Mathews both the heroism of America past and present and the corruption that too often tarnishes that heroism, one can never be sure that the deeply felt efforts of Mathews and others similar to him went entirely for naught. In ways that cannot be understood by others, such men often set a literary

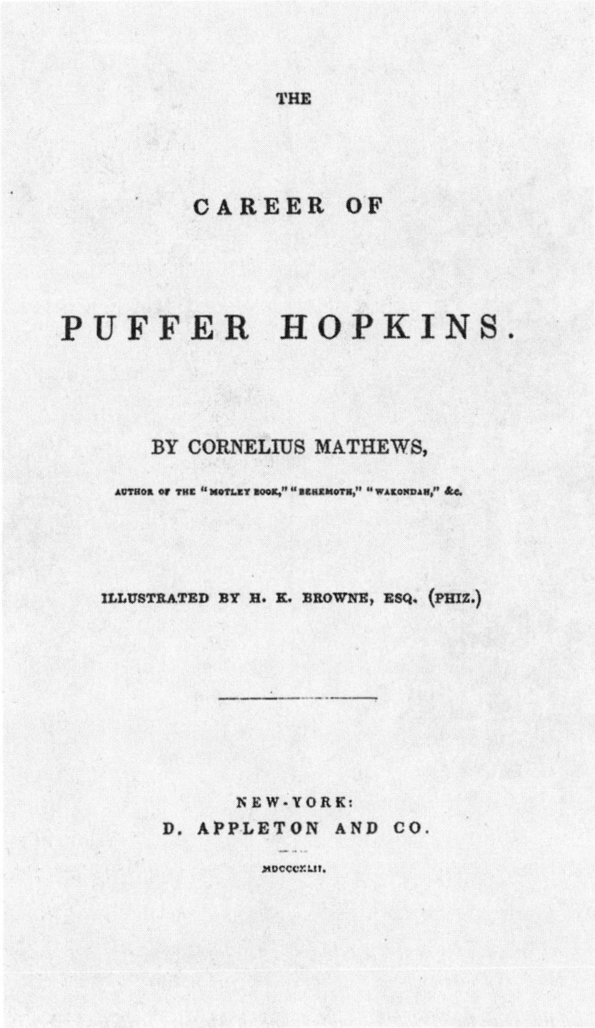

THE

CAREER OF

PUFFER HOPKINS.

BY CORNELIUS MATHEWS,

AUTHOR OF THE "MOTLEY BOOK," "BEHEMOTH," "WAKONDAH," &c.

ILLUSTRATED BY H. K. BROWNE, ESQ. (PHIZ.)

————————

NEW-YORK:
D. APPLETON AND CO.
MDCCCXLII.

Title page for Mathews's fictional exposé of New York City life and politics
(Houghton Library, Harvard University)

climate that enables other people of genius to find their own work.

Mathews was born in Portchester, New York (Westchester County), north of New York City, on 28 October 1817. He was the second son of Abijah and Catherine Van Cott Mathews. Shortly after Cornelius's birth his family moved to the city, and a lifelong involvement with the culture and politics of urban New York commenced. A bachelor throughout his life, Mathews graduated in 1834 from the University of the City of New York (now New York University) and was admitted to the bar in 1837. Though he contributed to *The American Monthly Magazine, The New-York Review,* and *The Knickerbocker* in the 1830s, he did not make a complete transition from the law to a career in literature until the early 1850s. From 1852 to 1856 he worked for *The Literary World,* owned by Evert A. and George L. Duyckinck.

An essential step to the development of a genuine American literature, Mathews believed, was the passage of an international copyright law. In *An Appeal to American Authors and the American Press, in Behalf of International Copy-right* (1842) and *The Better Interests of the Country, in Connexion with International Copy-right* (1843), he insisted that the absence of such a law would force American authors into unfair competition with cheap reprints of popular foreign books. The inevitable result would drive genuine American voices into poverty, leading either to their suppression or to their imitation of foreign authors. Such imitation, in turn, he was sure, drove the nation inexorably from the republican thought and virtues embodied by its forebears. Mathews's pamphleteering and speeches on behalf of international copyright were often too strident to be convincing. Although a distinctively American literature developed long

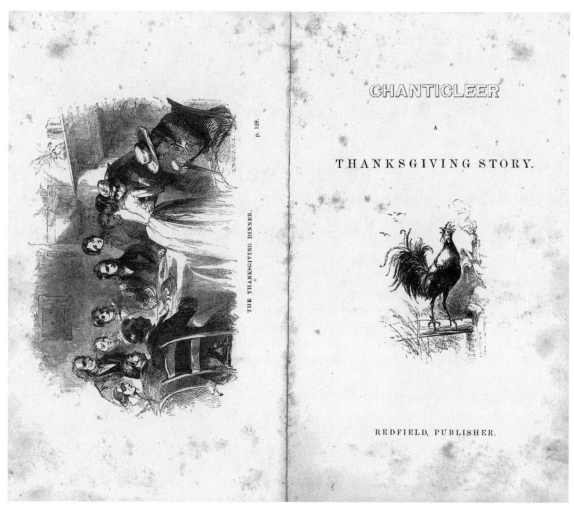

Frontispiece and decorated title page for one of the novels in which Mathews criticized his contemporaries for forgetting the values of their heroic ancestors (Leyburn Library, Washington and Lee University)

before the passage of an international copyright agreement in 1891, the validity of his insights is clearly attested to by the status of "poor devil authors": the dire poverty of Edgar Allan Poe, the financial difficulties of Nathaniel Hawthorne and Herman Melville, and the problems all three men had in reaching an audience all too ready to spoon up the soppy pabulum offered by some of the lesser English authors and their American progeny. For the light his case sheds on writing as an emerging profession, literary and cultural historians have studied the intersection of Mathews's career with the fortunes of these more significant figures.

As Mathews himself sought to create the sort of American literature he advocated, a major part of his effort was directed toward treating the American past in a grand, virtually epic manner, in order to impress upon his readers that their land was one hallowed by an heroic tradition. Thus, the novel *Behemoth: A Legend*

of the Mound-Builders (1839) and the long narrative poem *Wakondah; The Master of Life. A Poem* (1841), both dealing with the prehistoric Indians who inhabited the American continent, are crude attempts at epics showing the heroism that from the first marked America for greatness. Similarly, *Witchcraft: A Tragedy in Five Acts* (1852), a relatively successful poetic drama of the Salem witch trials that portrays a mother and son who bravely resist the hysteria about them, is calculated to instill in readers a sense of pride in their homeland. Two works set in Mathews's own day, *Big Abel, and the Little Manhattan* (1845) and *Chanticleer: A Thanksgiving Story of the Peabody Family* (1850), show that the present, for all of its shortcomings, is still not entirely divorced from a grand American past. In the former, Mathews presents the dynamic mid-nineteenth-century New York City as forever tied, whether most modern New Yorkers are conscious of it or not, to the heritage of earlier courageous inhabitants in the area, the Dutch and the Indians. In the latter, a contrived tale of Thanksgiving, the main character, who is the patriarch of a representative American family, is an aged Revolutionary War veteran, a visible reminder of the heroic history of the nation.

Feeling it his duty as an American writer to depict those shortcomings that he saw betraying the national heritage, Mathews frequently presented sharp indictments of some of the more unsavory aspects of his contemporary scene. His narrative of city life and New York politics, *The Career of Puffer Hopkins* (1842), appeared in the journal *Arcturus* from June 1841 to May 1842. His drama *The Politicians: A Comedy in Five Acts* (1840), many of the topical sketches in his humor magazines, and *Yankee Doodle* (1846–1847) and its sequel, the *Elephant* (1848), all satirize the corruption and demagoguery that pervert American political ideals. *Moneypenny; or, The Heart of the World: A Romance of the Present Day* (1849), a darkly comic mystery novel; his Thanksgiving tale, *Chanticleer;* and *False Pretenses; or, Both Sides of Good Society* (1856), a comedy of manners, all point out that Americans have fallen from the standards of their fathers not in their politics alone. Rather, as these works show, political failings are merely a manifestation of something more profound, a crisis in American values. Too many of his countrymen, Mathews believed, not only care merely for wealth and status, but readily sacrifice all principles and responsibilities to attain them.

He saw this crisis as a greater danger to the republic than even the poverty in which he knew many of his contemporaries to be mired; and in his poetic drama *Calmstorm, the Reformer: A Dramatic Comment* (1853), his *Poems on Man in His Various Aspects Under the American Republic* (1843), several articles in *Arcturus* (which he edited with Evert A. Duyckinck in 1841 and 1842), and his book *The Career of Puffer Hopkins,* Mathews evolved a social philosophy to deal with it. His philosophy eschews radical reform as disruptive and as little more than the tool of egotists seeking power and emphasizes instead a return to what Mathews saw as virtues of the American past— to principles, that is, of personal integrity, rigorous individualism, and staunch loyalty to homeland and one's fellow American individualists.

Though Mathews remained active in journalistic circles in the 1860s and 1870s, little substantial information about him has been added to the biographical record in the past century. He apparently supported himself by work in the theater and by contributions to periodicals in the decades after the masterworks of the American Renaissance by Poe, Melville, and Hawthorne had been produced.

Calling for a native American literature, arguing for the copyright law that would aid in its development, seeking in his own work to show how an American writer responsive to the heritage of his country and alert to its failings could work to forge a better nation, Cornelius Mathews committed his career to his homeland. His success was minimal. A little bit of urban local color here and there is mildly diverting, as are a joke or two that surprise the reader by coming off. Also, there is now and again a trenchant bit of social comment, but, as with the humor and good local color, too little to justify Mathews's efforts. Had he written less or taken more care or just had the requisite talent to be interesting, his efforts would have been better rewarded. As it is, one can do little but see Mathews as an inadequate fighter struggling, for the most part ineffectually, in a good cause.

References:

James J. Barnes, *Authors, Publishers and Politicians: The Quest for an Anglo-American Copyright Agreement 1815–1854* (Columbus: Ohio State University Press, 1974), pp. 78–83;

James Lester Busskohl, "*The Elephant,*" *American Humor Magazines and Comic Newspapers,* edited by David E. E. Sloane (New York: Greenwood Press, 1987), pp. 63–65;

James T. Callow, *Kindred Spirits: Knickerbocker Writers and American Artists, 1807–1855* (Chapel Hill: University of North Carolina Press, 1967);

Curtis Dahl, "Moby-Dick's Cousin Behemoth," *American Literature,* 31 (March 1959): 21–29;

Dahl, "Mound-Builders, Mormons, and William Cullen Bryant," *New England Quarterly,* 34 (June 1961): 178–190;

Lorne Feinberg, "*Yankee Doodle,*" *American Humor Magazines and Comic Newspapers,* edited by Sloane (New York: Greenwood Press, 1986), pp. 319–322;

Harrison Gray Fiske, "Obituary: Cornelius Mathews," *New York Mirror,* 6 April 1889, p. 6;

Robert W. Gladish, *Elizabeth Barrett Browning and the "Centurion": The Backgrounds to an Addition to the Elizabeth Barrett Browning Canon,* in *Baylor Browning Interests, No. 23* (Waco, Tex.: Baylor University Press, 1973);

Luther S. Mansfield, "Glimpses of Herman Melville's Life in Pittsfield: 1850–1851," *American Literature,* 9 (March 1937): 26–48;

Mansfield, "Melville's Comic Articles on Zachary Taylor," *American Literature,* 9 (January 1938): 411–418;

Perry Miller, *The Raven and the Whale: The War of Words and Wits in the Era of Poe and Melville* (New York: Harcourt, Brace, 1956);

Sidney P. Moss, "Poe, Hiram Fuller, and Duyckinck Circle," *American Book Collector,* 18 (October 1967): 8–18;

Moss, *Poe's Literary Battles: The Critic in the Context of His Literary Milieu* (Durham, N.C.: Duke University Press, 1963);

Moss, *Poe's Major Crisis: His Libel Suit and New York's Literary World* (Durham, N.C.: Duke University Press, 1970);

John P. Pritchard, *Literary Wise Men of Gotham: Criticism in New York, 1815–1860* (Baton Rouge: Louisiana State University Press, 1963);

Claude Richard, "Poe and 'Young America,'" *Studies in Bibliography,* 21 (1968): 24–58;

George O. Seilhmamer, *An Interviewer's Album: Comprising a Series of Chats with Eminent Players and Playwrights* (New York: Perry, 1881);

John Stafford, *The Literary Criticism of "Young America": A Study in the Relationship of Politics and Literature, 1837–1850* (Berkeley: University of California Press, 1952);

Allen F. Stein, *Cornelius Mathews* (New York: Twayne, 1974);

Daniel A. Wells, "'Bartleby the Scrivener,' Poe, and the Duyckinck Circle," *ESQ,* 21 (First Quarter 1975): 35–39;

Edward L. Widmer, *Young America: The Flowering Democracy in New York City* (New York: Oxford University Press, 1999);

Donald Yannella, "Foreword," in separate volume, photo-facsimile reprints of *Behemoth, Big Abel and the Little Manhattan,* and *The Career of Puffer Hopkins* (New York: Garrett, 1970);

Yannella, "*The Literary World,*" in *American Literary Magazines: The Eighteenth and Nineteenth Centuries,* edited by Edward E. Chielens (Westport, Conn.: Greenwood Press, 1986);

Yannella, "'Seeing the Elephant' in *Mardi,*" in *Artful Thunder: Versions of the Romantic Tradition in American Literature in Honor of Howard P. Vincent,* edited by Robert J. DeMott and Sanford E. Marovitz (Kent, Ohio: Kent State University Press, 1975), pp. 105–117;

Yannella, "Writing the '*Other Way*': Melville, the Duyckinck Crowd, and Literature for the Masses," in *A Companion to Melville Studies,* edited by John Bryant (Westport, Conn.: Greenwood Press, 1986), pp. 63–81;

Yannella, "*Yankee Doodle,*" in *American Literary Magazines: The Eighteenth and Nineteenth Centuries,* edited by Chielens (Wesport, Conn.: Greenwood Press, 1986), pp. 451–456.

Papers:

Cornelius Mathews's letters and manuscripts are held in the Duyckinck Family Papers and in other collections at the New York Public Library. Other holdings are at the Houghton Library, Harvard University; the Historical Society of Pennsylvania; the Boston Public Library; and the Library of Congress (Schoolcraft and Minnie Madden Collections).

Herman Melville

(1 August 1819 – 28 September 1891)

John Wenke
Salisbury University

See also the Melville entries in *DLB 3: Antebellum Writers in New York and the South* and *DLB 74: American Short-Story Writers Before 1880*.

BOOKS: *Narrative of a Four Months' Residence among the Natives of a Valley of the Marquesas Islands; or, A Peep at Polynesian Life* (London: John Murray, 1846); republished as *Typee: A Peep at Polynesian Life. During a Four Months' Residence in a Valley of the Marquesas* (New York: Wiley & Putnam, 1846); revised as *Typee: A Peep at Polynesian Life, during a Four Months Residence in a Valley of the Marquesas* (New York: Wiley & Putnam, 1846);

Omoo: A Narrative of Adventures in the South Seas; Being a Sequel to the "Residence in the Marquesas Islands" (London: John Murray, 1847); republished as *Omoo: A Narrative of Adventures in the South Seas* (New York: Harper, 1848);

Mardi: and A Voyage Thither, 3 volumes (London: Richard Bentley, 1849; 2 volumes, New York: Harper, 1849);

Redburn: His First Voyage. Being the Sailor-Boy Confessions and Reminiscences of the Son-of-a-Gentleman, in the Merchant Service, 2 volumes (London: Richard Bentley, 1849; New York: Harper, 1849);

White-Jacket; or, The World in a Man-of-War, 2 volumes (London: Richard Bentley, 1850; New York: Harper, 1850);

The Whale; or, Moby Dick, 3 volumes (London: Richard Bentley, 1851); republished as *Moby-Dick; or, The Whale* (New York: Harper, 1851);

Pierre; or, The Ambiguities (New York: Harper, 1852; London: Sampson Low, 1852);

Israel Potter: His Fifty Years of Exile (New York: G. P. Putnam, 1855; English piracy, London: George Routledge, 1855);

The Piazza Tales (New York: Dix & Edwards, 1856; London: Sampson Low, 1856);

The Confidence-Man: His Masquerade (New York: Dix & Edwards, 1857; London: Longman, 1857);

Herman Melville

Battle-Pieces and Aspects of the War (New York: Harper, 1866);

Clarel: A Poem and Pilgrimage in the Holy Land, 2 volumes (New York: G. P. Putnam, 1876);

John Marr and Other Sailors, with Some Sea-Pieces (New York: De Vinne Press, 1888);

Timoleon and Other Ventures in Minor Verse (New York: Caxton Press, 1891);

Billy Budd, and Other Prose Pieces, edited by Raymond Weaver, volume 13 of the Constable Standard Edition of Melville's *Complete Works* (London, Bombay & Sydney: Constable, 1924); *Billy Budd* republished in *Shorter Novels of Herman Melville* (New York: Liveright, 1928).

Edition: *The Writings of Herman Melville,* Northwestern-Newberry edition, edited by Harrison Hayford, Hershel Parker, and G. Thomas Tanselle, 15 volumes to date (Evanston, Ill.: Northwestern University Press / Chicago: Newberry Library, 1968–   ).

Herman Melville drew upon his adventurous travels on sea and land for the primary materials of his greatest fiction and poetry. Out of his experiences in the merchant service (1839), the whaling industry (1841–1843), and the United States Navy (1843–1844) emerged the storytelling impulse that led him to compose and publish *Narrative of a Four Months' Residence among the Natives of a Valley of the Marquesas Islands; or, A Peep at Polynesian Life* (1846). Titled *Typee: A Peep at Polynesian Life. During a Four Months' Residence in a Valley of the Marquesas* in subsequent editions, this wild tale of the narrator's life among a tribe of South Sea cannibals marked the high point of Melville's popularity and initiated his lifelong practice of plundering literary sources to augment the work of memory and invention. Following *Omoo: A Narrative of Adventures in the South Seas; Being a Sequel to the "Residence in the Marquesas Islands"* (1847), Melville rejected travel narrative in favor of an expansive, chaotic, allegorical romance. *Mardi: and A Voyage Thither* (1849) was a commercial failure, but its quest structure, lofty language, satirical content, philosophical imperatives, and wide-ranging allusions reflect Melville's ambition to make himself a writer for all the ages. Following *Redburn: His First Voyage. Being the Sailor-Boy Confessions and Reminiscences of the Son-of-a-Gentleman, in the Merchant Service* (1849) and *White-Jacket; or, The World in a Man-of-War* (1850), *The Whale; or, Moby Dick* (1851) dramatized Captain Ahab's vengeful hunt for the great white whale. Titled *Moby-Dick; or, The Whale* in subsequent editions, this masterwork fuses Ishmael's comedy of workaday struggle and Ahab's tragedy of "ungodly god-like" obsession. Exalted by his achievement, Melville plunged into his tale of a naive young man who mistakes the allure of incestuous desire for the demands of ideal truth. *Pierre; or, The Ambiguities* (1852) was a professional disaster from which Melville never recovered. After writing the unpublished novel "The Isle of the Cross," Melville produced such stellar magazine pieces as "Bartleby, the Scrivener. A Story of Wall-Street" (*Putnam's Monthly Magazine,* March–May 1853), "The Encantadas, or Enchanted Isles" (*Putnam's Monthly Magazine,* March–May 1854), and "Benito Cereno" (*Putnam's Monthly Magazine,* October–December 1855). *Israel Potter; or, Fifty Years of Exile. A Fourth of July Story* first appeared serially in *Putnam's Monthly Magazine* (July 1854–March 1855); the novel was then published in book form as *Israel Potter: His Fifty Years of Exile* (1855). In *The Piazza Tales* (1856) Melville collected six stories

that appeared originally in *Putnam's Monthly Magazine. The Confidence-Man: His Masquerade* (1857) was a commercial failure and became the last work of prose fiction he published in his lifetime.

Whereas Melville's prolific career as a fiction-writer consumed a mere eleven years, his career as a poet unfolded over the last thirty-four years of his life. In 1860 he tried and failed to publish his first volume of poems. Melville's most topical and politically timely work did not reach a large reading public, though it was reviewed or noticed in many American and British publications. *Battle-Pieces and Aspects of the War* (1866) is possibly the most expressive response to the Civil War written by an American author. Having ceased to court a readership, Melville continued to shape his vision within the rigors of metrical verse. Written in the evenings while Melville was employed as a customs inspector in New York City, the eighteen-thousand-line *Clarel: A Poem and Pilgrimage in the Holy Land* (1876) grew out of Melville's own travels twenty years before. *Clarel* tracks a Chaucerian band of pilgrims as they wander through an arid landscape. After retiring from government service on 31 December 1885, Melville turned his attention to an assortment of verse projects, publishing *John Marr and Other Sailors, with Some Sea-Pieces* (1888) and *Timoleon and Other Ventures in Minor Verse* (1891) and leaving in manuscript much poetry, including the unfinished collection "Weeds and Wildings with a Rose or Two." The prose headnote to a poem titled "Billy in the Darbies" grew over five years into *Billy Budd, Sailor: (An Inside Narrative).* At Melville's death the manuscript was left in a nearly finished state but was not published until 1924.

On 1 August 1819 Herman Melvill was born at 6 Pearl Street in New York City, the third child of Allan Melvill and Maria Gansevoort Melvill. Herman's grandfathers were Revolutionary War heroes: Thomas Melvill (born 1751) was a renowned member of the 1773 Boston Tea Party, and in 1777 General Peter Gansevoort (born 1749) led the defense of Fort Stanwix against the invading British forces of Colonel St. Leger. The child's patriotic heritage was matched by his aristocratic lineage. The Melvills claimed royal blood through their genealogical relationship to the Scottish Lords of Leven and Melvill. The Gansevoorts were related to the great Dutch families that had dominated upstate New York since the seventeenth century, among them the Van Rensselaers, the Van Schaicks, and the Van Vechtens. Herman's elder siblings were Gansevoort (born 6 December 1815) and Helen Maria (born 4 August 1817); his younger siblings were Augusta (born 24 August 1821), Allan Jr. (born 7 April 1823), Catherine (born 21 May 1825), Frances Priscilla (born 26 August 1827), and Thomas (born 24 January

Melville's maternal grandparents: General Peter Gansevoort in 1794 (painting by Gilbert Stuart; Munson-Williams-Proctor Institute, Museum of Art, Utica, New York) and Catherine Van Schaick Gansevoort circa 1820 (portrait by Ezra Ames; Gansevoort-Lansing Collection, Rare Books and Manuscripts Division, New York Public Library, Astor, Lenox and Tilden Foundations)

1830). Remarkably, all the Melvill children survived into adulthood.

Allan Melvill Sr., a French-speaking importer of dry goods, had aspirations to economic and cultural grandeur but was undone by financial ineptitude. An overreaching businessman, he led his wife and children on a decade-long decline from perennially unrealized anticipations of mercantile success to a humiliating, debt-ridden state of entangled financial insolvency. Until 1830, when his creditors finally sued, Melvill managed to mask impending ruin with an affluence made possible by borrowed money. Melvill drew most heavily from his father; his mother-in-law, Catherine Van Schaick Gansevoort; and his brother-in-law, Peter Gansevoort. In squandering vast sums, Melvill vitiated munificent inheritances that would have come following the deaths of his mother-in-law and father. On 10 October 1830 years of fiscal mismanagement culminated when Melvill sneaked out of New York by night to escape his creditors. At his side was eleven-year-old Herman, who helped his father carry off the household remainders. They were going to Albany to join the rest of the family and their furniture.

Despite his father's misadventures, Herman had a fine education prior to 1830. On 12 September 1825 he enrolled in the New York Male High School on Crosby Street. In a letter of 10 August 1826 to Peter Gansevoort, Allan Melvill described his second son as "very backward in speech and somewhat slow in comprehension." Herman was being measured against the standard set by his brilliant brother Gansevoort. In a 23 February 1828 letter to Peter Gansevoort, Melvill admitted his surprise "to know, that Herman proved the best Speaker in the introductory Department." Herman remained at the New York Male High School until 1 August 1829. Two months later Gansevoort and Herman enrolled in the Grammar School of Columbia College and attended at least through the following May. In a 20 May 1830 letter to his father, Melvill compared Gansevoort, "a distinguished classical Scholar," with Herman, "who I think is making more progress than formerly, & without being a bright Scholar, he maintains a respectable standing, & would proceed further, if he could be induced to study more." In what amounts to one of the great parental misjudgments of all time, Allan Melvill writes, "being a most aimiable [*sic*] of innocent child, I cannot find it in my heart to coerce him [Herman], especially as he seems to have chosen Commerce as a favorite pursuit, whose practical activity can well dispense with much book knowledge."

Following Melvill's financial collapse, Herman was in and out of school, depending on the family's ability to pay tuition. On 15 October 1830 Gansevoort and Herman enrolled at the Albany Academy, a classical school for college-bound students. According to David K. Titus in "Herman Melville at the Albany Academy" in *Melville Society Extracts* (May 1980), the curriculum included "Reading and Spelling; Penmanship; Arithmetic; English Grammar; Geography; Natural History; Universal, Grecian, Roman and English History; Classical Biography; and Jewish Antiquities." As Nathalia Wright makes clear in *Melville's Use of the Bible* (1949), the Bible was a primary text of Herman's youth. He also read widely in his father's well-stocked library. Like Redburn, Herman avidly read tales of Arabian nights as well as an 1822 six-volume London edition of the *Spectator*. In *Melville's Reading* (1988) Merton M. Sealts Jr. argues that in "Fragments from a Writing Desk" (*Democratic Press, and Lansingburgh Advertiser,* May 1839), Melville's first published fiction, are "tokens of his early familiarity with the writings of Shakespeare, Milton, Scott, Sheridan, Burke, Coleridge, Byron, and Thomas More." Although Herman's formal education was irregular—for example, he began his second year at the Albany Academy on 1 September 1831 only to be withdrawn in October for lack of funds—he absorbed a diverse body of materials that provided a prodigious foundation.

Though a financial failure, Allan Melvill Sr. was a loving father. His death was a devastating and irreparable loss to his wife and eight children. After suffering severe exposure while stranded on the ice-locked Hudson River, the forty-nine-year-old man fell deeply ill and knew his end was near. On 5 January 1832 he marked Psalm 55: "My heart is sore pained within me: and the terrors of death are fallen upon me." His physical ailments could only have been exacerbated by his dread of leaving his wife and children in such desperate straits. The fiscal wreck may even have driven him insane. His wife comments in the margin of their Bible: "This Chapter was mark'd a few days before my dear *Allan* by reason of severe suffering was depriv'd [sic] of his Intellect" (italics in original). On 11 January, Thomas Melvill Jr. describes his brother in a letter to Lemuel Shaw, Herman's future father-in-law: "I found him *very sick*—induced by a variety of causes—under great mental excitement—at times fierce, even *maniacal*." One can only imagine the horror that saturated the Melvill house in the weeks leading to Allan Melvill's death on 28 January 1832. Herman is not known to have written

directly about his father's death, but seventeen years later, the narrator of *Redburn* dismisses an idyllic memory from his childhood: "But I must not think of those delightful days, before my father became a bankrupt, and died, and we removed from the city; for when I think of those days, something rises up in my throat and almost strangles me."

Exactly two months after her husband's death, Maria Melvill signed a memorandum stipulating that Gansevoort was "carrying on the Fur, and Cap business in the City of Albany, on my account." So began the mother's campaign to resurrect the family fortunes through the heroic but futile efforts of her eldest son. Herman Melville (his mother began adding the *e* about this time) was relegated to a more servile role. Before June 1832, through the efforts of his Uncle Peter, Herman was hired as a clerk in the New York State Bank. When a cholera epidemic erupted, Maria fled Albany on 14 July 1832 with her eight children and arrived unannounced at the Melvill family farm south of Pittsfield, Massachusetts. On 18 July, Herman's status in his family was made clear when Uncle Peter called him back to the plague city. Herman returned and worked through the epidemic.

In late April or early May 1834 Herman left the bank to work as a clerk in his brother's fur and cap store, taking no vacation to Pittsfield that summer because Gansevoort determined that Herman was needed behind the counter. If the Pittsfield farm constituted Herman's temporary escape from oppression, then life as a clerk was synonymous with imprisonment. Frequently, Melville's protagonists decry the debilitating effects of servile drudgery. In *Moby-Dick,* for example, Ishmael describes the Manhattan landlubbers as "of week days pent up in lath and plaster—tied to counters, nailed to benches, clinched to desks." On Sunday they rush to the pier and gaze at the water. In another tale, the lawyer-narrator asks a troubled young man if he would like "a clerkship in a dry-goods store." Bartleby replies, "There is too much confinement about that. No, I would not like a clerkship, but I am not particular."

Despite the family's hardships, Herman pursued what education he could get—both in and out of the classroom. For part of 1835 he may have attended the Albany Classical School. On 29 January 1836 he joined Gansevoort in Albany's Young Men's Association for Mutual Improvement. On 1 September 1836 he returned to the Albany Academy after a five-year absence, enrolling in the Latin course. That fall he joined the Ciceronian Debating Society. But with Gansevoort's business deeply in debt, Herman was again withdrawn from school in March 1837. That summer, in the wake of business failure, Gansevoort went to

Melville's parents as painted by Ezra Ames, circa 1820: Allan Melvill (The Henry E. Huntington Library and Art Gallery, San Marino, California) and Maria Gansevoort Melvill (Berkshire Athenaeum)

New York City to study law, while Herman ran the Pittsfield farm. Following the harvest, Herman taught in a backwoods school before returning to Lansingburgh in January 1838 and rejoining the debating society. In *The Albany Microscope,* a paper published for young men, Herman enjoyed his first taste of having his words in print: he and other members of the debating society attacked one another with repeated volleys full of elevated language and strenuous outrage.

Such rhetorical play was one thing, but Herman needed a career. In November 1838 he began a course in surveying and engineering at the Lansingburgh Academy. After completing the course, he tried and failed to get a job on the Erie Canal. In May 1839 "Fragments from a Writing Desk" appeared in two installments in the *Democratic Press, and Lansingburgh Advertiser.* His literary debut, however, stands as a prelude to his first sea voyage. In June 1839 Melville left Manhattan on the *St. Lawrence,* a merchant ship bound on a round-trip voyage to Liverpool. From 4 July to 12 August he remained in Liverpool, working and living aboard ship but free to roam after 4:00 P.M. Following his return, Melville taught school in Greenbush before traveling the next summer with Eli Fly to Galena, Illinois, in hopes that Uncle Thomas Melvill might help him attain a position. Like his brother Allan, Thomas

Melvill was a chronic debtor. But unlike Allan, Thomas embezzled funds, got caught, and was fired. He could do little more for his nephew Herman than point him eastward.

Melville's most momentous journey began in Fairhaven, Massachusetts, on 31 December 1840. Having little or no money in his purse and nothing particular to interest him on shore, he signed on the whaling ship *Acushnet.* On 3 January 1841 Melville left for the Pacific Ocean. Just as his voyage on the *St. Lawrence* established the autobiographical basis for *Redburn,* his desertion from the *Acushnet* on 9 July 1842 initiated the adventures that later animated *Typee* and *Omoo.* At Nukuheva in the Marquesas, Melville and Richard Tobias (Toby) Greene escaped into the interior. What actually happened is not known, though Greene emerged a few days later, while Melville remained. After three weeks in the Typee valley, Melville made his way to the coast and signed on a Sydney, Australia whaler, the *Lucy Ann,* which sailed for Tahiti and the Society Islands. On 24 September 1842 some of the crewmen preferred not to do their duty. After being joined by Melville, these nonviolent mutineers were placed in indulgent confinement by acting British consul Charles Burnet Wilson. By mid October Melville had walked away from incarceration and traveled to the neighboring island of Eimeo with John Troy, the model for Dr. Long Ghost of *Omoo*. After a bit of farming, wandering, and beachcombing, Melville signed on 3 November 1842 for a single cruise on a Nantucket whaler, the *Charles and Henry*. On 27 April 1843 Melville was discharged at Lahaina in the Hawaiian Islands. On 18 May he arrived at Honolulu, where he worked as a pinsetter in a bowling alley and then on 1 July he took a position as a store clerk. On 18 August 1843 he signed on the navy frigate the *United States* as an ordinary seaman and gained the direct experience that he used six years later in *White-Jacket*. While cruising the Pacific and touching at Nukuheva and Tahiti and then along the western coast of South and Central America, Melville continued his practice from the *Lucy Ann* and *Charles and Henry* of telling animated tales about the Marquesan cannibals. On 3 October 1844 the *United States* arrived at the Boston Navy Yard. Before his discharge on 14 October Melville read old newspaper accounts of Gansevoort's growing notoriety as a rousing stump orator for Democratic presidential candidate James K. Polk. After a stay in Boston, where he visited relatives and friends and even regaled his future wife, Elizabeth Shaw, with polished tales of his exploits, Melville returned to Lansingburgh on 22 October. Sometime in November, at the urging of his sister Augusta, Melville began to translate his oral tale into a written text.

By early spring 1845 Harper and Brothers had found Melville's narrative implausible and refused to publish it. Gansevoort's 31 July 1845 appointment by President Polk as Secretary of the American Legation in London was the single most important contingency that made possible Melville's literary career. With hopes of securing a London publisher, Gansevoort carried the manuscript with him and offered it to John Murray, who doubted its authenticity. At home, Melville went back to work on his book, making extensive factual additions designed to enhance the verisimilitude of the whole. He drew upon William Ellis's *Polynesian Researches* (1833), Charles S. Stewart's *A Visit to the South Seas* (1831), Stewart's *Journal of a Residence in the Sandwich Islands* (1830), David Porter's *Journal of a Cruise Made to the Pacific Ocean* (1822), and George H. Von Langsdorff's *Voyages and Travels in Various Parts of the World* (1813). Melville did not begin his career as a self-professed fiction writer. Murray despised fiction and would have been appalled by Melville's creative liberties. In December 1845 Murray accepted the manuscript. On 21 February 1846 the *Narrative of a Four Months' Residence among the Natives of a Valley of the Marquesas Islands* was published in London. On 17 March, Wiley and Putnam of New York published a slightly censored version as *Typee: A Peep at Polynesian Life. During a Four Months' Residence in a Valley of the Marquesas.*

In *Typee* the narrator grows disgusted with the monotony of ship life and deserts with his friend Toby. Hoping to find a sequestered paradise but uncertain whether they will encounter the supposedly friendly Happar tribe or the infamously cannibalistic Typees, the wanderers lose themselves in a rainy mountain jungle and then blunder into Typee valley. In this tale Melville establishes his basic narrative device of conducting his protagonist through a change of worlds. The narrator (who comes to be called Tommo) leaves Western civilization and enters an ostensibly primitive world. Using a series of negatives, Tommo evokes the innate superiority of the valley to Western civilization: "There seemed to be no cares, griefs, troubles, or vexations, in all Typee. . . . There were no foreclosures of mortgages, no protested notes, no bills payable, no debts of honor in Typee . . . no beggars, no debtors' prison, no proud and hard-hearted nabobs in Typee; or to sum up all in one word—no Money."

Tommo's utopic depictions of non-Western life impel his polemical attacks on the colonization process. Tommo inveighs against the hand-in-glove fit between colonial and missionary imperatives. In Honolulu the natives are "civilized into draught horses, and evangelized into beasts of burden. . . . They have been literally broken into the traces, and are harnessed to the vehicles of their spiritual instructors like so many dumb brutes!" Central to the notorious success of *Typee* is Tommo's titillating account of his erotic adventures with Fayaway. The iconic image of naked Fayaway standing upright in a canoe using her shirt as a sail encapsulates the sexual allure of this distant exotic place. Such critics as Milton R. Stern in *The Fine Hammered Steel of Herman Melville* (1957) and Wai-chee Dimock in *Empire for Liberty: Melville and the Poetics of Individualism* (1989) have extensively explored the cultural, political, and ideological dimensions of the narrative.

Tommo's ostensible recovery of Eden, however, is seriously undercut, not only by his isolation within the confines of his own language and culture but also by lurking threats to his physical and psychological well-being. Uncertain whether apparent kindness might prefigure a cannibalistic feasting on his flesh, Tommo "saw everything, but could comprehend nothing." Melville not only dramatizes the limitations of the Western point of view but also reveals how Eden Regained is itself a self-gratifying, and fallacious, cultural fiction. As Tommo's longing for home grows, the Typee valley seems a hot spot of political intrigue and impending violence. Tommo fully awakens from his soporific immersion when Karky, the village artist, insists that Tommo's face be tattooed. If thus marked, Tommo would lose his mediatory position—his freedom to enjoy the valley's various fruits while retaining his Western identity.

Indeed, much criticism written on *Typee* turns on the complex issue of cultural affiliation. In fact, as John Samson points out in *White Lies: Melville's Narratives of Facts* (1989), the very name Tommo "has a meaning: it is a Marquesan verb signifying 'to enter into, to adapt well to.' The name indicates . . . that they wish him to enter into their society, but ironically Tommo not only fails to understand his newly given name, he never adapts." Tommo suspends himself between the wonders and horrors of alternative worlds. John Bryant argues in *Melville and Repose: The Rhetoric of Humor in the American Renaissance* (1993) that Melville also suspends the reader in a complex "rhetoric of deceit": "Tommo persuades us to embrace the savage mind, but once we are about to accept that sensual world, he suddenly disengages, leaving us alone with our freshly adopted beliefs."

The favorable British reviews of Melville's *Narrative of a Four Months' Residence among the Natives of a Valley of the Marquesas Islands* paved the way for the triumph of *Typee* in the United States. Reviewers admired the wild adventures, the evocation of lush verdure, the teasing erotica, and the delineation of strange native practices. As an anonymous Nathaniel Hawthorne remarks in the *Salem Advertiser* (25 March 1846), Melville "has that freedom of view—it would be too harsh to call it laxity of principle—which renders him tolerant of codes of morals that may be little in accordance with our own; a spirit proper enough to a young and adventurous sailor; and which makes his book the more wholesome to our staid landsmen." But for several reviewers, the specious authenticity of the book was troubling. Some were gently incredulous. In *The Harbinger,* "we cannot escape a slight suspicion that he has embellished the facts from his own imagination, in other words, that there is an indefinite amount of romance mingled with the reality of his narrative." In the 17 April 1846 issue of *Morning Courier and New-York Enquirer* the reviewer announces, "in all essential respects, it is a *fiction.*" Some questions were put to rest with the surprising emergence of Toby. Richard Greene contacted Melville from Buffalo, New York, and dutifully vouched for the "entire accuracy" of the work. But what evoked most fire was Melville's attacks on the missionaries. As Hershel Parker argues in *Herman Melville: A Biography* (1996), "The turning point in the American reception of *Typee* came with a review in the 9 April [1846] *New York Evangelist,* the principle organ of the Presbyterian church, and as such a fervent promoter of Protestant missions." The reviewer offers "severe condemnation" and protests Melville's "slurs and flings against missionaries and civilization." Melville's publisher, the Presby-

Melville's maternal uncle, Peter Gansevoort, who paid for the publication in 1876 of Melville's two-volume poem Clarel *(engraving by A. H. Ritchie)*

terian John Wiley, was aghast at the book that his partner—George Palmer Putnam—had signed. Wiley ordered that Melville expurgate it. On 6 August 1846 Wiley and Putnam released the "revised," heavily censored edition, which also included an epilogue, "The Story of Toby." With three versions of *Typee* in print, Melville's career was launched. But he never in his lifetime escaped the tag of a popular writer of sea yarns; he was always remembered, if remembered at all, as the "man who lived among the cannibals."

On 12 May 1846 Gansevoort Melville died in London. According to Dr. W. F. Chambers, Gansevoort's body was so diseased "as to prove that no human skill could have been effected in saving his life." This death was the second great disaster for the Melville family, possibly more psychologically devastating than Allan Sr.'s. Herman was now head of the family and implicitly responsible for his widowed mother, his four unmarried sisters, and his youngest brother. He was also thinking seriously of marriage. On or after 31 August 1846 Melville became engaged to Elizabeth Shaw, who was in Lansingburgh for an extended visit.

Since early 1846 Melville had been at work on the sequel to *Typee,* and in a 15 July 1846 letter, Melville offered *Omoo* to Murray: "It embraces adventures in the

South Seas (of a totally different character from 'Typee')." Melville emphasizes the authenticity of his account, though he fails to assuage Murray's continuing doubts. In fact, the publisher asked Melville for "documentary evidences" of having been in the Marquesas. In a 2 September 1846 letter Melville used Toby's emergence to buttress his credibility: "Dear Sir, how indescribably vexatious, when one really feels in his very bones that he has been there, to have a parcel of blockheads question it!" After assuring Murray that he was not one of the blockheads, Melville attempts to settle the issue: "Typee however must at last be beleived [sic] on its own account–they beleive [sic] it here now–a little touched up they say but *true*."

Melville touched up *Omoo*, as well, and it was published in London by Murray on 30 March 1847 and in New York by Harper and Brothers on 24 April 1847. Melville again drew on Stewart, Langsdorff, and especially Ellis, along with Michael Russell's *Polynesia* (1843) and the six-volume *Narrative of the United States Exploring Expedition* (1845). Whereas *Typee* was a brilliant amateur's slapdash creation, *Omoo* was the work of a man who considered himself a professional author. Despite the tragedy of Gansevoort's shocking death, which occurred in the midst of composition, Melville managed to infuse *Omoo* with a pervasive tone of lighthearted escapade. The lurking epistemological dilemmas of *Typee* give way to lively humor and risk-free adventure. In *Studies in Classic American Literature* (1923) D. H. Lawrence admires *Omoo* as "picaresque, rascally, roving. . . . Perhaps Melville is at his best." Though renewing his assault on the missionaries, Melville avoids symbolic dark forests. Christopher Sten in *The Weaver God, He Weaves: Melville and the Poetics of the Novel* (1996) follows Lawrence's lead and places *Omoo* in the tradition of Tobias Smollett's *Peregrine Pickle* (1751) and *The Adventures of Roderick Random* (1748), and Alain-René Lesage's *The Adventures of Gil Blas of Santillane* (1715–1735). Melville's wandering episodic plot follows the narrator's exploits on the *Julia*, which culminate in a bloodless mutiny. During the mutineers' mock incarceration in a paradisal prison, they enjoy the lazy self-indulgence denied to men before the mast. Upon his release, the narrator–who calls himself Paul–joins Dr. Long Ghost, and they wander the beaches and interior of Tahiti and Imeeo, actually following the path reported by Ellis in his *Polynesian Researches*. According to Sten, Melville's use of the picaresque depicts "lusty peripatetic characters with a powerful aversion to work–down-and-out types who live by their wits . . . take great pleasure in playing crude tricks, and excel . . . only at outfoxing an array of foolish authority figures." In *White Lies* Samson explores how Melville adapts "the idea of the sacred wanderer found in the missionaries' narratives" to dramatize a

"comic reduction of the sacred to the profane." Melville's desacralizing purpose, or what Samson identifies as a "pattern of profanation," has its greatest manifestation in repeated attacks on the missionaries, a remarkable fact insofar as Melville was completing *Omoo* even as he was involved in expurgating the revised American edition of *Typee*.

Omoo received favorable reviews, but it came under the lash for its incendiary polemics on the Christian missions. As with *Typee*, reviewers of *Omoo* did not distinguish between Melville and his roving narrator. The reviewer for the *London Athenaeum* (10 April 1847) lauds Melville's "*vraisemblance* of history" but recognizes the hand of a fabulist: "there are in the style and about the narrative indications of romance that suggest a power of prolonging these adventures to any extent for which a public may demand them." Whereas sympathetic reviewers praised Melville's fluent style and racy material, the negative reviewers–most notably, Horace Greeley in the *New-York Weekly Tribune*–castigated Melville for purveying blatant falsehoods and celebrating moral turpitude.

While waiting for *Omoo* to appear, Melville acquired J. Ross Browne's *Etchings of a Whaling Cruise* (1846) and informed Evert A. Duyckinck, editor of The New York *Literary World*, that he would review it; the essay appeared on 6 March 1847. Melville's essay on *Etchings of a Whaling Cruise* expresses self-reflexive critical categories that allow him to view his highly fictionalized books as literal narratives of fact. While celebrating the ocean as "the peculiar theatre of the romantic and wonderful," Melville laments how the "matter-of-fact details connected with nautical life" have vitiated "the poetry of salt water." Melville's identification of *Etchings of a Whaling Cruise* as "a book of unvarnished facts" reflects the degree to which he had come to see his own books as mundane journalistic exercises. To be considered the romancer he truly was irked Melville. He wanted to grow beyond the aesthetic confines of the travel narrative; he was itching to transfigure his Polynesian subject.

Melville began writing *Mardi* in mid May 1847 and did not complete it until late January 1849. The composition of *Mardi* was interrupted by his marriage to Elizabeth Shaw on 4 August 1847. After their subsequent honeymoon, the couple set up housekeeping on Fourth Avenue in New York City with Melville's brother Allan, his bride Sophia Thurston Melville, and Melville's mother and four unmarried sisters. Melville did not return to his manuscript in earnest until November 1847. His text grew and grew as his intentions expanded. Melville's daring experimentation was fueled by his eclectic reading in such romantic and poetic narratives as the ballads of Jean

Froissart; the James Macpherson sagas of Ossian, especially the epic *Fingal* (1752), the plays of William Shakespeare; Esaias Tegnér's translation of *Frithiof's Saga* (1825); George Gordon, Lord Byron's *The Island* (1823); and François Rabelais's *Gargantua and Pantagruel* (1844). Melville was also reading Platonic dialogues—certainly the *Republic, Phaedrus,* and *Phaedo*—as well as Sir Thomas Browne's *Religio Medici* (1835–1836). Melville admired Plato and Browne for their ability to set into motion a complex interplay of competing voices, thereby translating the process of thinking into the activity of writing. Melville encountered this same dialectical quality in Robert Burton's *Anatomy of Melancholy* (1801), Samuel Taylor Coleridge's *Biographia Literaria* (1847), Michel Eyquem de Montaigne's essays, and Rabelais's *Gargantua and Pantagruel.* In *Mardi* Melville attempted to discover new intellectual worlds that could generate new artistic domains.

After months of writing, Melville made his intentions known to a startled John Murray, the inveterate hater of fiction. In a letter of 1 January 1848 Melville described precisely the kind of book that Murray would never publish: "the plan I have pursued in the composition of the book now in hand, clothes the whole subject in new attractions & combines in one cluster all that is romantic, whimsical, & poetic in Polynisia [sic]." With his "rathar [sic] bold aim" Melville sought to actualize the truth-seeking possibilities of fiction. In late February 1849 Murray rejected *Mardi,* and John R. Brodhead, Gansevoort's friend and now Herman's London agent, offered it to publisher Richard Bentley. In opposition to his reader's report, Bentley accepted *Mardi* on 1 March 1849 and published it on 17 March 1849. In New York, Harper published the book on 7 April 1849.

As Melville makes clear in a 25 March 1848 letter to Murray, *Mardi* "opens like a true narrative . . . & the romance and poetry of the thing thence grow continuously, till it becomes a story wild enough I assure you & with a meaning too." *Mardi* is "wild," indeed, but its meaning has vexed readers since its publication. For example, in a 27 August 1850 letter to Duyckinck, Hawthorne described *Mardi* as "a rich book, with depths here and there that compel a man to swim for his life. It is so good that one scarcely pardons the writer for not having brooded over it, so as to make it a great deal better." Melville made *Mardi* the best book he could, but he did not control his materials. Put simply, Melville wanted to contain the world in this one book. *Mardi* begins with a scenario against which Melville's first philosophical quester will rebel. The narrator describes himself as sick and tired of the nautical life. He laments the boredom and tedium of his companions. The captain cannot "talk sentiment or philosophy." Nor can his shipmates "page me a quotation from

John Murray, who published Melville's first two books in England under the impression that they were nonfiction (Scottish National Portrait Gallery)

Burton on Blue Devils." Melville projects his own impatience with adventure yarns into a narrator who defines his aspirations in terms of intellectual fulfillment. He craves a world of expansive consciousness, an imagined "dream-land" somewhere to the west, "loosely laid down upon the charts." And so the narrator goes there.

After leaving the ship with a taciturn companion and alter ego named Jarl, the narrator re-creates their experiences "At sea in an open boat, and a thousand miles from land!" The title of chapter 9, "The Watery World Is All before Them," directly alludes to Book 10 of John Milton's *Paradise Lost* (1667), the point after the archangel Michael expels Adam and Eve from the Garden of Eden. Melville's narrator, however, does not enter the domain of fallen existence so much as he luxuriates in the possibilities of open fictional space. Nothing seems to be out there, so anything can be written. With so little going on, the narrator can always—as he surely does—spin meditative digressions. The narrator rejects the commonplace life of the ship and gives full play to the mind in motion. In chapter 13, for example, the sight of a strange floating creature evokes a foray in the voice of Browne: "Though America be discovered, the Cathays of the deep are unknown. And whoso crosses the Pacific might have read lessons to Buffon. The sea-serpent is not a fable; and in the sea, that snake is but a garden worm. There are more wonders than the wonders rejected, and more sights unrevealed than you or I ever dreamt of." In *Mardi* Melville makes a dramatic advance in his handling of narrative voice. He develops within one narrator two distinct voices that stand in dialectical tension. The narrator oscillates between speaking as a fraternal genialist who is associated with communal life, and as a solipsistic isolationist who locates himself in an ahistorical absolutistic context. These voices help Melville extend the possibilities of his fictional world, especially as the genialist and solipsist reflect metaphysical qualities of consciousness.

The major dramatic action of *Mardi*—the discovery and rescue of the maiden Yillah—estranges the narrator from his historical and cultural past. In the Yillah episodes Melville brings into full figure his first ideal absolutist. The high priest Aleema is conducting Yillah toward a sacrificial death. The narrator rescues the maiden, kills Aleema, and creates the dramatic occasion for Aleema's three sons to seek vengeance. The figure of Yillah fuses a host of literal and symbolic attributes. In *Melville's* Mardi: *A Chartless Voyage* (1952) Merrell R. Davis links Yillah's literary antecedents with Friedrich, baron de la Motte Fouqué's Undine; Thomas Moore's Lily; Friedrich Leopold von Hardenberg's Mathilde; Robert Southey's Oneiza; Coleridge's Geraldine; John Keats's Lamia; and also the enchanting fays of medieval legend. With her "reminiscences of her shadowy isle," Yillah also represents the Platonic realm of the soul's preexistence. An all-alluring ideal, she embodies a symbol of primordial perfection—once enjoyed, now regained, soon to be lost. When the narrator falls in love with Yillah, he reflects his own attraction to ideal possibility, even going so far as to assume the identity of Taji, a fabled demigod from the sun.

After arriving on the island of Odo, Taji loses Yillah. To find her, Taji enlists the help of four companions: King Media represents authority; Babbalanja represents philosophy; Yoomy represents poetry; and Mohi represents history. The questers travel the mythical archipelago of Mardi. Melville's allegorical plan fuels his appetite for intellectual play, improvisation, and dialectic; he presents the world as seen by these four characters. Though essentially disappearing as a character, Taji interrupts the action to offer three digressive soliloquies—"Time and Temples," "Faith and Knowledge," and "Dreams." The questers visit sixteen islands and pass many more. Each island presents specific dramatic circumstances. For example, they visit Juam, where the captive King Donjalolo destroys his body and mind in gluttonous excess. On Pimminee, the Tapparians legalistically prescribe the minutest affairs of life. On Diranda, the lords Piko and Hello stage deadly war games. On Vivenza, Melville satirizes a slaveholding republic much like the United States. The Juam episode exemplifies the intermittent brilliance of *Mardi*. Donjalolo anticipates the dandified Harry Bolton of *Redburn* and the self-contained Bartleby. In one imagistic extravaganza, the narrator summarizes Donjalolo's hyperbolic immurement: "And here, in this impenetrable retreat, centrally slumbered the universe-rounded, zodiac-belted, horizon-zoned, sea-girt, reef-sashed, mountain-locked, arbor-nested, royalty-girdled, arm-clasped, self-hugged, indivisible Donjalolo, absolute monarch of Juam:—the husk-inhusked meat in a nut, the innermost spark in a ruby; the juice-nested seed in a golden-rinded orange; the red royal stone in an effeminate peach; the insphered sphere of spheres."

The scattershot attempt at inclusiveness in *Mardi* leads frequently to discursiveness. The four characters argue over such subjects as the immortality of the soul, art, inspiration, Oro (God), preexistence, atavism, practical ethics, and authoritarianism. Melville stages especially well the intellectual gyrations of Babbalanja, who is most protean in exploring the "mystery of mysteries." Many readers, then and now, find the allegorical quest a tedious affair, a reaction that Melville himself seems to have expected. In the questers' discussion of Lombardo's epic "Koztanza," King Abrazza critiques the author in terms that describe Melville's achievement in *Mardi*: "The Koztanza lacks cohesion; it is wild, unconnected, all episode." For hundreds of pages, through countless dialogues, the questers resolutely do not find Yillah. The book seems endless largely because Melville refused to end it. Like Rabelais in *Gargantua and Pantagruel*, Melville spins new worlds out of his mind. For example, in early May 1848, Melville believed that *Mardi* was almost finished. But during the summer, stirred by momentous events erupting in the world, he added thinly disguised allegories of the European revolution of 1848 and U.S. politics.

The importance of *Mardi* resides in its ambitious attempt to contain human experience in the always too narrow confines of a literary text. Taji describes the magnitude of this venture: "Oh, reader, list! I've chartless voyaged. . . . Those who boldly launch, cast off all cables; and turning from the common breeze, that's fair for all, with their own breath, fill their own sails." The journey into "the world of mind" becomes a self-exhausting passage not to any "golden haven" but to the attenuated experience of insatiable desire: "So, if after all these fearful, fainting trances, the verdict be, the golden haven was not gained;—yet, in bold quest thereof, better to sink in boundless deeps, than float on vulgar shoals; and give me, ye gods, an utter wreck, if

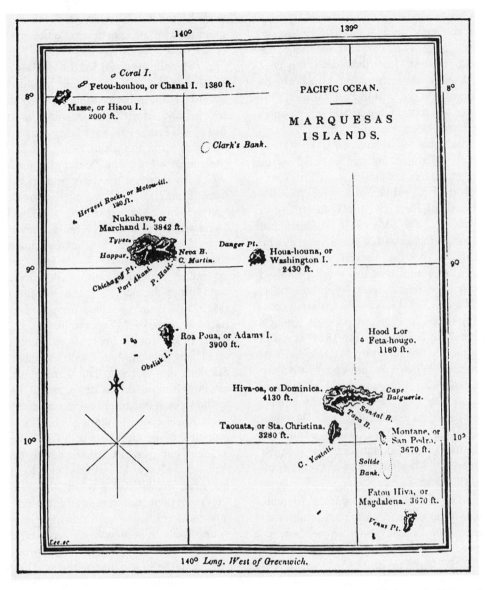

PACIFIC OCEAN.

M A R Q U E S A S
I S L A N D S.

Map of the setting for Melville's Narrative of a Four Months' Residence among the Natives of a Valley of the
Marquesas Islands *(1846), republished as* Typee *in the United States the same year
(courtesy of Special Collections, Thomas Cooper Library, University of South Carolina)*

wreck I do." Before he stumps the deck of the *Pequod,*
Ahab begins to speak in the defiant Promethean tones
of Taji. In *Mardi* Melville plants the "germinous seeds"
of his greatest fiction and poetry.

Following the completion of *Mardi,* Melville
entered a two-month period of recumbent self-satisfaction.
After mailing page proofs to Murray on 28 January
1849, which included a nonnegotiable demand for a two-
hundred-guinea advance, Melville went to Boston to
await the birth of his first child. Malcolm was born on 16
February 1849. Earlier, on 5 February, Melville had
heard Ralph Waldo Emerson speak on "Mind and Manners in the Nineteenth Century." At this time Melville
was immersing himself in Shakespeare's plays and pon-

dering the nature of literary genius. In a 3 March 1849
letter to Duyckinck, Melville included Emerson and
Shakespeare among "the whole corps of thought-divers,
that have been diving & coming up again with blood-shot
eyes since the world began." In his purchase of Pierre
Bayle's *An Historical and Critical Dictionary* (1710) Melville
found another great "thought-diver." In a 5 April 1849
letter to Duyckinck, Melville imagined himself presiding
over a three-way textual interchange: He said that he
had "bought a set of Bayle's Dictionary the other day,"
and that when he returned to New York, he intended "to
lay the great old folios side by side & go to sleep on them
thro' the summer, with the Phaedon in one hand & Tom
Brown in the other."

That *Mardi* was neither a critical nor a financial success soon became clear. In a 23 April 1849 letter to his father-in-law, Judge Lemuel Shaw, Melville discussed the mixed reviews: "I see that Mardi has been cut into by the London Atheneum, and also burnt by the common hangman in the Boston Post. However the London Examiner & Literary Gazette, and other papers this side of the water have done differently." Though wounded, Melville put on a stoical mask: "These attacks are matters of course, and are essential to the building of any permanent reputation. . . . But Time, which is the solver of all riddles, will solve 'Mardi.'" Whereas the reviewer for the 20 April 1849 edition of *New Bedford Mercury* lauds Melville's "unique but graphic description, mingled with a genial humor, philosophy, and original thought, altogether inimitable," reviewers more often found that this work promised nautical adventure but delivered metaphysical meandering. They saw *Mardi* for what it was–a collision of competing voices, intentions, and genres. George Ripley's review in the *New-York Tribune* (10 May 1849) is representative of those critics affronted by Melville's ardent embrace of romance: "We are . . . presented with a tissue of conceits, fancifully strung about the personages of the tale, expressed in language that is equally intolerable for its affectation and its obscurity. . . . [Melville] has failed by leaving his sphere, which is that of graphic, poetical narrative, and launching out into the dim, shadowy, spectral, Mardian region of mystic speculation and wizard fancies."

In the turbid wake of the failure of *Mardi,* Melville read the monetary signs of poor sales. That summer he did not doze over Plato, Bayle, and Browne. Instead, during six or more weeks in June and July 1848 he produced *Redburn,* a book based on his 1839 voyage to Liverpool. In August and September he managed the prodigious feat of composing *White-Jacket,* which was based on his experiences in the United States Navy in 1843–1844. Commenting to Shaw in a 6 October 1849 letter, Melville identified these books as "two *jobs,* which I have done for money–being forced to it, as other men are to sawing wood." In *Redburn* he repressed his "earnest desire to write those sort of books which are said to 'fail.'" Instead, he turned his attention to what he describes to Bentley as "a plain, straightforward, amusing narrative of personal experience," an entertaining tale with "no metaphysics, no conic-sections, nothing but cakes & ale." In *Redburn,* which was far more successful than the author ever admitted, Melville drew deeply from his experience of having lost his father and from his voyage as a green sailor. In *Melville's Early Life and Redburn* (1951), William H. Gilman provides the fullest account of biographical and textual intersections. The process of fictionalizing his own life issued not in

what he called a "nursery tale" but a penetrating dramatization of an experienced older man looking back on his own difficult youth.

Melville emerged from the wilds of *Mardi* with a highly refined gift for scenic compression. In consciously curbing his passion for metaphysics, Melville learned how objects can organize the thematic intensities of a scene. In *Redburn* he reveals a capacity to use things to evoke the young man's lost past. For example, the narrator casts the "old fashioned glass-ship . . . which my father, some thirty years before, had brought home from Hamburg" as an icon that expresses the fragility of his father's better days. The glass ship also stimulates the young boy's mind: "among . . . mazes of spun-glass I used to rove in imagination, till I grew dizzy at the main-truck." The past image retains its crystalline perfection only in memory; the process of time brings the father's death and the ship's dilapidation. Writing in his compositional present, the older narrator remarks, "We have her yet in the house, but many of her glass spars and ropes are now sadly shattered and broken,–but I will not have her mended." Speaking of a fallen "gallant warrior," he writes, "I will not have him put on his legs again, till I get on my own; for between him and me there is a secret sympathy."

Redburn stands among Melville's most autobiographical works–not because of its re-creation of mere incident but from its delineation of deeply felt emotional complexes. Coloring young Redburn's naiveté, for example, is a quality of obdurate misanthropy: "Talk not of the bitterness of middle-age and after life; a boy can feel all that, and much more, when upon his young soul the mildew has fallen; and the fruit, which with others is only blasted after ripeness, with him is nipped in the first blossom and bud. And never again can such blights be made good; they strike in too deep, and leave such a scar that the air of Paradise might not erase it." Shortly after his departure from home, driven by "demoniac feelings," he is angered when people on a Hudson River boat stare at his patched clothing. He points his gun at "the next gazer."

In style and incident *Redburn* owes much to Melville's reading of Washington Irving's *The Sketch Book* (1820), and the journey of his protagonist derives from Melville's familiarity with the tradition of the bildungsroman. The young man is educated into the manly world of work. After Wellingborough Redburn is nicknamed Buttons, he eschews aristocratic jargon in favor of ship-life talk. As he learns his tasks, Redburn casts off his bitterness and garners physical power. After helping to hoist "the stun'-sails to the top-sail yards," Redburn feels at one with the motion of the ship: "Every mast and timber seemed to have a pulse in it that was beating with life and joy; and I felt a wild

Oil painting by Asa W. Twitchell of Melville and a daguerreotype of his wife, Elizabeth Shaw Melville,
around the time of their marriage in 1847 (Berkshire Athenaeum)

exulting in my own heart, and felt as if I would be glad to bound along so round the world."

While in Liverpool, Redburn continues to grow in independence and self-possession. On the personal level he attempts to follow his father's outdated guide-book and realizes the stale, loosely Emersonian dictum: "Yes, the thing that had guided the father, could not guide the son." More dramatically successful is Red-burn's developing sense of social consciousness. Upon discovering a destitute mother and her three starving children, Redburn is disturbed by his inability to help them. His education also finds issue in Melville's sure-handed ability to project versions of his younger self into powerful character portraits. The displaced misanthropy of young Redburn appears full-blown in the figure of Jackson. Melville's first delineation of pri-mal depravity, Jackson is a "Cain afloat": he torments Redburn on the passage out and wastes away in sick-ness on the passage home. Redburn's youthful inepti-tude finds a counterpart in Harry Bolton. Unable to dispose of his aristocratic hauteur, Bolton fails to adapt to ship life.

On 2 July 1849 the Harpers agreed to publish *Redburn,* and on 18 August Melville sent the proofs to the American legation in London for delivery to Bent-ley, who moved quickly to protect his investment from piracy. In 1849 there was no international copyright law, and publishers were free to print any foreign book without compensating authors. The few British publish-ers of American books insisted on bringing the book out first in England in the fanciful belief that no other British publisher would pirate it. Given this uncertain state of affairs—one that would persist for half a cen-tury—American authors such as Melville had little chance of making much money. With *White-Jacket* com-pleted, Melville decided to take the Harper proof sheets to England and try to secure a contract with a large advance. On 11 October he sailed to England, prepared to stay away for nearly a year, making what he called in his journal a "grand circuit of Europe and the East." On the voyage Melville had the good luck to encounter the perfect companion. Like Melville, George J. Adler was coming off a strenuous period of intellectual exertion. Melville was fascinated by Adler's imposing scholarly mind. In his journal entry on 12 October 1849 Melville wrote, "He is author of a formidable lexicon, (German & English); in compiling which he almost ruined his health. He was almost crazy, he tells me, for a time. He is full of the German metaphysics, & discourses of Kant, Swedenborg, &c. He has been my principal companion thus far." The trip to England also gave Melville the chance to review his life. He could reexperience his feats as a sailor and rove at will in the rigging. Whereas he had worked on his first voyage as a green hand, he now traveled as a famous author. Prior to landing, as evinced by this journal entry on 4 November 1849, Melville was acutely aware of the change wrought during the last decade: "This time tomorrow I shall be on land, & press English earth after the lapse of ten years— *then* a sailor, *now* H.M. author of 'Peedee,' 'Hullabaloo' & 'Pog-Dog.'"

Once in London, Melville discovered new evidence of himself as an author. In a reading room he "happened to see 'Bentley's Miscellany' with something about Redburn . . . also saw Blackwood's long story about a short book. It's very comical—seemed so, at least as I had to hurry over it—in treating the thing as real. But the wonder is that the old Tory should waste so many pages upon a thing, which I, the author, know to be trash, & wrote it to buy some tobacco with." Melville was virtually alone in disparaging *Redburn*. On both sides of the Atlantic, reviewers hailed his return to adventure narrative. On 20 November 1849 the *Boston Post* reported, "It gives us pleasure to be able to praise this book, for we feared that the author had exhausted his vein, and that he might follow up his 'Mardi' with others of similar sort, to disgust rather than to amuse the public." N. P. Willis, the reviewer for *The New York Home Journal* and one of the few who saw *Mardi* as a great book, astutely distinguished between popular and literary reputation in a 24 November 1849 review: the "popularity of [*Redburn*] will far exceed any of the previous [books], though it will not perhaps raise the author's literary reputation from the pinnacle where Mardi placed it."

While in London, Melville went door to door on publisher's row, trying to sell *White-Jacket* for terms better than those proposed by Bentley—£200 but no advance. With rejections piling up, it became clear to Melville that he would not acquire sufficient funds to send money home and still travel extensively. In his journal on 17 November 1849 he noted, "The letter [from publisher Henry Colburn] simply declines my proposition . . . & on the ground, principally, of the cursed state of the copyright matter.—Bad news enough—I shall not see Rome—I'm floored—appetite unimpaired however."

Nor had Melville's taste for books diminished. On his book-buying rambles he revealed an inclination for four kinds of narrative—romance, autobiography, biography, and a fictional hybrid that combines personal narrative and biography. As he toured London, Melville took notes for his prospective retelling of Henry Turnbull's *Life and Remarkable Adventures of Israel Potter* (1824), which he had picked up by early fall 1849 in a cheaply printed chapbook. Of more pressing

import were acquisitions that influenced the composition of *Moby-Dick,* especially Thomas De Quincey's *The Confessions of an English Opium-Eater* (1822) and Mary Wollstonecraft Shelley's *Frankenstein, or The Modern Prometheus* (1849). He also purchased Johann Wolfgang von Goethe's *Autobiography* (1848), Jean-Jacques Rousseau's *Confessions* (1781–1788), and James Boswell's *Life of Johnson* (1839). With the disposition of *White-Jacket* on hold, Melville left England on 27 November and made a brief trip to France, Belgium, and Germany, returning to London on 13 December. On 15 December Melville accepted Bentley's offer before sailing home on 25 December from Portsmouth on the *Independence.*

White-Jacket; or The World in a Man-of-War was published in London by Bentley on 2 February 1850 and in New York by the Harpers on 9 March 1850. According to Willard Thorpe's "Historical Note" to the Northwestern-Newberry edition of *White-Jacket* (1970), "Melville appropriated passages from other writers, but the number of his extensive pillages for *White-Jacket* is exceeded only by those in *Moby-Dick*. These furnished him germinal ideas for scenes or factual information in at least thirty of his ninety-four chapters." Writing in the *New-Orleans Commercial Bulletin* (29 March 1850) Melville's friend Oakey Hall contended that *White-Jacket* "was dashed off in a score of sittings, yet possesses the air of Irving's elaboration." Such a performance is possible given what seems to have been Melville's compositional practice. In his 1996 biography of Melville, Parker speculates that Melville "spent two days or so laying out a set of sources for the next narrative sequence . . . then on the third day he wrote furiously." As reported by Thorpe, Melville's major sources include Nathaniel Ames's *A Mariner's Sketches* (1830); the United States Articles of War; Thomas Hodgskin's "Abolition of Impressment," in *The Edinburgh Review* (October 1824, pp. 154–181); Francis Jeffrey's review of *A Selection from the Public and Private Correspondence of Vice-Admiral Lord Collingwood* by G. L. Newnham Collingwood in *The Edinburgh Review* (May 1828, pp. 385–418); Samuel Leech's *Thirty Years from Home, or A Voice from the Main Deck . . .* (1843); *Life on Board a Man-of-War; Including a Full Account of the Battle of Navarino. By a British Seaman* (1829); *Life in a Man-of-War or Scenes in "Old Ironsides" During Her Cruise in the Pacific. By a Fore-Top-Man* (1841); William McNally's *Evils and Abuses in the Naval and Merchant Service, Exposed . . .* (1839); and *The Penny Cyclopaedia of the Society for the Diffusion of Useful Knowledge* (1833–1843).

White-Jacket is held together by a loosely structured narrative frame. Melville tells the story of a young man's homeward-bound cruise on the *Neversink,* a United States man-of-war. The first-person narrator dons a strange white jacket that becomes not only his name but also the ambiguous envelope of his identity.

of the book now in hand, whether the whole subject in new attractions & combining in one cluster all that is romantic, whimsical & poetic in Polynesia. It is yet a continuous narrative. I doubt not that — if it makes the hit I mean it to — it will be counted a rather bold aim, ~~& it another~~ but nevertheless, it shall have the right stuff in it, to redeem its faults, tho' they were legion.

All this to be sure, is confidential — & egotistical — decidedly the latter.

Upon the whole, allow me to suggest, that possibly, you may not form as high an idea of the book _now_, as when you may, when you see it.

And therefore, unless something unforeseen occurs, I may decide to allow the whole matter to rest where it is. And without seeking the _direct_ ness of any other London publisher, wait

Page from a 1 January 1848 letter Melville wrote to Murray concerning Melville's novel Mardi. *Murray rejected the work, which was published in 1849 by another London firm (courtesy of John Murray Ltd., London).*

The jacket separates the narrator from the masses and imbues him with a distinct nonuniform appearance. Just what this identity might be is not entirely clear, though the jacket seems designed to project the enigmatic public form behind which the narrator's truculent, often humorous, polemical self remains hidden. Unlike *Redburn, White-Jacket* does not delineate the protagonist's initiation into the social sphere. The narrator of *White-Jacket* is already at home in the world. His personal story depicts his relationship with his fellow foretopmen, especially the heroic Jack Chase and the poet Lemsford. There are two moments of intense personal crisis. One occurs when White-Jacket is found to be away from his station and comes close to being flogged. At the moment of greatest conflict he contemplates murdering the captain and then committing suicide. This imagined event focuses Melville's polemical exposé of the barbarous evil of flogging. In the second instance, White-Jacket tumbles from the yardarm into the sea. In imminent danger of drowning, he cuts himself out of his entangling jacket and rises to the surface, seemingly reborn. Never having suffered such a fall himself, Melville rewrote the scene from Ames's *A Mariner's Sketches*. Melville's sources and numerous redactions are extensively explored in Howard P. Vincent's *The Tailoring of Melville's White-Jacket* (1970).

Essentially, not only does Melville, through the narrator's journey, dramatize his polemical exposé of naval abuses and topical revelations about everyday ship life, but throughout the book he also presents the ship as a microcosm of the world: "As a man-of-war that sails through the sea, so this earth that sails through the air. We mortals are all on board a fast-sailing, never-sinking world-frigate, of which God was the shipwright; and she is but one craft in a Milky-Way fleet, of which God is the Lord High Admiral." This highly literate narrator is, like Ishmael in *Moby-Dick,* always on the hunt for resonant significations. Repeatedly, the narrator embarks on a series of essayistic excursions, whereby he ponders everyday objects and activities in metaphysical terms. In fact, White-Jacket defines philosophy as the ongoing, uncertain process of "concocting information into wisdom." The philosophical act is not a matter of propounding a priori truths but an engagement with the sullied complexities of lived experience: "For after all, philosophy—that is, the best wisdom that has ever in any way been revealed to our man-of-war world—is but a slough and a mire, with a few tufts of good footing here and there." The narrator's extensive and learned allusions imbue him with intellectual authority—an authority that supports him in his polemical and metaphysical excursions. Insistently, he *judges:* he parodies transcendentalism; he critiques the practice

of religion in a "castle of war"; and he mocks the chaplain's hypocritical intellectualism.

White-Jacket received almost unanimous praise. The reviewer for London's *John Bull* on 2 February 1850 lauds the author's maturity and depth: "[Melville] is no longer the wonder boy that used to give the rein to his wit and fancy, indulging . . . in that smart dare-devil style of remark which perverts, while it dazzles, the mind . . . the rattling youngster has grown into the thoughtful man." The reviewer for *The London Morning Post* (12 February 1850) admires Melville as "strikingly original. . . . The writer's superiority is the more marked from his not having drawn upon his imagination to the usual extent, but having given us incidents of real life." In the Boston *Daily Evening Transcript,* a reviewer on 25 March 1850 finds the new work "in the best vein of the author of 'Typee' and 'Omoo.'" The reviewer for the *New Bedford Mercury* (4 April 1850) offers a deft insight into the curious class inversions that animate Melville's sensibility: "[White-Jacket] is to the navy what Dana's book *[Two Years Before the Mast]* is to the merchant service—a revelation of the internal economy of a man-of-war, written by one by birth and breeding fitted to comprehend the feelings and sympathies of the quarter-deck; by position and experience part and parcel with the forecastle."

As the many reviews of *White-Jacket* appeared from late January through July 1850, Melville was hard at work on his new book. In a 1 May 1850 letter to Richard Henry Dana Jr., Melville made the first surviving mention of *Moby-Dick:* "About the 'whaling voyage'—I am half way in the work. . . . It will be a strange sort of a book, tho', I fear; blubber is blubber you know; tho' you may get oil out of it, the poetry runs as hard as sap from a frozen maple tree;—& to cook the thing up, one must needs throw in a little fancy, which from the nature of the thing, must be ungainly as the gambols of the whales themselves. Yet I mean to give the truth of the thing, spite of this." Although claiming to have been "half way in the work," Melville did not finish the book until late July 1851, fifteen months later. The disparity has established the chronological perimeters within which scholars have speculated on the genesis of the work. Melville's claim in the Dana letter apparently had reference to an early intention that was extensively modified and reshaped by the procreant processes of writing, reading, and living. In "'Unnecessary Duplicates': A Key to the Writing of *Moby-Dick*" (*New Perspectives on Melville* [1979]), Harrison Hayford suggests that the presence of duplicated elements—"two narrative starts, two whaling ports, two inns . . . two innkeepers, two beds and goings-to-bed, two comrades . . . two signings-aboard, two Quaker captain-owners and a third Quaker captain-in-command," among other replications—indicates the textual fusion of a vestigial narrative with its redesigned complement and extension. On this ur-voyage a narrator and his companion (probably Bulkington) might have gone to sea under a crusty, possibly peg-legged captain (Peleg). This narrative probably had close affinities with Melville's anatomical treatment of the man-of-war world in *White-Jacket*. The marvelous events of the sperm-whale fishery, especially the expository materials and action scenes associated with the cetological sections of *Moby-Dick,* may have supplied the basis upon which Melville imposed his new design. Sometime after 1 May 1850 Melville began telling his narrator's story about a maimed whaling captain and a great white whale based on several whaling legends, most notably the tale of Mocha Dick. At some point Melville called his narrator Ishmael.

What led Melville from a documentary fiction about whales to one of the greatest narratives ever written can only be seen as the consequence of many forces. First is Melville's experience of having written his first five books—with all their accumulated borrowing and transformation of sources—and his success in recasting his basic repertoire: the dramatic presentation of a tyro actor by his more experienced self; the collision of multiple cultures; the preoccupation with containing the world in a book; a penchant for using specific subjects to focus short chapters that combine action and exposition; a quest structure, specifically the transformation of quester Taji and ethereal Yillah, respectively, into angry Captain Ahab and magnificent Moby-Dick; the all-important adaptation of new source material; and the neighborly presence and example of Hawthorne.

Throughout the composition of *Moby-Dick,* Melville augmented his already compendious reading with new works. Howard P. Vincent in *The Trying-Out of Moby-Dick* (1948) provides the fullest examination of Melville's use of whaling sources. Of special note is Melville's acquisition of Thomas Beale's *The Natural History of the Sperm Whale* (1839), Owen Chase's *Narrative of the Most Extraordinary and Distressing Shipwreck of the Whale-Ship Essex* (1821), and William Scoresby's *An Account of the Arctic Regions . . .* (1820) and *Journal of a Voyage to the Northern Whale Fishery* (1823). Beyond the discernible presence of whaling sources, *Moby-Dick* includes a symphony of literary resonations. Along with sonorous rhythms of biblical phrasing, one finds pervasive echoes of Shakespearean language and recurrent expressions of Christian and Platonic idealism. Along with the specific impress of Emerson, De Quincey, Mary Shelley, and Thomas Carlyle, discussed in John Wenke's *Melville's Muse: Literary Creation and the Forms of Philosophical Fiction* (1995), Melville also relied heavily on Homer, Virgil, Milton, Greek tragedy, Christopher Marlowe, Montaigne, Browne, Byron,

Coleridge, and Wordsworth. As Thomas Vargish in his 1966 article "Gnostick Mythos in *Moby-Dick*" and Dorothy Metlitsky Finkelstein in *Melville's Orienda* (1961) make clear, the novel harbors a host of exotic philosophies, most notably Gnosticism, Zoroastrianism, and Hinduism. Melville's extensive adaptations of visual arts have only recently received careful attention, as witnessed in Sten's *Savage Eye: Melville and the Visual Arts* (1991), Robert K. Wallace's *Melville & Turner: Spheres of Love and Fright* (1992), Elizabeth A. Schultz's *Unpainted to the Last: Moby-Dick and Twentieth-Century American Art* (1995), and Douglas Robillard's *Melville and the Visual Arts: Ionian Form, Venetian Tint* (1997).

Despite the range and complexity of materials that impinged on the creation of *Moby-Dick,* the event most instrumental in driving Melville to the realization of literary greatness can be identified. On 5 August 1850, while on vacation at his cousin Robert Melvill's farm in Pittsfield, Melville met Hawthorne during a picnic excursion to Monument Mountain in the company of Evert Duyckinck and Cornelius Matthews. During this exhilarating day of scaling cliffs and quaffing champagne, even the usually reserved Hawthorne was reported in a 6 August 1850 letter by Duyckinck to his wife to have "looked wildly about for the great Carbuncle." The reclusive Hawthorne invited Melville to spend a few days with him and his family at their rented cottage in nearby Lenox. For his part Melville was so excited by Hawthorne that he quickly scanned a copy of Hawthorne's *Mosses from an Old Manse* (1846) and on 9 and 10 August 1850 he dashed off "Hawthorne and His Mosses" for publication in Duyckinck's *Literary World* on 17 and 24 August.

This essay is less a review of a four-year-old book that Melville barely read than a self-advertising manifesto announcing the emerging possibilities of American literature. Celebrating Hawthorne's "great power of blackness," Melville calls himself forth to assume the role of the American Shakespeare. He saw the forty-six-year-old Hawthorne as a kindred spirit, a compensatory presence, a personal muse, and a perfect audience. Perhaps Melville's lost father and lost older brother seemed to achieve stunning apotheosis in this new friend and artistic peer. Melville's essay and his letters to Hawthorne trumpet the exuberant dynamics of their friendship, especially Hawthorne's capacity to elicit from Melville the unmasked processes of his mind in motion. In these letters Melville wrote without reserve. They offer the clearest manifestation of the agitated energies impelling him to complete his "mighty book." For example, in a [16 April?] 1851 letter, Melville's description of "what so strongly characterizes" Hawthorne's work provides a self-reflexive summary of Melville's sense of his own mission as a

First two pages of Melville's copy of his contract with Harper and Brothers (Melville Collection, Houghton Library, Harvard University)

Melville shall be paid by the notes of the said Harper and Brothers at three months from those dates, or in cash interest off

Fifth: This agreement shall continue for seven years from the day of publication by said Harpers & Brothers at the expiration of which time the said Herman Melville shall have the right to the possession and complete ownership of the stereotype plates of the said work on paying to the said Harper and Brothers one half of their original cost deducting a fair valuation for the wear and tear they may have sustained in their use or injury from other causes: Upon which payment which may be made at anytime after the expiration of the said seven years the said stereotype plates shall belong to the said Herman Melville as his sole property.

Sixth. The said Harper and Brothers are to have the right to dispose of all copies of said work remaining on hand at the expiration of this agreement, they accounting upon the sale of said copies as herein provided.

Seventh. It is distinctly understood that this agreement refers solely to the publication of said work in the United States of America – In witness whereof the parties hereto have hereunto subscribed their names this twelfth day of September one thousand eight hundred and fifty one –

                    Harper & Brothers.

                    Herman Melville
                    per Allan Melville his atty

beleaguered artist, a defiant risk taker, and possibly a tragic martyr. By suggesting that Hawthorne expresses "the intense feeling of the visable [sic] truth," Melville sketches the outlines of Ahab's character and also defines the high office of the truth-telling writer: "By visable [sic] truth, we mean the apprehension of the absolute condition of present things as they strike the eye of the man who fears them not, though they do their worst to him,—the man who, like Russia or the British Empire, declares himself a sovereign nature (in himself) amid the powers of heaven, hell, and earth." Melville's letters were no doubt continuations of his and Hawthorne's expansive conversations. In his journal on 1 August 1851 Hawthorne wrote, "After supper, I put Julian to bed; and Melville and I had a talk about time and eternity, things of this world and of the next, and books, and publishers, and all possible and impossible matters, that lasted pretty deep into the night." As his letters, as evinced by this quote from 29 June 1851, make clear, Melville viewed his and Hawthorne's relationship as a spiritually and emotionally charged outpouring of "ontological heroics."

Given Hawthorne's presence in Lenox and Melville's lifelong love of the Berkshires, it is no wonder that Melville bought from John Brewster the farm adjacent to the Melvill estate. After moving his family to the farm he named Arrowhead, he settled into recasting his whaling book. With financial pressures mounting, driven especially by his inability to complete the down payment, Melville responded to the Harpers' refusal to tender him an advance by borrowing $2,050 from his Lansingburgh friend T. D. Stewart and using the money to escape foreclosure and make renovations. Like his father, Melville used borrowed money to weave a fragile, porous semblance of fiscal security. Nevertheless, by 1 August 1851, his thirty-second birthday, Melville had completed his greatest work. After 9 September he signed an agreement for Bentley to publish *The Whale,* though Melville's decision to change the title reached the publisher too late. On 18 October 1851 *The Whale* was published in London, lacking the "Epilogue." This odd accident gave British readers the impression that the first-person narrator went down with the ship. On 14 November 1851, less than a month after the birth of Melville's second child, Stanwix, *Moby-Dick; or, The Whale* was published in New York.

Despite exhaustive critical commentary and indefatigable scholarly investigation, this haunting masterwork continues to loom, through every rereading, as a strange mystery unfolding before one's eyes. In *Moby-Dick* "the flood-gates of the wonder-world swung open" and the reader was launched upon the deep. Melville wrote *Moby-Dick* so that it would seem to par-

ticipate in the reader's passing moment. The opening words of the narrative, "Call me Ishmael," evoke a conversational intimacy that positions the reader as an intellectual and emotional participant in two unfolding adventures—one adventure that *was* experienced by Ishmael "Some years ago—never mind how long precisely," and the other adventure enacted through the seeming spontaneity of Ishmael's mock-oral narrative. Much of the energy of the book derives from his attempt to explore the meaning of his voyage in the very activity of writing about it. Near the end of "Loomings," for example, while trying to comprehend why the Fates assigned him "this shabby part of a whaling voyage," Ishmael ponders, "yet, now that I recall all the circumstances, I think I can see a little into the springs and motives which being cunningly presented to me under varying disguises, induced me to set about performing the part I did." Ishmael fuses his retrospective, past-tense account with the (apparent) spontaneity of his compositional performance. What is Ishmael doing? He is writing a book in the guise of speaking it. He is, for example, not only dramatizing his meeting with kindly cannibal Queequeg and detailing his participation in Ahab's pursuit of cosmic vengeance, but he is also contemplating the multiple meanings of mundane, profane, and apocalyptic events. By taking the reader from Manhattan to New Bedford to Nantucket and then out to sea, Ishmael reveals a world growing increasingly strange, alluring, exotic, and dangerous.

Melville's structural principle cannot be summarized better than through Ishmael's self-referential claim: "a careful disorderliness is the true method." The first twenty-three chapters delineate Ishmael's journey to Nantucket, concluding when the multicultural crew "gave three heavy-hearted cheers; and blindly plunged like fate into the lone Atlantic." Throughout these early chapters, Ishmael not only meets Queequeg, but he also foregrounds three central elements of the book: the whale, Ahab, and the voyage. In evoking the whale, Ishmael presents in "Etymology" a late consumptive usher's list of lingual versions of the word *whale.* In "Extracts" Ishmael offers a sub-sub-librarian's collection of ostensibly "random allusions to whales." The reader immediately confronts two facts: any word is a relative sign; and the experience of whales finds issue in many literary texts, some of which are less inaccurate than others. Ishmael thereby directs the reader's attention to the basic semiotics of existence: how might one inscribe, though not fully know, the always partial meanings of experience? The ensuing search for any sperm whale and Ahab's quest for the great white whale assume the form of a language experience in which words, words, words chart the limitations of Ishmael's epistemological pursuit. Captain Ahab first

First page of a letter dated 29 January 1851 from Melville to his friend Nathaniel Hawthorne (Harry Ransom Humanities Research Center, University of Texas at Austin)

looms in the reader's imagination through Ishmael's conversation with Captain Peleg and Bildad and then through enigmatic predictions of Elijah, the cracked prophet of doom. A "grand, ungodly, god-like man," Ahab possesses "greatly superior natural force, with a globular brain and a ponderous heart"; he is one who has learned to speak "a bold and nervous lofty language." The voyage itself appears both as a "wonder-world" powerful enough to induce "mystical vibrations" and a "prospect [that] was unlimited, but exceedingly monotonous and forbidding; not the slightest variety that I could see." Ishmael leads the companionate reader to ponder the magnetic, mystical attraction of water, especially its capacity to reveal one's own alluring yet dangerous reflection: "And still deeper the meaning of that story of Narcissus, who because he could not grasp the tormenting, mild image he saw in the fountain, plunged into it and was drowned. But that same image, we ourselves see in all rivers and oceans. It is the image of the ungraspable phantom of life; and this is the key to it all." By imaging the sea as a double of the human self, the "story of Narcissus" symbolizes the human attempt to embrace the elusive Absolute. Throughout the narrative Ishmael marries empirical fact and metaphysical speculation, the phenomenal world of concrete objects and the noumenal world of ideal signification. In chapter 23, "The Lee Shore," Ishmael makes explicit the cosmic implications of "the lashed sea's landlessness": all deep, earnest thinking is but the intrepid effort of the soul to keep the open independence of her sea."

Once the *Pequod* is out to sea Ishmael brings together reciprocal narrative strategies. In *Hawthorne, Melville, and the Novel* (1976) Richard H. Brodhead examines the "suspenseful and linear story that leads toward a completion in Ahab's encounter with the white whale and a jerky, digressive, constitutionally incomplete narrative that traces Ishmael's effort to get to know the whale." In the chapter "The Quarter-deck" Ahab describes the metaphysical justification that impels his obsession. As Michael E. Levin argues in "Ahab as Socratic Philosopher: The Myth of the Cave Inverted" (1979), Ahab is an inverted Platonist. Like any Platonist, he sees the world as a sign of invisible forms. He believes, however, that malice—not beneficence—animates the "pasteboard masks" of material forms. Thus, Ahab's unwavering pursuit is designed to defeat the "unknown but still reasoning thing" that reveals its nature from behind "the unreasoning mask." To emphasize Ahab's forceful character, Ishmael often presents Ahab's scenes in dramatic form replete with stage directions. Indeed, Ahab is a histrionic figure, and the wide ocean is his egocentric theater. Consequently, the nine gams, or meetings, that the *Pequod* has with other ships underscore the linear structure of Ahab's dramaturgy. Each meeting anticipates that stunning moment late in the novel when Moby-Dick first appears.

As a self-empowering Prometheus, Ahab seeks to redeem his "whole race from Adam down." But given such a momentous and dangerous premise, Ahab should not be seen as a raving lunatic: he is a monomaniac—crazy about one thing. Every reader is charged to remember Captain Peleg's crucial, qualifying description: "stricken, blasted if he be, Ahab has his humanities." These "humanities" drive the linear plot and challenge him to enunciate greater justifications. Late in the novel Ahab expresses outrage over Pip's cosmic abandonment: "There can be no hearts about the snow-line. Oh, ye frozen heavens! look down here. Ye did beget this luckless child, and have abandoned him, ye creative libertines." In the chapter "The Symphony" Ahab looks into Starbuck's "human eye" and seems to waver in his fearful purpose.

Unlike Ahab, Ishmael wavers constantly. Though vowing to join Ahab's "fiery hunt," Ishmael possesses a flexible, humorous sensibility. He accepts the "universal thump" and considers a multitude of concerns. For example, he tirelessly details an encyclopedic anatomy of whaling. The many chapters on cetology provide documentary exhibitions of the whalemen's grueling workaday life. Whereas Ahab craves culmination, climax, and completion, Ishmael celebrates the seemingly endless quality of physical work. He also revels in his inability to achieve complete knowledge. Insistently, Ishmael casts himself and others as readers pondering inscrutable surfaces and sounding unfathomable depths. Ishmael's central epistemological activity emerges in repeated scenes of reading—from Ishmael's explication of the painting in The Spouter Inn, to his analysis of "The Whiteness of the Whale," to his attempts to interpret the hieroglyphic markings on the whale's body, to the self-reflexive tableau dramatized in the chapter "The Doubloon." Given the enormity of Melville's achievement, all *Moby-Dick* criticism seems to be little more than compendious endnotes to Ishmael's own recognition of the inadequacy of human investigation: When in the chapter "The Fountain," Ishmael is confronted by the apparently simple, though actually difficult, problem of knowing what spouts from the whale, he observes, "Still, we can hypothesize, even if we cannot prove and establish."

In mid October 1851, after completing the harvest on his farm, Melville began *Pierre; or, The Ambiguities* with an exuberant sense of possibility. He hoped that this new book would succeed in the vast, lucrative market catering to female readers of romances. In mid November he broke his rigid writing schedule and took Hawthorne to lunch in the Curtis Hotel in

Melville's first five books, published between 1846 and 1850

Lenox. There Hawthorne received a copy of the whaling book, opened it, and read the dedication, "In token of my admiration for his genius, This Book is inscribed to Nathaniel Hawthorne." A few days later in November Melville responded to Hawthorne's "joy-giving and exultation-breeding letter" and made the tactical blunder of dissuading Hawthorne from writing a review. *Moby-Dick* was blistered in some reviews for its heterogenous style, focus, and genre and blasted in others for its irreverence toward conventional religion. Like most writers, Melville took bad reviews more seriously than good ones. He was personally offended by Duyckinck's critical assault on the inconsistencies in the novel and his dismissive treatment of the metaphysical pursuits of the novel. Such attacks wounded Melville in ways that the predominant number of laudatory–even spectacular–reviews did not assuage. The reviewer for the *Spirit of the Times* (6 December 1851) was not alone in identifying the book as "a work of exceeding power, beauty, and genius." Despite evidence that *Moby-Dick* was reaching receptive readers, Melville was angered by Pittsfield gossip that vilified the book as "more than blasphemous."

Melville completed *Pierre* on the last day of 1851 and took the manuscript to New York City, where it was read by the Harpers in the early days of the new year. The mixed reviews and slow sales of *Moby-Dick* conspired with the Harpers' distress over the subject matter of *Pierre,* a book that Melville oddly referred to in the 8 January 1852 letter to Hawthorne's wife, Sophia, as "a rural bowl of milk." A young man from a wealthy upstate New York family believes he discovers his late father's illegitimate daughter. Overtly impelled by idealism but inwardly drawn by incestuous yearning, Pierre casts off his fair-haired fiancée, Lucy Tartan, in order to "champion" his supposed half sister–the beautiful, dark-haired, strange, and possibly insane Isabel. Pierre's rescue of Isabel takes the form of their fictitious marriage. This role is played out with disastrous consequences. Disowned by his haughty mother and banished from his ancestral home, Pierre moves to New York City with Isabel and Delly Ulver, a disgraced young woman. In the city, a morbidly transfigured Lucy Tartan joins the household. Having adopted a nunlike manner, she seems almost maniacal. At one point she paints a portrait of Pierre, which, when unveiled, finds him cast as a skeleton.

Throughout the novel the narrator delineates the limitations and essential folly of Pierre's version of philosophical idealism–his irrepressible resolution to risk everything on intimations derived from a naive sense of truth. Pierre's conscious mind works at cross-purposes to the shadowy recesses of his unconscious soul: "From without, no wonderful effect is wrought within ourselves, unless some interior, responding wonder meets it." Insistently, the narrator explores the province of fate, essentially the unwilled dictates of one's being. With the discovery of "infernal catacombs of thought" Pierre is overwhelmed: "He felt that what he had always before considered the solid land of veritable reality, was now being audaciously encroached upon by bannered armies of hooded phantoms, disembarking in his soul, as from flotillas of specter-boats." Pierre's idealistic mission has the effect of circumscribing personal power. Ultimately, he becomes "the fool of Truth, the fool of Virtue, the fool of Fate." In a world strafed by moral expediency, Pierre's incestuous compulsions and self-destructive philosophical awakenings challenge the practicability of Christian virtue.

In combining sexual dysfunction, metaphysical excursions, and apparent blasphemy, Melville seemed bent on smashing every icon he could find. Horrified by what they read, the Harpers still viewed Melville as a potentially profitable writer. But they attempted to cut their mounting losses, offering Melville a contract that would pay only 20¢ on the dollar after costs—down from their previous terms of 50¢ on the dollar. In a desperate attempt to escape the Harpers, Melville took the manuscript to Duyckinck, who less than a month before had slashed *Moby-Dick* in the *Literary World*. His pious sensibilities affronted, Duyckinck refused to help. Years passed before these friends fully reconciled. Stunned and angered, Melville exacted revenge. Over the next three weeks he expanded his manuscript by 150 pages and savaged the publishing establishment in general and his former friend in particular. The specious hinge that linked the new material to the once-finished narrative was the surprising announcement that Pierre had been a feted juvenile author. With this background established, Melville dramatizes the terrible consequences of Pierre's immature attempt to write a "Mature Book." In the expanded version, Melville (in the voice of the narrator) mocks Pierre as he slaves at his desk and castigates philosophers for daring to propose a "Talismanic secret" that might solve the riddles of existence.

Far from being the taut psychological exploration of a failed idealist that Melville had intended, the completed *Pierre* was a compendium of outlandish premises skittering wildly in collision. Melville's primal scream cured no ills; it merely undermined his professional standing. Like the Harpers, Richard Bentley was a businessman interested in limiting his losses. In a 4 March 1852 letter, Bentley informed Melville that he had lost £68 on *Mardi*, £76 on *Redburn*, £173 on *White-Jacket*, and £135 on *The Whale*. For *Pierre* Bentley offered publication with no advance, "yielding to you half the profits as they arrive." He also wished to expurgate the manuscript so that it might be "properly appreciated" in England. Since Melville rejected these terms, no English edition of *Pierre* exists, though Harper's London agent, Sampson Low, made available some copies of the American edition.

Except for friendly puffs from the *Lansingburgh Gazette* and *The New York Sun,* reviewers incinerated *Pierre*—and did so with venomous gusto. The *Boston Post* (4 August 1852) calls it "perhaps, the craziest fiction extant. It has scenes and descriptions of unmistakable power. . . . But the amount of utter trash in the volume is almost infinite—trash of conception, execution, dialogue and sentiment." In the *Boston Daily Times,* Charles Creighton Hazewell writes, "No man has more foolishly abused great original powers than the author of this singular work." Duyckinck did not take well to being skewered as the thinly disguised joint editor of *Captain Kidd Monthly*. In the *Literary World* on 21 August 1852 he describes the book as "a confused phantasmagoria of distorted fancies and conceits, ghostly abstractions and fitful shadows." A headline on 7 September 1852 in the *New-York Day-Book* blares, "Herman Melville Crazy."

Though *Pierre* destroyed Melville's reputation, he did not give up on being a novelist. While on a vacation in Nantucket with Judge Shaw in July 1852, Melville heard the story of Agatha Hatch, a woman who rescued and married a shipwrecked sailor, who then deserted her. Through the last half of 1852, while absorbing the hostile reception of *Pierre,* Melville tried to persuade Hawthorne to fictionalize the "Agatha" materials. In mid December Melville visited Hawthorne, who now lived in Concord, Massachusetts. In the last few years Hawthorne had written *The Scarlet Letter* (1850), *The House of the Seven Gables* (1851), *The Blithedale Romance* (1852), and, most recently, a campaign biography celebrating the life of his friend Franklin Pierce, the newly elected president of the United States. Reluctant to start a literary project, Hawthorne was waiting to receive his share of the spoils and soon did so in the form of a lucrative consulship to Liverpool. Melville took up the project himself and by late May 1853—the week his daughter Elizabeth was born—he completed the Agatha story and called it "The Isle of the Cross." Melville offered it to the Harpers, who refused to publish it; there is no record of Melville's submitting the work to another house. The fullest account of the circumstances relating to this lost (and probably destroyed) novel can be found in Parker's March 1990 article in *American Liter-*

ature, "Herman Melville's *The Isle of the Cross:* A Survey and a Chronology."

Following his failure to secure a consular appointment, Melville started writing short fiction in the spring of 1853. In the "Historical Note" to the Northwestern-Newberry edition of *The Piazza Tales and Other Prose Pieces* (1987) Sealts documents the probable order of composition, which does not correspond to the sequence of publication. In late spring and summer of 1853 Melville wrote "Cock-A-Doodle-Doo!," "The Happy Failure," "The Fiddler," and "Bartleby, the Scrivener." In December 1853 "Cock-A-Doodle-Doo!" appeared in *Harper's New Monthly Magazine* followed by "The Happy Failure" and "The Fiddler" in July and September 1854, respectively. "Bartleby, the Scrivener" was published in *Putnam's Monthly Magazine* in November and December 1853. By November, Melville was planning a new book, which he called "Tortoise Hunting Adventure," perhaps with the notion of returning to the vein of *Typee* and *Omoo*. On 24 November 1853 Melville wrote to the Harpers, claiming to have completed three hundred pages and requesting (and receiving) a $300 advance. With Melville's letter was a separate sheet in the hand of bookkeeper William Demarest listing the sale figures for Melville's novels: *Typee,* 1,779; *Omoo,* 6,328; *Mardi,* 2,544; *Redburn,* 4,316; *White-Jacket,* 4,145; *Moby-Dick,* 2,771; and *Pierre,* 1,916. But on 10 December 1853 another disaster occurred: the Harpers' warehouse burned, and the inventory was destroyed, though the plates of Melville's books survived. In a 22 May 1856 letter to Judge Shaw, Melville claimed that the fire cost him about $1,000.

In fall and winter Melville may have worked on his "tortoise" book, which he never finished. Material on tortoise hunting, however, does appear in "The Encantadas," which was published in *Putnam's* in March, April, and May 1854. By spring Melville had completed "Poor Man's Pudding and Rich Man's Crumbs," which was published in *Harper's* in June 1854, and "The Paradise of Bachelors and the Tartarus of Maids," which was paid for in May 1854 but not published in *Harper's* until April 1855. "The Lightning-Rod Man" and "The Two Temples" also belong to this period; the former tale was published in *Putnam's* in August 1854, and the latter was rejected with apologies by *Putnam's*. Following editor Charles F. Briggs's citation of the impious slant of the tale, Melville apparently did not try to place it elsewhere. "Jimmy Rose" and "The 'Gees" were written in late summer or fall of 1854, though "Jimmy Rose" did not appear in *Harper's* until November 1855 and "The 'Gees" was not published in *Harper's* until March 1856.

While still writing for the magazine market, Melville returned to the novel. In the spring and early

First American editions of Melville's masterpiece about Captain Ahab and the white whale (1851), the novel on the theme of incest that destroyed his reputation (1852), and his poems about the Civil War (1866)

summer of 1854 he worked on *Israel Potter,* which was published serially in *Putnam's* from July 1854 through March 1855. On 2 March 1855 Melville's fourth child and second daughter, Frances, was born. Having achieved such good results from *Israel Potter,* Melville moved next to recasting material from chapter 18 of Captain Amasa Delano's *Narrative of Voyages and Travels in the Northern and Southern Hemisphere* (1817). The result was *Benito Cereno.* It was written through the winter of 1854–1855, submitted to *Putnam's* by mid April, and then published in October, November, and December 1855. In spring 1855 Melville wrote "The Bell-Tower" and "I and My Chimney." "The Bell Tower" appeared in *Putnam's* in August 1855 and "I and My Chimney" appeared in *Putnam's* in March 1856. By fall 1855 Melville had sent to *Putnam's* "The Apple-Tree Table; or, Original Spiritual Manifestations," which appeared in May 1856. By February 1856 Melville had completed "The Piazza" as the lead story for a collection of tales and submitted to Dix and Edwards, who published *The Piazza Tales* in May 1856. (Sheila Post-Lauria gives an extended discussion of Melville's career as a magazine writer in *Correspondent Colorings: Melville in the Marketplace* [1996]).

By any artistic measure Melville's relatively brief immersion into the periodical market bore spectacular results. Scholars and critics have devoted most attention to "Bartleby, the Scrivener" and *Benito Cereno*. In "Bartleby, the Scrivener" the lawyer-narrator tells the strange story of a strange legal copyist who unsettled the lawyer's snug world with an intractable willfulness cast in the mildest tones: "I would prefer not to." For whatever reason, if any, Bartleby "would prefer not to" perform any task he did not wish to do, however appropriate or commonsensical the task might seem. The lawyer's narration of Bartleby's behavior has agitated a seemingly irreconcilable critical debate over the lawyer's status as narrator, employer, and human being as well as the cause and meaning of Bartleby's enigmatic reserve. Bartleby remains, in fact, the most impenetrable subject in all of Melville's fiction, though he has inspired a broad range of determinate explanations. He has been seen as an embodiment of the alienated and abused worker; the neglected and misunderstood artist; an archetypal lost soul; and even a version of Jesus of Nazareth. The frustrating history of "Bartleby" criticism—which is deftly summarized and critiqued in Stern's "Toward 'Bartleby the Scrivener,'" in *The Stoic Strain in American Literature* (1979)—reveals that no gestalt or paradigm brings to light the hidden recesses of Bartleby's psyche. Clearly, some pathology afflicts him. Indeed, Bartleby could be described (not explained) as clinically depressed, anorexic, and/or agoraphobic. Crucially, however, and central to Melville's strategy in the tale, Bartleby seems to know what he is about and at every point wills his oxymoronic negations. The scrivener's "cadaverously gentlemanly *nonchalance*" alternately stuns, teases, disgusts, enrages, exasperates, depresses, frightens, and amuses the lawyer (italics in original). This blustering and blundering man—the reader's only source of knowledge—dramatizes his failed attempt to find a language that can explain unspeakable misery.

If "Bartleby, the Scrivener" takes the reader toward the hidden involutions of unreachable, incurable pathology, then *Benito Cereno* conducts the reader through the benighted complacency of Captain Amasa Delano toward an encapsulation of the courtship by colonialism of apocalyptic destruction. After Delano's ship, the *Bachelor's Delight,* encounters the enigmatic *San Dominick,* showing no colors and drifting with the tides not far from Chile's southern coast, Melville delineates the complex intersection of the self-serving and facile innocence of America with the historical facts of New World slavery and the brutal realpolitik of colonization. On the *San Dominick* a slave uprising has occurred, and Delano is ideologically incapable of recognizing the key to the "spectacle of disorder" playing before him.

In reading this narrative, one must devote careful attention to Melville's complex point(s) of view. The third-person narrator depicts dramatic surfaces as they appear to the eye. These surfaces suggest the fact of a slave rebellion, but the narrator does not overtly state it. Indeed, the truth of the story—and the truth underlying ruthless power politics masquerading as divine right of rule—is actually concentrated in the figure carved on the stern piece of the *San Dominick:* "But the principal relic of faded grandeur was the ample oval of the shield-like stern-piece, intricately carved with the arms of Castile and Leon, medallioned about by groups of mythological or symbolical devices; uppermost and central of which was a dark satyr in a mask, holding his foot on the prostrate neck of a writhing figure likewise masked." As the story makes clear, human history depicts the recurrent process whereby the temporarily strong subdue the temporarily weak. Melville's tale dramatizes how civilization masks the disturbing ontological truth that all human beings are at least half beasts fully capable of extreme evil.

Melville's narrator knows the secrets of the *San Dominick* but does not tell. Instead, his account of dramatic surfaces segues into Delano's internal monologue, a self-congratulatory and racist misreading of Babo's carefully executed charade. The narrator enters the mind of Delano only and does so to indicate the self-deluding nature of the American's putative innocence. Adding to the interaction of these multiple points of view is the presence of the legal deposition. On the one hand, the deposition describes events that took place prior to the narrator's rigid concentration on the unfolding drama of the tale. Ostensibly, it propounds a reliable account of what happened. The deposition, however, is actually a culturally ordained version that justifies slavery. Little more than an egregious masquerade, the self-empowered legal structure determines meaning and value within the social hierarchy and imbues it with divine warrant. If one steps outside of Delano's mind—that is, if one steps outside the self-serving premises of the deposition—one sees Melville's vision of human society as little more than a collection of fictions designed to sustain the authority of a particular ruling class. Crucially, the fourth point of view of *Benito Cereno*

Melville's home, Arrowhead, near Lenox, Massachusetts (woodcut by W. Roberts)

can only be implied in Babo's "voiceless" silence. The prospective content of Babo's declaration of independence has no say within the hegemonic forms of American/Spanish inscription. Babo's tale, like Bartleby's unspoken truth, can only be pursued in the blank spaces of supposition and implication. In "Melville's Tales" (published in *A Companion to Melville Studies* [1986], edited by John Bryant), Johannes D. Bergmann addresses the volatile question of where Melville himself stands: "Many of the issues of the interpretation turn on the extent to which we can sort out the narrative points of view and determine or infer Melville's point of view."

Throughout his career as a magazine writer Melville was visited by poor health and continuous economic distress. In February 1855 he was debilitated from rheumatism and in June he suffered a severe attack of sciatica. His economic ills were far worse. A primary purpose of *The Piazza Tales* was to ward off financial ruin. Though reviews were laudatory, no record survives that indicates that this volume made any money. As a magazine writer Melville received top dollar–$5.00 per printed page–but his income was

insufficient to meet expenses. Essentially, the cost of borrowed money amounted to his undoing. In a 12 May 1856 letter to Judge Shaw, Melville summarized his financial problems. He owed Shaw $5,000; when he purchased Arrowhead, Melville had given Brewster a mortgage of $2,500 and had also borrowed an additional $2,050 from Stewart. For years Melville had defaulted on interest owed, and by 1 May 1856 the entire sum was due and Stewart was demanding to be paid. With Shaw's generous help and the sale of half the farm to neighbor George S. Willis, Melville managed to avert bankruptcy.

Whereas Melville clearly could not hope to earn a living by his writing, he nevertheless embarked on what became his last work of fiction to be published in his lifetime. By fall 1855 he was definitely working on *The Confidence-Man: His Masquerade* (1857) and may possibly have started as early as June 1855. He apparently completed this novel by early September 1856. Of those close to Melville, not a soul would have been pleased by this expenditure of authorial energy. The family's long-held belief was that the physical and emotional toll of writing was making him ill in body and mind. If he were to be cured, he needed to break the authorial habit. With *The Confidence-Man* completed, the family saw hopes of wrenching him from his seeming masochism. The cure would be extended travel. On 1 September 1856 Judge Shaw, in a letter to his son Sam, outlined the condition and prognosis: "I suppose you have been informed by some of the family, how very ill, Herman has been. It is manifest to me from Elizabeth's letters, that she has felt great anxiety about him. When he is deeply engaged in one of his literary works, he confines him[self] to hard study many hours in the day, with little or no exercise, & this specially in winter for a great many days together. He probably thus overworks himself & brings on severe nervous affections. He has been advised strongly to break off this labor for some time, & take a voyage or a journey, & endeavor to recruit." With approximately $1,500 borrowed from Shaw against his wife's inheritance, Melville planned a prolonged European and Middle Eastern tour—the very trip he had wished to make in 1849. With brother Allan arranging for the publication of *The Confidence-Man,* Melville left behind the strained domestic sphere and the fragments of his literary career. He looked forward to the balm of solitary travel. From his 11 October 1856 departure to 5 May 1857 when he was about to board a steamer for home, he kept a journal, probably with intentions of using his travels for future writing projects. His notes tend to be cryptic, often single words or clipped phrases designed to jog the memory and, perhaps, initiate a scene. There is no pretense of sequential narrative. In a 28 February 1857 entry, for example, Melville remarks, "At 12 M. was at Borghese villa. Extent of grounds—peculiar odors of Italian garden—Deep groves—cold splendor of villa—Venus & Cupid—mischevous [sic] look of C.—Thence to Villa Albani—along the walls—Antinous—head like moss-rose with curls & buds—rest all simplicity." Melville traveled from Scotland to York and then to Liverpool. On 11 November 1856 he visited Hawthorne at the consulate in Liverpool. The friends then repaired twenty miles north to Hawthorne's rented house in Southport. On 12 November Hawthorne took the day off and spent it with Melville. Melville writes in his journal: "Took a long walk by the sea. Sand & grass. Wild & desolate. A strong wind. Good talk." This experience inspired in Hawthorne the most authoritative and penetrating analysis of Melville ever written:

> we took a pretty long walk together, and sat down in a hollow among the sand hills . . . and smoked a cigar. Melville, as he always does, began to reason of Providence and futurity, and of everything that lies beyond human ken, and informed me that he had "pretty much made up his mind to be annihilated"; but still he does not seem to rest in that anticipation; and, I think, will

never rest until he gets hold of a definite belief. It is strange how he persists—and has persisted ever since I knew him, and probably long before—in wandering to and fro over these deserts, as dismal and monotonous as the sand hills amid which we were sitting. He can neither believe nor be comfortable in his unbelief; and he is too honest and courageous not to try to do one or the other. If he were a religious man, he would be one of the most truly religious and reverential; he has a very high and noble nature, and better worth immortality than most of us.

On 17 November, Melville, with his passport endorsed by Hawthorne, sailed from England and passed through The Straits of Gibraltar, stopping at Malta on his way to Constantinople. He traveled to Egypt. While in one of the pyramids he suffered a harrowing sense of claustrophobia and dread. For three weeks Melville toured the Holy Lands and absorbed experiences that he drew on fifteen years later when composing *Clarel.* Melville then visited Greece, Sicily, Naples, Rome, northern Italy, Switzerland, Germany, and the Netherlands before returning to England and departing for home on 5 May 1857.

On the day Melville was riding in a Venetian gondola—1 April 1857—*The Confidence-Man* was published in New York by Dix and Edwards and in London by Longman. The novel baffled readers and reviewers and earned the author no money. The reviewer for the *New-York Dispatch* (5 April 1857) dismissively summarizes the novel:

> It has all the faults of style peculiar to 'Mardi,' without the romance which attaches itself to that strange book. The Confidence Man goes on board a Mississippi steamboat and assumes such a variety of disguises, with an astonishing rapidity, that no person could assume without detection, and gets into the confidence of his fellow-passengers in such a manner as would tend to show that the passengers of a Mississippi steamboat are the most gullible people in the world, and the most ready to part with their money.

Though now generally considered one of Melville's greatest works, *The Confidence-Man* still baffles readers. There is no consensus regarding the genre of the book, the nature of the title character, or the thematic purpose of the book. As Bryant observes in *Melville and Repose,* "*The Confidence-Man* has been labeled allegory, 'new Novel,' comedy, picaresque, satire, romance, and even 'picaresque satiric romance.'" Not surprisingly, the narrative is all of these things part of the time. Throughout his fiction-writing career Melville produced literary hybrids; all of his works attempt to fuse eclectic forms.

Without question *The Confidence-Man* is rooted in—but not contained by—the satiric mode: the elusive nar-

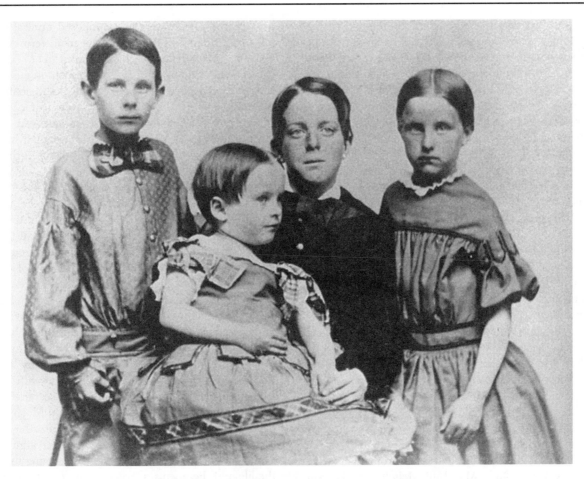

Melville's children: Stanwix, Frances, Malcolm, and Elizabeth

rator spins an elaborate web that exposes the folly of Melville's contemporary America. In *Satirical Apocalypse: An Anatomy of Melville's The Confidence-Man* (1996) Jonathan A. Cook details definite, probable, and possible analogues in Melville's expansive gallery of rogues and dupes. But *The Confidence-Man* might also be Melville's most single-mindedly metaphysical work. The satire, in fact, emerges in a series of philosophical dialogues moderated by a detached, retentive narrator who provides partial descriptions of dramatic surfaces and refuses to enter all but, possibly, one character's mind. The exception is Pitch, the Missouri Bachelor, whose interior monologue may have been overheard. The narrator is concerned less with the intricacies of "ontological heroics" than with dramatizing epistemological puzzles. With his cunning equivocation and knavish wordplay, the narrator halts the story three times to lecture the reader on the problematic relationship between fiction and life, language and truth. The novel anticipates postmodern preoccupations with the relation between object and sign, voice and writing, being and nonbeing.

This social satire cast in the form of metaphysical dialectic revolves around the indeterminate nature of the Confidence-Man himself. He makes his first appearance in the form of a placard-bearing mute, though some readers do not believe the mute is an avatar of the Confidence-Man. Essentially, there is no way of knowing. In the first half of the novel, the Confidence-Man apparently plays the following roles: the mute, the crippled Black Guinea, John Ringman (the man with the weed), the agent for the Seminole Widow and Orphan Asylum, Mr. Truman (the agent for the Black Rapids Coal Company), the herb doctor, and the man from the Philosophical Intelligence Office. Throughout the second half of the work, Frank Goodman (the Cosmopolitan) holds center stage and has prolonged conversational duels with Pitch, Charlie Noble, Egbert, and Mark Winsome. Unlike his earlier avatars, the Cosmopolitan does not extract a single cent from his interlocutors, though he diddles the barber out of the cost of a shave. On two occasions he pays money, seemingly with the purpose of playing the game of charity "to the life." Melville ends this novel of abiding irresolution with the cryptic suggestion, "Something further may follow of this Masquerade." A sequel seems to be advertised, but it never appeared. Melville may have planned one, but the concluding prospectus is more likely a mordant joke punctuating the end of his fiction-writing career.

Melville might have given up on prose fiction, but he never surrendered a literary life. In the fall of 1857 and winter of 1858 he lectured on "Statues in Rome" to audiences in New England, New York State, the Midwest, and Tennessee. In 1858–1859 Melville expounded on a more promising topic, "The South Seas." Nevertheless, he failed on the lecture stage. Though once admired for his animated oral narrations, he clearly did not fully give himself to the performative process. He had grown weary–if not contemptuous–of the need to satisfy a popular audience. He would rather talk about statues that his listeners had never seen than delight them with titillating descriptions of naked Fayaway and her naked friends. As he had noted long before in the 6 October 1849 letter to Judge Shaw, he preferred to write "the sort of books which are said to 'fail.' Pardon this egotism."

By July 1858 Melville started putting together another book that would fail, a collection of short poems that were probably responses to his recent travels. In May 1860 he finished this volume and left the problem of finding a publisher to his brother, his wife, and Duyckinck. On 31 May 1860 Melville sailed to San Francisco with his captain-brother Thomas on the clipper ship *Meteor*. During his passage Melville read much epic poetry, clearly with the intention of learning the craft. Upon his arrival in San Francisco, Melville found no bound volume awaiting him–only news that publishers had rejected his verse. Like "The Isle of the Cross," "Poems" is a lost work.

Following this disappointment, Melville repressed–or felt released from–the authorial urge. In February 1861 he attempted to gain a consulship. On 22 March, while in Washington to seek an appointment, he was called home by news of Judge Shaw's critical illness. Shaw died on 9 March. His will made it economically possible for Melville to rid himself of Arrowhead. Following his many ailments and injuries, Melville was no longer able to manage farm life. By November 1863 the family moved to East Twenty-sixth Street in New York.

Melville's response to the Civil War is well documented in Stanton Garner's *The Civil War World of Herman Melville* (1993). In this masterwork of biographical and historical reconstruction Garner tells the gripping tale of Melville's consumed relation and literary reaction to the national cataclysm. Garner dramatizes the personal and political milieu out of which *Battle-Pieces and Aspects of the War* emerged. According to Melville's

preface, the poems were not composed until after the fall of Richmond. They are arranged in terms of the chronology of the war. For example, "The Portent" depicts "the meteor of the war" in the pendulous figure of the hanged John Brown, a sign of the tragic inevitability of the war. "Misgivings" shifts from iconic portraiture to imagistic meditation. The coming war bursts "from the waste of Time / On the world's fairest hope linked with man's foulest crime." Throughout the subsequent poems Melville tells of battles–Shiloh, Antietam, and the Wilderness, to name a few–and offers meditations on individual men as well as more general circumstances of the war. Melville's abiding thematic context insistently critiques all idealized formulations about America. Like Whitman, Melville depicts the greatest horror of war through the deaths of young men. In "On the Slain Collegians," the speaker notes, "Each bloomed and died an unabated Boy." Significantly, Melville was the only major American writer to participate in a Civil War action. In April 1864 he traveled to the Virginia front to visit his cousin Henry Sanford Gansevoort, who served in the Army of the Potomac. On 14 April 1864 Melville rode with Union soldiers on an overnight expedition in search for the elusive, legendary guerrilla John Singleton Mosby. The eventual result of this brief immersion into the war is "The Scout Toward Aldie," which Garner argues is a "small-scale version of *Moby-Dick*." In bringing together the life and the poems, Garner examines a host of specific concerns: Melville's attraction to and repulsion from the new technology of mass slaughter; Hawthorne's gloomy retreat from life and his death on 19 May 1864 in New Hampshire; Melville's meeting with General Ulysses S. Grant; and the relationship of the 1863 New York Draft Riots to "The House-Top."

In August 1866 Harpers published *Battle-Pieces and Aspects of the War*. It was widely reviewed, though not a popular success. One thousand two hundred copies were printed. By February 1868, only 486 copies had been sold. *The New York Times* review on 27 August 1866 concentrates on Melville's prose supplement, in which the poet argues for cultivating an attitude of conciliation toward the South. The reviewer argues that the poems possess "marked poetic ability, although the unusual meters . . . give a stiffness." The *National Quarterly Review* of September 1866 finds the poetry weak and wishes Melville had used "plain prose." The *Philadelphia Inquirer* is prescient in its assessment on 3 September 1866, observing that the poems "possess considerable merit, and deserve a permanent place in our war literature."

On 5 December 1866 Melville finally received a government job, as a customs inspector in New York, a position he retained for nineteen years. Continuing the familiar family refrain that writing was hazardous to Melville's health, his mother celebrated the effects of regular occupation. She said in a letter to Catherine Gansevoort dated 11 March 1867 that Herman had been "much better since he has been compelled to go out daily to attend to his business." Cousin Catherine Gansevoort in a letter to her brother Henry on 19 March 1867 contended that "intercourse with his fellow creatures" was making him "less of a misanthrope."

Nevertheless, 1867 was a horrendous year for the family. Marital tensions were so extreme that Elizabeth thought herself, in the words of half brother Sam Shaw, "a much injured woman." Just what the injuries were remains a matter of speculation, though the documentary record most plausibly suggests that Elizabeth suffered emotional rather than physical abuse. In Shaw's letter (6 May 1867) to pastor Henry Bellows, he reports that Elizabeth believed her husband to be insane. There was a plan, never actualized, whereby Elizabeth would visit Boston and never return. This fractured household was made infinitely more miserable on 11 September when Malcolm, Melville's oldest son, shot himself in bed. The reasons for the suicide are not clear. But the previous night Malcolm had returned home late. The record does not indicate that he had been drinking or otherwise dissipated. Melville took away Malcolm's night key, after Malcolm returned late, a strange punishment to be handed out by a man who, at the age of eighteen, had been out on his own teaching school near Pittsfield. In a 12 September letter to his mother Sam Shaw reports, "In the morning he was found to be late and one of the girls went up and called him. He answered 'yes' but did not come down—Time went on and Herman advised Lizzie to let him sleep, be late at the office & take the consequences as a sort of punishment." That evening after work, Melville broke down the bedroom door and discovered his son dead with a pistol wound to the head. Though the original verdict of the coroner jury was "temporary insanity of Mind," the jurors later amended their findings to read, "We believe that his death was caused by his own hand, but not that the act was by premeditation or consciously done." The effect of Malcolm's suicide on Melville's work has not been fully assessed.

Gone were the days when Melville would, as he had with *Redburn,* finish a book in six weeks. The eighteen thousand lines of rhymed iambic tetrameter of *Clarel* gestated and unfolded slowly. By 31 January 1870 Melville was acquiring sourcebooks for *Clarel,* though Walter Bezanson speculates that by this time Melville had already written about 25 percent of the poem. Bezanson's groundbreaking "Introduction" to the 1960 Hendricks House edition of *Clarel* is reprinted as the "Historical and Critical Note" in the Northwestern-

Newberry edition, followed by Parker's "Historical Supplement." Major sources include W. H. Bartlett, *Forty Days in the Desert* (1848) and *The Nile Boat* (186–?); William Henry Davenport Adams, *The Buried Cities of Campania* (1869); John Macgregor, *The Rob Roy on the Jordan* (1870); and Arthur Penrhyn Stanley, *Sinai and Palestine in Connection with Their History* (1863). Melville's travel journal of 1856–1857 and the Bible were essential resources. An astute assessment of Melville's use of theology in the poem can be found in Stan Goldman's *Melville's Protest Theism: The Hidden and Silent God in Clarel* (1993).

While at work on the poem, Melville contended with a host of personal problems and losses. On 15 July 1868 his cousin Guert Gansevoort died. In April 1869 Stanwix, Melville's surviving son, left home and sailed for China on the *Yokohama.* He became more of a restless rover than his father ever was, at one point contemplating a walk from San Francisco to South Dakota. On 12 April 1871 Melville's cousin Henry Sanford Gansevoort died. On 9 February 1872 his brother Allan succumbed to tuberculosis. On 1 April his mother, Maria Gansevoort Melville, died at eighty-one. Later that year, on 9 November, the great Boston fire erupted, and Elizabeth Melville lost much of her income, which had amounted to $500 per year, more than a third of Melville's annual salary. An indication of financial trouble became manifest on 29 December 1873 when Elizabeth, unable to pay rent, gave up her pew in the Unitarian Church of All Souls.

By 1875 *Clarel* was finished. In August, Uncle Peter Gansevoort offered to pay the cost of publication, and on 4 January 1876 Melville completed arrangements with G. P. Putnam's Sons for the United States publication of *Clarel,* the very day that Peter Gansevoort died at age ninety-one. Melville's obsession with this book caused tremendous family stress. In a 2 February letter to Catherine Lansing, Elizabeth Melville describes her husband as being "in such a frightfully nervous state . . . that I am actually *afraid* to have anyone here for fear that he will be upset entirely. . . . If ever this dreadful *incubus* of a *book* (I call it so because it has undermined all our happiness) gets off Herman's shoulders I do hope he may be in better mental health." By 22 April Melville finally agreed to have his name printed on the title page. On 3 June *Clarel* was published. In a prose headnote he consigned this work to "whatever future awaits it."

Clarel—Melville's least read and least comprehended book—offers a culminating engagement with what Taji in *Mardi* calls "the world of mind." The poem revolves around the actions of Clarel, a young American divinity student. While waiting to marry

Pacific Ocean
Sep. 2d 1860

My Dear Bessie: I thought
I would send you a letter, that
you could read yourself — at
least a part of it. But here and
there I purpose to write in the usual
manner, as I find the printing style
comes rather awkwardly in a rolling ship.
Mamma will read those parts to you. We
have seen a good many
sea-birds. Many have follow
-wed the ship day after day.
I used to feed them with
crumbs. But now it has got
to be warm weather, the birds
have left us. They we about
as big as chickens — They were,
all over speckled — and they would

First page of a letter from Melville to his daughter Elizabeth (Houghton Library, Harvard University)

Ruth, Clarel makes a pilgrimage through the Holy Land. In the tradition of Melville's idealistic questers, Clarel seeks answers to the great mysteries of theology. An intellectual tyro, Clarel meets a host of prodigious figures. Rolfe and Ungar, for example, constitute projections of Melville's own sensibility. Rolfe embodies an Ishmaelean quality of accommodation: he combines "earnestness and levity," though he is cursed with a "hollow, Manysidedness." A former Confederate officer—"Too serious far to take a jest"—Ungar is an angry monomaniac. Despising contemporary America, especially its mercantile excess and spiritual vapidity, Ungar unleashes many diatribes. Of special note is Melville's re-creation of Nathaniel Hawthorne in Vine:

But who is he uncovered seen,
Profound in shadow of the tomb
Reclined, with meditative mien
Intent upon the tracery?
A low wind waves his Lydian hair;
A funeral man, yet richly fair—
Fair as the sabled violets be.

In *Clarel* the pilgrims wrangle over such issues as divine justice and human culpability; science and faith; and idealism and skepticism. Of all Melville's works, this epic poem lends itself least to concentrated assessment. Along with Bezanson and Goldman, other seminal works that deal with *Clarel* are Vincent Kenny's essay in Bryant's *A Companion to Melville Studies;* Bryan C. Short's "Form as Vision in Herman Melville's *Clarel*" in *American Literature* (January 1979); Shirley Detlaff's "Ionian Form and Esau's Waste: Melville's View of Art in *Clarel*" in *American Literature* (May 1982); and William Shurr's *The Mystery of Iniquity: Melville as Poet, 1857–1891* (1972).

Not surprisingly, most reviewers did not trouble themselves with sounding the depths of *Clarel.* The reviewer for the *New-York Tribune* on 16 June 1876 writes, "'Clarel,' we must frankly confess, is something of a puzzle, both in design and execution." The review in *The New York World* (26 June 1876) contends, "The philosophizing of the book is its least agreeable part." *The London Academy* on 19 August 1876 published one of the few appreciative reviews, though its description of the virtues of *Clarel* precisely reflects the reasons for the popular failure of the poem: It "is a book of very great interest, and poetry of no mean order. . . . We advise our readers to study this interesting poem, which deserves more attention than we fear it is likely to gain in an age which craves for smooth, short, lyric song, and is impatient for the most part of what is philosophic or didactic."

Sometime in the late 1870s Melville began two poems—"A Symposium of Old Masters at Delmonico's," later titled "At the Hostelry," and "A Morning in Naples," later titled "Naples in the Time of Bomba." He introduced these poems with prose headnotes. These "Burgundy Club Sketches," as they are now called, take a backward look at Melville's conversational experiences among the New York literati in the late 1840s. In *Melville and His Circle: The Last Years* (1996) William B. Dillingham explores the place of such imaginary voices in the biographical and literary life of Melville's last years. Dillingham sees the "Burgundy Club" as part of Melville's projected intellectual circle, a counter life in art that provided a self-stimulating refuge from his increasing sense of cultural alienation. Unpublished during Melville's lifetime, these sketches were part of a diverse body of work that was often retrospective, even nostalgic, as well as classicist in its conservative appreciation for ancient forms of architecture, poetry, and philosophy.

During this time Melville did not lack for evidence that the older generation was giving way to the new. Evert Duyckinck died on 13 August 1878. Melville's daughter Frances became engaged to Henry B. Thomas on 21 April 1878, and they were married on 5 April 1880. Melville's first grandchild, Eleanor Melville Thomas, was born on 24 February 1882, and his second grandchild, Frances Cuthbert Thomas, was born on 3 December 1883. Thomas Melville died suddenly on 5 March 1884 and his sister Frances died on 9 July 1885. Melville's customhouse life ended on 31 December 1885.

In retirement Melville devoted himself to a host of literary projects—mostly poetry and one significant work of prose fiction. His tendency was to write a poem and then introduce it with a prose sketch. Sometime in 1885 he wrote a poem about an old sailor awaiting, in chains, execution for his admitted involvement in a mutinous plot. His headnote to "Billy in the Darbies" metamorphosed over five years into *Billy Budd.* At Melville's death, the almost-finished novel was packed away in a bread box. In 1924 it was published as part of the Constable Edition of Melville's works. Whereas little evidence exists for the genesis and composition of *Clarel,* a massive amount of material on *Billy Budd* still awaits assimilation in Hayford and Sealts's genetic text of *Billy Budd,* the 1960 University of Chicago edition. Hayford and Sealts do not present a transcribed manuscript so much as a compilation and collation of successive fair-copy inscriptions, each started with the printer's eye in mind, each drawing Melville into further revision. Of special interest is that Captain Vere does not appear until relatively late in the compositional process. At the conclusion of the second transcription, young Billy is simply hanged for striking and killing Master-at-Arms John Claggart. This version ends with the narrator's summation: "Here ends a story not unwarranted by what sometimes happens in this [word undeciphered] world of ours–Innocence and infamy, spiritual depravity and fair repute." Billy's "innocence" becomes "infamy"; Claggart's "spiritual depravity" becomes "fair repute." In the extensive pencil draft version that Hayford and Sealts call stage x, Melville develops Vere and translates the moral into a vexing dramatization of incompatible imperatives. Until his death Melville was not simply tinkering with words and phrases but making decisive alterations that seem designed to thwart the determinate readings so characteristic of *Billy Budd* criticism. *Billy Budd* needs to be reexamined through the shifting crosslights cast by this genetic evidence. Rather than offering a grand final statement, *Billy Budd* stands among many writing projects that absorbed Melville's attention. He wrote everything for eventual publication, even paying for the issue of *John Marr and Other Sailors* in September 1888 and *Timoleon* in May or June 1891 in editions of twenty-five copies each. Had he lived, Melville would have published *Billy Budd* and "Weeds and Wildings with a Rose or Two," a collection of poems written for his wife.

Melville's undying authorial commitment was an affirmation of art and mind in the face of mutability and mortality. His son Stanwix died on 23 February 1886; his close friend and brother-in-law John Hoadley died on 21 October 1886. On 11 June 1888 Melville made out his will, leaving everything to his wife. On 14 December 1888 his older sister Helen died. Melville himself suffered increasing cardiac and pulmonary problems. With everything still to do–he once wrote to Hawthorne, "As long as we have anything more to do, we have done nothing"–Melville could not forestall his body's collapse. On 28 September 1891 he died of "Cardiac dilation, Mitral regurgitation . . . [and] Contributory Asthenia." On 2 October 1891 *The New York Times* offered a moving tribute:

> There has died and been buried in this city . . . a man who is so little known, even by name, to the generation now in the vigor of life that only one newspaper contained an obituary account of him, and this was but of three or four lines. Yet forty years ago the appearance of a new book by HERMAN MELVILLE was esteemed a literary event. . . . Whoever, arrested for a moment by the tidings of the author's death, turns back now to the books that were so much read and so much talked about forty years ago has no difficulty in determining why they were then read and talked about. His difficulty will be rather to discover why they are read and talked about no longer. The total eclipse now of what was then a literary luminary seems like a wanton caprice of fame.

Beginning in *Mardi* Melville made a practice of pondering ephemeral literary notoriety and its relation to time-honored greatness. In the spring of 1862, when his career lay wrecked behind him, Melville bought some books that explored the meaning of artistic excellence. His considered response can be found on a flyleaf to his edition of Giorgio Vasari's *Lives of the Most Eminent Painters, Sculptors, and Architects* (1850–1852). Melville lists his criterion for literary immortality:

> Attain the highest result.–
>   A Quality of Grasp.–
> The habitual choice of noble subjects.–
>   The Expression.–
> Get in as much as you can.–
>   Finish is completeness, fulness,
>   not polish.–
> Greatness is a matter of scale.–
>   Clearness & firmness.–
> The greatest number of the greatest ideas.

Full, unpolished expression–"A Quality of Grasp"–remained the province of all "thought-divers." As a close reading of the late poetry and prose attests, Melville never ran out of the greatest ideas, never tired of the demands of art, but like Plato, Shakespeare, Milton, and Hawthorne, he merely ran out of time.

Letters:

Correspondence, edited by Lynn Horth (Evanston, Ill.: Northwestern University Press / Chicago: Newberry Library, 1993), volume 14 of *The Writings of Herman Melville* (1968–   ).

Bibliographies:

Beatrice Ricks, *Herman Melville: A Reference Bibliography, 1900–1972, with Selected Nineteenth-Century Materials* (Boston: G. K. Hall, 1973);

Brian Higgins, *Herman Melville: A Reference Guide, 1931–1960* (Boston: G. K. Hall, 1987).

Biographies:

Leon Howard, *Herman Melville: A Biography* (Berkeley: University of California Press, 1951);

Jay Leyda, ed., *The Melville Log: A Documentary Life of Herman Melville, 1819–1891* (New York: Harcourt, Brace, 1951; with supplement, New York: Gordian Press, 1969);

Edwin Haviland Miller, *Herman Melville: A Biography* (New York: Braziller, 1975);

Stanton Garner, *The Civil War World of Herman Melville* (Lawrence: University Press of Kansas, 1993);

Hershel Parker, *Herman Melville: A Biography, Volume I, 1819–1851* (Baltimore: Johns Hopkins University Press, 1996);

Laurie Robertson-Lorant, *Melville, A Biography* (New York: Clarkson N. Potter, 1996).

References:

Johannes D. Bergmann, "Melville's Tales," in *A Companion to Melville Studies,* edited by John Bryant (New York: Greenwood Press, 1986), pp. 241–278;

Richard H. Brodhead, *Hawthorne, Melville, and the Novel* (Chicago: University of Chicago Press, 1976);

John Bryant, *Melville and Repose: The Rhetoric of Humor in the American Renaissance* (New York: Oxford University Press, 1993);

Jonathan A. Cook, *Satirical Apocalypse: An Anatomy of Melville's* The Confidence-Man (Westport, Conn.: Greenwood Press, 1996);

Merrell R. Davis, *Melville's* Mardi: *A Chartless Voyage* (New Haven: Yale University Press, 1952);

Shirley Detlaff, "Ionian Form and Esau's Waste: Melville's View of Art in *Clarel,*" *American Literature,* 54 (May 1982): 212–228;

William B. Dillingham, *Melville and His Circle: The Last Years* (Athens: University of Georgia Press, 1996);

Wai-chee Dimock, *Empire for Liberty: Melville and the Poetics of Individualism* (Princeton: Princeton University Press, 1989);

Dorothee Metlitsky Finkelstein, *Melville's* Orienda (New Haven, Conn.: Yale University Press, 1961);

William H. Gilman, *Melville's Early Life and* Redburn (New York: New York University Press, 1951);

Stan Goldman, *Melville's Protest Theism: The Hidden and Silent God in* Clarel (Dekalb: Northern Illinois University Press, 1993);

Harrison Hayford, "'Unnecessary Duplicates': A Key to the Writing of *Moby-Dick,*" in *New Perspectives on Melville,* edited by Faith Pullin (Kent, Ohio: Kent State University Press, 1979), pp. 128–161;

Brian Higgins and Hershel Parker, eds., *Herman Melville: The Contemporary Reviews* (New York: Cambridge University Press, 1995);

Vincent Kenny, *"Clarel,"* in *A Companion to Melville Studies,* edited by Bryant (New York: Greenwood Press, 1986), pp. 375–406;

D. H. Lawrence, *Studies in Classic American Literature* (New York: T. Seltzer, 1923);

Michael E. Levin, "Ahab as Socratic Philosopher: The Myth of the Cave Inverted," *American Transcendental Quarterly,* 41 (Winter 1979): 61–73;

Parker, "Herman Melville's *The Isle of the Cross:* A Survey and a Chronology," *American Literature,* 62 (March 1990): 1–16;

Sheila Post-Lauria, *Correspondent Colorings: Melville in the Marketplace* (Amherst: University of Massachusetts Press, 1996);

Douglas Robillard, *Melville and the Visual Arts: Ionian Form, Venetian Tint* (Kent, Ohio: Kent State University Press, 1997);

John Samson, *White Lies: Melville's Narratives of Facts* (Ithaca, N.Y.: Cornell University Press, 1989);

Elizabeth A. Schultz, *Unpainted to the Last:* Moby-Dick *and Twentieth-Century American Art* (Lawrence: University Press of Kansas, 1995);

Merton M. Sealts Jr., *Melville's Reading* (Columbia: University of South Carolina Press, 1988);

Bryan C. Short, "Form as Vision in Herman Melville's *Clarel,*" *American Literature,* 50 (January 1979): 553–569;

William Shurr, *The Mystery of Iniquity: Melville as Poet, 1857–1891* (Lexington: University of Kentucky Press, 1972);

Christopher Sten, *The Weaver God, He Weaves: Melville and the Poetics of the Novel* (Kent, Ohio: Kent State University Press, 1996);

Sten, ed., *Savage Eye: Melville and the Visual Arts* (Kent, Ohio: Kent State University Press, 1991);

Milton R. Stern, *The Fine Hammered Steel of Herman Melville* (Urbana: University of Illinois Press, 1957);

Stern, "Toward 'Bartleby the Scrivener,'" in *The Stoic Strain in American Literature,* edited by Duane J. Macmillan (Toronto: University of Toronto Press, 1979), pp. 19–41;

David K. Titus, "Herman Melville at the Albany Academy," *Melville Society Extracts,* 42 (May 1980): 4–10;

Thomas Vargish, "Gnostick Mythos in *Moby-Dick,*" *PMLA,* 81 (June 1966): 272–277;

Howard P. Vincent, *The Tailoring of Melville's* White-Jacket (Evanston, Ill.: Northwestern University Press, 1970);

Vincent, *The Trying-Out of* Moby-Dick (Boston: Houghton Mifflin, 1948);

Robert K. Wallace, *Melville & Turner: Spheres of Love and Fright* (Athens: University of Georgia Press, 1992);

John Wenke, *Melville's Muse: Literary Creation and the Forms of Philosophical Fiction* (Kent, Ohio: Kent State University Press, 1995);

Nathalia Wright, *Melville's Use of the Bible* (Durham: Duke University Press, 1949).

Papers:

Herman Melville's papers are housed in the New York Public Library. Other major holdings are located in the Newberry Library, Chicago; the Houghton Library, Harvard University; the Massachusetts Historical Society; the Lemuel Shaw Collection; and the Berkshire Athenaeum, the Herman Melville Memorial Room.

Mordecai M. Noah

(19 July 1785 – 22 March 1851)

Barbara Cantalupo
Pennsylvania State University–Lehigh Valley

BOOKS: *The Fortress of Sorrento: A Petit Historical Drama in Two Acts* (New York: D. Longworth, 1808);

Correspondence and Documents Relative to the Attempt to Negotiate for the Release of the American Captives at Algiers; Including Remarks on Our Relations with That Regency (Washington City, 1816);

Oration Delivered by Appointment Before Tammany Society of Columbian Order, Hibernian Provident Society, and Mason's Benevolent Societies: United to Celebrate the Forty First Anniversary of American Independence (New York: J. H. Sherman, 1817);

Discourse, delivered at the Consecration of the Synagogue of <in Hebrew: Holy Congregation, Remnant of Israel> in the City of New-York, On Friday, the 10th of Nisan, 5578, Corresponding with the 17th of April, 1818 (New York: C. S. Van Winkle, 1818);

Travels in England, France, Spain, and the Barbary States, In the Years 1813–14 and 15. By Mordecai M. Noah (New York: Kirk and Mercein; London: John Miller, 1819);

She Would Be a Soldier, or The Plains of Chippewa; An Historical Drama, in Three Acts (New York: D. Longworth, 1819);

Essays of Howard, on Domestic Economy, anonymous (New York: G. L. Birch, 1820); revised as *Gleanings from a Gathered Harvest* (New York: Charles Wells, 1845; reissued, 1847);

An Address Delivered Before the General Society of Mechanics and Tradesmen of the City of New-York, on the Opening of the Mechanic Institution: By M. M. Noah . . . To Which Is Added, The Remarks Made at the Request of the Mechanics' Society, On Laying the Corner Stone of that Edifice, By Thomas R. Mercein. A Member of the Society (New York: William Mercein, 1822);

Marion, or The Hero of Lake George: A Drama, in Three Acts, Founded on Events of the Revolutionary War (New York: E. Murden, 1822);

The Grecian Captive, or The Fall of Athens . . . As Performed at the New-York Theatre (New York: E. Murden, 1822);

Mordecai M. Noah (portrait by John Wesley Jarvis; Collection of Congregational Shearith Israel, New York City)

A Statement of Facts Relative to the Conduct of Henry Eckford, Esq. As Connected with The National Advocate (New York: J. W. Bell, 1824);

Prospectus of The Evening Star: *A New Daily and Semiweekly Paper, to be Published in the City of New-York, by M. M. Noah and Thomas Gill* (New York: Clayton & Van Norden, 1833);

Discourse on the Evidences of the American Indians Being the Descendants of the Lost Tribes of Israel. Delivered Before the Mercantile Library Association, Clinton Hall (New York: James Van Norden, 1837);

Discourse on the Restoration of the Jews: Delivered at the Tabernacle, Oct. 28 and Dec. 2, 1844 (New York: Harper, 1845);

A Letter Addressed to the Southern Delegates of the Baltimore Democratic Convention, on the Claims of the "Barnburners" to be Admitted to Seats in That Convention (New York, 1848);

Address, Delivered at the Hebrew Synagogue, in Crosby-Street, New York, on Thanksgiving Day, to Aid in the Erection of The Temple at Jerusalem (Kingston, Jamaica: R. J. De Cordova, 1849);

Address Delivered at the Re-Opening of the Apprentices' Library, and Reading Rooms, at the Mechanics' Hall, 472 Broadway, September 23d, 1850 (New York: Van Norden & Amerman, 1850);

A Literary Autobiography of Mordecai Manuel Noah. With an Introduction by George Alexander Kohut (N.p.: American Jewish Historical Society, 1897).

Collection: *The Selected Writings of Mordecai Noah,* edited by Michael Schuldiner and Daniel J. Kleinfeld (Westport, N.Y.: Greenwood Press, 1999).

PLAY PRODUCTIONS: *Paul and Alexis, or the Orphans of the Rhine,* Charleston, S.C., 1812; revised as *The Wandering Boys; Or, the Castle of Olival. A Melo-Drama, In Two Acts,* adapted by John Kerr and performed in London, Covent Garden, 1814 and New York, Park Theater, 16 March 1820;

She Would Be a Soldier, or The Plains of Chippewa; An Historical Drama, in Three Acts, New York, Anthony Street Theater, 21 June 1819; also performed as *The War of 1812, or She Would Be a Soldier,* New York, Barnum's Museum, 2 July 1866;

Yusef Caramalli, or The Siege of Tripoli, New York, Park Theater, 15 May 1820;

Marion, or The Hero of Lake George, New York, Park Theater, 25 November 1821;

The Grecian Captive, or The Fall of Athens, New York, Park Theater, 17 June 1822;

Natalie, or The Frontier Maid, Boston, Tremont Theater, 1 May 1840; New York, Park Theater, 18 May 1840.

OTHER: *Shakspeare Illustrated; or, The Novels and Histories on Which the Plays of Shakspeare are Founded. Collected and Translated from the Originals, by Mrs. Lenox* (Philadelphia: Bradford & Inskeep, T. & G. Palmer/New York: Inskeep & Bradford/Boston: W. M'Ilhenney/Baltimore: Coale & Thomas/Charleston, S.C.: E. Morford, 1809).

SELECTED PERIODICAL PUBLICATION—UNCOLLECTED: *Speech Delivered at the Laying of the Corner Stone of the City of Ararat, New York Evening Post,* 24 September 1825.

PERIODICALS EDITED: *National Advocate* (1817–1824);

New-York National Advocate (16 December 1824 – 17 July 1826);

New-York Enquirer (6 July 1826 – 23 May 1829);

New York Evening Star (1833–1840).

Described in Evert A. Duyckinck and George L. Duyckinck's *Cyclopedia of American Literature* (1855) as "the best newspaper paragraphist of his day," Mordecai M. Noah was also a newspaper editor and owner, a career politician (filling such posts as diplomat, judge, and sheriff), a strident promoter of the restoration of the state of Israel, one of the founding fathers of New York University, an advocate of American drama, and a successful playwright in his own right. In his "Autography" series in *The Messenger* (circa 1835–1836) Edgar Allan Poe refers to Noah's roles as playwright, essayist, and journalist: "Judge Noah has written several plays which took very well in their time, and also several essays and other works, giving evidence of no ordinary learning and penetration on certain topics. . . . He is better known, however, from the wit and universal *bonhomie* of his editorial paragraphs." Thomas Jefferson also praised Noah's writing in a 28 May 1818 letter to Noah: "I should not do full justice to the merits of your discourse, were I not, in addition, to that of it's *[sic]* matter, to express my consideration of it as a fine specimen of style & composition."

As Poe had noted, Noah's plays were well received, despite his description of himself as an amateur in an 11 July 1832 letter to William Dunlap: "While I was thus employed in occasional attempts at play-writing, I was engaged in editing a daily journal, and in all the fierce contests of political strife; I had, therefore, but little time to devote to all that study and reflection so essential to the success of dramatic composition." In addition to contributing to the American literary scene with his own work, Noah was an outspoken advocate of American literary talent, and in 1809, early in his writing career, he published *Shakspeare Illustrated; or, The Novels and Histories on Which the Plays of Shakspeare are Founded. Collected and Translated from the Originals, by Mrs. Lenox,* based on a 1753 work by Charlotte Lennox; with this volume and a proposed second one (which was never published), he had hoped to encourage American audiences to support works by American playwrights and turn away from the fascination with British theater, especially the plays of William Shakespeare. Ten years later, Noah helped found *The New-York Literary Journal and Belles-Lettres Repository* (1819–1821) to promote the publication and dissemination of literary efforts by American writers.

Mordecai Manuel Noah was born on 19 July 1785 in Philadelphia to Manuel Noah, a German immigrant, and Zipporah Phillips Noah. Noah's mother died when he was seven, shortly after his father had abandoned the family and fled to Europe because of financial difficulties.

Noah's wife, Rebecca Jackson Noah (portrait by John Wesley Jarvis; Collection of Congregational Shearith Israel, New York City)

Mordecai and his sister Judith were taken in by their maternal grandparents, Rebecca Machado and Jonas Phillips. Jonas Phillips, an outspoken defender of Jewish rights, had emigrated from Germany to Charleston, South Carolina, in 1756 as an indentured servant and had become a successful Philadelphia merchant, marrying the granddaughter of Dr. Samuel Nuñez, a Sephardic Jew. As Jonathan Sarna points out in his work on Noah, *Jacksonian Jew: The Two Worlds of Mordecai M. Noah* (1981), Mordecai Noah did not hesitate to promote this part of his ancestral heritage, becoming a "typical 'Sephardized' Jew," by "carefully" selecting "his ancestors. He displayed only those who enhanced his status."

Hoping to provide Noah with a stable income, his grandfather apprenticed him to a carver and gilder. Failing at this pursuit, Noah turned to sales before entering politics at the age of twenty-three. Having actively supported the successful election of Simon Snyder to the post of governor of Pennsylvania in 1808, Noah received his first patronage job, a post in the Pennsylvania militia; although he held this position for a short time, he was thereafter known as "Major Noah." Noah's livelihood depended, for the most part, on patronage jobs from federal appointments as consul to Tunis (1813) to Tammany Hall appointments as sheriff, judge, and newspaper editor.

Despite this pedestrian career track, Noah had been infatuated with the theater since early adolescence. In his 11 July 1832 letter to William Dunlap, Noah describes his early dedication to the stage, suggesting that his time at the theater helped him "avoid the haunts of taverns, and the pursuits of depraved pleasures, which too frequently allure and destroy our young men." Noah had attended Philadelphia's Chestnut Street Theatre on a daily basis, going home "gratified and improved." His avid involvement with the theater community led him to write, produce, and review plays.

Noah's first published play, *The Fortress of Sorrento: A Petit Historical Drama in Two Acts* (1808), described by Jonathan Sarna as "a thin melodrama" using "a well-worn motif—wife who dressed up as a man to save her husband from the hands of his enemies who had unjustly imprisoned him." The play was accepted by David Longworth's Dramatic Repository in exchange for a copy of all the plays that Longworth had published. This exchange provided Noah with a large collection of contemporary drama and the satisfaction of having one of his plays published, although *The Fortress of Sorrento* was never performed. His second play, *Paul and Alexis, or the Orphans of the Rhine* (performed 1812) written for Mrs. Charles Young, a popular actress of the day, and performed in Charleston was later adapted in 1814 by John Kerr and performed in Covent Garden as *The Wandering Boys; Or, the Castle of Olival. A Melo-Drama. In Two Acts* and, again, in New York at the Park Theater in 1820. The play was an adaptation of René-Charles Guilbert Pixèricourt's 1801 play *Le Pèlerin Blanc ou les Orphelins du Hameau* (The White Pilgrim, or the Orphans of Hameau). Like *The Fortress of Sorrento,* this play depends heavily on the devices of disguise and intrigue. An evil court attendant, hoping to take over the reign of the kingdom while the duke is away at battle, sets fire to the duchess's bedroom in an attempt to kill both her and her two sons. After many years, the duke, knowing a coup has occurred, returns in disguise at the same time as the two sons, who had been secretly saved from the fire by a trusted servant and raised in another village return to their home. In the end the duke triumphs, the sons are reunited with their father, and evil is suppressed.

Noah's first successful theatrical performance was the 21 June 1819 production at the New York Anthony Street Theater of *She Would Be a Soldier, or The Plains of Chippewa; An Historical Drama, in Three Acts* (published 1819). This play established Noah's place in American theater. As in his first play, *The Fortress of Sorrento,* one of the main characters disguises herself as a man and displays great fortitude, overcoming fear to follow her heart's allegiance. Though a well-worn conceit, such cross-dressing provided an opportunity for Noah to present a character who reflected his belief in woman's strength of character and virtue. In his *Discourse on the Restoration of the Jews: Delivered at the Tabernacle, Oct. 28 and Dec. 2, 1844* (1845), Noah's plea to American Christians to support his restoration efforts, he specifically calls for the support of the "first in zeal and true religion"—women—whom he characterizes as able to lead man "into the path of duty and high moral obligations. . . . all that she says and urges in the fulfillment of the most sacred duties drops like oily balsam upon the heart, soothes while it influences, and subdues while it controls."

This well-attended play projected, as well, an image of the Native American as an eloquent and commanding presence, reflecting Noah's belief that Native Americans are, in fact, one of the lost tribes of Israel. In his *Speech Delivered at the Laying of the Corner Stone of the City of Ararat*, published in the *New York Evening Post* (24 September 1825), Noah proclaims again his respect for Native Americans: "The Indians possess great vigour of intellect and native talent." The character of the Indian Chief in *She Would Be a Soldier* confronts the French officer, Pendragon, who had demanded that the Chief refer to the King of France "with proper awe, and not call him your father, but your gracious master," with this proud reply: "Young man, the Indian warrior knows no master but the Great Spirit, whose voice is heard in thunder, and whose eye is seen in the lightning's flash; free as air, we bow the knee to no man." In this play Noah also takes the opportunity to mock followers of fashion through the character Pendragon, the foppish officer of the French army. As a kind of ultimate embarrassment, he is forced by the Indian Chief's command to fight alongside him dressed in deerskin and painted face.

Encouraged by the success of *She Would Be a Soldier*, Noah wrote and produced *Yusef Caramalli, or The Siege of Tripoli* (1820), based on the Barbary Wars. No text is extant, but, according to Sarna, reviews of the 15 May 1820 performance at the Park Theater in New York suggest that this play was considered Noah's best: "Reviewers particularly noted the last scene in *Yusef Caramalli*, the grand ballet. Unfortunately, on the second performance of the play, the grand ballet gave way several hours later to a grand inferno. . . . the Park Theater was utterly destroyed."

The praise Noah received for this play encouraged him to write another based on a patriotic theme; this time he chose the Revolutionary War as the setting. *Marion, or The Hero of Lake George*, performed on 25 November 1821 in New York at Parker Theater and published in 1822, was dedicated to William Coleman, a strident critic of Noah's work, with these opening lines: "I dedicate this play to you—being the only critic of pretensions who abused it without having seen it performed." The

text of the dedication gives the reader a keen sense of Noah's feisty and flamboyant character, which was balanced, on the other hand, by widely acknowledged kindness and generosity. Sarna notes that, for example, Noah donated all of the money he earned from the benefit first performance of *Yusef Caramalli* to the actors and actresses associated with the play "corresponding to their losses and wants" following the fire at the Park Theater.

Marion focuses on an aspect of the American Revolution that personalizes the war: the pain and confusion divided loyalties caused for families. The play also pits individual integrity against governmental dictates. The hero, Marion, described as "an outlaw—proscribed—fighting in the mountains" is defended by Caleb, a farmer: "His estates were confiscated, because he displayed a courageous resistance to tyranny; he drew his sword for liberty, and earned the title of rebel.—Is he less a man, because an outlaw, and proscribed?" The plot revolves around the pursuit and capture of Marion and the conflict his allegiance presents for his betrothed's mother and brother, who side with the king of England. As in all of Noah's plays, good prevails. The play closes with the end of the revolution; Marion is freed, and vindicated. Marion's last speech predicts a happy ending: "At length the conflict's o'er; and the pains and perils of war will be succeeded by the blessings of peace and prosperity. Our country, free, sovereign, and independent; will pursue a steady march to glory and renown; and, when powerful and happy at home, feared and respected abroad, may future ages remember with pride and gratitude—the soldier of the revolution, and the struggle for freedom."

Noah's last published play, *The Grecian Captive, Or The Fall of Athens*, performed at the Park Theater, 17 June 1822, and published in 1822, is based on the French drama *Mahomet II*. Noah, focusing on the Greek struggle for independence from Turkey, changed the venue of the original play to Turkish-held Athens of 1820. As Sarna notes, "The tyrant Mahomet is transformed without any difficulty into the tyrant Ali Pacha. [Noah] also inserted two new characters: Alexander Ypsilanti, in the play as in real life the heroic leader of the Greek forces, and Burrows, an American officer." Noah's allegiances were with the Greeks in their struggle for independence, and this play applauds their effort. However, as Sarna notes, Noah made two innovations with this play that failed miserably: he gave printed copies of the play to the audience, causing great noise at each page turning, and he used live animals in the productions, including an elephant that, according to one of the performers, caused "an unexpected hydraulic experiment." As Sarna notes, "the play closed amid great confusion, and Noah blamed himself for imprudence."

Knowing that he would be unable to support himself in a theatrical career, Noah then turned to journalism. Under the pseudonym "Muly Mulak" he ran a series of articles for the *Charleston Times* described by Daniel J. Kleinfeld as using "a breezy, comic style for his mild, satiric pokes at American customs and fashions."

Noah's first serious journalism post came in 1817 as editor of the *The National Advocate,* published by his uncle Naphtali Phillips and sponsored by Tammany Hall's Bucktail faction, which had formed within the Democratic-Republican Party in opposition to the administration of Governor DeWitt Clinton. Noah transformed *The National Advocate* into a popular newspaper with his provocative style. According to Sarna, Noah "delighted in fierce controversy and scandalous revelations" during his term as editor of *The National Advocate.* Nevertheless, as an organ of Tammany Hall, the newspaper was necessarily partisan in its politics; pulled between party loyalty and his own desire for freedom of expression, Noah resigned in 1824 and, with E. J. Roberts, began publishing a competing newspaper, the *New-York National Advocate.* Because of irresponsible behavior on Roberts's part, the newspaper went into debt and closed two years later.

Noah then established, on his own, the *New-York Enquirer* with the motto: "A Free Press, The Ark of Public Safety"; the paper became known for investigative reporting and risk-taking politics. According to Sarna, Noah's journalistic efforts at the *New-York Enquirer* "contributed to the mood of popular dissatisfaction which eventually elected Andrew Jackson."

In 1833 Noah became editor of *The New York Evening Star,* a newspaper described by Sarna as "cautious and conservative." Although Noah "sought to maintain a foothold in the Jacksonian camp," his "ritualistic devotions to Andrew Jackson did not survive the bitter 1834 election. . . . By 1835, *The Evening Star.* . . . reminded readers about sordid aspects of Jackson's past that editor Noah had, just a few years earlier, striven mightily to cover up." Noah remained editor until *The Evening Star* closed in August 1840.

In 1838 the fifty-three-year-old Noah married seventeen-year-old Rebecca Jackson. In the thirteen years that they were married, the couple had seven children.

Noah did not produce any other significant plays until the May 1840 productions of *Natalie, or The Frontier Maid* in Boston and New York. In *Major Noah: American-Jewish Pioneer* (1936) Isaac Goldberg notes that the play was written for the French ballet star, Celeste, who "was the rage; the public could not get enough of her. Not only did she act three parts in Natalie alone, but she did a new fancy dance, also the trial dance from *La Bayadere.*"

Noah died of a stroke on 22 March 1851. His funeral, according to Sarna, was attended by "a large concourse of citizens—one of the largest to attend a New York funeral in years. . . . 'Representatives of the bench, the bar and the mart . . . doctors, authors, musicians, comedians, editors, mechanics, professional and non-professionals'" who heard the presiding rabbi's praise: "Mordecai Noah took upon himself the pleasing duty of proving to his country, that its children professing the Jewish faith were as able, as faithful, as zealous in her cause and service as any of her other children."

Bibliographies:

Jacob Blanck, *Bibliography of American Literature* (New Haven: Yale University Press, 1955), pp. 447–453;

Jonathan Sarna, "Bibliographical Essay," in his *Jacksonian Jew: The Two Worlds of Mordecai M. Noah* (New York: Holmes & Meier, 1981), pp. 215–225.

Biographies:

Robert Noah, "Mordecai M. Noah: Interesting Reminiscences of a Famous American Jew," *Reformer and Jewish Times,* 10 (15 November 1878);

Charles Daly, *The Settlement of the Jews in North America,* edited by Max J. Kohler (New York: P. Cowen, 1893);

A. B. Makover, *Mordecai M. Noah: His Life and Work from a Jewish Viewpoint* (New York: Bloch, 1917);

Isaac Goldberg, *Major Noah: American-Jewish Pioneer* (Freeport, N.Y.: Books for Libraries, 1936);

Robert Gordis, *Mordecai Manuel Noah: A Centenary Evaluation* (Philadelphia, 1951);

Jonathan Sarna, *Jacksonian Jew: The Two Worlds of Mordecai M. Noah* (New York: Holmes & Meier, 1981).

References:

Lewis Allen, "Founding of the City of Ararat on Grand Island by Mordecai M. Noah," *Publications of the Buffalo Historical Society,* 1 (1866): 305–328;

Allen, "The Story of the Tablet of the City of Ararat," *Publications of the Buffalo Historical Society,* 24 or 25 (1896): 113–144;

Lee M. Friedman, "Mordecai Manuel Noah as Playwright," *Historia Judaica,* 4 (1942): 154–161;

Leonard I. Gappelberg, "M. M. Noah and The Evening Star: Whig Journalism, 1833–1840," dissertation, Yeshiva University, 1970;

George Kohut, "A Literary Biography of Mordecai Manuel Noah," *Publications of the American Jewish Historical Society,* 6 (1897): 113–121;

Jonathan Sarna, "The Literary Contributions of Mordecai M. Noah, on the Bicentennial of His Birth," *Jewish Book Annual,* 42 (1984–1985): 189–198.

Frances Sargent Osgood

(18 June 1811 – 12 May 1850)

Mary De Jong
Pennsylvania State University, Altoona

BOOKS: *A Wreath of Wild Flowers from New England, By Frances Sargent Osgood* (London: Edward Churton, 1838; Boston: Weeks, Jordan, 1839);

The Casket of Fate (London: C. Whittingham, 1839; Boston: Weeks, Jordan, 1840);

The Snow-Drop: A New-Year's Gift for Children (Providence: Hiram Fuller, 1842);

May Queen (Boston: Henry Prentiss, 1842);

Lulu (Baltimore: F. D. Benteen, 1842);

Puss in Boots, and the Marquis of Carabas, Rendered into Verse (New York: Benjamin & Young, 1844);

Echo Song: I Know a Noble Heart! The Words by Mrs. Francis S. Osgood, music by Hermann S. Saroni (Philadelphia: George Willig, 1845);

The Flower Alphabet, in Gold and Colors (Boston: S. Coleman, 1845);

The Cries of New-York: with Fifteen Illustrations, Drawn from Life by a Distinguished Artist; The Poetry by Frances S. Osgood (New York: John Doggett, 1846);

A Letter about the Lions, Addressed to Mabel in the Country (New York: George P. Putnam; London: Putnam's American Agency, 1849);

I Wandered the Woodland, poetry by Osgood, music by Saroni (New York: William Hall, 1849);

Annie Ramsey: Ballad by the Author of Call Me Pet Names (Philadelphia: A. Fiot, 1852);

Lines to Mr. Dodson, Engraver of the Plate of Female Contributors to Graham's Magazine (Brooklyn, 1885);

Sketches For the Fair, anonymous (Boston: N.p., n.d.).

Collections: *Poems* (New York: Clark & Austin, 1846);

Poems (Philadelphia: Carey & Hart, 1850); republished as *Osgood's Poetical Works, Containing a Choice Selection of Sacred and Miscellaneous Poems* (Philadelphia: John F. Potter, n.d.).

OTHER: *The Poetry of Flowers and Flowers of Poetry: To Which Are Added, a Simple Treatise on Botany, with Familiar Examples, and a Copious Floral Dictionary,* edited by Osgood (New York: J. C. Riker, 1841);

The Floral Offering, a Token of Friendship, Edited by Frances S. Osgood. Illustrated with Ten Beautiful Bouquets of Flow-

Frances Sargent Osgood, circa 1842 (portrait by Samuel Osgood; from John Evangelist Walsh, Plumes in the Dust, *1980)*

ers Elegantly Coloured After Nature by I. Ackerman (Philadelphia: Carey & Hart, 1847).

SELECTED PERIODICAL PUBLICATIONS– UNCOLLECTED:

POETRY

"To [Edgar Allan Poe]," *Broadway Journal,* 2 (29 November 1845): 318;

"A Valentine, Affectionately Inscribed to Mrs. Mary E. Hewitt," *Knickerbocker,* 29 (February 1847): 128;

"Lines Suggested by the Announcement that 'A Bill for the Protection of the Property of Married Women Has Passed Both Houses of Our State Legislature,'" *New York Tribune,* 17 April 1848, p. [4];

"Song," *Godey's Lady's Book,* 40 (January 1850): 69;

"The Melancholy Jacques; or, a Dream of Life," *Sartain's Magazine of Literature and Art,* 6 (February 1850): 122.

FICTION

"The Maiden's Mistake," *Ladies' Companion,* 12 (November 1839): 36;

"Dora's Reward: Or the 'Ruse de Guerre,'" *Graham's Magazine,* 22 (June 1843): 357–362;

"The Wife," *Graham's Magazine,* 23 (December 1843): 268–271;

"Kate Melburne," *Ladies' National Magazine,* 5 (January 1844): 24–27;

"Florence Errington: 'An O'er True Tale,'" *Graham's Magazine,* 26 (February 1845): 54–56;

"Ida Grey," *Graham's Magazine,* 27 (August 1845): 82–84.

NONFICTION

"Pictures from a Painter's Life," *Ladies' Companion,* 16 (January 1842): 149–150;

"Life in New York: A Sketch of a Literary Soiree," *Graham's Magazine,* 30 (March 1847): 177–179;

"Kate Carol to Mary S[eward]," *Columbian Magazine,* 7 (May 1847): 203–306;

"Kate Carol to her *," *Sartain's Magazine of Literature and Art,* 1 (July 1847): 55–58;

"Reminiscences of Edgar A. Poe," *Saroni's Musical Times,* 1 (8 December 1849): 118–119.

Frances Sargent Osgood, a popular member of New York literary circles in the 1840s, achieved national recognition as a poet by satisfying the contemporary ideal of the woman poet and developing connections with editors, publishers, and fellow authors in Boston; Philadelphia; Providence, Rhode Island; Charleston, South Carolina; and New York. By the early twentieth century she had been relegated to a niche of literary history as a sentimentalist whose lyrical facility and personal charms led Edgar Allan Poe to praise her extravagantly. Recent scholars of women's poetry acknowledge her distinctive voice and examine her artful negotiation of social and literary conventions.

The sixth of seven children of Joseph Locke, a merchant, and his second wife, Mary (Ingersoll) Foster, Frances Sargent Locke was born in Boston 18 June 1811 and spent much of her youth in Hingham, Massachusetts. By her own account she was a happy, petted child. She was educated primarily at home but attended the prestigious Boston Lyceum for Young Ladies in 1828. With her family's encouragement she began writing in girlhood. Several of her verse narratives and addresses to relatives and friends, signed "Florence," were published in literary annuals and in periodicals, including the *Juvenile Miscellany* (Boston), *Ladies' Magazine* (Boston), and *Southern Rose* (Charleston).

In 1834, while composing poems in response to paintings at the Boston Athenaeum, Frances Locke met Samuel Stillman Osgood, a twenty-six-year-old artist who was exhibiting at the Athenaeum. He asked her to sit for a portrait and, as he worked, told her of his adventures at sea and on three continents. Locke later sketched some of Osgood's adventures in "Pictures from a Painter's Life" (January 1842). They were engaged before the portrait was finished and married on 7 October 1835. The couple soon proceeded to London in pursuit of Samuel Osgood's goal of studying art. During three and a half years in England he painted portraits of various notables and exhibited at the Royal Academy of Arts. Welcomed in circles of artists, authors, and visitors from America, Frances Osgood was acquainted with Eliza Cook, Mary Russell Mitford, and dramatist James Sheridan Knowles. Osgood's first daughter, Ellen Frances, born in July 1836, was a source of joy and a favorite literary subject. While contributing to English literary annuals and magazines, Osgood placed verses in American periodicals: the *Southern Rose;* its successor, *The Southern Rose Bud; The New York Mirror;* and *Godey's Lady's Book.*

A Wreath of Wild Flowers from New England, By Frances Sargent Osgood (1838) includes 137 of her poems. The most ambitious work in this volume is "Elfrida," a five-act blank-verse tragedy centered on a woman who fiercely desires to be queen. Poe and Sarah Josepha (Buell) Hale, editor of *Godey's,* commented that "Elfrida" has passages of considerable power; but Hale, like a reviewer for *The Ladies' Companion* of New York, stated that the poet's true "genius" was lyrical. Osgood took the hint, and literary critics have since focused on her short rhymed verse. Osgood was made popular by lyrics similar to "Miscellanous Poems" and "Juvenile Rhymes." Her lyrics include lines composed in response to pictures; dramatic monologues, some of which are in children's voices; ballads and other narratives chiefly about interpersonal relationships; verse letters; and tributes to relatives and friends. Memorable moments in the Osgoods' domestic life are captured in "The Child and the Watch" and "Ellen Learning to Walk."

Other themes and techniques characteristic of Osgood's later work are prominent in *A Wreath of Wild Flowers from New England.* "The Withered Flower and Broken Heart" portrays an innocent young woman—a common type in Osgood's poems and stories—arrayed for a dance before and after being slighted by the man she loves. The young woman's wilted rose is equated with her crushed feelings.

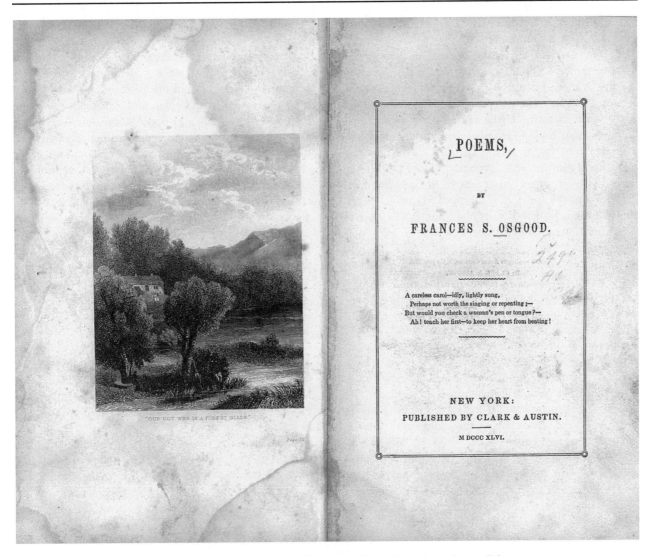

POEMS,

BY

FRANCES S. OSGOOD.

A careless carol—idly, lightly sung,
  Perhaps not worth the singing or repeating ;—
But would you check a woman's pen or tongue ?—
  Ah ! teach her first—to keep her heart from beating !

NEW YORK:
PUBLISHED BY CLARK & AUSTIN.
M DCCC XLVI.

"OUR COT WAS IN A FOREST GLADE"

Frontispiece and title page for Osgood's collection of 105 songs, dramatic monologues, dialogues,
and verse letters and narratives (Thomas Cooper Library, University of South Carolina)

Throughout Osgood's work, buds and blossoms are figures for women and children; flowers and gems represent emotions and abstractions. Her own penchant for spontaneity animates "The Spoilt Pupil of Fancy," spoken in the voice of a schoolgirl who "cannot bear to talk, and walk, / And look, and smile by rule." Formerly taught by the "pleasanter governess," Fancy, she is now subjected to Latin, bored with "haughty hum-drum Reason," and confronted with "Reality." This girl's impatience with mere facts is intended to be amusing. In contrast, the speaker of "The Warning," afraid that she has imagined the world to be brighter and better than it is, refuses to relinquish "the blessed illusion." Many of Osgood's poetic personae experience painful awakenings.

A Wreath of Wild Flowers from New England demonstrates Osgood's proficiency in a variety of verse forms, her expansive but musical style, and her reliance on favorite words and images. The work was well received in Britain; a second edition appeared in 1842 in London as well as Boston. American reviews sounded the keynotes of contemporary criticism of Osgood: her poems were beautiful, fluent, fanciful, and appropriately centered on "the affections." *The Ladies' Companion* (New York) and the *North American Review* (Boston) urged that the young author's effusions deserved careful revision.

While in London, Osgood also compiled a miniature volume of verse, *The Casket of Fate* (1839). One poem from the volume, "The Language of Gems," interprets precious stones as emblems of ideals, feelings, and qualities: the "rosy carnelian" suggests "Modesty's" blush; the carbuncle glows in darkness like "Faith." The rest of *The Casket of Fate* mainly consists of original verses that assign a gem and a fanciful meaning to each month.

The Osgoods returned to the United States in early summer 1839, determined to build successful careers. A second daughter, May Vincent, was born in Boston that July. The August issue of *The Ladies' Companion*–then featuring Lydia Huntley Sigourney, Ann Stephens, and Emma Embury–announced Osgood as a regular contributor. The magazine printed her writings steadily for the next three and a half years. In the early 1840s her lyrics also appeared in *Godey's* and the *Family Companion and Ladies' Mirror* of Macon, Georgia. In 1842 the couple settled in New York, the center of the American artistic community.

Frances Osgood expected and often received payment for her contributions to widely circulated periodicals. From May 1842 to early 1850 she frequently published poems and stories in *Graham's Magazine,* a flourishing monthly that paid its well-known contributors, including Osgood, liberally. In late 1843 she began writing for Charles Jacobs Peterson's *Ladies' National Magazine,* and from early 1844 to mid 1848 every volume of *The Columbian Magazine* included at least one of her compositions in prose or verse. In "To My Pen" (February 1846) the speaker wittily claims to be awed by the "twice twenty thousand eyes" that follow each "careless caper."

Osgood, like her acquaintances and like commentators who did not know her, maintained that poetry flowed freely through her pen, while she had a distaste for prose composition. The narrator of "Kate Melburne" (January 1844) bemoans the effort required to construct a plot when she "had rather be scribbling verses" and coaxes the reader to excuse this uninspired tale submitted for daily bread. Osgood's stories and sketches are variously developed, decorated, or filled out with lyrics. Perhaps she actually found versifying effortless. However, her productivity and demure self-promotion in personal and epistolary interactions with editors argue that she exerted herself for popular success. Her poems were published and copied not only in various periodicals and dozens of gift books but also in anthologies such as William Cullen Bryant's *Selections from American Poets* (1840) and mid-century collections of American "female poets" edited by Caroline May, Thomas Buchanan Read, and Rufus Wilmot Griswold.

The Poetry of Flowers and Flowers of Poetry: To Which are Added, a Simple Treatise on Botany, with Familiar Examples, and a Copious Floral Dictionary (1841), a gift book that Osgood edited, features colored plates and brief botanical and fanciful essays explicating the language of flowers–a genteel code propagated in many mid-nineteenth-century floral dictionaries. Osgood associates flowers and plants with emotions, abstractions such as absence, and nonverbal statements. By wearing white daisies, she explains, a lady can decorously convey the message "I will think of it" to a suitor who has proposed marriage. Along with "sentiments" selected from British and American poets she included more than a hundred of her own verses of varying lengths–some excerpted from earlier publications, others written specifically for this volume. Her lyrical "illustration" of the white daisy conventionally characterizes matrimony as the "changeless fate" that defines a woman's life. A few pieces signed "F. S. O." are comedic: "Let Me Go!" for example, portrays a pair of lovers barely able to conceal their mutual boredom. *The Poetry of Flowers and the Flowers of Poetry* flourished in a competitive market; there were several impressions of the first edition and at least a dozen reprints by 1869.

Osgood also wrote books for children's entertainment and instruction. *The Snow-Drop: A New-Year's Gift for Children* (1842), a collection of twenty-six of her own lyrics and verse narratives, is dedicated to her daughters, whom she affectionately sketches in "To My Readers." The illustrated *Puss in Boots, and the Marquis of Carabas, Rendered into Verse* (1844) retells the classic tale in both prose and verse. Her preface to *The Flower Alphabet, in Gold and Colors* (1845) states that her purpose is to meet the need for better verses and pictures for children. In this book "Little May" learns the alphabet on a journey guided by a fairy; each letter is adorned with an appropriate flower. Osgood composed brief humorous and moralistic verses for *The Cries of New-York: with Fifteen Illustrations, Drawn from Life by a Distinguished Artist; The Poetry by Frances S. Osgood* (1846), an illustrated directory of the city's working people–sweeper, match boy, baker, and others–with their street cries ("Rags! Rags! Any Rags to Sell"; "Ice! Rockland Ice!").

During their years in New York the Osgoods lived in boardinghouses and hotels, intermittently residing at the splendid Astor House, where they met merchants, tourists, booksellers, and writers–including Park Benjamin and Nathaniel Parker Willis. Frances Osgood entertained ladies and children in her parlor and corresponded with editors, literary and social acquaintances, and old friends, and continued her practice of communicating by means of verses that might be tucked into her portfolio, mailed, or printed.

The vibrant voice of Osgood's best published lyrics allowed contemporaries to feel that they knew her. Osgood's writing easily lends itself to autobiographical readings, if only because many lyrics and sketches narrated in the first person sound authentic. Osgood stated that she needed versifying as an emotional and imaginative outlet; she certainly used the written word to make connections with readers. Some of her publications are demonstrably based on personal experience. Constantly facing deadlines, however, and increasingly wary of exposing herself, she also appropriated conventions from literary annuals and magazines. Her sophistication and skill in creating personae, moreover, anticipate Emily Dickinson.

Contemporary scholars, lacking both a comprehensive biography and a complete bibliography of Osgood's work, have erroneously assumed that particular poems are records of readily identifiable events in Osgood's life, as is the case with critical readings of the poem "I Cannot Forget Him," in print by August 1844. At least three commentaries published since 1977 have misread the poem as a confession of Osgood's attachment to Poe, despite that the date of composition and initial publication antedate Osgood's first encounter with Poe, which occurred in 1845.

Like many of her contemporaries Osgood intimates that women write directly from the heart, a claim proffered on the title page of her *Poems* (1846). She also protested in "AH! Woman still" (April 1845) and later writings that women were not free to express what they felt or to do as they wished. In print and in person, she sometimes challenged social forms in the name of naturalness and candor. Trusting her own judgment and prizing her integrity, she took offense when her truthfulness was doubted or conduct questioned. But as an astute professional with dependent children she could not disregard respectability. She knew that readers tended to equate literary personae and narrators with their authors and, like fellow literary celebrities Willis and "Fanny Fern" (Sara Payson Willis), she sometimes encouraged that identification. By the mid 1840s, however, even some of the writings presented as nonfiction incorporate fictive elements and veils.

"Life in New York: A Sketch of a Literary Soiree" (March 1847) describes a fascinating figure who might be taken for Poe—except that his manner is "uncouth" and he is called "the ideal Yankee of the nineteenth century." Subtitles and epigraphs place "The Melancholy Jacques; or, a Dream of Life" (February 1850) and other late poems in literary contexts. Osgood states in her preface to *Poems* (1850) that some of the selections in that volume had been written for characters in her prose works. Griswold reinforced her disclaimer in his reviews of *Poems* and in his essay on her life and writings—but asserted in the same articles that certain of Osgood's poems truly expressed her essential self.

Unpublished letters of the early and mid 1840s document the Osgoods' intermittent financial difficul-

Osgood's husband, Samuel Stillman Osgood, circa 1850

ties and their extramarital relationships. When they visited Providence in summer 1842, Samuel made himself conspicuous by his attentiveness to twenty-four-year-old Elizabeth Newcomb (sister of Brook Farm boarder Charles King Newcomb). Newcomb's mother had almost given her consumptive daughter up for dead; nevertheless, she preferred that her daughter's gentleman callers be unmarried.

Ignoring or unaware of local gossip, Frances Osgood enjoyed the admiration of bookseller Hiram Fuller; their personal interaction and regular correspondence continued into 1843. To Fuller's chagrin, she responded to his recurrent claim that their relationship was not improper by showing to a mutual male friend the elaborately complimentary letters he had written her. Fuller probably did not know that she also shared his missives with female intimates who teasingly apologized to her for not writing "fuller" letters. In July 1845 Fuller, after having married and joined the editorial staff of *The New York Mirror*, helped Osgood find inexpensive, respectable New York lodgings to occupy without her husband. Later that year she dropped Fuller's acquaintance. He used *The New York Mirror* against her in 1846, snidely suggesting that Poe was overly familiar with "Mrs. Osgood's" prosody and serializing Thomas Dunn English's *1844; or, The Power of the "S. F.": A Tale: Developing the Secret Action of Parties During the Presidential Campaign of 1844,* a novel in which Poe is satirized and Osgood is caricatured as affected and childish.

Osgood's stories, like most other antebellum sentimental magazine fiction, focus on courtship, marriage, and friendship. Largely conventional, sometimes satirical, her stories occasionally reflect her own experience and desires. One such work is "Dora's Reward: Or the 'Ruse de Guerre'" (June 1843). A lady rejects a gifted young sculptor's proposal because he is "obscure." Received as a celebrity on returning from a sojourn in Europe, the artist marries his former model, Dora, who is invested with some of the childlike qualities ("innocence and purity") that Osgood idealized and that friends attributed to her.

The story's narrator also remarks that America patronizes foreign artists while neglecting native genius. This common plaint of American artists and authors had particular significance for the Osgoods. Orphaned at sixteen, Samuel had little formal education and no professional training; recurrent eye problems jeopardized his hard-won career. Traveling frequently in search of subjects, employment, and better health–such was the story told by the Osgoods' associates–he was absent for extended periods. While he was away Frances wrote, enjoyed friends and relatives, and tried, usually with success, to be–or appear to be–happy. Unable to stop speculation about the affectionate enthusiasm she inspired in male as well as female acquaintances, she provided a happy ending for "Dora's Reward": the artist comes home to the woman who would care for him even if he had not achieved wealth and fame. "The Wife" (December 1843) portrays a gentle, dignified woman neglected by a husband absorbed in his profession. Tempted by a lover, she resists adultery–but reveals ambivalence in "Oh, hasten to my side, I pray," a lyric addressed to the distant man she had married. This honorable poet-heroine is rewarded when her husband comes home to forgive and be forgiven.

The condition of the Osgoods' marriage has long intrigued students of Poe's life and literary criticism. Influential Poe scholars Sidney P. Moss and Thomas Olive Mabbott portray her as a coquette, whereas John Evangelist Walsh argues in *Plumes in the Dust: The Love Affair of Edgar Allan Poe and Fanny Osgood* (1980) that she was separated from Samuel in the mid 1840s and that Poe fathered her third child. Although the Osgoods' correspondence establishes that they lived apart at various times, no convincing evidence that they were estranged or that either committed adultery has come to light. Frances Osgood's reputation probably was not seriously compromised by the supposed relationship with Poe, given that her writings continued to be accepted by editors who valued their impeccable moral credentials.

Writings that she published in the mid 1840s do support the thesis that Osgood–disillusioned by intimate relationships (not exclusively marriage) and critical of herself as a gifted poet who was producing trifles–struggled to achieve independence and literary distinction. In "Florence Errington: 'An O'er True Tale'" (February 1845) a fragile heroine who shares Osgood's first pseudonym pines away, believing that her beloved husband is unfaithful. This story with a plot typical of sentimental fiction takes on additional meanings in light of Osgood's unconventional marriage and within the context of other stories and poems that portray dependency on any mortal idol as dangerous to the self. Claiming to prefer death to the loss of inspired self-expression, the "I" of "To the Spirit of Poetry" (January 1845) repeatedly implores the "only" essential "friend," the muse, "Leave me not yet" and resolves to make worthier use of the poetic gift. This prayer to an aesthetic and emotional holy spirit was chosen as the first lyric in her *Poems* of 1846.

By no means a wallflower, Osgood attended soirees for writers, artists, and intellectuals in the company of her husband, fellow poet Mary E. Hewitt, or other friends. At Anne C. Lynch's famous Saturday evenings and Valentine's Day parties in New York she interacted cordially with such lions as Margaret Fuller, Bayard Taylor, Horace Greeley, and Elizabeth Oakes Smith. Soon after meeting Poe in March 1845, she began submitting pseudonymous and signed lyrics to *The Broadway Journal,* his current editorial venture. As their friendship developed, they exchanged letters and met frequently at salons, including Lynch's, and in other settings. He published her submissions, copied her lyrics from other periodicals, and commented favorably on her work, including the romantic story "Ida Grey," published in *Graham's Magazine* in August 1845 and mentioned in the *New York Tribune* notice of that issue.

Ida, a childlike coquette who resembles Osgood physically and temperamentally, meets her soul mate–a genius comparable to Poe–after "his earthly nature" is already married. The hero declares that he and Ida are destined for each other, but she nobly retires to a convent, confident that they will spend eternity together.

Ideal love was a ubiquitous theme in nineteenth-century romantic literature. Osgood had previously written about failed romances, but her serious poems about love deferred for heaven appeared in print after her intense engagement with Poe. Contemporaries in literary networks that reached beyond New York heard of the poets' mutual admiration. Her eulogy beginning "I cannot tell *the world* how thrills my heart / To every touch that flies thy lyre along" quotes from Poe's "Israfel" (1831); signed with her own name, the poem appeared in *The Broadway Journal* on 29 November 1845. In December Poe printed his detailed, predominantly favorable review of her *Poems* (1846). He published three more essays on her work, including a complimentary sketch in his notorious series "The Literati of New York City" published in *Godey's Lady's Book* in May through October of 1846. Gossip about their relationship prompted Osgood to stop seeing him in early 1846. At Samuel Osgood's insistence, Elizabeth F. Ellet, another member of the literary coteries of New York, promised to stop spreading rumors. Ellet nevertheless resumed maligning Poe and Osgood and was confronted and silenced again in early 1849 by Griswold, Frances's new admirer and advisor. From mid 1846 to late 1849 Osgood published several poems and stories about rivalry, envy, slander, false friendship, and the temporal parting of poetic twin souls.

Her second major collection, the *Poems* of 1846, includes 105 songs, dramatic monologues, dialogues, verse letters, and narratives in tones whimsical, humorous, sentimental, homiletic, and monitory. Several selections idealize truth, female beauty and modesty, and that perennial in Osgood's garden, childlike innocence. Compared to *A Wreath of Wild Flowers from New England,* however, this volume projects a darker view of the social world. "Love's Mistake" observes that "Young Love" is attracted to Beauty, not Virtue; "She Says She Loves Me Dearly" expresses the shock of betrayal. Other poems, such as "To Sybil," admit that husbands do not behave like suitors while still others, such as "The Broken Lyre," acknowledge that love can be excruciating. Not remarkable for thematic originality, some of these poems are noteworthy for attitudes inconsistent with the sunny optimism for which Hale commemorated Osgood in *Woman's Record: or, Sketches of All Distinguished Women, From "The Beginning" Till A.D. 1850* (1853). Osgood's satirical pieces often expose hypocrisy and denial. The more conventional, ostensibly autobiographical "'Happy at Home'" (February 1842), opposing affectionate domesticity to "Luxury," "Fashion," and "Wealth," insists that the speaker neither needs nor desires to seek happiness elsewhere. "A Mother's Prayer in Illness" (October 1845) names Osgood's daughters, Ellen and May;

the world-weary speaker asks God to "take them first . . . and then me," lest they endure pain and learn distrust without their mother's loving protection. Unlike "'Happy at Home,'" "A Mother's Prayer in Illness" was not issued with sheet music. Fern quoted it in 1853 in a sentimental reflection on the early deaths of Osgood and her daughters. Other selections in Osgood's 1846 collection are self-critical: "Aspirations," "A Song" ("I turn'd from the monitor,—smiled at the warning"), and "To—" ("They tell me I was false to thee") reflect on the ruinous effects of devoting oneself to an unworthy person or object.

Characterizing Osgood as a well-known and esteemed woman poet, reviewers of the 1846 *Poems* praised her lyrics' "purity," liveliness, and unpretentiousness. *The Brooklyn Daily Eagle* of 17 January 1846 acknowledged her success as a "magazine writer" but admitted to finding her poems "girlish" rather than "womanly." The volume was popular enough to justify reprints in 1848, 1849, 1850, 1852, and 1861.

Osgood moved to Philadelphia in late 1846 with Sam, Ellen, May, and Fanny Fay, born in June 1846 and frail throughout her short life. *The Floral Offering, a Token of Friendship, Edited by Frances S. Osgood. Illustrated with Ten Beautiful Bouquets of Flowers Elegantly Coloured After Nature by I. Ackerman,* a second gift book, appeared in early 1847. This volume includes colored plates of bouquets, verses appropriate to the sentiments associated with each species, and a floral dictionary. Again relying largely on her own lyrics, Osgood also included some poems by close friends.

In 1847 she published six loosely connected prose sketches, four of them headed "Glimpses of a Soul." Narrated by "Kate Carol," these letters to friends such as Hewitt and "Grace Greenwood" (Sara Jane Clarke Lippincott) describe her three daughters and their home life; compliment Willis and Lydia Maria Child, her first patron; comment on her reading; and reflect on religion, duty, and the necessity of writing for pay. Like her stories, these sketches include lyrics, mostly her own. In all, she published at least forty-four prose works that have not been collected. Her stories were mentioned dismissively by Poe and Griswold but mildly praised by Hale and May; John S. Hart included "The Magic Lute" (November 1844) in *The Female Prose Writers of America* (1852). Recent critics have generally analyzed only her "Reminiscences of Edgar A. Poe" (December 1849) and commented briefly on the few stories as evidence of her fascination with Poe.

Several of Osgood's later publications and private letters reflect losses, disillusionments, and conflicts with people she cared for. Longing to escape

Osgood's daughters, May and Ellen, in 1851

life's difficulties, some speakers declare their reliance on God and faith rather than love and fancy. A fond mother's effort to accept her infant daughter's death (Fanny Fay died in October 1847) is movingly presented in "'Ashes of Roses,'" first published under Osgood's name in *The Home Journal* of New York (1 January 1848) with a sympathetic editorial headnote indicating that this poem, though "not written for publication," was being printed to ease "the hearts of those who have suffered the same bereavement." "The Starlight and Music of Home" (May 1848) abjures the hectic "world-life," where "radiant roses" conceal "the snake below," for "this still life" with her two surviving daughters, who comfort her by "talk of heaven and its *new* angel." Evaluated by the standards of domestic sentimentalism, Osgood was the ideal woman poet. By March 1848 she was racked by a cough, probably symptomatic of tuberculosis. But she worked on somber pieces in blank verse, some with rhymed passages in short meters; the latter poems appeared in magazines with subtitles indicating that they were parts of an

unfinished "story" or "novel." She also continued to write pleasing and satirical verses.

The wrapper of *A Letter about the Lions, Addressed to Mabel in the Country* (1849) looks like an envelope with a New York postmark. "Forwarded by G. P. Putnam," it is addressed in Osgood's hand to "Miss Mabel Montagu, Montpelier, Montgomery County, Massachusetts." This booklet offers a country cousin news of "this bewildering Babel" in which authors puff themselves; critics review books they do not read; and painters produce fake antiques. In ballad stanzas enlivened by puns and amusing rhymes, Osgood compliments or mildly satirizes contemporaries, among them "Fanny Forester" (Emily Chubbuck Judson), Sarah Helen Whitman, Evert Augustus Duyckinck, Griswold, "The Raven," landscape painter Thomas Cole, "illustrious illustrator" Felix Octavious Carr Darley, and "fearless" Samuel Osgood, "off again" to California.

Osgood's husband sailed for San Francisco in early February 1849–according to Griswold–to recover his health and make his fortune. The Osgoods corresponded during his yearlong absence; one of Sam's letters enclosed gold dust. Frances remained in New York, periodically visiting friends and relatives in Philadelphia and New England. Gossip dissuaded her from setting up housekeeping with Griswold (married but estranged from his wife) as a boarder. From January through June 1849 she was a regular contributor to *The Flag of Our Union,* a popular Boston monthly that generously paid successful authors. Hoping to regain her own health, she spent part of the summer of 1849 with friends at Saratoga Springs, New York. She visited the nearby grave of Margaret Davidson, revered in mid-century America as a child poet who died of consumption. Osgood's mother died 22 July 1849. On hearing that Poe had died 7 October 1849, she wrote "A Dirge" (13 October 1849) for *Saroni's Musical Times;* this tribute became the last song in her *Poems* of 1850. The speaker of "Alone" (November 1849) is "once more alone—and desolate," yet exults in newfound "self-reliance." Instead of "Love," the speaker now trusts "Faith" and "Courage."

Frances Osgood, still in need of affection and assistance, had given Griswold power of attorney in early 1849. He offered her manuscripts to editors, specifying the payments she would accept; he persuaded Carey and Hart to publish a new collection of her poems in a series of handsomely printed octavos by Bryant, Henry Wadsworth Longfellow, and Sigourney. Osgood's last book was anonymously edited and vigorously promoted by Griswold. Illustrated with ten plates, including engravings of Samuel Osgood's paintings of Frances, Ellen, and May, the *Poems* of 1850 includes 253 titles. According to Fannie Hunewell, 101 of these had already appeared in *A Wreath of Wild Flowers from New England* or the 1846 *Poems* or both. In addition to the varied lyric forms Osgood had previously employed, this volume includes effective pieces in blank verse. Griswold's influence is discernible in the conspicuous grouping of twenty-two "Sacred Poems." Griswold, an antifeminist, would not have been likely to demur if it was her choice to omit "Lines" (April 1848), her response to the recent passage of a law protecting married women's property rights in New York State. This signed poem in the *New York Tribune* asks, why don't "*all houses*" protect women's "fancies, tastes, affections," and "'warm illusions'"?

Osgood's last collection does include "Woman: A Fragment" (December 1848), which affirms that "fair woman" can be happy in her rigidly circumscribed domestic and social spheres if she can dress, laugh, "waltz and warble at her own sweet will."

Unlike "cold reformers" dissatisfied with "the sacred names of mother, sister, wife," Osgood's speaker gladly leaves to men the "sterner" occupations of sailor, warrior, blacksmith, and senator. The overt protest against "Decorum," "Fashion," and men's "tyrant power" is archly mitigated, or corroborated, in the last quatrain: "Woman is not unfair—the 'docile darling' merely wants '*her way!*'" First-person speakers in "It is this restless heart within" and "Song" (January 1850) assert without such coy or qualifying irony the need for freedom of will, movement, and expression.

A relatively expensive 466-page book, the *Poems* of 1850 did not sell as quickly as the publishers had expected, though it was widely and favorably reviewed. Commending her poems as "feminine" and herself as "womanly," critics agreed that she ranked among America's best and most popular women poets and predicted that this volume would secure her lasting fame. *The Literary World* (29 December 1849) suggested that she had written "too much" yet compared complaining of Osgood's "exuberance" to "criticising rosebuds for blooming prematurely into roses." *The Literary World* praised her for not venturing into subjects or harboring ambitions unsuitable for "her sex." The *Southern Quarterly Review* (April 1850) expressed reservations, finding the poetry immature but conceding that Osgood gushed "pleasantly." Her last collection was reprinted for the fourth time in 1850.

Previously unpublished poems by Osgood appeared in periodicals in late 1849 and early 1850. Like many authors afflicted with tuberculosis, during her final, rapid decline she was advised to stop writing. She found the prohibition difficult. In February 1850 her husband returned to New York in improved health and spirits and flush with his earnings from prospecting and painting. Sam carried her into their new home, where she died 12 May 1850, five weeks short of her thirty-ninth birthday.

The many periodicals that noticed Osgood's death assessed her work in terms characteristic of antebellum criticism of the successful woman poet: not a careful artist, she was a natural, graceful singer with a deservedly high rank among American women writers. Two essays by Griswold shaped her reputation for more than a century. The first was a sketch of her life and writings published in his own literary magazine, *International Monthly Magazine,* in December 1850 and reprinted in a commemorative gift book in Osgood's honor: *The Memorial: Written by Friends of the Late Mrs. Osgood and Edited by Mary E. Hewitt* (1851), reprinted as *Laurel Leaves: A Chaplet Woven by the Friends of the Late Mrs. Osgood, Edited by*

Mary E. Hewitt (1854). More influential was Griswold's controversial biography of Poe (1850) included in his edition of Poe's works. By incorporating Osgood's indulgent portrait of her friend as "that stray child of Poetry and Passion," Griswold encouraged readers to view her merely as the good angel of a deeply flawed genius, rather than a poet in her own right. Her currency as a popular poet and literary critics' patronage of artless poetesses dwindled during the late 1800s, to be obliterated by changing expectations for women's poetry and by the modernist reaction against domestic sentimentalism.

Frances Sargent Osgood's name was recognized exclusively by literary scholars and chiefly as the lady poet who charmed Poe until Emily Stipes Watts reclaimed her in *The Poetry of American Women from 1632 to 1945* (1977). Cheryl Walker examines her contribution to the "dominant female tradition" in *The Nightingale's Burden: Women Poets and American Culture Before 1900* (1982). Osgood is included in several anthologies of nineteenth-century women writers, including *American Women Poets of the Nineteenth Century: An Anthology* (1982), edited by Walker; *Nineteenth-Century American Women Writers: An Anthology* (1997), edited by Karen L. Kilcup; and *Nineteenth-Century American Women Poets: An Anthology* (1998), edited by Paula Bernat Bennett. Joanne Dobson argues in "Reclaiming Sentimental Literature" (1997) that sentimental writings–including poems by Osgood–can be responsibly and respectfully evaluated as literary texts.

Bibliography:

Frances Hunewell, *The Life and Writings of Frances Sargent Osgood,* M.A. thesis, University of Texas at Austin, 1924.

References:

Mary G. De Jong, "Lines from a Partly Published Drama: The Romance of Frances Sargent Osgood and Edgar Allan Poe," in *Patrons and Protegees: Gender, Friendship, and Writing in Nineteenth-Century America,* edited by Shirley Marchalonis (New Brunswick, N.J.: Rutgers University Press, 1988), pp. 31–58;

Joanne Dobson, "Reclaiming Sentimental Literature," *American Literature,* 69 (June 1997): 263–298;

Dobson, "Sex, Wit, and Sentiment: Frances Osgood and the Poetry of Love," *American Literature,* 65 (December 1993): 631–650;

Rufus Wilmot Griswold, "Frances Sargent Osgood," *International Monthly Magazine,* 2 (December 1850): 131–140;

Burton R. Pollin, "Poe and Frances Osgood, as Linked through 'Lenore,'" *Mississippi Quarterly,* 46 (Spring 1993):185–197.

Papers:

Correspondence and manuscripts of Frances Sargent Osgood are held by Harvard University, the Boston Public Library, and the American Antiquarian Society. The University of Virginia has a composition book from Osgood's school days.

James Kirke Paulding

(22 August 1778 – 6 April 1860)

Wayne R. Kime
Fairmont State College, West Virginia

See also the Paulding entries in *DLB 3: Antebellum Writers in New York and the South; DLB 59: American Literary Critics and Scholars, 1800–1850;* and *DLB 74: American Short-Story Writers Before 1880.*

BOOKS: *Salmagundi; or, the Whim-Whams and Opinions of Launcelot Langstaff and Others,* 20 parts, republished in 2 volumes, anonymous, by Paulding, Washington Irving, and William Irving (New York: D. Longworth, 1807–1808; London: L. M. Richardson, 1811);

The Diverting History of John Bull and Brother Jonathan, as Hector Bull-us (New York: Inskeep & Bradford / Philadelphia: Bradford & Inskeep, 1812; London: Sherwood, Neely & Jones, 1814);

The Lay of the Scottish Fiddle (New York: Inskeep & Bradford / Philadelphia: Bradford & Inskeep, 1813; London: James Cawthorn, 1814);

The United States and England: Being a Reply to the Criticism on Inchiquin's Letters. Contained in the Quarterly Review *for January, 1814* (Philadelphia: Bradford & Inskeep / New York: A. H. Inskeep, 1815);

Letters from the South, Written During an Excursion in the Summer of 1816, 2 volumes (New York: James Eastburn, 1817; revised and enlarged, New York: Harper, 1835);

The Backwoodsman (Philadelphia: M. Thomas, 1818);

Salmagundi, Second Series, 1819–1820, 2 volumes (Philadelphia: M. Thomas, 1819–1820);

A Sketch of Old England by a New-England Man, 2 volumes (New York: Charles Wiley, 1822; London: Sir Richard Phillips, 1822);

Koningsmarke, The Long Finne, A Story of the New World, 2 volumes (New York: Charles Wiley, 1823; London: Whittaker, 1823);

John Bull in America; or, The New Munchausen (New York: Charles Wiley, 1825; London: John Miller, 1825);

The Merry Tales of the Three Wise Men of Gotham (New York: G. & C. Carvill, 1826);

James Kirke Paulding (engraving by F. Halpin from a drawing by Joseph Wood, circa 1813)

The New Mirror for Travellers; and Guide to the Springs. By an Amateur (New York: G. & C. Carvill, 1828); revised and enlarged as *A Book of Vagaries; Comprising the New Mirror for Travellers and Other Whim-Whams, Being Selections from the Papers of a Retired Common-Councilman, Erewhile Known as Launcelot*

Langstaff . . . Edited by William I. Paulding (New York: Charles Scribner, 1868);

Tales of the Good Woman. By a Doubtful Gentleman (New York: G. & C. & H. Carvill, 1829);

Chronicles of the City of Gotham, from the Papers of a Retired Common Councilman (New York: G. & C. & H. Carvill, 1830);

The Dutchman's Fireside, 2 volumes (New York: J. & J. Harper, 1831; London: Henry Colburn & Richard Bentley, 1831);

Westward Ho! 2 volumes (New York: J. & J. Harper, 1832); republished as *The Banks of the Ohio* (London: A. K. Newman, 1833);

Sketch of the Early Life of Joseph Wood, Artist (Washington, D.C.: Temperance Association, 1834);

The Works of James K. Paulding, 15 volumes (New York: Harper, 1834–1839);

A Life of Washington, 2 volumes (New York: Harper, 1835);

Slavery in the United States (New York: Harper, 1836);

The Book of Saint Nicholas. Translated from the Dutch of Dominie Nicholas Ægidius Oudenarde (New York: Harper, 1836);

A Christmas Gift from Fairy Land (New York: D. Appleton, 1838);

The Old Continental; or, The Price of Liberty, 2 volumes (New York: Paine & Burgess, 1846);

The Puritan and His Daughter, 2 volumes (New York: Baker & Scribner, 1849; London: Putnam, 1849);

The Lion of the West Retitled The Kentuckian, or A Trip to New York; A Farce in Two Acts, . . . Revised by John Augustus Stone and William Bayle Bernard, edited by James N. Tidwell (Stanford: Stanford University Press / London: Oxford University Press, 1954).

OTHER: *The Bucktails; or, Americans in England,* in *American Comedies,* by Paulding and William Irving Paulding (Philadelphia: Carey & Hart, 1847), pp. 17–100.

SELECTED PERIODICAL PUBLICATIONS– UNCOLLECTED:

FICTION

"The Adventures of Henry Bird," *Analectic Magazine,* 6 (October 1815): 295–301;

"Cobus Yerks," in *The Atlantic Souvenir* (Philadelphia: Carey, Lea & Carey, 1828), pp. 192–206.

NONFICTION

"American Drama," *American Quarterly Review,* 1 (June 1827): 331–357;

"Dramatic Literature," *American Quarterly Review,* 8 (September 1830): 134–361.

James Kirke Paulding is best remembered today as a collaborator with the youthful Washington Irving in the *Salmagundi* papers, collected as *Salmagundi; or, the Whim-Whams and Opinions of Launcelot Langstaff and Others* (1807–1808), but a steady stream of his own writings came before the American public for almost a half century afterward. During a long and active lifetime he won reputation as a defender of the United States and its institutions against attacks by the British and as a pioneer in portraying American scenes, characters, events, and folkways in literature. Paulding wrote in several genres–informal essay, verse satire, short story, novel, travel account, biography, and drama. An astute and vocal observer of the political scene, he was for many years a prominent civil servant, rising to the secretaryship of the navy under President Martin Van Buren. Although an ardent nationalist, in his later years he was somewhat out of sympathy with his own time. He feared social change and distrusted banks, paper money, steam power, railroads, and the formation of great cities. For him, the peaceful state of agrarian society in the mid eighteenth century was a fondly imagined social ideal.

Paulding was born 22 August 1778 in Great Nine Partners, New York, one of nine children and the youngest son of William and Catharine Ogden Paulding. At the close of the Revolutionary War, William Paulding suffered severe financial reverses connected with his volunteer service as commissary general to the New York State militia, and the Paulding family became impoverished. James received little formal education, passing much of his boyhood wandering dreamily around the village of Tarrytown, New York, or else in reading whatever came to hand. As a child he was melancholy, painfully shy, and awkward in company–deficiencies that he overcame in adulthood even though he never lost his taste for solitude. Like Washington Irving, with whom he became acquainted during Irving's occasional visits to Tarrytown, Paulding developed a lifelong fondness for rural life and unspoiled nature.

At the age of eighteen Paulding moved to New York, where his brother William had secured employment for him in a public office. This change of residence brought Paulding into contact with his brother-in-law William Irving, a genial man of many talents whose home was a gathering place for young men of wit and ability. Paulding was soon taking part in the discussions, debates, and good times of this city-bred fraternity. He tried his hand at verse, and eventually under the pseudonym "Walter Withers" he began contributing *Spectator*-style essays to the *New York Morning Chronicle,* the same newspaper that printed the earliest writings of Washington Irving.

Paulding gained local prominence as an author when, between 24 January 1807 and 25 January 1808, he collaborated with Washington Irving and William Irving in *Salmagundi*, a series of twenty pamphlets that amused New Yorkers by its stylish satire of contemporary fads and follies. Brilliant, brash, and splendidly miscellaneous, *Salmagundi* gave pleasure both to its readers and to its creators. The three young men adopted a variety of pseudonyms for their contributions, but the shared authorship of the series soon became an open secret. Work on many of the individual pieces seems to have been truly collaborative. Paulding enjoyed his participation so much that in 1819–1820 he brought out a second *Salmagundi* series written by himself alone. However, this series lacked the sparkle of the original, and its limited success led some to compare him unfavorably to Washington Irving, whose *Sketch-Book* was being published serially at just that time.

In 1812 Paulding wrote the first of his several contributions to the acidulous war of words between the United States and England that raged for three decades thereafter. This prose narrative, *The Diverting History of John Bull and Brother Jonathan*, presents relations between England and America allegorically, as quarrels between members of a family—Britain, or "John Bull," was characterized as the paterfamilias, a pompous old fool. The following year Paulding wrote an even more bitter satire, *The Lay of the Scottish Fiddle*. This narrative in octosyllabic verse was a parody of Walter Scott's *The Lay of the Last Minstrel* (1805); Paulding's work portrayed with indignation the recent British attacks on American soil, including the burning of the White House and subsequently the town of Havre de Grace, Maryland. In 1813 Paulding also contributed sketches of American naval heroes to *The Analectic Magazine*, then under the editorship of Washington Irving. In 1814 Paulding enlisted in the New York militia and was commissioned a major.

Paulding's participation in the War of 1812 confirmed in him a nationalist spirit that continued to express itself through hostility toward England. The occasion of his *The United States and England: Being a Reply to the Criticism on Inchiquin's Letters. Contained in the Quarterly Review for January, 1814* (1815) was a contemptuous notice of *Inchiquin's Letters* (1810), by his countryman Charles Jared Ingersoll, in the anti-American London *Quarterly Review*. In this short book Paulding rebutted point by point the reviewer's abusive commentary on the United States and its citizenry. *A Sketch of Old England by a New-England Man* (1822) was another such counterattack, this time fictional. It reversed the familiar pattern of ignorant and biased British travelers who pretended in their published reports to profound familiarity with the entire American scene. In Pauld-

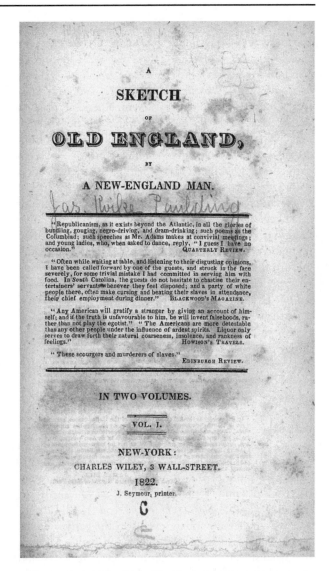

Title page for the U.S. edition of Paulding's fictional travel narrative, in which a sharp-tongued Yankee derides the English (Thomas Cooper Library, University of South Carolina)

ing's work the sneering traveler was a sharp-tongued, opinionated Yankee. *A Sketch of Old England* was an unusually unkind book even for Paulding, who relished controversy, and he later regretted its tone. The successor to this book, *John Bull in America; or, The New Munchausen* (1825), was another travesty of British travel writers, but its satire was of quite a different character. Written at intervals during five weeks while Paulding sought to care for his dying son, the work is deft and delightful—rich in caricature, diversified by tall tales, and pervaded by playful humor.

Paulding's literary activity on behalf of his country during wartime had attracted notice in Washington, and in 1815 he was appointed secretary to the Board of Navy Commissioners, beginning an association with the United States Navy that continued until 1841.

While living in the national capital, Paulding became friends with leading politicians, especially Southerners such as John Randolph and Henry Clay. A trip through Virginia resulted in *Letters from the South, Written During an Excursion in the Summer of 1816* (1817), a series of epistolary essays that comprises a sympathetic account of the landholding aristocracy—cultivated yet not ostentatiously so, hospitable, close to the land, and free from the dissipations of city life. Paulding, who was of Dutch extraction on his father's side, felt a deep identification with his childhood home along the Hudson River, but he was much interested in the peoples and customs of other regions. His *The Backwoodsman* (1818), a narrative in heroic couplets, celebrated the pioneer spirit that had manifested itself among immigrants beyond the mountains to Kentucky. Yet, in the same work he also wrote with understanding of the indigenous Indian peoples, troubled by the inexorable advance into their homeland of an alien civilization.

Paulding married Gertrude Kemble on 15 November 1818, and in 1823 he returned to New York, where he served until 1838 as navy agent and in his spare time became a professional writer. His wife had inherited funds that enabled him to write without anxiety for the commercial success of his books, but he pursued his new career energetically and with success. During his lifetime he earned more than $50,000 from authorship, an unusually large sum for that era. His initial work of the period, frankly inspired by the recent successes of James Fenimore Cooper, was *Koningsmarke, The Long Finne, A Story of the New World* (1823), an historical romance describing events in the early colonial period. This fast-paced tale of love and peril was set in the Swedish settlements along the Delaware River and featured a colorful assortment of characters—a despotic dominie, a half-addled Negro servant given to dire prophesies, Quakers, treacherous Indians, British soldiers, and the title character, "Long Finne."

In the later 1820s Paulding devoted most of his creative energy to writing short tales and sketches. He contributed more than seventy of these to newspapers, magazines, and annuals and collected several in volumes associated with a particular setting or group of characters. *The Merry Tales of the Three Wise Men of Gotham* (1826) was such a gathering; it portrayed early New York in a fictional guise while making light of Robert Owen's utopian theories. *Tales of the Good Woman. By a Doubtful Gentleman* (1829) recounted travelers' tales supposedly heard at The Good Woman, a fabled inn in New Jersey. *Chronicles of the City of Gotham, from the Papers of a Retired Common Councilman* (1830) again gave fictional form to bits of folklore connected with the Dutch colonies in America. Though loose in construction and uneven in quality, these tales convey at times a subtly realized sense of life as actually experienced, with a bittersweet sensitivity to human frailty and sorrow. Such authors as Edgar Allan Poe later wrote of Paulding with respect as an early practitioner of the short tale as an art form.

Paulding's gift as a humorist shines out in two books that appeared during these years. *The New Mirror for Travellers; and Guide to the Springs. By an Amateur* (1828) parodies popular guidebooks and, amid pleasant but often lengthy digressions, sketches the various social types to be seen along the Hudson River between New York and upstate resorts such as Saratoga Springs and Ballston-Spa. In this volume the brilliance of the original *Salmagundi* is again in evidence, modified by Paulding's easy impulse to linger. A second work, the winner in a contest to produce an original American play, was *The Lion of the West* (composed in 1830; published as *The Lion of the West Retitled The Kentuckian, or A Trip to New York A Farce in Two Acts* in 1954). It was performed in New York in 1830. Nimrod Wildfire, the hero of this lively comedy, was modeled on the eccentricities of Colonel David Crockett, the flamboyant congressman from Tennessee. To avoid giving offense to Crockett, Paulding denied having intended a specific portrait, but the likeness was nonetheless clear. The character of Nimrod Wildfire remained a prime feature in the repertory of the American actor James H. Hackett for two decades after.

Enjoying wide acclaim and writing with easy confidence, Paulding now resumed activity as a novelist, producing in succession two works that have been considered among his best. *The Dutchman's Fireside* (1831) describes scenes along the upper Hudson River during the French and Indian War. It portrays the troubled passage to manhood of Sybrandt Westbrook, an awkward, bookish youth whose travels bring him into contact with bluestocking New Yorkers, arrogant British soldiers, bloodthirsty Indians along the northern frontier, and most daunting of all, a young woman with whom he falls in love. Paulding portrays as one of Sybrandt's comrades and elder advisers an actual historical personage, Sir William Johnson, superintendent of the Six Iroquois Nations. However little this literary representation conformed to its original, the character of Sir William is a memorable mix of energetic woodsman's sagacity, worldly wisdom, and farsighted good nature. As his authority for depiction of American scenes and customs at this early period, Paulding drew upon Mrs. Anne Grant's *Memoirs of an American Lady* (1808), which he praised in the preface to *The Dutchman's Fireside* as "one of the finest sketches of early American manners ever drawn." *Memoirs of an American Lady* later served as a basis for James Fenimore Cooper's *Satanstoe* (1846).

The Dutchman's Fireside was followed by Westward Ho! (1832), a tale of the adventures in Kentucky of a Virginia family, the Dangerfields. In a manner that recalls his use of Grant's Memoirs of an American Lady, Paulding resorted to Timothy Flint's Recollections of the Last Ten Years, Passed in the Valley of the Mississippi (1826) to provide a realistic basis for his description of the frontier. However, Westward Ho! has been admired less for its success in representing remote locales than for its insightful portrayal of the psychological sufferings of Dudley Rainsford, the lover of the heroine Virginia Dangerfield. Though disjointed and disproportionate in its organization, Westward Ho! was a distinct popular success. Shortly afterward, Paulding's stature as an American author led the Harper publishing firm of New York to begin publishing a collected edition of his writings. Between 1834 and 1839 fifteen volumes of that edition were published, though the project was never completed.

In the mid 1830s Paulding became increasingly preoccupied by political issues that led him to write anonymous newspaper articles, but he also found time to complete two nonfictional works. A Life of Washington (1835), an adulatory biography written for the Harpers as a book for children, suffered from lack of detail but remained a standard account until supplanted by Irving's carefully documented Life of George Washington (1855–1859). Like A Life of Washington, Paulding's next book, Slavery in the United States (1836), was an openly patriotic work, though a different one, for it addressed in combative manner a topic of heated current controversy. The abolitionist cause, Paulding argued in this work, was ill conceived and potentially disastrous in its effects, for by promoting an early end to Negro slavery it threatened the survival of the United States. The abolitionists, he claimed, were ill informed about actual conditions in slaveholding regions, unrealistic in their belief that members of the Negro race would be benefited by being suddenly set free, and naive in their apparent belief that the constitutionally guaranteed property rights of a great body of American citizens could simply be set aside without dire consequences. Slavery in the United States set forth a detailed argument, but it was a fiercely polemical book.

Paulding's strong views, active involvement in contemporary affairs, and long federal service led to his appointment in 1838 as secretary of the navy, and in the three busy years that followed he had little time free for authorship. Other than gathering stories for reprinting in The Book of Saint Nicholas. Translated from the Dutch of Dominie Nicholas Ægidius Oudenarde (1836) and A Christmas Gift from Fairy Land (1838), he did not write for publication, so that his literary accomplish-

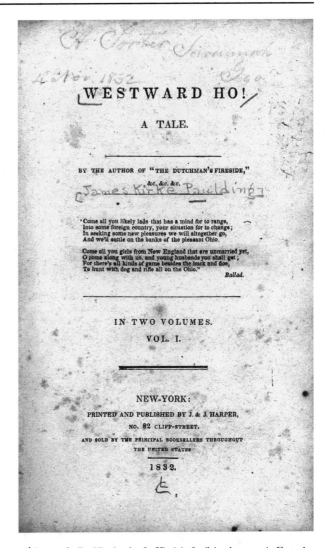

Title page for Paulding's tale of a Virginia family's adventures in Kentucky (Thomas Cooper Library, University of South Carolina)

ments faded somewhat from public view. A hostile notice of his collected works in 1839 marked the beginning of a decline in Paulding's literary reputation. In retaliation for a supposed slight, the New York poet and journalist N. P. Willis declared Paulding "quite dead and forgotten" as a writer, dismissing him as merely a "jackal" to Washington Irving. Paulding, who kept silence, was stoutly defended in print by others, but the damage was done.

For a time after his retirement in 1841 he continued to write for magazines, but his activity was now more desultory than before. In 1846 he purchased a rural estate near Hyde Park, New York, where he proposed to amuse himself as a gentleman farmer. During this decade he wrote two more novels, more for his own pleasure than in anticipation of renewed critical favor. The Old Continental; or, The Price of Liberty (1846) described events in Westchester County, New York,

Letter from Paulding to his former collaborator, Washington Irving (from The Letters of James Kirke Paulding, *edited by Ralph M. Aderman, 1962)*

during the Revolutionary War. Among many vivid scenes, it recounted one that had remained a cherished source of pride within the Paulding family, the capture in 1780 of Major John André, a British spy, by John Paulding and two of his comrades. Like Paulding's other book-length fictions, *The Old Continental* is often vivid in details and short passages but is slipshod in construction. His final volume, *The Puritan and His Daughter* (1849), begins by describing England in civil war in 1645 and follows Harold Habingdon, a devout Puritan, and his family to the New World, where he hopes to continue practicing his faith in its gospel purity. The subsequent fortunes of Habingdon involve conflict between his stern bigotry and the spirit of tolerance then prevailing in the colonies, especially in Virginia, where he immigrates. The novel was Paulding's personal favorite but is a feeble effort, unfulfilled in its thematic potential, weak in characterization, and uncharacteristically vague in its description of settings.

Having reached seventy-one years of age when *The Puritan and His Daughter* was published, Paulding continued to write, but not often for publication; he was content to live in obscure retirement. When he died on 6 April 1860, he had outlived his fame; nor, despite recent efforts to achieve an informed understanding of American literature prior to the Civil War, has that fame ever been renewed. Yet his writings do merit attention, for he was a versatile and lively presence on the national scene for many years. Although he often wrote too hastily and too lengthily, he won the respect of his contemporaries and produced a few works that remain among the finest of their era. James Kirke Paulding loved to write, and in testing his own powers he explored with originality and zest the possibilities of a national literature then in the process of defining itself.

Letters:
The Letters of James Kirke Paulding, edited by Ralph M. Aderman (Madison: University of Wisconsin Press, 1962).

Bibliographies:
J. Albert Robbins, "Some Unrecovered Poems of James Kirke Paulding: An Annotated Checklist," *Studies in Bibliography,* 3 (1950–1951): 229–240;

Ralph M. Aderman, "James Kirke Paulding's Contributions to American Magazines," *Studies in Bibliography,* 17 (1964): 141–151;

Michael John McDonough, "James Kirke Paulding: A Bibliographic Survey," *Resources for American Literary Study,* 15 (1985): 145–161.

Biographies:
William I. Paulding, *Literary Life of James K. Paulding* (New York: Charles Scribner, 1867);

Amos L. Herold, *James Kirke Paulding, Versatile American* (New York: Columbia University Press, 1926);

Larry J. Reynolds, *James Kirke Paulding* (Boston: Twayne, 1984).

References:
Ralph M. Aderman, "James Kirke Paulding as a Social Critic," *Papers on English Language and Literature,* 1 (1965): 217–229;

Amos L. Herold, "Paulding's Literary Theories," *Bulletin of the New York Public Library,* 66 (1962): 236–243;

Louis D. Owens, "James K. Paulding and the Foundations of American Realism," *Bulletin of the New York Public Library,* 79 (1975): 40–50;

Floyd C. Watkins, "James Kirke Paulding and the South," *American Quarterly,* 5 (1953): 219–230.

Papers:
Manuscripts, letters, and other papers of James Kirke Paulding are held in many libraries in the state of New York and elsewhere. The largest collections are in the New-York Historical Society, New York; the William R. Perkins Library, Duke University; the Henry E. Huntington Library, San Marino, California; the Berg Collection, New York Public Library; and the Library of Congress, Washington, D.C.

William Trotter Porter

(24 December 1809 – 19 July 1858)

James L. Gray
Indiana University of Pennsylvania

See also the Porter entries in *DLB 3: Antebellum Writers in New York and the South* and *DLB 43: American Newspaper Journalists, 1690–1872.*

BOOKS: *The Big Bear of Arkansas, and Other Sketches, Illustrative of Characters and Incidents in the South and Southwest,* edited by Porter (Philadelphia: Carey & Hart, 1845);

Instructions to Young Sportsmen, in All That Relates to Guns and Shooting by Lieut. Col. P. Hawker. . . . To Which Is Added the Hunting and Shooting of North America, with Descriptions of the Animals and Birds, edited by Porter (Philadelphia: Lee & Blanchard, 1846);

A Quarter Race in Kentucky, and Other Sketches, Illustrative of Scenes, Characters, and Incidents Throughout "The Universal Yankee Nation," edited by Porter (Philadelphia: Carey & Hart, 1846).

PERIODICALS EDITED: *St. Johnsbury, (Vt.), Farmer's Herald* (1829);

Norwich Vermont Enquirer, associate editor (1830);

Spirit of the Times (1830–1856);

American Turf Register and Sporting Magazine (1836–1856);

Porter's Spirit of the Times (6 September 1856–1858).

William Trotter Porter

William Trotter Porter is usually regarded as one of the most significant individuals in the development of what has come to be known as the "Humor of the Southwest." It would be easy to think of Porter in terms of anomalies. Porter was a New Englander by birth and a resident of New York City for most of his life. He did not intend to found a journal of humor; he did not write humor himself. Yet, *The New-York Spirit of the Times*—the journal he founded in New York City, owned for perhaps ten years, and edited for more than twenty—played a seminal role in the development of Southwestern humor. The two volumes he edited from *The Spirit of the Times*—*The Big Bear of Arkansas* (1845) and *A Quarter Race in Kentucky* (1846)—along with the journal itself brought national attention to most of the significant figures of the genre and the first publication for some writers.

Porter was born in Newbury, Vermont, the third son of Benjamin Porter and Martha Olcott. Both his father and his paternal grandfather, Asa Porter, thought of themselves as gentlemen and passed on an early love of horses and perhaps some social attitudes to Porter. After his father's death in 1818 Porter moved to Hanover, New Hampshire, where he, apparently reluctantly, received some education before being apprenticed to a printing firm in Andover, Massachusetts. Probably through the influence of his older brother Thomas O. Porter, he was brought into contact with Southern life. Norris W. Yates writes in *William T. Porter and The Spirit of the Times,* his 1957 biography of Porter:

Thus among the elements of Porter's early life and background we find the open-handed ways and liking for fine horses which one often associates with country gentlemen, a love of companionship, a dislike of academic routine and Calvinistic morality, a fondness for sport and the literature of sporting, and possibly an interest in things 'Southron.' These elements may or may not have directly influenced his mature life and work, but notice of them may at least help us to understand more readily the career of Porter and the *Spirit.*

Porter seems to have spent some years as a journeyman printer, was editor of the *Farmer's Herald* in St. Johnsbury, Vermont, in 1829 and associate editor of the *Norwich Vermont Enquirer* in Norwich, Vermont, the next year. He may also have done some teaching before arriving in New York City in 1830, where he worked as a printer and gave Horace Greeley his first New York job.

Porter was a convivial person, known for frequenting the gathering places, including saloons, in New York City and having many friends, especially among the New York literati and journalists. In addition to Greeley, George Wilkins Kendall, who became the editor of *The New Orleans Daily Picayune,* was among the earliest of these friends. Others included Nathaniel Parker Willis (with whom one of Porter's brothers founded a short-lived journal in 1839) and several of the members of his circle. Porter's biographer and brother-in-law, Francis Brinley, emphasizes Porter's social nature by reprinting an article about "Frank's," an establishment frequented by Porter and other "men about town," including Lewis Gaylord Clark, editor of *The New-York Knickerbocker,* a popular journal devoted to things English. An ardent fisherman and among the founders in 1842 of the New York Cricket Club, Porter had a particular interest in the breeding and raising of horses, a hobby that might be expected of him. Beginning in 1836 he made several trips to the South, where he visited family members and old friends and identified new contributors to his journal.

Porter and James Howe produced the first issue of *The Spirit of the Times* on 10 December 1831. Greeley helped prepare the first issues. Porter's desire was to found a sporting magazine, modeled on the pattern of *Bell's Life in London.* In that context, he featured reports and analyses of horse racing throughout the country, as well as material on other sporting activities. In his article "*Spirit of the Times,*" in *American Humor Magazines and Comic Periodicals* (1987), Lorne Fienberg quotes Porter's 1837 statement that "we are addressing ourselves to gentlemen of standing, wealth and intelligence" and asserts that "From its earliest issues, the editorial mission of *The Spirit of the Times* was the cultivation of the *ideal gentleman.*" In that context Porter early reprinted several major contemporary English writers, including Charles Dickens and William Makepeace Thackeray, who reflected gentle-

manly tastes. In the same spirit, Porter also reprinted selections from Americans James Fenimore Cooper, Washington Irving, and William Gilmore Simms. Throughout Porter's editorship, he continued to print sentimental pieces with some frequency. Despite his upper-class bias, Porter also clearly stated that he would not take political positions—quite possibly, Fienberg thinks, because he did not want to offend either his national or his Southern audience.

The first several years of *The Spirit of the Times* were not especially successful in the competitive world of New York City journalism; beginning at $3.00 per year for a subscription, then moving to $5.00, and in 1839 to $10.00—after he had purchased the *American Turf Register and Sporting Magazine*—it was more expensive than most. Though the exact dates Porter owned and edited the journal are difficult to sort out, especially before 1835, he clearly owned it from 1836 until mounting financial difficulties led him to sell it in 1842; the new owner reduced the subscription price to $5.00 annually in 1844. Although he remained editor in chief until 1856, Porter then surrendered editorial control and began a similar journal titled *Porter's Spirit of the Times,* but he died in 1858.

The focus emphasized by the subtitle of the magazine—a "Chronicle of the Turf, Agriculture, Field Sports, Literature and the Stage"—did not entirely disappear, but it did move over a period of years toward an increasing reliance on "correspondents" and "original contributions." Yates thinks that the effect on horse racing as a result of the panic of 1837 and Porter's several tours of the South beginning in 1836 were major factors in the change. Porter's continuing association, beginning in 1832, with George Wilkins Kendall, who became editor of *The Picayune,* and for whom Porter's brother George was an associate editor, was likely another factor. Walter Blair points out that Porter's "correspondents" frequently "embodied in their writings the matter and manner of the oral story." Blair describes the magazine as therefore often becoming "a medium for the swapping of tall tales." Yates sees a tension between the informal literary essay (especially the sporting narrative) made popular in England and "rougher freer style" of the "oral tale of the backwoods." He believes that the latter grew from the former as the generally upper-class authors described their social inferiors in the journal. As an obvious consequence, the characters in the narratives frequently mouthed opinions that their creators might not share, as well as used language and described actions that were not acceptable in more proper and mainstream literary forums. Porter often struggled with this latter tendency, sometimes rejecting material as too racy and even changing one sketch when he reprinted it in *A Quarter Race in Kentucky.* This positioning of inaccurate language (and sometimes improper behavior) as a characteristic of the

Illustration by F. O. C. Darley for The Big Bear of Arkansas,
and Other Sketches, Illustrative of Characters and
Incidents in the South and Southwest *(1845),*
edited by Porter. The pieces originally appeared in
Porter's journal, The Spirit of the Times.

lower classes clearly permitted the writers, the editor, and the readers to confirm their own superiority as individuals and to view the lower-class characters as clowns and entertainers. The frequently mentioned apolitical nature of the magazine may therefore be more than a little suspect. The obvious class attitudes in the narratives and Porter's oft-reiterated desire to publish material for the well-to-do in a periodical that aspired to be national perhaps suggest that Porter did not avoid political subjects only as a matter of principle. He might also have thought that his covert political positions, if made overt, would cost him subscribers and support. *The Spirit of the Times* became a major print outlet for most of those who have come to be known as the significant writers of Southwestern humor—Henry Clay Lewis (Madison Tensas), Johnson Jones Hooper, Sol Smith, Thomas Bangs Thorpe, William Tappan Thompson, Joseph M. Field, John S. Robb, Joseph Glover Baldwin, and George Washington Harris.

In these circumstances and with these writers, the stature of *The Spirit of the Times* increased, and the weekly in turn provided stature to its writers. *The Spirit of the Times* became a national weekly with a large circulation, though quite probably not the circulation of forty thousand that

Porter claimed at one point; selections from it, moreover, were widely reprinted in other journals. On 27 March 1841 Porter published the most famous tale in Southwestern humor, Thomas Bangs Thorpe's "The Big Bear of Arkansas." Johnson Jones Hooper, the creator of Simon Suggs, received his first national exposure from Porter. George Washington Harris for some years wrote intermittently for *The Spirit of the Times* and published his first Sut Lovingood tale there in 1854, near the end of Porter's tenure as editor. It is therefore not surprising that the Philadelphia publishing house of Carey and Hart asked Porter to edit a volume of sketches from *The Spirit of the Times* as early as the mid 1840s. These sketches rather quickly became two volumes, *The Big Bear of Arkansas* and *A Quarter Race in Kentucky*. For the two volumes Porter selected a total of fifty-four pieces by a wide variety of writers. Each volume sold out an original edition of four thousand copies and was reprinted frequently during the next few years. Yates points out that these were the third and fourth volumes of Southern and Western humor to be published in America, but eight of the authors included by Porter published volumes within two years. Porter's introduction to *The Big Bear of Arkansas* clearly indicates that by 1845 he was aware that he was involved in the development of a new kind of American writing.

In 1856 Porter left the editorship of *The Spirit of the Times* to become editor of *Porter's Spirit of the Times,* a new journal owned by George Wilkes. Increasing ill health and the death of the last of Porter's brothers in 1855 may have to some degree caused a further decline in Porter's health. Porter spent the last winter of his life at home among his books and with visits from his friends. He seemed to regain his health for a short while, but on 13 July he came down with a severe cold and congestion of the lungs; he died on 19 July 1858.

The new kind of American writing espoused by Porter had as one characteristic a changed attitude toward women and toward sentimentality. *The Spirit of the Times,* as Porter edited it, was directed almost entirely toward a masculine audience. Many of the narratives do not mention women, or do so only incidentally. Those stories that do mention women ordinarily treat them unsentimentally, and the male characters may be brutal toward women and treat them as sex objects. Fienberg perhaps takes one critical extreme when he characterizes "both its matter and its manner [as] defiantly masculine," given to debunking "myths about the chaste, genteel, and mannered young women whom they met in their parlor society, and courted to become their wives." They are the objects of bawdy stories, and their value lies in their ability to produce young. Other critics took a less extreme position, but most generally agreed with the notion that Porter's writers were assertively masculine in their attitudes. Yet, Porter, whose friendship with the ever-sentimental Willis has been noted, never quit publishing sentimental tales, and some of his correspondents, especially the soldiers, were often sentimental. In one famous instance, Porter revised a tale in *A Quarter Race in Kentucky* to make its conclusion sexually suggestive rather than overtly so. Yates reports that Porter in some instances rejected submissions as too racy. A 1993 essay by William E. Lenz titled "The Function of Women in Old Southwestern Humor: Re-reading Porter's *Big Bear* and *Quarter Race* Collections" examines Porter's two edited collections and finds the relationship between men and women in them to be more complex than earlier critics believed. Lenz sees women as "as an essential part of the tradition of Southwestern Humor," dominant in their "familial, domestic, or social situations" but likely to be either victimized or idealized when they appear "in the male domain."

The importance of William Trotter Porter and that of *The Spirit of the Times* might best be understood in the context of the development of Southwestern humor. Porter played an important role in the development of American realism and of a specifically American literature. Yet, when Ralph Waldo Emerson in the "American Scholar Address" (31 August 1837) and the "Divinity School Address" (15 July 1838) sought the new American writer—calling him a "poet"—Emerson never would have thought that in his "embrace of the common" and his desire to "know the meaning of . . . The meal in the firkin; the milk in the pan, the ballad in the street; the news of the boat . . . " that something similar to the pieces in *The Spirit of the Times* might contribute to the success of his search. What F. O. Matthiessen has named the "American Renaissance" had no place for Porter or for *The Spirit of the Times,* a circumstance Matthiessen seems to find disappointing. One part of the reason might have been the characteristic New England distaste for anything not of New England (Porter's own New England roots were of little importance). Another part might have been that the writers normally associated with Emerson had little of the sort of sense of humor exemplified in *The Spirit of the Times.* One perhaps surprising fact is that *The Spirit of the Times* is one of the few journals to review positively both Herman Melville's *Moby-Dick* (1851) and his *Pierre* (1852). *Moby-Dick* is one of the few novels of "Renaissance" figures to feature the kind of sense of humor that Porter published. The brief mention of *Pierre* may have been intended only as a kindness to the author of *Moby-Dick.* One can hardly imagine Porter's ideal Southern gentleman finding pleasure in *Pierre.* Whatever the reasons, as Kenneth S. Lynn demonstrates in *Mark Twain and Southwestern Humor* (1959), the humor that received its main impetus through Porter's journal was also at the center of the realistic movement that gave the

United States Mark Twain and much of the literature that was to follow.

Bibliography:

Norris W. Yates, *William T. Porter and* The Spirit of the Times (Baton Rouge: Louisiana State University Press, 1957), pp. 205–210.

Biography:

Francis Brinley, *Life of William T. Porter* (New York: D. Appleton, 1860).

References:

Walter Blair, *Native American Humor (1800–1900)* (New York: American Book Company, 1937), pp. 82–85;

Blair, "Traditions in Southern Humor," *American Quarterly,* 5 (1953): 132–142; reprinted in Walter Blair, *Essays on American Humor: Blair Through the Ages,* edited by Hamlin Hill (Madison: University of Wisconsin Press, 1993), pp. 15–24;

Lorne Fienberg, *"Spirit of the Times,"* in *American Humor Magazines and Comic Periodicals,* edited by David E. E. Sloane (New York: Greenwood Press, 1987), pp. 271–278;

William E. Lenz, "The Function of Women in Old Southwestern Humor: Re-reading Porter's *Big Bear* and *Quarter Race* Collections," *Mississippi Quarterly,* 46 (1993): 589–600;

Kenneth S. Lynn, *Mark Twain and Southwestern Humor* (Boston: Little, Brown, 1959);

F. O. Matthiessen, *American Renaissance: Art and Expression in the Age of Emerson and Whitman* (New York: Oxford University Press, 1941), p. 637;

Frank Luther Mott, *A History of American Magazines, 1741–1850* (New York: D. Appleton, 1930), pp. 480–481;

"William Trotter Porter," in *Appleton's Cyclopædia of American Biography,* volume 5, edited by James Grant Wilson and John Fiske (New York: D. Appleton, 1888), pp. 80–81;

Norris W. Yates, *"The Spirit of the Times:* Its Early History and Some of Its Contributors," *Papers of the Bibliographical Society of America,* 48 (1954): 117–148;

Yates, *William T. Porter and The Spirit of the Times: A Study of The Big Bear School of Humor* (Baton Rouge: Louisiana State University Press, 1957).

Papers:

The small number of William Trotter Porter's letters that exist and copies of *The Spirit of the Times* are scattered among three libraries.

George Palmer Putnam

(7 February 1814 – 20 December 1872)

Ezra Greenspan
University of South Carolina

See also the G. P. Putnam's Sons entry in *DLB 49: American Literary Publishing Houses, 1638–1899* and the George Palmer Putnam entries in *DLB 3: Antebellum Writers in New York and the South* and *DLB 79: American Magazine Journalists, 1850–1900.*

BOOKS: *Chronology; or, An Introduction and Index to Universal History, Biography, and Useful Knowledge; Comprising a Chronological, Contemporary, and Alphabetical Record, of Important and Interesting Occurrence, from the Earliest Period to the Present Time* (New York: Leavitt / Boston: Crocker & Brewster, 1833); revised and enlarged as *The World's Progress: A Dictionary of Dates. With Tabular Views of General History* (New York: Putnam, 1850; revised, 1851); republished as *Handbook of Chronology and History: The World's Progress, A Dictionary of Dates. With Tabular Views of General History* (New York: Putnam, 1852); republished as *The World's Progress: A Dictionary of Dates, with Tabular Views of General History* (New York: Barnes / Cincinnati: Derby, 1854); republished as *The World's Progress: A Dictionary of Dates; With Tabular Views of General History and a Historical Chart* (New York: Putnam, 1857); revised and enlarged as *Cyclopedia of Chronology; or, The World's Progress: A Dictionary of Dates, with Tabular Views of General History and an Historical Chart* (New York: Barnes & Burr, 1860); revised and enlarged as *The World's Progress: A Dictionary of Dates, Being a Chronological and Alphabetical Record of All Essential Facts in the Progress of Society, from the Creation of the World to the Inauguration of Lincoln* (New York: Putnam, 1864); revised and enlarged as *The World's Progress: A Dictionary of Dates: Being a Chronological and Alphabetical Record of All Essential Facts in the Progress of Society, from the Creation of the World to August, 1867* (New York: Putnam, 1867);

Leavitt, Lord & Co.'s Catalogue of Books in the Various Departments of Literature, Including Both Foreign and American Editions (New York: Leavitt, Lord, 1836);

George Palmer Putnam

The Tourist in Europe; or, A Concise Summary of the Various Routes, Objects of Interest, etc. in Great Britain, France, Switzerland, Italy, Germany, Belgium and Holland; with Hints on Time, Expenses, Hotels, Conveyances, Passports, Coins, etc.; Memoranda during a Tour of Eight Months in Great Britain and on the Continent, in 1836, as the Author of "An Introduction and Index to General History" (New York: Wiley & Putnam, 1838);

American Facts: Notes and Statistics Relative to the Government, Resources, Engagements, Manufactures, Commerce, Religion, Education, Literature, Fine Arts, Manners and Cus-

toms of the United States of America (London: Wiley & Putnam, 1845);

A Pocket Memorandum during a Ten Weeks' Journey to Italy and Germany (New York, 1848);

Catalogue of Foreign and American Books (New York: Putnam, 1850);

Catalogue of the Most Important Books Published During 1850, '51, and '52: A Supplement to Putnam's Book-Buyer's Manual (New York, 1852);

Supplement to The World's Progress, a Dictionary of Dates and Statistics (New York, 1852);

Catalogue of a Private Collection of Autograph Letters (New York: Putnam, 1858);

Before and after the Battle: A Day and Night in "Dixie" (New York, 1861);

Suggestions for Household Libraries of Essential and Standard Works (Exclusive of Scientific and Religious Works) (New York: Putnam, 1870); revised as *The Best Reading: Hints on the Selection of Books; on the Formation of Libraries, Public and Private* (New York: Putnam, 1873);

Studies of Irving, by Putnam, Charles Dudley Warner, and William Cullen Bryant (New York: Putnam, 1880).

OTHER: William Cullen Bryant, Daniel Webster, John W. Francis, George Bancroft, George W. Bethune, G. P. R. James, Francis L. Hawks, Samuel Osgood, Washington Irving, and others, *Memorial of James Fenimore Cooper,* edited by Putnam (New York: Putnam, 1852);

Popping the Question, and Other Tales: Embracing the Best Stories of the Best Authors; Now First Collected, edited by Putnam (Philadelphia: Peck & Bliss, 1858);

Ten Years of the World's Progress, Being a Supplement to the Work of That Title, edited by Putnam (New York: Putnam, 1861);

Letters from Europe Touching the American Contest: And Acknowledging the Receipt, from Citizens of New York, of Presentation Sets of the "Rebellion Record," and "Loyal Publication Society" Publications, edited by Putnam (New York: Loyal Publication Society, 1864);

Soldiers' and Sailors' Patriotic Songs, edited by Putnam (New York: Loyal Publication Society, 1864);

Benjamin Vincent, ed., *Haydn's Dictionary of Dates,* supplement by Putnam (New York: Putnam, 1867).

SELECTED PERIODICAL PUBLICATIONS—
UNCOLLECTED: "Recollections of Irving: By His Publisher," *Atlantic Monthly,* 6 (November 1860): 601–612;

"Rough Notes of Thirty Years in the Trade," *American Publishers' Circular and Literary Gazette,* new series 1 (15 July 1863): 242–245; (1 August 1863): 258–259; (15 August 1863): 290–292;

"Rough Notes of the English Book-Trade," *American Publishers' Circular and Literary Gazette,* new series 1 (15 October 1863): 418–419;

"Some Things in London and Paris—1836–1869," *Putnam's Magazine: Original Papers on Literature, Science, Art, and National Interests,* 3 (June 1869): 733–743;

"Leaves from a Publisher's Letter-Book," *Putnam's Magazine: Original Papers on Literature, Science, Art, and National Interests,* 4 (October 1869): 551–561; (December 1869): 675–682.

George Palmer Putnam was one of the leading American publishers of the nineteenth century. He was not only the founder of the firm of G. P. Putnam—later G. P. Putnam's Sons—but also the most active member of the trade in organizing publishing as a modern profession. He published works by many of the leading writers of the mid nineteenth century, including Washington Irving, James Fenimore Cooper, Nathaniel Hawthorne, Herman Melville, Edgar Allan Poe, Margaret Fuller, Susan Warner, and Thomas Carlyle. He opened the first overseas branch of an American publishing house and engaged for many years in the international and rare-book trades in both New York and London. He published or edited periodicals important to the development of American culture. He promoted and patronized American authors and fought for international copyright protection for their works. Finally, he helped bring the New York Book Publishers' Association into existence. Putnam was, however, not only a pioneering publisher but also a consequential figure in the professionalization of the related literary functions of authorship, editing, and bookselling, all of which he practiced over much of his career.

Putnam was born on 7 February 1814 in Brunswick, Maine, to Henry and Catherine Palmer Putnam. Both parents came from prominent Massachusetts families and were recent transplants to northern New England. Putnam's father, a Harvard-trained lawyer, failed in various pursuits before devoting much of his time during Putnam's boyhood to amateur authorship. He patronized the first printing shop in town, which was opened by Joseph Griffin in 1820, and a few months later he brought the manuscript for his first work to be printed there.

Putnam received his only formal education in the coeducational private school his mother operated in the family home. At eleven he was sent to Boston to apprentice in his uncle John Gulliver's carpet shop. The menial tasks of an errand and shop boy bored him, and in 1829 he obtained permission to leave his uncle's employ. He boarded a schooner for New York City, where he soon found a position as a clerk in the

Putnam's wife, Victorine Haven Putnam

the *Booksellers' Advertiser and Monthly Register of New Publications.* Putnam compiled this work, too, during his off-hours from Leavitt's store. He brought it out all through 1834, suspended it after the December number, then brought out one last issue in March 1836. The *Booksellers' Advertiser* was Putnam's first attempt to bring order and systematization to the largely provincial American publishing trade.

The reason for its termination was Putnam's departure from Leavitt on being offered a junior partnership with the bookselling and publishing firm of Wiley and Long at 161 Broadway. John Wiley wanted to play a larger role in the transatlantic book trade, and within a few weeks of being hired Putnam was off on an extended bookselling tour of Europe. Using London as his primary base of operations, Putnam not only forged connections for the firm with dozens of publishers and authors in Great Britain and on the Continent but also followed the current vogue for travel writing by keeping a notebook and then transcribing his impressions into a guidebook, *The Tourist in Europe; or, A Concise Summary of the Various Routes, Objects of Interest, etc. in Great Britain, France, Switzerland, Italy, Germany, Belgium and Holland; with Hints on Time, Expenses, Hotels, Conveyances, Passports, Coins, etc.; Memoranda during a Tour of Eight Months in Great Britain and on the Continent, in 1836* (1838).

Putnam returned to New York in the fall of 1836. Early the next year he succeeded George Long, who had retired, as Wiley's partner in the renamed firm of Wiley and Putnam. Putnam played a leading role in organizing a booksellers' dinner at the City Hotel to celebrate the achievements of American authors; it was held on 30 March 1837, with nearly three hundred in attendance.

A year later Putnam and Wiley opened a branch publishing house in London—the first such overseas expansion by an American firm. Putnam was put in charge of the London office, and he left New York in July on a venture that lasted for nearly ten years, interrupted by periodic returns to New York. During those years he used his strategic location in London and his connections with agents in major Continental book centers to buy rare books, magazines, and copies of current European works for sale, distribution, or republication in the United States. Only rarely did he publish works in England—the first seems to have been Poe's *The Narrative of Arthur Gordon Pym of Nantucket,* which appeared a few months after his arrival in London. He also played a large role in the composition and publication of *Wiley and Putnam's Literary News-Letter and Monthly Register of New Books, Foreign and American* (1841–1847), which is still a highly useful source of information on the

bookstore of George W. Bleecker. Bleecker published a monthly magazine, the *Euterpeiad: An Album of Music, Poetry and Prose,* and he sent his teenage clerk up the Hudson River to solicit subscriptions.

In 1831 Putnam moved to the larger establishment of Jonathan Leavitt, one of the city's most ambitious booksellers and publishers. During his five years with Leavitt he not only learned the profession of bookselling but also pursued two literary tasks that would have been daunting for a seasoned professional but were extraordinary for a teenage clerk. The first was the composition of *Chronology; or, An Introduction and Index to Universal History, Biography, and Useful Knowledge; Comprising a Chronological, Contemporary, and Alphabetical Record, of Important and Interesting Occurrence, from the Earliest Period to the Present Time* (1833), a reference work that Putnam compiled from notes he made during a course of self-study in standard works of history at the Mercantile Library in his after-work hours. Copublished by Leavitt in New York and Crocker and Brewster in Boston, it was a steady seller that Putnam's own publishing house later updated and kept in print into the twentieth century. The second was the establishment of the first trade journal in American publishing history:

book trade in the period. On 13 March 1841, on one of his visits to New York, he married sixteen-year-old Victorine Haven, one of his mother's students; they eventually had ten children.

During the last years of their partnership Wiley and Putnam launched two complementary series: the Library of Choice Reading brought prose works by leading British and Continental authors to American readers, while the Library of American Reading, published in New York and London, comprised works by such rising American authors as Poe, Melville, Hawthorne, Fuller, Bayard Taylor, and William Gilmore Simms. Putnam's *American Facts: Notes and Statistics Relative to the Government, Resources, Engagements, Manufactures, Commerce, Religion, Education, Literature, Fine Arts, Manners and Customs of the United States of America* was published in London in 1845, just after the debut of the two Library series. From his earliest years in New York, Putnam had assiduously collected data about American culture through library research, correspondence, and formal surveys, and he decided to use that information to try to explain the United States to a European audience. At the same time, the work provided American readers with a great deal of previously inaccessible information, and its narrative of material and cultural productivity became a central component of the developing American self-image.

Growing competition in the sale of European books in the United States and falling profits led Putnam to return to New York in the spring of 1847. First, however, he took a three-month farewell tour of the Continent with his wife, part of which they spent in the company of Fuller. As he had during his European tour a decade earlier, Putnam kept a diary of his impressions; it served as the basis of the privately published *A Pocket Memorandum during a Ten Weeks' Journey to Italy and Germany* (1848), much of which had been serialized in fifteen weekly installments in the *Literary World* from 7 August to 13 November 1847.

Putnam finished out the year with Wiley but went out on his own in early 1848, setting up shop a few doors down the block at 155 Broadway as G. P. Putnam. Within a few months he arranged to publish a revised author's edition of Irving's old works and all of his future ones; the agreement, which netted each man tens of thousands of dollars over the next decade, served as the cornerstone of Putnam's publishing house. He also proceeded quickly in 1848 to forge connections with a wide variety of established and rising authors, including Cooper, Poe, James Russell Lowell, Francis Parkman, and Catharine Maria Sedgwick. His initial year's list also included

one of the first standard reference sources in Americana, *Poole's Index*.

The early 1850s were years of fast-paced growth and prosperity for Putnam and the American publishing trade generally. Perhaps Putnam's personal high point was the decision he made, in concert with Charles Frederick Briggs, George William Curtis, and Parke Godwin, in late summer 1852 to publish a monthly magazine to serve as a showcase for American writing. From the first issue in January 1853 through the nearly two and a half years it remained under his control, *Putnam's Monthly Magazine of American Literature, Science, and Art* set a new standard for American literary journalism. Its first appearance nearly coincided with the publication for the 1852 Christmas season of one of Putnam's most important and enduring gift books, *Homes of American Authors*. The work identified a core group of outstanding contemporary American authors—Irving, Cooper, Sedgwick, Lowell, Simms, Ralph Waldo Emerson, Henry Wadsworth Longfellow, William Cullen Bryant, Nathaniel Hawthorne, Daniel Webster, William Prescott, and John Pendleton Kennedy—and demonstrated their professional success by describing the stately residences their works had presumably enabled them to purchase. The sketches of the authors and their homes were written by Briggs, Curtis, Godwin, Caroline Kirkland, Henry Tuckerman, George Hillard, Edward Everett Hale, Rufus Griswold, George Washington Greene, and George Washington Peck.

In the mid 1850s business reversals, most likely caused by embezzlement by John Leslie, the partner Putnam had taken in late 1852 to form G. P. Putnam and Company, undermined his ability to operate in the expansive style he had followed since going out on his own in 1848. Putnam kept the firm solvent by selling off the printing plates for many of its choice properties in 1854. In 1855 he sold the magazine to the new firm of Dix and Edwards.

Though beset by financial troubles, Putnam continued to play a central role in the profession. In 1855 he helped found the New York Book Publishers' Association and, under its auspices, a genuine trade journal, the *American Publishers' Circular and Literary Gazette* (the forerunner of *Publishers Weekly*). As secretary of the association he organized a lavish dinner in honor of American authors at the Crystal Palace on 27 September and gave the keynote speech, proudly pointing out the astronomical growth of American publishing and authorship: "Why, sir, the sheets from our book-presses alone, in a single year, would reach nearly twice round the globe; and if we add the periodicals and newspapers, the issues of our

Cover of a copy of the first issue of Putnam's first magazine that once belonged to William Makepeace Thackeray, who drew on it the sketches of an African American field-worker, Henry Wadsworth Longfellow, and George William Curtis (The Henry A. and Albert W. Berg Collection, New York Public Library)

presses in about eighteen months would make a belt, two feet wide, printed on both sides, which would stretch from New York to the Moon!"

In July 1857 further embezzlements by Leslie and the general downturn of the economy forced Putnam to declare bankruptcy. A generous settlement allowed him to reorganize his business within a few weeks, this time primarily as the publisher of Irving and Taylor. With renewed profitability from their works subsidizing his operations, he was able gradually to expand his publishing list in the years leading up to the Civil War.

Like the trade generally, Putnam entered the war era facing the loss of Southern markets, revocation of debts, and increasing costs of production caused by shortages of printmaking supplies. Nevertheless, during the first years of the conflict he kept up an active publishing list weighted toward war-related publications. The most important was the *Rebellion Record,* an illustrated weekly compendium that attempted to provide the fullest possible documentation of the war. An ardent supporter of the Republican Party since its founding and of the Union cause, he spent considerable effort trying to influence domestic and foreign public opinion by disseminating information and propaganda through the Loyal Publication Society, which he founded. After observing the first Battle of Bull Run he wrote *Before and after the Battle: A Day and Night in "Dixie"* (1861) as a corrective to reports that the Union army had retreated from the field in panicked disarray.

Following his appointment in 1862 as United States revenue collector for the Eighth District of New York, Putnam withdrew from active publishing and assigned his list to the firm of Hurd and Houghton. He planned to write a book, to be titled "Thirty Years Notes," in which he would tell not only the story of his own three decades in the profession but also that of the profession as a whole during the period. The Philadelphia publisher George W. Childs, whose opinion he consulted, thought that it would become "the booksellers' Bible." But Putnam backed away from his plan to write a book and instead published a short series of reminiscences titled "Rough Notes of Thirty Years in the Trade" in the *American Publishers' Circular and Literary Gazette* during the summer of 1863.

After being fired as tax collector by President Andrew Johnson in the fall of 1866 for his principled refusal to contribute money to Johnson's campaign, Putnam took back his plates and publication list and–with his oldest son, George Haven Putnam, as his junior partner–reopened for business in January 1867 at 661 Broadway as G. P. Putnam and Son. One of the highlights of these years was the resumption in January 1868 of the magazine, now called *Putnam's Magazine*. Also in 1868 Putnam was one of the prime movers in the founding of the International Copyright Association, which was formed to lobby Congress to pass a law protecting literary properties beyond national borders. In 1869 he wrote two series of professional reminiscences, "Some Things in London and Paris–1836–1869" and "Leaves from a Publisher's Letter-Book," for *Putnam's Magazine*. The magazine, however, was less successful than its predecessor had been, and Putnam was forced to abandon it in the summer of 1870. In that same year another son, John Bishop Putnam, became a partner in the firm, which was renamed G. P. Putnam and Sons. A long-time supporter of the fine arts and publisher of art books, Putnam played a leading role in founding the Metropolitan Museum of Art, which opened to the public on 22 February 1872 with Putnam as the honorary first superintendent.

A third son, Irving Putnam, entered the firm in 1872. The house continued its publishing and bookselling operations with little overall direction and on precarious, undercapitalized terms. George Palmer Putnam remained active in the business until his death on 20 December 1872. The following year the firm was renamed G. P. Putnam's Sons.

By that time the provincial world of American publishing that George Palmer Putnam had known as a teenage clerk was gone. Putnam, however, had not regretted the sweeping changes that time had brought. He had devoted his life to the professionalization of American writing and publishing, and he died with the satisfaction of having seen that mission largely accomplished.

Biographies:

George Haven Putnam, *A Memoir of George Palmer Putnam,* 2 volumes (New York: Putnam, 1903); revised as *George Palmer Putnam: A Memoir,* 1 volume (New York & London: Putnam, 1912);

Ezra Greenspan, *George Palmer Putnam: Representative American Publisher* (University Park: Pennsylvania State University Press, 2000).

Papers:

The largest archive of George Palmer Putnam's letters and manuscripts and of material pertaining to *Putnam's Monthly* is the George Palmer Putnam Collection at Princeton University. Other major archives are the Herbert Putnam Collection at the Library of Congress, the George Palmer Putnam Collection at the New York Public Library, and the George Haven Putnam Collection at Columbia University Library. Extensive files of Putnam's correspondence with specific authors are in the Bayard Taylor Collection at Cornell University Library and the Putnam-Asa Gray file at the Gray Herbarium Archives at Harvard University.

Anna Mowatt Ritchie

(12 September 1819 – 27 July 1870)

Anne Zanzucchi
University of Rochester

See also the Ritchie entry in *DLB 3: Antebellum Writers in New York and the South.*

BOOKS: *Pelayo, or The Cavern of Covadonga—A Romance,* as Isabel (New York: Harper, 1836);

Reviewers Reviewed: A Satire, as Isabel (New York: Harper, 1837);

Gulzara, or the Persian Slave (New York: S. French, 1841);

The Fortune Hunter, or the Adventures of a Man about Town: A Novel of New York Society, as Mrs. Helen Berkley (New York: J. Winchester, New World Press, 1844);

The Lady's Work-Box Companion: Being Instructions in All Varieties of Canvas Work (New York: J. Mowatt, 1844);

Life of Goethe: From His Autobiographical Papers and the Contributions of His Contemporaries, as Henry C. Browning (New York: J. Mowatt, 1844);

Evelyn; or a Heart Unmasked. A Tale of Domestic Life (Philadelphia: G. B. Zieber, 1845);

Armand; or the Child of teh People (New York: S. French, 1847); republished as *Armand; or the Peer and the Peasant. A Play in Five Acts* (New York: S. French, 1849);

Fashion; or, Life in New York. A Comedy in Five Acts (New York: S. French, 1849; London: W. Newbery, 1850);

Autobiography of an Actress; or, Eight Years on the Stage (Boston: Ticknor, Reed & Fields, 1854);

Mimic Life; or, Before and Behind the Curtain: A Series of Narratives (Boston: Ticknor & Fields, 1856);

Twin Roses: A Narrative (Boston: Ticknor & Fields, 1857);

Fairy Fingers: A Novel (New York: Carleton, 1865);

The Mute Singer: A Novel (New York: Carleton, 1866);

The Clergyman's Wife, and Other Sketches. A Collection of Pen Portraits and Paintings (New York: Carleton, 1867);

Italian Life and Legends (New York: Carleton, 1870).

Anna Mowatt Ritchie

Anna Mowatt Ritchie came from a socially prominent and wealthy New York family. Prior to her career as an actress, no one of her social rank in the United States had read publicly or worked in the theater. Though troubled by exhaustion and illness most of her life, she was a prolific writer and popular actress in both the United States and England. She began her career as a stage actress to save her husband James Mowatt from financial ruin, starring in Shakespearean and Restoration comedies and her own play *Fashion; or, Life in New York* (1849). Though she wrote articles, essays, and dramatic pieces throughout her life, *Fashion* and *Autobiography of an Actress; or, Eight Years on the Stage* (1854) are her most significant works. Throughout her lifetime Mowatt argued and demonstrated that women could have a public life.

When Anna Cora Ogden was born on 12 September 1819, the ninth of fourteen children, her family was living in Bordeaux, France. Mowatt's father, Samuel Gouverneur Ogden, was a successful merchant. He had helped to fund Colonel Smith's failed Miranda expedition in 1806, which was an attempt to secure Venezuela's independence from Spain. Ogden's shipping business later required him to move to France, where he met and married Eliza Lewis, the granddaughter of Francis Lewis, a signer of the Declaration of Independence.

In the early nineteenth century, performing plays at home was a popular pastime, one in which the Ogden children excelled. Anna Ogden's acting debut occurred at the age of five, when she played the judge in William Shakespeare's *Othello* (1622). When she was six years old, she and her family moved to New York. Ogden and her sister May were enrolled in a New York boarding school, Mrs. Okill's select academy for young ladies, where Anna Ogden continued to act and avidly read Shakespeare, developing a lifelong passion for literature. She also wrote, directed, and acted regularly for family occasions and birthdays, though always aware of the prejudices against a public stage life. In *Autobiography of an Actress* she describes attending a play with her father: "I did not quite forget that there must be some 'sin and wickedness' which I could not comprehend, and I believe I even asked my father to have the goodness to point out the 'harm.'"

Ogden was fourteen years old when she met her first husband, a lawyer named James Mowatt. Mowatt had first proposed to one of Ogden's older sisters, Charlotte, but Charlotte was already married. Soon after, he returned to find the sister who most resembled Charlotte and chose Anna. A year later Anna was promised by her father to be Mowatt's wife, on the condition that the couple wait two years. Mowatt became impatient and persuaded Anna to elope a few months later. The couple moved to Flatbush, Long Island.

Mowatt, in *Autobiography of an Actress,* describes this marriage as a staged performance. For example, to marry James she had to break family plans to perform *The Mourning Bride* (1791) for her father's birthday. In reaction, her father "told us that we should have a bridal ball instead, and, as I was still to be the heroine, I might enact the 'laughing bride.'" She then comments that "in my bridal robes, I appeared to be assuming a part quite as much as I should have done had we carried out our original intentions, and I had worn the costume of Almeira, the Mourning Bride." Mowatt later said in her autobiography: "In those days I seldom saw with my own eyes, or judged with my own judgment." Mowatt gained a sense of self later by having a public life.

Mowatt began her writing career at seventeen years of age, when she published an epic poem, *Pelayo, or The Cavern of Covadonga–A Romance* (1836), which critics censured. In response she challenged their criticisms in a verse satire called *Reviewers Reviewed: A Satire* (1837). In both cases she wrote under the pseudonym Isabel, a method she soon rejected. In 1838 Mowatt suffered from tuberculosis. To recover, she traveled through Europe for three years with her sister May. James Mowatt followed his wife to Paris when he began to suffer from partial blindness. While caring for him, she wrote a five-act play called *Gulzara, or the Persian Slave* (1841), which was later published in *The New World* and was favorably received by critics.

In the depression of the late 1830s James Mowatt had lost his investments, and by the time the couple returned to the United States, his fortune had been entirely lost. Within two weeks, however, Anna Mowatt developed a new career as a professional reader. Practicing for several hours a day, she prepared to read George Gordon, Lord Byron's "The Dream"; Sir Walter Scott's "The Lay of the Last Minstrel" (1895); and Epes Sargent's "The Missing Ship" and "The Light of the Lighthouse." She delivered three readings at the Masonic Temple in Boston.

Mowatt preferred reading in Boston because she confronted less prejudice there than in New York. Although New Yorkers attended her readings, they excluded her from social engagements and ignored her in public. She did, however, deliver a total of eight readings in the New York area–at the Stuyvesant Institute, the Lyceum in Brooklyn, and the Society Library. Reviewers had strong reactions to her readings, both negative and positive; their response reveals the kind of breakthrough her career choice was. The critic for *The Evening Post* claimed that her reading gave the poems "additional force and brilliancy from her mind and feeling" and "she evinced a power and volume of voice which would have pronounced it impossible for so young and delicate looking a being to possess." The *Ladies Companion; and Literary Expositor, a Monthly Magazine Embracing Every Department of Literature* censured her reading, for "if public readings must be given, I should read before an audience entirely of my own sex!" Mowatt's unconventional career choice was an opening for other women to enter into a similar profession. She notes this phenomenon in her memoirs, "My success gave rise to a host of lady imitators, one

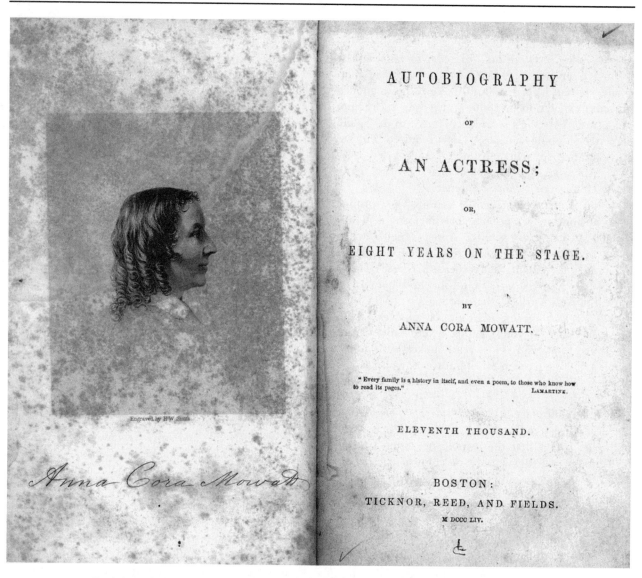

AUTOBIOGRAPHY

OF

AN ACTRESS;

OR,

EIGHT YEARS ON THE STAGE.

BY

ANNA CORA MOWATT.

" Every family is a history in itself, and even a poem, to those who know how
to read its pages."
LAMARTINE.

ELEVENTH THOUSAND.

BOSTON:
TICKNOR, REED, AND FIELDS.
M DCCC LIV.

Frontispiece and title page for Anna Mowatt's memoir of her theatrical career, published shortly before she married her second husband, William F. Ritchie (Thomas Cooper Library, University of South Carolina)

of whom announced 'Readings and Recitations in the Style of Mrs. Mowatt.'"

After suffering a fever, a lung hemorrhage, and exhaustion, Mowatt temporarily left the stage. This rest from public recitation proved to be a productive time for Mowatt because she was able to launch her writing career. She wrote, published, and sold books on knitting, cooking, and etiquette. She also wrote a two-volume domestic novel, *Evelyn; or a Heart Unmasked. A Tale of Domestic Life* (1845). Mowatt never had children of her own, but during this time she adopted three orphans.

In 1849 Samuel French published what became Mowatt's best-known piece, a comedy of manners called *Fashion; or, Life in New York*. According to Eric

Wollencott Barnes "the press reports, both in terms of space and allotted and liberality of encomiums, exceeded anything heretofore offered New Yorkers by way of dramatic criticism." Mowatt's contemporary J. W. S. Hows suggested that "It has created a sensation unexampled in theatricals and has decidedly established the fact that the time has arrived when a strictly American drama can be called into existence." In general the play received acclaim, with one notable exception—Edgar Allan Poe mockingly called *Fashion* a poor imitation of Richard Brinsley Sheridan's *The School for Scandal* (1780). Poe, however, did notice an important aspect of *Fashion*: the play uses the conventions of Restoration comedy to satirize nouveau riche Americans' imitation of

English manners, while asserting the importance of American morality. *Fashion* was also influenced by Mercy Otis Warren's *The Blockheads* (1776) and *The Motley Assembly* (1779), plays that satirize Americans' preference for European manners. Royall Tyler's *The Contrast: A Comedy in Five Acts* (1790) and William Dunlap's *The Father; or American Shandy-ism* (1789) are other earlier examples of American social satire. Despite Poe's criticism, *Fashion* was quite popular, going through many amateur productions in several locales, and is even occasionally performed today.

The satire focuses primarily on the frivolous Mrs. Tiffany, who, when she bankrupts her husband, protests, "It is totally and *toot a fate* impossible to convince you of the necessity of *keeping up appearances*. There is a certain display which every woman of fashion is forced to make!" She imitates European styles and manners, often as poorly as her pronunciation of French. Anything that resembles European fashion, Mrs. Tiffany accepts. This blind devotion provides opportunities for many follies; for example, she mistakes a French butler for a count.

Fashion also attempts to reveal larger social double standards. Mrs. Tiffany argues with Mr. Trueman over her African American servant, Zeke. Mr. Trueman continually calls him "nigger" while chastising Mrs. Tiffany for claiming "that liveries are all the fashion!" He replies, "The fashion, are they? To make men wear the badge of servitude in a free land—that's the fashion, is it? Hurrah, for republican simplicity!" Their contradictions probably were familiar and comic to an American audience.

Sargent recommended *Fashion* to the manager of the Park Theatre in New York, who quickly agreed to produce the play, since Sargent was a popular playwright and poet and because Mowatt had made a name for herself when she was a professional reader during 1841. *Fashion* premiered at the Park Theatre on 26 March 1845. The upper-class audience at the premiere was unprecedented in American theater. One audience member overheard the comment: "Now let's see if society here tonight will be magnanimous enough to applaudingly see and hear itself satirized." The audience apparently was not offended by Mowatt's satire, since *Fashion* became an instant success.

Three months after *Fashion* became a hit at the Park Theatre, Mowatt was encouraged to become an actress. Although she had gained high social standing from her family name and writing acclaim, she chose to act because that profession could pay the bills. She soon became a successful actress, starring in both English and American productions of *Fashion*. During the period of 1845 to 1853 she also starred in Shake-speare's comedies, Sheridan's *The School for Scandal*, and a sentimental drama by Edward Bulwer-Lytton, *The Lady of Lyons* (1838).

Fashion and *Armand; or the Peer and the Peasant. A Play in Five Acts* were both produced in London, where Mowatt often resided. When James Mowatt's health worsened, he went to Trinidad to recover while Anna Mowatt was busy with the third season of *Fashion* and *Armand* at the Royal Olympic Theatre. When she went to her husband, news reached her that the manager of the Olympic was arrested for embezzlement. The theater was closed and dispersed; hence, her engagements in London were over. This failed business venture, along with not receiving royalties for *Fashion,* prevented Mowatt from profiting financially from her plays—despite their popularity. James Mowatt suffered from poor health until his death in 1851.

Mowatt published her other well-known work, *Autobiography of an Actress,* in 1854. The book offers a vision of the acting world in the 1840s and early 1850s. She wrote this book with the hopes of paying her debts and to fulfill her promise to her late husband to describe her acting experiences. Overall, *Autobiography of an Actress* was well received. Elizabeth Cady Stanton argued for the importance of the autobiography as a reflection on the morality of working women. Nathaniel Hawthorne recommended her memoirs to his friend Richard Monckton Milnes. Some critics, however, retained their prejudice against women acting. For example, Mary Walker wrote in the *Evangelical Review* that she disagreed with Mowatt that "there was nothing in the theatrical profession itself which was absolutely conducive to immorality."

Still, *Autobiography of an Actress* remains one of Mowatt's most significant works as a personal and a social account of theater life. She uses stage language to describe various life events and to emphasize the dramatic quality of her breach of social convention. She openly challenges prejudices against women on stage by arguing that chastity and morality are not the result of any institution; rather they result from individual choice. She carefully constructs herself as a dedicated and moral wife, while asserting new professional options for women. The domestic, private sphere is not ideal; in fact, it, too, has become theatrical. This critique indicates that the notion of separate spheres is a false dichotomy. Her memoir also addresses a large, historical context. She describes her use of mesmerism to treat various illnesses and also discusses the importance of Emmanuel Swedenborg's ideas.

Shortly after the publication of her memoirs, Mowatt married William F. Ritchie, an editor of the

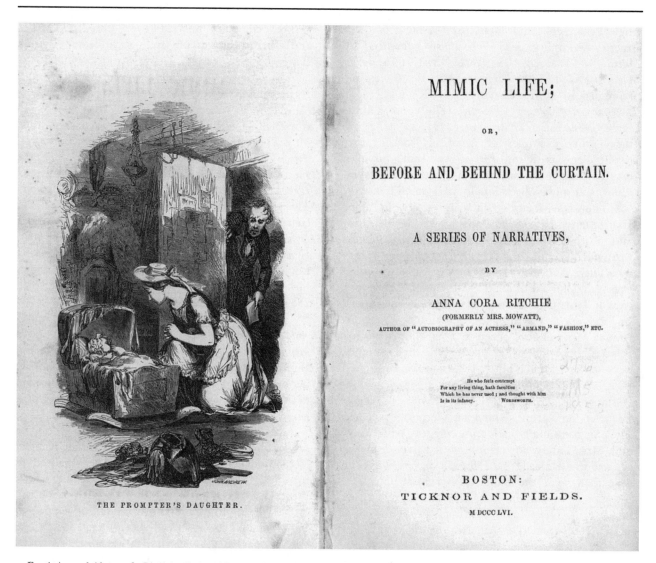

THE PROMPTER'S DAUGHTER.

MIMIC LIFE;

OR,

BEFORE AND BEHIND THE CURTAIN.

A SERIES OF NARRATIVES,

BY

ANNA CORA RITCHIE
(FORMERLY MRS. MOWATT),
AUTHOR OF "AUTOBIOGRAPHY OF AN ACTRESS," "ARMAND," "FASHION," ETC.

He who feels contempt
For any living thing, hath faculties
Which he has never used ; and thought with him
Is in its infancy. WORDSWORTH.

BOSTON:
TICKNOR AND FIELDS.
M DCCC LVI.

*Frontispiece and title page for Ritchie's collection of three novellas about actresses: "Stella," "The Unknown Tragedian," and "The Prompter's Daughter"
(Thomas Cooper Library, University of South Carolina)*

Richmond Examiner. She gained enough financial security to give up her acting career and moved to Richmond, Virginia, where she joined her husband's conservative, upper-class, social circle. A year and a half after her marriage Anna Ritchie published *Mimic Life; or, Before and Behind the Curtain: A Series of Narratives* (1856), a collection of three novellas: "Stella," "The Unknown Tragedian," and "The Prompter's Daughter." Clearly she and her publisher hoped to profit from her earlier success with *Autobiography of an Actress.* The opening pages of *Mimic Life* are filled with critics' praise for her earlier work, an advertising convention in the field of publishing. The *New Bedford Mercury* notes Mowatt's emphasis on public and private spheres, "It is with the greatest simplicity and candor of thought and expression, with the modesty

and true refinement which made her so beloved in private life, and respected in her successful career." The *Philadelphia Mail* calls her "one of the cleverest women living." *Mimic Life* is a fictional though somewhat biographical account of the theater culture during the antebellum period. Through *Mimic Life* Ritchie suggests that actresses can maintain morality and reveals how actors and actresses are exploited, thus defending her position as one of the first and few upper-class women in theater.

Of the three narratives, "Stella" most explicitly deals with this issue of chastity and the stage. Stella is a young, chaste, unmarried woman who suffers from the financial burden of her father's death, which leaves her to take care of her mother. Her brother, Ernest, is an actor whose success inspires her to reject the conventional women's work, domestic labor, to pursue a stage career. Her acting trainer, Mr. Oakland, warns her of dangers: "You do not know the difficulty of *representing in public that which is easy to feel, or simulate, in private*." She impresses Mr. Oakland with her "self-forgetful" ability–"the Protean changes of her sparkling countenance, her concentration of mind, the total self-forgetfulness, perforce dispelled his reluctance"–despite her wild and ill behavior. She becomes a brilliant actress because she can achieve "self-forgetfulness," but this blurring of private and public identities leads to later difficulties, and finally her death.

"Stella" suggests that moral character, rather than circumstance, causes a woman to lose her chastity. As Ernest expresses, "I do not believe *that through the consequences of the profession one chaste woman ever fell!*" This statement is a bold argument if one considers that at this time a stage actress's career was often compared to prostitution. Furthermore, this claim asserts that chastity is a result of individual choice and is not institutionally created.

Stella's foil, Miss Doran, competes with her to the extent that hatred and bitterness develop between them. The most remarkable instance of this hatred occurs when Miss Doran plants nails in the statue that Stella will hug during her Evadne performance. When Stella wraps her arms around the statue, she is pierced. Although this injury is not part of the script, she delivers an electrifying performance, enhanced by a speech that conveniently refers to blood. The figurative becomes literal, and Stella turns Miss Doran's sabotage into a personal triumph.

Meanwhile, a young playwright, Edwin Percy, pursues Stella. This romance offers hope: "His hand would snatch her from such desecration; the myrtle and the orange-blooms would woo her to forget the soul-bewildering laurel; love's tender breathings would fill her ears with richer music than thousand-tongued acclamations." Hope lies in the possibility of romance and a domestic life. Although this possible marriage seems like an escape, the stage is already a domestic sphere. Any distinction between a private, domestic life and the stage has been obscured by Stella's mothering nature. Already she has re-created the private sphere by mothering two stage children, Floy and Perdita. As close as she is from escaping the theater, tragedy occurs. During one of the performances Perdita's father is accidentally killed, sending Perdita and Stella into hysterics. Stella's next role is Ophelia, which she plays all too well: "her personation of the distraught Ophelia became painfully real." After this performance she

suffers from brain fever and dies, making her performance a reality. The blurring of distinctions between private and public life, illusion and reality, destroys this chaste character. The ending of the story poses a critique of the way mass entertainment exploits actors and provides a bleak commentary on the condition of women.

In "The Unknown Tragedian" the heroine, Elma, joins the theater to fulfill the wish of her dying mother, an actress who "loves her profession so passionately–it is enigmatical!" Although Elma dislikes the stage, she becomes an actress out of filial duty. Two noblemen, Lord Oranmore and Lord Edmonton, fall in love with her during one of her performances at the Dublin Theatre Royal. Lord Oranmore proposes and asks her to leave the stage, an offer that she declines because of her promise. Ritchie here uses prejudices against the theater as a critique of domestic life. Moreover, this comparison between private life and theater resembles points made in *Autobiography of an Actress*. Mortimer, the young playwright pursuing her throughout the story, suffers from mental illness. Dressed as Lear, he overhears her talking to her future husband, Edmonton, tragically telling him that she cannot marry because of her duty to care for Mortimer and to fulfill her mother's wish. While starring in *The Tragedy of Betram* Mortimer stabs himself, thus freeing Elma from her responsibilities toward the stage so she can marry Edmonton. The narrator asks after Elma's final performance, "Was Elma happy? Had she made a rich exchange? The answer was written upon her countenance in characters so luminous that even the blinded eyes of erring mortals could not misinterpret them."

In "The Prompter's Daughter" Susan, the wife of a hunchbacked prompter, Robin Truehart, tries to raise a child in the theater. The baby, Tina, becomes a prop in many plays and helps to humanize actors: "The child had been gifted with uncommon beauty; beauty of an ethereal, highly spiritual character." Tina has a purifying effect on the stage. As a child she joins Miss Amory's Sunday school but endures mockery once the children discover that she is from the theater. Even the kind Sunday-school teacher is prejudiced, as the narrator comments: "She adopted the social *fiction*–had become the dupe of that ignorant prejudice which caused her to look upon the temple of dramatic art with a half species of horror." Tina is later exploited by her manager, who cheats her out of pay by making her sign a contract, knowing his competitor will offer her more. Real-life tragedy occurs when Tina plays Ariel in *The Tempest*. For a flying effect she is drawn across the stage by wires. The wires get stuck in front of the lights, and before she can be saved, her feet are badly burned. Eventually she dies from the injury and fatigue. In grief her mother dies as well. The prompter remarks, "I bless the Lord for the strength he give me to yield up *both* my life's sole treasures, to his will!"–adding a sentimental tone to the tragedy.

Ritchie's marriage to her second husband was unhappy. She suspected he was having an affair with a slave and disagreed with his anti-Union stance. Ritchie and her husband separated, and she went to Paris in 1861, just before the American Civil War began. Her husband followed her, presumably to work out their marital problems, but she rejected the overtures, and he shortly returned to the United States. Like many American expatriates, Ritchie began to feel the immediacy of the war, so she also returned to the United States. Just before she left Paris she wrote *Fairy Fingers* (1865), a tale about an expert needlewoman. All of her heroines, with the exception of Evelyn, are working girls.

Although Anna Mowatt Ritchie suffered from various illnesses up until the end of her life, she continued to write prolifically. She died in Twickenham, England, on 27 July 1870.

Biographies:
Mary Forrest, *Women of the South* (New York: Charles B. Richardson, 1865);

Eric Wollencott Barnes, *The Lady of Fashion: The Life and Theatre of Anna Cora Mowatt* (New York: Scribner, 1954).

References:
Sally Burke, *American Feminist Playwrights: A Critical History* (New York: Twayne, 1996);

Dawn Keetley, "The Power of 'Personation': Actress Anna Cora Mowatt and the Literature of Women's Public Performance in Nineteenth-Century America," *American Transcendental Quarterly,* 10 (September 1996): 187–200;

Jeffrey H. Richards, "Chastity and the Stage in Mowatt's 'Stella'" *Studies in American Fiction,* 24 (Spring 1996): 87–100;

David W. Thompson, "Early Actress-Readers: Mowatt, Kemble, and Cushman," in *Performance of Literature in Historical Perspectives* (Lanham, Md.: University Press of America, 1983), pp. 629–635.

Papers:
The Anna Mowatt Ritchie Papers are located at Schlesinger Library, Radcliffe College. They include correspondence among Ritchie and members of the Sargent family, clippings, and an engraving of Ritchie.

Ann Sophia Stephens

(30 March 1810 – 20 August 1886)

Jennifer Hynes

See also the Stephens entries in *DLB 3: Antebellum Writers in New York and the South* and *DLB 73: American Magazine Journalists, 1741–1850.*

BOOKS: *The Queen of a Week* (New York: W. W. Snowden, 1839);

High Life in New York, as Jonathan Slick, Esq. (New York: E. Stephens, 1843; London: J. How, 1844);

Alice Copley: A Tale of Queen Mary's Time (Boston: "Yankee" Office, 1844);

David Hunt and Malina Gray (Philadelphia: G. R. Graham, 1845);

The Diamond Necklace, and Other Tales (Boston: Gleason's Publishing Hall, 1846);

The Tradesman's Boast (Boston: Gleason's Publishing Hall, 1846);

Henry Longford; or, The Forged Will. A Tale of New York City (Boston: F. Gleason, 1847);

The Red Coats; or, The Sack of Unquowa: A Tale of the Revolution (New York: Williams, 1848);

Fashion and Famine (New York: Bunce & Brother, 1854; London: Richard Bentley, 1854);

The Ladies' Complete Guide to Crochet, Fancy Knitting, and Needlework (New York: Garrett, 1854);

Zana; or, The Heiress of Clair Hall (London: Ward & Lock, 1854); republished as *The Heiress of Greenhurst: An Autobiography* (New York: E. Stephens, 1857);

The Old Homestead (New York: Bunce, 1855);

Myra, the Child of Adoption. A Romance of Real Life (New York: Beadle & Adams, 1856; London: Beadle, 1862);

Mary Derwent (Philadelphia: T. B. Peterson, 1858; London: Beadle, 1862);

Ahmo's Plot; or, The Governor's Indian Child (New York: Beadle, 1860; London: G. Routledge, 1866);

Malaeska; the Indian Wife of the White Hunter (New York: Irwin P. Beadle, 1860; London, 1861);

Victor Hugo's Letter on John Brown, with Mrs. Ann S. Stephen's Reply (New York: I. P. Beadle, 1860);

Sybil Chase; or, The Valley Ranche. A Tale of California Life (New York & London: Beadle, 1861); republished as *The Outlaw's Wife; or, The Valley Ranche* (New York: Beadle & Adams, 1874);

Esther: A Story of the Oregon Trail (New York: Beadle, 1862; London: E. F. Beadle, 1863); republished as *Kirk, the Guide. A Story of the Oregon Trail* (New York: Beadle & Adams, 1884);

Pictorial History of the War for the Union, 2 volumes (New York: J. G. Wells, 1862);

The Indian Princess (New York: Beadle & Adams, 1863);
published as *Mahaska, the Indian Princess. A Tale of
the Six Nations* (London: Beadle, 1863);

The Rejected Wife (Philadelphia: T. B. Peterson, 1863);
republished as *The Rejected Wife; or, The Ruling Passion* (Philadelphia: T. B. Peterson, 1876);

The Indian Queen (New York: Beadle & Adams, 1864);

The Wife's Secret (Philadelphia: T. B. Peterson, 1864);
republished as *The Wife's Secret; or, Gillian* (Philadelphia: T. B. Peterson, 1876);

Silent Struggles (Philadelphia: T. B. Peterson, 1865);

The Gold Brick (New York: Lupton, 1866; Philadelphia:
T. B. Peterson, 1866);

The Soldier's Orphans (Philadelphia: T. B. Peterson,
1866);

Doubly False (Philadelphia: T. B. Peterson, 1868);

Mabel's Mistake (Philadelphia: T. B. Peterson, 1868);

The Curse of Gold (Philadelphia: T. B. Peterson, 1869);

Ruby Gray's Strategy (Philadelphia: T. B. Peterson, 1869;
London & Halifax, 1878);

Wives and Widows; or, The Broken Life (Philadelphia: T. B.
Peterson, 1869);

Married in Haste (Philadelphia: T. B. Peterson, 1870);

A Noble Woman (Philadelphia: T. B. Peterson, 1871);

Palaces and Prisons (Philadelphia: T. B. Peterson, 1871);

The Reigning Belle: A Society Novel (Philadelphia: T. B.
Peterson, 1872);

Bellehood and Bondage (Philadelphia: T. B. Peterson,
1873);

Lord Hope's Choice (Philadelphia: T. B. Peterson, 1873);

The Old Countess; or, The Two Proposals (Philadelphia:
T. B. Peterson, 1873);

Phemie Frost's Experiences (New York: G. W. Carleton,
1874);

Bertha's Engagement (Philadelphia: T. B. Peterson, 1875);

Norston's Rest (Philadelphia: T. B. Peterson, 1877);

Lily. In Memoriam (New York: J. J. Little, 1884);

The Lady Mary. A Novel (New York: F. M. Lupton,
1887);

Rock Run; or, The Daughter of the Island (New York: F. M.
Lupton, 1893).

Collection: *The Works of Mrs. Ann S. Stephens,* 23 volumes (Philadelphia: T. B. Peterson, 1859–1886).

OTHER: *The Portland Sketch Book,* edited by Stephens
(Portland, Me.: Colman & Chisholm, 1836);

Frank Leslie's Portfolio of Fancy Needlework, edited by
Stephens (New York: Stringer & Townsend,
1855).

PERIODICALS EDITED: *Portland Magazine* (1834–
1836);

*Ladies' Companion; and Literary Expositor, a Monthly Maga-
zine Embracing Every Department of Literature,* associate editor (1837–1841);

Graham's Lady's and Gentleman's Magazine, associate editor
(1841–1842); *Lady's World,* co-editor (1842–
1849); as *Peterson's Magazine* (1849–1853);

Frank Leslie's Lady's Gazette of Fashion and Fancy Needlework
(1854–1856);

Mrs. Stephens New Monthly (1856–1858).

Ann Stephens is now remembered as the author
of the first Beadle Dime Novel, *Malaeska; The Indian
Wife of the White Hunter* (1860). During the mid nineteenth century, however, Stephens enjoyed a long lasting, lucrative career as one of the best known and
most respected American women writers. In addition
to serving as either editor or co-editor for six popular
magazines for more than twenty-six years, she wrote
some forty-five works of fiction and manuals on the
domestic arts. Some now credit Stephens as having
been one of the first generation of women writers to
assert themselves as professional writers, entering the
field of authorship for the sake of earning a good living rather than hiding behind a claim of literary phi-
lanthropy. Stephens made a name for herself as a
popular writer and editor as early as the 1830s and
grew to become one of the best-known American
women writers in both the United States and abroad.
By the time her most successful novels appeared in the
mid 1850s, Stephens's name was in such demand that
publisher Richard Bentley and *London Journal* editor
Howard Paul campaigned to secure advance copies of
her work for the British market. Stephens knew and
worked with important writers and editors in America
and England, from Charles Jacobs Peterson and Lydia
Huntley Sigourney to Charles Dickens and Edgar
Allan Poe. Her New York literary salon attracted the
most distinguished visitors to that city, and Henry
Clay wrote a laudatory poem, "On The Departure of
Mrs. Ann S. Stephens For Europe," in honor of her
1850 trip abroad.

Sarah Josepha Hale (Buell) lauded Stephens in
her entry for *Woman's Record* in 1855, commending
the "picturesque detail" and "easy flow of language"
in both her poetry and prose. Hale included a
lengthy passage of praise of Stephens by Peterson, in
which he cites the power of her description and gor-
geousness of her style. Just a few years later, the 1875
edition of Evert A. and George L. Duyckinck's *Cyclopaedia of American Literature* praised the energy of
Stephens's writing while it criticized some of her
urban stories for their excess realism and "questionable taste." While nineteenth-century readers enjoyed read-

ing Stephens's work, fastidious critics were not always sure they should.

Ann Sophia Winterbotham was born 30 March 1810 in Humphreysville (now Seymour), Connecticut, the third child of ten children born to Ann Wrigley and John Winterbotham, who was part owner and manager of a woolen mill co-owned by the Connecticut poet-patriot Colonel David Humphreys. When Ann was young, her mother died, and the child's maternal aunt, Rachel, became her stepmother. Winterbotham received her education at the local dame school and in South Britain, Connecticut. Her first published compositions, poetry, and prose appeared under pen names in various newspapers. In 1831 Winterbotham married a printer named Edward Stephens, of Plymouth, Massachusetts. After moving to Portland, Maine, the couple founded the *Portland Magazine* (1834–1836), a women's magazine including both reprinted material from other writers—a common practice in those days, when few periodicals boasted of wide readership—and their own work. Stephens acted as publisher while his wife served as editor. This apprenticeship taught Ann Stephens the workings of periodical publication and how to please the reading public. A poem she wrote for the 1 October 1834 issue of the *Portland Magazine,* "The Polish Boy," became popular and was often included in anthologies.

As a savvy professional writer, Stephens created stories and novels that caught the interest of a voracious reading public. She capitalized on a midcentury interest in historical romances, especially those dealing with American Indians, beginning with her prize-winning story, "Mary Derwent: A Tale of The Early Settlers" (1838), and continuing through her contributions to the Beadle Dime Novel series: *Malaeska; The Indian Wife of the White Hunter* (first serialized in 1839), *Ahmo's Plot; or, The Governor's Indian Child* (1860), *Mahaska, the Indian Princess. A Tale of the Six Nations* (1863), *The Indian Queen* (1864), and *Esther: A Story of the Oregon Trail* (1862). Her other historical romances tended to focus on British or European locations and characters and included the novels *Alice Copley: A Tale of Queen Mary's Time* (1844), *Zana; or, The Heiress of Clair Hall* (1854), and *Lord Hope's Choice* (1873). Stephens also excelled in the kind of domestic fiction that was being devoured by women readers at midcentury. Her best-selling novels in this genre included *Fashion and Famine* (1854) and *The Old Homestead* (1855), both of which foreshadow later realists' attempts to reproduce the suffering, poverty, and filth of modern urban life through graphic city scenes, which Stephens often contrasted with wholesome country settings. Stephens's body of work includes one overtly comic piece, her early satirical *High Life in New York* (1843), a spin-off from T. C. Hal-

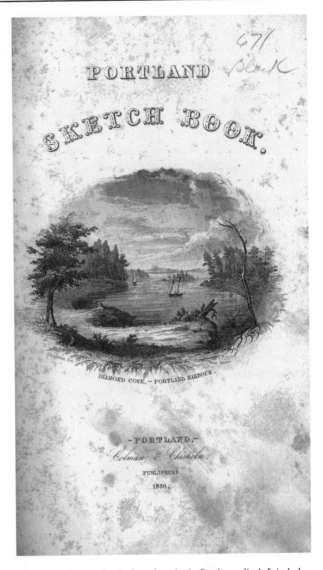

Decorated title page for the first of two books Stephens edited. It includes her poem "The Widowed Bride" and her short story "The Deserted Wife" (Thomas Cooper Library, University of South Carolina).

iburton's "Sam Slick" stories of a witty Yankee clock peddler. While many of her novels tend to be lumped into the category of sentimental women's fiction, Stephens was able to champion women's individuality while supporting a domestic feminism, which maintains separate gendered spheres, as later defined by Kathryn Kish Sklar in *Catharine Beecher: A Study in American Domesticity* (1975). In addition to writing novels, Stephens also wrote and compiled books dealing with needlework and cooking for a readership that placed as much importance on the domestic arts as on the literary arts.

Stephens included some of her own work in her first edited book, *The Portland Sketch Book* (1836). In addition to her poem "The Widowed Bride" and the short story "The Deserted Wife," the book includes regional pieces from authors such as Henry Wadsworth Longfellow, John Neal, Nathaniel Parker Willis, and Seba Smith, all of whom had also contributed to the *Portland Magazine* under Stephens's editorship.

When the Stephenses moved to New York in 1837, Edward Stephens took a job in the customs house for the annual salary of $1,200. Meanwhile, Ann Stephens took a position as associate editor of William W. Snowden's *Ladies' Companion; and Literary Expositor, a Monthly Magazine Embracing Every Department of Literature*. She retained the job through 1841. While working on the *Ladies' Companion* Stephens contributed to this magazine two pieces that later established her reputation. Her serialized story "Mary Derwent, A Tale of the Early Settlers" began in the May 1838 issue and won Stephens the top $200 prize in a writing contest. A romantic tale of a white woman who became the ruler of a Shawnee tribe of American Indians, the story demonstrated that Stephens was well aware of the contemporary reading public's interest in novels about American Indian characters. "Mary Derwent" deals loosely with the Wyoming Massacre of 1778, in which a large group of British-allied Iroquois attacked four hundred revolutionary soldiers. The focus of the novel is on several powerful women, including Queen Esther, a white woman taken captive as a child and later married to an American Indian chief, and Catharine Montour, a wealthy white woman also married to a powerful tribesman. *Mary Derwent* was later altered for T. B. Peterson's 1858 book publication, with the biracial woman, Tahmeroo, daughter of Catharine Montour, choosing to continue her life in the forest rather than to intermingle with whites. As Paola Gemme points out, between the 1830s and the 1850s Stephens apparently altered her view of the future of American Indians from espousing assimilation to acknowledging the value of separatism.

Stephens's historical novels dealing with relations between whites and American Indians followed a trend of such works that appeared during the same decades, including Catharine Maria Sedgwick's *Hope Leslie* (1827), Lydia Maria Child's *Hobomok* (1824), and James Fenimore Cooper's series of Leatherstocking Tales (1823–1841). Like these other books, Stephens's historical works include long descriptions of the natural setting, many battles between American Indians and white settlers, cross-cultural love, and the depiction of American Indians as "noble savages."

Stephens's other piece in the *Ladies' Companion* that later had a great impact on her career was *Malaeska*, serialized in 1839 and later published in 1860 as the first in the dime-novel series of the pub-

lishing firm Irving P. Beadle and Company under the title *Malaeska; The Indian Wife of the White Hunter*. The effects of an interracial marriage form the main interest of *Malaeksa*–tragic effects, since both the young white colonist and his American Indian bride, Malaeska, become outcasts from their respective societies and die young, while their proud Anglicized son kills himself upon discovering his interracial parentage. Alongside the tale of tragic interracial love stands repeated praise of feminine domestic usefulness over fashionable idleness–a moral lesson for young female readers.

The Stephens family grew during the early 1840s, with daughter Ann born in 1841 and son Edward born in 1845. Meanwhile, beginning in December 1841 Stephens worked alongside Poe on the editorial staff of *Graham's Magazine*. Stephens's story "The Two Dukes" appeared in the same issue of *Graham's Magazine* (January 1842) as did Poe's "An Appendix of Autographs." Although Poe claimed that Stephens was not actually involved in the editing of *Graham's Magazine*, he admitted her great popularity and included her name in his list of "the most noted among the living literati of the country."

Stephens's only foray into contemporary humor was her 1843 *High Life in New York*, a collection of articles reprinted from the *New York Daily Express*. Published by her husband and bearing the pseudonym Jonathan Slick, Esq.–a takeoff on T. C. Haliburton's "Sam Slick" persona–the book is a satire of New York society from the point of view of a country bumpkin. *High Life in New York* was reprinted several times in London and Stuttgart as well as in America.

One of Stephens's more interesting pieces of melodramatic fiction is the novel serialized in 1854 as *Zana; or, The Heiress of Clair Hall* and republished in 1857 as *The Heiress of Greenhurst: An Autobiography*. A surprising blend of woman's fiction and suspense, *The Heiress of Greenhurst* is written from the first-person point of view of the heroine, Zana. The story, taking place in Spain and England, follows the fortunes of Zana's gypsy mother, Aurore, as she forsakes her people in Spain to marry a British lord in secret. When the couple returns to England, Aurore submits to being hidden in a cottage by Lord Clare, who is ashamed of his exotic wife. Aurore tries to return to her home when Lord Clare finds a new love but is killed by her people. In contrast, the assertive Zana takes charge of her own fate, seeking vengeance on her father and his relatives for their treatment of Aurore. Secret love, death by stoning, a poisoning, and a final triumphant rise to power by the legitimate daughter made *The Heiress of Greenhurst* a page-turner and helped earn Stephens the title of melodramatist.

Stephens's *Fashion and Famine,* her first novel that clearly fits feminist critic Nina Baym's description of "woman's fiction"—popular fiction written by and for women during the mid nineteenth century—demonstrates Stephens's success in the popular style of the urban melodrama. Following the conventions of urban melodrama, *Fashion and Famine* pits its heroine, Ada, an innocent maiden with country roots, against the vice of the city, represented by her male seducer. Even after Ada has been transformed into a wealthy widow, she does not rest easy until she seeks out and vanquishes the villain. This task accomplished, the heroine turns her attention to caring for her honest, aging, rural parents and begins a home for virtuous, poor women. As Baym argues, *Fashion and Famine* is as much about Ada's need for self-fulfillment outside the realm of romantic love as it is about the struggle between vice and virtue.

Stephens's most popular novel, *The Old Homestead,* published in 1855, is another example of woman's fiction. *The Old Homestead,* which was dramatized in 1856 in a script written by Denman Thompson, focuses on the young heroine, Mary Fuller, daughter of a missing drunkard mother and dying father. When a charitable police officer takes in the newly made orphan, his career is ended by the jealous, hypocritical mayor. Thereafter, Mary and Isabel, the police officer's daughters, make their way through the city orphanage and to separate country homes. Again, the frivolous, dangerous nature of urban living—even when that living is done on fashionable holiday away from the city—is contrasted with the goodness and productivity of domestic country life. Both the narrative and Stephens's preface to *The Old Homestead* argue her belief in women's ability to provide needed charity and to cause social change on a grassroots level.

After her husband died in 1862, Stephens supported herself and her children by writing fiction; twenty-seven novels appeared in the last twenty-four years of her life. So popular were her novels that a twenty-three-volume uniform edition of her fiction, *The Works of Mrs. Ann S. Stephens,* was published by T. B. Peterson between 1859 and 1886. Stephens died on 20 August 1886 of nephritis at the home of her friend and publisher, Charles Peterson, in Newport, Rhode Island.

Critical opinion about Stephens through the first two-thirds of the twentieth century focused either on her financial success as a professional writer or on her importance as the author of the first Beadle Dime Novel. Fred Lewis Pattee in 1940

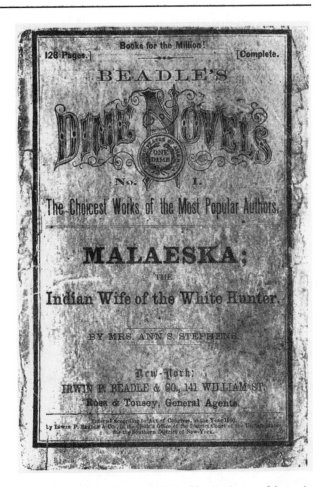

Cover for the 1860 dime-novel edition of Stephens's story of the tragic results of an interracial marriage (from the Benjamin Blom reprint, New York, 1971)

included Stephens in his list of members of the second flowering of New England writers, alongside such popular authors as Grace Greenwood, Fanny Fern, Caroline Lee Hentz, Sarah Josepha Hale, and Mary Jane Holmes. However, since Pattee's tone throughout *The Feminine Fifties* (1940) derides the sentimental style of many women of the period, his classification of Stephens as a melodramatic writer of ephemera is not surprising. In contrast, Helen Waite Papashvily in 1956 credited Stephens with a superior business sense that secured her position as a favorite American writer—even if, as Papashvily wrote, her work tended to be derivative of favorite plots and character types. In 1962 Madeleine B. Stern furthered Stephens's reputation by including her in a collection of historically important nineteenth-century women, noting her as the author of the first Beadle Dime Novel.

Present critical opinion, however, has turned to focus more closely on Stephens's work apart from the 1860 reprint of *Malaeska; the Indian Wife of the*

White Hunter. Because many of Stephens's works focus on the trials of a female heroine—whether she is of white, American Indian, or interracial ancestry—as that heroine struggles to secure a position in a world of dangers and temptations, Baym includes some of her work in her critique of women's fiction. While none of Ann Stephens's novels has found a place in the standard anthologies of American literature, she has become a fixture in guides and reference works on nineteenth-century women writers.

References:

Nina Baym, "Ann Stephens, Mary Jane Holmes, and Marion Harland," *Woman's Fiction: A Guide to Novels by and about Women in America, 1820–70,* second edition (Urbana & Chicago: University of Illinois Press, 1993), pp. 175–207;

Evert A. and George L. Duyckinck, *Cyclopaedia of American Literature,* 2 volumes (Philadelphia: William Rutter, 1875);

James Alfred Eastman, "Ann Sophia Stephens," M.A. thesis, Columbia University, 1952;

Juliann E. Fleener, "Ann Sophia Winterbotham Stephens," in *American Women Writers,* edited by Lina Mainiero (New York: Ungar, 1982), pp. 163–164;

Paola Gemme, "Rewriting the Indian Tale: Science, Politics, and the Evolution of Ann S. Stephens's Indian Romances," *Prospects: An Annual of American Cultural Studies,* 19 (1994): 375–387;

Sarah Josepha Hale, *Woman's Record* (New York: Harper, 1855);

Helen Waite Papashvily, *All the Happy Endings: A Study of the Domestic Novel in America* (New York: Harper, 1956);

Fred Lewis Pattee, *The Feminine Fifties* (New York & London: D. Appleton-Century, 1940);

Kathryn Kish Sklar, *Catharine Beecher: A Study in American Domesticity* (New Haven, Conn.: Yale University Press, 1975);

Ann S. Stephens, *Malaeska: The Indian Wife of the White Hunter,* introduction by Frank P. O'Brien (New York: Benjamin Blom, 1971);

Madeleine B. Stern, "The Author of the First Beadle Dime Novel: Ann S. Stephens, 1860," in her *We the Women: Career Firsts of Nineteenth-Century America* (New York: Schulte, 1962), pp. 29–54.

Papers:

Papers and letters by Ann Sophia Stephens may be found at the Boston Public Library, Brown University Library, the Connecticut Historical Society, the Historical Society of Pennsylvania, and the New York Historical Society. The New York Public Library holds a manuscript scrapbook.

John Lloyd Stephens

(28 November 1805 – 10 October 1852)

S. J. Wolfe
American Antiquarian Society

See also the Stephens entry in *DLB 183: American Travel Writers, 1776–1864.*

BOOKS: *Incidents of Travel in Egypt, Arabia Petraea, and the Holy Land,* 2 volumes, as "an American" (New York: Harper, 1837; revised and enlarged, 1838, 1839; London: R. Bentley, 1838);

Incidents of Travel in Greece, Turkey, Russia, and Poland, 2 volumes, as the author of *Incidents of Travel in Egypt, Arabia Petraea, and the Holy Land* (New York: Harper, 1838); republished as *Incidents of Travel in the Russian and Turkish Empires* (London: R. Bentley, 1839; revised and enlarged, 1847–1853);

Incidents of Travel in Central America, Chiapas, and Yucatan, 2 volumes (New York: Harper, 1841; London: John Murray, 1841);

Incidents of Travel in Yucatan, 2 volumes (New York: Harper, 1843; London: John Murray, 1843).

Edition: *Incidents of Travel in Central America, Chiapas, and Yucatan,* 2 volumes, edited by Richard L. Predmore (New Brunswick, N.J.: Rutgers University, 1949).

SELECTED PERIODICAL PUBLICATION–
UNCOLLECTED: "An Hour with Alexander von Humboldt," *Living Age,* 15 (October–December 1847): 151–153.

John Lloyd Stephens was the first popular American travel writer. He was born in Shrewsbury, New Jersey, 28 November 1805 to Benjamin and Clemence Lloyd Stephens. Although his parents were both natives of New Jersey, Stephens was brought up and educated in New York. He received his classical education in the schools of Mr. Boyle and the blind teacher Joseph Nelson. His education prepared him for early entry into college, and at the age of thirteen he entered Columbia College. Stephens was a favorite among the students, and although he entered low in class standing, he was at the head of his class at his graduation in 1822. Stephens then entered the New

John Lloyd Stephens

York office of Daniel Lord in order to read law. After a year with Lord, Stephens attended the Tapping Reeve Law School of Judge James Gould in Litchfield, Connecticut. Stephens returned to New York the following year and entered the law office of George W. Strong, where he remained, except for a brief absence, until he was called to the bar of New York City in 1827.

At the age of twenty, Stephens sought to satisfy his wanderlust by making a journey with a cousin to visit his aunt, who lived in Arkansas, then virtually a terra incognita. Having safely accomplished this visit, the two cousins decided not to return directly home and instead took a voyage down the Mississippi in a flatboat heading for New Orleans. After a few months Stephens returned from New Orleans by sea and resumed his study of law. He passed the bar examination in New York and practiced law there for eight years. He developed an ardent interest in politics, was a supporter of the Democratic Party, and gained a reputation as an occasional Tammany Hall speaker at Democratic Party meetings. He was noted for his strong advocacy of free trade and his strong opposition to monopolies. Stephens's earnest manner left no doubt of the courage of his convictions.

Stephens found the practice of law less than stimulating, however, and in the autumn of 1834 journeyed to Europe to improve his ill health. He bought passage on the packet *Charlemagne,* bound for Havre, France. He disembarked on the coast of England and went up to London; from there he crossed into France. Stephens progressed to the Mediterranean—visiting Italy, Greece, Turkey, and Russia—and returned to France by way of Poland and Germany.

His family expected him then to head back to New York, but instead he took passage aboard a steamer at Marseilles and headed for Egypt by way of the island of Malta. He landed at Alexandria and sailed up the Nile River as far as Thebes, where he became ill and was forced to return to Cairo for medical attention. Having regained his health, Stephens, traveling under the name Abdel Hassis—given him by the Bedouin tribesmen with whom he had become friendly—procured camels and set off toward the Red Sea. He spent several nights at Mount Sinai and then set out for Gaza. He detoured on the way, placing himself under the charge of a tribe of Arabs who accompanied him to the hidden city of Petra, Arabia. During this trip he again suffered several bouts of illness; he was so debilitated that he had to be carried reclining on the back of a camel. He recovered and finally made his way to the Dead Sea and wandered through Palestine. Stephens ended his trip with a stay of several weeks in Jerusalem. He returned home to New York in the latter part of 1836.

Charles Fenno Hoffman's *American Monthly Magazine* had published a series of letters that Stephens had written from Scio, Greece, and other places on his trip, describing his journeys. These letters were generally copied into the papers of the time and widely disseminated. The popularity of these accounts induced Stephens to think about expanding them into a more substantial description of his travels. He was indulged in this venture by the Reverend Francis L. Hawks, one of the editors of *The New-York Review.* Hawks had met Stephens in London in 1836 and urged him to write an account of his travels, similar to accounts Hawks was writing himself. The result was *Incidents of Travel in Egypt, Arabia Petraea, and the Holy Land* (1837), which was published in two volumes. Manuscript copies of lively chapters of the book were distributed by Harper for publication in the weeklies—a common publishing practice of the time—with the first of the chapters appearing as early as 1 April 1837 in *The New-Yorker.* Subsequent installments appeared in that magazine on 8 April, 22 April, 6 May, 13 May, and 27 May 1837. *The New-York Mirror* published excerpts on 1 April and 29 April 1837, as well as in the 3 June review. *The New York Knickerbocker* of May 1837 was still another newspaper publishing the titillating adventures. Reading the excerpts no doubt influenced readers to go out and buy the entire two-volume set.

The review of *Incidents of Travel in Egypt, Arabia Petraea, and the Holy Land* in *The American Monthly Magazine* for April 1837 stated:

> Most gladly do we welcome this new journeyer in those mystic climes, and we hesitate not to say that his work is one of the most entertaining books of travel that we ever perused. . . . There are no borrowed disquisitions—no appointed fits of rapture before celebrated objects that others have apostrophized; but the descriptions are thrown off with such a careless ease, a spirited freedom, that savours of any thing rather than bookmaking.

In a review of the third edition of this work in *The Christian Examiner and General Review* for March 1838, Henry Ware Jr. described the account as "written in a very sprightly manner." Ware added that the volumes included "a great deal of vivid description and entertaining narrative." Ware also apologized for not reviewing the first edition of the work, which had been excluded from publication because of time constraints. Ware, supportive of Stephens's desire to follow in the "track of chosen people out of Egypt," went on to chide Stephens gently for not having made a more thorough preparation in order to delete "inaccuracies and carelessness" in the history of the countries he was visiting and describing. Stephens was aware of his liberties and deficiencies in regard to history and later admitted that he could have been better prepared. The inaccuracies did not seem to matter to the reading public that eagerly bought the book and enjoyed it. The narrative may not have

*Page from the contract between Stephens and the English artist Frederick Catherwood agreeing to undertake the expedition
that resulted in* Incidents of Travel in Central America, Chiapas, and Yucatan *(1841), with text by
Stephens and illustrations by Catherwood (Bancroft Library, University of California at Berkeley)*

been learned, but it was truthful and intelligible to
the mass of readers.

Other reviews in *The New-York Review* for October 1837 and the *American Quarterly Review* for June
1837 were equally favorable. Reviews also appeared
in *The Biblical Repertory* (later *The Princeton Review*) and
the *North American Review* (January 1839), written by
Lewis Cass and accompanied by a map. The biggest
impression made on all the reviewers was Stephens's
description of the Dead Sea. *The New-York Review*
characterizes the work as "in some respects defi-
cient," although it also "presents some points of
moment to the geographers, to the antiquarian, and
more especially the theologian." The review ends

with the reviewer's hope that "it is not the last time
we shall hear from him. He is a traveller with whom
we should like to take other journeys."

The reviewer did not have long to wait. The
success of Stephens's first travel book was followed
almost immediately by *Incidents of Travel in Greece, Turkey, Russia, and Poland* (1838). Both works were popular in America and Europe, going through several
editions in the first years of publication and receiving
good reviews from both sides of the Atlantic. The
preface to the fourth 1838 American edition of *Incidents of Travel in Greece, Turkey, Russia, and Poland* states
that the "high mark of favor bestowed upon his work
by the public" made "it necessary, within less than

six weeks from the publication of the first to issue a fourth edition."

The Christian Review of June 1839 reported the book had an "easy, flowing and somewhat *piquant* style, and, by a happy blending of personal incident with general description, seldom fails in making us interested in all that he describes." The reviewer went on to praise Stephens's descriptions: "With sentiment enough to feel the power that comes from decaying monuments of ancient glory, he is yet liberal-minded enough to avoid any useless laments over the wrecks of foreign empires, or the rise of new ones in their place."

Stephens was a witty and intelligent man, a born raconteur who could vividly and charmingly describe his travels and keep his audience enthralled with his meticulous descriptions and good-natured humor. Almost overnight he became known as the "American traveler." Although he did not have the time to devote to becoming a learned antiquarian, he described accurately and precisely the manners, modes, customs, and relics of the places he visited. His enthusiasm for any project probably caused some rare opportunities to be offered to him. In 1839, for example, Stephens was recommended by Governor William Henry Seward for the appointment of Agent of New York State to Holland for the express purpose of gathering records of the colonial history of New York. The Whigs in the legislature opposed his nomination, and the post was conferred instead upon John Romeyn Brodhead.

Stephens made arrangements to visit Central America in the company of the acclaimed English artist Frederick Catherwood; their intention was to examine the remains of ancient art that were said to exist, all but forgotten, in the dense tropical forests. Their preparations were scarcely completed when William Leggett, who had been appointed minister to Central America, suddenly died. President Van Buren then gave Stephens the appointment of special ambassador to Central America and sent him on a confidential and hazy mission to negotiate a treaty with the governments there.

Stephens was encouraged in both endeavors by John B. Bartlett, who had read accounts of similar journeys by Antonio del Rio, Guillermo Dupaix, and Jean-Frédéric Waldeck, published in 1822 and 1838 respectively. Bartlett even managed to obtain a scarce copy of Waldeck's *Voyage pittoresque et archaeologique dans la province de Yucatan pendant des annees 1834–1836* (Picturesque and Archaeological Voyage into the Province of Yucatan from 1834–1836, 1838) for Stephens to take on the trip.

Not one to waste such an opportunity, Stephens, in the company of Catherwood, who also had some experience in archaeology, set out for Central America. Catherwood initially had some misgivings about combining business with pleasure but finally was persuaded to go along. The political confederation with which Stephens was to negotiate collapsed before he could achieve his primary mission. Stephens often joked that he traveled Guatemala looking for the confederation that he never could find and that his journeying enabled him to discover some things that would probably prove more interesting to his countrymen than mere diplomatic correspondence.

Stephens and Catherwood were the first Americans to excavate, view, and report upon the mysterious antiquities of the pre-Columbian Indians who had lived in that area. Stephens lacked the educational background to expound adequately on the ancient civilizations that had produced the marvels, but that lack did not stop him from writing about what he saw and experienced. He and Catherwood returned to New York, where Stephens produced the two-volume *Incidents of Travel in Central America, Chiapas, and Yucatan* (1841). The graphic accounts of the monuments, temples, pyramids, and other antiquities, illustrated handsomely with drawings taken—laboriously but accurately—on the spot by Catherwood's facile pencil and camera lucida, fueled a growing interest in archaeology and the prehistory of the American continents. One of the most delightful vignettes of these books is Stephens's description of his buying the entire ruined city of Copán for $50. The Mayanist Augustus Le Plongeon, among others, was inspired by the meticulous and detailed descriptions that Stephens had produced. When he undertook his own investigations, he reexamined the work of Stephens and challenged some of Stephens's identifications of ruins, attributing them instead to his own peculiar version of the history of the Maya.

A reviewer of the 1841 London edition of the book commented in the *London Quarterly Review* for December 1841 and March 1842 that "the present volumes have all the lively spirit and gay, healthy-minded tone of the former ones, with hardly a shade of their faults. There is more steadiness and reality in the tone of the narrative and the style is more chastened." The reviewer goes on to praise Stephens for the clear and concise language with which he wrote, "singularly free from American peculiarities" except for the "hideous vulgarism of 'left' used as a neuter verb." The review in the July 1841 *New-York Review* claimed the book "unites both literary and scientific merit of a higher order." The

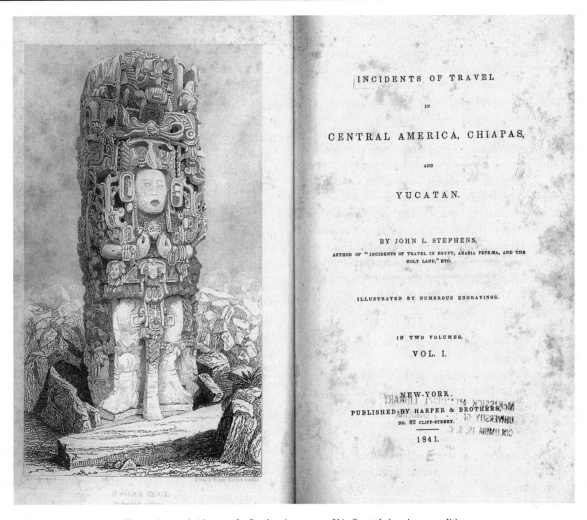

Frontispiece and title page for Stephens's account of his Central American expedition
(Thomas Cooper Library, University of South Carolina)

review also praised the style of the publisher, Harper Brothers, stating that the work "does honor to the publisher, and we are glad to see a specimen of typography from this press in all respects so highly creditable to them." J. G. Palfrey reviewed the work favorably for the October 1841 *North American Review;* the book was also reviewed in the July 1842 *Edinburgh Review*. Within four months of the first publication, American sales reached twelve thousand copies.

Stephens returned to Mexico in the autumn of 1841, again in the company of Catherwood, to excavate and explore as many of the ruins as he could. The fruits of this journey were published in two volumes in 1843 under the title *Incidents of Travel in Yucatan*. This account was favorably reviewed in several periodicals. Stephens and Catherwood had brought back artifacts, which were mounted in an exhibition in Catherwood's New York Rotunda,

where his panoramic painting of Jerusalem was also displayed. Although there is no direct evidence to support the case, Stephens was likely one of the investors in the Rotunda. The exhibition was destroyed by fire on 31 July 1842.

After this last expedition to Yucatán, William Hickling Prescott, historian of the ancient civilizations of Peru, tried to entice Stephens and Catherwood to make a similar discovery trip to South America. Catherwood had already committed himself to working in the West Indies for two years, so he and Stephens both declined to do the trip. Stephens then settled in New York and became more involved in the political scene. He was elected as a delegate to the 1846 New York Constitutional Convention. Stephens was nominated by the Democrats, but because of his popularity, he was also placed on the Whig ticket. He introduced and advocated the creation of a conciliation court that was eventually adopted by New York City.

In 1847 he turned his attention to the subject of ocean steam navigation and was active in organizing the Ocean Steam Navigation Company, a line of ocean-going steamships that traveled the seas between Bremen and New York and which was the first line to take advantage of government subsidies for mail steamships. Stephens was an investor and director of the company. Up until this time England had the monopoly on this mode of conveyance; the United States was deemed to have neither the capital nor the machinery to compete with England. The Ocean Steam Navigation Company built two ships, the *Washington* and the *Hermann*.

The steamer *Washington* carried Stephens as a member of the crew to Bremen on the ship's maiden voyage from New York to Germany. Stephens was exultant to be a participant in this successful venture and enthusiastically joined in the welcoming and congratulatory ceremonies at every stop. The *Washington* was greeted in Bremen with a cannon salute and many speeches. The successful trip made the United States a worthy competitor in the field of ocean steam navigation.

Stephens returned to England by way of Hamburg and Berlin and went to pay a visit to Baron von Humboldt in Potsdam. He considered Humboldt to be one of the greatest explorers, one whose investigations had stimulated his own desire to travel and explore the mysteries of the world. Stephens published an account of this visit as "An Hour with Alexander von Humboldt" in the *Living Age* (October–December 1847).

The venture was a success for a while but was eventually overshadowed by Edward K. Collins's subsidy steamship line. Stephens next turned his attention to the Hudson River Railroad, of which he was a vociferous and active supporter, giving a speech at the Merchant's Exchange in New York in its support.

Stephens's thirst for adventure never abated, and in 1849 he joined with William H. Aspinwall and Henry Chauncey to form the Panama Railroad Company, which was interested in building a railroad across the Isthmus of Panama. The company was formed in July 1849, with Stephens as vice president. In the autumn of that year he visited the isthmus and the country of Panama for the purpose of surveying the projected route. Catherwood joined him in 1850 and took charge of the project while Stephens went to Bogotá and concluded arrangements in New Granada that were favorable to the construction of the road. While returning to Bogotá, Stephens's mule slipped, and he suffered a severe fall that wrenched his spine. In agony he continued to Bogotá, where he took to his bed. Stephens managed

to continue his commission with the New Granadian Congress in spite of the pain. This accident, however, impaired his health and made him more susceptible to disease for the remainder of his life.

From Bogotá, Stephens was carried in a specially constructed chair, supported on pillows and carried by porters, to Cartagena, where he was placed on board a steamer bound for the United States. His illness did not stop him from making a whirlwind tour of Jamaica on the way. He was struck with the natural beauty of the island and with its emerging moral and social aspects in the wake of the abolishment of slavery on the island. He took copious notes, perhaps intending at some time to publish something on the subject.

Upon Stephens's return to New York, Thomas Ludlow, the president of the Panama Railroad Company, resigned, and Stephens was appointed president in his place. Stephens devoted all of his time and energies to this office. In the winter of 1850–1851 he went back to Panama and personally supervised the work being done on the railroad. In the spring of 1852 he returned to New York in seemingly good health, but in the space of six or eight weeks he was attacked by a liver disease that rapidly developed into an abscess. He lingered in great pain for about four months before he died on 10 October 1852. A monument to him was erected in Panama on the highest point of land overlooking the railroad he had helped to build.

By the time of John Lloyd Stephens's death, 21,000 copies of *Incidents of Travel in Egypt, Arabia Petraea, and the Holy Land*, 12,000 copies of *Incidents of Travel in Greece, Turkey, Russia, and Poland*, 15,000 copies of *Incidents of Travel in Central America*, and 9,750 copies of *Incidents of Travel in Yucatan* had been published. Stephens's sprightly and informative writings piqued the interest of many of his readers and instigated a literary turn of attention toward the Orient and other exotic locations. Most notable among the authors who were so influenced was Edgar Allan Poe, the "anonymous" reviewer of Stephens's first work in 1837 in *The New-York Review*. Stephens's influence on Poe's writings is clearly evident in *The Narrative of Arthur Gordon Pym*. There are passages in Poe's book that are strongly suggestive of *Incidents of Travel in Egypt, Arabia Petraea, and the Holy Land*, especially when Pym and Peters find themselves isolated on the barren plateau of Tsalal. The mysterious ruins and hieroglyphs of Tsalal may also have been drawn from Stephens's descriptions.

The reviewer of *Incidents of Travel in Yucatan* in the *Southern Literary Messenger* for August 1843 gives the best description of Stephens and his writings:

Catherwood's drawing of Casa de las Palomas, Uxmal, for the first volume of Stephens's Incidents of Travel in Yucatan *(1843)*
(Thomas Cooper Library, University of South Carolina)

We have followed Mr. Stephens joyfully, many long miles of his travels; but he has often left us as wearied as if we had gone on foot. He possesses many rare qualities for a journalist. He is not abstruse, he is social and good tempered, veracious and often humorous and racy. His descriptions are captivating, when not tedious, from minuteness and prolixity; and there is no balderdash of high wrought rhapsody and studied ecstacy. He is natural and candid. One of Mr. Stephens' greatest faults is his prolixity which has increased since he wrote his first work. The traveller is forced to tug through many tedious details to get at the pith, of which, it is true, there is a great deal, both juicy and sweet.

Stephens created a whole new type of travel literature, one that was observant, interesting, and could transport the reader to far off destinations as surely as if that person had accompanied him.

Biographies:

Victor Wolfgang Von Hagen, *Maya Explorer, John Lloyd Stephens and the Lost Cities of Central America and Yucatán* (Norman: University of Oklahoma Press, 1947);

Ann Sutton and Myron Sutton, *Among the Maya Ruins; The Adventures of John Lloyd Stephens and Frederick Catherwood* (Chicago: Rand McNally, 1967);

von Hagen, *Search for the Maya: The Story of Stephens and Catherwood* (Farnborough, U.K.: Saxon House, 1973);

Chuck Ennis and Pablo Bush Romero, *Siguiendo los Pasos de Stephens-Catherwood* (Mexico City: I. Vado, 1980).

References:

Frederick Catherwood, "Biographical Notice," in John Lloyd Stephens, *Incidents of Travel in Central America, Chiapas, and Yucatan* (London: A. Hall, Virtue, 1854), pp. iv–vi;

"The Late John L. Stephens," *Putnam's Monthly,* 1 (January 1853): 64–68;

Edgar Allan Poe, *The Imaginary Voyages,* edited by Burton R. Pollin (Boston: Twayne, 1981), pp. 24–25.

Papers:

The papers and correspondence of John Lloyd Stephens are located at the Bancroft Library of the University of California at Berkeley.

Richard Henry Stoddard

(2 July 1825 – 12 May 1903)

Peter C. Norberg
Saint Joseph's University

See also the Stoddard entries in *DLB 3: Antebellum Writers in New York and the South* and *DLB 64: American Literary Critics and Scholars, 1850–1880.*

BOOKS: *Foot-prints* (New York: Spalding & Shepard, 1849);

Poems (Boston: Ticknor, Reed & Fields, 1852);

Adventures in Fairy-land (Boston: Ticknor, Reed & Fields, 1853);

Songs of Summer (Boston: Ticknor, Reed & Fields, 1857);

Town and Country, and the Voices in the Shells (New York: Dix, Edwards, 1857);

The King's Bell (New York: Carleton, 1863; London: B. M. Pickering, 1864);

The Story of Little Red Riding Hood (New York: Gregory, 1864);

Abraham Lincoln: An Horatian Ode (New York: Bunce & Huntington, 1865);

The Children in the Wood, Told in Verse (New York: Hurd & Houghton, 1866);

The Book of the East, and Other Poems (Boston: Osgood, 1871);

A Century After: Picturesque Glimpses of Philadelphia and Pennsylvania (Philadelphia: Allen, Lane & Scott / Lauderbach, 1876);

Poet's Homes: Pen and Pencil Sketches of American Poets and Their Homes (Boston: Lothrop, 1877);

In Memory of William Cullen Bryant, 1794–1878 (New York: Evening Post Steam Presses, 1878);

Nathaniel Hawthorne (New York: Scribners, 1879);

The Poems of Richard Henry Stoddard. Complete Edition (New York: Scribners, 1880);

The Homes and Haunts of Our Elder Poets (New York: Appleton, 1881);

Henry W. Longfellow. A Memoir (London: Warne, 1882);

The Life of Washington Irving (New York: Alden, 1883);

Putnam the Brave (Cincinnati: Thomson, 1884);

The Lion's Cub; With Other Verse (New York: Scribners, 1890; London: Elkins Mathews, 1891);

Under the Evening Lamp (New York: Scribners, 1892);

Richard Henry Stoddard (from Stoddard's Recollections, Personal and Literary, *edited by Ripley Hitchcock, 1903)*

Recollections, Personal and Literary, edited by Ripley Hitchcock (New York: Barnes, 1903).

OTHER: *The Life, Travels and Books of Alexander von Humboldt,* edited by Stoddard (London: Low / New York: Rudd & Carleton, 1859);

The Last Political Writings of Gen. Nathaniel Lyon, edited by Stoddard (New York: Rudd & Carleton, 1861);

The Loves and Heroines of the Poets, edited by Stoddard (New York: Derby & Jackson, 1861);

The Late English Poets, edited by Stoddard (New York: Bunce & Huntington, 1865);

Melodies and Madrigals; Mostly from the Old English Poets, edited by Stoddard (New York: Bunce & Huntington, 1866);

Remember. A Keepsake, edited by Stoddard and Elizabeth Stoddard (New York: Leavitt & Allen, 1869);

The Female Poets of America, revised by Stoddard (New York: Miller, 1873);

Rufus Griswold, ed., *Poets and Poetry of America,* revised by Stoddard (New York: Miller, 1873);

Prosper Merrimee's Letters to an Incognita. With Recollections by Lamartine and George Sand, edited by Stoddard (New York: Scribner, Armstrong, 1874);

Anecdote Biographies of Thackeray and Dickens, edited by Stoddard (New York: Scribner, Armstrong, 1874);

Personal Reminiscences by Barham, Homes, and Hodder, edited by Stoddard (New York: Scribner, Armstrong, 1874);

Personal Reminiscences by Chorley, Planché, and Young, edited by Stoddard (New York: Scribner, Armstrong, 1874);

Personal Reminiscences by Cornelia Knight and Thomas Raikes, edited by Stoddard (New York: Scribner, Armstrong, 1875);

Personal Reminiscences by O'Keefe, Kelly, and Taylor, edited by Stoddard (New York: Scribner, Armstrong, 1875);

Edgar Allan Poe, *Poems,* complete, with an original memoir by Stoddard (New York: Widdleton, 1875);

Personal Reminiscences by Moore and Jerdan, edited by Stoddard (New York: Scribner, Armstrong, 1875);

Charles Cavendish Fulke Greville, *The Greville Memoirs; A Journal of the Reigns of George IV and William IV,* edited by Stoddard (New York: Scribner, Armstrong, 1875);

Personal Recollections of Lamb, Hazlitt and Others, edited by Stoddard (New York: Scribner, Armstrong, 1875);

The Life, Letters and Table-talk of Benjamin Robert Haydon, edited by Stoddard (New York: Scribner, Armstrong, 1876);

Personal Reminiscences. By Constable and Gillies, edited by Stoddard (New York: Scribner, Armstrong, 1876);

Elizabeth Barrett Browning, *Letters, Addressed to Richard Hengist Horne,* preface and memoir by Stoddard (New York: J. Miller, 1877);

Browning, *Mrs. E. B. Browning's Letters and Essays,* with a memoir by Stoddard (New York: J. Miller, 1877);

Anecdote Biography of Percy Bysshe Shelley, edited by Stoddard (New York: Scribner, Armstrong, 1877);

Poetical Works of William Cullen Bryant, edited by Stoddard (New York: Appleton, 1878);

John Doran, *Lives of the Queens of England of the House of Hanover,* preface by Stoddard (New York: Armstrong, 1880);

Wit and Wisdom of the Rev. Sydney Smith, edited by Evert A. Duyckinck, with a prefatory memoir of Duyckinck by Stoddard (New York: Armstrong, 1880);

Poems of William Wordsworth, edited, with an introduction, by Stoddard (New York: Johnston, 1881);

Henry Wadsworth Longfellow, *A Medley in Prose and Verse,* edited by Stoddard and William J. Linton (New York: Harlan, 1882);

English Verse, 5 volumes, edited by Stoddard and William J. Linton (New York: Scribners, 1883);

Readings and Recitations from Modern Authors, Being Pearls Gathered from the Fields of Romance, edited by Stoddard and Elizabeth Stoddard (Chicago & New York: Belford, Clarke, 1884);

Selections from Poetical Works of A. G. Swinburne, edited by Stoddard (New York: T. Y. Crowell, 1884);

Mayne Reid, *The Bush-boys; or The History and Adventures of a Cape Farmer and His Family in the Wild Karoos of Southern Africa,* edited, with a memoir, by Stoddard (New York: Knox, 1885);

Hippolyte Taine, *History of English Literature,* translated from the French by H. Van Lan, with a preface by Stoddard (New York: Worthington, 1889);

The Complete Poems of William Cullen Bryant, edited by Stoddard (New York: Stokes, 1894);

The Works of Lord Byron, with his Letters and Journals, and His Life by Thomas Moore, edited, with an introduction, by Stoddard (Boston: Nicolls, 1900);

Henry Cady Sturges, *Chronologies of the Life and Writings of William Cullen Bryant,* with a memoir by Stoddard (New York: Appleton, 1903).

Richard Henry Stoddard's poetry is not original; it did not have a significant influence on his contemporaries nor on the poets of future generations. It is still of interest, however, to scholars of nineteenth-century American culture. One can trace in Stoddard's career how the Romanticism of Henry Wadsworth Longfellow, John Greenleaf Whittier, William Cullen Bryant, and James Russell Lowell became the stock-in-trade of the literary establishment of New York during the middle of the century. As an editor of collections of British and American verse and various parlor-table compendia, Stoddard helped popularize the culture of Romantic and Victorian poetry, and as a poet, he prided himself on his ability to satisfy the desire for sentimental verse that he had helped to create. He is most often remembered today as the husband of Elizabeth Barstow Stoddard, whose Gothic, realist novels *The Morgesons* (1862) and *Two Men* (1865) are a scathing parody of the genteel manners that her husband worked so hard to cultivate. In their conventional appeal to a conventional audience, then, Stoddard's poems provide an accurate record of the middle-class tastes that made publishing a

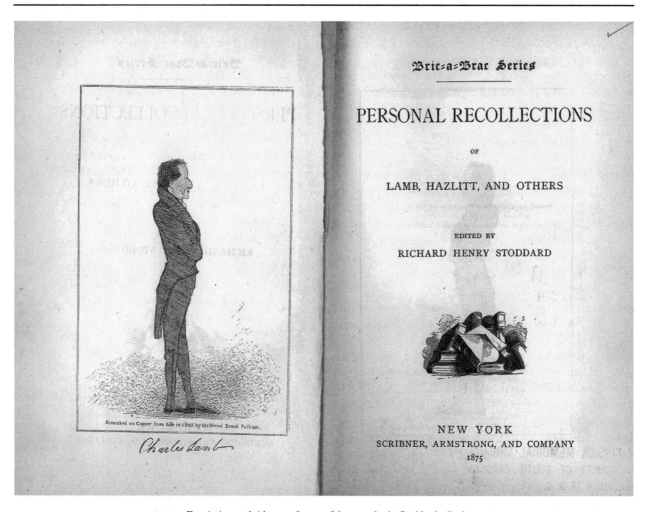

Frontispiece and title page for one of the many books Stoddard edited

business lucrative enough to support a professional class of writers, editors, and publishers. Stoddard worked hard to gain membership in this class, and, somewhat belatedly, he became a fixture in it.

Stoddard was born on 2 July 1825 in Hingham, Massachusetts. His childhood was a difficult one, filled with loss and financial instability. In 1828, when he was three years old, his father, Reuben Stoddard, a successful merchant sailor who worked his way up from deckhand to partner in the Hingham, Massachusetts, shipping firm for which he sailed, was lost at sea. His mother, Sophia Guerney Stoddard, unable to claim her husband's share in the vessel, was forced to rely on the charity of her in-laws to support herself; her son Richard Henry; his brother, Charles; and his sister, Mary. After the illnesses and deaths of Charles and Mary, however, the widow and Richard left Hingham to live with her parents in Abington, Massachusetts. There Richard received his first formal schooling. His education was soon interrupted, though, when he and his

mother moved to Boston, where she had found work sewing sailors' uniforms. She soon remarried, and when Richard was ten, the family moved to New York City to get what support they could from his stepfather's brother-in-law, who owned a restaurant there. Still, as Stoddard wrote in his *Recollections, Personal and Literary* (1903), "there was little to choose from" between his mother's and his stepfather's relatives, "for they were poor on both sides."

After first seeing her son put to work at the oyster bar of her brother-in-law's restaurant and then sent into the street to sell matches, Sophia insisted that he attend school and enrolled him in a private academy for "Young Gentleman and Ladies." However, the education he received there was minimal. In his *Recollections*, Stoddard recalled his instructor—a "Mr. Steele"—as a man who "knew absolutely nothing" and who kept the only textbook, *A Key to Daboll's Arithmetic,* in his desk "under the guarded safety of lock and key." Richard was soon withdrawn and sent to public school, where he immediately was placed in the highest class because his handwriting was "sufficiently legible." Stoddard, it seems, was for the most part self-taught. He was an avid reader from a young age; yet, the books available to him were few. Those that did come his way generally were cheap anthologies that reprinted popular fiction and poetry from British and American periodicals. These books were the only sort that Stoddard could afford, and he read a small library of them, beginning with John Peirpont's *The American First Class Book,* an elementary school reader that included selections from *Blackwood's Magazine* and Washington Irving's *Sketch Book* (1819–1820) as well as the first poem Stoddard claims to have read–fittingly, Nathaniel Parker Willis's "The Widow and Her Son." These anthologies served to educate Stoddard well in the sentimental tastes of the middle-class audience for whom he later wrote. They also helped him define the first principle of his aesthetic–that the purpose of poetry is entertainment, not instruction.

At fifteen, his parents took him out of school and sent him to work so that he could begin contributing his share to the family's meager income. For the next three years, he was employed successively as an errand boy, a legal copyist, a tailor's assistant, and a bookkeeper. In his free time, he continued to read voraciously the popular literature of his day, and after work he haunted bookstalls selling old books in order to add to his growing collection of British and American authors. This collection he further supplemented with volumes of the *Mirror Library,* a series that reprinted the readers' favorites from N. P. Willis and George P. Morris's *The New York Mirror.* He also began to read *The New World,* edited by Park Benjamin and Epes Sargeant, a publication he later praised as "admirable for what it was and was intended to be; namely, the speediest and cheapest reprint of the most popular British authors." At eighteen, Stoddard's mother apprenticed him to a blacksmith; however, the work proved too strenuous, and he was sent to work in an iron-molding factory instead, "casting fenders and frames for fireplaces." His job in the factory was tedious and tiring, but he had one consolation–"the day would end, night would come, and then I could write poetry."

His wide reading of the popular literature of his day decisively influenced his conception of the purpose of poetry and his ambitions as a poet. What he valued in his reading–the pleasure of diversion from his workday routine–he also cultivated in his writing. His early poem "Arcadian Idyll" provides a clear statement of his aesthetic. In a song sung by "the shepherd Lycidas" to "the Spartan poet"–and meant perhaps to dramatize the difference between his poetry and that of his friend Bayard Taylor–Stoddard writes that he is not the sort of poet who "to Wisdom turns," but instead "would be Pleasure's Poet till [he] died, / And die at last upon her burning heart."

While working at the iron-molding factory, Stoddard continued to write poetry in the evenings, and eventually he began to submit his work to publications such as *The Rover* and *The Union Magazine.* He diligently followed up his submissions in person, and through this persistence, he soon came to know many major and minor figures in the literary establishment of New York–including Seba Smith, Caroline M. Kirkland, Park Benjamin, N. P. Willis, and Rufus Griswold. Through these connections he was introduced to Bayard Taylor, who became a lifelong friend. At the time they met, Taylor was working as a copyeditor and sometime correspondent for the *New York Tribune.* His "Views Afoot," an account of his travels in Europe, had gained Taylor acclaim as an author, and Stoddard took some inspiration from Taylor's success. The two began to meet regularly on Saturday evenings to discuss their reading, their poetry, and their ambition as poets, and Taylor's encouragement likely led Stoddard to pay for the publication of his first volume of poems, *Foot-prints* (1849). In their studied use of conventional Classical allusions and Nature imagery, these early poems show clearly Stoddard's investment in the tropes and themes of Romanticism–elements that he and Taylor had absorbed together from their reading of John Keats, Percy Bysshe Shelley, Leigh Hunt, and George Gordon, Lord Byron, alongside their American counterparts Lowell, Longfellow, Whittier, and Bryant. *Foot-prints* was a commercial failure, but it won Stoddard the recognition of Griswold, who included Stoddard in his next edition of *Poets and Poetry of America.* In his biographical sketch, Griswold praised Stoddard as a working-class poet who "moulded his thoughts into the symmetry of verse, while he moulded the molten metal into shapes of grace." Stoddard later quipped that "a knowledge of foundries was not one of [Griswold's] strongpoints." Obviously for Stoddard a diligent pursuit of a career as a professional man of letters was a way out of the factory.

Through his contacts with New York editors, he was introduced to prominent authors–including Longfellow, Lowell, and Nathaniel Hawthorne. Their influence on his development as a poet, however, is less apparent than their influence on his career. Hawthorne was especially encouraging and went so far as to write a letter to President Franklin Pierce recommending Stoddard for a government appointment. However, the endorsement of Colonel T. J. Whipple was the one that in 1852 landed Stoddard a job in the New York Customs Office, where he later met Herman Melville. Stoddard may have played some small part in Melville's

Stoddard and his wife, Elizabeth Barstow Stoddard, in 1902 (photograph by Rockwood for the Authors Club)

mid-career transformation from novelist to poet. He twice helped Melville retain his post as a customs inspector; Stoddard also included a selection of Melville's Civil War poems in his 1873 revision of Griswold's *Poets and Poetry of America* (1842); and in his *Recollections,* he praised Melville as "one of our great unrecognized poets." Stoddard also met Edgar Allan Poe on a few occasions. While working for *The Broadway Journal,* Poe rejected Stoddard's poem "Ode on a Grecian Flute" and suggested that it was plagiarized because "it [was] too good at some points to be so bad at others." Stoddard may have held a grudge: "Misserimus," the poem he wrote in memory of Poe, damns with faint praise, "The summer-tide / Of his life was past, / And his hopes were fading, falling fast. / His faults were many, his virtues few, / A tempest with flecks of heaven's blue." Stoddard's characterization of Poe in *Recollections,* moreover, supports well Griswold's infamous biography.

Stoddard married Elizabeth Barstow in 1851, and the two moved to New York after Stoddard's 1952 appointment to the New York Customs Office. They were soon fixtures in a community of writers and artists that included Taylor, Edmund Clarence Stedman,

George H. Boker, and Thomas Buchanan Read. In this environment Elizabeth Stoddard first conceived of pursuing a career as a writer of the satiric realist novels *The Morgesons* (1862), *Two Men* (1865), and *Temple House* (1867). Not only was her husband supportive of her efforts, but his conscious efforts to cater to the conventional tastes of a wide, general readership also may have helped incite the parody in her novels of bourgeois domestic values and gender roles. His influence with Lowell—then editor of *The Atlantic Monthly*—led to the publication of Elizabeth Stoddard's first novel, but Stoddard feared that her unusual style and wit might prevent her from reaching a large audience. "She was not cursed with mediocrity," he once wrote, "but had the misfortune to be original."

The Stoddards' relationship was filled with fructuous tensions, and throughout the 1850s, 1860s, and 1870s, the two together pursued their dreams of literary success. Yet, while Elizabeth Stoddard's writing became increasingly introspective and personal, Stoddard's became ever more derivative of the popular models that he admired and whose success he hoped to reproduce. In *Songs of Summer* (1857), the ambitious lyricism of early poems such as "Ode,"

"Hymn to Flora," and "Arcadian Idyll" gives way to the formulaic sentimentalism found in "The Speech of Love" and "Invocation to Sleep." In *The Book of the East, and Other Poems* (1871), Stoddard is more experimental in his choice of subject matter, but the "Persian Songs," "Arab Songs," and "Chinese Songs" he turns out are little more than watered-down Orientalist vignettes, perhaps derived from French Orientalist works such as Gerard de Nerval's *Voyage en Orient* (1851), or Gustave Flaubert's *Salammbo* (1862), or even Taylor's successful *Poems of the Orient* (1854). While Taylor's poems are based on his personal experiences traveling in Egypt and the Middle East from 1851 to 1853, Stoddard's are simply a pastiche of popular Western images of the Orient. He never traveled outside of America. Among the "Other Poems" included with *The Book of the East,* however, are some realist sketches of courtship and domestic life—including "A Woman's Poem," "Within and Without," and "On the Town"—that make a useful point of comparison with the descriptions of gender roles and domestic life in Elizabeth Stoddard's *The Morgesons* and *Two Men.* In 1880 Scribners brought out *The Poems of Richard Henry Stoddard. Complete Edition.* Although this volume does not include Stoddard's late work—from 1880 until his death in 1903—it is the most complete collection of his major poetry, including all of his previously published volumes of poetry, as well as the occasional pieces and the pamphlet poems that established his reputation with the New York audience. Of especial interest are *The King's Bell* (1863), a narrative poem; *Abraham Lincoln: An Horatian Ode* (1865); and "Guest of the State (July 4, 1876)," a poem written in commemoration of the American centennial.

Stoddard may have made his most significant contributions to American poetic traditions not as a poet but as an editor, a biographer, and a writer of introductions and memoirs. He oversaw editions of Bryant, Longfellow, and Poe; wrote biographies of Hawthorne and Irving; and revised and expanded editions of Griswold's *Poets and Poetry of America* and *Female Poets of America* (1873). While contributing his small share to the formation of an American canon of poets, he also conditioned his audience to read this canon as coextensive with a history of English verse. He brought out collections such as *The Late English Poets* (1865), *Melodies and Madrigals: Mostly from the Old English Poets* (1866), and *English Verse* (1883), a five-volume set, as well as editions of the works of prominent Romantic and Victorian poets, including Wordsworth, Byron, and Algernon Charles Swinburne. Moreover, as editor of the widely read "Sans Souci" and "Bric-à-Brac" series, anecdotal biogra-

phies and personal reminiscences of popular authors, he was a great popularizer of the culture of Romantic and Victorian poetry. *The Loves and Heroines of the Poets* (1861) is especially interesting as an example of the extent to which Stoddard worked to codify the tastes of his audience. This volume compiles descriptions of women, both real and fictional, taken from famous poetry and attempts something like an historical classification of the female archetype in poetry—a critical project that may have been inspired by Stoddard's research for his biography *The Life, Travels and Books of Alexander von Humboldt* (1859). Yet, Stoddard's concern was less to establish on critical grounds the merits of British and American poets than to establish a commonality. He even went so far as to bring out a collection of pencil sketches of the homes of famous poets. As an editor, then, Stoddard familiarized his readers with the imagery and themes that he cultivated in his own poetry. For his efforts he gained a modest reputation as a poet among the literati of New York. In the last two decades of his life, his apartment on Fifteenth Street became somewhat of a literary salon, and in 1897 The Authors Club of New York held a dinner in his honor. The extent of his literary reputation during his life was most sympathetically given in Stedman's address on that occasion: "Our homage is rendered to the man who best preserves for us, in his living presence, the traditions of all that an English-speaking poet and book-fellow should be to constitute a satisfying type." Stoddard's genteel audience was well satisfied.

Because of his immersion in the conventional tropes of romantic sentimentalism, Stoddard never quite achieved a personal vision in his poetry. Although in his body of work one can find poems faintly reminiscent of Walt Whitman's realist descriptions of everyday life or of Emily Dickinson's poignant evocations of desire endlessly deferred, these soft echoes are lost among hundreds of formulaic love songs, such as "Head, or Heart," "The Dying Lover," or "The Lady's Gift." In the last analysis, Stoddard's career is an example of a lesson he drew in *Recollections* from the career of N. P. Willis: "its safer to be conventional than individual,—even among individual people, who, as a rule, are more satisfied with themselves than with others." His attendance on convention gained him some degree of self-satisfaction, but it also left his poetry lacking in emotional depth and power, and today his lyrical flights of sentiment only reflect the Gilded Age.

References:

"The Authors Club Dinner to Richard Henry Stoddard" (New York: The Mail and Express, 1897);

Edward Sculley Bradley, *George Henry Boker, Poet and Patriot* (Philadelphia: University of Pennsylvania Press, 1927), pp. 78–82;

Lawrence Buell and Sandra A. Zagarell, "Biographical and Critical Introduction," in Elizabeth Barstow Stoddard's *The Morgesons* (Philadelphia: University of Pennsylvania Press, 1984), pp. xi–xxv;

Richard Cary, *The Genteel Circle: Bayard Taylor and His New York Friends* (Ithaca, N.Y.: Cornell University Press, 1952);

Genius and Other Essays (New York: Moffat, Yard, 1911);

J. Gerald Kennedy, "Elegy for a 'Rebel Soul': Henry Clay Preuss and the Poe Debate," in *Poe and His Times,* edited by Benjamin Franklin Fisher (Baltimore, Md.: E. A. Poe Society, 1990), pp. 226–234;

R. Macdonough, "Stoddard's *Poems,*" *Scribner's Monthly,* 20 (September 1880): 686–694;

Herman Melville, *Correspondence,* in *The Writings of Herman Melville,* volume 14 (Evanston, Ill. & Chicago: Northwestern University Press and the Newberry Library, 1993), pp. 421–422;

Burton Pollin, "Poe as Misserimus," in *Discoveries in Poe* (Notre Dame: University of Notre Dame Press, 1970), pp. 200–204;

Merton M. Sealts Jr., "Melville and Richard Henry Stoddard," *American Literature,* 48 (November 1971): 359–370;

Edmund Clarence Stedman, *Poets of America* (Boston: Houghton, Mifflin, 1892);

"Stoddard's Elegiac Sonnet on Poe," *Poe Studies,* 19 (December 1986): 32–34;

John Tomsich, *A Genteel Endeavor: American Culture and Politics in the Gilded Age* (Stanford, Cal.: Stanford University Press, 1971), pp. 136–137, 150–156, 174–178.

Papers:

Large collections of Richard Henry Stoddard's manuscripts and other materials can be found in the Houghton Library, Harvard University; Cornell University Library; and the Library of the American Antiquarian Society.

Bayard Taylor

(11 January 1825 – 19 December 1878)

Katharine Mitchell
University of Mississippi

See also the Taylor entries in *DLB 3: Antebellum Writers in New York and the South* and *DLB 189: American Travel Writers, 1850–1915.*

BOOKS: *Ximena; or, The Battle of the Sierra Morena, and Other Poems* (Philadelphia: Hooker, 1844);

Views A-Foot; or, Europe Seen with Knapsack and Staff (New York: Wiley & Putnam, 1846; London: Wiley & Putnam, 1847); revised and enlarged as *Pedestrian Tour in Europe. Views A-Foot; or, Europe Seen with a Knapsack and Staff* (New York: Putnam, 1848);

Rhymes of Travel, Ballads and Poems (New York: Putnam, 1849);

The American Legend. A Poem Before the Phi Beta Kappa Society of Harvard University, July 18, 1850 (Cambridge, Mass.: J. Bartlett, 1850);

Eldorado; or, Adventures in the Path of Empire: Comprising a Voyage to California, via Panama; Life in San Francisco and Monterey; Pictures of the Gold Region, and Experiences of Mexican Travel, 2 volumes (London: R. Bentley, 1850; New York: Putnam, 1850);

A Book of Romances, Lyrics and Songs (Boston: Ticknor, Reed & Fields, 1852);

A Journey to Central Africa; or, Life and Landscapes from Egypt to the Negro Kingdoms of the White Nile (New York: Putnam, 1854); republished as *Life and Landscapes from Egypt to the Negro Kingdoms of the White Nile: Being a Journey to Central Africa* (London: Sampson Low, Son, 1855);

Poems of the Orient (Boston: Ticknor & Fields, 1855 [i.e., 1854]);

The Lands of the Saracen; or, Pictures of Palestine, Asia Minor, Sicily, and Spain (New York: Putnam, 1855 [i.e., 1854]); republished as *Pictures of Palestine, Asia Minor, Sicily, and Spain* (London: Sampson Low, 1855 [i.e., 1854]);

A Visit to India, China, and Japan in the Year 1853 (New York: Putnam / London: Sampson Low, Son, 1855);

Poems of Home and Travel (Boston: Ticknor & Fields, 1855);

Bayard Taylor

Northern Travel: Summer and Winter Pictures of Sweden, Lapland, and Norway (New York: Putnam, 1857); republished as *Northern Travel: Summer and Winter Pictures of Sweden, Denmark, and Lapland* (London: Sampson Low, 1858);

At Home and Abroad: A Sketch-Book of Life, Scenery and Men (New York: Putnam, 1859; London: Sampson Low, 1860);

Travels in Greece and Russia, with an Excursion to Crete (New York: Putnam, 1859; London, Sampson Low, 1859);

Humboldt. Lecture Delivered by Bayard Taylor, Before the Young Men's Christian Association, Schenectady, in the Methodist Church, Feb. 24, 1860 (N.p., 1860);

At Home and Abroad: A Sketch-Book of Life, Scenery and Men . . . Second Series, 2 volumes (New York: Putnam, 1862; London: Sampson Low, 1862);

The Poet's Journal (Boston: Ticknor & Fields, 1863 [i.e., 1862]; London: Sampson Low, 1863 [i.e. 1862];

Hannah Thurston: A Story of American Life (New York: Putnam, 1863; 3 volumes, London: Sampson Low, 1863);

John Godfrey's Fortunes: Related by Himself. A Story of American Life (New York: Putnam, Hurd & Houghton, 1864; 3 volumes, London: Sampson Low, Son & Marston, 1864);

The Poems of Bayard Taylor (Boston: Ticknor & Fields, 1865 [i.e., 1864]);

The Picture of St. John (Boston: Ticknor & Fields, 1866);

The Story of Kennett (New York: Putnam / Hurd & Houghton, 1866; 2 volumes, London, 1866);

Colorado: A Summer Trip (New York: Putnam, 1867);

By-Ways of Europe (New York: Putnam, 1869); republished as *Byeways of Europe* (London: Sampson Low, Son & Marston, 1869);

The Ballad of Abraham Lincoln (Boston: Fields, Osgood, 1870);

Joseph and His Friend: A Story of Pennsylvania (New York: Putnam, 1870; London: Sampson Low, Son & Marston, 1870);

Beauty and the Beast: A Story of Old Russia, And Tales of Home (New York: Putnam, 1872; London: Sampson Low, Marston, Low & Searle, 1872);

Diversions of the Echo Club; A Companion to the "Autocrat of the Breakfast-Table," anonymous (London: J. C. Hotten, 1872); republished as *The Echo Club, and Other Literary Diversions* (Boston: James R. Osgood, 1876);

The Masque of the Gods: In Three Scenes and in Verse (Boston: James R. Osgood, 1872);

Lars: A Pastoral of Norway (Boston: Osgood, 1873: London: Strahan, 1873);

Egypt and Iceland in the Year 1874 (New York: Putnam, 1874; London: Sampson Low, Marston, Low & Searle, 1875);

The Prophet: A Tragedy in Five Acts and in Verse (Boston: James R. Osgood, 1874);

A School History of Germany: From the Earliest Period to the Establishment of the German Empire in 1871 (New York: D. Appleton, 1874);

Home Pastorals, Ballads and Lyrics (Boston: James R. Osgood, 1875);

Boys of Other Countries: Stories for American Boys (New York: Putnam, 1876; New York & London: Putnam, 1884);

The National Ode: The Memorial Freedom Poem (Boston: W. F. Gill, 1877);

Prince Deukalion: A Lyrical Drama (Boston: Houghton, Osgood / Cambridge, Mass.: Riverside Press, 1878; London: Trübner, 1878);

Studies in German Literature, edited by Hansen-Taylor and Boker (New York: Putnam, 1879; London: Sampson Low, Marston, Searle, 1879).

Collections: *Critical Essays and Literary Notes,* with an introduction by George Henry Boker (New York: Putnam, 1880);

The Dramatic Works of Bayard Taylor (Boston: Houghton, Mifflin, 1880);

The Poetical Works of Bayard Taylor (Boston: Houghton, Osgood, 1880).

OTHER: *Hand-book of Literature and the Fine Arts,* edited by Taylor and George Ripley (New York: Putnam, 1852);

Cyclopædia of Modern Travel: A Record of Adventure, Exploration and Discovery, for the Past Fifty Years: Comprising Narratives of the Most Distinguished Travelers Since the Beginning of This Century, edited by Taylor (Cincinnati: Moore, Willstach, Keys, 1856); revised and enlarged as *Cyclopedia of Modern Travel: A Record of Adventure, Exploration and Discovery, for the Past Sixty Years: Comprising Narratives of the Most Distinguished Travelers since the Beginning of This Century,* 2 volumes (Cincinnati: Moore, Willstach, Keys, 1860);

Faust, A Tragedy by Johann Wolfgang von Goethe; the First Part, Translated, in the Original Metres, by Bayard Taylor (Boston: Fields, Osgood, 1871 [i.e., 1870]);

Faust, A Tragedy by Johann Wolfgang von Goethe; the Second Part, Translated, in the Original Metres, by Bayard Taylor (Boston: Osgood, 1871); republished as *Faust, Translated in the Original Metres,* 2 volumes (London: Strahan, 1871).

PERIODICAL EDITED: *Graham's American Monthly Magazine* (January 1841–18??).

A prolific travel writer, lecturer, novelist, playwright, and technically proficient poet, Bayard Taylor is best remembered today for his metrically faithful translation of Johann Wolfgang von Goethe's *Faust* (1808–1832), which was the best English translation of its time. Known by his peers as the "Great American Traveler," a term he despised, Taylor wrote travel narratives for several magazines and newspapers. The books he subsequently published about his travels around the world were at the time unprecedented in their exotic descriptions of other cultures and landscapes. Taylor always claimed that the only reason he wrote prose was to fund his true passion, writing poetry, but as a product of the genteel tradition, his poetry was characteristically sentimental, insipid in subject matter, full of romanticized language, and often imitative. Largely unread today, Taylor was popular in his own age for his revealing travel narratives and his dedication to expanding the readership of German literature and propagating its scholarship in America.

Born 11 January 1825 in the Quaker community of Kennett Square, Pennsylvania, Bayard Taylor was one of Joseph and Rebecca Taylor's six children who survived to adulthood. Taylor attended Bolmar Academy in West Chester, Pennsylvania, where his father moved the family in order to accept the position of county sheriff. Taylor's first poem was published in the local newspaper when he was just fifteen. When he was sixteen, his poem "Soliloquy of a Young Poet" appeared in the *Philadelphia Evening Post*. His formal education ended in 1842 when he became an apprentice to a printer in West Chester. He made his first literary acquaintance with Rufus W. Griswold, to whom he dedicated his first volume of self-published verse, *Ximena; or, The Battle of the Sierra Morena, and Other Poems* (1844), which he funded by selling subscriptions. In his 1896 biography of Taylor, Albert Smyth sums up the immature volume: "Too early publication is always a vain regret." This beginning, however, was not enough to stop Taylor from becoming one of the most prodigious authors of his era.

Even though his foremost ambition and greatest desire was to be a poet, Taylor early learned that he could earn more money by writing prose. At the age of nineteen Taylor set sail for London to make his grand tour. The two-year tour not only served as Taylor's college education but also profoundly impacted his worldview and determined his new career. Although the grand tour was a standard for many nineteenth-century male adolescents, Taylor's tour was unusual in that he wrote his way across Europe in order to fund his trip—a practice he maintained throughout his career. The trip was also funded by commissions he received to write travel letters for *The Saturday Evening Post,* the *United States Literary Gazette,* and the *New York Tribune.* Upon returning to the United States, Taylor published an account of his travels, *Views A-Foot; or, Europe Seen with Knapsack and Staff* (1846), which underwent six editions in its first year of publication, soliciting praise from Henry Wadsworth Longfellow and John Greenleaf Whittier, with whom Taylor formed long friendships. Immensely popular during a time when the reading population had a heightened interest in travel, the book conformed to the conventions of the travel narrative, and Taylor did little to vary from the "correct" attitudes and descriptions prescribed by the genre of the travel narrative. Although *Views A-Foot* created a stunning rep-

Taylor in the Bedouin costume he wore to lecture on his travels in Arabia (from Richmond Croom Beatty, Bayard Taylor: Laureate of the Gilded Age, *1936)*

utation for Taylor—twenty editions were printed over the course of a decade—he lamented that his reputation had not been founded upon his poetry. As he wrote in a letter to his good friend George Henry Boker, "I am not insensible that nine-tenths of my literary success (in a publishing view) springs from these very Views Afoot which I now blush to read. I am not known to the public as a poet, the only title I covet, but as one who succeeded in seeing Europe with little money." The struggle he felt between his enjoyment of his fame as a travel and prose writer and his desire to be a well-reputed poet was a lifelong dilemma for Taylor. Despite this conflict, Taylor continued to write, perhaps sacrificing the originality of his poetry by devoting so much time to the prose that afforded him the luxury of writing verse.

After a failed attempt at owning a local newspaper, the *Phoenixville Pioneer,* Taylor entered the New York literary world, receiving such jobs as editing *Graham's Magazine* and writing as New York correspondent for *The Saturday Evening Post*. In January 1848 Taylor found a position with Horace Greeley at the *New York Tribune*. The same year Taylor published a second book of verse, *Rhymes of Travel, Ballads and Poems* (1849), chiefly a collection of poems about his European travels, with additional ballads about California. In the preface to the collection, Bayard informed readers that the lines were the expression of "thoughts and emotions inspired by my journey at the time, often noted down hastily by the wayside." In 1849 the *Tribune* sent Taylor to California to report on the gold rush, a journey that led to his publication of *Eldorado; or, Adventures in the Path of Empire: Comprising a Voyage to California, via Panama; Life in San Francisco and Monterey; Pictures of the Gold Region, and Experiences of Mexican Travel* (1850), a popular, blindly optimistic, and descriptive book. Having carved out a niche for himself in the literary world, Taylor was honored to deliver his poem "The American Legend" before the Phi Beta Kappa Society of Harvard University on 18 July 1850, at the age of twenty-five.

On 24 October 1850 Taylor married his childhood sweetheart, Mary Agnew, after several delays owing to the severity of her tuberculosis and the frequency of his travels. She died 21 December, only two months after their marriage. Her death left Taylor bereaved and anxious to travel again in order to cope with his grief.

After his wife's death, Taylor immediately sought travel money again. He found a job for Putnam editing the *Hand-book of Literature and the Fine Arts* (1852) with George Ripley. During the summer of 1851 he left for Arabia on a two-year trip, an experience that deeply impressed him aesthetically and culturally. While traveling, Taylor had many experiences his abolitionist neighbors back home would have scorned, such as experimenting with hashish, done strictly "for the purpose of testing it." While he was traveling, a previously compiled volume of verse considered to be his first mature collection, *A Book of Romances, Lyrics and Songs* (1852), was published in America. The volume included such narrative poems as "Hylas" and "Kubleh, a story of the Assyrian Desert," which adhered to the same poetic conventions used by Herbert Spenser and William Morris.

Taylor was located in Constantinople, writing letters for American magazines, when he received a message from the New York *Tribune* requesting him to join Commodore Matthew Perry's expedition to Japan. Restricted from publishing the journals he recorded during the four-month expedition, he described his Asian adventures in a later book, *A Visit to India, China, and Japan in the Year 1853* (1855), a book praised for its firsthand account of Japan, which was relatively unexplored by the Western public.

The greatest impression of Taylor's personality and originality emerged during his lectures. While earning more travel money delivering lectures about his travels—a popular occupation for nineteenth-century authors—Taylor made an impressive display as a lecturer dressed in Bedouin costume and brandishing various artifacts from the Arabian culture. Taylor delivered more than two hundred lectures in 1854 alone, while still publishing three books during the lecture year. *A Journey to Central Africa; or, Life and Landscapes from Egypt to the Negro Kingdoms of the White Nile* (1854) along with *The Lands of the Saracen; or, Pictures of Palestine, Asia Minor, Sicily, and Spain* (1855) brought in $2,650 in sales by the end of the first year. *A Journey to Central Africa* was for the most part a rehash of previous travel narratives, but because Taylor succeeded in penetrating further into central Africa than most Americans or Englishmen had, the narrative promised readers excitement and adventure. *The Lands of the Saracen*, written in diary form, was a volume in his trilogy of African and Eastern travel books.

Another volume of verse about his experiences in the East, *Poems of the Orient* (1855), pleased readers with its exotic glimpses into a romanticized Orient. Unlike *The Lands of the Saracen, Poems of the Orient* was his "wonder book," although the poems themselves generally retained the imitative quality Taylor had cultivated as a poet of the genteel age. The notoriously vituperative Edgar Allan Poe praised the imagination and rhythm of the oriental poems. James Russell Lowell, however, perhaps sensing that in *Poems of the Orient* Taylor had stepped out of the genteel confines of his American culture during his world travels, warned him to "beware of becoming too deeply enamored of the sensuous in poetry." *Poems of the Orient* includes Taylor's best-known poem, "The Bedouin Song," a love story that has since been set to music several times—most often by college glee clubs.

In 1855 Taylor published his last volume of verse for the next several years, *Poems of Home and Travel*, most of which had been published previously. Taylor's eighth book to be published in an impressive four-year span was the *Cyclopedia of Modern Travel: A Record of Adventure, Exploration and Discovery, for the Past Fifty Years: Comprising Narratives of the Most Distinguished Travelers Since the Beginning of This Century* (1856). Consisting of 937 double-columned pages of fifty-five land-travel narratives—one of those being Taylor's—the compilation of the massive book was an appropriate endeavor for a man who had "traveled more and seen less than any man living." Sales for the volume were low, however.

Bedouin Song.

From the Desert I come to thee,
　　On a stallion shod with fire,
And the winds are left behind
　　In the speed of my desire.
Under thy window I stand,
　　And the midnight hears my cry.
I love thee, I love but thee,
　　With a love that never shall die,
　　　　Till the sun grows cold,
　　　　And the stars are old,
　　　　And the leaves of the Judgment Book
　　　　　　unfold!

Look from thy window, and see
　　My passion and my pain;
I lie on the sands below,
　　And I faint in thy disdain:
Let the night-winds touch thy brow
　　With the heat of my burning sigh,
And melt thee to hear the vow
　　Of a love that never shall die,
　　　　Till the sun grows cold,
　　　　And the stars are old,
　　　　And the leaves of the Judgment Book
　　　　　　unfold!

First page of the manuscript for Taylor's best-known poem (from The Poetical Works of Bayard Taylor
[Boston & New York: Houghton, Mifflin, 1907])

Although Taylor's ambition and passion was to write great verse, his travels and travel writing seemed to take precedence. While in Europe helping to settle his two sisters and youngest brother in Germany, Taylor traveled through Greece, Turkey, Poland, and Russia, and met his second wife, Marie Hansen, who was the niece of his host in Gotha. They married on 27 October 1857, and in 1858 their daughter, Lilian, was born. From these travels Taylor wrote several articles and letters back to American newspapers and magazines that he later revised as books, largely to raise money for his dream house, Cedarcroft. The resulting books were *Northern Travel: Summer and Winter Pictures of Sweden, Lapland, and Norway* (1857), republished as *Northern Travel: Summer and Winter Pictures of Sweden, Denmark, and Lapland* (1858), a narrative centering on the frigid weather and Taylor's distaste of Norwegians, and *Travels in Greece and Russia, with an Excursion to Crete* (1859), a book in which Taylor reflected on his disdain for the modern Greek's attitude toward race and rhapsodized over the remnants of glorious ages past. *At Home and Abroad: A Sketch-Book of Life, Scenery and Men* (1859) and a second series, *At Home and Abroad* (1862), are celebrated collections of humorous short pieces about more specific events and locations, such as a five-page anecdote about crossing the Atlantic Ocean.

As a confident and prosperous newlywed and an author with immense popularity and a large readership, Taylor followed the genteel tradition by using his earnings to erect Cedarcroft, a house he built near his family home in Kennett Square, on a two-hundred-acre plot of land that he had purchased several years earlier. In May 1860 Taylor and his family moved into the mansion, a symbol of his wealth, popularity, and position. The house cost him $17,000 to build and furnish, a hefty price for the mid 1800s, but a sum that would have been comfortably covered by his prosperous book sales and steady lecture-circuit income. Soon after the family's move into the house, however, the Civil War began, and Taylor's lecture invitations and book sales fell off. Taylor avidly delivered lectures and wrote magazine articles in which he spoke out against the civil rebellion, but he always revised his position depending upon where in the country he was lecturing. The elegant lifestyle he was living at Cedarcroft lost its sheen and feasibility as the war progressed. Taylor resigned his fantastic genteel dream in order to maintain the well-being of his small family. At one point, the Taylors were forced to live with Marie's family in Germany out of economic necessity.

Prosperity returned to Taylor in May of 1862 when he went to Persia with a new position, secretary to the legation of the minister. From this short-lived position he went on to St. Petersburg, Russia, where he served as chargé d'affaires, a relatively brief appointment. Taylor never stopped writing during these appointments. In between his economic crises and his dabbling in politics, he had been preparing himself for writing in yet another popular and lucrative literary genre—the novel. Before taking the position in St. Petersburg, Taylor had started a novel that he finished in Russia and saw published on his return to New York. In *Hannah Thurston: A Story of American Life* (1863), set in New York, the hero, Maxwell Woodbury, returns from traveling the world to take up residence in his childhood home, only to meet the women's liberation advocate Hannah Thurston and a host of slanderous and petty neighbors. Although *Hannah Thurston* was not an autobiographical novel, several elements, such as the characterization of the neighbors, reflect Taylor's life at Cedarcroft. The novel suffered because of Taylor's unwillingness to detach himself from the subject matter. Putnam sold 15,000 copies in the first four months, however, and translations appeared in Germany and Russia. Although a scathing *Atlantic Monthly* review decried Taylor's jovial references to drunkenness, Taylor was pleased by the reception of the novel with the literati, including positive criticism from Longfellow, Whittier, and Lowell. In a letter to Taylor, Nathaniel Hawthorne praised *Hannah Thurston:* "The book is an admirable one, new, true, and striking,—worthy of such a world-wide observer as yourself, and with a kind of thought in it which does not lie scattered about the world's highways."

In March 1864 Taylor began another novel, which he finished in August and published that November as *John Godfrey's Fortunes: Related by Himself. A Story of American Life.* Although not an actual sketch of the author's life, the first-person novel, rich in local color, echoes Taylor's literary and social experiences in New York. In October 1865 Ticknor and Fields reprinted *The Poems of Bayard Taylor,* originally published in 1852, and by March of 1866 *The Story of Kennett* had come out. An historical novel, *The Story of Kennett* is based on the life of a notorious highwayman from Chester County who is called Sandy Flash in the novel. Biographer Richmond Croom Beatty calls this novel Taylor's most readable because of the story's freshness and its "picturesque simplicity." In 1933 *The Story of Kennett* was successfully staged for a pageant in Kennett Square. Taylor's fifth and last novel, *Joseph and His Friend: A Story of Pennsylvania,* was published in 1870. *Beauty and the Beast: A Story of Old Russia, And Tales of Home* (1872), a volume of short stories and reprints of magazine stories, was mainly founded on the history and traditions of Taylor's home county of Chester. Although Taylor occasionally created unusual and lively characters brimming with the local color of Kennett Square, his charac-

CYCLOPÆDIA OF MODERN TRAVEL:

A RECORD OF

ADVENTURE, EXPLORATION AND DISCOVERY,

FOR THE PAST FIFTY YEARS:

COMPRISING

NARRATIVES OF THE MOST DISTINGUISHED TRAVELERS SINCE THE
BEGINNING OF THIS CENTURY;

PREPARED AND ARRANGED BY

BAYARD TAYLOR.

ILLUSTRATED WITH MAPS AND ENGRAVINGS.

CINCINNATI:
MOORE, WILSTACH, KEYS & CO.,
25 WEST FOURTH STREET.
NEW YORK:
HENRY W. LAW,
310 BROADWAY.

*Frontispiece and title page for Taylor's collection of fifty-five travel narratives by various authors, including one by Taylor himself
(Thomas Cooper Library, University of South Carolina)*

ters are wooden and contrived, while his plots rely on coincidence and fancy.

Taylor was an industrious reader and writer, able to accomplish large amounts of work quickly, as evidenced by his quick succession of publications. Like other authors who tried to produce so much material in a short time, the quantity took its toll on the quality and endurance of the works. Between 1858 and 1867 Taylor published eleven works and delivered more than six hundred lectures; whatever Taylor lacked in originality he made up for in sheer volume and presence.

Taylor managed to continue publishing verse, which was his true love and passion. In *The Genteel Circle: Bayard Taylor and His New York Friends* (1952), Richard Cary describes Taylor's verse as being a "playground of romantic figments, sentimental cliches, and genteel techniques." *The Poet's Journal* (1862) served as a record of Taylor's grief for his first wife and a celebration of familial life. In October of 1866 Taylor established himself in the ranks of his contemporaries by publishing a

narrative poem, running 3,200 lines, which he had been arduously working on for fifteen years. *The Picture of St. John* (1866) was, as customary, praised by the ring of friends, poets, and critics who congratulated each other's work in order to assure the prosperity of their own. Perhaps William Cullen Bryant's comments on the poem were genuine: "I congratulate you on having produced the best of your longer poems."

In 1869 Taylor published what he claimed was his last travel book, *By-Ways of Europe,* a collection of short pieces collected from a series of papers he wrote for the *Atlantic Monthly*. More polished than previous accounts, the pieces still follow Taylor's basic narrative formula. The most noteworthy element of *By-Ways of Europe* is the introduction, in which Taylor swears off traveling–a resolve that he followed only briefly. Throughout his career Taylor was intermittently writing for magazines and newspapers, reaping the monthly profits as well as those earned from publishing collections of these articles. Taylor's interests were straying

Taylor's painting of his home, Cedarcroft, near his childhood hometown of Kennett Square, Pennsylvania
(from Marie Hansen Taylor and Lilian Bayard Taylor Kiliani, On Two Continents, *1905)*

away from travel and the novel, and he managed to invest time and care into a translation of Goethe's *Faust,* the greatest manifestation of his growing interest in German literature.

Having conceived of the idea of producing *"the English Faust"* in the 1850s, Taylor started his translation in 1863 and completed it eight years later. In order to be as faithful as he could be to Goethe, Taylor tediously read all of the existing translations, commentaries, and histories about the masterpiece. He strove to translate the poem into its original meters while retaining the meaning. Taylor's commitment to maintaining the integrity of the meter was attacked by later critics, who considered the translation outdated. Taylor himself referred to the project as a labor of love. Taylor's eight-year emotional and intellectual investment in his dream project reaped nominal economic rewards. The reputation Taylor earned as translator, however, far outweighed his weak reputation as a poet. Taylor's admirable knowledge of German literature landed him, for the fall of 1869, the position of a nonresident professor of

German literature at Cornell University. He later delivered the same series of lectures around the country.

Having long since left his beloved Cedarcroft, Taylor returned to New York, where he took a desk job at the *New York Tribune* and continued to produce book after book. Taylor dabbled in several more literary genres, fancying himself a master of drama and pastoral poetry. Taylor traces the evolution of the human conception of a deity in *The Masque of the Gods: In Three Scenes and in Verse* (1872), a dramatic work rapidly written in four intense days. This play was followed by *Lars: A Pastoral of Norway* (1873); *Egypt and Iceland in the Year 1874* (1874); *The Prophet: A Tragedy in Five Acts and in Verse* (1874), a play with a Mormon setting and Mormon characters; and *Home Pastorals, Ballads and Lyrics* (1875). The most humorous and widely read of Taylor's works from this period was the playful *The Echo Club; and Other Literary Diversions* (1876), originally published anonymously in England as *Diversions of the Echo Club; A Companion to the "Autocrat of the Breakfast-Table,"* (1872). The work is an entertaining burlesque in which Taylor quite humorously and effectively imitated other popular authors. One poem, titled "Ode on a Jar of Pickles," made fun of Keats's "Ode on a Grecian Urn" (1820). Taylor's greatest occasional verse, *The National Ode: The Memorial Freedom Poem* (1877) was written for the centennial celebration of the United States and first read publicly on 4 July 1876 at the Continental Hotel in Philadelphia. Taylor was offered the opportunity to create the occasional poem after several other major poets, including Longfellow, Bryant, and Lowell, rejected the offer. The last volume published in Taylor's lifetime, *Prince Deukalion: A Lyrical Drama* (1878), was praised even by his critics. *Prince Deukalion* represents Taylor at the height of his metrical and rhythmical capabilities. A verse drama in four acts interspersed with songs and characters who speak in blank verse, *Prince Deukalion* celebrates the noble theme of the breadths and depths to which man travels to achieve his goals.

Taylor's intimate interest in German literature and culture and his previous experience in foreign affairs culminated in his appointment as minister to Germany in 1878. This position was ideal for a noted scholar in German literature, and Taylor was further interested in accepting the position because he was preparing to write biographies of Goethe and Friedrich von Schiller. Taylor fell ill, however, and was not able to perform his new duties. He suffered repeated illnesses while in Germany, where he died 19 December 1878. His body was sent back to his home at Kennett Square for burial. Several collections of his work were published posthumously, including *Critical Essays and Literary Notes* (1880), *The Dramatic Works of Bayard Taylor* (1880), and *The Poetical Works of Bayard Taylor* (1880).

Letters:

Marie Hansen Taylor and Horace Scudder, eds., *The Life and Letters of Bayard Taylor,* 2 volumes (Boston: Houghton, Mifflin, 1884);

John R. Schultz, ed., *Unpublished Letters of Bayard Taylor in the Huntington Library* (San Marino, Cal.: Huntington Library, 1937);

Charles Duffy, ed., *The Correspondence of Bayard Taylor and Paul Hamilton Hayne* (Baton Rouge: Louisiana State University, 1945);

Paul C. Wermuth, *Selected Letters of Bayard Taylor* (Lewisburg, Pa.: Bucknell University Press / London & Cranbury, N.J.: Associated University Presses, 1997).

Biographies:

Albert Smyth, *Bayard Taylor* (Boston: Houghton, Mifflin, 1896);

Marie Hansen Taylor and Lilian Bayard Taylor Kiliani, *On Two Continents: Memories of Half a Century* (New York: Doubleday, Page, 1905);

Richmond Croom Beatty, *Bayard Taylor: Laureate of the Gilded Age* (Norman, Okla.: University of Oklahoma Press, 1936).

References:

Richard Cary, *The Genteel Circle: Bayard Taylor and His New York Friends* (Ithaca, N.Y.: Cornell University Press, 1952);

John T. Krumplemann, *Bayard Taylor and German Letters* (Hamburg: Cram, De Gruyter, 1959);

Edmund Charles Stedman, *Poets of America* (Boston: Houghton, Mifflin, 1885);

Richard Henry Stoddard, *Recollections, Personal and Literary,* edited by Ripley Hitchcock (New York: A. S. Barnes, 1903);

Paul C. Wermuth, *Bayard Taylor* (New York: Twayne, 1973).

Papers:

The principal collections of Bayard Taylor's letters are in the Cornell University Library, Ithaca, New York, and the Huntington Library, San Marino, California.

Susan Warner
(Elizabeth Wetherell)
(11 July 1819 – 17 March 1885)

Susan M. Stone
Loras College

See also the Warner entries in *DLB 3: Antebellum Writers in New York and the South, DLB 42: American Writers for Children Before 1900,* and *DLB 239: American Women Prose Writers: 1820–1870.*

BOOKS: *The Wide, Wide World,* 2 volumes, as Elizabeth Wetherell (New York: Putnam, 1851 [i.e., 1850]; London: J. Nisbet, 1851);

Queechy, 2 volumes, as Wetherell (New York: Putnam, 1852; London: Nisbet, 1852);

American Female Patriotism: A Prize Essay, as Wetherell (New York: E. H. Fletcher, 1852);

Carl Krinken: His Christmas Stocking, by Susan Warner and Anna Warner, anonymous (New York: Putnam, 1854 [i.e., 1853]; London: Nisbet, 1854);

Mr. Rutherford's Children, 2 volumes, by Susan Warner and Anna Warner (New York: Putnam, 1854);

The Hills of the Shatemuc, 2 volumes, as the author of *The Wide, Wide World* (London: Sampson Low, Son, 1856; New York: Appleton, 1856); republished as *Rufus and Winthrop; or, The Hills of the Shatemuc* (London: Simpkin, Marshall, 1857); republished as *Rest, or, The Hills of the Shatemuc* (London: Milner & Sowerby, 1860); republished as *Hope's Little Hand* (London: Routledge, 1877); republished as *Hope and Rest* (London: Ward, Lock, 1890);

The Birthday Visit to Holly Farm, by Susan Warner and Anna Warner (London, 1860);

Say and Seal, 2 volumes, by Susan Warner and Anna Warner, as the author of *The Wide, Wide World,* and "Dollars and Cents" (London: Bentley, 1860; Philadelphia: Lippincott, 1860);

The Children of Blackberry Hollow (Philadelphia: American Sunday-School Union, 1861);

Hymns for Mothers and Children (Boston: Walker, Wise, 1861);

The Little Nurse of Cape Cod (Philadelphia: American Sunday-School Union, 1863);

Susan Warner

The Golden Ladder: Stories Illustrative of the Eight Beatitudes, by Susan Warner and Anna Warner, as the author of *The Wide, Wide World* (London: Nisbet, 1863 [i.e., 1862]; New York: Randolph, n.d.); republished in 8 volumes, as: *The Two School Girls and Other Tales,* by Susan Warner, anonymous

(New York: Carlton & Porter, Sunday-School Union, 1862 [i.e., 1863]; London: Routledge, 1864); *Althea. "Blessed Are They that Mourn: For They Shall be Comforted,"* by Susan Warner and Anna Warner, anonymous (New York: Carlton & Porter, Sunday-School Union, 1862 [i.e., 1863]); republished as *The Widow and Her Daughter* (London: Routledge, 1864); *Gertrude and Her Cat. "Blessed Are the Meek: For They Shall Inherit the Earth,"* by Susan Warner, anonymous (New York: Carlton & Porter, Sunday-School Union, 1862 [i.e., 1863]); republished as *Gertrude and Her Bible* (London: Routledge, 1864); *The Rose in the Desert. "Blessed are They Which Do Hunger and Thirst after Righteousness: For They Shall See God,"* by Susan Warner and Anna Warner, anonymous (New York: Carlton & Porter, Sunday-School Union, 1862, [i.e., 1863]; London: Routledge, 1864); *The Little Black Hen. "Blessed are the Merciful: For They Shall Obtain Mercy,"* by Susan Warner and Anna Warner, anonymous (New York: Carlton & Porter, Sunday-School Union, 1862 [i.e., 1863]; London: Routledge, 1864); *Martha's Hymn. "Blessed Are the Pure in Heart: For They Shall See God,"* by Susan Warner, anonymous (New York: Carlton & Porter, Sunday-School Union, 1862 [i.e., 1863]; republished as *Martha and Her Kind Friend Rachel* (London: Routledge, 1864); *The Carpenter's House. "Blessed are the Peacemakers: For They Shall be Called the Children of God,"* by Susan Warner, anonymous (New York: Carlton & Porter, Sunday-School Union, 1862 [i.e., 1863]); republished as *The Carpenter's Daughter* (London: Routledge, 1864); republished as *Little Nettie; or Home Sunshine* (London: F. Warne, 1872); *The Prince in Disguise. Blessed are They which Are Persecuted for Righteousness' Sake. For Theirs Is the Kingdom of Heaven,* by Anna Warner, anonymous (New York: Carlton & Porter, Sunday-School Union, 1862 [i.e., 1863]);

The Old Helmet, 2 volumes (New York: Carter, 1864 [i.e., 1863]; London: Nisbet, 1863);

Melbourne House, 2 volumes, as the author of *The Wide, Wide World* (New York: Carter, 1864; London: Nisbet, 1864);

The Word. Walks from Eden, as the author of *The Wide, Wide World* (New York: Carter, 1866 [i.e., 1865]; London: Nisbet, 1865);

The Word. The House of Israel. A Sequel to "Walks from Eden" (New York: Carter, 1867; London: Nisbet, 1867);

Gertrude and Lily, or, Good Resolutions (London: F. Warne, 1867);

Daisy: Continued from "Melbourne House," 2 volumes, as the author of *The Wide, Wide World* (Philadelphia: Lippincott, 1868; London: Nisbet 1868);

Daisy in the Field, as the author of *The Wide, Wide World* (London: Nisbet, 1869); republished as *Daisy. Continued from "Melbourne House,"* as the author of *The Wide, Wide World* (Philadelphia: Lippincott, 1869);

Sybil and Chryssa, Being a Sequel to "Mr. Rutherford's Children." And The Little Nurse of Cape Cod, by Susan Warner and Anna Warner (London & Edinburgh, 1869);

"What She Could," as the author of *The Wide, Wide World* (New York: Carter, 1871; London: Nisbet, 1871); republished with *Opportunities* (London: Nisbet, 1871);

Edith and Mary at the Holly Farm, as the author of *The Wide, Wide World* (London, 1871);

Opportunities. A Sequel to "What She Could," as the author of *The Wide, Wide World* (New York: Carter, 1871; London: Nisbet, 1871); republished with *"What She Could"* (London: Nisbet, 1871);

The House in Town. A Sequel to "Opportunities," as the author of *The Wide, Wide World* (New York: Carter, 1872 [i.e., 1871]; London: Nisbet, 1871);

Lessons on the Standard Bearers of the Old Testament. Third Grade for Older Classes (New York: Randolph, 1872; London: Nisbet, 1873);

"Trading." Finishing the Story of The House in Town (New York: Carter, 1873 [i.e., 1872]; London: Nisbet, 1873);

The Little Camp on Eagle Hill (London: Nisbet, 1873; New York: Carter, 1873); republished as *Giving Honour* (London: Nisbet, 1874);

Willow Brook: A Sequel to "The Little Camp on Eagle Hill," as the author of *The Wide, Wide World* (New York: Carter, 1874; London: Nisbet, 1874);

Sceptres and Crowns, as the author of *The Wide, Wide World* (Nashville: Publishing House of the Methodist Episcopal Church, South, Barber, & Smith, 1874; London: Routledge, 1875); republished with *The Flag of Truce* (London: Nisbet, 1875);

The Flag of Truce, as the author of *The Wide, Wide World* (New York: Carter, 1875); republished with *Sceptres and Crowns* (London: Nisbet, 1875);

Giving Trust. I. Bread and Oranges. II. Rapids of Niagara, as the author of *The Wide, Wide World* (London: Nisbet, 1875);

Bread and Oranges, as the author of *The Wide, Wide World* (New York: Carter, 1875);

The Rapids of Niagara, as the author of *The Wide, Wide World* (New York: Carter, 1876);

Wych Hazel, by Susan Warner and Anna Warner, as the author of *The Wide, Wide World* (London: Nisbet, 1876; New York: Putnam, 1876);

The Gold of Chickaree, by Susan Warner and Anna Warner (New York: Putnam, 1876; London: Nisbet, 1876);

The Glen-Luna Family: A Novel, as the author of *The Wide, Wide World* (London, 1877);

Pine Needles, as the author of *The Wide, Wide World* (London: Nisbet, 1877; New York: Carter, 1877); republished as *Needles and Old Yarns* (London: Simpkin, 1878); republished as *Pine Needles and Old Yarns* (Wakefield, U.K.: Nicholson, 1878);

Diana (New York: Putnam, 1877; London: Nisbet, 1877);

The Kingdom of Judah, as the author of *The Wide, Wide World* (New York: Carter, 1878; London: Nisbet, 1878);

The King's People, 5 volumes (New York: Carter, 1878)— comprises *Walks from Eden, The House of Israel, The Kingdom of Judah,* and *The Broken Walls of Jerusalem,* all by Susan Warner, and *The Star of Jacob,* by Anna Warner;

The Broken Walls of Jerusalem and the Rebuilding of Them, as the author of *The Wide, Wide World* (New York: Carter, 1879; London: Nisbet, 1879);

My Desire, as the author of *The Wide, Wide World* (New York: Carter, 1879; London: Nisbet, 1879);

The End of a Coil, as the author of *The Wide, Wide World* (New York: Carter, 1880; London: Nisbet, 1880);

The Letter of Credit, as the author of *The Wide, Wide World* (London: Nisbet, 1881; New York: Carter, 1882);

Nobody (London: Nisbet, 1882; New York: Carter, 1883);

Stephen M.D., as the author of *The Wide, Wide World* (New York: Carter, 1883; London: Nisbet, 1883);

A Red Wallflower, as the author of *The Wide, Wide World* (New York: Carter, 1884; London: Nisbet, 1884);

Daisy Plains, begun by Susan Warner and completed by Anna Warner, as the author of *The Wide, Wide World* (New York: Carter, 1885; London: Nisbet, 1885).

Edition: *The Wide, Wide World,* edited by Jane Tompkins (New York: Feminist Press of the City University of New York, 1987)—includes the previously unpublished final chapter.

OTHER: "How May an American Woman Best Show Her Patriotism?" *Ladies' Wreath: An Illustrated Annual,* edited by Mrs. S. T. Martyn (New York: J. M. Fletcher, 1851);

The Law and the Testimony, extracts from the Bible arranged by Susan Warner and Anna Warner (New York: Carter, 1853); republished as *The Law and the Testimony: Christian Doctrine* (London: Nisbet, 1853).

SELECTED PERIODICAL PUBLICATIONS– UNCOLLECTED: "Melbourne House," 46 parts, *Little American,* 1 (1 and 15 October 1862; 1 and 15 November 1862; 1 and 15 December 1862; 1 and 15 January 1863; 1 and 15 February 1863; 1 and 15 March 1863; 1 and 15 April 1863; 1 and 15 May 1863; 1 and 15 June 1863; 1 and 15 July 1863; 1 and 15 August 1863; 1 and 15 September 1863; 1 and 15 October 1863; 2 and 15 November 1863; 1 December 1863; 15 January 1864; 1 and 15 February 1864; 1 and 15 March 1864; 1 and 15 April 1864; 1 and 15 May 1864; 1 and 15 June 1864; 1 July 1864; 15 August 1864; 1 September 1864; 1 October 1864; 1 December 1864);

"Iceland," 5 parts, *Little American,* 1 (1 October 1862; 1 December 1862; 15 February 1863; 1 March 1863; 1 April 1863);

"The Seven Fairies," 5 parts, *Little American,* 1 (1 October 1862; 15 November 1862, 15 January 1863; 1 May 1863; 15 August 1863);

"Pigeontown," *Little American,* 1 (1 October 1862);

"Josie's Letters," 8 parts, *Little American,* 1–2 (1 October 1862; 1 and 15 December 1862; 1 October 1863; 2 and 15 November 1863; 1 December 1863; 1 February 1864);

"The Breakfast Table," 7 parts, *Little American,* 1–2 (1 October 1862; 15 November 1862; 1 January 1863; 1 February 1863; 1 April 1863; 15 November 1863; 1 December 1863);

"Little Lights," *Little American,* 1 (1 October 1862);

"The Chevalier Bayard," *Little American,* 1 (15 November 1862);

"The Grasses," 2 parts, *Little American,* 1 (15 November 1862; 15 March 1863);

"I Know How," *Little American,* 1 (1 December 1862);

"The Great Serpent," *Little American,* 1 (1 December 1862);

"Gates," *Little American,* 1 (15 December 1862);

"Children All Over the World," 4 parts, *Little American,* 1 and 2 (15 December 1862; 1 June 1863; 2 November 1863; 1 April 1864);

"The Old Man with the Two Flutes," *Little American,* 1 (15 December 1862);

"Bethlehem," *Little American,* 1 (1 January 1863);

"The Children's Dream," *Little American*, 1 (1 January 1863);

"The Ugly Knight," *Little American*, 1 (1 January 1863);

"The Experiences of the Rush Family," 6 parts, *Little American*, 1–2 (15 January 1863; 1 March 1863; 15 June 1863; 15 October 1863; 15 February 1864);

"The Midnight Alarm," *Little American*, 1 (15 January 1863);

"A Roseleaf," *Little American*, 1 (15 January 1863);

"The Strange Little Boy," *Little American*, 1 (1 February 1863);

"Mamma's Dressing Room," 2 parts, *Little American*, 1–2 (1 February 1863; 1 October 1863);

"The Wonderful Serpent," *Little American*, 1 (15 February 1863);

"The Black Art," *Little American*, 1 (15 February 1863);

"A Talking Party Among the Parrots: The Cockatoo," *Little American*, 1 (1 March 1863);

"Ready for Duty," *Little American*, 1 (15 March 1863);

"Chinese Visits," *Little American*, 1 (1 April 1863);

"The Robin's Breakfast," *Little American*, 1 (1 April 1863);

"Watch and Ward," *Little American*, 1 (15 April 1863);

"Mrs. Wren is Obliged to Build," *Little American*, 1 (15 April 1863);

"The Water-Cress Market," *Little American*, 1 (15 April 1863);

"Lamplighters of the World," 2 parts, *Little American*, 1 (1 May 1863; 1 June 1863); "May," *Little American*, 1 (1 May 1863);

"An Earl Who Loved His Country," *Little American*, 1 (1 May 1863);

"A Chinese Feast," *Little American*, 1 (1 June 1863);

"Truth," *Little American*, 1 (15 June 1863);

"A Concert–Beginning at Three, A. M.," *Little American*, 1 (15 June 1863);

"Workers in Wood," 4 parts, *Little American*, 1 (1 July 1863; 1 and 15 August 1863; 1 September 1863);

"Spring Doings," *Little American*, 1 (1 July 1863);

"The Indian Goose-Driver," *Little American*, 1 (1 July 1863);

"Feathers," *Little American*, 1 (1 August 1863);

"Shahweetah," 5 parts, *Little American*, 1 and 2 (1 August 1863; 15 October 1863; 15 January 1864; 1 February 1864; 1 October 1864);

"Distinguished," *Little American*, 1 (1 August 1863);

"Three French Knights," *Little American*, 1 (15 August 1863);

"The Fairy Greymantle," *Little American*, 1 (1 September 1863);

"The Seed-Bearing Grasses," *Little American*, 1 (1 September 1863);

"How People Live," 2 parts, *Little American*, 1–2 (1 September 1863; 15 June 1864);

"The Ship Worm," *Little American*, 1 (15 September 1863);

"The Sparrow," *Little American*, 1 (15 September 1863);

"The Flower-Girl," *Little American*, 1 (15 September 1863);

"The Ringing of Bells," *Little American*, 1 (15 September 1863);

"Mice!" *Little American*, 2 (1 October 1863);

"Masons of the World," 11 parts, *Little American*, 2 (1 and 15 October 1863; 2 and 15 November 1863; 1 December 1863; 15 January 1864; 1 and 15 March 1864; 15 April 1864; 15 May 1864; 1 September 1864);

"Moss," *Little American*, 2 (1 October 1863);

"The Link of Gold," *Little American*, 2 (15 October 1863);

"Deacon Broderick's House: Chapter 1," *Little American*, 2 (2 November 1863);

"Thanksgiving," 2 parts, *Little American*, 2 (15 November 1863; 1 December 1863);

"Christmas Eve," *Little American*, 2 (15 January 1864);

"Little Hands," *Little American*, 2 (15 January 1864);

"The Grain-Bearing Grasses," 4 parts, *Little American*, 2 (1 February 1864; 1 April 1864; 1 May 1864; 1 October 1864);

"Great Deeds," *Little American*, 2 (1 February 1864);

"Natural History," 4 parts, *Little American*, 2 (15 February 1864; 15 March 1864; 15 May 1864; 15 September 1864);

"History of a Needle," 5 parts, *Little American*, 2 (1 and 15 March 1864; 1 and 15 April 1864; 1 May 1864);

"The Sheep," *Little American*, 2 (1 March 1864);

"Safe–For Evermore," *Little American*, 2 (15 March 1864);

"Town Mouse and Country Mouse," 5 parts, *Little American*, 2 (15 April 1864; 1 and 15 May 1864; 1 and 15 June 1864);

"The Bouquet," *Little American*, 2 (1 May 1864);

"Thistle Work," *Little American*, 2 (15 May 1864);

"Dolls," *Little American*, 2 (1 June 1864);

"The Trumpets," *Little American*, 2 (1 June 1864);

"The Swans at a Watering Place," *Little American*, 2 (15 June 1864);

"Shadows," *Little American*, 2 (15 June 1864);

"Sheep Folds," *Little American*, 2 (1 July 1864);

"The Story of Hercules and Minerva," 4 parts, *Little American*, 2 (1 July 1864; 15 August 1864; 1 September 1864; 1 December 1864);

"Soldier Stories," 2 parts, *Little American*, 2 (1 July 1864; 15 August 1864);

"Shepherds," *Little American*, 2 (15 August 1864);

Warner's younger sister, Anna, who collaborated on some of her books

"Evening Prayer for the Children," *Little American,* 2 (15 August 1864);

"Gifts," *Little American,* 2 (1 September 1864);

"The Dove of Pompeii," *Little American,* 2 (1 October 1864);

"Fishers of the World: The Barnacle," *Little American,* 2 (1 November 1864);

"Shepherds in Early Times," *Little American,* 2 (1 November 1864);

"The Little Pilgrim," *Little American,* 2 (1 November 1864);

"The Little China Asters," *Little American,* 2 (1 November 1864);

"War in Old Times," *Little American,* 2 (1 December 1864).

PUBLICATION EDITED: *The Little American: A Series of Stories and Sketches for Young Folks,* edited by Susan Warner and Anna Warner (New York: 1862–1864).

Susan Warner, best remembered for her popular first two novels, *The Wide, Wide World* (1850) and *Queechy* (1852), was one of the few American women to write successfully for a living during the antebellum period. Attempting both to support her family and to impart Christian values to her predominantly young, female readers by way of believable characters, Warner wrote prolifically and profitably about those experiences she knew firsthand–financial hardship, spiritual uncertainty, moral growth, enduring friendship, and the loss of a parent.

Susan Bogert Warner, born 11 July 1819 in Manhattan, was the first of the two daughters of attorney Henry Whiting Warner and Anna Marsh Bartlett Warner. Although the girls' mother died in 1828, Henry Warner's sister Fanny came to live with them, and both Susan and her sister Anna Bartlett seem to have had a comfortable and enjoyable childhood. Because of their father's investments in real estate and the family's rapid financial ascendancy, Warner and her younger sister enjoyed a brief period of social affluence and elegant living. During the first eighteen years of her life, Susan Warner endeavored to master those arts that befitted her station. She studied French and Italian, learned singing and dancing, read from the works of Walter Scott, Maria Edgeworth, and Hannah More, and enjoyed evenings out at cotillions and concerts. After Henry Warner suffered tremendous losses during the panic of 1837–the first major economic depression in the United States–the family was forced to sell their St. Mark's Place town house and to retreat to their country home, a Constitution Island farmhouse on the Hudson River. In her time of crisis Warner turned to Christianity for solace.

Prompted by her aunt to earn money by writing a book, Warner drew upon both a serene sense of Christian devotion and the feelings she experienced when her mother died. The result of her efforts, written between 1848 and 1849, was her first novel, *The Wide, Wide World.* Because Warner was unsure of how her book would be received, she decided to publish under the pseudonym Elizabeth Wetherell. Her instincts about the semi-autobiographical tale proved correct: initial reaction to the novel was lukewarm. Several publishing companies, including Harper and Brothers and Robert Carter–which ultimately became Warner's principal American backer–rejected the manuscript. George Palmer Putnam, however, decided to take a chance on Warner's wholesome novel, perhaps because of his wife's enthusiastic endorsement of Warner's work.

Hoping to take advantage of the Christmas market, Putnam had 750 copies of *The Wide, Wide World* published in a two-volume set in December 1850. The edition was priced at $1.50 and sold beyond the publisher's expectations. Although response to the moralistic reversal-of-fortune novel was not immediate, *The Wide, Wide World* eventually became the first domestic novel that was an American best-seller. Largely well received by contemporary reviewers as a palatable blend of solidly characterized romance and didactic encouragement, Warner's first book enjoyed more than twenty domestic and foreign editions during its first three years in print. For eight decades, *The Wide, Wide World* did not go out of print. Including German, Dutch, French, and Polish translations, *The Wide, Wide World* has now been released in at least 131 authorized and unauthorized editions.

Comparable in success only to Harriet Beecher Stowe's *Uncle Tom's Cabin* (1851–1852) and Louisa May Alcott's *Little Women* (1868–1869)–the best-seller in which *The Wide, Wide World* is actually referred to as a March family favorite–Warner's first book appealed predominantly to girls and young women. Representative of and, perhaps, instrumental in the shaping of what is now referred to as the domestic or sentimental narrative, *The Wide, Wide World* offered a believable and likable character, Ellen Montgomery, a girl in search of spiritual, moral, and intellectual growth. For female readers seeking instruction in virtue and sensibility, young Ellen, who throughout the novel struggles to overcome her tears and emotions in an effort to arrive at emotional maturity, appeared as a role model. For others who had lost a parent, experienced a reversal of fortune, or removed to the country, Ellen was not only a reflection of their own lives, but also a source of comfort.

Despite the romantic trials and tribulations and the near desperate efforts at goodness and piety that occupy the plot, *The Wide, Wide World* offers a detailed, accurate glimpse at rural life that appealed to later-nineteenth-century reviewers such as Henry James. With both careful attention to minutiae and the realistic implementation of regional vernacular typically associated with postbellum writers such as Sarah Orne Jewett, Mary Eleanor Wilkins Freeman, and Susan Glaspell, Warner describes washing at the outdoor pump in winter, dyeing snow-white stockings slate gray using tree bark, making sausage and peeling apples at Miss Fortune's all-night bee, and hiking down a mountainside in the stinging darkness of a sudden snowstorm. Indeed, *The Wide, Wide World* offers multiple backdrops against which Ellen attempts to define herself and answer questions about her identity, family, spirituality, duty, and love.

Although fame came quickly for Warner, fortune was more elusive; the earnings from her first book were earmarked for settling accounts and repaying family debts. Financial necessity forced Warner to begin writing her second book, *Queechy*, immediately after proofreading *The Wide, Wide World*. Putnam published *Queechy* as a two-volume set attributed to Elizabeth Wetherell. This novel, which was almost as popular as Warner's first, enjoyed four editions its first year in print and almost sixty reprints and/or translations by various publishing houses in the United States, England, Australia, France, and Sweden. Like Ellen Montgomery, Fleda Ringgan, the heroine of the novel, is an orphan. Unlike Ellen, who leaves a life of luxury at ten years of age to take up residence with her all too provincial aunt, Fleda's new guardians treat her to several years of affluence. Before her sympathetic aunt and uncle are forced to retreat to the country town of Queechy, where she must wear an apron and dig potatoes for her dinner, Fleda travels abroad, studying and forming social connections in France. Like Warner, the heroine of *Queechy* is chagrined by her losses and turns to religion for comfort and guidance. Reassured that her faith, patience, and decorum will ultimately recompense her for her worldly sufferings, Fleda bears her burden, doing her part to keep the family from physical, social, and spiritual starvation. Yet humility does not erase all traces of her aristocratic behavior. On the contrary, Fleda, whose main task throughout the novel is to convert her future lover–a wealthy, older Englishman–to Christianity, believes that good bearing and fine manners are the moral rewards for religious piety and unwavering devotion. In essence, *Queechy* is a religious romance.

American Female Patriotism: A Prize Essay (1852), a short piece published during the same year as *Queechy,* is about another kind of female devotion. The essay–originally titled "How May an American Woman Best Show Her Patriotism?"–made its first appearance in 1851 as a short story for which Warner won an award of $50 from *The Ladies' Wreath: An Illustrated Annual.* In the work, a fictitious husband and wife discuss the many ways in which a woman might demonstrate her civic pride and patriotic support for her country, ultimately deciding that all pretensions of aristocratic behavior need to be erased and shunned by the American woman, save those concerning intellect and manners.

The Law and the Testimony (1853), like *American Female Patriotism,* attempts to offer instruction and guidance for its largely female audience. The book was Warner's only work of nonfiction to appear during the years immediately before the Civil War. Rather than the recipe for successful citizenship offered by *American Female Patriotism, The Law and the Testimony* offers its reader religious direction. Warner's didactic collection of thematically organized biblical Scriptures was prompted by and was most likely the partial result of

Frontispiece and title page for Warner's best-selling first novel (Widener Library, Harvard University)

her father's suggestion. According to Dorothy Hurlbut Sanderson in *They Wrote for a Living: A Bibliography of the Works of Susan Bogert Warner and Anna Bartlett Warner* (1976), Warner was told as a child that should she ever have a question about a particular topic, the best way of understanding that topic would be to gather together and examine all the evidences from the Bible on the subject. Although less popular than her novels, *The Law and the Testimony,* which is representative of Warner's religious enthusiasm, appeared in three different American and British editions.

Carl Krinken: His Christmas Stocking (1853), a children's book first published by Putnam, is usually attributed solely to Warner. Occasionally, however, it has been mistakenly considered a collaborative effort, most likely because *Carl Krinken* is also volume four of a series initiated by Anna Bartlett Warner called "Ellen Montgomery's Bookshelf." Although the sisters worked together on other literary endeavors, this tale and possibly the one written immediately after it, *Mr. Rutherford's Children* (1854), were the most successful in the collection of stories marketed as those held dear by Ellen Montgomery and Miss Alice in *The Wide, Wide World.* *Carl Krinken,* or *The Christmas Stocking* (1853), as it was

called abroad, is mentioned by Anna Bartlett Warner in the introduction to the original printing of the series as the only selection that was totally Susan Warner's creation; however, upon publication, *Mr. Rutherford's Children* is attributed to "the author of *Carl Krinken.*" *Carl Krinken* is a short work, but it is also an uplifting story of gratitude and appreciation. Respectably popular in the mid nineteenth century, *Carl Krinken* appeared as part of the "Ellen Montgomery's Bookshelf" collection five times and was published individually in the United States, England, and France under Susan Warner's name a total of twenty times between 1853 and 1877. In this holiday sketch Carl, an impoverished youth, learns to appreciate the meanings and intentions behind each seemingly insignificant gift in his not quite full Christmas stocking, thus realizing that the true spirit of Christmas is what makes him wealthy.

Mr. Rutherford's Children also explores the nature of goodness, respectful appreciation for one's physical and spiritual gifts, and the significance of family; however, the novel does so by showcasing two small New England girls. Although the work was published after *Carl Krinken, Mr. Rutherford's Children* was initially intended to be the first work in the "Ellen Montgomery's Bookshelf" series. Drawing on the popularity of *The Wide, Wide World,* Warner provides the juvenile reader an exemplary and didactic spin-off text. Chryssa and Sybil, the two orphaned sisters who are supposedly Ellen Montgomery's favorite heroines, learn the responsibilities associated with being upstanding young Christian women while participating in many minor adventures and exploring the wonders of the natural and man-made worlds.

Although both *Carl Krinken* and *Mr. Rutherford's Children* were popular and appeared in print in both the United States and Britain, other proposed volumes for the "Ellen Montgomery's Bookshelf" series, such as "The Breakfast Table," were never written, perhaps because Warner understandably wished to develop longer works with characters who were not connected to the larger-than-life protagonist of *The Wide, Wide World.*

Riding on the coattails of her first two novels, *The Hills of the Shatemuc* (1856), Warner's third novel, was initially quite popular, reportedly selling ten thousand copies on the first day the work was available for purchase. Ultimately, however, this fame was short-lived. First published by Appleton in the United States and now out of print for more than a century, the novel did not receive much contemporary critical attention. Instead of the rich detail and vivid description characteristic of her first two novels, *The Hills of Shatemuc* is a somewhat disjointed and superficial account of Winthrop Landholm's attempts to overcome his humble rural background, to complete law school, and to achieve social ascendancy. The biographical similarities between Winthrop Landholm and Warner's father, Henry Whiting Warner, are perhaps the most interesting aspects of this quickly forgotten romance.

A two-volume novel written by Warner and her sister Anna, *Say and Seal* (1860) is a mixture of religious didacticism, sentimental romance, brilliant characterization, and moral growth. Moreover, the novel offers a superb presentation of nineteenth-century New England society, one replete with brilliant examples of Yankee character and dialect that call to mind the intricate portraits painted by Jewett almost four decades later in *The Country of the Pointed Firs* (1896).

Although the plot is somewhat predictable, the Warners give skillful descriptions of both the countryside and the people in this picture of the inner workings of the village of Pattaquasset. Despite positive critical reviews in journals such as *Littell's Living Age* and *The Atlantic Monthly,* American readers had their minds on the more immediate matter of the Civil War. The story of John Endecott Linden, a young minister in training who teaches school in a small New England village and who converts his landlady's daughter–appropriately

named Faith Derrick–to Christianity while he is on leave from college, was, and still is, largely overlooked.

By the close of 1853 *The Wide, Wide World* and *Queechy* had made Susan Warner a famous author of domestic fiction; the two books had sold more than 104,000 copies. Warner, sometimes writing as Elizabeth Wetherell, published more than forty short stories, religious tracts, children's tales, and novels for adults before her death; she also wrote more than twenty works with Anna Warner. Most of Susan Warner's independent novels, however, such as *Wych Hazel* (1876), the two-volume *Melbourne House* (1864), and its sequels, *Daisy: Continued from "Melbourne House"* (1868) and *Daisy in the Field* (1869), were written during or after the Civil War and received little or no critical attention.

Wych Hazel, a novel that opens with James Russell Lowell's statement "We may shut our eyes, but we cannot help knowing that the skies are clear and grass is growing," is concerned with making the readers aware of and responsible for the world–both natural and human–around them. As is typical of Warner's works, the heroine is an orphan; however, in this tale, the main character, Wych Hazel Kennedy, is a wealthy socialite on the brink of womanhood. Under the supervision of her two wards, Mr. Falkirk and Mr. Rollo, Hazel learns to reject the fast-paced, superficial arena of her fellow social debutantes in favor of a more spiritually informed, family-oriented and community-centered existence. Finding herself frequently in sympathy with Mr. Rollo and his working-class friends, Hazel discovers that regardless of her wealth she cannot escape the ugliness of poverty or run from her obligations to those who live near her but are isolated in so many ways from her comfortable, insulated world. By purchasing and reforming a local mill and by embracing "work"–a constant topic in this novel–Hazel profits spiritually and personally, winning the admiration and respect not only of her employees but also of Mr. Rollo, who proposes marriage to her. Much like Alcott's *Work: A Story of Experience* (1873), *Wych Hazel* is a powerful novel that recommends community involvement, female alliances across classes, and the merits of work for women. Although it has a somewhat sentimental ending, *Wych Hazel* is a work that merits the attentions of modern feminist and cultural-studies scholars.

A later story that also reaped little critical notice, *Daisy Plains* (1885) offers the reader more than the expected struggles between selfishness and charity, immorality and Christianity, and materialism and education. Like *The Wide, Wide World, Mr. Rutherford's Children,* and many of Warner's other works, *Daisy Plains* follows the physical, emotional, and spiritual growth of various members of a single family. Yet this book, which revolves around the activities and journeys of

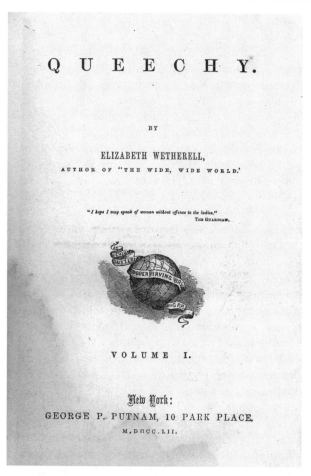

QUEECHY.

BY

ELIZABETH WETHERELL,

AUTHOR OF "THE WIDE, WIDE WORLD."

"I hope I may speak of woman without offence to the ladies."
THE GUARDIAN.

VOLUME I.

New York:
GEORGE P. PUTNAM, 10 PARK PLACE.
M.DCCC.LII.

Title page for Warner's religious romance, about a girl who descends from aristocratic luxury to rural poverty (Thomas Cooper Library, University of South Carolina)

the Thayers, also examines the relationships between and attitudes of their many acquaintances and neighbors. The novel takes place in a solid, rural New England town and—in a remarkably transcendental way—explores Ralph Waldo Emerson's preoccupations with nature as teacher, nurturer, provider, and reflection of God's divinity.

Although clearly intended for both adolescent and adult readers, *Daisy Plains* touches on two extremely serious topics not previously addressed at length by Warner—chattel and wage slavery. Mrs. Thayer, the "daughter of a Massachusetts farmer," finds, houses, and educates a runaway slave girl while living in Mississippi. Both at the time of and after her husband's death, Mrs. Thayer grapples with legal and moral issues, deciding ultimately to risk her own safety, social standing, and wealth in order to offer Mercy, the young woman of color, a safe haven. Mercy, an illiterate, proves through her comments about religion, her quickness in study and work, and her loyalty to the Thayers that Mrs. Thayer has done the right thing in helping

her. Mercy shows the reader that she is truly as good a human being and Christian as many whites, better than many, especially those whites such as the Southern slave trader who continually harasses the Thayers.

Mrs. Thayer's daughter, Helen—affectionately nicknamed "May"—also draws attention to various forms of social inequality. As do the protagonists in *Wych Hazel,* May visits prisons, poorhouses, factories, and mills, hoping to bring solace to those within by way of a shared prayer, a home-cooked meal, or a new job. The perfect example of charity and social consciousness, Helen gives all but a pittance of her own fortune to the less fortunate, electing as did her mother before her to forgo material comforts in exchange for the possibility of eternal wealth and rewards.

Although each of Warner's postbellum books—for example, the *Daisy* books, *Opportunities. A Sequel to "What She Could"* (1871), *The House in Town: A Sequel to "Opportunities"* (1872), *Sceptres and Crowns* (1874), *Diana* (1877), and *Wych Hazel*—enjoyed modest popularity, none compared with her antebellum successes, and Warner's following waned. Most likely, her initially refreshing formula—an orphaned girl gets religion, sacrifices her will, finds the perfect spouse, and regains her fortune and social standing—became predictable, thus alienating some of her once-substantial readership.

Susan Warner, who died 17 March 1885, is best remembered as one of the first women to capitalize upon the sentimental recipe of tears, trials, and transcendence, although many of Warner's more than thirty novels—*Daisy, Daisy in the Field, Diana, Melbourne House, The Old Helmet* (1864), *Queechy,* and *The Wide, Wide World*—remained consistently in print past the turn of the century, and two of her books, the first pair in print, continued to be popular until the 1930s. Until recently, however, modern literary scholars have scarcely considered Warner, except to find fault with her religious sentimentalism and her domestic didacticism. In the past two decades, perhaps because of an increasing interest in the relationship of women writers to the canon, critics have begun to explore her influence upon writing as a profession for women. Critics are also beginning to see beyond her superficial moralizing and instead are focusing on the rich, multivalent descriptions of landscape and character, thus situating Warner as a local colorist on the edge of realism.

Letters:

Olivia Egleston Phelps Stokes, *The Letters and Memories of Susan and Anna Bartlett Warner* (New York: Putnam, 1925).

Bibliographies:

Anonymous, "Bibliography of the Works of Susan Warner and Anna Bartlett Warner," *Fourth Report and Year Book of the Martelaer's Rock Association* (Highland Falls, N.Y.: Book Hill Press, 1923);

Dorothy Hurlbut Sanderson, *They Wrote for a Living: A Bibliography of the Works of Susan Bogert Warner and Anna Bartlett Warner* (West Point, N.Y.: Constitution Island Association, 1976).

Biographies:

Anna Bartlett Warner, *Susan Warner ("Elizabeth Wetherell")* (New York: Putnam, 1909);

Jane P. Tompkins, "Susan Warner," *Legacy: A Journal of Nineteenth-Century American Women Writers,* 2 (Spring 1985): 14–15;

Jane Weiss, "Susan Warner," *Nineteenth-Century American Women Writers: A Bio-Bibliographical Critical Sourcebook,* edited by Denise D. Knight (Westport, Conn.: Greenwood Press, 1997), pp. 452–462.

References:

Mabel Baker, *The Warner Family and the Warner Books* (West Point, N.Y.: Constitution Island Association, 1971);

Nina Baym, *Woman's Fiction: A Guide to Novels by and about Women in America, 1820–1870* (Ithaca, N.Y. & London: Cornell University Press, 1978), pp. 150–165;

Edward Halsey Foster, *Susan and Anna Warner* (Boston: Twayne, 1978);

Catharine O'Connell, "'We Must Sorrow': Silence, Suffering, and Sentimentality in Susan Warner's *The Wide, Wide World,*" *Studies in American Fiction,* 25 (Spring 1997): 21–39;

Grace Overmyer, "Hudson River Bluestockings–The Warner Sisters of Constitution Island," *New York History,* 40 (April 1959): 137–158;

George Haven Putnam, "The Warner Sisters and the Literary Association of the Hudson River Valley," in *Fourth Report and Year Book of the Martelaer's Rock Association, 1920–23* (Highland Falls, N.Y.: Book Hill Press, 1923), pp. 16–57;

Jane P. Tompkins, "The Other American Renaissance," in *The American Renaissance Reconsidered: Selected Papers from the English Institute, 1982-83,* edited by Walter Benn Michaels and Donald E. Pease (Baltimore, Md.: Johns Hopkins University Press, 1985), pp. 34–57;

Cynthia Schoolar Williams, "Susan Warner's *Queechy* and the Bildungsroman Tradition," *Legacy: A Journal of Nineteenth-Century American Women Writers,* 7 (Fall 1990): 3–16;

Susan S. Williams, "Susan Warner, Her Readers, and the Assumption of Authorship," *American Quarterly,* 42 (December 1990): 565–586.

Walt Whitman

(31 May 1819 – 26 March 1892)

Ed Folsom
University of Iowa

and

Kenneth M. Price
University of Nebraska–Lincoln

See also the Whitman entries in *DLB 3: Antebellum Writers in New York and the South; DLB 64: American Literary Critics and Scholars, 1850–1880,* and *DLB 224: Walt Whitman: A Documentary Volume.*

BOOKS: *Franklin Evans; or The Inebriate: A Tale of the Times* (New York: J. Winchester, 1842);

Leaves of Grass, anonymous (Brooklyn, N.Y.: Fowler & Wells, 1855; revised second edition, 1856; revised third edition, Boston: Thayer & Eldridge, 1860–1861 [i.e., 1860]; revised fourth edition, New York: William E. Chapin, 1867; revised fifth edition, Washington, D.C.: J. S. Redfield, 1871; revised "Author's Edition," Camden, N.J., 1876; revised sixth edition, Boston: James R. Osgood, 1881–1882 [i.e., 1881]; republished, Philadelphia: Rees Welsh, 1882); revised and enlarged as *Leaves of Grass: Including Sands at Seventy . . . 1st Annex, Good-Bye My Fancy . . . 2d Annex, A Backward Glance o'er Travel'd Roads, and Portrait from Life* (Philadelphia: David McKay, 1892);

Drum-Taps (New York: Peter Eckler, 1865);

Poems by Walt Whitman, edited by William Michael Rossetti (London: John Camden Hotten, 1868);

Democratic Vistas (Washington, D.C. [i.e., New York]: J. S. Redfield, 1871);

After All, Not to Create Only (Boston: Roberts, 1871);

Passage to India (Washington, D.C. [i.e., New York]: J. S. Redfield, 1871);

As a Strong Bird on Pinions Free. And Other Poems (Washington, D.C.: J. S. Redfield, 1872);

Memoranda During the War (Camden, N.J.: The Author, 1875–1876 [i.e., 1876]);

Two Rivulets, including Democratic Vistas, Centennial Songs, and Passage to India (Camden, N.J.: The Author, 1876);

Walt Whitman, circa 1860 (Feinberg Collection, Library of Congress)

Specimen Days & Collect (Philadelphia: Rees Welsh, 1882–1883 [i.e., 1882]);

Specimen Days in America (London: Walter Scott, 1887);

Complete Poems & Prose of Walt Whitman, 1855–1888: Authenticated & Personal Book (Handled by W. W.), Portraits from Life, Autograph (Camden, N.J.: Whitman, 1888);

Democratic Vistas, and Other Papers (London: Walter Scott, 1888);

November Boughs (Philadelphia: David McKay, 1888);

Good-Bye My Fancy: 2d Annex to Leaves of Grass, anonymous (Philadelphia: David McKay, 1891);

Complete Prose Works (Philadelphia: David McKay, 1891);

Calamus: A Series of Letters Written during the Years 1868–1880 by Walt Whitman to a Young Friend (Peter Doyle), edited by Richard Maurice Bucke (Boston: Laurens Maynard, 1897);

The Wound Dresser: A Series of Letters Written from the Hospitals in Washington during the War of the Rebellion, edited by Bucke (Boston: Small, Maynard, 1898);

Notes and Fragments, edited by Bucke (London, Ont.: Printed for the editor by A. Talbot & Co., 1899);

The Complete Writings of Walt Whitman, 10 volumes, edited by Bucke, Thomas B. Harned, and Horace L. Traubel (New York: Putnam, 1902);

An American Primer, edited by Traubel (Boston: Small, Maynard, 1904);

Walt Whitman's Diary in Canada, edited by William Sloane Kennedy (Boston: Small, Maynard, 1904);

Lafayette in Brooklyn (New York: George D. Smith, 1905);

Criticism: An Essay (Newark, N.J.: Carteret Book Club, 1913);

The Gathering of the Forces: Editorials, Essays, Literary and Dramatic Reviews and Other Material Written by Walt Whitman as Editor of the Brooklyn Daily Eagle *in 1846 and 1847,* 2 volumes, edited by Cleveland Rodgers and John Black (New York: Putnam, 1920);

The Uncollected Poetry and Prose of Walt Whitman, 2 volumes, edited by Emory Holloway (Garden City, N.Y.: Doubleday, Page, 1921);

The Half-Breed and Other Stories, edited by Thomas Ollive Mabbott (New York: Columbia University Press, 1927);

Pictures: An Unpublished Poem, edited by Holloway (New York: June House, 1927);

The Eighteenth Presidency! (Montpelier, France: Causse, Graille & Castelnau, 1928);

Walt Whitman's Workshop, edited by Clifton Joseph Furness (Cambridge, Mass.: Harvard University Press, 1928);

A Child's Reminiscence, edited by Mabbott and Rollo G. Silver (Seattle: University of Washington Book Store, 1930);

I Sit and Look Out: Editorials from the Brooklyn Daily Times, edited by Holloway and Vernolian Schwarz (New York: Columbia University Press, 1932);

Walt Whitman and the Civil War: A Collection of Original Articles and Manuscripts, edited by Charles I. Glicksberg (Philadelphia: University of Pennsylvania Press, 1933);

New York Dissected, by Walt Whitman: A Sheaf of Recently Discovered Newspaper Articles by the Author of Leaves of Grass, edited by Holloway and Ralph Adimari (New York: Rufus Rockwell Wilson, 1936);

Walt Whitman's Backward Glances, edited by Sculley Bradley and John A. Stevenson (Philadelphia: University of Pennsylvania Press, 1947);

Faint Clews and Indirections: Manuscripts of Walt Whitman and His Family, edited by Silver and Clarence Gohdes (Durham, N.C.: Duke University Press, 1949);

Walt Whitman of the New York Aurora, edited by Joseph Jay Rubin and Charles H. Brown (State College, Pa.: Bald Eagle Press, 1950);

Walt Whitman Looks at the Schools, edited by Florence Bernstein Freedman (New York: Columbia University Press, 1950);

Whitman's Manuscripts: Leaves of Grass *(1860): A Parallel Text,* edited by Fredson Bowers (Chicago: University of Chicago Press, 1955);

An 1855–56 Notebook toward the Second Edition of Leaves of Grass, edited by Harold W. Blodgett and William White (Carbondale: Southern Illinois University Press, 1959);

Walt Whitman's Civil War, edited by Walter Lowenfels (New York: Knopf, 1960);

"Kentucky"–Walt Whitman's Uncompleted Poem, edited by Harry W. Warfel (Lexington: University of Kentucky Library Associates, 1960);

The People and John Quincy Adams, edited by White (Berkeley Heights, N.J.: Oriole Press, 1961);

The Collected Writings of Walt Whitman, 21 volumes to date, edited by Gay Wilson Allen and others (New York: New York University Press, 1961–1984; New York: Peter Lang, 1998–)—comprises *The Correspondence of Walt Whitman,* 6 volumes, edited by Edwin Haviland Miller (New York: New York University Press, 1961–1977); *The Early Poems and the Fiction,* edited by Thomas L. Brasher (New York: New York University Press, 1963); *Prose Works 1892: Specimen Days; Collect and Other Prose,* 2 volumes, edited by Floyd Stovall (New York: New York University Press,

1963, 1964); *Leaves of Grass: Comprehensive Reader's Edition,* edited by Blodgett and Sculley Bradley (New York: New York University Press, 1965); *Daybooks and Notebooks,* 3 volumes, edited by William White (New York: New York University Press, 1977); *Notebooks and Unpublished Prose Manuscripts,* 6 volumes, edited by Edward F. Grier (New York: New York University Press, 1984); *The Journalism,* volume 1: *1834–1846,* edited by Herbert Bergman, Douglas A. Noverr, and Edward J. Recchia (New York: Peter Lang, 1998);

Walt Whitman's Memoranda during the War; and, Death of Abraham Lincoln: Reproduced in Facsimile, edited by Roy P. Basler (Bloomington: Indiana University Press, 1962);

Walt Whitman's Blue Book: The 1860–61 Leaves of Grass, *Containing His Manuscript Additions and Revisions,* 2 volumes, edited by Arthur Golden (New York: New York Public Library, 1968);

Walt Whitman's Autograph Revision of the Analysis of Leaves of Grass *(for Dr. R. M. Bucke's* Walt Whitman*),* edited by Quentin Anderson and Stephen Railton (New York: New York University Press, 1974);

The Walt Whitman Archive: A Facsimile of the Poet's Manuscripts, 3 volumes, edited by Joel Myerson (New York: Garland, 1993);

The Sacrificial Years: A Chronicle of Walt Whitman's Experiences in the Civil War, edited by John Harmon McElroy (Boston: David R. Godine, 1999).

Editions: *Leaves of Grass: The Poems of Walt Whitman,* edited by Ernest Rhys (London: Walter Scott, 1886);

The Eighteenth Presidency! edited by Edward F. Grier (Lawrence: University of Kansas Press, 1956).

Widely considered the most influential and innovative poet of America, Walt Whitman was born in West Hills, a village near Hempstead, Long Island, on 31 May 1819 to Walter and Louisa Van Velsor Whitman. His father had been born just after the end of the American Revolution and had known and admired Thomas Paine. Walt Whitman was, thus, part of the first generation of Americans who were born in the newly formed United States. Pride in the emergent nation was rampant, and Walter Sr.–after giving his first son, Jesse (born in 1818), his own father's name, his second son his own name, his daughter Mary (born in 1822) the name of his wife's grandmothers, and his daughter Hannah (born in 1823) the name of his own mother–turned to the heroes of the Revolution and the War of 1812 for the names of three of his other sons: Andrew Jackson (born in 1827), George Washington (born in 1829), and Thomas Jefferson (born in 1833).

Only the youngest son, Edward (born in 1835), who was mentally and physically handicapped, carried a name that tied him to neither the family's nor the country's history.

Trained as a carpenter but struggling to find work, Walter Sr. had taken up farming by the time Whitman was born. When Whitman was almost four, his father moved the family to Brooklyn, across from "Mannahatta," as Whitman later called New York in his celebratory writings about the city. One of Whitman's favorite stories about his childhood concerned the time the Marquis de Lafayette visited New York and, selecting the six-year-old Walt from the crowd, lifted him up and carried him. Whitman came to view this event as a kind of laying on of hands: the French hero of the American Revolution anointing the future poet of democracy in the energetic city of immigrants where the nation was being invented day by day.

Whitman's father was of English stock and his mother of Dutch and Welsh descent. The combination led to what Whitman always considered a fertile tension in the children between a smoldering, brooding Puritanical temperament and a sunnier, outgoing Dutch disposition. Whitman's father was stern and hot-tempered, perhaps an alcoholic; Whitman respected but never felt a great deal of affection for him. On the other hand, a special bond existed between Whitman and his mother, and the long correspondence between them records a kind of partnership in attempting to deal with the family crises that mounted in later years.

The Whitmans moved around Brooklyn frequently as Walter Sr. tried, mostly unsuccessfully, to cash in on the city's quick growth by speculating in real estate–buying an empty lot, building a house, moving the family into it, then trying to sell it at a profit and start the process over again. Whitman frequently rode the ferries back and forth across the East River to New York City, an experience that is reflected in his 1856 poem "Crossing Brooklyn Ferry." The daily commute suggested to him the passage from life to death and back to life and also the passage from poet to reader to poet via the vehicle of the poem.

One of Whitman's greatest poems, "Out of the Cradle Endlessly Rocking," is, on one level, a reminiscence of his boyhood visits to the Long Island farm of his grandparents Major Cornelius Van Velsor and Amy Williams Van Velsor and of how his desire to be a poet arose in that landscape. Whitman's experiences as a young man alternated between the city and the Long Island countryside, and he was attracted to both ways of life. His poetry is often marked by shifts between rural and urban settings.

Whitman's formal education consisted of six years in the Brooklyn public schools (which was far

Whitman's parents, Walter Whitman Sr. and Louisa Van Velsor Whitman (left: from Henry Bryan Binns, A Life of Walt Whitman, *1905; right: from Randall H. Waldron, ed.,* Mattie: The Letters of Martha Mitchell Whitman, *1977)*

more schooling than either of his parents had received). At eleven he began working as an office boy for some prominent Brooklyn lawyers; they gave him a subscription to a circulating library, where his self-education began. Whitman absorbed an eclectic and wide-ranging education by reading the works of Sir Walter Scott, James Fenimore Cooper, and other romance novelists; attending the theater, where he fell in love with William Shakespeare's plays, especially *Richard III;* hearing lectures by such speakers as Frances Wright, the Scottish radical emancipationist and women's rights advocate; visiting museums; and engaging everyone he met in conversation and debate. He always recalled the first great lecture he heard, when he was ten: it was given by the radical Quaker leader Elias Hicks, an acquaintance of Whitman's father and a close friend of Whitman's grandfather Jesse. While most other major writers of his time received highly structured classical educations at private institutions, Whitman forged his own rough and informal curriculum of literature, theater, history, geography, music, religion, and archaeology.

In the summer of 1831 Whitman became an apprentice printer on the *Long Island Patriot,* a liberal working-class newspaper in Brooklyn. He soon began contributing to the newspaper and experiencing the exhilaration of getting his own words published. In 1832 he moved to the *Long Island Star,* also in Brooklyn. The rest of his family moved back to the Hempstead area in 1833, leaving the fourteen-year-old Whitman alone in the city. His first signed article, in the upscale *New York Mirror* in 1834, expressed amazement that people were still alive who could remember "the present great metropolitan city as a little *dorp* or village; all fresh and green as it was, from its beginning" and told of a slave, "Negro Harry," who at his death in 1758 at age 120 could remember New York "when there were but three houses in it." Late in his life Whitman could still recall the excitement of seeing this article in print: "How it made my heart double-beat to see *my piece* on the pretty white paper, in nice type."

By the time he was sixteen Whitman was a journeyman printer and compositor, working in various printing shops in New York City; he always retained a typesetter's concern for how his words looked on a page, the typeface in which they appeared, and the effects of various spatial arrangements. But then two of New York's worst fires wiped out the major printing and business centers of the city, and Whitman joined his family at Hempstead in 1836.

Rebelling at his father's attempts to get him to work on the new family farm, Whitman spent the next five years teaching school in at least ten Long Island towns. Rooming in the homes of his students, he taught three-month terms to classes that sometimes held more than eighty students ranging in age from five to fifteen for up to nine hours a day for little pay. He recorded his disdain for the unenlightened country people among whom he lived during this time in a series of letters, discovered in the 1980s, to a friend, Abraham Leech: "Never before have I entertained so low an idea of the beauty and perfection of man's nature, never have I seen humanity in so degraded a shape, as here," he wrote from Woodbury on 11 August 1840. "Ignorance, vulgarity, rudeness, conceit, and dulness are the reigning gods of this deuced sink of despair."

The little that is known of Whitman's teaching, most of which comes from recollections by a few former students, suggests that he employed what were then progressive techniques: encouraging students to think aloud rather than simply recite, involving them in educational games, joining them in baseball and card games, and refusing to resort to corporal punishment. He used his own poems, which were rhymed, conventional verses that indicated nothing of the innovative poetry to come, as texts in his classroom. One of the poems in the first edition of *Leaves of Grass* (1855), titled "There Was a Child Went Forth" in later editions, can be read as a statement of Whitman's educational philosophy: it celebrates unrestricted extracurricular learning, an openness to experience and ideas that allows for endless absorption of variety and difference–the kind of education Whitman had given himself. He was always suspicious of classrooms, and his great poem "Song of Myself" is generated by a child's question, "What is the grass?" Whitman spends the rest of the poem ruminating about this question as he discovers the complex in the seemingly simple, the cosmos in himself–an attitude that is possible only when one puts "creeds and schools in abeyance."

Whitman kept active intellectually during his teaching years by taking part in debating societies and political campaigns. Inspired by Wright, who came to the United States to support Martin Van Buren in the presidential election of 1836, he became an industrious worker for the Democratic Party and campaigned for Van Buren's successful candidacy.

Whitman interrupted his teaching in 1838 to try his luck at starting his own newspaper, *The Long Islander,* to cover the towns around Huntington. He bought a press and type and hired his brother George as his assistant; but the paper failed within a year, and he reluctantly returned to the classroom. Two years later he abruptly quit teaching for good. A persistent rumor is that Whitman committed sodomy with one of his students in Southold and was run out of town in disgrace, never to return; but it is not possible to prove that he ever taught there, and he did visit Southold in later years: in the late 1840s and again in the early 1860s he wrote some journalistic pieces about the town that carry no hint that he had had a bad experience there. It is far more likely that Whitman gave up teaching simply because he was temperamentally unsuited for it.

Whitman returned to New York City and began writing fiction. About twenty newspapers and magazines published his stories between 1840 and 1845, including the *American Review* (later renamed the *American Whig Review*) and the *Democratic Review,* one of the nation's most prestigious literary magazines. His first published story, "Death in the School-Room (A Fact)," which appeared in the *Democratic Review,* grew out of his teaching experience and includes direct editorializing: the narrator hopes that soon the "many ingenious methods of child-torture will be gaz'd upon as a scorned memento of an ignorant, cruel, and exploded doctrine." The tale has a surprise ending: the teacher flogs a student he thinks is sleeping, only to make the macabre discovery that he has been beating a corpse. "The Shadow and the Light of a Young Man's Soul," published in the *Union Magazine* for June 1848, offers a barely fictionalized autobiography: the hero, Archibald Dean, leaves New York because of the great fire to take charge of a small district school, a move that makes him feel "as though the last float-plank which buoyed him up on hope and happiness, was sinking, and he with it." Other stories are concerned with friendships between older and younger men, the latter of whom are frequently weak or in need of defense because they are misunderstood by, and at odds with, authority figures.

Whitman published five stories in the *Democratic Review* between January and September 1842. That year Park Benjamin, editor of the New York paper *The New World,* decided that Whitman was the perfect candidate to write a novel to capitalize on the booming temperance movement. Whitman had worked as a printer for Benjamin in 1841; the two had quarreled, leading Whitman to write "Bamboozle and Benjamin" (*New York Aurora,* 24 March 1842), an article attacking the irascible editor whose practice of rapidly printing advance copies of novels, typically by English writers, threatened the development of native authors and the profits of American publishing houses. But both men

Whitman's birthplace in West Hills, near Hempstead, Long Island (from Henry Bryan Binns, A Life of Walt Whitman, *1905)*

were willing to overlook past differences to seize a good financial opportunity.

In an extra number in November 1842 Benjamin's *New World* published Whitman's *Franklin Evans; or The Inebriate: A Tale of the Times,* about a country boy who, after falling prey to drink in the big city, causes the deaths of three women. The work, in its fascination with "fatal pleasure"–Evans's name for the strong attraction most men feel for sinful experience, be it drink or sex–is typical of the temperance literature of the time in bringing in sensationalism under a moral guise. Whitman's treatment of sex, however, is unpersuasive and seems to confirm a remark he had made two years earlier: that he knew nothing about women either by "experience or observation." The novel is, nonetheless, one of the earliest explorations in American literature of the theme of miscegenation. It succeeded despite being a patched-together concoction of new writing and previously composed stories; around twenty thousand copies were sold–more than of anything else Whitman published in his lifetime. In his old age he described *Franklin Evans* to his friend Horace Traubel as "damned rot–rot of the worst sort" and

claimed that he completed it in three days, composing some of it in the reading room of Tammany Hall, inspired by gin cocktails (on another occasion he said that he was buoyed by a bottle of port). He began another temperance novel, "The Madman," within months of finishing *Franklin Evans,* though he soon abandoned the project. Earlier he had published two stories–"Wild Frank's Return" (in the *Democratic Review,* November 1841) and "The Child's Champion" (in the *New World,* also in November 1841) –that also turn on the consequences of excessive drinking. His later poetry refers again and again to the awful "law of drunkards," "the livid faces of drunkards," "those drunkards and gluttons of so many generations," the "drunkard's breath," the "drunkard's stagger," and "the old drunkard staggering home."

In 1842–1843 Whitman, like many journalists of the period, moved in and out of positions on an array of newspapers, including the *New York Aurora,* the *New York Evening Tattler,* the *New York Statesman,* and the *New York Sunday Times.* He cultivated a fashionable appearance: William Cauldwell, an apprentice who knew him as lead editor at the *Aurora,* said that Whitman "usually wore a frock coat and high hat, carried a small cane, and the lapel of his coat was almost invariably ornamented with a boutonniere." His editorial topics ranged from criticism of police roundups of prostitutes to denunciation of Bishop John Hughes for trying to use public funds to support parochial schools.

Whitman left Manhattan in 1845 for steadier work in the somewhat less competitive journalistic environment of Brooklyn. Though he is often regarded as a New York writer, his residence and professional career in the city thus actually ended a decade before the first appearance of *Leaves of Grass*. He continued to shuttle back and forth to Manhattan via the Fulton ferry and drew on the city for the subject matter of his writing.

Opera was one of the attractions that encouraged Whitman's frequent returns to New York City. He began attending performances, often accompanied by his brother Jeff, in 1846, a practice that was disrupted only by the onset of the Civil War (and even during the war he went to the opera whenever he got back to New York). The coloratura soprano Marietta Alboni sent him into raptures, and his poem "To a Certain Cantatrice" addresses her as the equal of any hero. He once said after attending an opera that the experience was powerful enough to initiate a new era in a person's development. Opera provides both structure and contextual clues to the meaning of "Out of the Cradle Endlessly Rocking."

From September 1845 to March 1846 Whitman composed two or three editorials a week for the *Long Island Star;* from 5 March 1846 to 18 January 1848 he served as editor of the *Brooklyn Eagle*. He published little of his own poetry or fiction during these years, but he introduced literary reviewing to the *Eagle* and commented, if often superficially, on writers such as Thomas Carlyle and Ralph Waldo Emerson. He also wrote editorials on issues such as street lighting, politics, and banking. But he claimed that what he valued most was not the ability to promote his opinions but the "curious kind of sympathy . . . that arises in the mind of a newspaper conductor with the public he serves. He gets to *love* them."

Whitman was adamant in his editorials that slavery not be allowed into the new western territories, because he feared that whites would not migrate to areas where their labor was devalued by competition from slaves. He expressed outrage at practices that furthered slavery, such as laws that made possible the importation of slaves by way of Brazil. Like Abraham Lincoln, he consistently opposed slavery, even though he knew—again like Lincoln—that the more extreme abolitionists threatened the Union itself. He finally lost his position as editor of the *Eagle* because the publisher,

Isaac Van Anden, sided with conservative proslavery Democrats.

On 9 February 1846 Whitman met J. E. McClure during intermission at the Broadway Theatre in New York. McClure and his partner, A. H. Hayes, were planning to launch a paper, the *Crescent,* in New Orleans. On the spot McClure hired Whitman to edit the paper and provided him with an advance to cover his travel expenses to New Orleans. Whitman's brother Jeff went with him to work as an office boy on the paper. The journey by train, steamboat, and stagecoach was Whitman's first excursion outside the New York City–Brooklyn–Long Island area.

In New Orleans, Whitman wandered around the French Quarter and the old French market, attracted by "the Indian and negro hucksters with their wares" and the "great Creole mulatto woman" who sold him the best coffee he had ever tasted. He enjoyed "exquisite wines, and the perfect and mild French brandy" in "splendid and roomy bars" that were packed with soldiers who had recently returned from the war with Mexico, many of them recovering from wounds. He was entranced by the mix of languages—French, Spanish, and English—in the cosmopolitan city and began to see the possibilities of a distinctive American culture emerging from the melding of races and backgrounds. But the city was not without its horrors: slaves were auctioned within an easy walk of where the Whitman brothers were lodging at the Tremont House. Whitman never forgot the experience of seeing humans on the selling block, and he kept a poster of a slave auction in his room for many years as a reminder that such dehumanizing events occurred in the United States. He later incorporated a slave auction into his poem "I Sing the Body Electric."

One experience that Whitman did not have in New Orleans was the romance with a beautiful Creole woman that was first imagined by his biographer Henry Bryan Binns in 1905 and elaborated on by others who were eager to identify heterosexual desires in the poet. The published versions of his poem "Once I Pass'd Through a Populous City" seem to recount a romance with a woman, though the manuscript reveals that he initially wrote it with a male lover in mind.

Whitman thought that New Orleans agreed with him better than New York, but Jeff suffered from dysentery and homesickness. Furthermore, the *Crescent* owners exhibited what Whitman called a "singular sort of coldness" toward their new editor; they probably feared that he would embarrass them because of his unorthodox ideas, especially about slavery. Whitman's sojourn in New Orleans lasted only three months, but it produced a few lively sketches of life in the city and at least one poem. In "Sailing the Mississippi at Midnight" the steamboat journey becomes a symbolic journey of life:

> Vast and starless, the pall of heaven
> Laps on the trailing pall below;
> And forward, forward, in solemn darkness,
> As if to the sea of the lost we go.

Whitman wrote such conventional poems, often echoing William Cullen Bryant and, at times, Percy Bysshe Shelley and John Keats, through much of the 1840s. Bryant and the "graveyard school" of English poetry probably had the most important impact on his sensibility, as can be seen in his pre–*Leaves of Grass* poems "Our Future Lot," "Ambition," "The Winding-Up," "The Love that is Hereafter," and "Death of the Nature-Lover." The poetry of these years is artificial in diction and didactic in purpose, rarely inspired or innovative. By the end of the decade, however, Whitman had undertaken serious self-education in the art of poetry, which he conducted in a typically unorthodox way: he clipped essays about and reviews of leading British and American writers. His marginalia in these articles demonstrate that he was learning to write not in the manner of his predecessors but against them.

The mystery about Whitman in the late 1840s is the speed of his transformation from an unoriginal and conventional poet. He abruptly abandoned conventional rhyme and meter and began finding beauty in the commonplace but expressing it in an uncommon way. His earliest known notebook may have been started as early as 1847, though much of it probably dates from the early 1850s. This extraordinary document includes early articulations of some of Whitman's most compelling ideas. Passages on "Dilation," on "True noble expanding American character," and on the "soul enfolding orbs" are memorable prose statements that express the newly expansive sense of self that Whitman was discovering, and one finds him here setting the tone and expressing the ideas that allowed for the writing of *Leaves of Grass*.

On 16 July 1849 the publisher Lorenzo Fowler of the Brooklyn firm Fowler and Wells performed a phrenological analysis of Whitman that resulted in a flattering–and in some ways quite accurate–description of his character. In addition to bolstering Whitman's self-confidence, the reading of the bumps on his skull gave him some key vocabulary, such as "amativeness" and "adhesiveness," phrenological terms delineating forms of sexual affection, for *Leaves of Grass*.

At this time of poetic transformation Whitman's politics–especially his racial attitudes–also underwent a profound alteration. Blacks become central to his poetry and to his understanding of democracy. Note-

book passages assert that the poet has the "divine grammar of all tongues, and says indifferently and alike How are you friend? to the President in the midst of his cabinet, and Good day my brother, to Sambo among the hoes of the sugar field." His first notebook lines written in the free-verse manner of *Leaves of Grass* focus on the fundamental issue dividing the United States, seeking to bind opposed categories, to link black and white, and to join master and slave:

> I am the poet of the body
> And I am the poet of the soul
> And I am
> I go with the slaves of the earth equally with the masters
> And I will stand between the masters and the slaves,
> Entering into both so that both will understand me alike.

The audacity of the final line remains striking. While most people were lining up on one side or another, Whitman placed himself in the space–sometimes violent, sometimes erotic, always volatile–between master and slave. His extreme political despair led him to replace what he named the "scum" of corrupt American politics in the 1850s with his own persona: a shaman, a culture healer, an all-encompassing "I."

That "I" became the main character of *Leaves of Grass,* the explosive book of twelve untitled poems that Whitman wrote in the early 1850s and for which he set some of the type in the print shop of James and Andrew Rome, designed the cover, and oversaw all other details. When Whitman wrote "I, now thirty-six years old, in perfect health, begin," he announced a new identity for himself, and his novitiate came at a quite advanced age for a poet. Keats had died ten years before reaching that age; George Gordon, Lord Byron had died at exactly that age; William Wordsworth and Samuel Taylor Coleridge had produced *Lyrical Ballads* (1798) in their twenties; Bryant had written "Thanatopsis" (published 1817), his best-known poem, while still in his teens; and most other great Romantic poets Whitman admired had done their most memorable work early in their adult lives. In contrast, by the time Whitman reached his mid thirties he seemed destined, if he were to achieve fame in any field, to do so as a journalist or, perhaps, as a writer of fiction; no one could have guessed that he would suddenly begin to produce work that has led many to view him as America's greatest and most revolutionary poet.

The mystery that has intrigued biographers and critics over the years has been what prompted the transformation: did Whitman undergo a spiritual illumination that opened the floodgates of a radical new kind of poetry, or was this poetry the result of a carefully calculated strategy to blend journalism, oratory, popular music, and other cultural forces into an innovative

THE NEW WORLD.

PARK BENJAMIN,
EDITOR

J. WINCHESTER,
PUBLISHER.

"No pent-up Utica contracts our powers; for the whole boundless continent is ours."

EXTRA SERIES.   OFFICE 30 ANN-STREET.   NUMBER 34

VOL. II....No. 10.   NEW-YORK, NOVEMBER, 1842.   PRICE 12½ CENTS.

Original Temperance Novel.

Entered according to Act of Congress, in the year 1842,

BY J. WINCHESTER,

In the Clerk's Office of the Southern District of New York.

FRANKLIN EVANS;

OR

THE INEBRIATE.

A TALE OF THE TIMES.

BY WALTER WHITMAN

INTRODUCTORY.

THE story I am going to tell you, reader, will be somewhat aside from the ordinary track of the novelist. It will not abound, either with profound reflections, or sentimental remarks. Yet its moral—for I flatter myself it has one, and one which it were well to engrave on the heart of each person who scans its pages—will be taught by its own incidents, and the current of the narrative.

Whatever of romance there may be—I leave it to any who have, in the course of their every-day walks, heard the histories of intemperate men, whether the events of the tale, strange as some of them may appear, have not had their counterpart in real life. If you who live in the city should go out among your neighbors and investigate what is being transacted there, you might come to behold things far more improbable. In fact, the following chapters contain but the account of a young man, thrown by circumstances amid the vortex of dissipation—a country youth, who came to our great emporium to seek his fortune—and what befell him there. So it is a plain story; yet as the grandest truths are sometimes plain enough to enter into the minds of children—it may be that the delineation I shall give will do benefit, and that educated men and women may not find the hour they spend in its perusal, altogether wasted.

And I would ask your belief when I assert that, what you are going to read is not a work of fiction, as the term is used. I narrate occurrences that have had a far more substantial existence, than in my fancy. There will be those who, as their eyes turn past line after line, will have their memories carried to matters which they have heard of before, or taken a part in themselves, and which, they know, are *real*.

Can I hope, that my story will do good? I entertain that hope Issued in the cheap and popular form you see, and wafted by every mail to all parts of this vast republic; the facilities which its publisher possesses, giving him the power of diffusing it more widely than any other establishment in the United States; the mighty and deep public opinion which, as a tide bears a ship upon its bosom, ever welcomes anything favorable to the Temperance Reform; its being written *for the mass*, though the writer hopes, not without some claim upon the approval of the more fastidious; and, as much as anything else, the fact that it is as a pioneer in this department of literature—all these will give "THE INEBRIATE," I feel confident, a more than ordinary share of patronage.

For youth, what can be more invaluable? It teaches sobriety, that virtue which every mother and father prays nightly, may be resident in the characters of their sons. It wars against Intemperance, that evil spirit which has levelled so many fair human forms before its horrible advances. Without being presumptuous, I would remind those who believe in the wholesome doctrines of abstinence, how the earlier teachers of piety used parables and fables, as the fit instruments whereby they might convey to men the beauty of the system they professed. In the resemblance, how reasonable it is to suppose that you can impress a lesson upon him whom you would influence to sobriety, in no better way than letting him read such a story as this.

It is usual for writers, upon presenting their works to the public, to bespeak indulgence for faults and deficiences. I am but too well aware that the critical eye will see some such in the following pages; yet my book is not written for the critics, but for THE PEOPLE; and while I think it best to leave it to the reader's own decision whether I have succeeded, I cannot help remarking, that I have the fullest confidence in the verdict's being favorable.

And, to conclude, may I hope that he who purchases this volume, will give to its author, and to its publisher also, the credit of being influenced not altogether by views of the profit to come from it? Whatever of those views may enter into our minds, we are not without a strong desire that the principles here inculcated will strike deep, and grow again, and bring forth good fruit. A prudent, sober, and temperate course of life cannot be too strongly taught to old and young; to the young, because the future years are before them—to the old, because it is their business to prepare for death. And though, as before remarked, the writer has abstained from thrusting the moral upon the reader, by dry and abstract disquisitions—preferring the more pleasant and quite as profitable method of letting the reader draw it himself from the occurrences—it is hoped that the New and Popular Reform now in the course of progress over the land, will find no trifling help from a "TALE OF THE TIMES."

First page of Whitman's temperance novel, which was published as an entire issue of the magazine

American voice like the one for which Emerson had called in "The Poet" in his *Essays: Second Series* (1844?) "Our log-rolling, our stumps and their politics, our fisheries, our Negroes, and Indians, our boasts, and our repudiations, the wrath of rogues, and the pusillanimity of honest men, the Northern trade, the Southern planting, the Western clearing, Oregon and Texas, are yet unsung," Emerson wrote. "Yet America is a poem in our eyes; its ample geography dazzles the imagination, and it will not wait long for metres." Whitman began writing poetry that seemed to record everything for which Emerson had called, and he began his preface to the first edition of *Leaves of Grass* by paraphrasing Emerson: "The United States themselves are essentially the greatest poem."

The romantic view of Whitman is that he was suddenly and impulsively inspired to write the poems that transformed American poetry; the more pragmatic view holds that he devoted himself in the five years before the publication of *Leaves of Grass* to a disciplined series of experiments that gradually led to the intricate structuring of his singular style. The evidence supports both theories. Few manuscripts for the poems in the first edition of *Leaves of Grass* remain, leading many to believe that they emerged in a fury of inspiration. On the other hand, the manuscripts that do exist indicate that Whitman meticulously worked and reworked his poems and carefully oversaw every aspect of the production of his book, issuing detailed instructions to the typesetters. Whitman seems, then, to have been both inspired poet and skilled craftsman, at once under the spell of his newly discovered and intoxicating free-verse style but also remaining in control of it. For the rest of his life he added, deleted, fused, separated, and rearranged poems as he produced six distinct editions of *Leaves of Grass*. Emerson once described Whitman's poetry as "a remarkable mixture of the Bhagvat Ghita [sic] and the *New York Herald*," and that odd joining of the scriptural and the vernacular, the transcendent and the mundane, captures the simultaneously magical and commonplace, sublime and prosaic quality of Whitman's work. It was work produced by a poet who was both sage and huckster and who was concerned as much with the sales and reviews of his book as with the state of the human soul.

Whitman paid the costs of production of the 795 copies of the book out of his own pocket; he had them bound at various times as his finances permitted. He always recalled the book as appearing, fittingly, on the Fourth of July—a kind of literary Independence Day. His joy at getting the book published was, however, diminished by the death of his father on 11 July. Though Whitman and Walter Sr. had never been particularly close, they had only recently traveled together

to the old Whitman homestead in West Hills. His father's death, along with his older brother Jesse's absence in the merchant marine—and, later, Jesse's mental instability—meant that Whitman had to become the substitute father for the family. Because of Walter Sr.'s drinking and growing depression, Whitman had already taken on some adult responsibilities—buying boots for his brothers, for instance, and holding the title to the family house as early as 1847.

Even with these growing family burdens, however, Whitman managed to concentrate on his new book. Just as he had overseen all the details of its composition and printing, he supervised its distribution by Fowler and Wells and tried to control its reception. Whitman later claimed that the first edition sold out, but, in fact, the sales were poor. He sent copies to several well-known writers—including John Greenleaf Whittier, who, legend has it, threw it into the fire—but the only one who responded was Emerson, who recognized in Whitman's work the spirit, tone, and style for which he had called. "I greet you at the beginning of a great career," Emerson wrote on 21 July, noting that *Leaves of Grass* "meets the demand I am always making of what seemed the sterile & stingy Nature, as if too much handiwork or too much lymph in the temperament were making our western wits fat & mean." Whitman's poetry, Emerson believed, would get the country into shape, helping to work off its excess of aristocratic fat.

Whitman's poetry in the book is cast in unrhymed long lines with no identifiable meter; the voice is haranguing, mundane, and prophetic, a combination of oratory, journalism, and the Bible—an absorptive and accepting voice that wants to catalogue the vast diversity of the country and hold it all in a unified identity. "Do I contradict myself?" Whitman asks confidently toward the end of the long poem he later titled "Song of Myself." "Very well then . . . . I contradict myself; / I am large . . . . I contain multitudes." This new voice spoke confidently of union at a time of division, and it spoke with the assurance that everything, no matter how degraded, could be celebrated as part of itself: "What is commonest and cheapest and nearest and easiest is Me." Whitman's work echoes with the speech of the American urban working class and reaches deep into the various corners of nineteenth-century culture, reverberating with the nation's stormy politics, its motley music, its new technologies, its fascination with science, and its evolving pride in an American language that was forming as a tongue distinct from British English.

Whitman did not put his name on the title page of the book—an unconventional act suggesting that the author believed that he spoke not for himself but for

Frontispiece engraving of Whitman by Samuel Hollyer in Leaves of Grass *(1855)*

America. (His name did not appear on a title page of *Leaves of Grass* until the 1876 "Author's Edition," and then only because he signed each copy as it was sold.) But opposite the title page was a portrait of Whitman, an engraving by Samuel Hollyer from a daguerreotype taken by the photographer Gabriel Harrison in the summer of 1854. The most famous frontispiece in literary history, it shows Whitman from head to just above the knees; he is dressed in workman's clothes, shirt open, hat cocked to the side, standing insouciantly and fixing the reader with a challenging stare. It is a pose that indicates Whitman's redefinition of the role of poet as the democratic spokesperson who no longer speaks only from the intellect and with the formality of tradition and education; the new poet pictured in Whitman's book speaks from and with the whole body and writes outside, in nature, not in the library. Whitman called his work "al fresco" poetry, indicating that it was written outside the bounds of convention and tradition.

Within a few months of the publication of the first edition of *Leaves of Grass* Whitman was at work on the second. While in the first edition he had allowed his long lines to stretch across the page by printing the book on large paper, the second edition was what he

later, in conversation with Traubel, called his "chunky fat book," his earliest attempt to offer the reader what he thought of as the "ideal pleasure": "to put a book in your pocket and [go] off to the seashore or the forest." On the spine of this edition, which was published and distributed by Fowler and Wells (though the firm carefully distanced itself from the book by proclaiming that "the author is still his own publisher"), Whitman emblazoned one of the first "blurbs" in American publishing history: without asking Emerson's permission, he printed in gold the opening words of Emerson's letter to him: "I greet you at the beginning of a great career," followed by Emerson's name. He also appended to the volume several reviews of the first edition, including three he wrote himself along with a few negative ones, under the heading "Leaves-Droppings." At the end of the book he printed Emerson's entire letter (again, without permission) and a long reply—a kind of apologia for his poetry—addressed to "Master." Although he sometimes downplayed the influence of Emerson on his work, at this time, he later recalled, he had "Emerson-on-the-brain."

With four times as many pages as the first edition, the 1856 *Leaves of Grass* added twenty new poems—including the powerful "Sun-Down Poem," later called "Crossing Brooklyn Ferry"—to the twelve in the 1855 edition. The original twelve had been untitled in 1855, but Whitman was doing all he could to make the new edition look and feel different: small pages instead of large, a fat book instead of a thin one, and long titles for the poems instead of none at all. The untitled introductory poem from the first edition that was eventually named "Song of Myself" was called "Poem of Walt Whitman, an American" in 1856; and the poem that later became "This Compost" appeared as "Poem of Wonder at the Resurrection of The Wheat." Some titles, like the poems themselves, incorporated rolling catalogues: the poem that was later titled "To a Foil'd European Revolutionaire" appeared in 1856 as "Liberty Poem for Asia, Africa, Europe, America, Australia, Cuba, and The Archipelagoes of the Sea." As if to counter criticism that he was not really writing poetry at all—the review in *Life Illustrated* (28 July 1855), for example, called Whitman's work "lines of rhythmical prose, or a series of *utterances* (we know not what else to call them)"—Whitman put the word "Poem" in the title of all thirty-two pieces in the 1856 edition. But despite his efforts to remake his book, the results were the same: sales of the thousand copies that were printed were even poorer than for the first edition.

In May 1857 Whitman went to work for the *Brooklyn Daily Times,* a Free Soil newspaper; in the summer of 1859, once again, a disagreement with the newspaper's owner led to his dismissal. Meanwhile, he was forging literary connections. Emerson had come to visit at the end of 1855–they had gone back to Emerson's room at the elegant Astor Hotel, where Whitman, dressed as informally as in his frontispiece portrait, was denied admission. It was the first of many meetings the two men had over the next twenty-five years, as their relationship turned into one of grudging mutual respect mixed with suspicion. In 1856 Henry David Thoreau and Bronson Alcott visited Whitman's home; in his journal Alcott described Thoreau and Whitman as each "surveying the other curiously, like two beasts, each wondering what the other would do." Whitman also befriended visual artists such as the sculptor Henry Kirke Brown, the painter Elihu Vedder, and the photographer Gabriel Harrison. He got to know several women's rights activists and feminist writers, some of whom became ardent readers and supporters of *Leaves of Grass;* he became particularly close to Abby Price, Paulina Wright Davis, Sarah Tyndale, and Sara Payson Willis. (Under the pseudonym Fanny Fern, Willis wrote a popular newspaper column and many books, including *Fern Leaves from Fanny's Portfolio* [1853]–the cover of which Whitman had imitated for the first edition of *Leaves of Grass.*) Their radical ideas about sexual equality had a growing impact on Whitman's poetry. He also knew many abolitionist writers, including Moncure Conway, and wrote vitriolic attacks on the Fugitive Slave Law and the moral bankruptcy of American politics, notably the pamphlet *The Eighteenth Presidency!* (1928). But these pieces were not published in Whitman's lifetime and remain vestiges of a career–stump speaker and political pundit–with which he flirted but that he never pursued.

Whitman also began in the late 1850s to become a regular at Pfaff's saloon, a favorite gathering place for bohemian artists in New York. There Whitman the former temperance writer began a couple of years of unemployed carousing. At Pfaff's he mingled with figures such as Henry Clapp, the influential editor of the antiestablishment *Saturday Press,* who helped publicize Whitman's work in many ways, including publishing an early version of "Out of the Cradle Endlessly Rocking" on 24 December 1859. At Pfaff's, Whitman also became friends with many writers, some well known at the time, including Ada Clare, Fitz-James O'Brien, George Arnold, and Edmund Clarence Stedman. There, too, he met the young William Dean Howells; Howells recalled many years later that Whitman had already become something of a celebrity, even if his fame was largely the infamy resulting from what many considered to be his obscene writings ("foul work" filled with "libidinousness," scolded *The Christian Examiner* in November 1856). Whitman and Clare, the "queen of Bohemia" (she had an illegitimate child and

proudly proclaimed herself an unmarried mother), became two of the most notorious figures at the beer hall, flouting convention and decorum.

Also at Pfaff's, Whitman joined the "Fred Gray Association," a group of young men anxious to explore new possibilities of male-male affection. It may have been at Pfaff's that Whitman met Fred Vaughan, a young Irish stage driver and an intriguing mystery figure to Whitman biographers. Whitman and Vaughan clearly had an intense relationship at this time, but Vaughan soon married; he went on to have four children and only sporadically kept in touch with Whitman. The sequence of homoerotic love poems called "Live Oak, with Moss" that became the heart of the "Calamus" cluster in the 1860 edition of *Leaves of Grass* record despair over the failure of the relationship.

Within a year of the appearance of the 1856 edition Whitman had written nearly seventy new poems. He continued to have them set in type by the Rome brothers and other printer friends; apparently he assumed that he would inevitably be publishing them himself, since no commercial publisher had indicated an interest in his book. But there was another reason Whitman set his poems in type: he always preferred to deal with his work in printed form rather than in manuscript and often made revisions directly on the printed versions of his poems. For him poetry was a *public* act, and until a poem was in print he did not truly consider it a poem. Manuscripts were never sacred to Whitman, who often discarded them.

In February 1860 Whitman received a letter from William Thayer and Charles Eldridge, whose aggressive new Boston publishing house specialized in abolitionist literature; they wanted to publish the next edition of *Leaves of Grass.* Whitman readily agreed, and Thayer and Eldridge invested heavily in the stereotype plates for Whitman's idiosyncratic book: more than 450 pages of varied typefaces and odd decorative motifs. Whitman traveled to Boston in March to oversee the printing.

Whitman is a major part of the reason that America's literary center moved to New York in the second half of the nineteenth century; but in 1860 the superiority of Boston was evident in its influential publishing houses; its important journals, including the new *Atlantic Monthly;* and its venerable authors, including Henry Wadsworth Longfellow, whom Whitman met while he was in town. And, of course, Boston was the city of Emerson, who came to see Whitman shortly after his arrival. As they strolled together on the Boston Common, Emerson tried to persuade Whitman to remove from his book the new "Enfans d'Adam" cluster of poems (after 1860 Whitman dropped the French version of the name and called the cluster "Children of

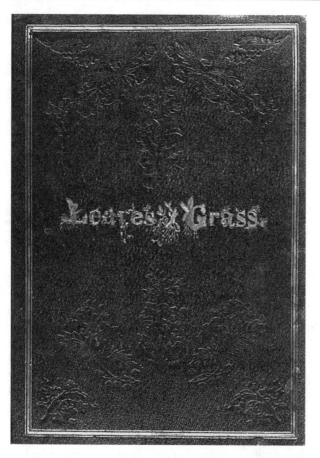

Leaves

of

Grass.

Brooklyn, New York:
1855.

Binding and title page for the first edition of Whitman's poems. He helped to set the type for the ninety-five-page book, which was published by Fowler and Wells.

Adam"), which portrayed the human body more explicitly and in more direct sexual terms than any previous American poems had. Whitman believed, as he later recalled, "that the sexual passion in itself, while normal and unperverted, is inherently legitimate, creditable, not necessarily an improper theme for poet." "*That,*" insisted Whitman, "is what I felt in my inmost brain and heart, when I only answer'd Emerson's vehement arguments with silence, under the old elms of Boston Common," he wrote in "A Memorandum at a Venture" (1882). The body was Whitman's theme, and he would not shy away from any part of it: the genitals and the armpits were as essential to the fullness of identity as the brain and the soul, just as in a democracy the poorest and most despised citizens were as important as the rich and famous. So he ignored Emerson's advice and published the "Enfans d'Adam" poems in the 1860 edition along with the "Calamus" cluster; the first cluster celebrated male-female sexual relations, the second the love of men for men. *Leaves of Grass* did not set out to shock but to make the reader more aware of the body that he or she inhabited, to convince the reader

that the body and the soul were conjoined and inseparable—just as Whitman's ideas were physically embodied in the ink and paper that the reader held in his or her hands.

Whitman called the "Calamus" poems his most political work—"The special meaning of the *Calamus* cluster," he wrote in the preface to the 1876 edition, "mainly resides in its Political significance"—since in these poems he was advocating a new kind of intense affection between males and thereby countering the masculine competitiveness encouraged by the developing democratic society and the emerging capitalistic economy. Whitman was inventing a language of homosexuality, and the *Calamus* poems became influential in the development of gay literature. On their first appearance, however, these poems did not cause as much sensation as "Enfans d'Adam"/"Children of Adam," because their sensuality was confined to handholding, hugging, and kissing; the "children of Adam" poems evoked a more explicit genital sexuality. Only later in the century, when homosexuality began to be regarded in medical and psychological circles as aberrant, did the

"Calamus" poems begin to be read by some as dangerous and "abnormal" and by others as brave early expressions of gay identity.

Whitman's remade self-image is evident in the frontispiece for the 1860 edition. It was the only time Whitman used this portrait, an engraving based on a painting by his friend Charles Hine. Whitman's friends called it the "Byronic portrait," and Whitman—with coiffure and cravat—does look more like the conventional image of a poet than he ever did before or after.

With the 1860 edition of *Leaves of Grass* Whitman began the incessant rearranging of his poems in various groupings that often alter their meaning and significance. In addition to "Calamus" and "Enfans d'Adam," this edition included the clusters "Chants Democratic and Native American" and "Messenger Leaves" and one with the same title as the book: "Leaves of Grass." The 1860 edition also included the first book publications of "Starting from Paumanok," here called "Proto-Leaf," and "Out of the Cradle Endlessly Rocking," here called "A Word Out of the Sea," along with more than 120 other new poems. Whitman revised many of his older poems, including "Song of Myself," which is here titled "Walt Whitman." He also numbered the verses throughout the book, creating a biblical effect: he conceived of his project as the construction of a "New Bible," a new covenant that would convert America into a true democracy.

The first printing of one thousand copies of the 1860 edition was quickly exhausted, and Thayer and Eldridge promptly ordered an additional printing of at least one thousand and perhaps as many as three thousand or four thousand copies. The edition received many reviews, most of them positive—particularly those by women, who were more exhilarated than offended by Whitman's candid images of sex and the body and welcomed his attempt to sing "The Female equally with the Male," as he put it in the poem "One's-Self I Sing."

Whitman's stay in Boston—the first extended period he had been away from New York since his trip to New Orleans twelve years earlier—was a transforming experience. He was surprised to see African Americans treated much more fairly and as equals than they were in New York: they shared tables with whites at restaurants, worked next to whites in printing offices, and served on juries. He met some abolitionist writers who became close friends and supporters, including William Douglas O'Connor and John Townsend Trowbridge, both of whom later wrote at length about him.

When Whitman returned to New York at the end of May, his mood was ebullient. He was a recognized author: the Boston papers had run feature stories about his visit to the city, and photographers had asked to take his picture—not only did he have a growing notoriety, but he also was a striking physical specimen: more than six feet in height—especially tall for the time—with long, already graying hair and beard. All summer he read reviews of his work in prominent newspapers and journals. And in November his young publishers announced that his new book of poems, to be titled "Banner at Day-Break," was forthcoming.

But the deteriorating national situation made any business investment risky, and Thayer and Eldridge compounded the problem with some bad business decisions. At the beginning of 1861 they declared bankruptcy and sold the plates of *Leaves of Grass* to the Boston publisher Richard Worthington. Worthington continued to publish pirated copies of the 1860 edition for decades. The large number of copies that Thayer and Eldridge had printed, combined with Worthington's piracy, made the 1860 edition the most widely available version of *Leaves of Grass* for the next twenty years and diluted the impact, as well as depressing the sales, of Whitman's own new editions.

In February 1861 Whitman saw Lincoln pass through New York on the way to his inauguration. In April, on the way home from an opera performance, he bought a newspaper and read that Southern forces had fired on Fort Sumter. Whitman, like many others, thought that the struggle would be over in sixty days or so. A few days after the firing on Fort Sumter, Whitman recorded in his journal his resolution "to inaugurate for myself a pure perfect sweet, cleanblooded robust body by ignoring all drinks but water and pure milk—and all fat meats late suppers—a great body—a purged, cleansed, spiritualised invigorated body." It was as if he sensed the need to break out of his newfound complacency, to cease his Pfaff's beer-hall habits and bohemian ways, and to prepare himself for the challenges that faced the divided nation.

Whitman's brother George immediately enlisted in the Union army; his accounts of his experiences provided Whitman with many insights into the nature of the war and into soldiers' feelings. Whitman's chronically ill brother Andrew also enlisted but served for only three months in 1862. His other brothers—the hot-tempered Jesse; the recently married Jeff, on whom fell the burden of caring for the extended family, including his own infant daughter; and the mentally feeble Eddy—did not serve. Nor did Whitman, who was in his early forties when the war began.

During the first year and a half of the Civil War, Whitman remained in the New York City area, writing a series of twenty-five lengthy articles, titled "Brooklyniana," about the history of Brooklyn for the *Brooklyn Daily Standard*. He had been visiting Broadway Hospital for several years, comforting injured stage drivers and

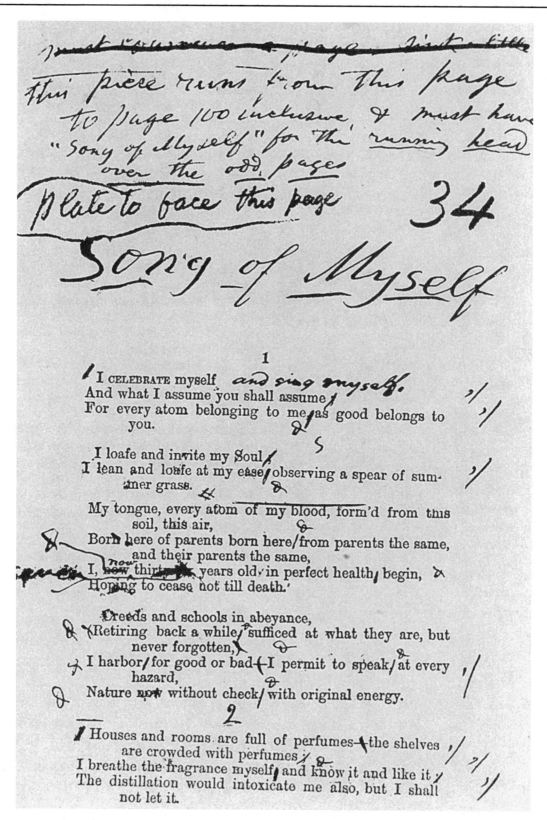

Whitman's revisions of "Song of Myself" for the 1881 edition of Leaves of Grass. *Whitman usually revised his published poetry by marking up earlier printed versions of it (Richard Maurice Bucke sale, American Art Association, 15–16 April 1936).*

ferryboat workers (serious injuries were common in the chaotic New York transportation industry at the time). While he enjoyed his friendships with literary figures, his true preference in companions was always for working-class men, especially those who worked on the omnibuses and ferries—"all my ferry friends," as he called them in his autobiographical work "Specimen Days," published along with other miscellaneous prose writings in the volume *Specimen Days & Collect* (1882). He reveled in the process of travel, instead of worrying about destinations: "I cross'd and recross'd, merely for pleasure," he wrote of his trips on the ferry. He remembered fondly the "immense qualities, largely animal" of the colorful omnibus drivers, whom, he said, he enjoyed "for comradeship, and sometimes affection" as he rode "the whole length of Broadway" listening to the stories of the driver and conductor or "declaiming some stormy passage" from one of his favorite Shakespeare plays.

As the Civil War began taking its toll, wounded soldiers joined the transportation workers as patients Whitman saw on his frequent rounds. The soldiers came from all over the country, and their reminiscences of home taught Whitman about the breadth and diversity of the growing nation. He developed an idiosyncratic style of informal personal nursing, writing down stories the patients told him, giving them small gifts, writing letters for them, and holding and kissing them. His purpose, he wrote, was "just to help cheer and change a little the monotony of their sickness and confinement," though he found that the soldiers' effect on him was as rewarding as his on them: the wounded and maimed young men aroused in him "friendly interest and sympathy," and he said some of "the most agreeable evenings of my life" were spent in hospitals. He wrote about the soldiers in a series, "City Photographs," for the *New York Leader* in 1862.

Whitman once said that if he had not become a writer, he would have been a doctor. He developed close friendships with many of the physicians at Broadway Hospital, even occasionally assisting them in surgery. His fascination with the body, so evident in his poetry, was intricately bound to his attraction to medicine and to the hospitals, where he learned to face bodily disfigurations and gained the ability to see beyond wounds and illness to the human personalities that persisted through the pain and humiliation.

With the nation locked in an extended war, all of Whitman's deepest concerns and beliefs were under attack. *Leaves of Grass* had been built on a faith in union, wholeness, the ability of a self and a nation to contain contradictions and absorb diversity; now the United States had come apart, and Whitman's project was in danger of becoming an anachronism. *Leaves of Grass* had

been built, too, on a belief in the power of affection to overcome division and competition; his "Calamus" vision was of a "continent indissoluble" with "inseparable cities" all joined by "the life-long love of comrades." But now fathers were killing sons, sons, fathers; brothers, brothers. Whitman's prospects for his "new Bible" that would bind a nation, build an affectionate democracy, and guide a citizenry to celebrate its unified diversity were shattered in the fratricidal conflict that engulfed America.

In December 1862 the name "G. W. Whitmore" appeared in the newspaper casualty roster from Fredericksburg. Fearful that the name was a garbled version of George Washington Whitman, Whitman immediately set out for Virginia to try to find his brother. His pocket was picked on the crowded platform as he changed trains in Philadelphia, leaving him penniless for the rest of his journey to Washington. There he encountered O'Connor, the abolitionist writer he had met in Boston, who loaned him money. After futilely searching for George in the nearly forty Washington hospitals, Whitman took a government boat and an army-controlled train to the battlefield at Fredericksburg to see if George was still there. He found George's unit and discovered that his brother had received only a superficial facial wound. But Whitman's relief turned to horror when, as he wrote in his journal, outside a mansion converted into a field hospital he came upon "a heap of amputated feet, legs, arms, hands, &c., a full load for a one-horse cart." They were "human fragments, cut, bloody, black and blue, swelled and sickening." Nearby were "several dead bodies . . . each cover'd with its brown woolen blanket." The sight continued to haunt this poet who had so confidently celebrated the physical body—who had claimed that the soul existed only *in* the body, that the arms and legs were extensions of the soul, the legs moving the soul through the world and the hands allowing it to express itself. The young American males on whom he had staked the future of democracy were being dismembered.

After telegraphing his family that he had found George, Whitman decided to stay with his brother for a few days instead of returning to New York. He assisted in the burial of the dead still lying on the battlefield, where eighteen thousand Northern and Southern troops had been killed or wounded on 13 December (the next day Robert E. Lee, sickened by the carnage, had declined to attack General Ambrose Burnside's Union troops, even though they were in a vulnerable position).

Although Whitman had already written some of the poems that he eventually published in his Civil War collection, *Drum-Taps* (1865)—notably the "recruitment" poems, such as "Beat! Beat! Drums!" and "First O

Songs for Prelude," that evoked the frightening yet exhilarating energy of cities arming for battle—only after he encountered the horrifying aftereffects of a real battle did the powerful war poems begin to emerge. In the journal he kept at George's camp, Whitman noted a "sight at daybreak—in a camp in front of the hospital tent on a stretcher, (three dead men lying,) each with a blanket spread over him—I lift up one and look at the young man's face, calm and yellow,—'tis strange! (Young man: I think this face of yours the face of my dead Christ!)" This journal sketch, like many others, was gradually transformed into a poem that later appeared in *Drum-Taps:*

> A sight in camp in the daybreak gray and dim,
> As from my tent I emerge so early sleepless,
> As slow I walk in the cool fresh air the path near by the hospital tent,
> Three forms I see on stretchers lying, brought out there untended lying,
> Over each the blanket spread, ample brownish woolen blanket,
> Gray and heavy blanket, folding, covering all.
> . . . .
> Then to the third—a face nor child nor old, very calm, as of beautiful yellow-white ivory;
> Young man I think I know you—I think this face is the face of the Christ himself,
> Dead and divine and brother of all, and here he lies again.

The journal entry and poem offer a glimpse into how Whitman began restructuring his poetic project after the Civil War began. He was still writing a "new Bible," reexperiencing the Crucifixion in Fredericksburg. But this crucifixion does not redeem sinners and create an atonement with God so much as it posits divinity in everyone and mourns senseless loss: the death of this one young man amid the thousands of deaths is as significant as any death in history. And the massive slaughter of young soldier-Christs, he thought, would create for all who survived the war an obligation to construct a nation worthy of their great sacrifice.

During the time he spent with George's unit Whitman often went into the makeshift hospital outside of which he had seen the pile of amputated limbs. "I do not see that I do much good to these wounded and dying," he wrote in his journal, "but I cannot leave them." He found himself particularly attracted to a nineteen-year-old Confederate from Mississippi whose leg had been amputated. Whitman visited him regularly in the battlefield hospital and continued to visit him after the soldier was transferred to a Washington hospital. "Our affection is an affair quite romantic," he wrote. The intimate expressions of manly friendship that he had described in the "Calamus" cluster in 1860 became generalized in the poet's many close relation-

ships with injured soldiers over the next three years. Letters from these soldiers clearly indicate the intensity of the love that they felt for Whitman, and Whitman's letters demonstrate that the affection was reciprocated. The language of this correspondence is partly that of lovers, partly that of friends, partly that of son to father and father to son—many of the letters to Whitman are addressed to "Dear Father"—and partly that of calm, wise, old counselor to confused, scared, and half-literate young men.

It is not known when Whitman decided to stay in Washington, D.C. Like virtually all of the abrupt changes in his life—quitting teaching, going to New Orleans and to Boston, and, years later, deciding overnight to settle in Camden, New Jersey—this one came with no planning, advance notice, or preparation. He was a profoundly unsettled person, who seemed able to shuck obligations and relationships without much regret; in "Song of the Open Road" he said, "The long brown path before me leading wherever I choose. . . . I will scatter myself among men and women as I go."

> Allons! We must not stop here,
> However sweet these laid-up stores, however convenient this dwelling we cannot remain here,
> However shelter'd this port and however calm these waters we must not anchor here,
> However welcome the hospitality that surrounds us we are permitted to receive it but a little while.

Perhaps the decision was made while he was nursing the wounded and developing his relationship with the Mississippi soldier in the field hospital: that was when he wrote to his mother that he might seek employment in Washington and to Emerson to ask for letters of recommendation to the secretary of state and the secretary of the treasury. It may have been made on the trip back to Washington in early January 1863, when he was put in charge of a trainload of casualties who were being transferred to hospitals in the capital. While the wounded were being moved to a steamboat for the trip up the Potomac, Whitman wandered among them, comforting them and writing down and promising to send their messages to their families. Perhaps by the time he got to Washington, determined to stay a few days to visit wounded soldiers from Brooklyn, he knew at some level that he would have to remain there for the duration of the war.

Whitman's Boston connections served him well in Washington: he got the letters of introduction from Emerson, a room in O'Connor's boardinghouse, and, through Eldridge, the publisher of the 1860 *Leaves of Grass* who was serving as assistant to the army paymaster, a part-time job as a copyist in the paymaster's office. O'Connor and his wife, Nellie, provided Whitman's meals, and the poet began receiving contributions from his brother Jeff and others in Brooklyn who heard of his work in the hospitals. Whitman used his funds to buy candy, tobacco, flavored syrup, and books for the wounded soldiers, and he soon became a familiar figure in the hospitals. Prematurely gray and looking a decade or two older than his forty-three years, Whitman must have seemed to the soldiers–many of whom were still in their teens–a tattered Saint Nick handing out treats and bringing good cheer. Though he admired the Christian Commission, an agency organized by several churches that recruited volunteers to help in the hospitals, Whitman acted independently. He had nothing but contempt for the U. S. Sanitary Commission, the government body charged with nursing the soldiers back to health and returning them to battle: these functionaries kept their distance from the soldiers and worked primarily for pay. Whitman always insisted that he gained more from the soldiers than they received from him; he considered his years of hospital service "the greatest privilege and satisfaction . . . and, of course, the most profound lesson of my life," he wrote in "Specimen Days."

The nation's capital was in a chaotic state in 1863, with unpaved streets and many half-completed government buildings, including the Capitol itself. Lincoln insisted that construction proceed at full pace, and some of the newly constructed buildings were almost immediately turned into hospitals. The U.S. Patent Office became a hospital in 1863, and Whitman noted the irony of the "rows of sick, badly wounded and dying soldiers" surrounding the "glass cases" displaying the inventions that had created modern warfare.

Whitman's job in the paymaster's office occasionally required him to go on trips to visit troops, as when he traveled to Analostan Island in July 1863 to help issue paychecks to the First Regiment U.S. Colored Troops. He was "well pleas'd" with their professional conduct and strong demeanor, and he was struck by the names of the black soldiers as the roll was called–George Washington, John Quincy Adams, Daniel Webster, James Madison, John Brown. The heritage of the United States, Whitman realized, was being carried forward by a much more diverse citizenry: the African American soldiers, like Whitman's own brothers, bore the names of the nation's proud past. The war, for all of its destruction, was clearing the space for a broader American identity.

Meanwhile, the news from Whitman's family was not good: Andrew was extremely ill; Jesse was increasingly violent and had even threatened Jeff's daughter; and his sister Hannah was being abused by her husband. At his mother's plea, Whitman went back to New York for a visit toward the end of 1863. There he saw

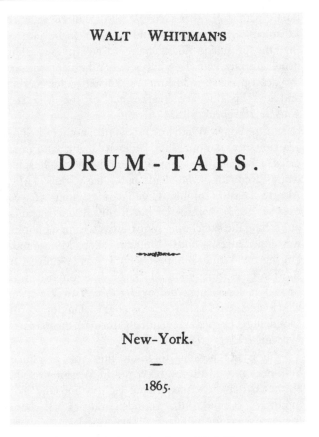

Title page for Whitman's volume of Civil War poems

Andrew for the last time: Andrew died on 3 December, leaving behind two children and a pregnant alcoholic wife who later became a prostitute. The family problems were of deep concern to Whitman, but he felt compelled to return to his soldier friends in Washington, to whom he wrote regularly during the weeks he was in New York.

One day while heading to the hospitals Whitman met John Burroughs, an aspiring young writer who had started frequenting Pfaff's beer hall in New York a couple of years previously in the hope of meeting Whitman. The encounter led to one of the most enduring friendships of Whitman's life; he spent most Sundays at the home of Burroughs and Burroughs's wife, Ursula, who also became one of his closest friends. Burroughs and O'Connor later wrote–with a good deal of help from Whitman himself–some of the earliest lengthy treatments of the poet, and despite some arguments with Whitman over the years, both remained unwavering supporters.

Whitman also met the photographer Alexander Gardner, whose pictures record the striking toll the war took on Whitman's appearance. The photographs show a tired, somber, yet determined Whitman, who seems to be absorbing the soldiers' pain. The war was taking a toll on other faces: Whitman often watched Lincoln's carriage pass by, and he noted in his journal that the president "looks more careworn even than usual–his face with deep cut lines." Whitman repeated the description in a 30 June 1863 letter to his mother and in "'Tis But Ten Years Since" in the *New York Graphic* (28 February 1874).

One day Whitman ran into another Boston acquaintance, the publisher James Redpath, who organized a fund-raising campaign for the poet's hospital work. Redpath, who had published Louisa May Alcott's account of her Civil War nursing, *Hospital Sketches* (1863), considered but finally decided against publishing the sketches Whitman was writing about his war experiences, a book Whitman called "Memoranda During the War." Whitman's book was composed of short articles, many of which he had published in Brooklyn newspapers and in *The New York Times,* for which he served as an occasional Washington correspondent. The pieces eventually formed the basis of "Specimen Days" (1882).

It is not possible to know how many soldiers Whitman nursed during his years in Washington; he estimated that he visited "from eighty thousand to a hundred thousand of the wounded and sick." Walking the wards was for him like walking America: every bed contained a representative of a different region, city, or town, and way of life. He loved the varied accents and diverse physiognomies. "While I was with wounded and sick in thousands of cases from the New England States, and from New York, New Jersey, and Pennsylvania, and from Michigan, Wisconsin, Ohio, Indiana, Illinois, and all the Western States, I was with more or less from all the States, North and South, without exception." In the hospital wards he crossed boundaries otherwise not easily crossed: "I was with many rebel officers and men among our wounded, and gave them always what I had, and tried to cheer them the same as any. . . . Among the black soldiers, wounded or sick, and in the contraband camps, I also took my way whenever in their neighborhood, and did what I could for them." With all those he met, he both sought and offered love, as he told Redpath in a 6 August 1863 letter: "What an attachment grows up between us, started from hospital cots, where pale young faces lie & wounded or sick bodies. The doctors tell me I supply the patients with a medicine which all their drugs & bottles & powders are helpless to yield."

After the burst of creativity in the mid and late 1850s that had resulted in the vastly expanded 1860 *Leaves of Grass,* Whitman had not written many poems until he got to Washington. There the daily encounters with soldiers opened a fresh vein of creativity that produced a poetry more modest in ambition and muted in

its claims, a poetry in which death was no longer indistinguishable from life–in "Song of Myself" Whitman had written, "Has any one supposed it lucky to be born? I hasten to inform him or her it is just as lucky to die, and I know it"–but was revealed as horrifying, grotesque, and omnipresent. Whitman was writing poems about the war, but he almost never wrote about battles; instead, he described the aftereffects of warfare: moonlight illuminating the dead on the battlefields, churches turned into hospitals, the experience of dressing wounds, an encounter with a dead enemy in a coffin, the nightmares of soldiers who had returned home. The poems were so different from any in *Leaves of Grass* that Whitman assumed that they could never be joined in the same book with the earlier ones, so he gathered them, along with the ones Thayer and Eldridge had planned to publish as "Banner at Day-Break," into a book he called *Drum-Taps*–the title evoking both the beating of the drums that accompanied soldiers into battle and the beating out of "Taps," the death march sounded at the burial of soldiers (originally played on the drums instead of the trumpet).

The year 1864 began with one of Whitman's closest soldier friends, Lewis Brown, with whom he had imagined living after the war was over, having a leg amputated; Whitman watched the operation through a window at Armory Square Hospital. In February and March he traveled to the Virginia battlefront to nurse soldiers in field hospitals. In April he stood for three hours watching General Burnside's troops march through Washington until he could pick out his brother George. Whitman fell in beside George and gave him news from home. It was the last time Whitman saw his brother before George was captured by Confederate troops in the fall.

During the early summer Whitman began to complain of a sore throat, dizziness, and a "bad feeling" in his head. Physician friends persuaded him to go back to Brooklyn for a rest. Whitman took the *Drum-Taps* manuscript with him, hoping to publish it while he was there.

In Brooklyn, Whitman could not stop doing what had become both a routine and a reason for his existence: he visited wounded soldiers in New York–area hospitals. He also reestablished contacts with old friends from the Pfaff's beer-hall days and explored some new saloons with them. He wrote articles for *The New York Times* and other papers and took care of pressing family matters, including the commitment of Jesse to the Kings County Lunatic Asylum, where he died six years later. The year ended with the arrival at the Whitman family home of George's personal items. George had been sent to the Libby Prison in Richmond, Virginia; later he was sent to military prisons in

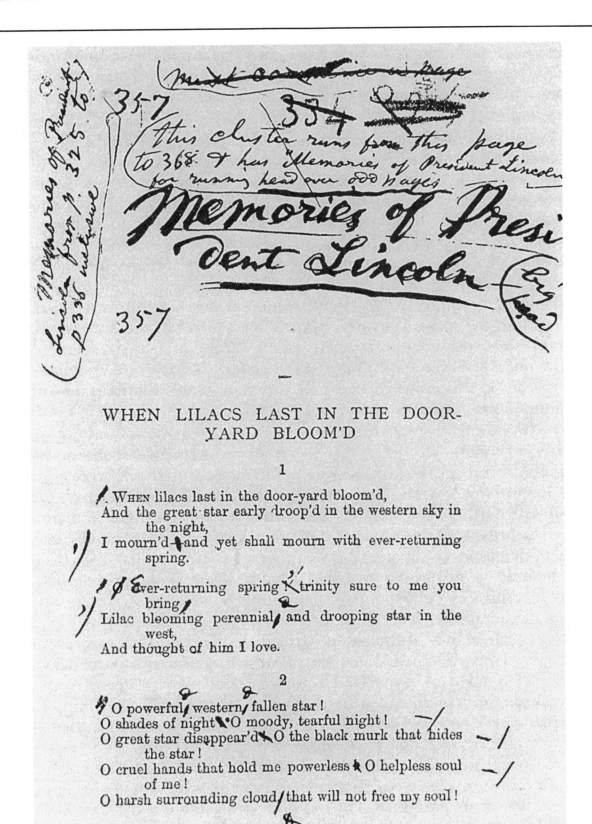

Whitman's revisions of one of his Lincoln poems for the 1881 edition of Leaves of Grass *(Richard Maurice Bucke sale, American Art Association, 15–16 April 1936)*

Salisbury, North Carolina, and in Danville, Virginia. In the hope of effecting George's release Whitman began a campaign in newspaper articles and letters to government officials for an exchange of prisoners between the Union and the Confederacy. Union generals opposed the idea because they believed that it would benefit the South by returning troops to an army that was in desperate need of men.

At the beginning of 1865 O'Connor helped arrange a clerkship for Whitman in the Indian Bureau of the Department of the Interior. Whitman carried his *Drum-Taps* manuscript back to Washington, hoping that his increased income might allow him to publish the book, and moved to a new apartment in the home of what he called a "secesh" landlady. At the Indian Bureau (his desk was in the U.S. Patent Office Building, which he had visited when it was used as a temporary hospital) he met delegations of Indian tribes from the West. He had already included Indians in his poems of America; in "Proto-Leaf" in the 1860 edition of *Leaves of Grass,* for example, he catalogued "the red aborigines" and celebrated their "charging the water and the land with names" (Whitman preferred the Indian name "Paumanok" to "Long Island" and often argued that aboriginal names for American places were superior to those imported from Europe). The impact of Whitman's experiences at the Indian Bureau is apparent in such later poems as "Osceola" and "Yonnondio," which mourn what Whitman believed was the inevitable loss of native cultures.

George Whitman was released from the Danville prison in February and returned to the family home in March. Whitman got a furlough from the Indian Bureau to see George; while he was in Brooklyn he signed a contract with a New York printer on 1 April for the publication of *Drum-Taps*. He was still in Brooklyn eight days later, when Lee surrendered at Appomattox, and five days after that, when Lincoln was assassinated at Ford's Theatre in Washington. When he heard the news about Lincoln he went to console himself in his mother's dooryard, where the lilac bushes were blooming, and the scent of the lilacs became viscerally bound for him to the memory of Lincoln's death. *Drum-Taps* had already been delivered to the printer, but before the book was set in type he was able to add a brief poem about Lincoln's death, "Hush'd Be the Camps To-day." His powerful elegies to Lincoln– "When Lilacs Last in the Dooryard Bloom'd" and the uncharacteristically rhymed and metered "O Captain! My Captain!"–were written after the book was in press. Whitman, therefore, had them printed as "Sequel to Drum-Taps" when he went back to Washington. In October he returned to Brooklyn to oversee the collat-

ing and binding of "Sequel to Drum-Taps" with *Drum-Taps*.

One stormy night, while riding the streetcar home after dinner at John and Ursula Burroughs's apartment, Whitman began talking with the conductor, a twenty-one-year-old Irish immigrant and former Confederate soldier named Peter Doyle. Doyle later recalled that Whitman was the only passenger, and "we were familiar at once–I put my hand on his knee–we understood. . . . From that time on, we were the biggest sort of friends." The friendship lasted for the rest of Whitman's life and was the most intense and romantic one the poet ever had. Doyle's widowed mother and his siblings came to be a second family for Whitman. Whitman continued to visit soldiers in Washington hospitals during the first few years after the war, but he focused his attention increasingly on this young former artilleryman from the South. Like so many of Whitman's closest friends, Doyle had only a rudimentary education and was from the working class. These young men were reflections of Whitman's own youthful self, and he saw his poetry as speaking for them, putting into words what they could not. For Whitman, Doyle represented America's future: healthy, witty, handsome, good-humored, hard-working, enamored of good times, he gave Whitman's life some energy and hope during an otherwise bleak time. They rode the streetcars together, drank at the Union Hotel bar, took long walks outside the city, and quoted poetry to each other (Whitman recited Shakespeare; Doyle, limericks). As Whitman's health deteriorated in the late 1860s and early 1870s, Doyle nursed and offered comfort to the poet, just as Whitman had to so many wounded soldiers. And just as Whitman had picked up the germs of many of his poems from the stories soldiers had told him, he got from Doyle–who had been at Ford's Theatre the night John Wilkes Booth shot the president– the narrative of the assassination that he used for the Lincoln lectures that he delivered regularly in later years.

Only in 1870 did the Doyle-Whitman relationship encounter severe problems. In some of the most intriguing and often-discussed entries in all of Whitman's notebooks, the poet records a cryptic resolution: "TO GIVE UP ABSOLUTELY & for good, from the present hour, this FEVERISH, FLUCTUATING, useless UNDIGNIFIED PURSUIT of 16.4–too long, (much too long) persevered in,–so humiliating." Critics eventually broke Whitman's code, in which *16* stands for *P* and *4* for *D,* and realized that Whitman was writing about his relationship with Doyle. Whitman goes on to urge himself to "Depress the adhesive nature / It is in excess–making life a torment / Ah this diseased, feverish disproportionate adhesiveness / Remember

Fred Vaughan." Vaughan, who probably inspired the "Calamus" poems, shared many traits with Doyle, and Whitman came to be jealous of both men when they did not return his love with the fervor he demanded. Soon after meeting Doyle, Whitman had revised the "Calamus" sequence to remove the darker poems that expressed despair at being abandoned. In 1870 the dark emotions reappeared, though this time Whitman and his partner managed to work through the trouble. They never lived together, though Whitman dreamed of doing so, and, while their relationship never regained the intensity it had in the mid 1860s, Doyle and Whitman continued to correspond, and Doyle visited Whitman regularly for two decades after the poet moved to Camden.

In May 1865 a new secretary of the interior, James Harlan of Iowa, was sworn in and immediately set out to clean up the department, issuing a directive to abolish nonessential positions and to dismiss any employee whose "moral character" was questionable. Harlan was a former U.S. senator, a Methodist minister, and president of Iowa Wesleyan College, and when he saw the copy of the 1860 *Leaves of Grass* that Whitman kept in his desk so that he could revise his poems during slow times at the office, he was appalled. On 20 June, Whitman, along with some other Department of the Interior employees, received a dismissal notice. Whitman turned to O'Connor, who was working in the Treasury Department, and O'Connor, at some risk to his own career, contacted the assistant attorney general, J. Hubley Ashton. Ashton talked with Harlan, who not only refused to rescind the dismissal order but also announced his intention to prevent Whitman from getting work in any other government agency. Ashton talked Harlan out of interfering with Whitman's appointment outside of the Department of the Interior, then convinced Attorney General James Speed to hire Whitman. Whitman became a clerk in the attorney general's office the next day. He liked the work better—he aided in the preparation of requests for pardons from Confederates and later copied documents for delivery to the president and cabinet members—and held the job until he gave it up because of ill health in 1874.

The flap over Whitman's firing seemed to be over in a day, but O'Connor, a highly regarded editor, novelist, and journalist, could not control his rage at Harlan and wrote a diatribe of nearly fifty pages against the moralistic secretary of the interior and his "commission of an outrage": the unceremonious dumping of Walt Whitman, "*the Kosmical man— . . . the* ADAMUS *of the nineteenth century—not an individual, but* MANKIND." O'Connor excoriated Harlan and sanctified Whitman, offering a ringing endorsement of the poet's work and

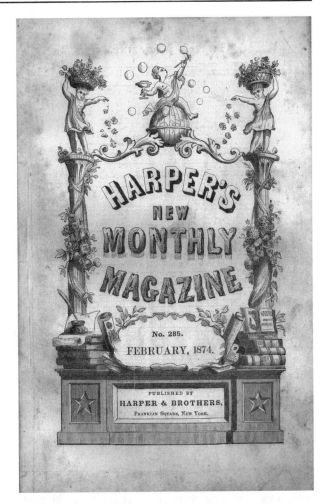

Cover for the journal that includes Whitman's "Song of the Redwood Tree," collected in Two Rivulets (1876) as one of the "Centennial Songs" (Joel Myerson Collection, Special Collections, Thomas Cooper Library, University of South Carolina)

life, emphasizing his hospital work and his love of country, and locating any indecency in Harlan's "horrible inanity of prudery," not in the poetry itself. Whitman offered O'Connor advice and suggestions on the piece, which O'Connor titled *The Good Gray Poet*—creating an epithet that attached itself to Whitman from then on. The pamphlet was published at the beginning of 1866 and played a major role in changing the public perception of Whitman from the outrageous, immoral, indiscriminate, and radical poet of sex to the saintlike, impoverished, aging singer of strong American values.

Around this time Whitman visited George Washington's home in Mount Vernon, perhaps looking for some stable point in a national history that seemed to be spinning out of control. He attended some of the Congressional debates on Reconstruction but was unable to make up his mind on the questions of citizenship and suffrage for the newly freed slaves. He attended baseball games; the new sport was quickly becoming the national game as returning Civil War soldiers, who had learned to play it in military camps, began organizing teams in various parts of the country. Whitman was the first to call it "America's game," telling Traubel years later that it had the "snap, go, fling, of the American atmosphere" and was as important to "the sum total of our historic life" as America's laws and Constitution.

Taking a leave from his job, Whitman spent August and September 1866 in New York overseeing the printing of a new edition of *Leaves of Grass*. The book appeared near the end of the year, though the title page is dated 1867. It is the most carelessly printed and chaotic of all the editions. Whitman bound the book in five distinct formats: the revised *Leaves of Grass* alone; *Leaves of Grass* plus *Drum-Taps; Leaves of Grass, Drum-Taps,* and "Sequel to Drum-Taps"; all of these, along with another new cluster, "Songs Before Parting"; and *Leaves of Grass* and "Songs Before Parting" only. He always believed that the history of *Leaves of Grass* paralleled his own history and that both histories embodied the history of America in the nineteenth century; thus, the 1867 edition can be read as his first tentative attempt to absorb the Civil War into his book. His sewing of the printed pages of *Drum-Taps* and "Sequel to Drum-Taps" into the back of some of the copies creates a jarring textual effect: pagination and font fracture as Whitman adds his poems of war and division to his poems of absorption and nondiscrimination. The Union has been preserved, but this stripped and undecorated volume–the only edition of *Leaves of Grass* supervised by Whitman that does not include a portrait of the poet–manifests a kind of forced reconciliation, a recognition that everything now has to be reconfigured.

Whitman kept rearranging, pruning, and adding to *Leaves of Grass* to try to solve the structural problems of the 1867 edition. The book took a radically new shape when the fifth edition appeared; known as the 1871–1872 edition because of the varying dates on the title–page, it was actually first printed in 1870. This complex edition, which, like the 1867 one, appeared in several versions, reveals Whitman's attempt fully to absorb the Civil War and its aftermath into his book as the *Drum-Taps* poems are given their own "cluster" but are also scattered into other parts of *Leaves of Grass,* and the war experience bleeds out into the rest of the poems in sometimes subtle small additions and changes. The edition includes some revealing clusters of poems that disappear in the much-better-known 1881 arrangement: "Marches Now the War is Over" and "Songs of Insurrection" capture the charged historical moment of Reconstruction to which this edition responds.

Whitman was aided in the development from the 1867 to the better-integrated 1870 edition by William Michael Rossetti's *Poems by Walt Whitman* (1868), the first British edition of Whitman's work. Rossetti's arrangement of the poems helped Whitman to see how *Drum-Taps* could be integrated into the larger project of *Leaves of Grass*. Rossetti believed, however, that Whitman's poetry had to be expurgated for the sensibilities of British readers, and as work on the English edition progressed Whitman took various positions on Rossetti's suggestions for censoring his verses. At one point he seemed to grant permission through his friend Conway to substitute other words for "father-stuff" and "onanist," but in a 3 December 1867 letter he told Rossetti that "I cannot and will not consent, of my own volition, to countenance an expurgated edition of my pieces." Rossetti's diplomatic approach was to alter no words in Whitman's poems, though he often changed the titles; instead, if he thought that a poem might offend too many readers or provoke the censors, he omitted it altogether. Rossetti regarded Whitman as one of the great poets of the English language and hoped that his selection of the poems would lead to a printing of Whitman's complete works in England. *Poems by Walt Whitman,* comprising approximately half of the 1867 *Leaves of Grass,* made English friends for Whitman who later helped sustain him financially and advanced his reputation on both sides of the Atlantic.

In 1870 Whitman also published *Democratic Vistas* and *Passage to India* (the title pages of both works carry the date 1871). *Passage to India,* a collection of seventy-five poems, one-third of them new, was intended as a follow-up to *Leaves of Grass* that would inaugurate an emphasis in Whitman's poetry on the "Unseen soul" and, thus, complement his earlier songs of the "Body and existence." Poor health eventually forced Whitman to curtail the plan. The title poem celebrates the work of engineers, especially the global linking accomplished by the transcontinental railroad, the Suez Canal, and the Atlantic cable. (Whitman's enthusiasm for engineering accomplishments was magnified because of his pride in his brother Jeff, who had moved west in 1867 to become the chief engineer in charge of building and overseeing a waterworks for St. Louis–a "great work–a noble position," Whitman had exclaimed in a 29 April 1867 letter to Jeff). For Whitman, modern material accomplishments were most important as means to better understanding of the "aged fierce enigmas" at the heart of spiritual questions. "Passage to India" is grand in conception and has had many admirers, but the rhetorical excesses of the poem–apparent in its heavy reliance on exclamation marks–reveal a poet not so much at odds with his subject matter as flagging in inspiration.

Whitman's celebration of engineers, architects, and machinists in "Passage to India" prompted the organizers of the 1871 exposition of the American Institute, a large industrial fair, to invite him to deliver the opening poem. Whitman gladly accepted the $100 payment and the publicity that would follow from distribution of a pamphlet by Roberts Brothers, a Boston publisher. Assured publicity was welcome because his recent work had garnered few reviews. He hoped to benefit fully, and he prepared copies of his poem, "After All Not to Create Only" (later called "Song of the Exposition"), for release to the New York dailies. Reports on the effectiveness of Whitman's reading are mixed: some accounts indicate that the poet could not be heard over the workmen constructing exhibits, while other reports describe a "good elocutionist" greeted by long applause. There was, however, enough sarcasm in the press reports to make the event less than a thoroughgoing success.

If "Passage to India" and "After All Not to Create Only" were celebratory—perhaps at times naively so—*Democratic Vistas* mounted sustained criticism of Reconstruction era failures. Based in part on essays that had appeared in *The Galaxy* in 1867 and 1868, *Democratic Vistas* responds to Thomas Carlyle's racist diatribe *Shooting Niagara: And After?* (1867). Carlyle's "Great Man" view of history made him impatient with democracy and opposed to efforts to expand the franchise in either the United States or England: the folly of giving the vote to blacks, he contends, is akin to that of going over Niagara Falls in a barrel. Whitman acknowledges the "appalling dangers of universal suffrage in the U.S." because of the "people's crudeness, vices, caprices"; he gazes piercingly at a society "canker'd crude, superstitious and rotten," in which the "depravity of our business classes . . . is not less than has been supposed, but infinitely greater." But, contrasting these current problems with "democracy's convictions" and "aspirations," he provides a ringing endorsement of democracy as intertwined with the fate of the United States—the two, in fact, are "convertible terms." Crucial to Whitman's program for strengthening democracy are what he calls "personalism"—a form of individualism—and the nurturance of an appropriate "New World literature."

A series of blows turned 1873 into one of the worst years of Whitman's life. On 23 January he suffered a stroke; in February his sister-in-law Mattie, Jeff's wife, died of cancer; in May his mother's health began to fail. Partially paralyzed with weakness in his left leg and arm, Whitman arrived in Camden, New Jersey, three days before his mother's death on 23 May. He returned to Washington at the beginning of June, hoping to resume his job. But by the middle of the month he was back in Camden to stay, moving into a working-class neighborhood with his brother George and George's wife, Lou.

One can glimpse Whitman's emotional state in "Prayer of Columbus," published in *Harper's Magazine* in March 1874: it depicts Christopher Columbus—resembling Whitman himself—as a battered, wrecked, paralyzed old man, misunderstood in his own time. Gradually, however, the poet's spirits improved as he warmed to Camden. Among the city's advantages was its location across the Delaware River from Philadelphia, a city with a thriving intellectual and artistic community. Thomas Eakins at the Pennsylvania Academy of the Fine Arts made Whitman the subject of a memorable portrait and of many photographs, and he produced other work, including the painting *Swimming* (1883), informed by Whitman's vision. Whitman had long been interested in photography, and Philadelphia was the home of the country's oldest photographic society and of the journal *Philadelphia Photographer*.

Not long after his stroke Whitman expanded and reworked some of his newspaper articles and notebook entries to compose *Memoranda During the War* (1876). The book was published at the end of Reconstruction, when a rise in immigration and racial conflict strained national cohesion and, to Whitman's mind, lent urgency to his argument that affectionate bonds between men constituted the vital core of American democracy. The prose in the volume is taut, concise, detailed, and unflinching. Although the Civil War had received more press coverage than any previous conflict, Whitman worried that its true import would be lost, that what he called "the real war" would never be remembered. He lamented the lack of attention being paid to the common soldiers and to the fortitude and love he had seen in his many visits with soldiers in the hospitals.

Whitman hoped that the Centennial Commission would ask him to write the national hymn, but five others were asked before Bayard Taylor accepted. Whitman celebrated the nation's centennial by bringing forth the variously labeled "Author's Edition" or "Centennial Edition" of *Leaves of Grass*. It was, technically, a republication of the 1870 edition with intercalations: he pasted four new poems on blank sections of pages and included two portraits, the old Hollyer engraving that he had used as his 1855 frontispiece and a new one by William Linton of a recently taken photograph. The companion volume, *Two Rivulets* (1876), collects his Reconstruction writings; in one section, poetry and prose are printed on the top and bottom halves of the pages, respectively. The three publications make up a complex, multifaceted Centennial offering that provides trenchant commentary on the century-old country,

SEQUEL TO DRUM-TAPS.

(SINCE THE PRECEDING CAME FROM THE PRESS.)

WHEN LILACS LAST IN THE DOOR-YARD BLOOM'D.

AND OTHER PIECES.

WASHINGTON.
1865-6.

Title page for the 1865 addendum to Whitman's Civil War poems, which was published after the assassination of President Abraham Lincoln and includes the memorial poems "When Lilacs Last in the Door-Yard Bloom'd" and "O Captain! My Captain!"

mixes indictment and praise, and offsets despair at failure with hope for the future.

Whitman's centennial publications were more successful financially than his previous work, in part because of a transatlantic debate that dramatically increased his visibility. Whitman helped spark the controversy with "Walt Whitman's Actual American Position," a third-person contribution to the *West Jersey Press* on 26 January 1876 that offered an exaggerated account of his neglect: it argued that he was systematically excluded from American magazines and that leading poets snubbed him when compiling anthologies of poetry. Among those to whom Whitman sent the article were Rossetti in England, Edward Dowden in Ireland, and Rudolph Schmidt in Denmark. The British journalist-critic Robert Buchanan, famous for his essay on the pre-Raphaelites, "The Fleshly School of Poetry" (1871), entered the fray, sharply criticizing the treatment of Whitman in American letters to the *Daily News*

(London) on 13, 16, and 17 March; Taylor led the other side, defending the American literati's treatment of Whitman in editorials in the *New York Tribune* on 28 March and 12 and 22 April. The editor of *Appleton's Monthly Magazine* commented in the April issue that the whole thing smacked of an "advertising trick" by Whitman and his allies to market his works. In fact, the debate did increase sales of Whitman's works; Whitman said that English subscribers to the 1876 *Leaves of Grass* and to *Two Rivulets* "pluck'd me like a brand from the burning, and gave me life again."

English interest in Whitman had been building since the publication of Rossetti's *Poems by Walt Whitman*. One of the many readers drawn to Whitman through this book was Anne Burrows Gilchrist, the widow of Alexander Gilchrist, who, after her husband's death in 1861, had completed his biography of William Blake (1863). Gilchrist wrote a series of letters to Rossetti that formed the basis for her insightful essay, "A Woman's Estimate of Walt Whitman," published in *The Radical* in 1870. Gilchrist and Whitman corresponded for six years, with ardor on her side and caution on his; then, surprisingly, the poet sent her a ring. With this gift Whitman meant to signal not romantic love but the loving friendship he was ready to share with Gilchrist. In September 1876 Gilchrist crossed the Atlantic, convinced that she was destined to bear the children of the "tenderest lover." After some initial awkwardness, the two developed a warm friendship. She remained in the United States for eighteen months, during which time Whitman visited almost daily and sometimes lived at the Gilchrist house. He developed close ties to Gilchrist's four children, particularly her son Herbert, a painter, who sketched and painted several portraits of Whitman.

By this time Whitman and Doyle were seeing less and less of one another, and Harry Stafford soon displaced Doyle as the poet's "darling son." When Whitman met him in 1876, Stafford was an emotionally unstable eighteen-year-old who did odd jobs at the *Camden New Republic*. Stafford's family regarded Whitman as a mentor and were pleased with the poet's interest in the young man. Staffords' mother was especially solicitous as Whitman, after his stroke, strove to nurse himself back to health at the Staffords' farm near Timber Creek, about ten miles from Camden, using a self-imposed idiosyncratic but effective regimen of physical therapy, including wrestling with saplings and taking mud baths. The nature of Whitman's relationship with Stafford remains mysterious. It is known that the two wrestled together (leaving John Burroughs to record in his diary his dismay at the way they "cut up like two boys"); that a friendship ring Whitman gave Stafford went back and forth many times, with anguished rhetoric; and that they shared a room when traveling. Whitman and Stafford also discussed attractive women, as the poet had with Doyle. The two maintained a friendly relationship after Stafford married in 1884.

Whitman was regarded as a figure of pivotal importance by English writers, intellectuals, shopkeepers, and laborers who were struggling to establish a positive image of homosexuality in a culture that increasingly categorized it as morbid and criminal. One of these men, Edward Carpenter, visited Whitman in Camden in 1877 and again in 1884. Carpenter influenced various artists, intellectuals, and sexual radicals through the example of his decades-long relationship with a working-class man, George Merrill, and through his writings, including his Whitman-inspired poem *Towards Democracy* (1883), his essays, and *Days with Walt Whitman* (1906), his memoir of his association with Whitman and analysis of Whitman's work and influence. Carpenter helped spread word of Whitman to the English labor movement, which employed the poet's language of comradeship to advocate a more egalitarian society. In 1882 Oscar Wilde drank elderberry wine with the poet, enthused over his Greek qualities, and declared that there is "no one in this great wide world of America whom I love and honor so much."

In 1881 a mainstream Boston publisher, James R. Osgood and Company, decided to bring out *Leaves of Grass* under its imprint. As had been the case more than twenty years earlier, when Thayer and Eldridge offered him respectable Boston publication, Whitman anticipated the benefits of high visibility, wide distribution, and institutional validation. Once again, however, things soon went awry. Oliver Stevens, the Boston district attorney, wrote to Osgood on 1 March 1882, "We are of the opinion that this book is such a book as brings it within the provisions of the Public Statutes respecting obscene literature and suggest the propriety of withdrawing the same from circulation and suppressing the editions thereof." The New England Society for the Suppression of Vice endorsed this view, and many reviews also predicted trouble for the book. Osgood attempted to strike a compromise, and Whitman, thinking that the changes might involve only ten lines "& half a dozen words or phrases," worked to find a way around the ban. But his position stiffened once he realized how extensive the changes would have to be. The offending passages appeared in "Song of Myself," "From Pent-Up Aching Rivers," "I Sing the Body Electric," "A Woman Waits for Me," "Spontaneous Me," "Native Moments," "The Dalliance of the Eagles," "By Blue Ontario's Shore," "To a Common Prostitute," "Unfolded Out of the Folds," "The Sleepers," and "Faces." In most of those poems particular passages or words were found offensive, but the district attorney insisted that "A Woman Waits for Me" and "To a Common Prostitute" had to be removed altogether. On 23 March, Whitman wrote Osgood, "The list whole & several is rejected by me, & will not be thought of under any circumstances." Osgood ceased selling *Leaves of Grass* and gave the plates to Whitman, who took them to the Philadelphia publisher Rees Welsh. Rees Welsh printed around six thousand copies of the book, and sales, initially at least, were brisk. Within the Rees Welsh company David McKay was particularly supportive of Whitman; McKay soon founded his own firm and began publishing Whitman's works. The suppression controversy helped to end a period of estrangement between Whitman and O'Connor, who came to his old friend's defense.

The year *Leaves of Grass* was banned in Boston, Whitman wrote "A Memorandum at a Venture," which appeared in the *North American Review* in June. Whitman argues that the "current prurient, conventional treatment of sex is the main formidable obstacle" to the advancement of women in politics, business, and social life. Whitman's depictions of women have received a fair amount of criticism. D. H. Lawrence, for example, claimed in the *Nation and Athenaeum* (23 July 1921) that Whitman reduced women to "Muscles and wombs." It is true that *Leaves of Grass* emphasizes motherhood, but the women Whitman most celebrated were those who challenged traditional ways, including Margaret Fuller, Frances Wright, George Sand, and Delia Bacon. Elizabeth Cady Stanton was troubled by the skewed understanding of women's sexuality suggested by "A Woman Waits for Me," even as she endorsed Whitman's insistence in the same poem that women must "know how to swim, row, ride, wrestle, shoot, run, strike, retreat, advance, resist, defend themselves." Many women of his day wrote him letters of appreciation for the liberating value of his poetry, and writers such as Kate Chopin, Charlotte Perkins Gilman, and Edith Wharton admired his work both because of what he said about women and because his vision of comradeship based on mutuality and equality lent itself—whatever the nature of his own relationships may have been—to a critique of hierarchical relations between men and women.

"Specimen Days" was published as a prose counterpart to the 1881 edition of *Leaves of Grass*. Whitman described it as the "most wayward, spontaneous, fragmentary book ever printed;" and as an autobiography, it is certainly anomalous. Whitman sheds little light on the development of the first edition of *Leaves of Grass*, which remains a central mystery. After a brief section on his family background, he moves rapidly past his "long foreground" to focus, relying heavily on material

Page from a manuscript for an essay Whitman included in Specimen Days & Collect *in 1882*
(William F. Gable sale, American Art Association, 10-11 March 1924)

from *Memoranda During the War,* on the Civil War. Aware that no other major writer could match his direct and extensive connection to the war, he continues to argue that the hospitals were central to the war just as the war itself was definitional for the American experience. He then shifts to nature reflections evoked by the Stafford farm. He also describes his 1879 trip to attend the twenty-fifth-anniversary celebration of the settlement of Kansas and to visit his brother Jeff in St. Louis. Whitman journeyed as far as the Rockies, finding in the landscape a grandeur that matched his earlier imaginings of it and a ruggedness that justified his approach to American poetry. Consistently in "Specimen Days" Whitman keeps his standing in the national pantheon in mind. In sections such as "My Tribute to Four Poets" and the accounts of the deaths of Emerson, Longfellow, and Carlyle he seeks to establish a newly magnanimous position in relation to his key predecessors, praising fellow poets he once derided as "jinglers, and snivellers, and fops." Long largely ignored by critics, "Specimen Days" is now being read as an eccentric and experimental prose counterpart to Whitman's radically new poetry.

Whitman seized another opportunity to formulate his life story when the Canadian Richard Maurice Bucke began to plan the first full-length biography of the poet, which was published as *Walt Whitman* in 1883. Bucke had first read Whitman in 1867 and had been immediately enthralled. His initial overtures toward Whitman had been rebuffed when Whitman failed to answer his letters. When the two men met in the late 1870s, however, they began an important friendship and literary relationship. Bucke's own life blended science and mysticism: he was superintendent of the largest mental asylum in North America and the author of *Man's Moral Nature* (1879) and later wrote *Cosmic Consciousness* (1901). For Bucke, Whitman's achievement of illumination put him near the head of a group including Moses, Buddha, Socrates, Jesus, and Wordsworth. Whitman visited Bucke in Ontario for four months in the summer of 1880, providing information for the biography. Nonetheless, even though Whitman drafted parts of the work and edited much that Bucke wrote, he did not think that the book created a truthful portrait. Whitman contributed to the distortions by excising some of Bucke's better insights, such as his recognition of Whitman's motherly nature and his observations of the intimate friendship the poet struck up with a Canadian soldier while traveling with Bucke.

Beginning in the late 1870s and continuing for about a decade, Whitman regularly gave lectures on Lincoln. The lectures were the closest he came to fulfilling his early dream of being a wandering lecturer. Despite his personal misgivings about the conventional-

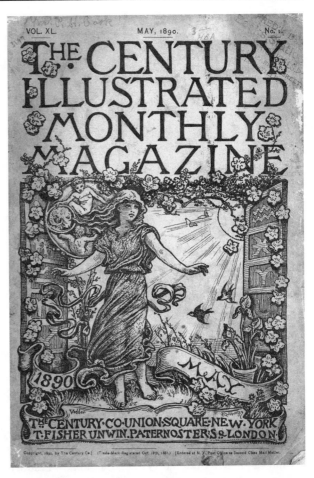

Cover for the journal in which "A Twilight Song" was first published (Joel Myerson Collection, Special Collections, Thomas Cooper Library, University of South Carolina)

ity of the poem, he usually closed with "O Captain! My Captain!"

Whitman had been living with his brother George; but when George retired and moved the family to a farm outside of town, Whitman refused to leave Camden. With what he had saved from the royalties from the 1881 edition of *Leaves of Grass,* combined with a loan from the publisher George W. Childs, he bought "a little old shanty of my own," and in March 1884 he moved into the only home he ever owned. Lacking a furnace and in need of repairs, the two-story frame house at 328 Mickle Street suited him well, he said. Visitors noted that the poet resided in a sea of chaotic papers.

In 1885 Thomas Donaldson, a Philadelphia lawyer, procured a horse and buggy for Whitman by asking thirty-five men to donate $10 each. Bill Duckett, a teenager who boarded with Whitman and his housekeeper, Mary O. Davis, often acted as Whitman's driver. It is doubtful that Duckett's relationship with Whitman was anything like those the poet had had with Doyle, Vaughan, or Stafford. Whitman was, however, photographed with the youth in one of the same kind of pictures, akin to wedding poses, in which he appears with Doyle and Stafford. Eventually, the friendship with Duckett soured, and Davis took Duckett to court for nonpayment of his boarding bill; the young man claimed that he owed nothing, since Whitman had invited him into the house.

In later editions of *Leaves of Grass* Whitman retained the structure of the 1881 edition, relegating the poetry written after that year to appendices—or, as he called them, annexes—to the main book. Typically, new material first appeared in separate publications, such as *November Boughs* (1888). This volume comprises sixty-four new poems gathered under the title "Sands at Seventy" and prose works previously published in periodicals, including "Father Taylor (and Oratory)," "Robert Burns as Poet and Person," and "Slang in America." *Good-Bye My Fancy* (1891) is also a miscellany of prose and verse; Whitman republished thirty-one poems from that book as the "second annex" to the 1892 edition of *Leaves of Grass.* Whitman lacked the poetic power of his early years, but he was still capable of writing engaging poems such as "Osceola," "A Twilight Song," and "To the Sun-Set Breeze."

In the late 1880s Horace Traubel, who had known Whitman since the poet moved to Camden, became a daily visitor at Whitman's home. Traubel was unmatched in his dedication to the poet and in his belief that all that Whitman said was memorable: he kept meticulous notes of his daily conversations with Whitman and published three large volumes of them as *With Walt Whitman in Camden* (1906, 1908, 1914); six more volumes (1959, 1964, 1982, 1992, two in 1996) were published after Traubel's death. He believed that his hybrid identity—one of his parents was a Jew, the other a Christian—left him especially suited to interpret Whitman, a poet of inclusiveness. Traubel, who worked in a bank until he had to resign because of his socialist views, frequently urged Whitman to affirm a faith in socialism. After Whitman's death, he was one of the three executors of Whitman's estate and a staunch defender of the poet's reputation. He became editor of the *Conservator,* a journal dedicated to continuing Whitman's message. Traubel was the key figure among Whitman's American disciples, a group sometimes disparagingly referred to as the "hot little prophets." Although Traubel—married and with a child—had at least one intense love affair with a man, he was characteristic of Whitman's American followers in resisting the association of Whitman's reputation with homosexuality, going so far as to refer to same-sex love as "muck and rot."

The American disciples had counterparts in England. J. W. Wallace was the leader of a group of socialists in Lancashire, known as "Bolton College," who ardently admired Whitman. Wallace came to Camden in the autumn of 1891 to see the "prophet" of a new religion of socialism. Other notable members of the group were Fred Wild, a cotton-waste merchant, and Dr. John Johnston, a general practitioner. Johnston corresponded with the poet, photographed him, and, with Wallace, wrote about him in *Visits to Walt Whitman in 1890–1891 by Two Lancashire Friends* (1918). Wallace's group was confident of its place in history: "*We* stand in closest relation to Walt Whitman—the divinely inspired prophet of world democracy," Johnston and Wallace wrote in *Visits to Walt Whitman* (1918).

Though Whitman never gave up looking to the United States for his most enthusiastic audience, he welcomed the continuing support from English readers. He found some support he received there, however, ill advised and trying. The poet, student of sexuality, and classical scholar John Addington Symonds began in the 1870s a decades-long questioning of Whitman about the meaning of the "Calamus" cluster: did it authorize carnal relations between men? Fascinated by the powerful same-sex attachment depicted in *Leaves of Grass,* Symonds was hesitant to explicate the poems without reassurance from Whitman; but the poet refused to provide it. (Symonds's hesitancy can be explained as an aftereffect of his earlier disastrous exposure of the affair of Dr. Charles Vaughan, headmaster of Harrow, with a student, Symonds's friend Alfred Pretor.) Symonds pressed Whitman so much that in a 19 August 1890 letter the poet concocted a lie of grand proportions: "Tho' always unmarried I have had six children—two are dead—One living southern grandchild, fine boy, who writes to me occasionally. Circumstances connected with their benefit and fortune have separated me from intimate relations." Whitman was similarly coy with Traubel, repeatedly suggesting that he had a great secret to divulge and repeatedly deferring the telling of it. Whitman was more interested in cultivating sexual mystery than clarity, and he was not going to reduce his life or thought to narrow and distorting labels or answers, especially on anyone else's terms.

Whitman continued writing, "garrulous," as he said, to the very end, but he worried that "Ungracious glooms, aches, lethargy, constipation, whimpering *ennui,* / May filter in my daily songs." The "Deathbed Edition" of *Leaves of Grass,* technically a republication of the 1881 edition with supplemental material, appeared in 1892. The first printing was bound in paper to make sure a copy reached the poet before his death. In this edition *Leaves of Grass* takes its final shape as authorized by the poet. He closed the book with an expanded version of "A Backward Glance O'er Travell'd Roads," an essay that had appeared earlier, in parts, in *The Critic* and in *The New York Star*.

Beset by an array of ailments, Whitman seemed to endure his final months through sheer force of will. For some time he had been making preparations for the end. He had a large mausoleum built in Camden's Harleigh Cemetery on a plot given to him in 1885, shortly after the cemetery opened. The tomb was paid for in part by Whitman with money donated to him so that he could buy a house in the country, and in part by Thomas Harned, one of his literary executors. (Eventually, his siblings Hannah, George, Louisa, and Edward and their parents were reinterred in the tomb, on which the inscription reads simply "Walt Whitman.") The poet composed his last will and testament on 24 December 1891; in an 1873 will he had bequeathed his silver watch to Doyle, but with Doyle largely absent from his life he gave that watch to Stafford and a gold one to Traubel.

Whitman was nursed in his final illness by Frederick Warren "Warry" Fritzinger, a former sailor. Whitman liked Fritzinger's touch, which blended masculine strength and feminine tenderness. The poet's last words were addressed to Fritzinger: "Shift, Warry," a request to be moved in bed. Whitman died on 26 March 1892, his hand resting in Traubel's. The cause of death was miliary tuberculosis, with other contributing factors. The autopsy revealed that one lung had completely collapsed and the other was working only at one-eighth capacity; his heart was "surrounded by a large number of small abscesses and about two and half quarts of water." Daniel Longaker, Whitman's physician in the final year, noted that the autopsy showed Whitman to be free of alcoholism and syphilis. He emphatically rejected the "slanderous accusations that debauchery and excesses of various kinds caused or contributed to his break-down."

In "Poets to Come" Whitman claimed: "I am a man who, sauntering along without fully stopping, turns a casual look upon you and then averts his face, / Leaving it to you to prove and define it, / Expecting the main things from you." That "casual look" has had an uncanny impact as countless writers have sought to complete Whitman's project and, thereby, to know themselves better. The responses have been varied, ranging from indictments to accolades. Poetic responses to Whitman sometimes fall into his cadences and in other ways mimic his style, but many poets have understood, with William Carlos Williams, that the only way to write like Whitman is to write unlike him. To an unusual degree, however, his legacy has not been lim-

Whitman in 1886 with Bill Duckett, his friend, choachman, and general assistant (Bayley Collection, Ohio Wesleyan University)

ited to the genre in which he made his fame. Beyond poetry, Whitman has had an extensive impact on fiction, movies, architecture, music, painting, dance, and other arts.

Whitman has enjoyed great international renown. Perhaps William Faulkner can match Whitman's impact in South America, but no American writer, including Faulkner, has had a comparable influence in as many parts of the world. *Leaves of Grass* has been translated in complete editions in Spain, France, Germany, Italy, China, and Japan, and partial translations have appeared in all major languages but Arabic. Whitman's importance stems not only from his literary qualities but also from his standing as a prophet of liberty and revolution: he has served as a major icon for socialists and communists but has also been invoked occasionally by writers and politicians on the far right, including the National Socialists in Germany. Whitman's influence internationally has been most felt in liberal circles, where he is regarded as a writer who articulated the beauty, power, and always incompletely fulfilled promise of democracy.

"My book and the war are one," Whitman once said. He might have said as well that his book and the United States are one. Whitman has been of crucial importance to minority writers who have talked back to him–extending, refining, rewriting, battling, endorsing, and sometimes rejecting the work of a writer who strove so insistently to define national identity and to imagine an inclusive society. Critics sometimes decry Whitman's shortcomings and occasional failure to live up to his own finest ideals. But minority writers from Langston Hughes to June Jordan and Yusef Komunyakaa have, with rare exceptions, warmed to an outlook extraordinary for its sympathy, generosity, and capaciousness. Whitman's absorption by people from all walks of life justifies his bold claim of 1855 that "the proof of a poet is that his country absorbs him as affectionately as he has absorbed it." More than a century after his death, Whitman is a vital presence in American cultural memory. Television shows depict him. Musicians allude to him. Schools, bridges, truck stops, apartment complexes, parks, think tanks, summer camps, corporate centers, and shopping malls bear his name. One can look for him, just as he said one should, under one's boot-soles.

Letters:

Letters Written by Walt Whitman to His Mother from 1866 to 1872, edited by Thomas B. Harned (New York: Putnam, 1902);

The Letters of Anne Gilchrist and Walt Whitman, edited by Harned (New York: Doran, 1918);

Whitman and Rolleston: A Correspondence, edited by Horst Frenz (Bloomington: Indiana University Press, 1951);

The Correspondence of Walt Whitman, 6 volumes, edited by Edwin Haviland Miller (New York: New York University Press, 1961–1977);

Selected Letters of Walt Whitman, edited by Miller (Iowa City: University of Iowa Press, 1990);

The Correspondence of Walt Whitman: A Second Supplement with a Revised Calendar of Letters Written to Whitman, edited by Miller (Iowa City: Walt Whitman Quarterly Review Press, 1991);

"The Correspondence of Walt Whitman: A Third Supplement with Addenda to the Calender of Letters Written to Whitman," edited by Ted Genoways, *Walt Whitman Quarterly Review,* 18 (Summer–Fall 2000): 1–59.

Bibliographies:

Emory Holloway and Henry S. Saunders, "Whitman," in *The Cambridge History of American Literature,* volume 2, edited by William P. Trent and others (New York: Putnam, 1918), pp. 551–581;

Frank Shay, *The Bibliography of Walt Whitman* (New York: Friedmans, 1920);

Carolyn Wells and Alfred F. Goldsmith, *A Concise Bibliography of the Works of Walt Whitman* (Boston: Houghton Mifflin, 1922);

Gay Wilson Allen, *Twenty-Five Years of Walt Whitman Bibliography: 1918–1942* (Boston: F. W. Faxon, 1943);

Allen, *Walt Whitman Handbook* (Chicago: Packard, 1946);

Library of Congress, *Walt Whitman: A Catalog Based upon the Collections of the Library of Congress* (Washington, D.C.: Government Printing Office, 1955);

Evie Allison Allen, "A Checklist of Whitman Publications 1945–1960," in *Walt Whitman as Man, Poet, and Legend,* by Gay Wilson Allen (Carbondale: Southern Illinois University Press, 1961), pp. 179–260;

James T. Tanner, *Walt Whitman: A Supplementary Bibliography 1961–1967* (Kent, Ohio: Kent State University Press, 1968);

William White, *Walt Whitman's Journalism: A Bibliography* (Detroit: Wayne State University Press, 1969);

Roger Asselineau, "Walt Whitman," in *Eight American Authors,* edited by James Woodress, revised edition (New York: Norton, 1971), pp. 225–272;

Gay Wilson Allen, *The New Walt Whitman Handbook* (New York: New York University Press, 1975);

Gloria A. Francis and Artem Lozynsky, *Whitman at Auction, 1899–1972* (Detroit: Gale, 1978);

Jeanetta Boswell, *Walt Whitman and the Critics: A Checklist of Criticism, 1900–1978* (Metuchen, N.J.: Scarecrow Press, 1980);

Scott Giantvalley, *Walt Whitman, 1838–1939: A Reference Guide* (Boston: G. K. Hall, 1981);

Donald D. Kummings, *Walt Whitman, 1940–1975: A Reference Guide* (Boston: G. K. Hall, 1982);

Ed Folsom, "Whitman: A Current Bibliography," *Walt Whitman Quarterly Review* (1983–   ); reformatted as an annual on-line bibliography, in *The Walt Whitman Hypertext Archive,* edited by Kenneth M. Price and Folsom, <http://jefferson.village.virginia.edu/whitman/> (1995–   );

Michael Winship, "Walt Whitman, 1819–1892," in *Bibliography of American Literature,* volume 9, edited by Winship and Jacob Blanck (New Haven: Yale University Press, 1991), pp. 28–103;

Joel Myerson, *Walt Whitman: A Descriptive Bibliography* (Pittsburgh: University of Pittsburgh Press, 1993).

Biographies:

William Douglas O'Connor, *The Good Gray Poet: A Vindication* (New York: Bunce & Huntington, 1866);

John Burroughs, *Notes on Walt Whitman as Poet and Person* (New York: American News, 1867);

Richard Maurice Bucke, *Walt Whitman* (Philadelphia: McKay, 1883);

William Clarke, *Walt Whitman* (London: Swan Sonnenschein, 1892);

Thomas Donaldson, *Walt Whitman, the Man* (New York: Harper, 1896);

William Sloane Kennedy, *Reminiscences of Walt Whitman* (London: Alexander Gardner, 1896);

Elizabeth Porter Gould, *Anne Gilchrist and Walt Whitman* (Philadelphia: McKay, 1900);

Henry Bryan Binns, *A Life of Walt Whitman* (London: Methuen, 1905);

Edward Carpenter, *Days with Walt Whitman* (London: George Allen, 1906);

Bliss Perry, *Walt Whitman* (Boston: Houghton, Mifflin, 1906);

Horace Traubel, *With Walt Whitman in Camden, March 28–July 14, 1888* (Boston: Small, Maynard, 1906);

Traubel, *With Walt Whitman in Camden, July 16–October 31, 1888* (New York: Appleton, 1908);

James Thomson, *Walt Whitman: The Man and the Poet* (London: Dobell, 1910);

W. C. Rivers, *Walt Whitman's Anomaly* (London: George Allen, 1913);

Traubel, *With Walt Whitman in Camden, November 1, 1888–January 20, 1889* (New York: Kennerley, 1914);

Walt Whitman, as Man, Poet and Friend, edited by Charles N. Elliot (Boston: Badger, 1915);

John Johnston and J. W. Wallace, *Visits to Walt Whitman in 1890–1891 by Two Lancashire Friends* (New York: Egmont Arens, 1918);

Leon Bazalgette, *Walt Whitman*, translated by Ellen Fitzgerald (Garden City, N.Y.: Doubleday, Page, 1920);

Elizabeth Leavitt Keller, *Walt Whitman in Mickle Street* (New York: Kennerley, 1921);

John Bailey, *Walt Whitman* (New York: Macmillan, 1926);

Emory Holloway, *Whitman: An Interpretation in Narrative* (New York: Knopf, 1926);

Cameron Rogers, *The Magnificent Idler: The Story of Walt Whitman* (Garden City, N.Y.: Doubleday, Page, 1926);

Harrison S. Morris, *Walt Whitman: A Brief Biography with Reminiscences* (Cambridge, Mass.: Harvard University Press, 1929);

Clara Barrus, *Whitman and Burroughs: Comrades* (Boston: Houghton Mifflin, 1931);

Edgar Lee Masters, *Whitman* (New York: Scribners, 1937);

Babette Deutsch, *Walt Whitman: Builder for America* (New York: Messner, 1941);

Frances Winwar, *American Giant: Walt Whitman and His Times* (New York: Harper, 1941);

Hugh I'Anson Faussett, *Walt Whitman: Poet of Democracy* (New Haven: Yale University Press, 1942);

Henry Seidel Canby, *Walt Whitman: An American* (Boston: Houghton Mifflin, 1943);

Frederik Schyberg, *Walt Whitman*, translated by Evie Allison Allen (New York: Columbia University Press, 1951);

Gay Wilson Allen, *The Solitary Singer: A Critical Biography of Walt Whitman* (New York: Macmillan, 1955; revised edition, New York: New York University Press, 1967);

Traubel, *With Walt Whitman in Camden, January 21–April 7, 1889*, edited by Sculley Bradley (Carbondale: Southern Illinois University Press, 1959);

Roger Asselineau, *The Evolution of Walt Whitman: The Creation of a Personality* (Cambridge, Mass.: Harvard University Press, 1960);

Holloway, *Free and Lonesome Heart: The Secret of Walt Whitman* (New York: Vantage, 1960);

Gay Wilson Allen, *Walt Whitman* (New York: Grove, 1961);

James E. Miller Jr., *Walt Whitman* (New York: Twayne, 1962; revised, 1990);

Traubel, *With Walt Whitman in Camden, April 8–September 14, 1889*, edited by Gertrude Traubel (Carbondale: Southern Illinois University Press, 1964);

Adrien Stoutenburg and Laura Nelson Baker, *Listen America: A Life of Walt Whitman* (New York: Scribners, 1968);

Barbara Marinacci, *O Wondrous Singer! An Introduction to Walt Whitman* (New York: Dodd, Mead, 1970);

Thomas L. Brasher, *Whitman as Editor of the* Brooklyn Daily Eagle (Detroit: Wayne State University Press, 1973);

Justin Kaplan, *Walt Whitman: A Life* (New York: Simon & Schuster, 1980);

Walter H. Eitner, *Walt Whitman's Western Jaunt* (Lawrence: Regents Press of Kansas, 1981);

Traubel, *With Walt Whitman in Camden, September 15, 1889–July 6, 1890*, edited by Gertrude Traubel and William White (Carbondale: Southern Illinois University Press, 1982);

Paul Zweig, *Walt Whitman: The Making of the Poet* (New York: Basic Books, 1984);

Whitman in His Own Time, edited by Joel Myerson (Detroit: Omnigraphics, 1991);

Philip Callow, *From Noon to Starry Night: A Life of Walt Whitman* (Chicago: Ivan R. Dee, 1992);

Traubel, *With Walt Whitman in Camden, July 7, 1890–February 10, 1891,* edited by Jeanne Chapman and Robert MacIsaac (Carbondale: Southern Illinois University Press, 1992);

Philip W. Leon, *Walt Whitman and Sir William Osler: A Poet and His Physician* (Toronto: ECW, 1995);

Catherine Reef, *Walt Whitman* (New York: Clarion, 1995);

David S. Reynolds, *Walt Whitman's America: A Cultural Biography* (New York: Knopf, 1995);

Traubel, *With Walt Whitman in Camden, February 11, 1891–September 30, 1891,* edited by Chapman and MacIsaac (Oregon House, Cal.: W. L. Bentley, 1996);

Traubel, *With Walt Whitman in Camden, October 1, 1891–April 3, 1892,* edited by Chapman and MacIsaac (Oregon House, Cal.: W. L. Bentley, 1996);

Gary Schmidgall, *Walt Whitman: A Gay Life* (New York: Dutton, 1997);

Joann P. Krieg, *A Whitman Chronology* (Iowa City: University of Iowa Press, 1998);

Jerome Loving, *Walt Whitman: The Song of Himself* (Berkeley: University of California Press, 1999);

Roy Morris Jr., *The Better Angel: Walt Whitman in the Civil War* (New York: Oxford University Press, 2000).

References:

Philip Akers, *The Principle of Life: A New Concept of Reality Based on Walt Whitman's* Leaves of Grass (New York: Vantage, 1991);

Marion Walker Alcaro, *Walt Whitman's Mrs. G: A Biography of Anne Gilchrist* (Rutherford, N.J.: Fairleigh Dickinson University Press, 1991);

Gay Wilson Allen, *The New Walt Whitman Handbook* (New York: New York University Press, 1975);

Allen, *A Reader's Guide to Walt Whitman* (New York: Farrar, Straus & Giroux, 1970);

Allen, *Walt Whitman as Man, Poet, and Legend* (Carbondale: Southern Illinois University Press, 1961);

Allen, ed., *Walt Whitman Abroad: Critical Essays from Germany, France, Scandinavia, Russia, Italy, Spain, and Latin America, Israel, Japan, and India* (Syracuse, N.Y.: Syracuse University Press, 1955);

Allen and Ed Folsom, eds., *Walt Whitman and the World* (Iowa City: University of Iowa Press, 1995);

Newton Arvin, *Whitman* (New York: Macmillan, 1938);

Harold Aspiz, *Walt Whitman and the Body Beautiful* (Urbana: University of Illinois Press, 1980);

Roger Asselineau, *The Evolution of Walt Whitman: The Creation of a Book* (Cambridge, Mass.: Harvard University Press, 1962);

Asselineau and William White, eds., *Walt Whitman in Europe Today: A Collection of Essays* (Detroit: Wayne State University Press, 1972);

Mark Bauerlein, *Whitman and the American Idiom* (Baton Rouge: Louisiana State University Press, 1991);

Christopher Beach, *The Politics of Distinction: Whitman and the Discourses of Nineteenth-Century America* (Athens: University of Georgia Press, 1996);

Joseph Beaver, *Walt Whitman: Poet of Science* (New York: King's Crown Press, 1951);

Joan D. Berbrich, *Three Voices from Paumanok: The Influence of Long Island on James Fenimore Cooper, William Cullen Bryant, Walt Whitman* (Port Washington, N.Y.: Ira J. Friedman, 1969);

Dennis Berthold and Kenneth M. Price, eds., *Dear Brother Walt: The Letters of Thomas Jefferson Whitman* (Kent, Ohio: Kent State University Press, 1984);

Henry Bryan Binns, *Walt Whitman & His Poetry* (London: Harrap, 1915);

Stephen A. Black, *Whitman's Journey into Chaos* (Princeton: Princeton University Press, 1975);

Harold Blodgett, *Walt Whitman in England* (Ithaca, N.Y.: Cornell University Press, 1934);

Harold Bloom, ed., *Walt Whitman* (New York: Chelsea House, 1985);

Helena Born, *Whitman's Ideal Democracy* (Boston: Everett, 1902);

Arthur E. Briggs, *Walt Whitman: Thinker and Artist* (New York: Philosophical Library, 1952);

Richard Maurice Bucke, *Cosmic Consciousness* (New York: Dutton, 1923);

Bucke, Horace Traubel, and Thomas B. Harned, eds., *In Re Walt Whitman* (Philadelphia: McKay, 1893);

John Burroughs, *Whitman: A Study* (Boston: Houghton, Mifflin, 1896);

Edwin H. Cady and Louis J. Budd, eds., *On Whitman: The Best from American Literature* (Durham, N.C.: Duke University Press, 1987);

Marina Camboni, ed., *Utopia in the Present Tense: Walt Whitman and the Language of the New World* (Rome: Il Calamo, 1994);

E. Fred Carlisle, *The Uncertain Self: Whitman's Drama of Identity* (East Lansing: Michigan State University Press, 1973);

Edward Carpenter, *Some Friends of Walt Whitman: A Study in Sex-Psychology* (London, 1924);

George Rice Carpenter, *Walt Whitman* (New York: Macmillan, 1909);

David Cavitch, *My Soul and I: The Inner Life of Walt Whitman* (Boston: Beacon, 1985);

Sherry Ceniza, *Walt Whitman and Nineteenth-Century Women Reformers* (Tuscaloosa: University of Alabama Press, 1998);

V. K. Chari, *Whitman in the Light of Vedantic Mysticism: An Interpretation* (Lincoln: University of Nebraska Press, 1965);

Richard Chase, *Walt Whitman* (Minneapolis: University of Minnesota Press, 1961);

Chase, *Walt Whitman Reconsidered* (New York: Sloane, 1955);

Leadie M. Clark, *Walt Whitman's Conception of the American Common Man* (New York: Philosophical Library, 1955);

Graham Clarke, *Walt Whitman: The Poem as Private History* (London: Vision, 1991);

Keith V. Comer, *Strange Meetings: Walt Whitman, Wilfred Owen and the Poetry of War* (Lund, Sweden: Lund University Press, 1996);

Thomas Edward Crawley, *The Structure of* Leaves of Grass (Austin: University of Texas Press, 1970);

Hans-Günther Cwojdrak, *Walt Whitman: Dichter und Demokrat Amerikas* (Hamburg: Phönix-Verlag, 1946);

Robert Leigh Davis, *Whitman and the Romance of Medicine* (Berkeley: University of California Press, 1997);

Basil de Selincourt, *Walt Whitman: A Critical Study* (London: Secker, 1914);

James Dougherty, *Walt Whitman and the Citizen's Eye* (Baton Rouge: Louisiana State University Press, 1993);

Geoffrey Dutton, *Whitman* (New York: Grove, 1961);

Edwin Harold Eby, *A Concordance of Walt Whitman's* Leaves of Grass *and Selected Prose Writings,* 5 volumes (Seattle: University of Washington Press, 1949–1955);

Betsy Erkkila, *Walt Whitman among the French* (Princeton: Princeton University Press, 1980);

Erkkila, *Whitman the Political Poet* (New York: Oxford University Press, 1989);

Erkkila and Jay Grossman, eds., *Breaking Bounds: Whitman and American Cultural Studies* (New York: Oxford University Press, 1996);

Robert D. Faner, *Walt Whitman and Opera* (Philadelphia: University of Pennsylvania Press, 1951);

Ed Folsom, *Walt Whitman's Native Representations* (Cambridge: Cambridge University Press, 1994);

Folsom, ed., *Walt Whitman: The Centennial Essays* (Iowa City: University of Iowa Press, 1994);

Folsom, Jim Perlman, and Dan Campion, eds., *Walt Whitman: The Measure of His Song* (Minneapolis: Holy Cow! 1981; revised edition, Duluth, Minn.: Holy Cow! 1998);

Byrne R. S. Fone, *Masculine Landscapes: Walt Whitman and the Homoerotic Text* (Carbondale: Southern Illinois University Press, 1992);

Florence Bernstein Freedman, *William Douglas O'Connor: Walt Whitman's Chosen Knight* (Athens: Ohio University Press, 1985);

José Gabriel, *Walt Whitman: La Voz Democrática de América* (Montevideo, Uruguay: Deibo, 1944);

Kenneth F. Gambone, ed., *Remembering Walt Whitman* (N.p.: Walnut Leaf, 1992);

William Gay, *Walt Whitman: His Relation to Science and Philosophy* (Melbourne, Australia: Firth & M'Cutcheon, 1895);

Arthur Golden, ed., *Walt Whitman: A Collection of Criticism* (New York: McGraw-Hill, 1974);

Mauricio González de la Garza, *Walt Whitman: Racista, Imperialista, Antimexicano* (Mexico City: Colección Malaga, 1971);

Douglas Grant, *Walt Whitman and His English Admirers* (Leeds, U.K.: Leeds University Press, 1962);

Ezra Greenspan, *Walt Whitman and the American Reader* (Cambridge: Cambridge University Press, 1990);

Greenspan, ed., *The Cambridge Companion to Walt Whitman* (Cambridge: Cambridge University Press, 1995);

Walter Grünzweig, *Constructing the German Walt Whitman* (Iowa City: University of Iowa Press, 1995);

Grünzweig, *Walt Whitmann: Die deutschsprachige Rezeption als interkulturelles Phänomen* (Munich: Fink, 1991);

William N. Guthrie, *Walt Whitman, Camden Sage* (Cincinnati: Robert Clarke, 1897);

Jessica Haigney, *Walt Whitman and the French Impressionists* (Lewiston, Me.: Edwin Mellen Press, 1990);

Will Hayes, *Walt Whitman: The Prophet of the New Era* (London: C. W. Daniel, 1921);

Ronald Hayman, *Arguing with Walt Whitman* (London: Covent Garden Press, 1971);

Milton Hindus, ed., Leaves of Grass: *One Hundred Years After* (Stanford, Cal.: Stanford University Press, 1955);

Hindus, ed., *Walt Whitman: The Critical Heritage* (London: Routledge & Kegan Paul, 1971);

C. Carroll Hollis, *Language and Style in* Leaves of Grass (Baton Rouge: Louisiana State University Press, 1983);

Guiyou Huang, *Whitmanism, Imagism, and Modernism in China and America* (Selinsgrove, Pa.: Susquehanna University Press, 1997);

George B. Hutchinson, *The Ecstatic Whitman: Literary Shamanism and the Crisis of the Union* (Columbus: Ohio State University Press, 1986);

Matthew F. Ignoffo, *What the War Did to Whitman* (New York: Vantage, 1975);

William Sloane Kennedy, *The Fight of a Book for the World* (West Yarmouth, Mass.: Stonecroft Press, 1926);

M. Jimmie Killingsworth, *The Growth of* Leaves of Grass: *The Organic Tradition in Whitman Studies* (Columbia, S.C.: Camden House, 1993);

Killingsworth, *Whitman's Poetry of the Body: Sexuality, Politics, and the Text* (Chapel Hill: University of North Carolina Press, 1989);

Martin Klammer, *Whitman, Slavery, and the Emergence of* Leaves of Grass (University Park: Pennsylvania State University Press, 1995);

Bettina L. Knapp, *Walt Whitman* (New York: Continuum, 1993);

George Knox and Henry Lawton, eds., *The Whitman-Hartmann Controversy: Including Conversations with Walt Whitman and Other Essays* (Bern: Herbert Lang, 1976);

Lawrence Kramer, ed., *Walt Whitman and Modern Music* (New York: Garland 2000);

Joann P. Krieg, *Whitman and the Irish* (Iowa City: University of Iowa Press, 2000);

Krieg, ed., *Walt Whitman: Here and Now* (Westport, Conn.: Greenwood Press, 1985);

David Kuebrich, *Minor Prophecy: Walt Whitman's New American Religion* (Bloomington: Indiana University Press, 1989);

Donald D. Kummings, ed., *Approaches to Teaching Whitman's* Leaves of Grass (New York: Modern Language Association, 1990);

Kummings and J. R. LeMaster, eds., *Walt Whitman: An Encyclopedia* (New York: Garland, 1998);

Kerry C. Larson, *Whitman's Drama of Consensus* (Chicago: University of Chicago Press, 1988);

Harry Law-Robertson, *Walt Whitman in Deutschland* (Giessen: Munchowsche Universitäts, 1935);

R. W. B. Lewis, ed., *The Presence of Walt Whitman* (New York: Columbia University Press, 1962);

Haniel Long, *Walt Whitman and the Springs of Courage* (Santa Fe, N.Mex.: Writers' Editions, 1938);

Jerome Loving, *Emerson, Whitman, and the American Muse* (Chapel Hill: University of North Carolina Press, 1982);

Loving, *Walt Whitman's Champion: William Douglas O'Connor* (College Station: Texas A&M University Press, 1978);

Loving, ed., *Civil War Letters of George Washington Whitman* (Durham, N.C.: Duke University Press, 1975);

Artem Lozynsky, ed., *Richard Maurice Bucke, Medical Mystic: Letters of Dr. Bucke to Walt Whitman and His Friends* (Detroit: Wayne State University Press, 1977);

Luke Mancuso, *The Strange Sad War Revolving: Walt Whitman, Reconstruction, and the Emergence of Black Citizenship, 1865–1876* (Columbia, S.C.: Camden House, 1997);

Ivan Marki, *The Trial of the Poet: An Interpretation of the First Edition of* Leaves of Grass (New York: Columbia University Press, 1976);

Robert K. Martin, ed., *The Continuing Presence of Walt Whitman: The Life after the Life* (Iowa City: University of Iowa Press, 1992);

F. O. Matthiessen, *American Renaissance: Art and Expression in the Age of Emerson and Whitman* (New York: Oxford University Press, 1941);

Maurice Mendelson, *Life and Work of Walt Whitman: A Soviet View* (Moscow: Progress Publishers, 1976);

Charles R. Metzger, *Thoreau and Whitman: A Study of Their Aesthetics* (Seattle: University of Washington Press, 1961);

Diane Wood Middlebrook, *Walt Whitman and Wallace Stevens* (Ithaca, N.Y.: Cornell University Press, 1974);

Edwin Haviland Miller, *Walt Whitman's Poetry: A Psychological Journey* (Boston: Houghton Mifflin, 1968);

Miller, *Walt Whitman's "Song of Myself": A Mosaic of Interpretations* (Iowa City: University of Iowa Press, 1989);

Miller, ed., *The Artistic Legacy of Walt Whitman: A Tribute to Gay Wilson Allen* (New York: New York University Press, 1970);

Miller, ed., *A Century of Whitman Criticism* (Bloomington: Indiana University Press, 1969);

James E. Miller Jr., *A Critical Guide to* Leaves of Grass (Chicago: University of Chicago Press, 1955);

Miller, Leaves of Grass: *America's Lyric-Epic of Self and Democracy* (New York: Twayne, 1992);

Miller, Karl Shapiro, and Bernice Slote, *Start with the Sun: Studies in the Whitman Tradition* (Lincoln: University of Nebraska Press, 1960);

Katherine Molinoff, *Some Notes on Whitman's Family: Mary Elizabeth Whitman, Edward Whitman, Andrew and Jesse Whitman, Hannah Louisa Whitman* (Brooklyn, N.Y.: Printed for the author, 1941);

Michael Moon, *Disseminating Whitman: Revision and Corporeality in* Leaves of Grass (Cambridge, Mass.: Harvard University Press, 1991);

S. Musgrove, *T. S. Eliot and Whitman* (Wellington: New Zealand University Press, 1952);

O. K. Nambiar, *Walt Whitman and Yoga* (Bangalore, India: Jeevan, 1966);

Tenney Nathanson, *Whitman's Presence: Body, Voice, and Writing in* Leaves of Grass (New York: New York University Press, 1992);

James Nolan, *Poet-Chief: The Native American Poetics of Walt Whitman and Pablo Neruda* (Albuquerque: University of New Mexico Press, 1994);

Ron Padgett, ed., *The Teachers & Writers Guide to Walt Whitman* (New York: Teachers and Writers Collaborative, 1991);

Roy Harvey Pearce, ed., *Whitman: A Collection of Critical Essays* (Englewood Cliffs, N.J.: Prentice-Hall, 1962);

Isaac Hull Platt, *Walt Whitman* (Boston: Small, Maynard, 1904);

Vivian Pollak, *The Erotic Whitman* (Berkeley: University of California Press, 2000);

Kenneth M. Price, *Whitman and Tradition: The Poet in His Century* (New Haven: Yale University Press, 1990);

Price, ed., *Walt Whitman: The Contemporary Reviews* (Cambridge: Cambridge University Press, 1996);

T. R. Rajasekharaiah, *The Roots of* Leaves of Grass: *Eastern Sources of Walt Whitman's Poetry* (Rutherford, N.J.: Fairleigh Dickinson University Press, 1970);

Hans Reisiger, *Walt Whitman* (Berlin: Suhrkamp, 1946);

Nathan Resnick, *Walt Whitman and the Authorship of the Good Gray Poet* (Brooklyn, N.Y.: Long Island University Press, 1948);

David Reynolds, ed., *A Historical Guide to Walt Whitman* (New York: Oxford University Press, 2000);

Richard H. Rupp, ed., *Critics on Whitman* (Coral Gables, Fla.: University of Miami Press, 1972);

John E. Schwiebert, *The Frailest Leaves: Whitman's Poetic Technique and Style in the Short Poem* (New York: Peter Lang, 1992);

Esther Shephard, *Walt Whitman's Pose* (New York: Harcourt, Brace, 1938);

Charley Shively, ed., *Calamus Lovers: Walt Whitman's Working Class Camerados* (San Francisco: Gay Sunshine, 1987);

Shively, ed., *Drum Beats: Walt Whitman's Civil War Boy Lovers* (San Francisco: Gay Sunshine, 1989);

Geoffrey M. Sill, ed., *Walt Whitman of Mickle Street: A Centennial Collection* (Knoxville: University of Tennessee Press, 1994);

Sill and Roberta K. Tarbell, eds., *Walt Whitman and the Visual Arts* (New Brunswick, N.J.: Rutgers University Press, 1992);

Jan Christian Smuts, *Walt Whitman: A Study of the Evolution of a Personality,* edited by Alan L. McLeod (Detroit: Wayne State University Press, 1973);

John Snyder, *The Dear Love of Man: Tragic and Lyric Communion in Walt Whitman* (The Hague: Mouton, 1975);

Floyd Stovall, *The Foreground of* Leaves of Grass (Charlottesville: University Press of Virginia, 1974);

John Addington Symonds, *Walt Whitman: A Study* (London: Routledge, 1893);

M. Wynn Thomas, *The Lunar Light of Whitman's Poetry* (Cambridge, Mass.: Harvard University Press, 1987);

Erik Ingvar Thurin, *Whitman between Impressionism and Expressionism* (Lewisburg, Pa.: Bucknell University Press, 1995);

Oscar L. Triggs, *Browning and Whitman: A Study in Democracy* (Chicago: University of Chicago Press, 1893);

W. H. Trimble, *Walt Whitman and* Leaves of Grass (London: Watts, 1905);

John Townsend Trowbridge, *My Own Story* (Boston: Houghton, Mifflin, 1903);

Randall H. Waldron, ed., *Mattie: The Letters of Martha Mitchell Whitman* (New York: New York University Press, 1977);

William English Walling, *Whitman and Traubel* (New York: Boni, 1916);

James Perrin Warren, *Walt Whitman's Language Experiment* (University Park: Pennsylvania State University Press, 1990);

Howard Waskow, *Whitman: Explorations in Form* (Chicago: University of Chicago Press, 1966);

Charles B. Willard, *Whitman's American Fame* (Providence, R.I.: Brown University Press, 1950);

James Woodress, ed., *Critical Essays on Walt Whitman* (Boston: G. K. Hall, 1983).

Papers:

The largest collection of manuscripts, proofs, and printed works relating to Walt Whitman is at the Library of Congress. Other significant collections are at the Duke University Library, the Harry Ransom Humanities Research Center at the University of Texas at Austin, and the Clifton Waller Barrett Library of American Literature in Special Collections at the University of Virginia Library.

Nathaniel Parker Willis

(20 January 1806 – 20 January 1867)

Kathleen Healey
Colby-Sawyer College

See also the entries on Willis in *DLB 3: Antebellum Writers in New York and the South; DLB 59: American Literary Critics and Scholars, 1800–1850; DLB 73: American Magazine Journalists, 1741–1850; DLB 74: American Short-Story Writers Before 1880;* and *DLB 183: American Travel Writers, 1776–1864.*

BOOKS: *Sketches* (Boston: S. G. Goodrich, 1827);

Fugitive Poetry (Boston: Pierce & Williams, 1829);

Poem Delivered Before the Society of United Brothers, at Brown University, on the Day Preceding Commencement, September 6, 1831 With Other Poems (New York: Harper, 1831);

Melanie and Other Poems, edited by Barry Cornwall (London: Saunders & Otley, 1835; enlarged edition, New York: Saunders & Otley, 1837);

Pencillings by the Way, 3 volumes (London: John Macrone, 1835; Philadelphia: Carey, Lea & Blanchard, 1836; revised and enlarged, London: George Virtue, 1842; revised and enlarged, New York: Morris & Willis, 1844);

Inklings of Adventure, 3 volumes (London: Saunders & Otley, 1836; New York: Saunders & Otley, 1836);

Al'Abri, or, The Tent Pitch'd (New York: Samuel Colman, 1839); enlarged as *Letters from Under a Bridge, together with Poems* (London: George Virtue, 1840; New York: Morris & Willis, 1844);

Bianca Visconti; or, the Heart Overtasked. A Tragedy in Five Acts (New York: Samuel Colman, 1839; republished as *Dying to Lose Him; or, Bianca Visconti* in *Two Ways of Dying for a Husband* (London: Hugh Cunningham, 1839);

Tortesa the Usurer (New York: Samuel Colman, 1839; republished as *Dying to Keep Him; or, Tortesa the Usurer* in *Two Ways of Dying for a Husband* (London: Hugh Cunningham, 1839);

American Scenery; or, Land, Lake, and River. Illustrations of Transatlantic Nature, 2 volumes, from drawings by William H. Bartlett (London: George Virtue, 1840; New York: R. Martin, 1840);

Nathaniel Parker Willis

Loiterings of Travel, 3 volumes (London: Longman, Orme, Brown, Green & Longmans, 1840; republished as *Romance of Travel; Comprising Tales of Five Lands,* volume 1 (New York: Samuel Colman, 1840);

Canadian Scenery, Illustrated, from drawings by Bartlett; (London: George Virtue, 1842);

The Scenery and Antiquities of Ireland, Illustrated, from drawings by Bartlett; by Willis and J. Stirling Coyne (London: George Virtue, 1842);

The Sacred Poems (New York: Morris, Willis, 1843);

Poems of Passion (New York: Morris, Willis, 1843);

The Lady Jane, and Other Humourous Poems (New York: Morris, Willis, 1844);

Lecture on Fashion, Delivered Before the New-York Lyceum, June, 1844 (New York: Morris, Willis, 1844);

Dashes at Life with a Free Pencil (New York: Burgess, Stringer, 1845; revised, London: Longmans, Brown, Green & Longmans, 1845);

The Complete Works of N. P. Willis (New York: J. S. Redfield, 1846);

The Prose Works of N. P. Willis (Philadelphia: Carey & Hart, 1849);

Rural Letters and Other Records of Thought at Leisure, Written in the Intervals of More Hurried Literary Labor (New York: Baker & Scribner, 1849; London: Wiley, 1849);

People I Have Met; or, Pictures of Society and People of Mark, Drawn under a Thin Veil of Fiction (New York: Baker & Scribner, 1850; London: Bentley, 1850);

Life Here and There; or, Sketches of Society and Adventure at Far-Apart Times and Places (New York: Baker & Scribner, 1850; London: Bohn, 1850);

Hurry-Graphs; or, Sketches of Scenery, Celebrities and Society, Taken From Life (New York: Charles Scribner, 1851; London: Bohn, 1851);

Summer Cruise in the Mediterranean, on Board an American Frigate (New York, 1853; London & Edinburgh: T. Nelson, 1853);

Fun Jottings; or, Laughs I Have Taken a Pen To (New York: Charles Scribner, 1853; republished as *Laughs I Have Put a Pen To,* London: Samuel Rowe, 1854);

A Health Trip to the Tropics (New York: Charles Scribner, 1853; London: Sampson Low, 1854);

Famous Persons and Places (New York: Charles Scribner, 1854);

Out-Doors at Idlewild; or, The Shaping of a Home on the Banks of the Hudson (New York: Charles Scribner, 1855; London: Trübner, 1855);

The Rag-Bag. A Collection of Ephemera (New York: Charles Scribner, 1855; London: Trübner, 1855);

Paul Fane; or, Parts of a Life Else Untold (New York: Charles Scribner, 1857; London: Sampson Low, 1857);

The Convalescent; His Rambles and Adventures (New York: Charles Scribner, 1859; London: Bohn, 1859).

PLAY PRODUCTIONS: *Bianca Visconti; or, the Heart Overtasked. A Tragedy in Five Acts,* New York, 1837; *Tortesa the Usurer,* New York, 1839.

PERIODICALS EDITED: *Youth's Companion* (Boston) (16 April 1827–1857);

American Monthly Magazine (Boston) (April 1829 – July 1831);

Corsair (New York) (16 March 1839 – 7 March 1840);

Dollar Magazine (New York) (1841–1842);

New Mirror (New York) (8 April 1843 – 28 September 1844);

New York Evening Mirror (7 October 1844–1859);

New York Weekly Mirror (12 October 1844 – 18 January 1845);

National Press (New York) (14 February 1846 – 14 November 1846); renamed *Home Journal* (21 November 1846–1867).

OTHER: *The Legendary, Consisting of Original Pieces, Principally Illustrative of American History, Scenery, and Manners,* edited by Willis (Boston: Samuel G. Goodrich, 1828; London: Kennett, 1829);

The Token; A Christmas and New Year's Present, edited by Willis (Boston: Samuel G. Goodrich, 1828);

The Opal: a Pure Gift for the Holy Days, edited by Willis (New York: John C. Riker, 1844);

The Sacred Rosary: A Select Volume of Serious Poetry, compiled and edited by Willis (New York: Morris & Willis, 1844);

A Library of the Prose and Poetry of Europe and America, compiled and edited by Willis and G. P. Morris (New York: Paine & Burgess, 1846);

The Gem of the Season, for 1850, edited by Willis (New York: Leavitt, 1850);

The Works of the Late Edgar Allan Poe: With Notices of His Life and Genius, by N. P. Willis, edited by Willis, James Russell Lowell, and Rufus W. Griswold, 2 volumes (New York: J. S. Redfield, 1850);

Memoranda of the Life of Jenny Lind, edited by Willis (Philadelphia: Robert E. Peterson, 1851);

Trenton Falls, Picturesque and Descriptive . . . Embracing the Original Essay of John Sherman, edited by Willis (New York: George P. Putnam, 1851);

The Thought-Blossom: A Memento, edited by Willis (New York: Leavitt & Allen, 1854).

Nathaniel Parker Willis was an astute magazine editor and one of the most versatile writers of his era. A prolific poet, magazine writer, and travel writer, Willis also wrote a novel and two plays. In addition, he edited several leading magazines and earned a reputation as a literary critic. One of the most outstanding features of Willis's career as an editor was his ability to know the public's reading tastes and to deliver skillfully what the public wanted. He brought the world of gossip, fashion, and high society to eager middle-class readers. At the same time, Willis

Willis's father, Nathaniel Willis, circa 1830 (painting by Chester Harding; from Thomas N. Baker, Sentiment & Celebrity: Nathaniel Parker Willis and the Trials of Literary Fame, *1999)*

up. Surrounded by the prominent families of Boston, Willis was preoccupied with his own lack of social standing and his desire to emulate his associates. This concern with social standing found its way into his writing later in his career. Willis's father encouraged the young Willis to write poetry and publish it.

Willis studied at the Boston Latin School and later at Andover in order to prepare to enter Yale University. While at Yale, Willis immersed himself in reading literature and also continued to write poetry of a scriptural nature, publishing his works in *The Boston Recorder* under the pseudonym "Roy." Some of his poems also appeared in *The Christian Examiner* and *The Connecticut Journal.* In 1826 Willis won a prize from *The Boston Recorder* for his poem "The Sacrifice of Abraham," and the following year he won a $50 prize for poems submitted to the *Philadelphia Album.* Also in 1827 he won a prize for his poem "Absalom." Willis graduated from Yale College in 1827, serving as the class valedictorian poet.

After graduation, Willis settled in Boston and acquired editorial experience, serving an apprenticeship under Samuel P. Goodrich on *The Legendary.* Willis also edited *The Token; A Christmas and New Year's Present,* a gift-book annual, in 1828, securing the works of authors such as Lydia Sigourney and John Neal. In 1829 Willis founded *The American Monthly Magazine,* a cultural periodical patterned after the literary and political magazines of England. The journal included a discussion of nonpartisan politics as well as literary criticism. Willis was a man of high social aspirations and also was known as a "natty" dresser. He carefully cultivated an editorial persona in *The American Monthly Magazine* of a man of fashion, humor, and refinement, chatting to his readers in a comfortable manner. Willis's articles and editorials reveal the breadth of his knowledge of literature and the arts as well as his interest in traveling. The pages of *The American Monthly Magazine* also included some of Willis's own material, such as poems and fictional pieces.

While Willis was a skilled and energetic editor, he had little business sense. Consequently, the magazine, because of increasing debt, folded shortly after the July 1831 issue. Willis left Boston and moved to New York because of his financial problems and also because the atmosphere in Boston was unfriendly toward him after he had incurred the wrath of other journalists and magazinists such as Joseph Buckingham, William Snelling, and Lydia Maria Child.

In New York, Willis found a much more congenial atmosphere and also the friendship of George Pope Morris, editor of *The New-York Mirror* since 1823. Morris had admired Willis's work, and in the

also wrote many essays about travel and nature. He brought the quiet joys of country life and the beauties of American scenery to a middle-class audience eager to experience nature in a romanticized pastoral setting.

Willis was born on 20 January 1806 in Portland, Maine. He came from a family of writers and editors. His grandfather had owned *The Boston Independent Chronicle* as well as newspapers in the frontier towns of western Virginia during the eighteenth century, and Willis's father had founded the *Eastern Argus* in Portland, Maine, in September 1803. Eventually, Willis's father became a Calvinist clergyman, combining his new vocation with his background as a journalist to found a religious newspaper. This venture was unsuccessful, and the elder Willis moved his family from Portland to Boston and established *The Boston Recorder* in 1816. Later, Willis's father founded the *Youth's Companion and Sabbath School Recorder,* a magazine for children that was published into the twentieth century.

The elder Willis's religious and journalistic careers had a strong influence on Nathaniel, as did the social milieu of Boston while Willis was growing

summer of 1831 he invited Willis to join him as co-editor of *The Mirror*. *The Mirror* was a magazine with a growing circulation that attempted to appeal to a broad audience. Its aim was to offer a combination of instructive literary pieces and amusement. Willis continued to write his chatty editorials on society and the world at large. He also encouraged Morris to send correspondents abroad to report upon events, persons, and places. This venture was successful for both *The Mirror* and Willis.

Willis set sail for Europe in October 1831 and began sending letters back to *The Mirror* after arriving in Le Havre, France, on 3 November. After these letters appeared in *The Mirror*, Willis collected, edited, and published many of them plus other material acquired during his travels abroad in *Pencillings by the Way* (1835). In these letters to *The Mirror*, Willis maintained the relaxed and friendly persona evident in his editorials, recording his experiences in a clear, impressionistic style. Willis stayed in Paris for six months, traveling to Italy on 16 April 1832. During his travels, Willis found he had a penchant for viewing art and visited many museums. The art and architecture he observed abroad complemented his literary sketches and stories. As Willis sketched people and locales with his pen, he drew on the details and scenes gleaned from artworks to bring his literary works to life. Willis's travels included stops in Greece, Turkey, Switzerland, and England. While in England, Willis published some of his sketches and short stories in various British periodicals; many of the stories and sketches later appeared in *The Mirror*. He also met Mary Leighton Stace, the woman who became his wife. The couple was married on 1 October 1835 and honeymooned in Paris. They eventually had a daughter, Imogen, who was born in 1842. Willis's travel letters—139 in all—were printed in *The Mirror* between 13 February 1832 and 14 January 1836.

Willis's popular travel sketches yielded *The Mirror* an increase in circulation. Many readers enjoyed stories about other countries, the private lives of members of the haut monde of London and New York, and the affairs of foreign literary figures. However, Willis's own prejudices and often outspoken commentaries left his editor to fend off attacks from various groups. For example, Willis criticized the wealth of the Roman Catholic cardinals in Rome, thus incurring the wrath of Catholic readers in America. At another time, Willis angered an extremist Protestant group. Willis was also accused of lacking good taste in some of what he published about certain people in British society. Morris refused to defend his roving reporter, an act that led to future

discord between the two editors. In 1839, after Willis wrote another scandalous story—this time about a British writer—Morris wrote a public apology. Consequently, Willis severed ties with *The Mirror*. Upon leaving *The Mirror*, Willis became co-editor of the journal *The Corsair* with Timothy O. Porter. The life of the journal was short. In 1840 it folded because of lack of financial support.

Throughout his years as an editor, Willis continued to write poetry. His poems may be classified as "sacred," "sentimental," and "occasional." His early poems were adaptations of biblical events, some of which appeared in *The American Monthly Magazine*. Earlier volumes of his poems include *Sketches* (1827) and *Fugitive Poetry* (1829). The 1837 edition of his verses, *Melanie and Other Poems*, included reprints of earlier works. Willis's poetry reflects the influence of English poets, revealing that Willis was well acquainted with the works of writers from the Elizabethan era through the early nineteenth century. In his own works, Willis followed the style of the eighteenth- and nineteenth-century Romantic poets, especially the works of George Gordon, Lord Byron. In Willis's "Melanie," for example, the narrator of the story, Rodolph de Brevern's son, is a Byronic hero, melancholy in temperament. The narrator travels to Italy with his sister, Melanie, who falls in love with a painter, Angelo. The brother becomes jealous yet accepts their love. At the moment the sister is to marry Angelo, a nun appears and states she is Angelo's mother and that Angelo is Melanie's half brother. The poem imitates Byron's works in tone, setting, and human relationships of the characters. Byron's influence is evident in many of Willis's poems, including "Lady Jane," a long poem similar to Byron's *Don Juan* (1819–1824) in elements of social and literary satire. Like other Romantics, Willis also often wrote of the beauties of nature and personal feelings. In "The Spring is Here," for example, Willis praises life close to nature: "We pass out from the city's feverish hum / To find refreshment in the silent woods; / and nature that is beautiful and dumb, / Like a cool sleep upon the pulses broods—." While readers today might find Willis's poetry unreadable, in its sentimentality and romanticism it appealed to the readers of his day, especially those who read the journals for which he wrote.

During the 1830s Willis successfully composed and staged two plays: *Bianca Visconti; or, the Heart Overtasked. A Tragedy in Five Acts* (first performed 1837; first published 1839) and *Tortesa the Usurer* (first performed 1839; first published 1839). Influenced by the popular Romantic traditions of his day as well as his many trips to various countries, the plays are

Willis's mother, Hannah Parker Willis, 1831 (oil painting by Chester Harding; Collection of the family of Hannah Locke Carter)

tragic and historical, written in blank-verse form. Both plays were first performed in New York. Willis won an award for *Bianca Visconti.*

The plot of *Bianca Visconti* centers on the character of Francesco Sforza, a man of "natural nobility." The play opens as Sforza learns he cannot marry his betrothed, Bianca Visconti, because her father, a count, feels Sforza is of low birth. The marriage takes place, but Sforza fears Bianca does not love him because he is not courtly enough. Sforza leaves her, and Bianca, deeply in love with him, mourns. The play includes political intrigue and plots to kill Sforza, who is a military hero. Once Bianca's father dies, she reveals her plan to give the crown to Sforza, an action that leads to another attempt on his life, planned by Giulio, the heir to the count's estate. Bianca, who has learned of the plot, saves Sforza by drugging Giulio and leaving him where Sforza usually sleeps. Thus, Giulio is killed in Sforza's place. However, Bianca loses her mind once Giulio is assassinated. She regains her sanity after Sforza is crowned but dies before he feels sorry for what he has done to her. As in his fiction, Willis is concerned in *Bianca Visconti* with the effects of social caste on human relationships. He juxtaposes true nobility of spirit with social ideals about birth and wealth and

demonstrates the damage that occurs from snobbery. Willis's experiences while traveling also play a significant role in the drama.

Tortesa the Usurer was also a successful play, derived from an Italian source as well as the works of William Shakespeare. In the play, Tortesa is engaged to Count Falcone's daughter, Isabella. Her father opposes the marriage but agrees to the match in order to gain lands and social position. The play has an intricate plot with confusion over love relationships. Isabella, for example, loves Angelo, a painter, who loves her in return. But another character, Zippa, also loves Angelo. Isabella feigns her death so that she does not have to marry Tortesa. Eventually, Tortesa duels with Angelo for the love of Isabella. At the end of the play Angelo marries Isabella and Tortesa marries Zippa. Willis reveals Tortesa's natural nobility toward the end of the play, demonstrating again that an individual's true worth comes from the spirit. In theme the play is about love conquering all, and thus it had a great appeal to contemporary audiences. Edgar Allan Poe, in a review of the play, noted it was "by far the best play from the pen of an American author." He found that despite some flaws, it was a good play, natural and truthful "in sentiment and language."

In 1840 Willis contracted with the British publisher George Virtue to write short essays for William H. Bartlett's book of landscape sketches, *American Scenery; or, Land, Lake, and River. Illustrations of Transatlantic Nature.* This project enabled Willis to realize his long-held desire to assemble "as much as possible of that part of the American story which history has not yet found leisure to put into form, and which romance and poetry have not yet appropriated—the legendary traditions and anecdotes. . . ." The landscapes depicted in *American Scenery* were favorites with American and European tourists—Niagara Falls, the Palisades, the Hudson River, the Highlands, the Susquehanna, and the Natural Bridge in Virginia. Other views included popular sites in America, such as Yale University, the Erie Canal, Mt. Vernon, and the White House. *American Scenery* was a popular coffee-table book that brought the scenery of America into middle-class homes.

By April 1843 Willis and Morris had resolved their differences and began work on a new venture, *The New Mirror. The New-York Mirror* had collapsed earlier in 1843. As with *The New-York Mirror,* the two editors approached their new journal with creativity and a good sense of what the public wanted to read. However, the costs of mailing the magazine were high. Despite a growing circulation rate, Willis and Morris ended *The New Mirror* in September 1844 and created the *New York Evening Mirror* and the *New York Weekly Mirror,* both newspapers that would have considerably lower postal rates than magazines. Upon the publication of their new newspaper, Willis and Morris invited a third man, Hiram Fuller, to become a partner. As with their earlier journalistic ventures, the focus of *The Evening Mirror* and *The Weekly Mirror* was literary and cultural, with a great deal of reporting about fashion and society. The newspapers appealed to American middle-class readers' interest in fashionable society and their desire to be cultured and refined.

Willis's wife, Mary, died in childbirth in 1845, and Willis, overcome with grief, once again traveled to Europe to act as correspondent for the new newspapers. However, Morris left the newspapers while Willis was in Europe, reportedly because Willis and Morris had learned that Fuller had been involved in an illegal activity. The *Evening Mirror* and *Weekly Mirror* are significant not only because of their connection to Willis but also because Walt Whitman may have worked for one of the newspapers for two or three weeks in October 1844. Edgar Allan Poe also joined the staff of the *Evening Mirror,* working as a subeditor and as a "mechanical paragraphist" until January 1845. In addition, Poe wrote and obtained materials for various columns in the *Evening Mirror.* Both Willis and Morris had a congenial relationship with Poe, often praising his works in their journals.

On 1 October 1846 Willis married Cornelia Grinnell, with whom he eventually had four children. Also in 1846, after Willis and Morris left the *Evening Mirror* and the *Weekly Mirror,* they edited a new newspaper named the *National Press.* Eight months later, they renamed the newspaper *The Home Journal,* which described better the contents of the periodical. The aim of the journal was to provide entertainment, news, and culture to be shared by families in their homes. The intention of the journal was to instruct and refine, and also to include society news. Eventually, *The Home Journal* moved to the barest reporting of serious news—focusing instead upon news of society and the fashionable world. In subject matter and tone, the newspaper was decidedly apolitical, insuring its popularity among readers of all political interests. The *Home Journal* also attempted to cater to the interests of female readers. Lives of society women were discussed, as were issues of manners, propriety, diet, and dress.

In addition, *The Home Journal* published the work of New Yorkers and included essays on the geography and history of the city. For example, issues of the newspaper included the works of Washington Irving, as well as commentaries about his life

Willis's first wife, Mary Leighton Stace Willis, in the early 1840s (Houghton Library, Harvard University)

and work, and the writing of Knickerbocker poets such as William Cullen Bryant. Poets who were not from New York—such as Henry Wadsworth Longfellow, Oliver Wendell Holmes, and John Greenleaf Whittier—also were featured in the newspaper. *The Home Journal* was successful until the Civil War, delivering amusement and culture to a broad audience.

In addition to his work as an editor, Willis was a prolific writer of short stories from the beginning of his career in the 1820s until he published his novel, *Paul Fane; or, Parts of a Life Else Untold* (1857). Willis's short stories are too numerous to treat in detail, but they have been compared to the work of Irving, especially in Willis's use of his travel experiences in his fiction. Willis wrote about the locales he saw during his travels, but he also wrote about the people he observed, their manners, and their customs. Not surprisingly, considering his youthful sense of social inferiority, many of Willis's stories are about society and social caste. Willis aspired to high social standing, yet he also despised the rigid social hierarchy he saw around him. Many of his short works are con-

1847 letter from Willis to Edgar Allan Poe, who worked for Willis's New York Evening Mirror *from September 1944 until January 1845 (from Richard Henry Stoddard, ed.,* The Works of Edgar Allan Poe, *volume 1 [London: Routledge, 1896])*

cerned with English high life and American fashionable life. The majority of the stories are romances, and many demonstrate Willis's sense of humor.

The years following the creation of the *National Press* and *The Home Journal* were the busiest of Willis's career. While he focused his energies upon his co-editorship of *The Home Journal,* he also continued to be a productive writer. During the 1850s and 1860s, he devoted much of his time to writing letter-essays and columns. Willis often was battling illness during this time, but he still wrote his weekly letters from Europe, Washington, the West Indies, Idlewild, or any other place in which he was traveling or recuperating. Many of his travel and contemplative essays were published in book form along with his short stories, poems, and sketches. Among these works are his books *Rural Letters and Other Records of Thought at Leisure, Written in the Intervals of More Hurried Literary Labor* (1849), *Letters from Under a Bridge, together with Poems* (1840), *Hurry-Graphs; or, Sketches of Scenery, Celebrities and Society, Taken From Life* (1851), *A Health Trip to the Tropics* (1853), *Famous Persons and Places* (1854), *Out-Doors at Idlewild; or, The Shaping of a Home on the Banks of the Hudson* (1855), and *The Convalescent; His Rambles and Adventures* (1859). *Rural Letters,* for example, included many letters that Willis had sent to Morris's *National Press* (New York) from various fashionable places such as Sharon Springs and Trenton Falls. In addition, the work includes many personal essays, reflective in nature, about places Willis lived, especially his home in Glenmary, Pennsylvania. These passages reveal Willis's feelings about his retreats and his interest in and love for the natural world. Similarly, Willis's *Out-Doors at Idlewild* includes a series of letters written from his home in Cornwall, New York, on the banks of the Hudson River.

Willis's book *Hurry-Graphs; or, Sketches of Scenery, Celebrities and Society, Taken From Life,* was a collection of travel essays sent to *The Home Journal* from various places in New England. In this work, Willis sketched the people and places of America, bringing to his readers vivid portraits of what he saw. Like other writers of his time, Willis drew on his knowledge of art and painterly techniques. For example, at one point in *Hurry-Graphs,* he noted that the people on Cape Cod were good subjects for painters. Willis had an appreciation for the beauty of nature and an eye for detail that he brought to his travel sketches.

During the 1850s Willis became involved in several publicized incidents that tarnished his already colorful reputation. One was the sensational divorce of Edwin and Catharine Forrest; Willis was named as one of Catharine Forrest's lovers. Eventually she was cleared of her involvement with various men, including Willis, but his connection to this dramatic melee remained in the public's memory. Following the Forrest scandal, Willis's sister Sara Willis Parton, in 1854, under the pseudonym "Fanny Fern," wrote her novel *Ruth Hall* (1855), in which she characterized Willis in an unflattering manner. Sara, then a widow, had suffered great financial and personal setbacks and had appealed to Willis to help her find publication for her writing. Willis refused to help his sister, stating that she had no chance to become a successful writer. Sara was hurt and enraged by his treatment but also determined to forge her career, a career that became quite successful. Willis appears in her novel, *Ruth Hall,* as Hyacinth Ellet, a self-serving and foppish editor with no redeeming qualities. Despite her use of a pseudonym, Sara's true identity was known by many, who also knew that the events in *Ruth Hall* were thinly veiled truth. Willis's relationship to Hyacinth Ellet became public knowledge, once more making Willis the target of gossip and intrigue.

In 1856 Willis wrote his only novel, *Paul Fane,* which was published in 1857. In this work, Willis brought together many of the themes and ideas he had dealt with in shorter pieces and sketches. The title character of the novel, Paul Fane, at his father's request, attends college to become a minister but really wishes to study art. Paul meets a woman, Mildred Ashly, who looks upon him as an inferior, leading Paul to contemplate the rigid social stratification based upon inheritance and blood. Paul travels to Italy to study art but also to contemplate further his position in society. In Italy, Paul meets many people of high society, including a princess, who talks about social issues and art with Paul. Paul once again meets the Ashly family, who all compliment his work but still see him as a social inferior. The novel includes romance and intrigue, for Paul is in love with a young woman, Sybil Paleford, who is being pursued by Mildred Ashly's brother, Arthur. Paul also disguises himself as a "Mr. Evenden" in order to paint a picture for Mildred Ashly's sister, Florence. Eventually Paul achieves recognition for his art in England but decides to return to America.

Paul Fane is, in many ways, Willis's autobiography. The main character is a young man whose father, like Willis's, wishes him to study for the ministry; yet the son pursues an artistic career instead. The novel deals with the themes evident in many of Willis's earlier stories and reflects his concern about social distinctions and class. Willis critiques a society that looks down upon others of different social standing who demonstrate true or "natural" nobility. Paul Fane is an individual with a noble spirit who, despite social standing, is superior to those deemed to be greater because of artificial social distinctions. Like Henry James, Willis attempted to define the relationship of America to Europe.

Despite frequent bouts with illness, Nathaniel Parker Willis remained active as editor and contributor to the *Home Journal* until his death. He died on his sixty-first birthday, 20 January 1867.

Biographies:

Henry E. Beers, *Nathaniel Parker Willis* (Boston: Houghton, Mifflin, 1885);

Kenneth L. Daughrity, "The Life and Works of Nathaniel P. Willis, 1806–1836," dissertation, University of Virginia, 1935;

Kenneth B. Taft, *Minor Knickerbockers* (New York: American Book, 1947).

References:

Cortland P. Auser, *Nathaniel P. Willis* (New York: Twayne, 1969);

Thomas N. Baker, *Sentiment & Celebrity: Nathaniel Parker Willis and the Trials of Literary Fame* (New York: Oxford University Press, 1999);

Richard P. Benton, "The Works of N. P. Willis as a Catalyst of Poe's Criticism," *American Literature,* 39 (1967): 315–324;

Charles A. Huguenin, "Nathaniel Parker Willis: His Literary Criticism of His Contemporaries," dissertation, St. John's University, 1940;

Edgar Allan Poe, "N. P. Willis," in *Complete Works of Edgar Allan Poe,* edited by James A. Harrison, volume 8 (New York: Putnam, 1902);

Robert E. Spiller, *The American in England* (New York: Henry Holt, 1926);

Sandra Tomc, "An Idle Industry: Nathaniel Parker Willis and the Workings of Literary Leisure," *American Quarterly,* 49 (December 1997): 780–805;

James Grant Wilson, *Bryant and His Friends: Some Reminiscences of the Knickerbocker Writers* (New York: Fords, Howard & Hulbert, 1886).

Papers:

Small holdings of Nathaniel Parker Willis's papers and correspondence are located in many libraries in the United States. The largest collection of Willis's manuscripts can be found at the Historical Society of Pennsylvania in Philadelphia. Other sizable collections include the Cornwall Public Library, Cornwall-on-Hudson Branch, Cornwall-on-Hudson, New York; the Beinecke Rare Book Room and Manuscript Library, Yale University; the New York Public Library; the Harry Ransom Humanities Research Center, University of Texas at Austin; and the Rare Book and Manuscript Library, Columbia University.

Samuel Woodworth
(Selim)
(13 January 1785 – 9 December 1842)

Anita G. Gorman
Slippery Rock University

BOOKS: *New-Haven, a Poem, Satirical and Sentimental, with Critical, Humorous, Descriptive, Historical, Biographical, and Explanatory Notes,* as Selim (New York: Printed for the author, 1809);

Beasts at Law, or Zoologian Jurisprudence; A Poem, Satirical, Allegorical, and Moral. In Three Cantos, translated from the Arabic of Sampfilius Philoerin, Z.Y.X.W. &c., &c. Whose Fables Have Made So Much Noise in the East, and Whose Fame Has Eclipsed That of Aesop (New York: Harmer, 1811);

The First Attempt, or, Something New: Being a Picture of Truth, Drawn From the Nature of Things As They Really Exist (New York: Halcyon, 1811);

Quarter-Day; or, The Horrors of the First of May: A Poem by the Author of Beasts at Law (New York: S. Woodworth, 1812);

Bubble & Squeak; or, A Dish of All Sorts. Being a Collection of American Poems, Published in New-York; Comprising Quarter-Day, or The Horrors of the First of May; Beasts at Law, or Zoologian Jurisprudence; The Fatal Amour; The Desponding Lovers, and The Capture and Shipwreck of the U.S. Brig Vixen (New York: Printed for the booksellers, 1814);

Champions of Freedom; or, The Mysterious Chief, a Romance of the Nineteenth Century, Founded on the Events of the War, Between the United States and Great Britain, Which Terminated in March, 1815 (New York: Charles N. Baldwin, 1816);

The Poems, Odes, Songs, and Other Metrical Effusions, of Samuel Woodworth (New York: Abraham Asten & Matthias Lopez, 1818);

The Deed of Gift: A Comic Opera in Three Acts (New York: C. N. Baldwin, 1822);

An Excursion of the Dog-Cart: A Poem by an Imprisoned Debtor (New York: William Bonker Jr., 1822);

La Fayette; or, The Castle of Olmutz. A Drama, in Three Acts, as Performed at the New-York Park Theatre, with Unbounded Applause (New York: Circulating Library and Dramatic Repository, 1824);

Samuel Woodworth (Clifton Waller Barrett Library, University of Virginia)

The Forest Rose; or, American Farmers (New York: Circulating Library and Dramatic Repository, 1825);

The Life and Confession of James Hudson, Who Was Executed on Wednesday the 12th of January, 1825 at the Falls of Fall Creek, for the Murder of Logan, an Indian Chief of the Wyandott Nation, To Which Is Added an Account of His Execution. The Whole Written and Published at the Request of the Deceased (Indianapolis: Gazette, 1825);

Ode for the Canal Celebration: Written at the Request of the Printers of New-York (New York: Clayton & Van Norden, 1825);

The Widow's Son; or, Which Is the Traitor? (New York: Circulating Library and Dramatic Repository, 1825);

Melodies, Duets, Trios, Songs and Ballads (New York: J. M. Campbell, 1826); revised as *Melodies, Duets, Trios, Songs, and Ballads, Pastoral, Amatory, Sentimental, Patriotic, Religious and Miscellaneous. Together With Metrical Epistles, Tales and Recitations* (New York: Elliot & Palmer, 1830; revised edition, New York: Elliot & Palmer, 1831);

Ode Written for the Celebration of the French Revolution, in the City of New-York, Nov. 25, 1830 (New York: James Conner, 1830);

Festivals, Games, and Amusements, Ancient and Modern, by Horatio Smith, With Additions by Samuel Woodworth (London: Colburn & R. Bentley, 1831; New York: J. & J. Harper, 1832);

Poetical Works of Samuel Woodworth, edited by Frederick A. Woodworth (New York: Scribner, 1861).

PLAY PRODUCTIONS: *The Deed of Gift,* Boston, The Boston Theatre, 25 March 1822;

La Fayette; or, The Castle of Olmutz, New York, Park Theatre, 23 February 1824;

The Forest Rose; or, American Farmers, New York, Chatham Theatre, 6 October 1825;

The Widow's Son; or, Which Is the Traitor? New York, Park Theatre, 25 November 1825;

The Cannibals; or, The Massacre Islands, New York, Bowery Theatre, 20 February 1833;

Blue Laws; or, Eighty Years Ago, New York, Bowery Theatre, 15 March 1833;

The Foundling of the Sea, New York, Bowery Theatre, 16 May 1833.

OTHER: *The Complete Coiffeur; or, An Essay on the Art of Adorning Natural, and of Creating Artificial, Beauty,* as John B. M. D. Lafoy (New York: Stereotyped for the proprietors, 1817);

A Narrative of Four Voyages to the South Sea, North and South Pacific Ocean, Chinese Sea, Ethiopic and Southern Atlantic Ocean, Indian and Antarctic Ocean, as Benjamin Morrell (New York: J. & J. Harper, 1832).

PERIODICALS EDITED: *Fly; or Juvenile Miscellany* (Boston) (16 October 1805 – 2 April 1806);

Belles-Lettres Repository (New Haven: 5 March 1808 – 16 April 1808);

Halcyon Luminary, and Theological Repository (New York) (January 1812 – December 1813);

New York War, edited by Woodworth (27 June 1812 – 6 September 1814);

New York Republican Chronicle (31 December 1817 – 25 July 1818);

New York Republican Chronicle & City Advertiser (4 March 1818 – 25 July 1818);

New York Ladies' Literary Cabinet (15 May 1819 – 5 August 1820);

Literary Casket, and Pocket Magazine (New York) (April 1821 – November 1821);

New-Jerusalem Missionary, and Intellectual Repository (May 1823 – April 1824);

New-York Mirror, and Ladies' Literary Gazette (2 August 1823 – 10 July 1824);

New York Parthenon, or, Literary and Scientific Museum (22 August 1827 – 8 December 1827).

Though largely forgotten in the twentieth and twenty-first centuries, Samuel Woodworth—journalist, poet, song lyricist, playwright, and editor—actively participated in the literary life of the United States during the nineteenth century and helped foster an American culture separate from that of England. The author of the first hit musical in American history, the writer of one of the best-loved nineteenth-century song lyrics, and a pioneer journalist, Woodworth praised the joys of agrarian life and of republicanism.

The fourth child of Benjamin Woodworth, a farmer and soldier in the American Revolution, and Abigail Bryant Woodworth, Samuel Woodworth was born in Scituate, Massachusetts, on 13 January 1785. His father—a sailor, carpenter, and farmer—failed to provide adequately for his family, and young Woodworth suffered from poor health, poverty, and little educational opportunity. When he was fourteen, he lived for the winter with the Reverend Nehemiah Thomas, under whose supervision he learned English and Latin grammar and read the classics, "but the unprofitable employment of writing verses, considerably retarded his more useful pursuits," according to a "Sketch of the Author's Life" by publishers Abraham Asten and Matthias Lopez, included in the 1818 collection of Woodworth's poems. Next Woodworth moved to Boston, where he became an apprentice to Benjamin Russell, editor of the *Columbian Centinel,* wrote for Boston magazines, and edited a juvenile paper, *The Fly* (named for the area over a theatrical stage housing overhead lights and other equipment), together with John Howard Payne, who later made a name as a writer, actor, and composer of the well-known lyric, "Home, Sweet Home." Woodworth also published poetry under various pseudonyms, most frequently Selim. In New Haven in 1808, he started *The Belles-Lettres Repository,* serving, in his own words, as "editor, publisher, printer, and very often, the carrier" of a publication that lasted less than two months.

After working in Boston, New Haven, and Baltimore, Woodworth moved in 1809 to New York City, where on 24 September 1810 he married Lydia Reeder, with whom he eventually had ten children. He earned some notice with the publication of three long satiric poems—*New-Haven, a Poem, Satirical and Sentimental, with Critical, Humorous, Descriptive, Historical, Biographical, and Explanatory Notes* (1809), *Beasts at Law, or Zoologian Jurisprudence; A Poem, Satirical, Allegorical, and Moral. In Three Cantos* (1811), and *Quarter-Day; or, The Horrors of the First of May: A Poem by the Author of Beasts at Law* (1812)—and began a printing business in 1811, which gave him some brief profit. From 1812 to 1814 Woodworth published *The New York War,* a weekly newspaper that reported events during the War of 1812. At this time Woodworth also edited *The Halcyon Luminary, and Theological Repository,* a monthly publication espousing Swedenborgianism. By 1815, having amassed debts of $15,000, he had to give up his own print shop and worked for a time in the printing shop of Charles N. Baldwin. Woodworth's 1816 novel, *The Champions of Freedom; or, The Mysterious Chief, a Romance of the Nineteenth Century, Founded on the Events of the War, Between the United States and Great Britain, Which Terminated in March, 1815,* combined fiction with facts about the War of 1812. The mysterious chief is a mythic Miami Indian killed in the battle of Fallen Timbers, the battle in which Major Willoughby loses his hand and drops the sword George Washington had presented him. When Willoughby wishes he had a son to inherit the sword, the chief's body speaks and says that he does in fact have a son. Mrs. Willoughby, at that very moment, is dying while giving birth to a son, who becomes the hero of the novel; the plot later reveals that the chief, who reappears at each of the crises in the hero's life, represents the spirit of Washington.

In the spring of 1817 Baldwin and Abraham Asten began to publish the *New York Republican Chronicle,* a semiweekly newspaper; Woodworth at first was put in charge of the literary department and by December had been named editor, a position that lasted just over six months; at that time Baldwin's business failed. *The Poems, Odes, Songs, and Other Metrical Effusions, of Samuel Woodworth,* published in 1818, presents Woodworth's verse in categories such as "Patriotic" and "Amatory." The book was favorably reviewed by a few critics. Competent and conventional, the verse praises family life and romantic love, as well as the nation—as in the "Inauguration Ode," written in honor of President James Monroe, which reads, in part:

> While the vassals of Tyranny rivet their chains
>   By birth-day effusions, and base adulation,
> Let freemen express, in their holiday strains,
>   The voice of a people—the choice of a nation.
>   Let laureats sing for the birth of a king,

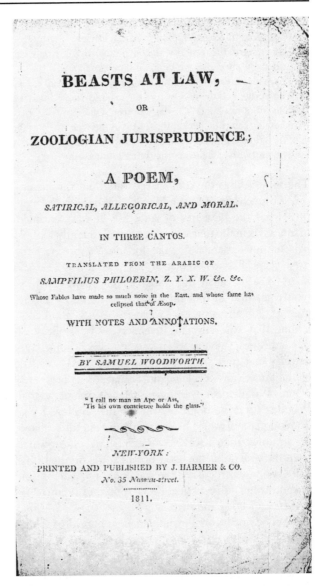

Title page for Woodworth's book-length satiric poem, supposedly based on a shorthand account by William Sampson of the trial of the Reverend William Parkinson on charges of committing assault and battery on Mrs. Eliza Wintringham in New York City

> 'Tis ours to rejoice for the first fruits of spring;
> For still shall the Fourth Day of March ever yield
> A harvest of glory in Liberty's field.

Woodworth's most famous song, "The Bucket," now known as "The Old Oaken Bucket," was published in the *New York Republican Chronicle* on 3 June 1818, reprinted in several publications, and linked to at least three musical settings. The melody most frequently associated with the lyric remains "Araby's Daughter" by George Kiallmark, an English violinist and composer. The first verse illustrates that the poetry is conventional while the subject matter is original:

How dear to this heart are the scenes of my childhood,
When fond recollection presents them to view,
The orchard, the meadow, the deep tangled wildwood,
And ev'ry lov'd spot which my infancy knew.
The wide-spreading stream, the mill that stood near it,
The bridge and the rock where the cataract fell;
The cot of my father, the dairy house by it,
And e'en the rude bucket that hung in the well.
The old oaken bucket, the iron-bound bucket,
The moss-cover'd bucket that hung in the well.

The song praises the cool, sweet water and the memories the poet has of his childhood, his father's "plantation," and the pleasures of rural life. It was reprinted many times in the nineteenth century, frequently anthologized, and remained popular for more than one hundred years. Samuel Kettell, in his *Specimens of American Poetry* (1829), called the song "a very happy performance, natural in thought and expression, and distinguished for the musical sweetness of its numbers," adding that "the engaging liveliness and simplicity of this little strain have made it very popular." Some controversy surrounds the origin of the poem. The Daughters of the American Revolution in Scituate, Massachusetts, where Woodworth was born, related the story that Woodworth came home on a warm day in New York, drank a glass of water from the pump, and after enjoying it, noted that it was not as refreshing as the water from the well at his boyhood home; at the urging of his wife, Woodworth created the song out of his memories. A contrasting story circulating in 1860 and reported in *The Home Journal*, the successor to *The New-York Mirror*, had Woodworth complimenting a man named Mallory, a New York hotelman, on the taste of the wine at the hotel, with Mallory responding that a cold drink from the farm wells of childhood would have been even more delicious. The true inspiration for this work, Woodworth's best known, remains obscure.

From 4 March 1818 through 25 July 1818 Woodworth worked as the editor of the daily *New York Republican Chronicle & City Advertiser*. His "Funeral Ode on the Obsequies of Montgomery" was recited in New York City on 4 and 18 July in the same year at the Pavilion Theatre, and on 10 July 1818 his song "Freedom's Jubilee" was sung; these mark the first public performances of Woodworth's work.

Woodworth edited several other journals, among them the *New York Ladies' Literary Cabinet* (1819–1820), a weekly in which the first of his serial novels, *Magnanimity*, appeared from May to October 1819; this story of Solon Woodville, a minister's son corrupted by the reading of novels, finds a parallel in a group of supposedly autobiographical essays written by Woodworth using the pseudonym Perry Doolittle in *The New-York Mirror* in 1833–1834. How much is based on Woodworth's life is difficult to determine. Both Doolittle and Woodville read romances to their detriment; both neglect their work on the farm; both fall in love with young women named Sophia; both are shy; and both use pretty cousins to camouflage their real love interests. From 22 January to 29 July 1820, Woodworth ran his second serial novel, *Resignation,* in the *Ladies' Literary Cabinet;* the novel, a Gothic romance, features a penniless heroine later revealed to be an heiress, escape from a brothel, a mysterious stranger revealed eventually as the heroine's father, and the prorepublican, antiaristocratic stance championed by Woodworth throughout his work. Forced to leave the unprofitable *Ladies' Literary Cabinet,* one of the first American periodicals to target a female audience, he next began *The Literary Cabinet,* a publication that lasted about one year.

Though not as well known as "The Bucket," Woodworth's song "The Hunters of Kentucky," originally called "New Orleans," enjoyed a great deal of popularity for decades and was still sung by folk-song enthusiasts well into the twentieth century. Noah Ludlow, a traveling player, received a copy of the song in 1821 and performed it, in his words, to "tremendous applause" and a standing ovation: "I had to sing the song three times that night before they would let me off." Using the tune "O Miss Bailey," the song praises the leadership of Andrew Jackson and the bravery of the Kentucky riflemen during the War of 1812. It begins,

Ye gentlemen and ladies fair,
  Who grace this famous city,
Just listen, if ye've time to spare,
  While I rehearse a ditty;
And for the opportunity,
  Conceive yourselves quite lucky,
For 'tis not often that you see,
  A hunter from Kentucky.
Oh! Kentucky, the hunters of Kentucky,
  The hunters of Kentucky.

The song even found its way into James Fenimore Cooper's 1827 novel *The Prairie;* bee-hunter Paul Hover whistles the "'Kentucky Hunters' as diligently as if he had been hired to supply his auditors with music by the hour."

In September 1821, Woodworth won second prize for a poem entered in a contest commemorating the reopening of the Park Theatre, destroyed by fire a year earlier. This prize poem, spoken by actress Mrs. Barnes before the theatrical performance on 3 September, displays Woodworth's patriotic and theatrical fervor. It reads, in part:

Ye generous freemen, who in danger stand
The shield and bulwark of your happy land;
Who, mid the sweeter luxuries of peace,

Behold your greatness and your arts increase,
Whose liberal minds throw lustre on the age,
Oh! still protect and patronize the stage;
That bright auxiliar in Refinement's cause,
Which raised proud Greece to what at length she was;
Invited forth and scattered unconfined
The boundless treasures of a Shakespeare's mind,
And taught the vulgar barbarous sons of strife
The gentler courtesies that sweeten life.

In 1821 Woodworth published a miniature journal, *Literary Casket and Pocket Magazine,* and on 25 March 1822 his first full-length theatrical production, *The Deed of Gift,* a type of operetta (with seven songs set to popular tunes), was performed in Boston and published in the same year. The play, which was not profitable, involves a young man whose inheritance is stolen by his brother and restored by the clever disguise and actions of his beloved. On 2 August 1823 Woodworth founded *The New-York Mirror, and Ladies' Literary Gazette* with George Pope Morris. Woodworth edited *The Mirror* for a short time but left in 1824 for reasons unknown, though he continued to contribute to the magazine and remained friends with Morris, who continued his association with *The Mirror* for forty years. Unfortunately, none of Woodworth's journalistic efforts turned the handsome profits that accrued to *The Mirror,* one of the most successful magazines in American literary history. During this period, he again edited a Swedenborgian periodical, this time *The New-Jerusalem Missionary, and Intellectual Repository,* which lasted less than a year. His second theatrical production, *La Fayette; or, The Castle of Olmutz,* had its New York premiere on 23 February 1824, a date marking George Washington's birthday and the impending return of Lafayette to the republic he helped bring about; it was also published that year. "Received," according to *The Mirror,* "with decided and deserved approbation," the play was performed half a dozen times in the next two years, including a gala performance on 9 September 1824 during Lafayette's visit to New York. The plot details the efforts of a German physician and an American to rescue Lafayette in 1792 from a German prison and includes a romance between the American and the daughter of the Austrian general who is keeping Lafayette a prisoner; with the exception of the romantic plot, the story is historically quite accurate. Woodworth's third theatrical effort, *The Forest Rose; or, American Farmers,* which debuted on 6 October 1825 at New York's Chatham Theatre, remains his most famous and successful play, even though, as the author confesses in the preface to the edition published in 1825, it was written in some haste. The plot concerns a country girl pursued by a foppish English villain. The heroine seems to agree to an elopement, but the villain is led to capture a servant instead. The heroine in the

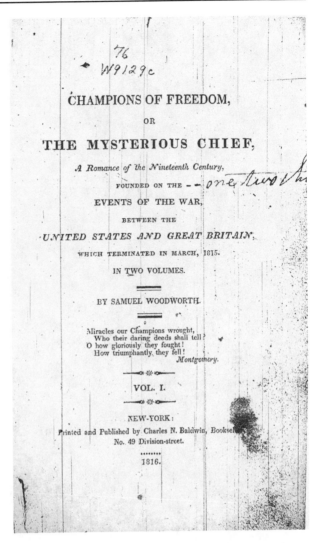

Title page for Woodworth's 1816 novel, in which an Indian chief utters a prophecy after being killed in the War of 1812

end is matched with her true love, a stalwart American farmer. Praised by critics as an "acquisition to our dramatic stock," the major appeal of the play lies in its promotion of America and in the character of Jonathan Ploughboy, the first stage Yankee enthusiastically received by theater audiences; Jonathan is a rustic, simple, awkward man who also shows shrewdness and ingenuity and provides much of the humor in the play. *The Forest Rose* strongly supports rural life over urban life, champions America over Britain, and concludes with a nine-stanza ode to the "Lords of the Soil."

Among the actors who performed the role of Jonathan Ploughboy were George Handel Hill, Danforth Marble, and Joshua Silsbee. *The Forest Rose* was first presented as a second feature to Edward Bulwer-Lytton's comedy *The Lady of Lyons* (first performed in 1838). For thirty-five years, however, *The Forest Rose* sustained popularity in its own right, playing in New York,

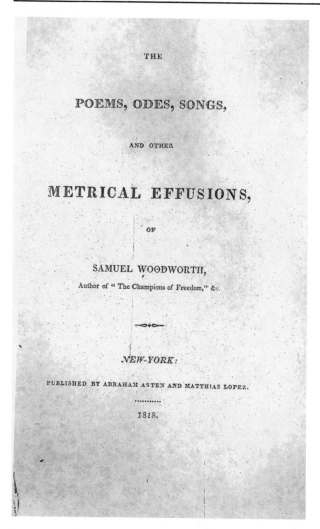

THE

POEMS, ODES, SONGS,

AND OTHER

METRICAL EFFUSIONS,

OF

SAMUEL WOODWORTH,

Author of " The Champions of Freedom," &c.

NEW-YORK:

PUBLISHED BY ABRAHAM ASTEN AND MATTHIAS LOPEZ.

1818.

Title page for Woodworth's 1818 collection of patriotic and romantic verse, published in the same year that his most famous work, the song "The Old Oaken Bucket," appeared in the New York Republican Chronicle

Philadelphia, New Orleans, St. Louis, Mobile, and California. Even the English enjoyed the play when it was produced at London's Adelphi Theatre, with Josh Silsbee playing Jonathan Ploughboy for ninety-nine performances. *The Forest Rose* was the first hit show of the American theater.

Less than a month after the premiere of *The Forest Rose*, another Woodworth play, *The Widow's Son; or, Which Is the Traitor?* opened in New York on 25 November 1825 at the Park Theatre. *The Widow's Son*, a drama about "Crazy Peg" Darby's espionage on behalf of Washington, lasted for only a few performances. Margaret Darby, whose husband died in General Wolfe's defeat in Quebec, came to America from Ireland with their sons. Her son William was arrested for Royalist tendencies and deserted the American forces to give plans for Fort Montgomery to General Clinton. The

widow's reaction to this event affected her economic, social, and mental health; she was soon living in a rocky glen, telling fortunes for a living, and known as the "Witch of Blagge's Cove"; these details are narrated in an introduction to the play published in 1825. The plot centers on Margaret's son and her concern for him; at the end of the play, the son is killed fighting a duel with an English officer and thereby is reconciled with his mother. Oral Sumner Coad, writing in the *Sewanee Review* in 1919, said of *The Widow's Son:* "The play is badly built; the scene shifts with the frequency of a moving-picture film, the interest is not properly centralized about the main characters, and there is an excess of incident."

Woodworth's collection, *Melodies, Duets, Trios, Songs and Ballads,* was published in 1826. In 1827 Woodworth functioned as an editor for the last time–at *The New York Parthenon, or, Literary and Scientific Museum,* a literary magazine that survived for only sixteen weeks. When his 1830 collection, *Melodies, Duets, Trios, Songs, and Ballads, Pastoral, Amatory, Sentimental, Patriotic, Religious and Miscellaneous. Together With Metrical Epistles, Tales and Recitations* was published, the critic for *The Mirror,* commenting that "the poetry of a people is a correct transcript of their national character," added that Woodworth's poems reflected the American character, "as it abounds with sentiments of patriotism, descriptions of rural pleasures and enjoyments, and the endearments of domestic relations."

During 1833 Woodworth's *The Cannibals; or, The Massacre Islands* was produced, though not published; the play was based on the *Narrative of Four Voyages* (1832) by Benjamin Morrell, a book ghostwritten by Woodworth with the help of notes provided by Morrell. In the same year, *Blue Laws; or, Eighty Years Ago,* an unpublished farce, debuted on 15 March and lasted for five performances. The third Woodworth play produced in 1833, *The Foundling of the Sea,* was entered in a contest sponsored by actor George Handel Hill. Although the judges of the contest decided that no entry deserved a reward, Hill himself presented the prize of $400 to Woodworth and performed in the productions in both Philadelphia and New York. This unpublished play takes place at a spa, where a widower from Boston visits his friend, whose daughter is courted by two William Smiths. The heroine's life is saved by Zachariah Dickerwell, a Yankee peddler revealed to be the long-lost son of the man from Boston.

Plagued by financial uncertainty for most of his life, Woodworth gave up his literary career and from 1835 to 1836 worked as a clerk in the Boston Navy Yard until his deteriorating eyesight put an end to gainful employment. On 6 February 1837 he endured the first of several paralytic strokes, forcing him to spend the rest of his life as an invalid. Two theatrical benefits in the fall of 1837 provided him with some income, and he continued to contribute essays and poetry to assorted periodicals. An anonymous 1839 volume of religious essays, *Sunday Morning Reflections,* often attributed to Woodworth, includes excerpts from earlier Woodworth writings and espouses the Swedenborgianism that commanded his allegiance for his entire adult life. He died in New York City on 9 December 1842. In 1864, Woodworth's son, Selim E. Woodworth, a naval commander stationed in San Francisco, removed his father's body to Laurel Hill Cemetery in San Francisco. With the passing of new cemetery regulations at the beginning of the twentieth century, Woodworth family members had the remains cremated, "leaving the tomb, now the sport of winds, in the cemetery to await the wreckers," according to *The San Francisco Chronicle* (1 July 1937).

Today, although even his most famous work, "The Old Oaken Bucket," has nearly been forgotten, Samuel Woodworth ought to be remembered for his role in editing and publishing many American periodicals, for promoting a national literature, for enhancing the American theater, and for writing two lyrics that gave pleasure for more than one hundred years.

References:

Oral Sumner Coad, "The Plays of Samuel Woodworth," *Sewanee Review,* 27 (April 1919): 163–175;

Samuel Kettell, *Specimens of American Poetry with Critical and Biographical Notices* (Boston: Goodrich, 1829);

Richard Moody, ed., *Dramas from the American Theatre 1762–1909* (New York: Houghton Mifflin, 1969);

Burton R. Pollin, "The 'Narrative' of Benjamin Morrell: Out of 'The Bucket' and into Poe's 'Pym,'" *Studies in American Fiction,* 4, no. 2 (1976): 157–172;

Thomas Robert Price, "Samuel Woodworth and Theodore Sedgwick Fay: Two Nineteenth-Century American Literati," dissertation, Pennsylvania State University, 1970;

Arthur Hobson Quinn, *A History of the American Drama: From the Beginning to the Civil War* (New York: Harper, 1923);

Kendall B. Taft, "Samuel Woodworth," dissertation, University of Chicago, 1937;

Taft, "Samuel Woodworth," part of a dissertation, University of Chicago, 1938;

Taft, ed., *Minor Knickerbockers: Representative Selections, with Introduction, Bibliography, and Notes* (New York: American Book, 1947);

George M. Young, "The Author of 'The Old Oaken Bucket,'" *New England Magazine,* 5 (September 1891–February 1892): 661–662.

Papers:

Some of Samuel Woodworth's papers are in the Special Collections Department, University of Virginia Library, Charlottesville. Research notes, photographs, and copies of manuscripts concerning Samuel Woodworth and assembled by Kendall B. Taft are housed at the Library of the New York State Historical Association, Cooperstown.

Books for Further Reading

The following selective list should be of interest to those who want to read further about antebellum literature in New York and the South. The list is limited, for the most part, to works that deal with American literature from 1815 to 1865. Those who wish additional suggestions may consult *Eight American Authors,* edited by James Woodress; *Fifteen American Authors Before 1900,* edited by Robert A. Rees and Earl N. Harbert; *Articles in American Literature,* 3 volumes, edited by Lewis Leary; the annual *PMLA* bibliography; the annual bibliography in *Mississippi Quarterly;* and *American Literary Scholarship: An Annual.*

Aaron, Daniel. *The Unwritten War: American Writers and the Civil War.* New York: Knopf, 1973.

Adams, Grace and Edward Hutter. *The Mad Forties.* New York: Harper, 1942.

Alderman, Edwin A. and Joel Chandler Harris, eds. *A Library of Southern Literature,* 17 volumes. New Orleans & Atlanta: Martin & Hoyt, 1908–1923.

Bain, Robert, Joseph M. Flora, and Louis D. Rubin Jr. *Southern Writers: A Biographical Dictionary.* Baton Rouge: Louisiana State University Press, 1979.

Barnes, James J. *Authors, Publishers and Politicians: The Quest for an Anglo-American Copyright Agreement 1815–1854.* Columbus: Ohio State University Press, 1974.

Bartlett, Irving H. *The American Mind in the Mid-Nineteenth Century.* New York: Crowell, 1967.

Baym, Nina. *American Women Writers and the Work of History, 1790–1860.* New Brunswick, N.J.: Rutgers University Press, 1995.

Baym. *Novels, Readers, and Reviewers: Responses to Fiction in Antebellum America.* Ithaca, N.Y.: Cornell University Press, 1984.

Baym. *Woman's Fiction: A Guide to Novels by and about Women in America, 1820–1870,* second edition. Urbana: University of Illinois Press, 1993.

Bell, Michael Davitt. *The Development of American Romance: The Sacrifice of Relation.* Chicago: University of Chicago Press, 1980.

Bender, Thomas. *New York Intellect: A History of Intellectual Life in New York City, from 1750 to the Beginnings of Our Own Time.* Baltimore: Johns Hopkins University Press, 1988.

Bender. *Toward an Urban Vision: Ideas and Institutions in Nineteenth-Century America.* Lexington: University of Kentucky Press, 1975.

Blair, Walter. *Native American Humor.* San Francisco: Chandler, 1960.

Bode, Carl. *Antebellum Culture.* Carbondale, Ill.: Southern Illinois University Press, 1969.

Bradbury, Malcolm. *Dangerous Pilgrimages: Transatlantic Mythologies and the Novel*. New York: Viking, 1996.

Braden, W. W., ed. *Oratory in the Old South: 1828–1860*. Baton Rouge: Louisiana State University Press, 1970.

Bradshaw, S. E. *On Southern Poetry Prior to 1860*. Richmond: B. F. Johnson, 1900.

Branch, E. Douglas. *The Sentimental Years 1836–1860*. New York: Appleton-Century, 1934.

Brooks, Van Wyck. *Chilmark Miscellany*. New York: Dutton, 1948.

Brooks. *The Times of Melville and Whitman*. New York: Dutton, 1947.

Brooks. *The World of Washington Irving*. New York: Dutton, 1944.

Brown, Herbert Ross. *The Sentimental Novel in America, 1789–1860*. Durham: Duke University Press, 1940.

Callow, James T. *Kindred Spirits: Knickerbocker Writers and American Artists, 1807–1855*. Chapel Hill: University of North Carolina Press, 1967.

Calverton, V. F. *The Liberation of American Literature*. New York: Scribners, 1932.

Camfield, Gregg. *Necessary Madness: The Humor of Domesticity in Nineteenth-Century American Literature*. New York: Oxford University Press, 1997.

Cash, W. J. *The Mind of the South*. New York: Knopf, 1941.

Chai, Leon. *The Romantic Foundations of the American Renaissance*. Ithaca, N.Y.: Cornell University Press, 1987.

Charvat, William. *Literary Publishing in America: 1790–1850*. Philadelphia: University of Pennsylvania Press, 1959.

Charvat. *The Profession of Authorship in America, 1800–1870*, edited by Matthew J. Bruccoli. New York: Columbia University Press, 1992.

Chielens, Edward, ed. *American Literary Magazines: The Eighteenth and Nineteenth Centuries*. New York: Greenwood Press, 1986.

Coultrap-McQuin, Susan. *Doing Literary Business: American Women Writers in the Nineteenth Century*. Chapel Hill: University of North Carolina Press, 1990.

Cunliffe, Marcus. *The Literature of the United States*. London & Baltimore: Penguin, 1954.

Current-Garcia, Eugene. *The American Short Story through 1850*. Boston: Twayne, 1985.

Davidson, James Wood. *The Living Writers of the South*. New York: Carleton, 1869.

Day, Martin S. *History of American Literature from the Beginning to 1900*. Garden City, N.Y.: Doubleday, 1970.

Dekker, George. *The American Historical Romance*. Cambridge: Cambridge University Press, 1987.

Derby, J. C. *Fifty Years among Authors, Books, and Publishers*. New York: Carleton, 1884.

Dormon, James H., Jr. *Theater in the Antebellum South*. Chapel Hill: University of North Carolina Press, 1967.

Douglas, Ann. *The Feminization of American Culture*. New York: Knopf, 1977.

Duyckinck, Evert A. and George L. Duyckinck, eds. *Cyclopaedia of American Literature,* 2 volumes. New York: Scribner, 1855.

Eaton, Clement. *The Growth of Southern Civilization, 1790–1860.* New York: Harper, 1961.

Eaton. *The Mind of the Old South,* revised edition. Baton Rouge: Louisiana State University Press, 1967.

Eggleston, George Cary. *Recollections of a Varied Life.* New York: Holt, 1910.

Ekirch, Arthur A., Jr. *The Idea of Progress in America, 1815–1860.* New York: Columbia University Press, 1944.

Elliott, Emory, ed. *Columbia Literary History of the United States.* New York: Columbia University Press, 1988.

Faust, Drew Gilpin. *A Sacred Circle: The Dilemma of the Intellectual in the Old South, 1840–1860.* Baltimore: Johns Hopkins University Press, 1978.

Feidelson, Charles. *Symbolism and American Literature.* Chicago: University of Chicago Press, 1953.

Feller, Daniel. *The Jacksonian Promise: America, 1815–1840.* Baltimore: Johns Hopkins University Press, 1995.

Ferguson, Robert A. *Law and Letters in American Culture.* Cambridge, Mass.: Harvard University Press, 1984.

Floan, Howard R. *The South in Northern Eyes 1831 to 1861.* Austin: University of Texas Press, 1958.

Flora and Bain. *Fifty Southern Writers Before 1900: A Bio-Bibliographical Sourcebook.* New York: Greenwood Press, 1987.

Foster, Edward Halsey. *The Civilized Wilderness: Backgrounds to American Romantic Literature, 1817–1860.* New York: Free Press, 1975.

Freidel, Frank, ed. *Harvard Guide to American History,* revised edition, 2 volumes. Cambridge, Mass.: Harvard University Press, 1974.

Gaines, Francis Pendleton. *The Southern Plantation: A Study in the Development and the Accuracy of a Tradition.* New York: Columbia University Press, 1924.

Garvin, Harry R. and Peter C. Cariofol, eds. *American Renaissance: New Dimensions.* Lewisburg, Pa.: Bucknell University Press, 1983.

Gilmore, Michael T. *American Romanticism and the Marketplace.* Chicago: University of Chicago Press, 1985.

Gohdes, Clarence. *American Literature in Nineteenth-Century England.* New York: Columbia University Press, 1944.

Goldfarb, Russell M. and Clare R. *Spiritualism and Nineteenth-Century Letters.* Rutherford, N.J.: Fairleigh Dickinson University Press, 1978.

Grammer, John M. *Pastoral and Politics in the Old South.* Baton Rouge: Louisiana University Press, 1996.

Grey, Robin. *The Complicity of Imagination: The American Renaissance, Contests of Authority, and Seventeenth-Century English Culture.* New York: Cambridge University Press, 1997.

Gross, Theodore L. *The Heroic Ideal in American Literature.* New York: Free Press, 1971.

Guarneri, Carl J. *The Utopian Alternative: Fourierism in Nineteenth-Century America.* Ithaca, N.Y.: Cornell University Press, 1991.

Gustafson, Thomas. *Representative Words: Politics, Literature, and the American Language, 1776–1865*. New York: Cambridge University Press, 1992.

Haralson, Eric L., ed. *Encyclopedia of American Poetry: The Nineteenth Century*. New York: Garland, 1998.

Harris, Neil. *The Artist in American Society; The Formative Years, 1790–1860*. New York: Braziller, 1966.

Harris, Susan K. *19th-Century American Women's Novels: Interpretive Strategies*. New York: Cambridge University Press, 1990.

Hart, James D. *The Popular Book: A History of America's Literary Taste*. New York: Oxford University Press, 1950.

Hoffman, Daniel. *Form and Fable in American Fiction*. New York: Oxford University Press, 1961.

Holliday, Carl. *A History of Southern Literature*. New York: Neale, 1906.

Holman, C. Hugh. *The Immoderate Past: The Southern Writer and History*. Athens: University of Georgia Press, 1977.

Howard, Leon. *Literature and the American Tradition*. Garden City, N.Y.: Doubleday, 1960.

Howe, Daniel Walker. *The Political Culture of the American Whigs*. Chicago: University of Chicago Press, 1979.

Hubbell, Jay B. *The South in American Literature, 1607–1900*. Durham: Duke University Press, 1954.

Hubbell. *Southern Life in Fiction*. Athens: University of Georgia Press, 1960.

Hudson, Arthur Palmer. *Humor of the Old Deep South*. New York: Macmillan, 1936.

Inge, M. Thomas, ed. *The Frontier Humorists: Critical Views*. Hamden, Conn.: Archon, 1975.

Jehlen, Myra. *American Incarnation: The Individual, the Nation, and the Continent*. Cambridge, Mass.: Harvard University Press, 1986.

Jones, Howard Mumford. *O Strange New World: American Culture, The Formative Years*. New York: Viking, 1967.

Joyce, William L., David D. Hall, and John B. Hench, eds. *Printing and Society in Early America*. Worcester, Mass.: American Antiquarian Society, 1983.

Kammen, Michael. *A Season of Youth: The American Revolution and the Historical Imagination*. New York: Knopf, 1978.

Kasson, Joy S. *Artistic Voyagers: Europe and the American Imagination in the Works of Irving, Allston, Cole, Cooper, and Hawthorne*. Westport, Conn.: Greenwood Press, 1982.

Kaul, A. N. *The American Vision: Actual and Ideal Society in Nineteenth-Century Fiction*. New Haven: Yale University Press, 1963.

Kelley, Mary. *Private Woman, Public Stage: Literary Domesticity in Nineteenth-Century America*. New York: Oxford University Press, 1984.

Kerr, Howard, John W. Crowley, and Charles L. Crow. *The Haunted Dusk: American Supernatural Fiction, 1820–1920*. Athens: University of Georgia Press, 1983.

Knight, Denise, ed. *Nineteenth-Century American Women Writers: A Bio-Bibliographical Sourcebook*. Westport, Conn.: Greenwood Press, 1997.

Knight, Grant C. *American Literature and Culture*. New York: Long & Smith, 1932.

Kolb, Harold H., Jr. *A Field Guide to the Study of American Literature*. Charlottesville: University Press of Virginia, 1976.

Kramer, Aaron. *The Prophetic Tradition in American Poetry, 1835–1900*. Rutherford, N.J.: Fairleigh Dickinson University Press, 1968.

Kramer, Michael P. *Imagining Language in America: From the Revolution to the Civil War*. Princeton: Princeton University Press, 1992.

Lavernier, James and Douglas R. Wilmes. *American Writers Before 1900: A Biographical and Critical Dictionary*. Westport, Conn.: Greenwood Press, 1983.

Lawrence, D. H. *Studies in Classic American Literature*. New York: Viking, 1961.

Leary, Lewis. *American Literature: A Study and Research Guide*. New York: St. Martin's Press, 1976.

Lee, A. Robert, ed. *The Nineteenth-Century American Short Story*. New York: Barnes & Noble, 1986.

Lehmann-Haupt, Hellmut, and others, *The Book in America: A History of the Making and Selling of Books in the United States*, second edition. New York: R. R. Bowker, 1951.

Leisy, Ernest Erwin. *American Literature: An Interpretative Survey*. New York: Crowell, 1929.

Lemelin, Robert E. *Pathway to the National Character, 1830–1861*. Port Washington, N.Y.: Kennikat, 1974.

Leverenz, David. *Manhood and the American Renaissance*. Ithaca, N.Y.: Cornell University Press, 1989.

Levin, Harry. *The Power of Blackness: Hawthorne, Poe, Melville*. New York: Vintage, 1950.

Levine, Lawrence. *Highbrow/Lowbrow: The Emergence of Cultural Hierarchy in America*. Cambridge, Mass.: Harvard University Press, 1988.

Lewis, R. W. B. *The American Adam: Innocence, Tragedy and Tradition in the Nineteenth Century*. Chicago: University of Chicago Press, 1955.

Lively, Robert A. *Fiction Fights the Civil War: An Unfinished Chapter in the Literary History of the American People*. Chapel Hill: University of North Carolina Press, 1957.

Loving, Jerome. *Lost in the Customhouse: Authorship in the American Renaissance*. Iowa City: University of Iowa Press, 1995.

Marchalonis, Shirley, ed. *Patrons and Protégées: Gender, Friendship, and Writing in Nineteenth-Century America*. New Brunswick, N.J.: Rutgers University Press, 1988.

Martin, Terence. *The Instructed Vision: Scottish Common Sense Philosophy and the Origins of American Fiction*. Bloomington: Indiana University Press, 1961.

Martin. *Parables of Possibility: The American Need for Beginnings*. New York: Columbia University Press, 1995.

Marx, Leo. *The Machine in the Garden: Technology and the Pastoral Ideal in American Culture*. New York: Oxford University Press, 1964.

Matthiessen, F. O. *American Renaissance: Art and Expression in the Age of Emerson and Whitman*. New York: Oxford University Press, 1941.

Michaels, Walter Benn and Donald Pease, eds. *The American Renaissance Reconsidered.* Baltimore: Johns Hopkins University Press, 1989.

Miller, Perry. *Nature's Nation.* Cambridge, Mass.: Harvard University Press, 1967.

Miller. *The Raven and the Whale: Poe, Melville, and the New York Literary Scene.* Baltimore: Johns Hopkins University Press, 1997.

Minnigerode, Meade. *The Fabulous Forties, 1840–1850.* Garden City, N.Y.: Garden City Publishing Company, 1924.

Mitchell, Donald Grant. *American Lands and Letters–Leather-Stocking to Poe's "Raven."* New York: Scribners, 1899.

Moses, Montrose J. *The Literature of the South.* New York: Crowell, 1910.

Moss, Elizabeth. *Domestic Novelists in the Old South: Defenders of Southern Culture.* Baton Rouge: Louisiana State University Press, 1992.

Mott, Frank Luther. *Golden Multitudes: The Story of Best Sellers in the United States.* New York: Macmillan, 1947.

Mott. *A History of American Magazines,* 5 volumes. Cambridge, Mass.: Harvard University Press, 1938–1968.

Nilon, Charles. *Bibliography of Bibliographies in American Literature.* New York: R. R. Bowker, 1970.

Nye, Russel Blaine. *Society and Culture in America, 1830–1860.* New York: Harper & Row, 1974.

Osterweis, Rollin G. *Romanticism and Nationalism in the Old South.* New Haven: Yale University Press, 1949.

Paine, Gregory L., ed. *Southern Prose Writers: Representative Selections.* New York: American Book Company, 1947.

Papashvily, Helen Waite. *All the Happy Endings: A Study of the Domestic Novel in America.* New York: Harper, 1956.

Parks, Edd Winfield. *Antebellum Southern Literary Critics.* Athens: University of Georgia Press, 1962.

Parks. *Segments of Southern Thought.* Athens: University of Georgia Press, 1938.

Parks, ed. *Southern Poets: Representative Selections.* New York: American Book Company, 1936.

Parrington, Vernon Louis. *The Romantic Revolution in America, 1800–1860.* New York: Harcourt, Brace, 1927.

Pattee, Fred Lewis. *The Development of the American Short Story: An Historical Survey.* New York: Harper, 1935.

Pattee. *The Feminine Fifties.* New York: Appleton-Century, 1940.

Pattee. *The First Century of American Literature, 1770–1870.* New York: Appleton-Century, 1935.

Pearce, Roy Harvey. *The Continuity of American Poetry.* Princeton: Princeton University Press, 1961.

Pearce. *Savagism and Civilization: A Study of the Indian and the American Mind.* Baltimore: Johns Hopkins University Press, 1967.

Pease. *Visionary Compacts: American Renaissance Writings in Cultural Context.* Madison: University of Wisconsin Press, 1987.

Petter, Henri. *The Early American Novel.* Columbus: Ohio State University Press, 1971.

Porte, Joel. *The Romance in America: Studies in Cooper, Poe, Hawthorne, and James.* Middletown, Conn.: Wesleyan University Press, 1969.

Price, Kenneth and Susan Belasco Smith, eds. *Periodical Literature in Nineteenth-Century America.* Charlottesville: University Press of Virginia, 1995.

Pritchard, John Paul. *Literary Wise Men of Gotham: Criticism in New York, 1815–1860.* Baton Rouge: Louisiana State University Press, 1963.

Quinn, Arthur Hobson. *American Fiction: An Historical and Critical Survey.* New York: Appleton-Century, 1936.

Quinn, ed. *The Literature of the American People: An Historical and Critical Survey.* New York: Appleton-Century-Crofts, 1951.

Reynolds, David S. *Beneath the American Renaissance: The Subversive Imagination in the Age of Emerson and Melville.* New York: Knopf, 1988.

Reynolds, Larry. *European Revolutions and the American Literary Renaissance.* New Haven: Yale University Press, 1988.

Richardson, Robert, Jr. *Myth and Literature in the American Renaissance.* Bloomington: Indiana University Press, 1978.

Riegel, Robert E. *Young America 1830–1840.* Norman: University of Oklahoma Press, 1949.

Riley, Sam G. *Magazines of the American South.* New York: Greenwood Press, 1986.

Ringe, Donald A. *American Gothic: Imagination and Reason in Nineteenth-Century Fiction.* Lexington: University of Kentucky Press, 1982.

Rogers, Edward R. *Four Southern Magazines.* Richmond, Va.: Williams, 1902.

Rosenthal, Bernard. *City of Nature: Journeys to Nature in the Age of American Romanticism.* Newark: University of Delaware Press, 1980.

Rourke, Constance. *American Humor: A Study of the National Character.* New York: Harcourt, Brace, 1931.

Rowe, John Carlos. *Through the Custom-House: Nineteenth-Century American Fiction and Modern Theory.* Baltimore: Johns Hopkins University Press, 1982.

Rubin, Louis D., Jr., ed. *A Bibliographical Guide to the Study of Southern Literature.* Baton Rouge: Louisiana State University Press, 1969.

Rubin, ed. *A History of Southern Literature.* Baton Rouge: Louisiana State University Press, 1985.

Rubin and Holman, eds., *Southern Literary Study: Problems and Possibilities.* Chapel Hill: University of North Carolina Press, 1975.

Rutherford, Mildred L. *The South in History and Literature.* Atlanta: Franklin-Turner, 1907.

Samuels, Shirley. *Romances of the Republic: Women, the Family, and Violence in the Literature of the Early American Nation.* New York: Oxford University Press, 1996.

Sanford, Charles L. *The Quest for Paradise: Europe and the American Moral Imagination.* Urbana: University of Illinois Press, 1961.

Sartain, John. *Reminiscences of a Very Old Man 1808–1897*. New York: Appleton, 1899.

Saum, Lewis. *The Popular Mood of Pre-Civil War America*. Westport, Conn.: Greenwood Press, 1980.

Seldes, Gilbert. *The Stammering Century*. New York: John Day, 1928.

Simpson, David. *The Politics of American English 1776–1850*. New York: Oxford University Press, 1986.

Simpson, Lewis. *The Man of Letters in New England and the South: Essays on the History of the Literary Vocation in the United States*. Baton Rouge: Louisiana State University Press, 1973.

Slotkin, Richard. *Regeneration Through Violence: The Mythology of the American Frontier*. Middletown, Conn.: Wesleyan University Press, 1973.

Smith, Henry Nash. *Democracy and the Novel: Popular Resistance to Classic American Writers*. New York: Oxford University Press, 1978.

Smith. *Virgin Land: The American West as Symbol and Myth*. Cambridge, Mass.: Harvard University Press, 1970.

Spencer, Benjamin T. *The Quest for Nationality: An American Literary Campaign*. Syracuse: Syracuse University Press, 1957.

Spengemann, William C. *The Adventurous Muse: The Poetics of American Fiction, 1789–1900*. New Haven: Yale University Press, 1977.

Spiller, Robert E. and others, *Literary History of the United States,* fourth edition, revised. New York: Macmillan, 1974.

Spiller, ed. *The American Literary Revolution, 1783–1837*. Garden City, N.Y.: Anchor, 1967.

Stafford, John. *The Literary Criticism of "Young America": A Study in the Relationship of Politics and Literature 1837–1850*. Berkeley: University of California Press, 1952.

Stauffer, Donald Barlow. *A Short History of American Poetry*. New York: Dutton, 1974.

Stem, Madeleine B. *Heads & Headlines: The Phrenological Fowlers*. Norman: University of Oklahoma Press, 1971.

Strong, George Templeton. *The Diary of George Templeton Strong,* edited by Allan Nevins and Milton Halsey Thomas, 4 volumes. New York: Macmillan, 1952.

Sundquist, Eric. *To Wake the Nations: Race in the Making of American Literature*. Cambridge, Mass.: Harvard University Press, 1993.

Taft, Kendall B., ed. *Minor Knickerbockers*. New York: American Book Company, 1947.

Taylor, William R. *Cavalier and Yankee: The Old South and the American National Character*. New York: Braziller, 1961.

Tompkins, Jane. *Sensational Designs: The Cultural Work of American Fiction, 1790–1860*. New York: Oxford University Press, 1985.

Trent, William P. *A History of American Literature 1607–1865*. New York: Appleton, 1903.

Tyler, Alice Felt. *Freedom's Ferment: Phases of American Social History from the Colonial Period to the Outbreak of the Civil War*. Minneapolis: University of Minnesota Press, 1944.

Van Doren, Carl. *The American Novel, 1789–1939*. New York: Macmillan, 1955.

Von Frank, Albert J. *The Sacred Game: Provincialism and Frontier Consciousness in American Literature.* Cambridge: Cambridge University Press, 1985.

Voss, Arthur. *The American Short Story: A Critical Survey.* Norman: University of Oklahoma Press, 1973.

Waggoner, Hyatt H. *American Poets from the Puritans to the Present.* Boston: Houghton Mifflin, 1968.

Walker, Cheryl. *The Nightingale's Burden: Women Poets and American Culture Before 1900.* Bloomington: Indiana University Press, 1982.

Watson, Ritchie Devon. *The Cavalier in Virginia Fiction.* Baton Rouge: Louisiana State University Press, 1985.

Watts, Emily Stipes. *The Poetry of American Women from 1632 to 1945.* Austin: University of Texas Press, 1977.

Weisbuch, Robert. *Atlantic Double-Cross: American Literature and British Influence in the Age of Emerson.* Chicago: University of Chicago Press, 1986.

Welter, Barbara. *Dimity Convictions: The American Woman in the Nineteenth Century.* Athens: Ohio University Press, 1976.

Welter, Rush. *The Mind of America, 1820–1860.* New York: Columbia University Press, 1975.

Wendell, Barrett. *A Literary History of America.* New York: Scribners, 1900.

Widmer, Edward L. *Young America: The Flowering of Democracy in New York City.* Oxford: Oxford University Press, 1999.

Williams, Stanley T. *The Beginnings of American Poetry (1620–1855).* Uppsala, Sweden: Airnquist & Wiksells, 1951.

Wilson, Edmund. *Patriotic Gore: Studies in the Literature of the American Civil War.* New York: Oxford University Press, 1962.

Woodward, C. Vann. *The Burden of Southern History,* revised edition. Baton Rouge: Louisiana State University Press, 1968.

Yellin, Jean Fagan. *The Intricate Knot: Black Figures in American Literature, 1776–1863.* New York: New York University Press, 1972.

Zboray, Ronald J. *A Fictive People: Antebellum Economic Development and the American Reading Public.* New York: Oxford University Press, 1993.

Ziff, Larzer. *Literary Democracy: The Declaration of Cultural Independence in America.* New York: Viking, 1981.

Contributors

Barbara Cantalupo . . . . *Pennsylvania State University–Lehigh Valley*

Boyd Childress . . . . *Auburn University*

Clifford E. Clark Jr. . . . . *Carleton College*

Michael Cody . . . . *East Tennessee State University*

Jonathan A. Cook . . . . *Northern Virginia Community College, Alexandria*

Angela Courtney . . . . *Fairfield University*

Valerie DeBrava . . . . *Williamsburg, Virginia*

Mary De Jong . . . . *Pennsylvania State University, Altoona*

Heyward Ehrlich . . . . *Rutgers University, Newark*

Benjamin F. Fisher . . . . *University of Mississippi*

Ed Folsom . . . . *University of Iowa*

Frank Gado . . . . *Enfield, New Hampshire*

Joseph F. Goeke . . . . *University of South Carolina*

Anita G. Gorman . . . . *Slippery Rock University*

James L. Gray . . . . *Indiana University of Pennsylvania*

Ezra Greenspan . . . . *University of South Carolina*

George Egon Hatvary . . . . *St. John's University*

Kathleen Healey . . . . *Colby-Sawyer College*

Jennifer Hynes . . . . *Kingsport, Tennessee*

Emily A. Bernhard Jackson . . . . *Brandeis University*

Wayne R. Kime . . . . *Fairmont State College, West Virginia*

Camille A. Langston . . . . *Northwest Vista College*

Jo Ann Manfra . . . . *Worcester Polytechnic Institute*

Michael C. Mattek . . . . *Marquette University*

Katharine Mitchell . . . . *University of Mississippi*

Peter C. Norberg . . . . *Saint Joseph's University*

Kenneth M. Price . . . . *University of Nebraska*

Stephen Railton . . . . *University of Virginia*

Karen S. H. Roggenkamp . . . . *University of Minnesota, Twin Cities*

Richard Dilworth Rust . . . . *University of North Carolina–Chapel Hill*

Susan M. Stone . . . . *Loras College*

Bruce I. Weiner . . . . *St. Lawrence University*

John Wenke . . . . *Salsibury University*

Peter Lamborn Wilson . . . . *New Paltz, New York*

S. J. Wolfe . . . . *American Antiquarian Society*

Donald Yannella . . . . *Barat College*

Anne Zanzucchi . . . . *University of Rochester*

Cumulative Index

Dictionary of Literary Biography, Volumes 1-250
Dictionary of Literary Biography Yearbook, 1980-2000
Dictionary of Literary Biography Documentary Series, Volumes 1-19
Concise Dictionary of American Literary Biography, Volumes 1-7
Concise Dictionary of British Literary Biography, Volumes 1-8
Concise Dictionary of World Literary Biography, Volumes 1-4

Cumulative Index

DLB before number: *Dictionary of Literary Biography,* Volumes 1-250
Y before number: *Dictionary of Literary Biography Yearbook,* 1980-2000
DS before number: *Dictionary of Literary Biography Documentary Series,* Volumes 1-19
CDALB before number: *Concise Dictionary of American Literary Biography,* Volumes 1-7
CDBLB before number: *Concise Dictionary of British Literary Biography,* Volumes 1-8
CDWLB before number: *Concise Dictionary of World Literary Biography,* Volumes 1-4

H

O

Cumulative Index

S

W

ISBN 0-7876-4667-9

90000

9 780787 646677